technicians at a recently opened military-communi_____ __hool in
Guatemala. And now that the Reagan A_____ Jimmy
Carter's military embargo, the Guat_____ side in
American-made trucks, jeeps and h____
   Still, Reagan can hardly mend rel_____ ment
that seems to have made murder an of _____ _____ people
have been killed since 1978, and the _____nt estimates that 300
more are murdered each month. The morning papers are full of reported kill-
ings by *desconocidos* (unknowns). Most murders seem to be the work of
right-wing death squads like the Secret Anti-Communist Army, widely assumed to be covert agents of the government. A U.S. missionary, John
Arnold Miller, was killed two weeks ago, the seventh cleric murdered in
fourteen months. And in the village of Uspantán last week 53 peasants were
rounded up and beheaded. The government blamed guerrillas, but the evidence was skimpy. "There are no political prisoners in Guatemala," former
Vice President Francisco Villagrán Kramer once remarked. "Only political
murders."
   **'Hydra':** The wholesale killing has not yet daunted the regime's guerrilla
opponents. Earlier this month the four principal guerrilla groups announced
they had joined in a "Guatemalan National Revolutionary Unity." Within
hours of the declaration Guatemala City was almost blacked out by a series of
bomb blasts—evidence that unification may work to the advantage of the estimated 3,000 to 5,000 guerrillas. They may also be bolstered by assistance
and training from Communist-bloc countries. Last summer the government
discovered more than 25 guerrilla safe houses stocked with Chinese and
Soviet-bloc weapons, including a cache of U.S. M-16 rifles whose serial
numbers matched those left behind in Vietnam. In 1981 there were 383 reported clashes with guerrillas—almost four times as many as the year before.
"We have been able to pacify some regions," says Col. Jaime Rabanales
Reyes. "But the guerrillas are like a hydra—their heads always show up in
some other place."
   The choices facing the United States in Guatemala are few and unpleasant.
Washington can hardly hope for a centrist political solution: the same Christian Democrats the United States supports in El Salvador continue to be deci-
mated in Guatemala. In the last eighteen months 238 Christian Democratic
leaders have disappeared. Some diplomats think the extreme right is de-
stroying the moderate center precisely to preclude the sort of "reformist" solution that the United States advocates in El Salvador. Ultimately the polari-
zation serves the cause of the leftist revolutionaries. The growing strength of
the left conceivably could persuade the United States to back yet another Central American dictatorship—this one, in Guatemala, the most brutal of them
all.

LARRY ROHTER in Guatemala City

# Strategies of
# Discourse Comprehension

# Strategies of
# Discourse Comprehension

*Teun A. van Dijk*

Department of General Literary Studies
Section of Discourse Studies
University of Amsterdam
Amsterdam, The Netherlands

*Walter Kintsch*

Department of Psychology
University of Colorado
Boulder, Colorado

1983

ACADEMIC PRESS
*A Subsidiary of Harcourt Brace Jovanovich, Publishers*
New York   London
Paris   San Diego   San Francisco   São Paulo   Sydney   Tokyo   Toronto

ACADEMIC PRESS, INC.
111 Fifth Avenue, New York, New York 10003

*United Kingdom Edition published by*
ACADEMIC PRESS, INC. (LONDON) LTD.
24/28 Oval Road, London NW1 7DX

Library of Congress Cataloging in Publication Data

Dijk, Teun Adrianus van, Date
    Strategies of discourse comprehension.

    Bibliography: p.
    Includes index.
    1. Discourse analysis--Psychological aspects.
2. Comprehension. I. Kintsch, Walter, 1932–
II. Title.
P302.D472  1983  401'.41          82–22671
ISBN  0–12–712050–5

PRINTED IN THE UNITED STATES OF AMERICA

83 84 85 86     9 8 7 6 5 4 3 2 1

# Contents

*Chapter 3*
# The Notion of Strategy in Language and Discourse Understanding

*Chapter 4*
# Propositional Strategies

*Chapter 5*
# Local Coherence Strategies

*Chapter 6*
# Macrostrategies

*Chapter 7*
# Schematic Strategies

*Chapter 8*
# Production Strategies

*Chapter 9*
# Strategies for the Use of Knowledge

*Chapter 10*
# The Cognitive Model

# Preface

There has been a surge of interest in discourse comprehension in recent years. The time has come to analyze and study scientifically what we all do with great facility every day when we are reading a newspaper article, studying a chapter in a textbook, or participating in a conversation. The scientific approaches that have been used in studying this subject matter are equally diverse, ranging from linguistic analysis to sociological field studies, computer understanding of text to psychological laboratory experiments on comprehension and memory for text. Obviously, no single work can do justice either to the breadth of the field or to the variety of methods used in studying it. We are trying to present here a broadly based, general, but coherent approach to the investigation of discourse phenomena, grounded on the notion that discourse understanding is strategic. Just as strategies, usually unconscious and often automatic, have been shown to play an important role in sentence understanding, we propose to identify a set of discourse strategies that people use in forming the multilevel representations that are involved in discourse comprehension and memory.

The present theory is the result of a scientific collaboration between the two authors that goes back several years, starting with a joint paper on story understanding in 1975 and leading to the publication of our initial model of discourse comprehension in 1978. The 1978 model is the direct predecessor of the present theory, which not so much replaces our former work, but extends and elaborates on it. We worked in our previous model with some useful but ultimately inadequate approximations, which we have tried to replace here with more detailed and realistic analyses. Specifically, we attempt to sketch the way knowledge is used in discourse comprehension, rather than bypass this central component with statistical approximations.

The theory assumes that a verbal input is decoded into a list of atomic propositions which are organized into larger units on the basis of some knowledge structure to form a coherent text base. From this text base a macrostructure is constructed which represents the most essential information in the text base. Not only the comprehender's knowledge, but also beliefs and goals play a crucial role in this process. In parallel with this hierarchical textbase a situation model is elaborated, which integrates the comprehender's existing world knowledge with the information derived from the text that is being processed. Thus, the end product of comprehension is a multilevel processing record, which includes memory traces of the actual linguistic input, of the meaning of the text both at a local and global level, and of the effect the text had on the comprehender's world knowledge. The on-line processing strategies that produce this structure are the primary concern of this book.

Our goal in writing this book has been to provide an at least tentative sketch of these processes and their strategic underpinnings. Our emphasis has been on establishing a reasonably complete, comprehensive framework, rather than working out the myriad fine details involved. After a brief overview, we review the relevant literature, emphasizing those aspects we feel to be most crucial to our own concerns. Then, in Chapters 4–9, we take up the various levels of representations individually examining in some detail the strategies used in their construction. What we offer in these chapters are analytic discussions of the issues involved, rather than fully formalized, explicit models. Our hope is, of course, that such models can be constructed eventually on the foundation we have provided here. Finally, we consider some problems peculiar to discourse production, and we end the book with a discussion of some psychological processing characteristics of discourse comprehension, including knowledge use, cognitive resource constraints, and memory. The concept of situation model, which is new to our theory, is used throughout to separate textual *processes* from the use that is made of the *information* conveyed by the text for whatever purposes.

Most of the chapters also contain reports of psychological experiments that were performed to test various aspects of our theory. We have no illusions about the difficulty of evaluating a theory as complex as ours, especially one which is not yet stated formally and explicitly in all the necessary detail; but we feel that the studies reported here manage to throw some light on difficult and controversial issues in discourse comprehension.

## ACKNOWLEDGMENTS

Eileen Kintsch edited the entire manuscript, and we are most grateful to her for smoothing over the differences in our writing styles and for helping us to improve the quality of this book at all levels. Special thanks also go to P. Bochert, whose typing skills and patience are much appreciated. We also owe a debt of gratitude to a number of our students who collaborated with us on the experimental studies reported in this book and who permitted us to present their work here: Ugo Racheli, Raymond Guindon, Craik Yarbrough, and Randy Fletcher at the University of Colorado, and Paul Leseman and Frank Lemmens at the University of Amsterdam. Last but not least we acknowledge the support of various granting agencies which made possible this work as well as the intercontinental collaboration of the two authors. Travel funds for Teun van Dijk were provided on several occasions by The Netherlands Organization for the Advancement of Pure Research (ZWO). The work of Walter Kintsch from which this book evolved was supported by Grant MH-15872 from the National Institute of Mental Health. Research performed for the Office of Naval Research under Contract N00014-78-C-0433 also significantly influenced the development of the present model. Finally, we thank the Center for Advanced Study at Stanford, which gave Walter Kintsch the opportunity to complete this book, with support from NIMH Grant 5T32MH14581-06 and the Spencer Foundation.

# Chapter 1

# Toward a Model of
# Strategic Discourse Processing

## 1.1. THE STUDY OF DISCOURSE

### 1.1.1. Historical Background

Several disciplines in the humanities and the social sciences have recently shown an increasing interest in the study of discourse. This development, which really began around 1970, is not without historical sources however. Over 2000 years ago, classical poetics and rhetorics already provided structural models for texts, such as poetry, drama, and legal or political discourse (Wellek, 1955; Wimsatt & Brooks, 1957; Lausberg, 1960; Corbett, 1971). The conceptual sophistication of classical rhetorics remained unmatched until the development of structuralism in linguistics, poetics, and anthropology in the late 1960s, after the earlier example of the so-called Russian Formalists (Erlich, 1955) and the Czech Structuralists between the world wars (Ihwe, 1972; Culler, 1975). Thus, the work of the Russian anthropologist Vladimir Propp (1928) on the Russian folktale provided an example for the structural approach to narratives which was taken up more than 30 years later, mainly in France, by anthropologists and literary scholars such as Lévi-Strauss, Barthes, Bremond, Todorov, Greimas, and others, and which finally emerged within psychology, in the work on story grammars (Rumelhart, 1975; van Dijk, 1980a). Although these various classical and structuralist theories do not meet the current methodological standards of explicitness in linguistics and psychology, many of the theoretical notions remain relevant today.

## 1.1.2. Textlinguistics

Until the 1970s modern linguistics in America rarely looked beyond the sentence boundary. The prevailing generative transformational paradigm focused on phonological, morphological, syntactic, and later also semantic, structures of isolated, context- and text-independent sentences, ignoring the early programmatic call for discourse analysis by Harris (1952). Interest in the linguistic study of discourse was restricted to less prominent linguistic schools, such as tagmemics (Pike, 1967; Grimes, 1975; Longacre, 1976), which developed discourse analytic methods mainly for descriptive field work on indigenous languages. European linguistics, especially in England and Germany had remained somewhat closer to the structuralist tradition which had less respect for the boundaries of linguistics itself in general, and of the sentence unit in particular (Halliday, 1961; Hartmann, 1964, 1968; Harweg, 1968; Petöfi, 1971; van Dijk, 1972; Dressler, 1972; Schmidt, 1973). Indeed, some of these linguistic studies of discourse were at the boundaries of grammar, stylistics, and poetics (Leech, 1966; Crystal & Davy, 1969). Initially, the more theoretical claims and proposals based on the assumption that a grammar should also account for the systematic linguistic structures of whole texts, thereby becoming a text grammar, remained in a programmatic stage, still too close to the generative paradigm for comfort. Soon, however, both text grammars and the linguistic study of discourse in general developed a more independent paradigm, finally spreading from Europe to the United States (van Dijk, 1977a; van Dijk & Petöfi, 1977; Dressler, 1978; Sinclair & Coulthard, 1975; Coulthard, 1977, and many other studies; see de Beaugrande & Dressler, 1981, and de Beaugrande, 1980, for a survey and introduction).

More or less parallel with this development, American linguistics had itself shown an increasing tendency toward text- and context-dependent grammatical analysis, after the earlier tagmemic work, especially within so-called functional paradigms (Givón, 1979a).

## 1.1.3. The Social Sciences and Discourse Analysis

The study of discourse became relevant in particular as soon as it was recognized, also around 1970, that language studies should not be restricted to the grammatical analysis of abstract or ideal language systems, but, rather, that actual language use in the social context should be the empirical object of linguistic theories. Thus, sociolinguistics not only became interested in the study of social variation of language use, but also paid increasing attention to various forms of language use, such as verbal dueling and storytelling (Labov, 1972a, 1972b).

Some of this sociolinguistic work became intertwined with a similar development in anthropology and ethnography, where earlier structural analyses of myths, folktales, riddles, and other forms of verbal art gave way to a broader analysis of communicative events in various cultures (Gumperz & Hymes, 1972; Bauman & Sherzer, 1974; Sanches & Blount, 1975).

Finally, this general tendency toward a study of naturally occurring speech could also be observed in microsociology, where the ethnomethodological attention paid to everyday interaction soon focused on conversational interaction as well (Sudnow, 1972; Sacks, Schegloff, & Jefferson, 1974; Schenkein, 1978). In fact, conversation analysis soon became so popular that it virtually was identified with discourse analysis, and its influence in recent linguistics has been considerable (Franck, 1980; Coulthard & Montgomery, 1981).

At the moment, it is hard to make strict disciplinary distinctions within the study of discourse, which seems to emerge more and more as an independent, interdisciplinary field, in which purely linguistic or grammatical methods and theories mingle with those from ethnography, microsociology and, as we will see, from psychology.

## 1.1.4. Psychology and Artificial Intelligence

Following the prevailing generative transformational trend, psychology and psycholinguistics were hesitant to recognize the relevance of discourse to the study of language processing. Early psycholinguistic models in the 1960s were restricted to the syntax and, later, the semantics, of isolated sentences (Clark & Clark, 1977; Fodor, Bever, & Garrett, 1974).

Again, the early 1970s brought a breach in this paradigm. The growing interest in semantic memory resulted in the use of discourse materials and the first steps toward a cognitive model of discourse understanding (Kintsch, 1972, 1974; Bower, 1974; for a survey of other work, see Chapter 2). At the same time, educational psychology realized that learning often takes place on the basis of texts, which also contributed to the quickly developing interest in memory for discourse (Rothkopf, 1972; Meyer, 1975). Thus, we witnessed in psychology a general revival of earlier work on discourse within the gestalt tradition, notably that of Bartlett (1932), which had only occasionally inspired psychologists during the intervening 40 years (Cofer, 1941: Gomulicki, 1956; Paul, 1959; Slamecka, 1959; Pompi & Lachman, 1967).

This revival, not only of discourse comprehension but also of various schema theories, took place in artificial intelligence as well. In this area, the year 1972 brought a decisive paradigm shift (Winograd, 1972; Charniak, 1972; Simmons, 1972). The computer-simulated understanding of language required the development of programs for the automatic processing of texts. Crucial to this research was the modeling of world knowledge necessary for the understanding of stories, for example. Thus, Bartlett's notion of schema was taken up again in a more explicit fashion under such labels as "schema," "scenario," "frame," and "script," in order to account for the role of world knowledge representations in discourse understanding and other complex cognitive tasks (Schank & Colby, 1973; Minsky, 1975; Bobrow & Collins, 1975; Norman & Rumelhart, 1975; Schank & Abelson, 1977).

Ten years have elapsed since these early studies in linguistics, psychology, artificial intelligence, and the social sciences. Whereas the earlier approaches often developed in a more or less autonomous and parallel way, we now witness an increasing integration of the many theoretical proposals. Within the wide new field of cognitive science, the interdisciplinary study of discourse has seen the publication of numerous books and papers, the foundation of two specialized journals (*Discourse Processing*, 1978; *Text*, 1981), and the regular occurrence of conferences or sessions within larger conferences. There have been numerous mutual contacts between linguistics and psychology, between linguistics and microsociology, and between psychology and ethnography.

In our initial work on cognitive models for discourse comprehension (Kintsch & van Dijk, 1975, 1978; van Dijk & Kintsch, 1978) we attempted to integrate several proposals from these earlier approaches to discourse, in particular from our own work in these areas. Thus, the general memory model was developed from previous work on semantic memory (Kintsch, 1970, 1972), whereas the various textual structures, such as local and global coherence, macrostructures, and superstructures, were analyzed for their role in processing in terms of earlier textlinguistic work (van Dijk, 1972, 1977a) and its influence in psychology (Kintsch, 1974).

Although this interdisciplinarily inspired model of discourse comprehension has been steadily extended and refined over the past years, both by ourselves and, often independently and into other directions, by others (see the survey of this work in Chapter 2), the model presented in this book should be considered both as a further extension of this earlier work as well as a new direction in the cognitive modeling of discourse processing. Whereas our earlier model could still be characterized as predominantly *structural*, we now propose a more dynamic, process-oriented, on-line model, an approach we want to call *strategical*.

## 1.2. BASIC ASSUMPTIONS

Having sketched some of the historical background of our model, we shall now present an informal outline of its basic assumptions. These assumptions not only inspire the major theoretical notions and components of the model, but also establish the necessary relationships with other models of discourse use in linguistics and the social sciences. In the next main section of this chapter we give an overview of the major components of the model, which the following chapters will systematically treat in further theoretical and experimental detail.

### 1.2.1. Cognitive Assumptions

Suppose someone witnesses a car accident. We assume that such a person constructs a mental representation of that accident, and that his or her understanding of the observed events consists in that process of construction and its memorial consequences. Now, suppose that another person hears a story about the same accident. We assume that understanding such a story also involves the construction of a mental representation of the story. Of course, a representation of the accident itself and a representation of the story about the accident will not be identical. In the latter case, we will have a representation of the speaker's already coded version of the accident (Hörmann, 1976). But, the common characteristic of both cognitive processes is that the person who witnesses the accident and the person who listens to the story each constructs a representation in memory, on the basis of the visual and the linguistic data, respectively. We will call this the *constructivist* assumption of our model.

Next, we will assume that both the witness of the accident and the listener of the accident story do not merely represent the visual and the verbal data, such as the movements of objects or persons (events) or the sounds uttered when the story is told, but also, or rather, an interpretation of the events and the utterance (Loftus, 1979). In both cases they construct a meaning: The events are interpreted as 'an accident', and the story utterance is interpreted as a story about an accident. We will call this the *interpretative* assumption of the model. In fact, we will be nearly exclusively dealing with this semantic aspect of discourse processing.

We will further assume that the construction of a representation of the accident or of the accident story, and in particular of the meaning of the input data, takes place more or less at the same time as the processing of the input data. In other words, we assume that the witness and the listener in our example do not first process and store all input data of the respective events, and only afterward try to assign meaning to these. That is, understanding takes place on-line with the processing of input data, gradually, and not post hoc. Using the computer metaphor, we will call this the *on-line* assumption of discourse processing (Marslen-Wilson & Tyler, 1980).

Persons who understand real events or speech events are able to construct a mental representation, and especially a meaningful representation, only if they have more general knowledge about such events. In order to interpret some events as an accident, they must know something about the usual traffic events and actions in which cars and drivers are involved, and for stories they must have more general knowledge about stories and about their relationship to the events that they tell of. Similarly, the two persons may interpret the events in the light of previous experiences with similar events, experiences that may have led to the more general knowledge about them. In addition to this knowledge, the listener and the witness may have other cognitive information, such as beliefs, opinions, or attitudes regarding such events in general, or motivations, goals, or specific tasks in the processing of these events. More generally, then, we will assume that understanding involves not only the processing and interpretation of external data, but also the activation and use of internal, cognitive, information. Since this information can be considered as cognitive presuppositions of the construction process, we will call this the *presuppositional* assumption of the model.

As we will see in somewhat more detail in what follows, accidents and stories will not simply be observed and understood *in vacuo,* but as parts of more complex situations or social contexts. Understanding them therefore also means that the person uses or constructs information about the relationships between the events and their situations. That is, the understander now has three kinds of data, namely, information from the events themselves, information from the situation or context, and information from the cognitive presuppositions. This information may be combined in an effective way, such that a mental representation of the event is constructed as soon as possible and as well (as meaningfully, usefully, etc.) as possible. This may mean, for instance, that the observer of an accident even constructs meanings derived from his or her presuppositional information for which the external data are lacking, and the same is true for the listener of the story: He or she may have expectations about what may be told before actually having heard it, and this may facilitate the understanding process when he or she actually does get the relevant external information. There is no fixed order, at each point, between input data and their interpretation: Interpretations may be constructed and only later matched with input data. We see that persons have the ability to flexibly make use of various kinds of information, that the information may be processed in several possible orders, that the information that is interpreted can be incomplete, and that the overall goal of the process is to be as effective as possible in the construction of the mental representation. We will call this the *strategic* assumption of the model. Whereas the other assumptions have already received due attention in previous discourse-processing models, this strategic assumption will be the focus of the present book. We will see that it is inextricably linked with the other assumptions, especially with the on-line assumption about complex information processing of events and discourses.

We can now conclude that the major dimensions of our model are based on the assumption that discourse processing, just like other complex information processing, is a strategic process in which a mental representation is constructed of the discourse in memory, using both external and internal types of information, with the goal of interpreting (understanding) the discourse. Of course, these very general assumptions have many corollaries and implications. Thus, the constructivist assumption has as an important corollary that gradual, on-line, construction is possible only on the basis of a structural analysis and synthesis process, in which, at various levels, meaningful units can be distinguished, as can ways in which these units can be combined into more complex units. This and other corollaries and implications of our assumptions will be spelled out in the appropriate chapters of this book.

### 1.2.2. Contextual Assumptions

We already suggested that discourses such as stories do not occur *in vacuo*. They are produced and received, by speakers and listeners, in specific situations within a wider sociocultural context. Hence, discourse processing is not merely a cognitive event, but also a social event. This is obvious, of course, but here we will assume, first of all, that the social dimensions of discourse interact with the cognitive ones. In other words, the cognitive model should also provide for the fact that discourse, and hence the process of understanding a discourse, is functional in the social context. We will call this the (social) *functionality* assumption. The first cognitive implication of this assumption is that language users construct a representation not only of the text but also of the social context, and that these two representations interact.

More specifically, we assume that a story about an accident is told and understood in a process of communication, in which a listener acquires information from the speaker, in this case about some accident (and about the way the speaker has coded this accident in his or her memory). This communicative assumption may mean, among other things, that the listener does not merely attempt to construct his or her own representation of the story, but matches this interpretation with a representation of the assumptions about what the speaker intended the listener to understand.

Because intentions are involved in discourse, we deal not only with linguistic objects, but also with the results of some form of social action. Thus, when telling a story a speaker will engage in the social act, a speech act, of asserting something, or warning the listener about something. The form and the interpretation of the story may be a function of this intended speech act function of the utterance act. We will call this the *pragmatic* assumption of a model of discourse processing. The cognitive implication of this assumption is, for instance, that a person who interprets a story will also construct a representation of the possible speech acts involved, by assigning a specific function or action category to the discourse utterance, and hence to the speaker. In this case, the listener will evaluate the discourse on a number of points relative to the intended pragmatic functions: This story may be pragmatically appropriate as a speech act only if some contextual conditions match with some textual properties.

Next, it should be assumed that the interpretation of a discourse as a specific speech act (or series of speech acts) is embedded within an interpretation of the whole interaction process taking place between the speech participants. Both the speaker and the listener will have motivations, purposes, or intentions when engaging in verbal interaction, and the same holds for the further actions with which the verbal actions are related in the same situation. Hence, the pragmatic assumption should be generalized to an *interactionist* assumption. Again, this means that we assume that language users construct a cognitive representation of the verbal and nonverbal interaction taking place in the situation. This would imply, for instance, that the representation of the discourse in memory will depend on the assumptions of the listener about the purposes (goals) and further underlying motivations of the speaker, as well as on the listener's own goals and motivations when listening to a story.

Finally, as we have already suggested, the interaction in which the processing of discourse is embedded is itself part of a social situation. The speech participants may have certain functions or roles; there may be differences in location or setting; and there may be specific rules, conventions, or strategies governing possible interactions in such a situation. One cannot say just anything in any situation: Possible actions, hence possible goals and hence possible discourses, are constrained by the various dimensions of the situation. The accident story may be told in a bar, to a friend at home, or perhaps to a stranger on the bus, but would not be a permissible speech act during an exam. In order to be able to understand a story, therefore, we have to link its pragmatic function with the general interactional constraints as determined by, or as determining, the social situation; and this is possible only if, again, we specify in our model how the social situation is cognitively represented. In more concrete terms: The interpretation of the meaning and the functions of the accident story will be different when told in informal contexts to our friends than when told, by a witness, in a court trial related to the accident. Hence, we will ultimately have to take into account a *situational* assumption about discourse processing. This may include, as presuppositions, general norms and values, attitudes, and conventions about the participants and the interactions in some situation.

It goes without saying that these various contextual assumptions about discourse processing can be independently formulated within sociological models of language use. Yet, our general functional assumption suggests that the process of understanding also involves these various kinds of contextual information, that representations are constructed of the speech act, the communicative interactions, and the whole situation, and that these representations will strategically interact with the understanding of the discourse itself. Hence, understanding is no longer a mere passive construction of a representation of a verbal object, but part of an interactive process in which a listener interprets, actively, the actions of a speaker.

It will not be our main task to investigate the nature of the representations and the interpretation processes of such contextual information, but we will take them into account when formulating the processes of discourse understanding.

### 1.2.3. Limitations

We cannot possibly investigate the details of all assumptions set forth. Hence, against the background of the more general assumptions defining the basis of the model, we will specify only some of its components. Although we present some general ideas about the ways these various components of the model interact, we will assume that the components can be spelled out more or less independently (Simon, 1969). The three major limitations of our model are therefore the following:

1. *Linguistic parsing:* We do not fully model the processes by which linguistic input is analyzed (or synthesized) and semantically interpreted; for the most part, we limit the model to the processing of semantic information.
2. *Knowledge representation and use:* We will not completely spell out the knowledge base—or other cognitive information, such as beliefs or opinions, tasks, and goals—which provides the information necessary for the various semantic operations of discourse understanding; knowledge specified will be ad hoc and intuitive, and we will only focus on some aspects of the processes of knowledge use.

3. We will also neglect the systematic representation of *contextual informa-tion* in discourse processing, such as relevant speech acts, interaction, and situation; again, this information will be provided ad hoc when necessary in the formulation of semantic processes.

Since we formulate more or less general hypotheses about the relationships between our semantic component and the other components, and because at certain points we do specify in detail how the components interact, we hope that the formulation of the principles of the semantic model is sufficiently constrained by the implications of the other components.

In addition to its theoretical incompleteness, the model also has a number of more empirical limitations. We have been talking so far about discourse processing in general, using the example of story comprehension. However, discourse process-ing also involves participating in a conversation, skimming the newspaper, giving a lecture, reading a textbook, or writing a police report. Hence, we have provisionally assumed that principles of discourse processing can be formulated at a level that encompasses these various *discourse types*. Obviously, each discourse type will involve linguistic and cognitive differences, but we will only occasionally take these into account.

Furthermore, the *language users* involved may be very different. They may have different knowledge, beliefs, and opinions, have different social roles, they may be children or adults, male or female, have a different education, and so on. Again, we will for the moment abstract from these differences, and hope to provide a framework within which they can easily be filled in.

Finally, there are also different kinds, styles, or *modes of comprehension*. We have noted the possibility of skimming a newspaper story. On the other hand, we may also actively study or even learn by heart some part of a textbook, we may read a text with much or with little attention, we may be distracted by other contextual information or not, and so on. We will also abstract from these differences, and act as if the language user processes all information, constructs a complete representa-tion, and stops the construction of the representation as soon as it satisfies a number of conditions, for example, those of local and global (macrostructural) coherence. However, our strategic approach would expressly provide for the possibility that language users often do process information incompletely or incorrectly and yet feel that they understand the text. Similarly, we limit the model to an account of proper semantic understanding. We have already stressed that understanding of the prag-matic or interactional aspects of the discourse will not be fully spelled out, but this also involves neglecting other personal relationships or experiences of the listener, as well as the listener's social or ideological understanding of the discourse or the understanding of the person producing the discourse, which would involve attribut-ing various motivational or personality structures.

There is no unitary process of comprehension, but variable comprehension processes in different situations, of different language users, of different discourse types. We will assume, though, that our model is general and flexible enough to allow later specification of these various differences. In the following we will not apologize for the theoretical or empirical incompleteness or limitations of our model every time this excuse would be relevant. Nor do we want to stress at each point that the comprehension process we model is rather idealistic. The limitations spelled out in this section should be considered as the boundary conditions for the model throughout this book.

## 1.3. AN OVERVIEW OF THE MODEL

### 1.3.1. General Properties

Many models of language and language use, both in linguistics and in psychology, account for linguistic objects in terms of the *levels* of morphonology, syntax, semantics, and pragmatics. Although such a level-by-level description may be relevant in a more abstract analysis, it does not seem particularly relevant from the point of view of processing models. One of the major assumptions has been that in a cognitive model of discourse understanding and production, information from these various levels interacts in an intricate way. Thus, semantic interpretation does not simply follow full syntactic analysis, but may already occur with an incomplete surface structure input, whereas further syntactic analysis may use information from the semantic and pragmatic levels. Although we will certainly make use of different kinds of information, such as syntactic units or semantic units, our model operates on more complex chunks. Thus, we will analyze discourse processing from the word units on the lower level, up to the unit of overall themes or macrostructures. For the understanding and integration of these different units, various kinds of information may be used. In this way, we may use words, perhaps thematic words, in order to construct macrostructures, and we may use macrostructures in the understanding of words.

Our model is not level oriented but *complexity* oriented: We go from the understanding of words, to the understanding of clauses in which these words have various functions, and then to complex sentences, sequences of sentences, and overall textual structures. But even so there is continual feedback between less complex and more complex units: Understanding the function of a word in a clause will depend on the functional structure of the clause as a whole, both at the syntactic and at the semantic level. This means that instead of a conventional structural model of processing, we operate with a *strategic* model.

The notion of comprehension strategy was introduced in 1970 by Bever in the context of sentence processing. Several other researchers have employed the notion since then, but it did not receive the central role we would like to reserve for it in our model. Earlier notions of strategy were often restricted to particular levels, such as syntactic analysis. We would like to extend the notion, first of all, from the sentence level to the discourse level. Second, we want to use it for processing across several levels of the discourse input, as well as for both textual and contextual information, and for both external and internal information.

Strategic processes contrast with algorithmic, rule-governed processes. An example of the latter is a generative grammar, which produces a structural description of a sentence by syntactic parsing rules. This process may be complex, long, and tedious, but it guarantees success as long as the rules are correct and are applied correctly. In a strategic process, there is no such guaranteed success and no unique representation of the text. The strategies applied are like effective working hypotheses about the correct structure and meaning of a text fragment, and these may be disconfirmed by further processing. Also, strategic analysis depends not only on textual characteristics, but also on characteristics of the language user, such as his or her goals or world knowledge. This may mean that a reader of a text will try to reconstruct not only the intended meaning of the text—as signaled by the writer in various ways in the text or context—but also a meaning that is most relevant to his or her own interests and goals.

Strategies are part of our general knowledge; they represent the procedural knowledge we have about understanding discourse. They are an open set. They need to be learned, and overlearned, before they can become automatized. New types of discourse and forms of communication may require the development of new strategies. Whereas some of the strategies, such as those of word and clause comprehension, are acquired at a relatively early age, others, such as those of gist inferring, are acquired rather late. Some strategies, such as the schematic strategies of understanding the structure of psychological articles, may only be acquired with special training.

Formally, strategies can be represented as productions (Newell, 1973). If certain conditions are satisfied, a certain action is to be taken. Such conditions will often involve a combination of information from various sources. In Chapter 3, we will discuss this notion of strategy in more detail.

The overall strategy, which we will decompose into a series of more specific strategies, to be studied in the appropriate chapters of this book, has as its goal the construction of a *textbase*. Such a textbase is the semantic representation of the input discourse in episodic memory. This overall strategy of constructing a textbase is successful for a language user as soon as the textbase satisfies a number of minimal criteria, such as those of local and global coherence. It follows that two major substrategies consist in the establishment of this kind of local and global coherence.

Textbases will be defined in terms of *propositions* and relations among propositions. Although there are other, formally equivalent, ways to represent meaning, we will follow this well-known representation format, borrowed from linguistics and philosophy. However, we will assign more structure to propositions than has been usual in logic, following functionalist proposals from linguistics (Fillmore, 1968; Dik, 1978, 1980; Givón, 1979b).

A major feature of our model is the assumption that discourse understanding involves not only the representation of a textbase in episodic memory, but, at the same time, the activation, updating, and other uses of a so-called *situation model* in episodic memory: this is the cognitive representation of the events, actions, persons, and in general the situation, a text is about. Once again, there are historical precedents for such a notion (e.g., Johnson-Laird, 1980).

A situation model may incorporate previous experiences, and hence also previous textbases, regarding the same or similar situations. At the same time, the model may incorporate instantiations from more general knowledge from semantic memory about such situations. In Chapter 10 we will give a number of arguments for this kind of double representation in episodic memory. If in the following chapters we specify the strategies used in the construction of a semantic textbase in episodic memory, it is understood that this representation is continually matched with 'what we already know about similar situations', that is, with the episodic model. This process is important, because it allows us to limit a textbase to information expressed or implied by the text itself, without having to interpolate into it large amounts of activated knowledge. This episodic and semantic knowledge will be assumed to be integrated into the more complete situation model with which the textbase is continuously compared. This means that understanding is restricted to an evaluation of the textbase not only with respect to local and global coherence, but also with respect to its corresponding situation model. In this way, we know not only what the text means conceptually, but also what it is about referentially. In other words, here we are introducing into cognitive psychology the well-known distinction in philosophy between *intensional* (meaning) semantics and *extensional* (referential) semantics. One obvious advantage of the presence of situation models is the possibility for the language user to assign such fundamental notions as truth and falsity to discourses.

Another general property of the model is its overall *control system*. For the processing of each discourse, this control system is fed by specific general information about the type of situation, type of discourse, overall goals (of the reader/listener and of the writer/speaker), by the schematic superstructure and the macrostructures (gist, themes) of the text, or by plans in the case of production. This control system will supervise processing in short-term memory, activate and actualize needed episodic and more general semantic knowledge, provide the higher order information into which lower order information must fit, coordinate the various strategies, decide which information from short-term memory should be moved to episodic memory, activate the relevant situation models in episodic memory, guide effective search of relevant information in long-term memory, and so on. The control system guarantees that all strategies are geared toward producing information, such as semantic representations (but also pragmatic and other interactional and contextual representations), that is consistent with the overall goals of understanding. The control system incorporates all the information that is needed for processing in short-term memory but that the short-term buffer need not and cannot itself keep in store at each step. Using the compartmental metaphor for the modeling of memory, we will assume that this control system has a specific localization in episodic memory (if we do not want to speak of a more or less separate control memory) such that its information is accessible both to short-term memory and long-term memory processes. In Chapter 10 we will be more specific about these various functions of the memory stores, but we assume throughout that strategies operate under the general monitoring of the control system.

Finally, the model crucially involves large amounts of *knowledge,* both episodic and more general and abstract knowledge as represented in semantic memory. We will assume that fast access and effective retrieval of this knowledge is vital for strategic discourse comprehension, and that such effective retrieval is possible only if knowledge is well organized, for example, according to the many schemalike proposals made in artificial intelligence and various psychological theories in the last few years. However, as already mentioned, we will not present a complete representation format for knowledge. On the whole, we will assume that there *are* various forms of organization, but that these forms are more flexible than rigid frames or scripts. For our purposes, then, we will pay special attention to the *strategies* of knowledge *use.* Instead of a more or less blind activation of all possible knowledge, in the understanding of a word, a clause, or the construction of a global theme, we assume that the use of knowledge is strategic, depending on the goals of the language user, the amount of available knowledge from text and context, the level of processing or the degree of coherence needed for comprehension, which are criteria for strategic knowledge use monitored by the control system. Details of these strategies are given in Chapter 9, but again the following chapters will presuppose a permanent flow of knowledge between long-term memory and short-term memory in order to support the specific comprehension strategies.

What has been said for knowledge also is assumed to hold for other presupposed cognitive information, such as beliefs, opinions, and attitudes. Again, we do not propose any concrete representation models, but it is obvious that most discourse understanding will involve personal beliefs and evaluations. Without these, certain kinds of local and global coherence might not be established at all because they may presuppose personally held beliefs (e.g., about causality) or opinions. Further work on discourse processing will have to take into account the role of these kinds of "hot cognition" (Abelson, 1979; Carbonell, 1978; van Dijk, 1982a; Wegman, 1981).

Within the framework of these more general properties of our model, we can now summarize its various components.

### 1.3.2. Propositional Strategies

The first step of our semantic model involves the strategic construction of propositions. This step, of course, presupposes surface structural decoding of phonetic or graphical strings, the identification of phonemes/letters, and the construction of morphemes, but we will not provide an account of these purely surface strategies. For our purposes, it is sufficient to stress that word recognition strategically depends on underlying semantic interpretation, generating expectations about possible meanings, and hence possible word classes, as well as on the overall syntactic structure of the clause. (For further details about these processes, see Chapter 2.)

Propositions, then, are constructed in our model on the basis of word meanings, activated from semantic memory, and syntactic structures of clauses. In principle, we will assume that there is a strategic one-to-one relationship between propositions and clauses: One clause expresses one proposition. This means, however, that our propositions must be *complex,* according to the usual models from logic or philosophy. Word meanings will usually correspond to what is called an *atomic proposition.* A one-clause sentence like

(1) *The fascists have won the elections in El Salvador.*

would be analyzed into the following atomic propositions:

(2)     (i)   FASCISTS($x_1$)
        (ii)  HAVE WON ($x_1$, $x_2$)
        (iii) ELECTIONS ($x_2$)
        (iv)  IN ($x_2$, $x_3$)
        (v)   EL SALVADOR ($x_3$)

However, a linguistically and cognitively adequate representation of the meaning of (1) cannot be rendered by the list—or a conjunction of the atomic propositions—in (2). The respective concepts or atomic propositions have complex relational structures, or roles, in which words like *fascists* have the role of agents, as is signaled by first position occurrence and grammatical subject in syntactic structure. Hence, we assume that these atomic propositions are organized in a *propositional schema,* involving these structural relations or functions. Such a schema is a strategical unit: It allows a fast analysis of surface structures into a relatively fixed and simple semantic configuration. Thus, a first occurrence grammatical subject noun, or a pronoun, when denoting a person, will be strategically assigned the agent position in such a schema, even before the rest of the clause has been analyzed.

Similarly, complex sentences will be analyzed as complex propositional schemata, in which propositions may be coordinated or mutually embedded under the relevant functional category. In this case, again, surface ordering and hierarchy of clauses will be strategical indications for the ultimate organization of these complex propositional schemata, although other semantic information, for example, from previous sentences or the overall macrostructure, may assign a different structure to the semantic representation of the sentence. In Chapter 4 we will discuss a number of strategies used in this kind of clause and sentence interpretation within texts and contexts.

### 1.3.3. Local Coherence Strategies

Whereas most sentence-based psycholinguistic models of language understanding will stop at this point, our discourse processing model has as its next task the establishment of meaningful connections between successive sentences in a discourse. We summarize the set of strategies involved here under the more general heading of *local coherence* strategies. That is, we assume that the major task of understanding at this point is the construction of local coherence. The main abstract condition on local coherence is that the complex propositions, expressed by the respective clauses or sentences, denote *facts* of some possible world that are related, conditionally or by inclusion (van Dijk, 1977a). Hence, in a cognitive model, the strategic establishment of local coherence requires that the language user search as effectively as possible for potential links among facts denoted by the propositions. Often facts thus related feature identical referents, namely, individual objects or persons. One possible strategy, therefore, is to look for those arguments in a proposition which corefer with one of the arguments of the previous proposition. The argument repetition strategy of our previous work (Kintsch, 1974; Kintsch & van Dijk, 1978) essentially attempted to capture this strategy. But it is only one possible aspect of a more complex local coherence strategy, which requires that whole propositions, and hence whole facts, be connected. Clause ordering, explicit connectives, and knowledge from long-term memory will provide the means of deciding this overall connection between the propositions.

The establishment of local coherence takes place in short-term memory under the general monitoring of the control system, and hence under the scope of a macroproposition. In our previous discourse-processing model (Kintsch & van Dijk, 1978) we assumed that local coherence establishment took place after the complete processing of the clauses or sentences involved. The present strategic model, however, tries to account for the plausible assumption that language users establish coherence as soon as possible, without waiting for the rest of the clause or sentence. They immediately attempt to link, by coreference, for instance, first noun phrases, and hence underlying concepts (atomic propositions), with related concepts in the previous proposition, according to the information from the functional structure of the previous proposition, the topic–comment structure in the subsequent clauses (see Givón, 1979b), or the provisionally assumed role of the concept in the currently processed clause. In Chapter 5 we will formulate a number of these local coherence strategies and report some relevant experimental results.

### 1.3.4. Macrostrategies

A central component of our model is a set of macrostrategies. Such strategies infer macropropositions, of the same structure as the propositions mentioned earlier, from the sequence of propositions expressed, locally, by the text. Macropropositions may again, in a similar strategic way, be connected into sequences. Moreover, by reapplying the relevant inference strategies, we may have several levels of macropropositions, together forming the *macrostructure* of a text. Such a macrostructure is the theoretical account of what we usually call the gist, the upshot, the theme, or the topic, of a text.

In contrast to the abstract macrorules as defined in our earlier work (van Dijk, 1977a, 1980b; Kintsch & van Dijk, 1978), macrostrategies are flexible and have a heuristic character. A language user need not wait until the end of a paragraph, chapter, or whole discourse before being able to infer what the text or the text fragment is about, globally speaking. In other words, it is plausible that with a minimum of textual information from the first propositions, the language user will make guesses about such a topic. These guesses will be sustained by various kinds of information, such as titles, thematic words, thematic first sentences, knowledge about possible ensuing global events or actions, and information from the context. Again we see that an expedient strategy will operate on many kinds of information, which individually are incomplete or insufficient to make the relevant hypothetical assumption. In Chapter 6 we will discuss some of these macrostrategies.

### 1.3.5. Schematic Strategies

Many discourse types seem to exhibit a conventional, and hence culturally variable, schematic structure, an overall form that organizes the macropropositions (the global content of the text). Thus, stories are usually assigned a narrative schema, consisting of a hierarchical structure of conventional categories, such as Setting, Complication, and Resolution. Argumentations and psychological research reports also have their own schemata. Such schemata we will call the *superstructure* of the text, because the term schema is too general and too vague for our purpose. A superstructure provides the overall syntax for the global meaning, the macrostructure, of the text.

Language users manipulate superstructures in a strategic way. They will try to activate a relevant superstructure from semantic memory as soon as the context or the type of text suggests a first cue. From then on, the schema may be used as a powerful top-down processing device for the assignment of relevant superstructure categories (global functions) to each macroproposition—or sequences of macro-propositions—and will at the same time provide some general constraints upon the possible local and global meanings of the textbase. In Chapter 7 some of these strategies will be studied in more detail. There it will also be shown that they cannot simply be reduced to local or even global semantic strategies for the processing of information about human action, as has been proposed by several researchers in artificial intelligence.

### 1.3.6. Production Strategies

Although our model is mainly concerned with discourse comprehension, a complete discourse-processing model should also include a production component. In an abstract discourse theory it does not matter whether the structures are specified by analysis or synthesis, because rules can be formulated both ways as mappings between semantic representations and surface structure expressions and their ordering. In a cognitive model, however, and especially in a strategic model, we cannot simply invert the direction of the mapping. At each point of the comprehension of the production process, the listener and the speaker have access to different kinds of information, so that the relevant strategies will also be different. To wit, a reader or listener will have to figure out in complex ways what the topic of the discourse is, whereas the speaker in many cases, except in some forms of spontaneous conversation, already knows the topic of the discourse to be produced.

Hence, the major task for a speaker is the construction of such a macrostructure as a semantic discourse *plan,* composed of elements from general knowledge and, especially, from elements of the situation model (including a model of the hearer— and his or her knowledge, motivations, past actions, and intentions—and of the communicative context). With this macroplan, the next main task is to strategically execute, at the local and linear level, the textbase, choosing between explicit and implicit information, establishing but also appropriately signaling local coherence, and finally formulating surface structures with the various semantic, pragmatic, and contextual data as controlling input. In accordance with the nature of the comprehension strategies, we will also have to assume here that local proposition formation and local surface structure formulation do not come after the formation of full semantic macrostructures or local propositions, respectively. Speakers will probably start to formulate sentences before the full semantic representation of the sentence has been formed, and the same will hold at the more global level, so that partial or previously formed macrostructures may be changed due to local information constraints. This will especially be the case in conversation and in those monologues which involve contextual feedback from hearers, or parallel observation of ongoing events or actions.

At present we know very little about specific production strategies. However, although these operations and their ordering will be different from those used in comprehension, it does not seem plausible that language users have two completely different and independent systems of strategies. This would even be inconsistent with our general assumption that understanding is not purely passive analysis, but a constructive process. Thus, the important role of top-down processing in understanding also involves partial planning of (expectations about) structures and meanings of sentences and whole texts. Without entering into much detail, in Chapter 8 we will sketch some of the strategic features of a production model. Such a model will at the same time account for the *reproduction* dimension of discourse processing, as in retrieving textual information in recall tasks.

### 1.3.7. Other Strategies

Although we have discussed some major types of strategy in discourse comprehension, these are certainly not the only ones. Both in production and in comprehension we also have a number of *stylistic* strategies. These allow language users to make strategic options between alternative ways of expressing more or less the same meaning or denoting the same referent, under the controlling scope of text type and context information (type of situation, degree of informality, categories of speech participants, and overall goals). Thus, a language user will also have the task of establishing some form of stylistic coherence, selecting or interpreting words from the same register and indicators of the same personal or social situation. For a listener, this means in particular the strategic use of stylistic markers to infer many properties of the speaker or the social context, such as anger, love, cooperation, dominance, or class membership, information that is vital for successful interaction (Sandell, 1977).

Similarly, we may distinguish *rhetorical strategies,* in both the production and the comprehension of rhetorical structures (figures of speech, among others). Whereas the main function of stylistic variation is to signal relations between the discourse and the personal and social context of speaking, rhetorical structures are used to enhance the effectiveness of the discourse and the communicative interaction. Hence, they are strategic by definition because they are only used to better realize the goals of the verbal interaction, such as comprehension, acceptance of the discourse, and successfulness of the speech act.

As such, they do not lead to the construction of semantic representation, but they help in this process. Figures of speech may attract attention to important concepts, provide more cues for local and global coherence, suggest plausible pragmatic interpretations (e.g., a promise versus a threat), and will in general assign more structure to elements of the semantic representation, so that retrieval is easier.

Parallel to the proper verbal interaction that they accomplish when uttering a discourse, language users also have to strategically process *nonverbal information,* such as gestures, facial expressions, proximity, body positions, and so on. Again, these will seldom lead independently to semantic representations in their own right (such as 'an angry face' implies 'The speaker is angry'), but will in general facilitate the strategies of discourse understanding and production. Gestures and facial expressions will suggest which speech act is involved, which further semantic implications should be drawn from local propositions, which are the referents of deictic expressions (Marslen-Wilson, Levy, & Tyler, 1982), and what concepts should be specially attended to, all of which again are markers of possible macrostructures. That is, the properties of nonverbal interaction provide important information for nearly all strategies that we will discuss in this book, as well as for the strategies of interaction in general (Goffman, 1967, 1969; Kendon, Harris, & Key, 1975; Kendon, 1981; Scherer & Ekman, 1982).

These strategies are relevant especially in dyadic discourse types, such as everyday conversations. Both at the textual and the paratextual (nonverbal) level, therefore, there will be a set of specific *conversational strategies,* including moves involving the social and interactional functions of discourse units, such as speech acts or propositions. The system of turn taking, usually formulated in terms of rules, would in a cognitive model require reformulation in terms of expedient strategies of participants in the allocation and appropriation of speaker turns. Besides information from the ongoing utterance, such as syntactic boundary signals or semantic closure of complex propositions, such turn-taking strategies would involve nonverbal information such as direction of gaze, gestures, pauses, or concomitant actions of the participants, in combination with more general social properties of participants and the specific context (who has the right—and the power—to keep or take the floor?) (see Sudnow, 1972; Sacks, Schegloff, & Jefferson, 1974; Schenkein, 1978; Franck, 1980).

The stylistic, rhetorical, nonverbal, and conversational or other interactional strategies briefly mentioned here cannot be treated in this book. It is obvious, however, that at many points they run parallel to or add to the strategies we do discuss, especially because they make semantic interpretation more effective. Due to disambiguation, or marking of personal motivations and intentions of speakers, for example, they help to establish the function of the discourse within the interactional context or the adequate performance and comprehension of speech acts. Current work, especially in nonverbal interaction and conversation, should therefore be reformulated from the perspective of a strategic cognitive model, so that what has been analyzed in a more structural way, or what has been already done on interactional strategies, can be given a solid cognitive basis.

## 1.4. CONCLUSIONS

This chapter has sketched the interdisciplinary backgrounds as well as the major assumptions of our model. It outlines the macrostructure of this book, namely, the various components of a strategic approach to discourse processing. However, it also stresses what the model cannot and will not spell out at the moment, such as surface structure parsing and full knowledge representation. Furthermore, it suggests many ways in which the model could be and should be extended in the future: the role of beliefs, opinions, and attitudes; the nature and the role of stylistic, rhetorical, conversational, and interactional strategies; and, in general, the embedding of the model into a broader model of strategic verbal interaction in the social context. On the other hand, we have briefly suggested how such a social model should at the same time have a cognitive basis, for example, by representing social contexts, situations, participants, and interactions in the cognitive model we propose. Indeed, the strategies we formulate for the semantic interpretation of discourse may well be good examples for a further theory about the understanding, the planning, and hence the participation in interaction. Whereas there is still a theoretical gap between a linguistic theory of language and discourse, on the one hand, and a theory of social interaction on the other, our cognitive model provides a potential link between these two theories. Since we translate abstract textual structures into more concrete, on-line, cognitive processes of a strategic nature, and at the same time would do so for the abstract structures of interaction and social situations, we are able to combine them in a complex way into a model of discourse interaction. Filling in these programmatic statements is, of course, a nontrivial task and a challenge for the future development of an interdisciplinary cognitive science.

# Chapter 2

# Observations on the Status of Experimental Research on Discourse Comprehension

A thorough, comprehensive review and evaluation of the rapidly expanding research on discourse processing would take us too far away from the main concerns of this book. Instead, we shall try to present here a highly selective and biased review. We want to make some points that are important for the understanding of the matters on which this book will be focused, and we want to examine some of the details of the psychological background from which our work derives. Thus, we shall discuss the research on discourse comprehension as we see it from the vantage point of our own work, and emphasize those trends that we perceive to be important for providing a perspective on that work, either in terms of historical antecedents and parallels or as contrasts.

## 2.1. PERCEPTUAL PROCESSES: LETTER AND WORD IDENTIFICATION

Although our own model completely neglects the perceptual components of the comprehension process, we need to make a few remarks about the research in this area. It is a comparatively well-developed field of research, with a rich empirical data base and a history of instructive theoretical controversies. Some of the problems that we shall be concerned with later on have well-studied analogues at this level. The theoretical framework developed in these studies of letter identification and word recognition also forms the basis for our approach to higher level comprehension processes.

### 2.1.1. Top-down Effects

The most basic result that is of importance for us here is that the perception of letters is influenced by our knowledge about words; that the recognition of words is influenced by the sentence context in which they are presented; and that sentence processing itself is determined by the status of the sentence in a text, as we shall see later. Thus, reading[1] is not simply a sequence of processes starting with feature detection and letter identification, and continuing through word recognition and sentence parsing to more global discourse processing. Instead of a sequence of bottom-up processing, we have a situation in which higher level processes affect the lower ones; that is, we have top-down effects with which to contend. This situation is far from simple, and we shall have to analyze more closely the evidence for the claims just made and the theoretical models that have been proposed to grapple with all this complexity.

Nearly a hundred years ago Cattell (1886) observed that when letter strings were presented on a tachistoscope, subjects were able to report more letters when the letters formed a word than when they did not. Although these results were replicated many times (Huey, 1908), their implications were never quite clear. Since subjects in these experiments had to report whole letter strings, it is possible that the effects which were observed so reliably had nothing to do with perception per se, but could be ascribed to postperceptual processes. Although subjects reported the letters they had seen immediately, some forgetting may still have occurred, and words are easier to retain than random strings of letters. In addition, if perception is fragmentary, subjects in the word condition have a great advantage because they can often guess missing letters in a word, whereas no such guessing is possible with random letter strings.

Thus, it was not really known whether or not Cattell's data implied that familiar words somehow facilitated the perception of the letters they contained. In 1969 Reicher—and many others since then—showed that they did indeed. Reicher presented target letters tachistoscopically under three conditions: as part of a word, as part of an unpronounceable nonword, or in isolation, always followed by a patterned mask. Only one of the letters was then tested by a two-alternative forced choice test which was designed so that both of the alternatives formed familiar words. For instance, suppose the target letter was *C;* the presentation strings then might be *CAR, CTA,* or *C* alone, and on the test the subject had to decide whether a *C* or an *H* was presented. Even under these conditions, subjects performed better when the target letter was part of a word than when it was part of a nonword or alone. Neither differential guessing nor differential forgetting can explain these results. It appears that being part of a word made the letter easier to see.

The situation with respect to word recognition is similar. It is clear that context affects word recognition. Words are easier to perceive when they are part of a meaningful sentence (Tulving & Gold, 1963, and studies thereafter) or part of a

---

[1]Most of the studies discussed here are concerned with reading, but similar arguments could be made about listening.

meaningful text (Wittrock, Marks, & Doctorow, 1975). To account for these results, several authors have proposed two-process theories, where a bottom-up, data-driven analysis process interacts with a top-down, knowledge-driven hypothesis-testing process. The basic idea is that context effects have two sources (Stanovich & West, 1981). On the one hand, there is an automatic facilitation of perception. Context automatically activates some pathways, and this activation benefits the perception of words that use these pathways, without cost to words that do not. On the other hand, there is controlled hypothesis testing. Hypothesizing a particular word benefits perception if the hypothesis turns out to be correct, but interferes with perception if it is incorrect. (The cost–benefit model of Posner & Snyder, 1975, was applied to this problem by Stanovich & West, 1981.)

### 2.1.2. Good and Poor Readers

The full complex nature of the interaction between these top-down and bottom-up processes becomes apparent if one looks at the contrast between good and poor readers in these terms. What exactly distinguishes a good reader from a bad reader? One popular suggestion is that the good reader is more adroit at exploiting the regularities and redundancies inherent in language and does not bother much with laborious bottom-up decoding letter by letter or word by word. Thus, Goodman (1976) referred to reading as a "psycholinguistic guessing game," and Smith (1973) argued that reading instruction should rely as little as possible on decoding skills. Indeed, there is a great deal of evidence that good readers are more skilled at exploiting higher order constraints in a text. Perfetti and Roth (1981), for instance, have shown that good readers' hypotheses about a word more fully reflect all the relevant information in a text. Meyer, Brandt, and Bluth (1980) observed that good readers were more responsive to rhetorical structure than were poor readers. Several other studies with similar results could be cited, all showing that good readers are better top-down processors; they are good because they know how to use context[2] more efficiently.

However, we immediately run into a paradox: Context effects are most pronounced in poor readers! If one looks at the occurrence of semantically appropriate substitution errors in reading, they are more likely to be found in poor readers than good readers (e.g., Kolers, 1975). The greatest facilitation of word recognition by meaningful context is observed with poor readers, not with good readers (e.g., Perfetti, Goldman, & Hogaboam, 1979). Furthermore, it is simply not true that good readers take decoding lightly; they fixate almost every content word (Just & Carpenter, 1980), and they do it so carefully that they are better able than poor readers to detect misspellings and visual irregularities in a word (McConkie & Zola, 1981). It has been found over and over again that the best discriminator between

---

[2]In Chapter 1 we have distinguished between (con)*textual* factors and the general situational context. In the research we review here the situational context is often not considered explicitly and the term context is taken to refer to the verbal context of a sentence or word.

good and poor readers is performance on simple letter and word identification tasks (see Perfetti & Lesgold, 1977, for representative results). What is really wrong with poor readers is that they recognize isolated words inaccurately and too slowly, and compensate for their lack in decoding skills with context-dependent guessing or hypothesis testing. Therefore, they depend very much on contextual cues, and, if these are absent or misleading, their performance suffers. Good readers with their superior decoding skills can decode letters and words rapidly in a bottom-up fashion, and therefore do not normally need to resort to guessing strategies. In this view, context effects are only symptoms; what is really at issue are the speed and accuracy of context-free word recognition operations (Stanovich & West, 1981).

Thus, we have two findings which appear contradictory at first sight: Context effects are most notable with poor readers, but good readers are better at exploiting context cues. But there is no paradox here. Good readers are simply better than poor readers, both when it comes to decoding skills and to guessing skills (Carr, 1981). They form better, more sophisticated, hypotheses during reading. They do not have to resort continuously to hypothesis-testing processes (as poor readers are forced to do because of their deficient decoding skills), but when they do, they do it well. Frederiksen (1981), among others, reports data that show this very clearly. In one of his experiments, subjects were given a sentence with the last word missing. They were then shown a target word which they were required to pronounce. If the target word fit into the context sentence, pronunciation latencies were reduced compared to a condition where isolated words had to be read. If the sentence strongly constrained the target word, both good and poor readers showed large priming effects (savings of about 125 msec); if the context was only weakly constraining, however, there was a priming effect for good readers but not for poor readers. Good readers were still able to exploit weak contexts. Somehow, they prepared for a large number of possible target words. Poor readers under these conditions were able to generate only a few candidates for the target word and hence were usually unprepared. For them, the weak context simply was not enough. Frederiksen theorizes that poor readers generate contextually relevant lexical items via a slow, controlled serial process, whereas good readers have available a parallel automatic process that produces a much greater pool of items. Perhaps, however, both good and poor readers rely on automatic spreading activation type processes, except that the good readers do so with more success because they can afford to devote more resources to this process. In contrast, the resources of the poor readers are exhausted by the decoding process and hence the activation for them is weak and reaches too small a pool of items.

In another experiment, Frederiksen (1981) collected pronunciation onset times for words and pseudowords of different orthographic structures. He found, for instance, that pronunciation latencies for three-syllable strings were greater than for two-syllable strings, resulting in a substantial correlation between structurally matched word and pseudoword pairs. However, when the words were presented in a strongly constraining context, that correlation went to zero for the good readers, but not for the bad readers: The good readers were able to develop task-specific response strategies that completely bypassed orthographic analysis, whereas the poor readers who show the lowest skill in decoding could not give it up.

### 2.1.3. Theories of Word Recognition

The brief review given here certainly does not do justice to the complexity and richness of the word recognition literature, but perhaps it is sufficient to indicate (a) that matters are complex, indeed, and (b) that there is rhyme and reason to the seeming chaos. Such a state of affairs is a challenge to theorists, and they have lived up to it rather well. Theories of word recognition, starting with the Pandemonium model of Selfridge and Neisser (1960) and Morton's logogen model (Morton, 1969) have been successively refined, up to the most recent generation of models (Adams & Collins, 1979; Perfetti & Lesgold, 1977; McClelland & Rumelhart, 1981; Stanovich, 1980).

These new models are all interactive models. The evidence against the traditional view of reading as extricating-information-from-text is overwhelming, as we have just seen, ruling out pure bottom-up models. Pure top-down models have never really existed, strictly speaking, because pure top-down processing is psychologically absurd. The question is how to conceptualize the interactions. Without discussion of any specific model here, some common principles can be determined. First, there is the notion of a logogen or word demon as a place where evidence regarding a word (or letter) is accumulated. Any stimulus input activates in parallel a number of letter and word logogens, as shown in Figure 2.1 which is taken from McClelland and Rumelhart (1981). Note that in this particular model there are both inhibitory and facilitory connections. Note, furthermore, that in this model features do not directly feed into word logogens. Conceivably, the feature 'horizontal-bar-on-top' might have a direct facilitory connection with ABLE, TRAP, etc., and inhibitory connections with other words—all too many such connections, indeed. Similarly, why not have TRIP facilitate the detection of the feature 'vertical-bar-in-center', etc.? The question that arises, then, is what is the architecture of such systems, what interacts with what?[3]

There is good reason to believe that the general form of a word analysis system is that of a cascade rather than a strict hierarchy (McClelland, 1979). In a cascade, output from a particular level feeds not only into adjacent levels, up or down, but also, possibly, to more distant higher and lower levels. In a completely interacting system every level is allowed to interact with every other. The complexity of such a system would be horrendous, and much of it probably wasted. It is an empirical question which levels in a system interact, and how (though theoretical simulations might provide important clues concerning calculational feasibility and efficiency).

Researchers have just begun to ask such questions and to develop the models that are essential for answering them. A great deal of progress has been made,

---

[3]Other important components of the model, such as the mathematics of the activation and response generation processes, are of no direct interest here.

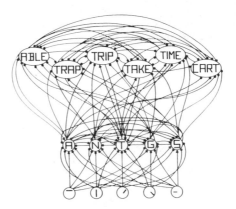

**Figure 2.1.**   A few of the neighbors of the node for the letter *T* in the first position in a word, and their interconnections. (From J. L. McClelland & D. E. Rumelhart, An interactive activation model of context effects in letter perception. *Psychological Review,* 1981, *88,* 375–407. Copyright 1981 by the American Psychological Association. Reprinted by permission of the author.)

though, and the framework that has evolved appears to be a useful and enduring one. It also appears to be a general one, in that the same type of model that has been proposed for word recognition processes is also suitable for modeling comprehension processes at other levels. In what follows, we shall expand this picture to include other levels of comprehension.

### 2.1.4. Implication

Before leaving word recognition, however, some general observations need to be made about the status of research in that area. First, we note that we have obtained a lot of useful information about the process of word identification in reading from some very artificial laboratory studies, using tasks quite unlike "real reading." Reading is most certainly not tachistoscopic word recognition. Carr (1981) points out that in naming or lexical decision tasks meanings are activated by the input to the human information-processing system very early in the course of the interaction between that system and a word. A word needs to be seen only for 30–40 msec for a full semantic activation (though, of course, no responses can be made in that time—responses occur only 500–1500 msec after a word's onset). Fixations during reading typically last for about 200–300 msec. From the standpoint of word identification, most of that time appears wasted—but, then, reading is not just word identification; it is that plus a lot more. Thus, the difference between reading and word identification must not be overlooked, yet the experimental work on word identification has proved to be very informative and has greatly increased our understanding of reading.

Second, it bears mentioning that although we are talking about the process of word identification, this is not a single process, nor is it a unitary skill. Rather, there are a number of separate components representing perceptual and linguistic sub-processes (Frederiksen, 1977). Gross oversimplification and distortion results unless the full complexity of the system is taken into account.

Finally, we have to face openly some of the consequences of dealing with such complex systems. Note that we have discussed experiments in which good readers were better users of context, experiments in which they did not use context, experiments in which poor readers relied most heavily on context, and so on—and somehow the same theory accounted for all these diverse, not to say contradictory, results! Do we have here a vacuous supertheory that simply "explains" everything? Surely, the theory that explains everything explains nothing. The problem is, however, that people actually do all these diverse and contradictory things. Indeed, the most general law of behavior seems to be that people will do almost everything and its opposite, given the right conditions. A theory, therefore, has to take into account this diversity and be ready to explain $X$ as well as not-$X$. It is nonvacuous insofar as it specifies the precise conditions under which $X$ and not-$X$ occur, or under which an observation is evidence for $X$ or its opposite. An observation may have many causes, and it may confirm $X$ under some circumstances and not-$X$ under others. Theories have to be complex because the world is complex, but they must not be arbitrary. We mention this dilemma here in talking about other people's theories, but we shall meet it again in our own work.

## 2.2. SYNTACTIC–SEMANTIC PARSING

In considering how people parse discourse we are still below the level at which our model operates, but once again it is important to inquire what we know about such processes to see how our own proposals might fit (or not fit) into a more general model of comprehension.

When people communicate via language, their normal purpose (except in some specific situations, e.g., literary ones) is to communicate some semantic content and/or a pragmatic message. The former is predominant in written communication (though never exclusive), whereas in some types of conversations the semantic content may be subordinated to pragmatic goals. Syntax, phonology, morphology, and nonverbal expressions, in either case, serve in a supporting role. Complex semantic contents can only be expressed or understood clearly with the help of syntax, and syntax can make language communication more efficient.

### 2.2.1. The Phrase as a Processing Unit

Discourse comprehension (or production) always operates under the constraints imposed by the limits of the human information-processing system. Limitations imposed by the capacity of short-term memory are particularly serious ones in processing the continuous flow of a discourse. One cannot retain everything one reads or hears for very long, and thus it becomes crucial to know when to discard what. The syntactic phrase structure of a text provides an important clue for how to chunk it into reasonable units. Thus, one function of syntactic cues in a text is to permit effective short-term monitoring (at this level of analysis—additional considerations enter at the propositional level and macrolevel).

There is a great deal of psychological evidence that readers and listeners are sensitive to the phrase structure of sentences and chunk sentences accordingly. Most of this evidence is well known and has been reviewed repeatedly (e.g., Kintsch, 1977a), so that we shall do no more here than cite a few seminal studies. Thus, the famous click studies, for all the controversies that surrounded them, in the final analysis show pretty clearly that readers segment text at phrase boundaries (e.g., Garrett, Bever, & Fodor, 1966). As far as short-term memory is concerned, Jarvella (1971) and others have shown that readers hold the final phrase in short-term memory, dumping it when they arrive at a clause boundary. Jarvella employed a free recall paradigm, while Caplan (1972) arrived at the same conclusion using a recognition test. Through an analysis of the transition errors made between words, Johnson (1965) could show that most errors made in learning a sentence occur at major clause boundaries. For perception as well as memory, it seems clear that at this level of analysis the clause is the functional psychological unit. As we look at the problems involved more closely, we shall have to modify this blunt claim somewhat (Section 2.2.3), because we shall see that it is not the clause boundaries themselves that are important, but the ways in which people use them in their processing.

## 2.2.2. Parsing Strategies

The question arises of how people detect clause boundaries in a sentence, and how they derive its syntactic structure. One class of theories holds that they rely on linguistic rules: People have implicit knowledge of linguistic rules, which they apply in parsing a sentence. What these rules are varies with the particular theorists; thus, in some classical examples they were phrase structure rules, as in Yngve (1961), or transformational rules, as in Miller and McKean (1964). Alternatively, the parsing may be done on the basis of strategies. We shall discuss the strategy concept in much more detail in the next chapter. Here, the relevant contrast is between a closed, logical system of rules, the application of which will, sooner or later, guarantee the correct parsing of whatever input string was used, and an open, nondeterministic, fuzzy system employing strategies.

Strategy theories of sentence comprehension were introduced by Bever (1970), and have been more recently discussed by Clark and Clark (1977). The reason for introducing strategies was that some of the rule systems that linguists were using to parse sentences were implausible as psychological process models: The calculations involved, the resources demanded, simply exceeded human processing limitations. Strategies were simpler. They did not guarantee the right result, or even a unique result, but it was plausible that people could parse sentences on the basis of strategies. Very soon, evidence was compiled showing that people really do operate that way.

Again, there is no point in systematically reviewing the literature, because the basic findings have been discussed elsewhere (e.g., Clark & Clark, 1977). Instead, we shall merely present some illustrations of parsing strategies that have been identified by various authors, as well as some of the relevant experimental evidence.

STRATEGY EXAMPLE 1. *Whenever you find a function word, begin a new constituent larger than one word* (Clark & Clark, 1977), which has the specific subcase: *Whenever you find a determiner (a, the), begin a new noun phrase* (Bever, 1970). A parser using this strategy can be tricked into making mistakes, as the following "garden path" sentence shows: *The old man the boats.* The determiner *the* sets up an expectation for a noun phrase, *old man* is interpreted accordingly— and then has to be reinterpreted when the second noun phrase comes in, because NP + NP does not yield S (we expect a VP after a NP). This reinterpretation disrupts the comprehension process.

STRATEGY EXAMPLE 2. Another subcase of the same general strategy is *Whenever you find a relative pronoun (that, which, who, whom), begin a new clause* (Clark & Clark, 1977). This strategy implies that sentences in which relative clauses are signaled by a relative pronoun will be easier to parse than sentences without such a signal. It has been shown experimentally that this is indeed the case, at least for self-embedding sentences. In one relevant experiment, for instance, Fodor and Garrett (1967) had subjects paraphrase sentences such as

(1)    *The pen which the author whom the editor liked used was new.*
(2)    *The pen the author the editor liked used was new.*

The relative pronouns were clearly helpful to the subjects, as indicated by their ability to paraphrase sentences like (1) faster and better than sentences like (2). Similarly, Hakes and Foss (1970) showed that when subjects were asked to detect a particular phoneme in a sentence they were listening to, their reaction times were slower for sentences of the second type than for sentences of the first type. This observation is taken as evidence that when the sentences lacked relative pronouns, subjects had to apply more of their resources to the parsing task, and had less left over for the secondary phoneme detection task.

STRATEGY EXAMPLE 3. *Try to attach each word to the constituent that came just before.* Kimball (1973) and Clark and Clark (1977) provide an interesting example for this memory-saving strategy. Consider the following sentence:

(3)    *The dog that was rabid came from New York.*

Here the strategy works fine; the relative clause *that was rabid* gets properly attached to *the dog.* But we run into a problem in Sentence (4):

(4)    *The dog came from New York that was rabid.*

The strategy tells us to attach the relative clause to *New York;* this does not work semantically, and we have to reinterpret the sentence. In Sentence (5), the situation is worse yet:

(5)     *The dog bit the fox that was rabid.*

If the speaker of (5) intended the dog to be rabid, the strategic comprehension process will misinterpret (5): *that was rabid* will be attached to *fox,* and this time there is no semantic safeguard to prevent the misinterpretation.

STRATEGY EXAMPLE 4. *Use semantic constraints to identify syntactic function* was one of the original five strategies described by Bever (1970); it was subsequently elaborated and refined by Clark and Clark (1977). This strategy is a very important one, and in extreme cases it allows the construction of propositional representations directly from the sentence, bypassing syntactic analysis altogether. If we want to say *Dog bites man,* we can do without syntax (though we need it for the more interesting *Man bites dog*). In other cases, although the syntactic cues are there, they are simply not used, as when 2- and 3-year-old children treat the following sentences all alike:

(6)     *The cat chased the mouse.*
(7)     *The mouse was chased by the cat.*
(8)     *The mouse chased the cat.*
(9)     *The cat was chased by the mouse.*

The children know that the cat chases the mouse—and that is what all of these sentences mean to them (Strohner & Nelson, 1974).

STRATEGY EXAMPLE 5. *Select the grammatical subject of an initial sentence as the preferred referent for a pronoun occurring in a following sentence.* This is one of several strategies identified by Frederiksen (1981) for establishing the referents of anaphora. Consider the following:

(10)     *Modern advertising does not, as a rule, seek to demonstrate the superior quality of the product.*
(11)     *The superior quality of the product is not, as a rule, what modern advertising seeks to demonstrate.*
(12)     *It plays up to the desire of Americans to conform, to be like the Joneses.*

The reading times for (12) are faster when (12) follows (10) so that the *it* refers to the subject of the preceding sentence, then when it follows (11) where this is not the case. We shall show in what follows (Experiment 2, Section 5.5) that this subject strategy is only one of several strategies used in pronoun identification, and apparently not the dominant one: Agent role, recency, and especially topicality must also be considered.

Of course, there are interactions among strategies. For instance, another strategy that readers use in identifying pronoun referents is a minimum distance principle—roughly, *try the closest noun phrase*. If that were the dominant strategy, the *it* in (12) would be easier to identify following (11), where the·referent *modern advertising* comes at the end of the sentence, than following (10), where it is at the beginning. It is probably quite easy to bias subjects in favor of another strategy (e.g., through the establishment of an experimental set in favor of a particular kind of anaphoric relationship), and thus to obtain experimental results that are exactly the opposite of Frederiksen's.

To avoid misunderstandings, it should be emphasized that the term strategy is used in all this work without any connotations of consciousness or intentionality.[4] On the contrary, comprehension strategies are generally unconscious. Strategic behavior is neither necessarily controlled nor necessarily automatic in the sense of Shiffrin and Schneider (1977). Like other behaviors, it varies from controlled (i.e., slow, sequential, resource demanding) to automatic (fast, parallel, effortless) as a function of stage of practice. The child, in the process of acquiring a strategy, uses it quite differently than does the mature speaker of the language. For the latter, what were once demanding tasks have become fully automated with very low resource demands—unless, of course, the smooth operation of strategies is blocked (as in the garden path sentences), and attention-demanding, controlled, repair processes are required.

It is important to realize that although strategic systems are nondeterministic, open ended, and highly context sensitive, theories that have these properties may nevertheless be stated with precision and the objectivity required for a scientific theory. A favored way to model sentence parsing is as an Augmented Transition Network (Woods, 1970; Wanner & Maratsos, 1977). There is nothing in this formalism that says that it must inherently be either rule based or strategy based. Either kind of model could be implemented as an ATN model (Kaplan, 1972). Alternatively, parsing can be modeled as a production system (J. R. Anderson, 1976). Again, production systems are neutral with respect to the strategy-versus-rule issue.

In our discussion of the word recognition literature in the previous section of this chapter, we concentrated on the interactive nature of the process. Top-down, predictive, hypothesis testing was shown to combine with bottom-up, stimulus driven, analysis. This is just as much the case when it comes to parsing a sentence. Because strategies function as predictors, they induce top-down processing. Thus, if you find a determiner, look for a noun phrase; if you have identified a verb, search for its corresponding arguments; if you have a content word with a conjunction at the beginning of a clause (such as *Mary and*), look for another content word of the same kind as the first one (*Bill*). Thus, an interactive processing model with top-down and bottom-up components is just as appropriate for the parsing level as it was for the word identification level of comprehension.

---

[4]These matters are discussed more fully in the next chapter. We merely anticipate here a few crucial points which are relevant in the present context.

## 2.2.3. Sentence Processing in Discourse

We end this review of the sentence parsing literature with a caveat. We have learned a lot from these studies, but if we are interested in discourse comprehension we must beware of taking for granted the relevance of sentence grammars and psychological experiments using sentence lists. Understanding sentences as part of a discourse is a different process from understanding sentences in isolation. Irrespective of the particular form of the sentence, what may be important is how well the sentence can be integrated semantically with the previous discourse (Haviland & Clark, 1974; Huggins & Adams, 1980). How fast we can read a sentence depends on its discourse context (Haberlandt, 1980; Sanford & Garrod, 1981). How much difficulty fourth-graders have with various syntactic forms depends on the context in which they are used; there are very few forms children cannot understand in at least some context (Lesgold, 1974).

We are interested in the strategies people use when they read a text—a book chapter for an exam, or a story for their entertainment. These strategies may be quite different from the ones subjects adopt in a psychological experiment. In order to have a well-controlled experiment, the experimenter typically arranges an artificial, underdetermined situation in which to study the subjects' strategies. Such situations are new to the subject; his or her normal strategies fail precisely because the experimental material has to be well controlled, which means that the usual redundancies on which these strategies rely have been removed from the text. Hence, the subject falls back on general problem-solving strategies and devises on the spot some procedure that works. The trouble is that this procedure may be entirely task specific and of no general interest as far as normal discourse processing is concerned. Thus, if we observe in the laboratory how people identify anaphora when they are given lists of sentence pairs in which certain well-controlled anaphoric relationships are built in, we might identify such strategies as minimum distance or subject preference, as mentioned earlier. But we need additional evidence to determine whether and to what extent these strategies are used in reading a text, or in producing a discourse. We might be left with quite the wrong conclusions from such experiments (and give quite the wrong advice to educators, textbook writers, etc.). Karmiloff-Smith (1981), for instance, has observed how children of various ages and skill levels use pronouns in producing a story. In this situation, the strategies for anaphoric reference that have been identified from sentence experiments play a negligible role. Basically, the strategies these children use are discourse determined. Thus, at a certain age level, children may reserve the pronoun for the hero of the story (if there is only one); later, when they use a pronoun to refer to someone/something else, they add an identifying noun phrase (e.g., "he–the one with the balloons"); if a story has two main characters, yet another strategy for pronoun use is employed, and so on. Studying sentences in isolation may tell us something, but it is also possible that it will mislead us. (See also Marslen-Wilson, Levy, & Tyler, 1982, as well as Chapter 5 of this volume.)

## 2.3. AMBIGUITY

Neither words nor sentences are mapped into meanings one-to-one, and psycholinguistic research, from the very beginning, has been fascinated by the issue of ambiguity. It is an important issue, indeed, and a complex one, and we shall have to examine it in some detail to determine how our model is to deal with the ambiguities that are inherent in the use of language. We shall first start with a discussion of the identification of ambiguous words, which does not really concern our model directly, but which will form an important background for the treatment of ambiguity in the construction of sentence and discourse meanings.

### 2.3.1. Lexical Decisions

Introspections about sentence ambiguity are quite compelling. If we hear on the radio

(13)     *Three masked gunmen robbed a bank yesterday.*

we are not aware of the alternative meaning of *bank* as river bank. If someone says in the supermarket

(14)     *These brown ones over there, they are cooking bananas.*

we are not aware of an alternative parsing with *are cooking* as the verb and *bananas* as the object. This suggests an intelligent word recognition mechanism that somehow uses the context in (13) to retrieve the right meaning of *bank* without even considering alternatives. In parsing (14), the fact that *they* is deictically identified as brown objects immediately precludes the alternative parsing of the syntactically ambiguous second phrase requiring an animate subject. So much for intuition. What are the facts?

In the case of lexical retrieval, they flatly contradict intuition. When people read a lexically ambiguous word in a text they retrieve all of its meanings, contextually appropriate or not. A choice is then made among these alternatives, and the inappropriate meanings are rapidly deactivated. There is considerable converging evidence on this issue, but the clearest results are those of Swinney (1979). Swinney used a cross-modality priming task, in which the primary task of a subject is to listen to a text presented over earphones, and later to answer some questions about it, to make sure it was properly comprehended. In parallel with this, the subject performs a lexical decision task: On a screen in front of the subject, letter strings are presented from time to time, and the subject has to react as fast as possible by pressing one key if the letters form a word and another key if they do not. It is well known that in such a task priming effects occur: The subject is faster at deciding that something is a word if it is closely related to a word presented auditorily at the same time. Thus, if the subject hears *On the flower sat a large yellow butterfly which. . . .* and the word *insect* is presented visually simultaneously with *butterfly*, *insect* is identified as a word more rapidly than appropriate control words that are not related to *butterfly*. There will be a savings of around 40 msec, which is called a priming effect.

Swinney used lexically ambiguous words in this task. He showed that, for example, when subjects hear the sentence

(15)     *The house crawled with cockroaches and bugs were everywhere.*

words presented visually at the termination of *bugs* were primed equally whether they were related to the contextually appropriate meaning of *bug* as insect or to the inappropriate meaning of spying device. Thus, in (15), both *spider* and *spy* would be primed by *bugs*. However, if a delay is introduced between *bugs* and *spider* or *spy*, only the contextually correct meaning will exert a priming effect. After about 500 msec, only *spider* is primed by *bugs*, but not *spy*.

Thus, when a lexically ambiguous word is encountered during reading, all meanings of the word (though not their *full* meanings, presumably) are activated momentarily and offered to a context-based decision process for selection. The selection of the appropriate meaning is made quite rapidly, and inappropriate alternatives are suppressed without ever reaching the threshold of awareness.

Actually, this is precisely what psychologists should have suspected all the time because it is also how perception works. The perceptual system prefers to process all kinds of information rather than filtering out everything that is not relevant at the moment. The whole flux of stimulation around us is continuously monitored at an unconscious level. Unconscious does not necessarily mean superficial, and a lot of evidence exists today that this unconscious perceptual processing extends to the level of meaningfulness. However, only a small subset of what is taken in is selected for further processing and ever becomes a conscious percept. The capacity limitations of human information processing do not limit the perceptual processes per se, but have to do with consciousness and memory. Psychologists only became aware of this important fact about human information processing, as the history of theories of attention shows, in the time between Broadbent's filter model (Broadbent, 1958) and current all-processing theories (Shiffrin & Geisler, 1973). Kintsch (1977a) describes this shift in our conception of the nature of capacity limitations in some detail. Word identification is a kind of perception. It works as a parallel system that fully analyzes the input for all possible interpretations and then picks out what it needs. It does not make shrewd guesses early on, but uses all the information available and only later decides. The cost is a lot of brute force calculation—as it is elsewhere in the perceptual system. The benefit is that the final decisions are made in a fully informed maneuver, and hence are more likely to be the correct ones.

### 2.3.2. Multiple Paths in Sentence Parsing

Do we understand sentences in the same manner as we perceive words? That is, do we work on many possible parsings in parallel, or do we make the kind of early commitments introspection suggests? The answer is at present unknown. There are no a priori reasons why sentence parsing has to work the same way as word recognition. Indeed, there are some good arguments why it should be different. Lexical items are relatively fixed chunks in memory and their retrieval is highly automatized. But we do not automatically retrieve sentences, let alone discourse meanings; rather, we construct them. It may not be very expedient to construct many irrelevant alternatives. In fact, if we did so for all contexts, we might invite a combinatorial explosion. It is quite possible that the higher mental processes differ from perception in this respect.

It is equally possible, however, that the parsing process relies on extensive calculations in much the same way that perceptual processes do. Woods (1980) strongly advocates this view from a computational standpoint. He describes various methods used in artificial intelligence for exploring multiple evaluations of a sentence, such as backtracking, where, while one alternative is being explored, information relevant for others is carefully retained for possible later use, or separate virtual processing, where alternatives are followed up in parallel, until a choice among them can be made on the basis of some higher level plausibility judgment.

It is certainly impossible to understand sentences on the basis of local information alone. Consider the following sentence (cited after Woods, 1980):

(16)    *The city council refused to grant the women a parade permit because*

$$they \begin{Bmatrix} feared \\ \\ advocated \end{Bmatrix} violence.$$

With either verb in penultimate position the sentence is readily understood. But how do we pick one referent for *they* with *feared* and another one with *advocated?* The strategies that we have discussed thus far at best provide the right candidates (subject bias in one case, and minimum distance in the other), but to actually make the identification, quite extensive additional computations must be involved. Local constraints alone are insufficient: Either the council or the women can fear as well as advocate. Thus, it would seem that in understanding (16) all possible pronoun referents are computed and the one that makes sense globally is eventually adopted, much the way ambiguous content words are treated. Indeed, there is direct evidence that people compute all possible referents for a pronoun. Frederiksen (1981) reports that sentences with an ambiguous pronoun take much longer to read than unambiguous target sentences (277 msec/syllable versus 208 msec/syllable). All alternative referents for a pronoun (i.e., nouns that agree in gender and number) are retrieved when a pronoun is encountered, and a selection is then made that fits the semantic constraints of the text.

Parsers operating in this manner will necessarily have to do a large amount of computation. Nevertheless, even if computations are cheap, there must be some limit to how much can be computed. One suggestion that we would like to offer is that clause boundaries serve as decision points: Alternatives are explored in parallel within a clause, but when a major boundary is reached, a selection is made and the nonselected alternatives are discarded. Bever, Garrett, and Hurtig (1973) have argued that this is indeed the case. They showed that although people find it harder to complete ambiguous phrases such as

(17)     *Although flying airplanes can . . .*

than they do suitable unambiguous control phrases (MacKay, 1966), this is no longer true when they are given still ambiguous but completed clauses, such as

(18)     *Although flying airplanes can be dangerous, he . . .*

After having crossed the clause boundary, people are apparently left with only one reading of (18). Clark and Clark (1977) point out that the reason clause boundaries are so important may simply be due to that fact that most strategies deal with constituents no larger than the clause. In most cases, local information is probably sufficient, hence the psychological effects of clause boundaries. As we have seen, however, local constraints are not always powerful enough, and comprehension still proceeds smoothly as in (16), or local constraints can be misleading and disrupt comprehension as in garden path sentences.

Whether a clause boundary forms an effective decision point in a sentence appears to depend on several factors. If a clause is very short, there is very little incentive for segmenting the discourse at that point and erasing computations (Carroll & Bever, 1976). The deciding factor, however, appears to be whether the processing strategy employed requires information from beyond the clause. If a clause is semantically complete, it acts as a processing unit; if the semantic interpretation cannot be completed within the clause, the clause boundary is ineffective. An experiment by Marslen-Wilson, Tyler, and Seidenberg (1978) using a rhyme-monitoring procedure showed this quite clearly. Subjects were asked to monitor sentences for words rhyming with a given target word, and the latency of their detection response was taken as a measure of the accessibility of the sentence in memory. When subjects were asked to monitor the following two sentences for a word that rhymes with *doubt*, their latencies were longer in (19b) than in (19a):

(19)     a. *Although Mary rarely cooks trout, when she does it is delicious.*
         b. *Although Mary rarely cooks, trout is one thing she prepares well.*

In (19a) the rhyming word *trout* comes at the end of the phrase and is therefore highly constrained and detected more rapidly than in (19b) where it follows a segmentation point in the sentence. The clause boundary in (20b), however, is quite ineffective (monitor for a word that rhymes with *bats*):

(20)     a. *Even though they are quite small cats, they need a lot of space.*
         b. *Even though they are quite small, cats need a lot of space.*

*Cats* is detected equally fast in either context, showing that the clause boundary in (20b) did not have the same effect as in (19b). The difference is that (20b) is not semantically complete. Computations cannot be finished and erased at the clause boundary because *they* still needs to be identified. As Clark and Clark suggested, it is not the clause boundary per se, but people's processing strategies that are important.

What happens when we comprehend larger discourse units? Do people compute alternative macrostructures, eventually settling on the most promising one? Introspectively, we appear to be committed to one interpretation, and if we suddenly realize a text is about something quite different than we thought, we experience a conscious, effortful reconstruction not unlike the one in garden path sentences.[5] But too much reliance on introspection would clearly be foolish in this case and definitive experimental results are not available as yet. Thus, we simply note that the theory of comprehension advocated here explicitly assumes that only a single alternative is followed up at a time in organizing a text. Our organizational strategies choose a single knowledge proposition in terms of which to organize the semantic units of a text. Once the choice is made, the process is committed to it, until conditions are ripe for a new choice. There is no parallel exploration of alternative text organizations. Although this is clearly different from what happens at the word identification level, such a model is not implausible. Brute force computations may be the best solution when there are relatively few retrievable alternatives, as in word disambiguation, but it is hard to see how it could be employed at the higher levels of analysis without totally overwhelming the system. It may very well be the case that at this level perception is different from comprehension. We do not know that it is, but working out in some detail one of the alternatives should help us to decide this tricky but important issue one way or another.

## 2.4. SEMANTIC UNITS: PROPOSITIONS

In order to study the semantic components of discourse processing, some representation of the content of elementary meaning units is required. Linguists, computer scientists, and psychologists have developed a number of conventions for the representation of meaning involving propositional units. Differences between the various systems are often not very important (e.g., it is merely a matter of convenience whether graphic network representations are used or list-based representations). Among the early developments within linguistics we mention Vendler (1967), Weinreich (1966), van Dijk (1972), as well as the influence of case grammar, such as Fillmore (1968) and Stockwell, Schachter, and Partee (1973). Procedural representations were favored by Miller and Johnson-Laird (1976) and Winograd (1972), among others. Graphic networks of one kind or another were used by Norman and Rumelhart (1975), Schank (1975), Woods (1975), and de Beaugrande (1980), for instance. Proposition lists were introduced by Kintsch

---

[5]Reading a text at more than one level, that is, constructing a complex macrostructure, is something else again, as are explicit alternatives in a macrostructure, such as might be formed in reading a mystery novel.

(1974), Frederiksen (1975), Meyer (1975), Anderson and Bower (1973), Anderson (1976), Clark and Clark (1977), and Kieras (1981a), to cite just some of the major examples. Manuals for propositionalizing text have been provided by Turner and Greene (1978) and Bovair and Kieras (1981). As all of these systems are largely equivalent (except for the use of decomposition, as will be discussed in what follows), and most of the differences are based on essentially arbitrary decisions which these authors were forced to make, it would be of little use to compare and contrast these various systems.

Although there are problems with any such system, and an irreducible degree of arbitrariness, propositional analyses have worked very well in practice. In our experience, people learn to propositionalize texts quickly, and the interjudge reliability in such analyses is reassuringly high. For many purposes, such as scoring recall data (for which several of these procedures were originally developed), or providing a representation for the semantic level of analysis in the processing model to be discussed in the succeeding chapters of this book, propositional analyses have served very well. One must, however, guard against the view that they are all-purpose representations, and, in particular, provide ''the'' representation of meaning. They are no more than a tool—indeed, a rather primitive one—useful for certain purposes and useless for others. Logic and formal semantics, specifically, need quite different tools which, however, are as little suited to our purposes as the propositions used in text analyses are to theirs. Every branch of science develops a representation language suited to its own goals. ''The'' representation of meaning is an elusive and deceptive goal (see Kintsch, 1982c, for further discussion).

Ideally, of course, one would have an explicit processing model that would take text as its input and derive a semantic representation such as the one discussed here. There are several parsers today that are able to do that in some restricted domains (e.g., Winograd, 1972; Schank, Goldman, Rieger, & Riesbeck, 1975; Woods & Brachman, 1978; Anderson, 1976; Simmons, 1978). As yet there is no system able to parse arbitrary English text reliably. However, the necessary components for a successful parser are being brought together, and with a better understanding of the cognitive principles involved; thus, the time may be approaching when a truly successful general parser can be developed.

### 2.4.1. Propositions as Psychological Processing Units

Although it is not yet entirely clear how to construct a good parser, it is widely accepted that the output to be obtained from such a parser will be a semantic representation of the kind discussed here. Psychological research in the last few years has provided a sound basis for such an expectation. The semantic units which were devised mostly on the basis of linguistic considerations have been shown to function as psychological processing units. Four lines of converging evidence support this conclusion.

1. *Cued recall studies.* Lesgold (1972), Wanner (1975), and Anderson and

Bower (1973)—the last with mixed results—have all shown that words from the same proposition are more effective recall cues than words from different propositions of a sentence. Thus, in the following sentence

(21)     *The mausoleum that enshrined the czar overlooked the square.*

*overlooked* will be a better recall cue for *mausoleum* than for *czar*, in spite of its greater physical proximity to the latter.

    2. *Free recall studies.* Buschke and Schaier (1979), Goetz, Anderson, and Schallert (1981), Graesser (1981), and Kintsch (1974) have reported evidence that propositional units tend to be recalled as a whole. The particularly extensive experiment by Goetz *et al.* will serve as illustration. In this experiment, subjects were given blocks of eight sentences to read and recall immediately afterward. In each block, three of the sentences were single-proposition sentences (e.g., *The customer wrote the company a complaint*) and three were three-proposition sentences (e.g., *The famous professor lectured in the classroom*), with the last two sentences in the block serving as a short-term memory buffer. Six different types of three-proposition sentences and three different types of one-proposition sentences were studied. Over 94% of the words recalled from the three-proposition sentences arose from the recall of complete constituent propositions. In other words, if any part of a proposition was recalled, the whole proposition was recalled. Interestingly, Goetz *et al.* also included sentences in which the propositions did not form such well-integrated semantic units as in the preceding examples. Thus, they used sentences like *The comedian supplied glassware to the convicts,* or *The bedraggled intelligent model sang.* Preformed associations or familiarity play little or no role with these sentences; nevertheless, holistic recall was just as strong as with the familiar, well-integrated sentences (89%). What is processed as a propositional unit gets recalled together, irrespective of semantic plausibility and familiarity.

    3. *Reading time and recall.* How fast people read and what they can recall depends, inter alia, on the propositional structure of sentences. Forster (1970) showed that if words are presented one by one at a rate of 16 words per second, subjects were able to report more words from one-proposition sentences than from two-proposition sentences. All sentences in his experiment were six words long. To cite his most extreme examples, subjects were able to recall 4.41 words on the average when they saw sentences of the form *The kitten climbed over the fence,* but only 3.09 words from sentences like *The truck Susan was driving crashed.*

    Kintsch and Keenan (1973) gave subjects sentences to read that were approximately equal in length but varied in the number of propositions. The subjects pressed a button as soon as they were finished reading each sentence and then attempted to recall it as well as they could, not necessarily verbatim. Sentence (22) is an example of a sentence with four propositions; sentence (23) contains eight propositions:

(22)     *Romulus, the legendary founder of Rome, took the women of the Sabine by force.*

(23)     *Cleopatra's downfall lay in her foolish trust in the fickle political figures of the Roman world.*

The more propositions subjects were able to store in memory (as assessed by the immediate recall test), the more encoding time was required. Reading times increased from about 10 sec for (22) to 15 sec for (23): About 1.5 sec of additional reading time was required for the recall of each additional proposition. For longer paragraphs, as much as 4.5 sec additional reading time was necessary for recalling each proposition. However, with the longer paragraphs, forgetting and retrieval problems enter the picture, so that the value of 1.5 sec per proposition is probably a more accurate estimate of the rate at which propositions are encoded when reading simple texts.

Graesser, Hoffman, and Clark (1980) replicated the finding of Kintsch and Keenan (1973) that reading time increases as a linear function of the number of propositions in a sentence, but obtained substantially lower estimates of encoding times. They found that subjects needed only 117 msec to interpret a proposition[6] and argue that the estimates obtained by Kintsch and Keenan are inflated. With sentence length held constant, few proposition sentences introduce more new arguments than many-proposition sentences, and the time to foreground new arguments is therefore confounded with the encoding time per proposition in the Kintsch and Keenan experiment. In the Graesser *et al.* study, the number of new arguments was factored out statistically. It, too, was found to be a significant contributor to reading time (see also Kintsch, Kozminsky, Streby, McKoon, and Keenan, 1975), as were number of words, syllables, and letters, familiarity, and especially narrativity. Studies in which number of propositions and number of new arguments are experimentally manipulated are indispensable for obtaining accurate estimates for encoding times per proposition and new arguments (the results of multiple regression analyses have to be considered with caution, too, because they depend on how this analysis is performed).

4. *Priming studies.* While the three groups of studies reviewed thus far strongly suggest that propositions are important psychological processing units, each one taken separately can be criticized on grounds of experimental design. Basically, the problem is that in each case different sentences are compared that vary in the number of propositions, but that necessarily also vary in many other ways—the choice of lexical items, syntax, familiarity, semantic integration, etc. One can try to control these factors, but the possibility of confounding is always there. Ratcliff and McKoon (1978) have developed a procedure that avoids these criticisms. They showed that priming effects on recognition latencies could be used to investigate the structure of discourse. On each trial they showed their subjects four sentences for 7 sec each. The sentences were of five different types, based on one or two propositions. After reading these sentences, the subjects were given a recognition test with single words from the sentences and unrelated distractor words. The subject's task

[6]Haberlandt, Berian, and Sandson (1980) observed values in a comparable range (68–157 msec).

was to respond as fast as possible by pressing either a "yes" or a "no" button, depending on whether or not the word had been seen before. In this task, a reliable priming effect can be observed: If a subject has seen a word from a given sentence (and correctly responded with the yes button) and another word is presented from the same sentence, the mean reaction time for correct responses is only $561 \pm 3$ msec, compared to $671 \pm 4$ msec when the word is from a different sentence. Thus, a sentence priming effect of 110 msec is obtained. What is important here is that this priming effect is greater (111 msec) when the two words come from the same proposition than when they come from different propositions (91 msec). This amounts to a $20 \pm 7$ msec within-proposition priming effect—not a large effect, but given the extremely small standard error a highly reliable one. Ratcliff and McKoon could show that it is indeed the propositional structure that accounts for this priming effect, and not such surface features as physical distance. Sentence (21) is actually one of their examples, and the point they make is that *square* is a better prime for *mausoleum* (the within-proposition condition) than for *czar* which is much closer to *square* in the surface structure. They were also able to show (McKoon & Ratcliff, 1980a) that these priming effects were not confounded by preexisting semantic relations: Propositional units were just as effective when they were poorly integrated semantically as when familiar semantic bonds were involved. Automatic rather than controlled processes were shown to be involved in priming (Ratcliff & McKoon, 1981).

We conclude that the evidence for the psychological reality of propositional units is overwhelming. The nature of these units appears to be pretty close to what Kintsch (1974) argued for, though some details of that system appear to be in need of revision (e.g., Goetz *et al.,* 1981). Even researchers who formerly rejected the notion of propositional processing units have come around to accepting it (Anderson, 1980).

### 2.4.2. Semantic Decomposition

One distinctive feature of the Kintsch (1974) system is the use of complex semantic concepts as predicates and arguments of the propositions rather than decomposition into semantic primitives. Philosophers (Katz & Fodor, 1963), linguists (Lakoff, 1970), computer scientists (Schank, 1972), and psychologists (Miller & Johnson-Laird, 1976) often view understanding a sentence as recovering its representation at the level of semantic primitives. Thus, understanding *John is a bachelor* means representing it as *John is an unmarried man.* The underlying metaphor of such semantic analyses comes from chemistry: Just as chemical compounds are structures composed of relatively few chemical elements, so complex semantic concepts are analyzed into their semantic primitives. This strategy worked well for linguists in the case of classical phonology, where phonemes could be decomposed into distinctive features. It is unquestionably the case that semantic concepts can also be analyzed into more elementary constituents—linguists do it all the time, and even our normal comprehension processes often involve decomposition, for example, when we correctly answer a question about John's marital status after hearing that he is a bachelor. The problem is whether such decomposition is an obligatory feature of comprehension. Is the psychological lexicon based upon some closed set of semantic primitives so that understanding is synonymous with the recovery of these primitives, or does each word in the lexicon function as its own internal representation for purposes of comprehension, a representation which may be elaborated on demand through meaning postulates?

Many theoretical arguments can be made against the dominant view that regards comprehension as a process of semantic decomposition (e.g., Kintsch, 1974), but empirically the issue was until recently quite undecided. Although some experimental evidence was available that suggested that people did not necessarily decompose complex semantic concepts into their primitives during comprehension (Kintsch, 1974; Fodor, Fodor, & Garrett, 1975), the design of these experiments was not entirely conclusive. Kintsch (1974) showed, for instance, that the processing load imposed by semantically complex concepts was no higher than that imposed by simple concepts, as measured by a phoneme-monitoring task, but as this experimental design depended on statistically accepting a null-hypothesis, the interpretation of his results can be challenged. More recently, however, Fodor, Garrett, Walker, and Parkes (1980) have provided definitive results that speak against the decomposition hypothesis. For example, one of the sentence types they investigated was causative constructions such as *John killed Mary*. If *kill* is treated as a unitary semantic concept, the structure of this sentence would be represented in the notation of Kintsch (1974) by

(24)     (KILL, JOHN, MARY)

If *kill* is decomposed we have

(25)     P1 (CAUSE, JOHN, P2)
         P2 (DIE, MARY)

Do people treat this sentence in the manner suggested by (24) or by (25)?

Fodor *et al.* devised a rating procedure, where subjects are asked to rate the degree of relatedness between words. They first showed that this procedure was sensitive enough to reflect the difference in propositional structure of *John expected Mary to leave* and *John persuaded Mary to leave:*

(26)     P1 (EXPECT, JOHN, P2)
         P2 (LEAVE, MARY)
(27)     P1 (PERSUADE, JOHN, MARY, P2)
         P2 (LEAVE, MARY)

Subjects rated *John* and *Mary* to be more strongly related in the *persuade* sentence where *John* and *Mary* are part of the same proposition than in the *expect* sentence where they are in separate propositions. The question is, now, how do subjects rate

*John* and *Mary* in the sentence pair *John killed Mary* and *John bit Mary?* If they treat *John killed Mary* as (24), there should be no difference, in contrast to the *expect–persuade* pair; if they treat it as (25), the same difference as between *persuade* and *expect* should emerge. The results, not only in this case but also with several analogous paradigms, were clear: The rated degree of relationship on *killed* and *bit* sentences did not differ, contradicting obligatory semantic decomposition.

## 2.5. COHERENCE

### 2.5.1. Argument Repetition and Levels Effects in Free Recall

What are the principles according to which coherence is formed? As a first approximation, Kintsch (1974), Kintsch and van Dijk (1978), and others have suggested a principle of argument repetition. Two propositions are related if they share a common argument. Coherence is thus reduced to referential ties, which is certainly an oversimplification, but attractive in its simplicity. Argument repetition may often be merely an accidental by-product of some more basic coherence relationship among propositions (e.g., a causal relationship, or participation in the same script), but at least it serves to index the existence of a relationship in an objective, easily identifiable way. Reducing coherence to argument repetition thus provides a convenient first approximation.

The psychological importance of shared reference among propositions has been demonstrated repeatedly (e.g., Haviland & Clark, 1974; Kintsch & Keenan, 1973; Kintsch et al., 1975; Manelis & Yekovich, 1976). Haviland and Clark, for instance, showed that sentences were read more rapidly if they shared a common referent with a preceding sentence. It took people less time to read and comprehend *The beer was warm* in the context of (28), where there is a common referent between sentences, than in (29) where there is no common referent and readers have to make a bridging inference:

(28)    *George got some beer out of the car. The beer was warm.*
(29)    *George got some picnic supplies out of the car. The beer was warm.*

However, demonstrations that argument repetition alone is not the whole story are easy to obtain (e.g., Haberlandt & Bingham, 1978).

The relationships among propositions in textbases constructed entirely on the principle of argument repetition turn out to be quite predictive of recall. Specifically, in short paragraphs, if one selects intuitively a superordinate proposition and constructs a textbase hierarchy by subordinating to that proposition all propositions that share an argument with it, and then puts at the third level all propositions that share an argument with the second-level propositions, and so on, the resulting structures predict recall very well. In Kintsch and Keenan (1973), for instance, recall of the top-level propositions was above 90% and decreased monotonically from there to about 60% for the lowest (fifth) level. Similar results have been obtained by Kintsch et al. (1975), and, although levels were not always defined in quite the same way, by Meyer (1975, 1977), Britton, Meyer, Hodge, and Glynn (1980), Manelis (1980), and Yekovich and Thorndyke (1981). Hierarchical text-bases, even when they are constructed purely on the basis of such a simple criterion as argument repetition, predict free recall rather well, in that superordinate propositions are recalled much better than more subordinate ones.

### 2.5.2. The Kintsch and van Dijk (1978)
### Processing Model

As the model that we are going to describe in the succeeding chapters of this book is an extension, elaboration, but also a modification, of the Kintsch and van Dijk (1978) model, we need to describe this model here in some detail.

A reader or listener cannot construct a textbase only after all the evidence is available at the end of a paragraph (chapter, book), but must do so in real time and with a limited short-term memory capacity. In the 1978 model we assumed that a reader accumulates semantic units until a sentence or major clause boundary occurs (Miller & Kintsch, 1980, formalized this aspect of the model). At that point, a coherent structure is built on the basis of the pattern of argument repetition among the semantic units in the text. Semantic units are added level by level, as described earlier, to the fragment of the already existing textbase still available in short-term memory. If no superordinate units are available in short-term memory, a new superordinate is chosen from the current input. This choice itself was outside the scope of the 1978 model and had to be made on the basis of intuition. Bridging inferences were used when necessary. The coherence graph that was constructed at the end of each processing cycle contained, in general, too many semantic units to be fully retained in short-term memory during subsequent processing cycles. It was assumed that the capacity of the short-term memory buffer for holding previous textual material was limited to $s$ semantic units, where $s$ was a free model parameter to be estimated from the data. In different studies, estimates of $s$ between 1 and 4 semantic units were obtained. The selection of propositions to be retained at each cycle was made on the basis of the leading-edge strategy, which favored the selection of semantic units high in the textbase hierarchy. In case of ties, recency was made the basis for selection. As the process thus moved from cycle to cycle, important superordinate propositions were frequently retained, sometimes for more than one additional cycle. A very general principle of memory thus could be used to account for the differential recall of semantic units: We remember what we process, and if superordinate propositions are processed more because they are the ones most likely to be selected for retention in the short-term memory buffer from one cycle to the next, superordinate propositions will also be recalled more. Thus, a processing explanation was obtained for the structural effect first observed by Kintsch and

Keenan (1973) that the level of a semantic unit in the textbase hierarchy determines the likelihood of its recall.[7]

This simple model predicts recall just as well as the structural model discussed earlier. Typically, correlations show $r = .8$ are obtained between predicted and observed recall frequencies for the semantic units of a text (e.g., Kintsch & van Dijk, 1978; Kozminsky, Kintsch, & Bourne, 1981; Miller & Kintsch, 1980; Spilich, Vesonder, Chiesi, & Voss, 1979; Vipond, 1980).[8] Probably, if one just asked people to tell how well each semantic unit of a text would be remembered, their intuitions would also be as good as the model, but it makes a difference that such predictions can be derived from an at least partially explicit formal model.

Besides predicting recall, the model was also very useful in analyzing the readability of texts. Readability is taken here to mean the relative ease with which texts can be read and remembered, as indicated by such measures as reading time per proposition recalled on an immediate test (Kintsch & Vipond, 1979; Miller & Kintsch, 1980). A significant achievement of the model in this respect is that it permits us to quantify aspects of the text comprehension process that were neglected by traditional readability formulas. Such formulas (for a fuller discussion see Kintsch & Vipond, 1979) are able to deal only with relatively superficial surface variables, primarily word frequency and sentence length, which although important are certainly not the whole story. The Kintsch and van Dijk (1978) model introduced two additional determinants of readability: the number of bridging inferences required to construct a coherence graph, and the number of memory reinstatements that occur in processing it. The need for reinstating a text proposition that is no longer available in the short-term memory buffer occurs when the textual input on a given cycle is unrelated to the propositions still held in the short-term buffer. In such cases, the model assumes that the reader searches episodic text memory for possible antecedents to the current propositional input. If a proposition is found that shares an argument with the current input, it is reinstated in short-term memory, thus providing a coherence link between what was read before and the new input. If reinstatement searches are unsuccessful, a bridging inference is assumed to occur. Both reinstatement searches and inferences are assumed to be resource-consuming operations and therefore likely sources of reading difficulty. Experimental evidence showed that this was indeed the case: Reinstatements do make a text harder to read. Note that the need for reinstatements varies with different readers (the bigger a

---

[7]Cirilo and Foss (1980) questioned this processing explanation. They showed that words belonging to superordinate propositions tend to be focused for a longer time already at first reading, suggesting that their recall advantage is not, or is not entirely, due to reprocessing on succeeding cycles. However, since they used rather long texts, their results may be caused by macroprocesses which overlay the microprocesses as will be shown in what follows. The fact that the largest number of regressive eye movements during reading target superordinate propositions supports the Kintsch and van Dijk model (Mandel, 1979).

[8]In computing this correlation, the macrostructure of the text, to be discussed in what follows, is also taken into account.

reader's short-term memory capacity, the fewer occasions there will be for rein-statements).

Although the number of inferences and reinstatement searches are clearly important for readability, they still do not tell the whole story. Counting only the number of bridging inferences that are required is quite unsatisfactory because there are many different types of inferences varying widely in difficulty and resource demands. The model is too simple. This simplicity was an asset initially because it permitted us to obtain testable empirical predictions at an early stage of develop-ment of the model, but more realistic assumptions have to be made if we are to overcome the limitations of the 1978 formulation of the model. The readability predictions of that model are interesting, but do not exhaust the full potential of the approach; the recall predictions are reasonably accurate, but still involve an intuitive component. To go beyond the 1978 version of our model, we have to relax our most restrictive assumption: Coherence can no longer be regarded simply in terms of argument repetition. Following earlier theoretical work of van Dijk (e.g., van Dijk, 1977a), we have now developed a much richer and linguistically and psychologi-cally more adequate model of how coherent textbases are constructed (see es-pecially Chapter 5).

## 2.6. KNOWLEDGE STRUCTURES

During comprehension, readers pull out from their general store of knowledge some particular packet of knowledge and use it to provide a framework for the text they are reading. That is, they use information from semantic memory to organize the text they read in order to form a new episodic memory trace (analogous to the subject in a traditional memory experiment who organizes a categorized word list on the basis of his or her knowledge about semantic categories in forming a new episodic trace for the list).

### 2.6.1. Causes and Goals

If we ask ourselves what sort of knowledge sources readers use in this process, the easy answer is: almost any we can think of. There are some particularly impor-tant types of knówledge, though, which deserve special discussion. Causal relations in the physical world and the goals, plans, and intentions of human actors play a predominant role and have received much attention in the literature.

Causal relations exist between states and events in the physical world. Knowl-edge about them is often crucial for interpreting a text (Norman & Rumelhart, 1975; Schank, 1975; Schank & Abelson, 1977; Warren, Nicholas, & Trabasso, 1979). Typically, a text leaves some crucial causal relationship implicit, and readers have to supply this missing link from their own knowledge. As it turns out, people are often not very good at this task, and arrive at misrepresentations that grossly distort the actual causal relations in the system (Stevens, Collins, & Goldin, 1979; Graesser, 1981). The causal model that people use is very different from the unambiguous, contradiction-free system of science (for an interesting exploration of a naive, nonscientific causal structure see Gladwin, 1970). Indeed, even experts arguing in their own domain may reason at multiple, mutually inconsistent levels (Stevens *et al.*, 1979).

Human actions involve relations akin to physical causality, but people are much more adept at dealing with goals, plans, and intentions than with causal relations among physical states and events. This, of course, does not mean that naive action theory is any more consistent and scientific than naive physics (Charniak, 1977; Schank & Abelson, 1977; Wilensky, 1978). Knowledge about human action is employed in story understanding, stories being texts about human actions. Stories can be analyzed as problem-solving tasks, where the protagonist faces some problem in the pursuit of his or her goals and has to find a way around it (Rumelhart, 1975). The events in a story that are directly on the path of relationships between the protagonist's initial state and goal state form the backbone of the story, and are thus considered particularly important by the reader and are recalled best (Black & Bower, 1980; de Beaugrande & Colby, 1979; Lehnert, 1980a). However, discourse understanding may rely on many other knowledge sources in content areas other than physical causality and human action. We mention as examples work by the Yale group on beliefs (Abelson, 1979), attitudes (Schank, Wilensky, Carbonell, Kolodner, and Hendler, 1978), and emotion (Lehnert, 1980a), as well as research in social cognition concerning personality and social role (e.g., Cantor & Mischel, 1977).

### 2.6.2. Schemata

It does not appear to be useful, however, to classify knowledge structures by content area, as they seem to be organized in packets that cut across content. Knowledge structures are variously called schemata (Rumelhart & Ortony, 1977), frames (Minsky, 1975), scripts (Schank & Abelson, 1977), or MOPs (Schank, 1979). Basic to all these notions is the intuition that knowledge must be organized in packets, that it cannot be represented simply as one huge interrelated network of nodes, but that there must be subsets of that network that can function as wholes.

A person's knowledge about taking a bus might be an example of such a knowledge unit—the 'bus' schema. According to Rumelhart and Ortony (1977), a schema is characterized by several distinct properties. The schema has variables that in any particular instantiation may be filled with constants. For instance, there are certain actor roles (driver, passenger) that may be bound by particular persons. Schemata also have other schemata embedded in them; thus, the details of paying the fare on the bus are handled by an embedded 'paying' schema. Schemata may vary widely in abstractness, as is seen by comparing the relatively concrete 'bus' schema (or script) with a general schema for causality or with some of the more abstract rhetorical schemata to be discussed in what follows. Finally, schemata are descriptions, not definitions. The 'bus' schema contains information that is normally valid, plus perhaps some specific details that apply to particular buses, but there is no specification of necessary and sufficient conditions. Instead, normal conditions from many different content areas are combined, having to do with goals, consequences, geographic routes, the physical nature of buses, implications concerning social status, attitudes toward public transport, and whatever else.

In succeeding chapters of this book, we shall explore the nature of such knowledge structures and how they are used in discourse comprehension. There are many unsolved problems. Although there is wide agreement today as to the need for some such concept like "schema," exactly how to build a knowledge structure incorporating this notion is another matter. The problem is how to get a knowledge base to deliver nicely prepackaged schemata, while at the same time retaining its flexibility and context sensitivity. It is simply not the case that every time we need the 'bus' schema, we want the same package. Rather, in each new context, it is a subtly different complex of information that becomes relevant.

The problems of schema use that shall concern us can be subsumed under the headings of identification and application. We shall describe strategies for identifying and activating relevant schemata in the course of discourse processing. Once selected, the schema performs various functions. First of all, it provides the reader with a basis for interpreting the text. A coherent textbase is obtained by binding the semantic units derived from the textual input to the conceptual skeleton provided by the knowledge schema. Textbases are the result of this marriage between schema knowledge and text.

However, schemata not only provide a coherent framework for the semantic units of a text, they also provide a basis for more active, top-down processes. Missing information can be assigned default values if it appears insignificant, or it can be actively looked for in the text. Deviations from the schema either may be accepted and registered, or, if they appear to be major ones, may become the basis for a problem-solving effort trying to account for them. As we shall see in the next section, many of the inferences made in discourse comprehension are schema driven.

The schema notion is very widely used today, from theories of letter perception to those of macrostructure formation. On the one hand, this makes it possible to begin formulating a truly general, comprehensive theory of discourse perception and comprehension, along the lines of Adams and Collins (1979), of which our own work could form a part. On the other hand, the notion of schema is so general that it says little more than that knowledge may be schematically organized. We cannot indiscriminately reduce discourse processes to such a vague notion: As we shall show in what follows, we must distinguish various kinds of schema-based process—macrostructures and superstructures and knowledge representations in long-term memory are by no means the same, and collapsing them under the notion of "schema" produces nothing but confusion. However, we believe that schema theory can overcome this danger of vagueness and overgenerality by making the kind of distinctions we advocate with respect to discourse processes in such areas as perception and action as well: Local and global coherence, macrostructures, and superstructures are potentially as useful in these areas as they are in discourse processing.

## 2.7. INFERENCES

Inferences play a crucial role in discourse comprehension and have received their share of attention in the literature. Several classification schemes have been proposed outlining numerous different types of inferences (e.g., Crothers, 1979; de Beaugrande, 1980) as they can be determined on the basis of linguistic analysis. On the other hand, a great deal of research has also been devoted to the question of what inferences people actually make on the basis of a text, when they are asked to do so. The question-answering method developed by Graesser (1981) provides a wealth of information concerning this problem.

One aspect that distinguishes text-based inferences is the degree of certainty with which they can be made. Some inferences appear to be necessary consequences of the text, whereas others we are less certain about and still others we would regard as no more than plausible or possible conjectures. Thus, if we hear *George is older than Sue,* we are quite convinced that 'Sue is younger than George', or if we hear *Sue forgot her raincoat,* we take it for granted that she does not have it. *All p are q; p, therefore q* has the ring of inevitability, but when used in concrete instances, common sense might tell us that the conclusion is not all that certain: *All clams on the beach are edible; John found a clam on the beach; therefore it is edible*—some people might still hesitate. Lexical inferences range from certainty (*John killed Sue—Sue is dead*) to plausibility (*Sue punched John— She used her fist*) to the faintest possibility (*Sue is ill—with peritonites*). Script-based inferences are in general merely plausible, not necessary (if John took the bus to the airport, we assume he paid for his ticket, but who knows?). Conversations are full of plausible inferences: *It is cold in here* probably is a request to turn up the furnace, but it may just be an admiring remark from one fellow-energy-saver to another (Rescher, 1976).

### 2.7.1. When Bridging Inferences Are Made

The biggest problem with discourse inferences is to determine when they are made: Are they part of comprehension proper, or do they occur optionally after comprehension? It is clear that not all possible inferences can actually be made (the dangers of the resulting computational explosion has been described by Rieger, 1977). The question therefore is, how can one distinguish those inferences that must occur as an integral part of discourse comprehension proper?

One class of inferences that appear to be necessary during comprehension are are the bridging inferences required for the coherence of the text (Kintsch, 1974; Clark, 1977; Miller & Kintsch, 1980). Attempts were made to show that such inferences occur during comprehension by demonstrating that bridging inferences are verified as quickly as statements explicitly mentioned in the text.[9] It is claimed that when people verify a sentence, they access a matching memory trace. As bridging statements are verified equally rapidly whether they had to be inferred or not, one can conclude that in either case a memory trace existed in memory. If the statement was presented explicitly in the text, the memory trace that was accessed was the proposition derived from it. If the statement had to be inferred, an inference-generated proposition was accessed. If no such proposition had been inferred during comprehension, an inference would have had to be generated in response to the verification demand, which presumably would have extended the time needed to make the verification. As no such effect on verification times was observed, it was concluded that the inferred proposition had been there all the time (Keenan & Kintsch, 1974; Baggett, 1975; McKoon & Keenan, 1974). A premise of this argument—that memory look-up always precedes the inference—may, however, be wrong. As Reder (1982a) has shown, subjects may be using inferences about the plausibility of statements in preference to a memory search. Quick and easy plausibility judgments appear to be less resource demanding than memory searches (see also Den Uyl & van Oostendorp, 1980). If that is true, of course, verification times for inferred and explicit bridging statements would not differ (except, again, for the effects introduced by the ready availability of surface features in short-term memory for explicit sentences), but this result would not tell us when such inferences were made.

Other methods have also been used to investigate when inferences are made, but the experimental difficulties here are considerable. We have already mentioned the study by Haviland and Clark (1974) where sentences that required a bridging inference were shown to have longer reading times than sentences that did not. Although it is certainly possible that this increased reading time was used to make the bridging inference, we have no assurance that this was so; it is also possible that the longer reading time merely reflects the reduced comprehensibility of the test sentence: The subjects are slow because they realize something is missing, but they are not necessarily inferring what the missing element is (McKoon & Ratcliff, 1980b).

Cued recall experiments have shown over and over again that subjects are able to make inferences: In general, cues that represent inferable information are just as good retrieval cues as cues that represent information explicitly stated in the text (see Anderson & Ortony, 1975, for a representative example). However, that fact has no bearing on the issue of interest here, namely, when the inferences are made.

On the other hand, in the special case of inferring the instruments that go habitually with certain verbs, there is evidence that the inferences do not occur during comprehension, though they are readily made when needed (Singer, 1981;

---

[9]This is true if the verification test is delayed sufficiently to assure that surface features of the text which would otherwise facilitate the verification of explicitly presented statements are no longer available in memory (Kintsch, 1974; Baggett, 1975).

Corbett & Dosher, 1978). Thus, when subjects hear *The worker pounded the nails* they do not infer *with a hammer,* though they can and will do so if there is a reason for it.

Today, the most promising experimental technique for investigating inferences during comprehension is the priming method as used to study anaphoric inferences by McKoon and Ratcliff (1980b). One would hope that it would eventually allow us to answer the questions raised here more definitely than is now possible.

To summarize our present state of ignorance, one could say that we are fairly confident today that bridging inferences are indeed an integral part of the comprehension process, though the final evidence is lacking. In this book, we are proposing to look at inferences during comprehension in a rather different way from the one that has characterized research heretofore. We propose (see especially Chapter 10) that inferences are not a part of the textbase proper but pertain to a different, nontextual, level of analysis, the situation model. The textbase is a representation of the text as it is. Bridging inferences and other types of inferences belong to the situation model constructed on the basis of that textbase *and* knowledge. What is inferred are therefore not propositions in the textbase but links in the situation model. This shifts the analysis of inferences in discourse processing from the linguistic level to the conceptual level, and may permit us to arrive at more clear-cut answers than have been possible so far.

## 2.7.2. Elaborative Inferences

Elaborative inferences are another important type of inference, and we are even less certain about their role in text comprehension. Elaborative inferences occur when the reader uses his or her knowledge about the topic under discussion to fill in additional detail not mentioned in the text, or to establish connections between what is being read and related items of knowledge.

It seems that elaborative inferences do not necessarily occur during comprehension, but when they are made (e.g., because subjects were instructed to elaborate) they may have quite beneficial effects on text memory. That elaboration can be helpful for remembering has been known for some time. Consider the well-known paired associate experiment of Bobrow and Bower (1969). Subjects were given noun pairs to learn by rote and managed to learn 29% of them. Their success rate was precisely doubled when they were instructed to elaborate the noun pairs by inserting between the nouns a suitable connecting verb. Anderson and Reder (1979) report similar results. Although elaboration is necessarily more complex when it comes to discourse comprehension, the basic findings are the same. Reder (1980b) found beneficial effects when subjects were elaborating simple texts on the basis of applicable script knowledge. Mayer (1980) gave subjects instructions on how to use a computer and found several ways of inducing active, elaborative processing, which again proved beneficial. Thus, at least certain kinds of elaborative inferences during comprehension, especially those that produce a tighter integration between the text and the reader's own knowledge structure, result in better learning.[10] Elaborative inferences also occur during the reproduction of a text, of course, where they are often used to cover up an inability to recall details of the original text (Kintsch & van Dijk, 1978). Thus elaborations can also distort a text. The source of elaboration is some knowledge schema that is being used to interpret the text, and, if there is a misfit between the schema and the text, it is possible that the text will be adjusted to make it conform better to the schema. The classical work of Bartlett (1932) was concerned with this phenomenon.

A particular kind of elaboration that may be very important for memory involves imagery. It is known at least since Yuille and Paivio (1969) that concrete texts (not just words!) are easier to recall than abstract texts, presumably because they invite more elaborations via imagery. Without wanting to enter the controversy about what exactly is implied by the use of imagery in remembering, we suggest that there may be a rich and rewarding field for future studies of learning from texts.

In addition to bridging inferences and elaborate inferences, it might be useful to mention restructuring as a third category of local inferences that seems to be important in discourse comprehension. Schnotz, Ballstaedt, and Mandl (1981) obtained protocols from subjects summarizing and recalling a text and observed instances where text elements from different places in the text were combined in novel ways, creating interpretations that presumably were not intended or foreseen by the writer of the text. It is not clear when such restructuring occurs, nor what its precise role is in text comprehension. In every way our knowledge about inferences in comprehension is as yet inadequate.

## 2.8. MACROSTRUCTURES

Macrostructures are also the product of inferential processes. However, the inferences involved in the generation of macrostructures can be distinguished from those discussed in the preceding section because they are reductive and serve to reduce a text to its essential communicative message. Macrostructures were designed to capture the intuitive notion of the "gist" of a discourse. The theory of macrostructures has been explored extensively (Bierwisch, 1965; van Dijk, 1972, 1977a, 1977b, 1980b). Whereas the textbase represents the meaning of a text in all its detail, the macrostructure is concerned only with the essential points of a text. But it, too, is a coherent whole, just like the textbase itself, and not simply a list of key words or of the most important points. Indeed, in our model the macrostructure consists of a network of interrelated propositions which is formally identical to the microstructure. A text can be reduced to its essential components in successive steps, resulting in a hierarchical macrostructure, with each higher level more con-

---

[10]However, we are far from understanding these matters fully: In some cases, elaboration is quite useless for learning—a simple, stripped-down summary of the important points of a text proves just as good or better than the full, elaborated original (Reder & Anderson, 1980, 1982; Reder, 1982b)!

densed than the previous one. In a book, for instance, the top level of the macro-structure may simply be expressed by the title of the book, with the next level corresponding to some subjective table of contents. Each chapter would then be broken down into subsections and sub-subsections, eventually arriving at the text-base itself. The textbase thus may be regarded as the lowest level of the macrostructure—the basis from which it evolves. Hence, theoretically, microstructure and macrostructure may "collapse," as in one-sentence discourses.

In general, the macrostructure of a book that exists in a reader's mind as the memorial record of his or her interaction with the text will be rather sketchy, of course. Furthermore, it will represent only one of a set of possible macrostructures. Each reader, with particular goals and knowledge background, interacts with the text in a new way, producing a distinct macrostructure. The set of possible macro-structures will have much in common, since, after all, all macrostructures are derived from the same text, but to the extent that knowledge differences exist among readers and that their reading goals are not the same, different reading episodes will result in different macrostructures. In the extreme case, when a text is being read for a very unusual and specific purpose, the macrostructure may be far removed from the one intended by the author. The set of possible macrostructures is, indeed, a fuzzy one. The goals of a theory of macrostructure can only be to predict some prototypical macrostructures for some common reading goals, or to explain post hoc what happened in individual cases.

As with bridging inferences, elaborations, and the like, the question arises of when reductive inferences occur. Are they an integral part of text comprehension, or do they occur in response to some specific task demand, such as to summarize or recall the text? Furthermore, assuming that macrostructure formation is a necessary and integral part of comprehension, when in the process of reading or thereafter does it occur? In a study by Schnotz, Ballstaedt, and Mandl (1981), it was observed that subjects appeared unable to distinguish what was macrorelevant in a text when they tried to summarize it right away after reading it once. They included large numbers of elaborations and restructurings in their summaries. On a second try, on the other hand, these elaborations were largely excluded and the length of the summary was reduced by more than half. Indeed, the first summary these subjects produced looked more like a free recall protocol than a summary. There is at least a suggestion here that in the early stages of processing (i.e., during first readings) readers are concerned mainly with forming a coherent textbase and the local inferences involved in that process; reductive inferences may be postponed for later. At least that was the case with the rather difficult essay text studied by Schnotz *et al.*—macroprocesses may be more on line with less demanding texts such as stories. In Section 6.6 we take up this issue in more detail.

## 2.8.1. Structural, Syntactic, and Semantic Signals

The comprehension strategies which are used to form macrostructures depend on the presence of certain signals in the text that indicate to the listener or reader the text elements that are to be considered as macrorelevant. Among those, certain kinds of structural signals have been investigated in some detail by psychologists and educational researchers. A review of this work has been provided by Ballstaedt, Mandl, Schnotz, and Tergan (1981). Some well-known examples are, for instance:

1. Titles (Bransford & Johnson, 1972; Dooling & Mullet, 1973; Schallert, 1976; Kozminsky, 1977; Schwarz & Flammer, 1981)
2. Subtitles, headings, and captions (Evans, 1974)
3. Initial appearance of sentences (Thorndyke, 1977; Meyer, 1977; Kieras, 1978, 1980c, 1981b, 1981c)
4. Summaries (Hartley & Davies, 1976; van Dijk & Kintsch, 1977; Kintsch & Kozminsky, 1977)
5. Advance organizers (Meyer, 1979)
6. Questions and reminders (Rothkopf, 1970)

In one form or another, these signals have all been shown to facilitate comprehension, although not all of these studies make a clear distinction between local comprehension processes and macrostructure formation, which is presumably the locus of the effects observed in these studies.

The way in which syntactic signaling devices indicate importance has been studied extensively by Jones (1977) and van Dijk (1980b). Typically, syntactic signals have local effects, but local signals can assume a global role if they add up, repeatedly pointing to a particular piece of information. Thus, Kieras (1981b) has demonstrated that readers choose a noun more frequently as a paragraph topic when it occurs repeatedly as a sentence subject, with other factors such as mere frequency of mention and semantic content controlled.

Frequency of mention can be a sign of macrorelevance in itself, however. Perfetti and Goldman (1974) showed that merely by mentioning something repeatedly in a discourse, subjects can be led to believe that this item plays an important role in the macrostructure of the discourse.

## 2.9. SCHEMATIC SUPERSTRUCTURES

In principle, any kind of knowledge source may be involved in forming macrostructures, just as in the case of microstructures: Human action schemata may provide the basis for organizing a novel, specialized professional knowledge the basis for a scientific report. There are, however, special types of schemata that are peculiar to macrostructures, the superstructures (van Dijk, 1980). Superstructures are schemata for conventional text forms; knowledge of these forms facilitates generating, remembering, and reproducing macrostructures. Not all text types have such conventional forms, but when one exists it seems to play a considerable role in processing.

### 2.9.1. Story Grammars and the Narrative Schema

The form that has been most widely explored in the literature is that of simple, traditional stories (Propp, 1928; Lévi-Strauss, 1960, 1963; Barthes, 1966; Greimas, 1966; Todorov, 1968; van Dijk, 1972; Bremond, 1973; for an introduction and survey, see Gülich & Raible, 1977). A story is built around an actor and certain functions, which are the major actions of a story that change it from one state to another (such as marriage, betrayal, etc.). Although actors in a simple story remain constant, functions change throughout. In looking at folktales, Propp originally thought of functions as fixed and limited, but later investigators noted their flexible nature. Only the category to which an action belongs is fixed in a story, not the function itself. The actions in a story fall into the categories of exposition, complication, and resolution (Labov & Waletsky, 1967). Expositions introduce the actors and the situation; the complication brings in some remarkable, interesting event; the resolution returns the story to a new stable state. Simple, one-episode stories of the exposition–complication–resolution form can be elaborated by concatenating episodes, permitting categories to overlap (so that the resolution of one episode becomes the exposition of the next), or embedding one episode within another framelike episode (e.g., a complication may become expanded into a whole series of episodes).

This knowledge about the conventional form of the text type 'story' is the story schema. In comprehension, the story schema guides the formation of the macrostructure, that is, the main events of the story are assigned to the schematic categories described here (Kintsch & van Dijk, 1975; van Dijk & Kintsch, 1978). Note that the schema itself is not a macrostructure—it is just a mold for forming one.

In forming the macrostructure of a story, much more than the story schema is involved, however. In particular, our knowledge about human goals and actions is absolutely necessary for story understanding. A recent attempt to account for all of these factors in story understanding led to the development of story grammars—and to a rather fierce debate about the adequacy and cognitive relevance of such "grammars." On the one side there are the story grammarians, who postulate that narrative structures do have processing reality (Johnson & Mandler, 1980; Mandler, 1978; Mandler & Johnson, 1977, 1980; Rumelhart, 1975, 1980; Thorndyke, 1977; Stein & Glenn, 1979). The opposing view is held by those psychologists and scholars from artificial intelligence who claim that such structures are theoretical artifacts which can or should be explained away or modeled in terms of the structure of actions, emphasizing such notions as motivation, purpose, intention, and goal (e.g., Black & Bower, 1980; Bruce, 1980; Schank & Abelson, 1977; Thorndyke & Yekovich, 1980). Black and Wilensky (1979) have argued that there is no theoretically interesting way of formulating grammars for narrative structures, and that the actual grammars proposed both in psychology and the theory of discourse cannot be called grammars. As a specific type of action discourse, stories should be accounted for instead in terms of action structural categories, which have real psychological relevance because they organize the planning and execution of action.

In our opinion, the truth resides on both sides, and we will list a number of arguments to show why this is the case. As discussion has focused mainly on narrative superstructures, we will for the moment take these as a characteristic example. However, one should bear in mind that a refutation of the cognitive relevance of schematic superstructures in order to be persuasive should also be extended to other kinds of superstructures. Obviously, these cannot all be reduced to action-theoretical notions.

We would like to argue that specific narrative schematic structures and action structures are both necessary to account for story processing, for the following reasons:

1. Stories are a subset of the set of action discourses: They are concerned with human actions and hence will be about the properties of human actions, such as motivations, plans, aims or purposes, and goals (van Dijk, 1976). It is obvious that in any semantic theory of such discourses these notions should be made explicit. In a cognitive model, likewise, understanding a story also means understanding what a story is about; thus, understanding a story does indeed partially involve understanding human action.

2. A philosophical or cognitive account of human action must be general in nature. In an overall cognitive model of information processing, knowledge about the structure of action need not feature in a semantics of action discourse, in a model of narratives, and in a model of understanding and planning real actions as well. We have a general knowledge base concerning the structure of actions, and this knowledge is used in a variety of tasks. This means that a specific account of human action is necessary neither in story grammars nor in the goal-oriented models of stories and story understanding. If Ockham should use his razor, it should be here.

3. Stories are action discourses, indeed, but not all action discourses are stories. We may have descriptions of actions in police protocols, ethnographic studies, or manuals for repairing one's car. Stories, apparently, are a subset of the set of action discourses. In our culture, for instance, they are about interesting events and actions, they may involve funny, dangerous, unexpected, uncommon events, and they require human participants, in particular a narrator. Thus, stories have a number of specific semantic and pragmatic constraints distinguishing them from other action discourses.

4. For each culture these semantic and pragmatic constraints may become conventionalized. This means that participants not only recognize specific story properties, but also become normative about them: If there is no interesting event or action in a story, we do not call it a story, or we think the story is not yet finished, that it has no point, or that it may be a story from another culture. The narrative categories that have been proposed in the literature are precisely the theoretical reconstructions of such constraints: All stories do, in principle, that is, canonically,

have a Setting, an interesting Complication, and a Resolution featuring what the participants did in that complicating situation. For specific story types further categories are possible. It may be assumed that for each culture, members do learn some cognitive variant of these categorical constraints on the semantic structure of stories, and use these during understanding and retrieval. That some part of the story should feature an interesting event or action is not an inherent part of action structure. Most of our everyday actions are not interesting and would not qualify as referential objects for storytelling.

5. Although stories are about actions, and therefore story understanding presupposes knowledge about general and more particular, cultural or stereotypical, features of action, what we should emphasize is that knowledge about action is not the same as knowledge about action discourse. Action discourses are descriptions (or ascriptions, or prescriptions) of actions—and also of situations, objects, persons, and so on. It is well known that not all aspects of actions can or should be described in such discourse. For pragmatic reasons only the unknown, interesting things and their actual background need be told. That is, sometimes details will be supplied, other times the description will skip many actions or describe them only in very general terms. The ordering of action propositions may not be identical with that of the actions themselves. In other words, what is really interesting in a linguistic or cognitive theory of stories is not so much a theory of action, but rather a theory of action description. Thus, such factors as degree of completeness, level of description, ordering, style, perspective or point of view, etc. become relevant.

These arguments have led us to assume that schematic superstructures for certain discourse types, such as stories, may be acquired during socialization, and that they play a role in the understanding, the representation, and the retrieval of discourse. That is, we assume that language users know, implicitly and to some extent also explicitly, which categories and which schemata are involved, and that they use these to further organize the linguistic structure of the discourse. For stories this means that the narrative pattern organizes the semantic macrostructures, by assigning narrative functions to macropropositions.

### 2.9.2. The Guiding Role of the Narrative Schema in Macrostructure Formation

Our compromise position with respect to the story grammar controversy fits the available data rather well. When it comes to story recall and comprehension, both action schemata and narrative superstructures are important.

There is good evidence today that episodes function as psychological units in story comprehension as well as recall (Black & Bower, 1979; Mandler, 1978; Thorndyke, 1978). These episodes can usually be formed both on the basis of narrative categories, as suggested by Kintsch and van Dijk (1975) and the story grammarians, and on the basis of the content of the story (e.g., Black & Bower, 1980). It is hard to disentangle the structure of human action from that of stories, but in some of the studies discussed in what follows this has been achieved to varying extents.

The hierarchical structures generated by story grammars predict recall, in that superordinate nodes tend to be recalled better than subordinate nodes (Thorndyke, 1977), but the semantic content of these nodes may override structural effects (Black & Bower, 1980). Similarly, the recurrent observation (Mandler & Johnson, 1977; Haberlandt, Berian, & Sandson, 1980) that some narrative categories are better recalled than others (beginning, attempt, and outcome are usually recalled better than goal and ending) is difficult to interpret. Goals and endings are readily inferable if the rest of the story is known, and may therefore simply be omitted in recall. Furthermore, actions are usually more salient than states by themselves, quite apart from their narrative functions. This cannot, however, be the sole explanation of the results obtained, as was demonstrated by Poulson, Kintsch, Kintsch, and Premack (1979). These authors showed young children (4- and 6-year-olds) pictures which told a story, and asked the children to describe the pictures as they saw them, and later to recall them. The pictures were shown either in their proper order forming a story, or in scrambling order so that the children could not form a coherent story from what they saw (though they tried). A comparison of how well a picture was recalled when it formed part of a story and when it was perceived outside the story context permits one to gauge the effects of story structure per se, as the semantic content of the picture is the same in both conditions. Certain pictures were recalled better when they were part of a story than when they were seen in isolation. These were the pictures belonging to the resolution category. As they often depicted states, and were in general not very exciting pictorially (e.g., a boy sitting with a dog, as opposed to a fox chasing the dog), they were not very well recalled by themselves. But when they formed the resolution of a story, recall was significantly superior due to their important narrative function, though the fact that it was part of a human action schema (the boy wanted to get his lost dog back) may also have contributed to the superior recall.

Cirilo and Foss (1980) reported an experiment analogous to the Poulson *et al.* study, in which the same sentence was embedded in different parts of stories. Thus, semantic content was controlled while narrative function varied. It was found that subjects took longer to read the critical sentence when it played an important role in the text (according to Thorndyke's story grammar) than when it was placed in a subordinate position. Further evidence that reading times for sentences are affected by their narrative role was reported by Haberlandt, Berian, and Sandson (1980), who relied on statistical control rather than on experimental manipulation. Their subjects read stories sentence by sentence. Haberlandt *et al.* were interested in exploring the boundary hypothesis: When subjects arrive at an episode boundary they must engage in macroprocessing, and hence sentences at the conclusion of an episode should be read more slowly, above and beyond sentence-level factors influencing reading times. Various cues in the text indicate to the reader that a category boundary has been reached (e.g., Kintsch, 1977b) and serve as signals for coding operations at the macrolevel. Haberlandt *et al.* used multiple regression to predict reading times for sentences, and then showed that the pattern of residuals could be accounted for quite well by this boundary effect. The word- and sentence-level factors that they used in their predictions were number of words in the sentence, number of propositions, number of new arguments, frequency of content words, rated importance of the sentence, and serial position. They could show that narrative function played a role in addition to all these other factors, in that sentences at episode boundaries were read especially slowly when they were part of a story, though not when read in isolation.

Thus, there exists a wealth of information suggesting that story structure plays an important role in discourse processing, over and beyond other factors. However, because narrative categories tend to be confounded with human action schemata, the interpretation of these results is not entirely unambiguous. It is therefore necessary to investigate texts whose semantic content and rhetorical form are less interwoven. So far, relatively little has been done with nonnarrative texts, though important beginnings have been made (Kieras, 1978; Olson, Duffy, & Mack, 1980; Olson, Mack, & Duffy, 1981; Otto & White, 1982). In Chapter 7, we shall report some further results with description texts that provide clear-cut support for the cognitive reality of superstructures and their role in macrostructure formation.

## 2.10. OUTLOOK

We have now done two things: In Chapter 1 we have sketched the model we want to develop and outlined its general intellectual background. In the present chapter we have looked in somewhat more detail at the status of the experimental research on discourse comprehension. Our purpose was not to provide a comprehensive review of that work, but rather to determine where and how our own work fits in. Our model cannot possibly deal with every component of discourse comprehension. It must necessarily be selective and even within its domain we cannot treat adequately all relevant aspects. However, it is necessary to view our model against the background of knowledge that has accumulated about all aspects of discourse processing. At the minimum, we require that our model does not contradict current knowledge whenever that knowledge is relevant to it, and that it is constructed in such a way that it is conceivable in principle that it could sometime be extended to those components of discourse processing that are at present neglected.

The emphasis in our model is on strategic processes in higher order discourse comprehension. That is, we are concerned with the formation of a coherent propositional textbase and its macrostructure, rather than with lower order perceptual processes or linguistic parsing processes. However, our discussion of the empirical results concerning these lower order processes in Sections 2.1–2.4 of this chapter makes the point that principles like the ones that are central to our model might very well also apply to the perceptual and linguistic processing levels that are neglected in our model. This continuity is apparent in two ways. First, the notion of strategy can be used fruitfully—and in some cases already has been—to account for lower levels of comprehension processes as well as for the higher levels which are our main concern in this book. Second, we have in the concept of schema a theoretical notion that has proven to be useful at levels of analysis as far apart as letter perception and semantic superstructures. In part, this merely reflects the vagueness with which this concept is sometimes used. However, we have argued (and shall try to substantiate these claims further in the chapters to come) that theoretical substance can be given to the schema concept, and that together with the notion of strategy it is basic to an understanding of comprehension processes in general and discourse comprehension in particular. Thus, although our model is only a fragment, there is reason to be optimistic that it will prove compatible with other models being developed for those aspects of comprehension processes that we neglect.

The second half of this chapter dealt with research results that bear directly on the assumptions our model makes about comprehension. It is the empirical-experimental background of our model, just as important for its development as the theoretical-linguistic background discussed in Chapter 1. Unfortunately, experimental research on many of the topics mentioned in these sections is still in its early stages and sometimes inconclusive. One important function our model can fulfill is to serve as a framework for further experimental research in this area. In the remaining chapters of this book we fill in various missing details, but much more remains to be done along those lines before we have an adequate experimental data base to evaluate our model decisively against alternative approaches, formulated and as yet unformulated ones.

The experimental research we have discussed here deals, roughly speaking, with the strategic aspects of discourse comprehension. Another data base which also has been of great importance for the design decisions we made in developing our model has not been alluded to here at all. That is the work on memory. Our model is a processing model, and memory and processing constraints play a crucial role. As we shall emphasize throughout this book (but especially in Chapters 9 and 10), the process of comprehension cannot be understood without taking seriously what we know about memory and information processing. The interplay between information active in short-term memory and information retrieved from the long-term store, and the control function exercised by the situation model that is generated in memory in parallel with the text representation, are central to our conception of discourse comprehension. However, it is not necessary to review the memory literature in the same detail as we have reviewed here the comprehension literature. Compared to the latter, the field of memory is much more advanced and a certain consensus exists with regard to the major memory phenomena that have been studied in the laboratory. It will therefore be sufficient for our purposes to merely remind the reader of the major features of current memory theory when the occasion arises.

# Chapter 3

# The Notion of Strategy in Language and Discourse Understanding

## 3.1. INTRODUCTION

The survey of discourse-processing models given in the previous chapter has shown that these models have a number of serious shortcomings. Not only are they incomplete, as many theories are, but, more importantly, their general orientation as cognitive models is misguided: Their focus has been on problems of representation rather than on the dynamic aspect of processing. What we want to know is how textual representations in memory come about, how they are constructed step by step by the hearer or reader, and what strategies are used to thereby understand a discourse.

In this chapter we will explore the notion of strategy as applied to the processing of discourse. For simplicity we will use the term *discourse strategies* to refer to the various strategies used in the production, comprehension, and reproduction of discourse. We will discover that part of these strategies may be called linguistic, especially those that link textual and sentential surface structures with underlying semantic representations. But other strategies are more generally cognitive and involve the use of world knowledge, the use of episodic knowledge (memories in the strict sense), and the use of other cognitive information, such as opinions, beliefs, attitudes, interests, plans, and goals.

Before we consider in detail in the following chapters the major strategies involved in the processing of discourse, it is necessary to get some insight into the notion of discourse strategy in particular and into that of strategy in general. What precisely are strategies? What is the difference between rules and strategies, between heuristics and strategies? Are there any differences between general cognitive strategies and more specific linguistic or textual strategies, or are the latter just special instances of the former? In other words: if people go about interpreting a scene, a sequence of events, or pictures of events, do they use strategies of comprehension that are similar to those used in understanding a discourse? Besides this conceptual analysis of the notion of strategy and its relevance for a cognitive model, we will want to know whether strategies are ordered (e.g., hierarchically) and what kind of processing should be postulated to account for them.

Our answers to these questions will be partial: It is not our aim to provide a general theory of strategy, but we do want to specify the notion in more detail than has been usual in linguistics and psychology. The study of comprehension strategies is difficult, however, because some of the more or less explicit models of strategy analysis in problem solving and decision making cannot be applied directly to the very fast and highly automatized strategies used in language understanding. Furthermore, only certain kinds of discourse strategies are open to empirical assessment via protocol analysis, which raises the general problem of experimental tests for strategic discourse models.

## 3.2. THE NOTION OF STRATEGY

Although the notion of strategy has been used in many studies in cognitive science, it is very rarely defined. As a metaphor it has been borrowed from military science (Greek *strategia* means 'military command'), where it is used to denote the organization of military actions to reach a particular military goal. The term has also been used in political science, economics, and in other disciplines involved with complex, goal-directed actions. Simon (1967) has used the term "design," which seems to lie between our notion of strategy and our notion of plan. The term strategy has been used extensively in the theory of decision making (e.g., by Edwards & Tversky, 1967; Lee, 1971; and Moore & Thomas, 1976). In all those cases the concern is not merely with reaching a goal, but with reaching it in some optimal way (e.g., quickly, effectively, or with low cost).

### 3.2.1. Action Theory

A strategy involves human *action,* that is, goal-oriented, intentional, conscious, and controlled behavior (van Dijk, 1977a, 1980b). Actions are a specific kind of event. They imply changes in the world—they establish these changes or prevent them from occurring. Hence, they are particular ways of changing states of affairs into other states of affairs, changes that are the consequences of bodily doings, whereas the doings in turn are controlled by cognitive information, such as purposes and their underlying desires, wants, preferences, decisions, or other motivational structures. The final state, as intended by the agent, is the result of an action. If the results are in accordance with the intentions of the agent, we say that the action is weakly successful. In general, though, agents will not only want to bring about results, that is, final states of actions (e.g., an open door as the final state of the action of opening a door), but have more far-reaching purposes. They want the action (and its result) to bring about some desired goal: a state or event that is a consequence of the action (we open doors not just to open them, but usually to leave or enter, or to let somebody else leave or enter). Such consequences may, of course, be beyond the control of the agent. In that respect we say that our actions may fail: They may not achieve the goal we aimed at. If they do achieve their goal, we say that they are strongly successful. Cognitively speaking, we will assume that intentions are representations of doings plus their result, and that purposes or aims are representations of wanted consequences of an action. These cognitive representations allow us to monitor our doings and actions. The analysis of each state of the environment (the action domain) may be compared to the cognitive representation of what we wanted.

Actions are usually complex. That is, we do something, or a number of things, in order to achieve a certain result. Even a relatively simple action like opening a door involves several successive and concomitant actions, of which some will be automatized, that is, not governed by conscious intent nor individually subordinated to a general purpose. Sequences of actions, thus, may have intermediate results or goals and final results or goals.

Similar definitions may be given for *interactions*. In this case, several agents are involved, each with their own doings and actions, and hence with their own intentions and purposes for their respective results and goals. Interactions may be said to be coordinated if the agents involved have identical intermediate or final results and goals. Moving a heavy table together, playing chess, or going to the movies together are in this way coordinated. The actions themselves may be partially different, but some intermediate or final results and goals may be the same. Obviously, this kind of coordination in general presupposes mutual knowledge or beliefs about each other's respective purposes and intentions.

The complexity of action or interaction sequences will in general require some form of higher organization. That is, we make global *plans* to be able to execute such complex (inter-)actions. A plan may be defined as a cognitive macrostructure of intentions or purposes. It is a hierarchical schema dominated by a *macroaction* (van Dijk, 1980b; Schank & Abelson, 1977). Eating in a restaurant, making a trip by plane, or building a house are such macroactions. At a more local level these are performed by the execution of a number of more detailed actions. The macroaction is the global conceptual structure organizing and monitoring the actual action sequence. It defines the global final results and goals.

Final results and goals can often be realized in a number of alternative ways. There are often several courses of action or interactions that may lead to the same final result or goal. In Figure 3.1 we give a tree diagram to represent such a course of action. It should be read from left to right, where each branching represents a different alternative to reach a next state (intermediary result) of the specific course of action (path). The initial state of the course of action is characterized here only by the fact that a state of affairs $p_1$ does *not* hold. The general, overall purpose is to act such that $p_1$ will be realized as a consequence of the action sequence. In the final

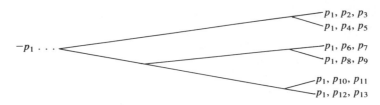

**Figure 3.1.**   A schematic representation of alternative courses of action.

states we read that $p_1$ (in the alternative possible worlds) has been realized as a consequence of the actions. The final states, however, are not only characterized by $p_1$, but also by other properties ($p_2$, $p_3$, etc.). It may be that the agent does not want these to be realized as consequences of the action. In that case the alternatives are reduced to those paths that lead to $p_1$ plus those other properties that are at least not inconsistent with the wishes of the agent. If one of these other properties is also wanted, then the path that leads to a state that leads to both will be chosen. In that case we speak of an optimal goal, that is a goal that contains at least $p_1$ plus a maximum of further properties $p_2$, $p_3$, . . . that are also wanted.

However, going from the initial to the final state along different paths will seldom be equally easy. That is, some actions will take more time, effort, money, or will involve unwanted intermediary states. The sum of these will, as in economic decision theory, be called the cost of each action. A rational agent will in such cases try to reach an optimal goal along the lowest cost path, that is, in the easiest way. Often things will not be so clear-cut: Optimal goals may be reached only via high cost paths. The agent will then have to decide, by comparing costs and goals (a means–end analysis), what his or her preferences are: easy actions with minimal goal attainment (i.e., at least $p_1$), or maximizing the goal with further cost.

Finally, it should be borne in mind that goals are merely consequences of actions and hence beyond the control of the agent. In other words, they will obtain with only some degree of probability, depending on other circumstances of each state in the action sequence. Thus, some action sequences will almost certainly lead to $p_1$, whereas others have a high chance of failing (not in Figure 3.1, where each path leads to $p_1$). In many cases, these intermediary circumstances may not be known to the agent, so that each path choice will depend on the knowledge and beliefs of the agent about the possible outcomes, consequences, and circumstances of each action. Hence, some paths may be riskier, that is, have lower accumulated probabilities of leading to the desired goal. Again, the agent will then have to choose between relatively risky or certain paths, as compared to relatively optimal final goals.

## 3.2.2. Strategies

Against this background of notions from the theory of action we may now define the notion of strategy. We have seen that strategies involve actions, goals, and some notion of optimality: Intuitively, a strategy is the idea of an agent about the best way to act in order to reach a goal. For our purposes we will, indeed, take a strategy to be a cognitive representation of some kind, just as a plan was defined as a cognitive representation of some macroaction. Now, whereas a plan is a global concept of the macroaction and its final result or goal, a strategy is a global representation of the means of reaching that goal. This overall means will dominate a number of lower level, more detailed, decisions and actions. Thus, if the strategy is globally characterized by the concept FAST, then at each point that action will be taken that leads most quickly to the next stage, and thus to the final goal. If the strategy is OPTIMAL GOAL, then at each point a decision will be made to execute those further actions that lead not only to $p_1$, but also to a maximum number of other desired properties of the state of affairs aimed at. Similarly, we may have a SURE strategy, which involves always choosing the action alternative that most probably leads to the wanted results, intermediary and final goals, or a CHEAP strategy which does so at lowest cost. Combinations are, of course, possible, for example, CHEAP–FAST, or SURE–EXPENSIVE.

Note the difference between a plan and a strategy. A plan is merely a global representation of an action, for example, 'Taking a plane to New York'. A strategy, however, is a global mental representation of a style, that is, of a way of doing this global action in the most effective way (e.g., with low cost, minimum risk, etc.). Taking a charter flight would be an action appropriate for the CHEAP strategy of accomplishing the global action, although such a choice may involve loss of time, changing planes, booking long in advance, lack of freedom to alter one's plans, etc. Thus, according to our definition, a strategy is not a detailed representation of some action sequence. The reason for this is that, in general, very complex (inter-)actions have many as yet unknown intermediary circumstances and results, so that detailed (microstructure) planning in advance is impossible. A strategy is merely a global instruction for each necessary choice to be made along the path of the course of action: whatever happens, always choose the cheapest, fastest, surest, etc., alternative. Just like plans, strategies may, of course, be changed along the way: A CHEAP strategy may turn out to be so time consuming or risky that the final goal can hardly be reached within some desired time limit, or with some desired degree of confidence. For the rest of the action sequence an agent may then change to a less CHEAP, but faster or surer, strategy.

In general, plans and strategies will be represented together, as the content and style of a global action defining an action sequence. The precise representation format does not matter here, nor do the exact cognitive processing aspects, to which we will turn later. At this point, the notion of strategy is still very general and abstract. We merely assume that a strategy is a cognitive representation of some kind, that it pertains to complex action sequences, that it is linked to the notion of plan, and that it, therefore, must also be a macronotion: It pertains to a global way of deciding, in advance, which kinds of action alternatives will be taken along a course of actions. A plan is macroinformation that decides the possible actions contained in a global action, and a strategy is the macroinformation that determines the choice at each point of the most effective or rational alternative.

It hardly needs saying that in everyday life we perform many actions without much of a strategy: We may decide at each point which kind of decision to make—although even this lack of a strategy may be characterized as a strategy (WAIT-AND-SEE). Strategies become necessary as soon as the end goals become extremely important, or the means very costly or risky (e.g., in governing countries or big organizations, or in making important life decisions).

Each local choice of action may conform more or less to the global strategy. We will say that a course of action is strategically coherent if its component actions are always consistent with the global strategy. This may mean that we have degrees of strategic coherence. We may deviate more or more often from the global strategy. Before we try to focus the notion of strategy on cognition and language use, some further concepts should be introduced that are closely related to the notion of strategy.

First, we introduce the notion of *move.* A move in a sequence of (inter-)actions is an action—which itself may be complex, or even a subsequence of actions—but taken from a specific point of view. This point of view we will call functional. Thus, a move may be an action that is functional with respect to the desired final goal of the action sequence: Taking an airplane thus may have as moves going to the airport and boarding the plane. But, in general an agent will also accomplish many actions that are not functional in this way (buying a newspaper, having a drink, chatting with a fellow passenger, etc.). In other words, a move is any action that is accomplished with the intention of bringing about a state of affairs that directly or indirectly will (probably) lead to a desired global goal. For some global actions nearly every action may also be a move, for example, in playing chess or in conversation. According to our definition of strategy, a move thus is not a part of a strategy, but part of an action sequence or global action that is dominated by a plan (including a representation of a final goal) and a strategy. Moves, thus, are bound actions, in contrast to free, optional actions, which may or may not be performed and which do not influence the rest of the course of action. A strategy is defined as a cognitive unit dominating only the moves of an action sequence and not each action. For instance, traveling to New York with the CHEAP strategy will influence the choice of a charter flight but not, for instance, the choice of having a drink at the airport before leaving even if not having a drink would make the whole trip slightly cheaper. Such a choice is strategically free.

Next, we consider the notion of *tactics,* which sometimes is used as a synonym for strategy. We will, however, reserve the notion of tactics to denote an organized set, a system, of strategies. That is, a strategy applies, just like a plan, to a particular action sequence, and hence to a particular goal to be reached. Just as the various plans of our life may be organized by increasingly larger plan systems including more or less general life goals, we may also have systems of strategies which in the same way can be defined as more or less general life-styles (Schank & Abelson, 1977). Tactics, hence, will be relevant for relatively large segments or periods of our lives and actions. Studying psychology, for instance, may involve a tactic that includes a strategy for studying hard, a strategy that leads to a maximum number of final goal properties (lack of specialization so that it may be easier to find a job afterward), a strategy to make many friends or a few good friends among our costudents, etc. A tactic is not any set of strategies, but a set that has organization: Some strategies will depend upon others. Studying hard may mean that making many friends will be difficult due to lack of time for social interaction. Bad tactics typically involve conflicting strategies.

Whereas a tactic may apply to a global action, such as studying psychology, it may also be used to define a global *style* of action. For instance, a CHEAP tactic will typically determine for an agent the choice of CHEAP strategies for specific action sequences. Such overall systems may be related to what is traditionally called the personality of the agent: To be thrifty involves among other things a general constraint on strategies to try to reach one's goals by the cheapest possible course of action.

Another relation exists between strategies and *rules* (von Wright, 1963; Lewis, 1969; Collett, 1977). Whereas rules are more or less general conventions of a social community regulating behavior in a standard way, strategies are particular, often personal, ways of using the rules to reach one's goals. Rules have been explicitly or implicitly established as norms for possible or correct actions and therefore are related to sanctions which are applicable when rules are broken. Thus we have rules defining games, such as the rules of chess which define the possible moves that may be made in the game, and rules of traffic which determine the traffic actions that can or should be performed. Similarly, rules of language determine which utterances count as correct within a given language system. So, whereas rules are more general, relatively fixed, prescriptions of correct behavior, strategies pertain to ways of *effective* behavior in a certain situation for an individual to reach a goal. Rules, thus, define the possible moves, whereas strategies determine which choices are made among the possible moves so that the aims of the agent are realized optimally. Later we will come back in somewhat more detail to the interplay between rules and strategies of language use and discourse understanding.

Whereas rules define the possible moves, the execution of these moves may be either via strategies or via *algorithms*. An algorithm guarantees that the rules, if applied correctly, will eventually produce a solution. Arithmetic calculations are good examples of commonly used algorithms: If the procedures of an algorithm are followed faithfully, step by step, the desired end result will be obtained. However, it may take very long to obtain that result, or it may be very expensive to execute the steps of the algorithm, so that for all practical purposes the algorithm is useless. One may know how to compute the result, but given human limits on time and resources, it nevertheless is unobtainable. Strategic approaches have to take over at this point. Strategic moves are only intelligent guesswork and, unlike algorithmic moves, carry no guarantees, but they make it possible to solve complex problems given the time and the resources available. The risk is, of course, that they may fail or result in errors. A good strategy is something that works most of the time, whereas an algorithm always works—but only in principle, not in real situations. Strategies are intelligent but risky; algorithms rely on blind, methodological application of rules.

Finally, another notion often used in relation to, or even as a synonym for, strategies is that of *heuristics*. We will take a heuristic as a system of discovery procedures, that is, as actions that are intended to acquire knowledge about conditions that may enable an agent to reach a certain goal, typically in the context of problem solving. A heuristic involves typical kinds of strategies, namely, those strategies that aim at the acquisition of knowledge in a context in which this knowledge cannot be obtained in automatic, obvious ways. Just as with strategies in general, this means that we may want to find the desired information in a FAST, but perhaps not very SURE way, or choose a path that is rather complicated but that has a higher probability of yielding the necessary information. In this way, we give a global or overall characterization of a heuristic: It is a general way of proceeding, a schema for finding something. An alternative way of defining the notion would be to apply it more locally, at the microlevel. In that case, it would define the full set of intended actions that will be performed to find some information (e.g., as represented in a flow diagram). However, we will use both the notion of strategy and the notion of heuristics to denote only higher level macroschemata for action. The reason for this is that in general, due to circumstances, actions of other agents, or ignorance about the possible outcomes or consequences of our actions, we are unable to plan in advance each detailed action. At most we may have beforehand an idea of what kind of action we will choose at each point in a course of action.

A classic example of the use of heuristics occurs in scientific investigation. In order to be able to formulate some regularity or law, we may systematically observe a number of phenomena, or we may first try to derive the regularity from other regularities and then check our hypothesis with the facts, or we may employ a combination of these heuristics. In this example we have a preset schema that controls the way we will look for an answer.

## 3.3. COGNITIVE STRATEGIES

The notion of strategy we have discussed here applies to actions in the strict sense, that is, to overt, intended doings of humans. In psychology, however, the notion is used also in a more specialized way, to denote cognitive behavior of some kind. The use of the notion of action, and hence of strategy, is notoriously problematic in this case. We may, of course, speak of mental acts, in which case these would be open to strategic control. Thinking and problem solving are well-known examples: We have an explicit goal to be reached, the solution of a problem, and there may be specific operations, mental steps, to be performed to reach that goal. These steps are under our conscious control and we may be at least partly able to verbalize them, so that we can analyze the strategies followed in solving the problem.

Similarly, many of the overt action strategies described in the previous section presuppose thinking: We have defined strategy in terms of properties of global plans, that is, cognitive representations of action sequences and their goals. This means that our desires or wants are compared to what we know about our abilities, about the action context, about possibilities or probabilities of outcomes, about actions of others, and so on. In other words, a strategy will in general be the result of a mental process involving much information. As soon as this mental process is consciously controlled, orderly, such that each mental step yields the information necessary for the next mental step, we may also speak of mental strategies.

However, there are many cognitive activities that do not seem to have this conscious, orderly, controlled nature. If we look at a landscape, at a movie, or read a text, then we may very well have the overall goal of comprehending, but it can hardly be said that we have explicitly controlled strategies to reach that goal. Yet there is a sequence of mental operations that allow us to reach that goal, and these may also be more or less effective. We may also say that we follow a strategy of GOOD understanding or a strategy of FAST understanding.

Before we turn to more specific language-understanding strategies in the next section, let us briefly examine the nature of the more explicit and verbalizable strategies of problem solving, for example, as discussed by Newell and Simon (1972). Although the notion of strategy is used on several occasions in Newell and Simon (1972), there is no explicit definition of it. A strategy will in general involve higher levels of information processing, that is, the high-level strategic attempts of a problem solver. For instance, a subject will try to analyze a problem into sub-problems if it is rather complex and if it has no obvious, direct solutions. The product of $7 \times 5$ may be drawn directly from memory, whereas $7 \times 35$ will be computed by most subjects according to the rules of arithmetic. Another general strategic procedure is to compare means and end, that is, to analyze the nature of the goal, the final state to be reached by the problem-solving process, and the kind of steps that may lead there. Third, if a subject does not know how to reach some point from a starting point, he or she may apply the general strategy of working backward from those intermediary or end points that are known, a strategy also applied in cases where errors were made. A very well-known strategy for cases in which no information at all is available is the trial-and-error strategy. Apart from such very general properties of strategies, Newell and Simon (1972:62) represent a strategy as a production system, which involves rules that have on the left of an arrow the information now at hand (e.g., the situation in a game of tic tac toe or chess) and on the right the specific move to take at each point of the game. Later (pp. 282ff.) the authors give a more general definition independent of a particular task and of a particular production system. Thus, apart from analyzing the problem into sub-problems, a subject will try to obtain new information when needed, will integrate new information found into the knowledge set, will go back to previous correct (not disconfirmed) states of the problem in case an error is reached, will check new information with old information, etc. It is easy to complement this list of general strategies with others. We may assume, for example, that at each point of a problem (which may be represented by a graph such as the one given in Figure 3.1), a subject will perform forward searches of alternatives in terms of their probability of success: Steps that are deemed most likely to lead to a goal will be preferred or explored first. If probability of success is believed to be equal, the shortest or easiest action or operation will be taken. In interactive strategy situations, for example, those of games like chess, other global strategies will become relevant, such as assumptions about intended actions and hence also about strategies of other participants, or specific attack or defense strategies such as limiting the choices of other participants, turning a defense move at the same time into an attack move, and so on.

Important for our discussion is that strategies in these cases also involve stepwise, complex acts (although these acts are mental) that lead to a certain goal, and that at each point or state of a problem several options are possible and at the same time limited knowledge is available about context, consequences, actions, and other participants. In rather complex problems, part of these strategies may be consciously intended. Yet, part of them will also be more or less automatized, as in standard problems, or at least not explicitly intended. From the preceding discussion it is not completely clear whether strategies have only an overall, planned nature. Some of the examples seem to identify strategies with more local decision procedures for taking next moves. We will, however, provisionally assume, according to our earlier hypothesis, that strategies have a higher level, general nature, namely, as specific properties of plans that control the local steps in problem solving.

## 3.4. LANGUAGE STRATEGIES

As part of the cognitive strategies we will now focus on the more specific strategies of language use, that is, strategies that are applied by language users in the production and comprehension of verbal utterances or speech acts of a natural language. Apart from a few general remarks, this section will review some of the sentence-based, grammatical strategies of language users, whereas the following section and the rest of this book will concentrate on discourse strategies.

First, we again have the general question of whether the notion of strategy is appropriate in this case. To a greater extent than complex problem solving, the production and comprehension of verbal utterances is an automatized activity. Unless an utterance has specifically difficult, problematic, or unusual properties, production and comprehension is not monitored at each step by the language user. If we do not know the meaning of a word, we may apply the strategy of asking somebody, consulting a dictionary, or guessing the meaning of the word from context, and if a sentence structure is particularly complex, we may—in written communication—backtrack and start reading again. Similarly, in discourse, we may have texts that are so complex that various external aids, such as schemata, summaries, or notes, are necessary to control the meaning of the text in production or comprehension. But such devices are rather special: Understanding and speaking are usually almost automatic processes.

There is also another problem. Unlike the kinds of strategies, both overt and implicit, that we have discussed thus far, language production and understanding are not really problem-solving strategies. There is no single goal, the goal is not a final state, nor is the goal well defined (we do not know if or when we have reached it), unless we take the act of production or comprehension itself to be the relevant global action whose final state—deciding that we have done enough toward producing or understanding the utterance—corresponds to the goal. Thus, language production and comprehension, if a problem at all, is a continuous task, consisting of many small-scale problems that together define the problem as a whole.

Yet, it makes sense to speak of strategies of language use anyway, although those strategies in most cases will not be preprogrammed, intended, conscious, or verbalizable by the language user. Rather, we should say, they are strategies of the cognitive system, usually beyond the conscious control of the language user. Also, they apply to sequences of mental steps that perform a number of tasks. These tasks are different in nature and scope—for example, identifying sounds or letters, constructing words, analyzing syntactic structures, and understanding sentential or textual meanings. This means that the total task, namely, the production or understanding of the utterance—as part of the even larger task of participating in some form of communicative social interaction—is a complex task that is performed if each component task has been performed. Whereas some of these tasks are well defined (e.g., identifying a sound, letter, or word, or analyzing a syntactic structure), others are much less clear-cut, especially the semantic tasks of interpreting sentences or whole texts. It is a notoriously difficult problem both for linguistics and for psychology to determine what a semantic representation is: how much, how deep, how elaborate, should such a representation be, and how much of episodic memories or general world knowledge should it include? Understanding language is a fuzzy task, and the communicative context will determine how much fuzziness is allowed for appropriate understanding and communication. Thus, we know that some subtasks belong to the overall task (e.g., understanding words and sentences), whereas others are much less obviously related to the task (e.g., understanding backgrounds or ideologies, or associating personal memories when reading a newspaper story).

The reasons, then, that we may still speak of strategies when referring to specific kinds of cognitive processing in using language may be summed up as follows:

1. In both the production and comprehension of verbal utterances as speech acts in some communicative context, the language user is confronted with the execution or understanding of an action.
2. Such an action has a rather well-defined initial state or starting point.
3. The action has an end point or goal, although this goal will often be fuzzy: In addition to having said or having read something, which are rather well-defined final goals, we have meaning or intending something, and understanding such meanings or intentions, or understanding in an even broader sense.

4. The task is complex. It consists of a number of subtasks that must be fulfilled.
5. The solution of the task occurs step by step: We cannot produce or understand an utterance by accomplishing just one task.
6. In general, the component tasks are not obvious: Information may be lacking or not readily available, and alternative routes (options) are possible.

These are some general criteria that allow us to speak of strategies when language use is concerned. Later we will see that the nature of the strategies is indeed sufficiently general to make the notion interesting. If we chose a strict definition of strategy we would apply the notion of strategy only to complex overt actions. Then, perhaps, listening and interpreting would not be considered an action at all but just some activity that cannot be controlled in a stepwise fashion as actions can. In this case, the notion of language strategy becomes a metaphor, applying not only to mental acts, as in difficult problem solving, but also to mental activities, such as the processes in the production or understanding of language. Instead of strategies of an agent, or language user, we would then speak of strategies of a system. Just like agents, such systems should exhibit the crucial notion of effectiveness that we have taken as the explanandum of a theory of strategies. Thus, language strategies are being postulated because we assume that the language user as an agent *and* his or her cognitive system will try to perform their tasks as quickly, as well, as easily, as cheaply, etc., as possible.

There is another reason to speak of strategies when dealing with language use. We postulate language strategies as a complement to an account of verbal behavior in terms of *rules*. Rules of language, for instance, those of a grammar, whether explicitly formulated or not, have by definition a general nature. For some level of the utterance, it is specified what the possible, or correct, structures are, for example, those of phonology, morphology, or syntax; or what the possible meanings or functions are, as in semantics and pragmatics. A rule has a general and abstract nature, and represents, in rather idealistic terms, what language users in general do or what they implicitly or explicitly think they do or should do. Opposed to this are the possible uses of the rule, which may depend on context, on the particular language user, or on communicative goals, and which are variable. Whereas rules of language account for some rather general norm, that is, formulate what is held to be correct by language users of a certain group in certain contexts, a language strategy accounts for what is effective, for example, for producing or understanding correct utterances in a certain way. One of the main reasons why strategies are necessary in addition to the rules of language lies in the specific processing features of natural language utterances:

1. Language users have limited memory, and, especially, a limited short-time memory capacity.
2. Language users cannot process many different kinds of information at the same time.

3. Production and understanding of utterances is linear, whereas most of the structures the rules pertain to are hierarchical.
4. Production and understanding require not only linguistic or grammatical information, but other information as well, for example, information about the context, episodic memories, knowledge of the world, intentions, plans and goals, and so on.

So, whereas rules are abstract and are therefore formulated a posteriori for complete structures, at various levels, and for various scopes, strategies are necessary to allow a language user to accomplish the task of production or understanding linearly, at several levels, simultaneously taking into account different kinds of information, and with limited knowledge. Rules are not formulated for this kind of complex task, but strategies should be such that they satisfy the various conditions formulated here. As we go along, we will add some further characteristics of language strategies.

## 3.5. GRAMMATICAL STRATEGIES

We use the term *grammatical strategies,* or sentence strategies, although it should be kept in mind that these are not strategies that are formulated by the grammar, but cognitive strategies that are used to produce or understand structures that are specified by the rules of the grammar.

It is at this point that the difference between the notions of rule and strategy become most obvious. Even if we accept the hypothesis that a grammar is a theoretical—and hence general, abstract, and idealized—reconstruction of the language rules known by language users, there is still a crucial difference between grammatical rules on the one hand and strategies on the other.

Typically, rules apply to structures taken as complete entities, a posteriori. For both synthetic and analytic types of rules in sentence grammars or cognitive models, the categories and units are typically structural. They characterize a syntactic sentence structure as a whole. Thus, a NP–VP categorical analysis of a sentence pertains to the sentence as a whole (or to a clause as a whole), and not to serially processed linguistic units, that is, to units as they are understood or processed by a language user in real time. Strategies pertain to the latter kind of linear processing, that is, to information that a language user processes fragmentarily. This does not mean that strategies do not also imply higher level structures, or that parallel processing would be excluded in a cognitive model of language use, but rather that the data are processed in real time. Once the relevant data are processed, a language user may use rules to check whether the strategies have been correctly applied.

From this latter aspect we see that strategies and rules are not independent. In fact, this would be highly uneconomical for the cognitive system. We may assume, thus, that the categories and units on which they operate are roughly the same. If we know the units to which rules apply, it would be strange indeed if strategies did not make use of the same units also, at least in part. In other words, a language user will generally try to respect word boundaries in applying fast strategies for the semantic interpretation of a sentence, although there are times when he or she will jump to a conclusion about the meaning of a word after having analyzed only part of it. This is possible, for instance, in cases of well-founded expectations about meanings of words as derived from the meaning of the previous part of the text or from the context. In this example we witness a typical further characteristic of grammatical strategies: They are not limited to the use of rule-governed information from the cognitive grammar and its specific levels, units, or categories (e.g., morphology or syntax), but will at the same time use information from other levels or even from the communicative context. Furthermore, strategies appear to be hypothetical, probabilistic: They make fast but effective guesses about the most likely structure or meaning of the incoming data. These guesses may, of course, be wrong. In that case, the grammatical rules will establish—on second analysis—the correct structure or meaning. Another interaction between rules and strategies may be called schematical. Although theoretically and also empirically all or most of our sentences will be unique, especially if they are rather long, it goes without saying that many of them will show grammatical patterns that are very similar or identical. This means that a language user, after years of experience, may form schemata for these linguistic patterns. The schemata themselves are, of course, developed on the basis of rules, but their use is strategic: As soon as data are analyzed that conform to the terminal categories of the schema, then the sentence will be analyzed according to the schema. Here we witness an intermediary phase between rules and strategies, namely, a kind of preprogramming of rules, to be strategically applied as soon as the input data appear to be standard. From this perspective, psycholinguistics in the last 10 years has developed a number of hypotheses about effective grammatical strategies or schemata for the production, and especially the understanding, of sentences. Although experimental confirmation of these hypotheses has proven to be notoriously difficult, and although sometimes conflicting results have been obtained, there are a number of strategies that are fairly well established, as indicated in the previous chapter.

If we forget for a moment the phonological and morphological strategies and focus upon syntactic strategies for sentence understanding, we find that earlier models of sentence recognition, namely, those closely linked to the framework of transformational grammar, should be discarded as plausible models of sentence processing (Fodor, Bever, & Garrett, 1974). That is, models that somehow—through analysis by analysis or analysis by synthesis—try to match an input string of lexical items to structures generated by grammatical rules, quickly run into trouble. Even for moderately complex sentences the number of possible structural descriptions (trees) is astronomically high, and effective search among such possible structures would be impossible. Fodor, Bever, and Garret (1974:328ff.) opt for a model that is less close to the grammar, although it is still level specific. The model gives a strategy for syntactic analysis—a strategy that does not at the same time operate on or with other kinds of information, such as semantic, contextual, or epistemic (world knowledge) information. It is assumed that analysis is clausal: A language user first tries to discover the clauses of a sentence, by interpreting clause boundary signals of various kinds. These clauses are assumed to be the surface representation of underlying sentoids of the deep structure (the authors still differentiate between surface and deep structure for syntactic description and understanding). Information about the internal structure of each clause is then gathered in the short-term memory buffer, and as soon as the clause has been interpreted, this information is erased from the store so that new information can be stored. The relations between the interpreted clauses can then be established. Each clause will be strategically interpreted by a ''canonical-sentoid'' analysis of the NP–VP–(NP) type, whereas a lexical strategy determines which relations exist between the clauses. For example, some verbs are known to often have *that*-complements, for instance, *see, hear, suppose,* or *doubt,* and similar observations might be made for connectives such as *although, because,* or *but.* But this is still much too simplistic; the strategy would fail in many cases. Because *that* may not always occur in the surface structure, we must have a strategy for recognizing whether a verb is part of a main or a subordinated clause (e.g., by assuming that a first verb, after an NP, will be the verb of the main clause, unless there is a mark for subordination in the surface structure).

Important for our discussion is the conclusion of the authors (p. 369) that the sentence recognition device, that is, the system of strategies used in understanding a sentence, is not closely bound to the system of grammatical rules, but that the system has its own cognitive properties.

Although this model is already notably distant from a transformational-grammar-based recognition model, it still carries some of the distinctive properties of transformational grammar. Mainly, it is, as we already suggested, still syntactically based: It tries to establish syntactic structures before even looking at the semantic or pragmatic information available to a language user. Yet it is precisely that information that yields powerful expectations about the meaning of a sentence and therefore also about the correct surface analysis of a sentence. Moreover, morphophonemic surface signals for syntactic structures are few and often difficult to perceive in natural speech. Hence, a semantically and pragmatically based system of strategies seems to be more effective, or as Clark and Clark (1977) put it:

> Listeners usually know a lot about what a speaker is going to say. They can make shrewd guesses from what has just been said and from the situation being described. They can also be confident that the speaker will make sense, be relevant, provide given and new information appropriately, and in general be cooperative. Listeners almost certainly use this sort of information to select among alternatives parses of a sentence, to anticipate words and phrases, and sometimes even to circumvent syntactic analyses altogether. Just how is not very clear [p. 72].

Clark and Clark (1977:72ff.) therefore make a distinction between two very basic principles, which we might take as characterizing two kinds of strategies—the *reality principle* and the *cooperative principle.* The reality principle pertains to the close relationships that exist between meaning, reference, and (our knowledge about) possible states of affairs in the world. Since we make intelligent guesses about a situation or event a speaker is referring to, we also have some idea about what the speaker could possibly mean, that is, we have a range of possible semantic readings for the sentence. These assumptions may, in turn, be matched with strategic analyses at the syntactic level—if these latter are still needed at all. The cooperative principle—as adopted from Grice (1967)—assumes that speakers in general try to make sense, want to be cooperative, and do this by being truthful, being clear, saying no more nor less than is meant, and trying to be relevant. Hence, the first principle can be called semantic and the second pragmatic. Apart from the general principles of cooperation, we may have expectations about the possible speech acts of a speaker (a promise, a threat), depending on an analysis of the context (see van Dijk, 1981a). This, in turn, presupposes specific meanings (propositions) of sentences and clauses, whereas we also have information about a still wider interactional, social, and cultural context. From those we may infer expectations about possible speech acts, about possible meanings, about possible themes (see Section 6 on discourse, in this chapter), about style (e.g., as dependent on the social and personal contexts), and hence about matching surface structures. Hence, the two principles mentioned by Clark and Clark (1977) may be formulated in a still broader framework, a framework that is still further away from grammar, involving world knowledge, and knowledge about the social, personal, and cultural contexts of communication. We may assume that there is a hierarchy in these systems and their concomitant strategies: Interactional strategies will probably dominate pragmatic ones, pragmatic (speech act) comprehension strategies the semantic ones, and the semantic strategies the syntactic and other surface structure strategies of analysis.

This assumption about the hierarchical ordering of strategy systems of language understanding should be handled with care, however. It does not mean that a language user will always and for each sentence first apply all interactional, pragmatic, etc., strategies. Sometimes the knowledge about the wider context is not relevant, or is already established and functioning only as a background monitoring device. And, more importantly, it may be more effective to try to assemble some directly available information from the utterance than to scan the wider contextual possibilities. As we have assumed, strategies are flexible, they use several kinds of information at the same time, and they adapt to continuing changes in the ongoing utterance and context. To establish which speech act is now being performed, the hearer will, of course, make a systematic analysis of the interactional context— determining a class of possible speech acts—but at the same time will try to get semantic or even surface structure information that manifests or signals the speech act in the utterance: Verbs, tenses, syntactic structure, and propositional content can all be used to decide what the speech act is that is now being performed. The hierarchy should thus be understood as a device that effectively narrows the scope of the operation of following strategies. If a specific context makes the speech act of a command highly unlikely, we will not even try, on first analysis, to semantically understand or syntactically parse the sentence according to a strategy that relates form and meaning with such a speech act. And, conversely, if the broader (higher) level yields a rather probable hypothesis about the relevant speech act, then the rest of the analysis may directly focus on the meaning and reference content—if that cannot be predicted from a semantic strategy operating on world knowledge. In other words, a hierarchical ordering of language understanding strategies has two complementary basic features: It narrows down the scope for the operation of lower-level strategies, or it provides possible direct guesses which may make the operation of further strategic analysis partly unnecessary, at least until conflicting information is encountered.

Returning briefly to semantic strategies of sentence understanding, we observe that Clark and Clark (1977:73ff.) use the reality principle to limit the scope of possible meanings for sentences, and we next assume that a schematic analysis of the sentence or clause takes place that is like the semantic counterpart of the clause analysis for syntax we have met earlier. A language user will first look for a (main) verb, interpret that as an expression of an underlying predicate, and then search for the surface structure elements that express the normal categories (arguments) that go with the verb. Thus, the verb or predicate *to hit* will require an agent, an object, and possibly an instrument. These may be expressed by noun phrases in surface structure. Moreover, there is for each language a preferential ordering for such noun phrases (see also Dik, 1978, 1980), such that the agent-expressing noun phrase will typically be the subject of the sentence, which will often be realized first.

We see that semantic strategies may be schematic, in the sense that they make use of canonical semantic structures of propositions, and that these strategies will cooperate with surface structure information, whereas both are controlled by our knowledge of the actual or wider (social, cultural) contexts: who is now agent in this context, who could be agent, what kind of actions are possible or probable, etc.— and the same for other possible participants in an event a sentence is referring to.

From this brief discussion of some of the strategies and principles used in cognitive models for the understanding of language we may first of all conclude that strategies are indeed a fundamental component of our cognitive ability to use (understand and produce) language utterances. Second, these strategies are parts of sets that are ordered hierarchically. Third, the strategies are flexible, operate at several levels at the same time, use incomplete information, and combine bottom-up (inductive) and top-down (deductive) ways of processing information. And, fourth, they are context sensitive: Depending on the attention, interests, goals, beliefs, attitudes, or opinions of the language user, and depending on the actual interactional and social context—as cognitively represented by the language user— the strategies may be changed. For instance, sometimes it will be more important to establish what kind a speech act is being performed by a speaker, on other occasions the precise semantic content of a speech act may be more relevant, and, on yet other occasions the specific surface structure or style may be most relevant and hence focused upon.

One basic way in which the principles and strategies mentioned here are context sensitive is in their dependence on text or discourse. That is, a speech act or meaning conveyed by a clause or sentence will typically depend on those occurring earlier in the same monological or dialogical discourse. Just as it is highly unlikely that word recognition strategies operate independently of sentence recognition strategies, sentence strategies will be very much dependent on textual strategies. Given that phonology and syntax are somewhat more closely linked to sentential structures—although there are also phonological and syntactic constraints across sentence boundaries-we may expect textual strategies to influence the semantic and pragmatic strategies of the sentence level. In the following section we will give a survey of some arguments regarding discourse strategies of different kinds and their relationship to sentence-understanding strategies. In later chapters we will then treat some of these textual strategies in more detail.

## 3.6. DISCOURSE STRATEGIES

Strategies for the production and comprehension of discourse are similar to those used in the comprehension of sentences. Language users always manipulate surface structures, word, phrase, and clause meanings, pragmatic information from the context, as well as interactional, social, and cultural data. That is, a language user will try to effectively assess the meanings of (parts of) the discourse, corresponding reference, pragmatic functions or speech act values of (parts of) the discourse, as well as other interactional, social, and cultural functions. Hence, a number of the fundamental principles are those we have already discussed. Moreover, as we have also observed, sentence strategies are closely linked to discourse strategies: The production and comprehension of sentences depends on textual information of a larger scope or of a higher level. Conversely, the semantic and pragmatic interpretation of the discourse will have sentential information as input. This is precisely as it should be. One of the fundamental properties of strategies is that they are not independent, contrary to many grammatical rules.

Yet, there are a number of discourse strategies that need to be formulated in their own right, in part because sentence strategies may in turn depend on them. Clark and Clark (1977:76) give an example of this interdependence.

(1)     a. *Claire and Kent climbed Mt. McKinley last summer.*
        b. *She photographed the peak, and he surveyed it.*

To establish the meaning and reference of (1b), and in particular that of its referring phrases *she, the peak, he,* and *it,* a language user does not have to make a large-scale search in memory for the possible referents of these expressions: The previous sentence immediately yields the information needed; search for appropriate referents can, in this example, be strategically limited to the small set of referents introduced by this previous part of the discourse. Of course, the strategy becomes much more complex when there are several sentences preceding and when the referents must be sought in larger chunks of previous discourse. Also, the strategy as is may not be powerful enough. Consider, for example, the following continuation sentences:

(1)      b'. *They didn't like it very much.*
            b''. *It was their last holiday.*

Here the reference of *it* cannot easily be established by coreference with *Mt. McKinley:* In (1b') *it* may refer to the mountain, but also to the climbing; in (1b'') *it* may be taken to refer to the whole previous event or as an empty pronoun introducing *holiday* (as in *It was a very cold day*). We see that even for a very simple discourse and for a limited problem, the establishment of (co)reference, we soon get into a rather thorny issue. Moreover, in our example taken from Clark and Clark it should also be stressed that a simple search for appropriate referents is not enough. The interpretation of the *the peak* will also require some information from world knowledge, namely, the fact that a mountain has a peak. This implicit information, signaled by the definite noun phrase *the,* is assumed by the speaker to be known to the hearer. The strategy therefore also requires searching relevant knowledge of the world and drawing correct inferences from it.

Even from this initial example we can conclude that semantic discourse strategies involve at least the following principles:

1. Both meaning and reference information needed to interpret a sentence may be searched for in the representation of one or more previous sentences.
2. Part of the information for semantic interpretation must be sought for in or inferred from general world knowledge.
3. Search in both cases will also depend on the meaning of the (rest of) the sentence being interpreted.

A more general principle dominating these principles is the very assumption that in successive sentences of a discourse the referring phrases may be coreferential and that, more generally, two successive sentences are coherent.

Extensive work in text linguistics and the psychology of discourse comprehension (see Chapter 2) has resulted in the formulation of rules and conditions for this kind of discourse coherence, both in terms of semantics and pragmatics and in terms of world knowledge. It has been assumed that in addition to this structural approach we now also need a system of strategies as used by speakers and hearers to establish, construct, discover, or recognize this fundamental property of discourse.

In order to formulate such strategies we should first realize what coherence intuitively means for language users. If predicated of a sentence, it may mean, for instance, that it is a normal, possible, understandable, or correct continuation with respect to already produced/read/heard parts of ongoing discourse. More specifically, coherence may be taken as a condition on good semantic (meaning and reference) continuation of a sentence with respect to previous discourse. In other words, it must be possible for the language user to establish semantic relations between a sentence and previous discourse. On the other hand, coherence may also be taken as predicated not of a sentence, but of pairs, triples, . . . , *n*-tuples of sentences or of fragments or the whole of a discourse. In that case, the intuitive notion involved is that of unity: The respective sentences belong together, can appropriately be used together as one whole and in one utterance. And, third, coherence may also be predicated of a sentence relative to this whole. In that case, the sentence fits well into the whole discourse. Coherence conditions have been discussed in more detail in van Dijk (1977a).

We have seen in Chapter 2 that these intuitive notions that underlie discourse strategies can be theoretically represented in terms of local and global semantic properties of a discourse, that is, in terms of semantic relations between sentences and in terms of rules relating sentences or $n$-tuples of sentences with semantic macrostructures.

The question now is how to reformulate these conditions and rules in terms of strategies. Furthermore, we must determine what other textual strategies are involved in the production and comprehension of discourse—surface structure strategies, as well as the more general strategies of knowledge use and the use of contextual information (speech act, interaction, personal, social, and cultural situation). Although it is impossible to be complete, we will draw a list of the kinds of strategies that may be used in the processing of discourse. Only some of these strategy classes will be studied in more detail in the following chapters. It should therefore be borne in mind that the strategies we discuss later are intimately tied to the other kinds of strategies listed in this section. Note that the names of the strategy classes and subclasses are a convenient shorthand, so that we can easily refer back to them in the rest of the book without explaining in detail what kind of strategy is involved. We will follow the hierarchy discussed earlier, that is, we will start with the strategy types of the largest scope, in other words, those strategies that are most fundamental to understanding in general, both of language and of other semiotic practices, of interactions, events, and objects. Our formulation, however, will be focusing on the relevance of these strategies to the processing of discourse. In particular, we shall restrict the specification to strategies of understanding, although similar strategies may be formulated for production.

Finally, it should be stressed that the various strategies are of a cognitive nature. They operate on cognitively represented information actualized from long-term memory. The cultural and social information discussed earlier is assumed to have been acquired through learning processes (general knowledge) or to be representations of actual social situations.

### 3.6.1. Cultural Strategies

Cultural strategies are those strategies that pertain to the effective selection of cultural information that is relevant to the comprehension of the discourse. These strategies may be speaker or hearer oriented. That is, a hearer/reader may use the information about the cultural background of the speaker/author or the production conditions of a discourse, or may address the information of his or her own cultural background and the specific understanding, or reception conditions, of a discourse. Often, especially in everyday conversation, the two perspectives will coincide: Speaker and hearer belong to the same culture of the same time period. Speaking with members of another culture, or reading myths, stories, or documents of other cultures or of the same culture from a different period, requires a differentiation in cultural strategies (Bauman & Sherzer, 1974; Chafe, 1979). We may assume that hearer-oriented cultural strategies will dominate the speaker-oriented ones: Even if we are able to address knowledge or beliefs about the cultural backgrounds of the speaker of another culture we will tend to do so from the perspective of our own cultural background. This means that understanding discourse from other cultures may be a process that is marked. Whereas for our own culture comprehension automatically presupposes information about the culture, understanding discourse from other cultures requires specific processing of knowledge or beliefs we have about these other cultures or at least assumptions about various kinds of differences we do not know about.

Cultural strategies have a very wide scope. They involve knowledge about different geographical areas and locations, different social structures, institutions, and events, different communicative events, different languages, different discourse types, different speech acts, different superstructures (e.g., different narrative schemata), different local and global coherence conditions, different styles and rhetorics, different symbolic or ritual values and functions, different knowledge, beliefs, opinions, attitudes, ideologies, norms, and values as well as their implicit or explicit use in the production of the discourse, a different conceptual ordering of the world and society (and hence different lexicons), and, finally, different objects of reference. Even if this list is not complete, we see already that all aspects of discourse understanding are directly or indirectly affected by the kind of strategic uses of cultural information. Not only on a trivial level may the language itself be different, but also surface structure, style, coherence conditions, themes, discourse types, meanings, and pragmatic and interactional functions are influenced by cultural background. Understanding a discourse according to these cultural strategies hence means that we relate all these levels and dimensions with what we know about the communicative features of the culture of the speaker.

Marked (i.e., different culture) cultural strategies typically involve partial understanding. Most hearers or readers will only have limited knowledge about the other culture, so that sometimes guesses must be made about precise word meanings, coherence conditions, implicit beliefs, and pragmatic or interactional functions of the discourse.

We may now summarize these points into a most general principle or superstrategy dominating these cultural strategies: Understand the discourse, both textually and contextually, according to what you (the hearer) believe to be the cultural context of the communicative situation in which or for which the discourse has been produced or used. Under this principle, we will then use strategies that enable us to know, for instance, that telling a story in another culture, and in a specific social context, may not only mean that the speaker wants to amuse the listener, but may also, perhaps, be intended to make a reproach, to give advice, or to reaffirm basic norms of a group or teach its history. Another example is the derivation of macrostructures (themes) from the discourse. These are sensitive to what in a certain culture is believed to be important, relevant, interesting, or otherwise prominent information in discourse. Lack of appropriate cultural information of this type may mean that we think the discourse has no point, or that we do not understand why a story is interesting (Kintsch & Greene, 1978). Specifically, we need to know which sequences of events or actions and their descriptions can be taken to manifest a higher level event or action which does not have a comparable conceptualization in our culture.

### 3.6.2. Social Strategies

Part of the cultural strategies mentioned here pertain to more specific social strategies. That is, we must assume in understanding a discourse that it is produced and used within a larger social context or at a more local social occasion (Sudnow, 1972; Scherer & Giles, 1979). These social strategies involve information about the general social structure of a group, about institutions, roles, or functions of participants, discourse genres of institutions or social occasions, style differences related to social structure, occasion, or social members, possible speech acts that can be performed on those occasions and by those members, and the social norms, conventions, values, or ideologies of those members. In other words, we must apply different strategies when understanding a discourse produced by the government, a bank, a judge in the courtroom, a student in our class, a friend in a bar, or our child at the breakfast table. The strategic nature of the understanding process lies in the fact that we activate different kinds of expectations about possible interactional functions (intentions), speech acts, global themes, discourse types, coherence, styles, etc. From a government or bank we do not expect stories, but laws, documents, or reports—discourse types we, in turn, do not expect from friends or family members in everyday conversation. Also the status of the discourses may be different with regard to the intended rights, duties, or ensuing actions: We must obey the law, but not a request from a stranger. We know, similarly, that we must obey an order of a judge or policeman on duty but not an order by the same person in an off-duty situation.

These examples show that a language understander has a strategy to limit the interpretation of many aspects of the discourse to rather restricted sets. Assumptions may be made about the intended social function (status) of the discourse, about the possible speech acts, possible macrostructures, possible discourse types, and possible styles of the discourse. Apart from different institutions or context types, these expectations may depend on assumptions about the member categories in these social contexts, that is, on whether we are communicating with a man or a woman, a child or an adult, a young or an old person, a friend or a stranger, a rich or a poor person, with people having more or less power or status than we, and so on.

### 3.6.3. Interactional Strategies

The more general social and cultural strategies provide the basic background information for the specific strategies used in communicative situations. The hearer or reader of a discourse is now not an observer of the social or cultural contexts, but a direct participant in the communicative relationship: The discourse is addressed to, intended for, him or her. We also assume that the communicative process is a form of social interaction and at the same time a coherent part of larger interaction sequences. This may mean that the discourse, as an act, is meant to affect further verbal or nonverbal actions or their conditions, such as the knowledge, beliefs, opinions, or motivations of the hearer.

To understand a discourse strategically as an action in an ongoing social interaction sequence means that the hearer makes assumptions about the intentions, purposes (represented goals), wishes, preferences, beliefs, opinions, attitudes, ideology, emotions, and personality of the speaker. This information may be drawn from episodic memory already established on other occasions about the speaker, or be inferred from the representation of the actual social context and communicative situation. Thus, from an obviously lost stranger in our town, heading for us and speaking to us, we may expect a request for information about the location of streets or buildings. Wishes, purpose of speaking, and intention of the speech act may be inferred even before we hear the particular request. We know that the speaker assumes that we can and will give that information, that is, that the action is meant to lead to specific other actions. Hence, an interactional strategy for discourse understanding means that a hearer derives effective expectations from the global or local social context with respect to the interactive intentions, goals, and motivations of the speaker as they relate to cognitive or actional changes of the hearer.

Just as was the case for the more general social and cultural strategies, interactional strategies may yield or require information from all discourse levels: a specific range of possible speech acts, possible themes, or a specific style. In case of the stranger, we may expect a request as a speech act, a theme about being lost and location, and polite style. These expectations will monitor the more specific discourse analysis strategies.

Similarly, the understanding strategy at this level will make assumptions about the interactional function of the discourse. Thus, the discourse may be understood—given beliefs about the social situation and the personality of the speaker—as an attack, a defense, as aggressive, as helping, as cooperative, as obstructive, or as facilitating with respect to the interactional sequence. In this respect the strategy may involve assumptions about the interactive strategies of the speaker, that is, the strategies to be specified in a production model of discourse.

### 3.6.4. Pragmatic Strategies

One specific type of interactional strategies are the pragmatic strategies. Whereas the other strategies mentioned thus far have a more general nature (i.e., they govern comprehension processes in general), pragmatic strategies are bound to natural language. Although the notion of pragmatics is often used vaguely to denote all contextual aspects of language use, we will limit it to the subtheory of linguistics that is concerned with the study of language utterances as speech acts. A speech act can be loosely defined as the social action that is performed by a speaker when producing an utterance in some specific context. Promises, threats, and congratulations are such social actions, performed by language users. These speech acts are said to be appropriate if a number of contextual conditions are satisfied. These conditions pertain to the wants, beliefs, and intentions of the speaker and to a limited number of social relations between speaker and hearer, such as rank and familiarity. In particular, a pragmatic theory specifies what properties of an utterance can be related to its specific pragmatic function as a speech act: Surface structure and semantic structure (e.g., time, action, and reference to speaker or hearer) may thus constrain the possible speech acts.

A cognitive model of pragmatics should, among other things, specify how the utterances of a language user can be comprehended as specific speech acts (van Dijk, 1981a; Chapter 9.). How does a hearer know that an utterance such as *Can you lend me that book?* can be taken, in a specific context, as a request?

We assume that a language user, apart from applying pragmatic rules, needs strategies to accomplish this rather complex task. At the discourse level, this means that a language user is able to infer from text and context not only which speech acts are performed by the individual sentences of the discourse, but also the pragmatic status of the discourse as a whole—that is, what possible macrospeech acts are being performed. The reason to assume that strategies are necessary here, both for sentences and for discourse, is that it seems likely that a hearer will in general not wait until the end of the utterance to infer what speech act is being performed. Especially for longer discourses, this would seem highly improbable. After a few sentences, the hearer can often guess what the speaker is driving at—pragmatically speaking—, that is, what he or she is intending and doing (e.g., promising something, making a request, or making an accusation). An early guess of this kind will enable the hearer to design his or her own strategies for appropriate production.

Hence, pragmatic discourse strategies involve several tasks; the hearer must decide (*a*) what speech acts are being performed by the individual sentences or clauses of the discourse, (*b*) what pragmatic relations exist between these local speech acts, (*c*) what global (or macro-) speech act is being performed by larger parts of the discourse or by the discourse as a whole, (*d*) what the relations are between local and global speech act sequences, and (*e*) what the relations are between the global speech acts. It is obvious that these are fairly complex tasks which require elaborate cognitive computing.

We assume that pragmatic strategies, which link textual structures with context, especially the interactional context, combine two kinds of information, namely, properties of the utterance and properties of the pragmatic context (for details, see van Dijk, 1977a, 1981a). Our hierarchical treatment of discourse comprehension strategies implies that the contextual information has priority. This is indeed plausible: A systematic analysis of the relevant context may enable a language user to make intelligent guesses about the possible speech acts that can be expected from a speaker. From the stranger-in-town example of the previous section, we may conclude that certain contexts greatly limit the possible speech acts (e.g., to a request, rather than an assertion or accusation). If we know what the social situation is, if we can infer what the wishes and intentions of an agent-speaker are, and if we know what our relation with the speaker is, we can often already guess what is going to happen even before the speaker actually performs the speech act.

We further assume that the hearer's search through available social and interactional information in order to predict possible speech acts is not arbitrary but systematic. There are many social properties of the context that are not relevant for the interpretation or evaluation of a speech act. Therefore, we use the term pragmatic context to denote those contextual features that are relevant for pragmatic interpretation. Whereas sex differences will in general not systematically define different appropriateness conditions for speech acts (there are no speech acts, in our culture, that are used only by men or only by women), relationships of power or familiarity do define such conditions (commands, for instance, are appropriately given only by superiors, and many types of congratulations or compliments require at least some degree of mutual acquaintance). Similarly, the pragmatic context will be scanned for a restricted number of cognitive properties of the speaker, such as his or her actual wishes, purposes, and intentions, on the one hand, and beliefs and evaluations, on the other. Thus, in a request, we must presuppose that a speaker wants something done by us, which in turn presupposes that we assume that the speaker believes that we can and are willing to do this. In accusations and congratulations, we assume that the speaker has some negative or positive evaluation about our past actions. We see that some assumptions about the past, actual, and future action context and about some cognitive states of the speaker relative to this context already allow us to make rather well-specified inferences about possible speech act types.

Although in some cases this kind of systematic contextual search allows a hearer to make a good guess about the speech act that is going to be performed, usually the hearer will need more information. This information, of course, will have to come from the utterance itself. Again we assume that the pragmatic strategies involved will not blindly scan all the structural information of the discourse processed so far. It is much more effective to search a partial textual representation as it is being processed in short-term memory for specific pragmatic signals. These signals may be both superstructural and semantic: A specific intonation may distinguish assertions from requests and questions, or praise from accusations; word order, as well, indicates differences between assertions and questions or requests; action verbs in general will indicate action-related speech acts, such as promises, threats, accusations, or requests; tense and time will indicate past, future, or present actions, which is relevant to distinguish between promises and excuses, or between threats and accusations. Similarly, references (*I, you*) to speaker and hearer will determine the agents or other participant roles in these actions, whereas expressions such as *rather, like,* and other opinion words may indicate evaluations or preferences of the speaker, defining advice, congratulation, or accusations. We have no idea which specific order or hierarchy will be followed by these textual pragmatic comprehension strategies. According to our hierarchy hypothesis, it would be the most informative information that is scanned first, which would be the semantic information. Yet, this information can only be acquired, at least in part, through surface structure interpretation. So, the very use, say, of pronouns such as *I* and *you* as first mentioned NPs or subjects will already give some information about participant relations in the action described, and hence possibly on the speech act being performed. However, this strategy will probably work only in a few cases and will usually require at least partial interpretation of the predicate: A sentence beginning with *I* . . . may express nearly any speech act. Yet, a sentence beginning with *I am* . . . will very often be an assertion, and *I want* . . . very often a request, question, or command, whereas *You are* . . . merely will define the class of evaluative speech acts, which includes such different ones as accusations, praise, congratulations, or compliments. Hence, although some partial surface and semantic processing will sometimes yield indications of possible speech act classes, we will in general need the full clausal (propositional) structure in order to decide what the speech act is. This is natural because, first of all, relevant pragmatic intonation includes a clause or sentence as a whole, relevant time and place indicators may sometimes occur at the end, and the further participants in the event or action may also occur rather late in clause or sentence (at least in English).

The second class of pragmatic strategies will need to link thus interpreted speech acts into coherent sequences. That is, the hearer will assume not only that the meanings and references of the various sentences of a discourse are meaningfully related, but also that the speech acts being performed by their utterance are as well. Strategies governing speech act sequences may be understood in the light of a broader theory of planning and understanding action and interaction sequences in general. Just as we understand successive actions of agents to be meaningfully related, for example, with respect to some goal, we make the assumption that successive speech acts are related. Consider sequences such as the following:

(2)      a. *You've done a swell job.*
         b. *I'll pay you double.*
(3)      a. *It is cold in here.*
         b. *Can you please shut the window?*

Performed by the same speaker, each of these two examples of speech act sequences can be coherently understood by a hearer if it is assumed that the speech act performed first is a condition for the production, and hence for the comprehension, of the speech act that follows. Thus, praise may establish a situation in which a speaker may feel indebted to a hearer, which is a situation in which a promise may be appropriate. Similarly, an assertion about some want, lack, or need may be a condition for the appropriate request that follows. In both examples, a hearer may make strategic guesses about the possible pragmatic functions of the first speech act, or rather about its possible pragmatic consequences. These are expectations about what the agent-speaker will or can do next. Thus, the hearer may expect that a particular assertion about needs or wants will be followed by a request. In fact, this is so often the case that the very use of such an assertion may count as an indirect request: Sentence (3a) may be used to make a request in a context in which the source of cold (open window) is believed by the speaker to be known to the hearer (Clark, 1979, 1983).

Relevant to our discussion is the fact that hearers apparently have strategies for an effective preanalysis of speech acts and speech act sequences. Such strategies are possible because of the general motivational (wants, wishes, preferences) and goal-directed nature of action and interaction, and hence also of speech acts. Also, a hearer likewise knows about possible production strategies of speakers. A difficult request or an embarrassing accusation may often be introduced by an assertion or excuse (*I am sorry, but . . .*). Finally, language users will apply strategies to derive global speech acts from speech act sequences. That is, they may know that in a conversation a sequence consisting of greeting, question, assertion, assertion, assertion, (request), and greeting may function as a global request. A long letter, consisting perhaps only of assertions and requests (*We have your son. . . . Will you please pay. . . .*), may function as a global threat. As we assumed earlier, a hearer need not hear a whole discourse before knowing or being able to guess what the global pragmatic point is. That is, the initial speech acts of a text or conversation will be interpreted as possible components in a global speech act, which need not be directly expressed in the text. We have seen that assertions about lack of money and about the need to pay some amount soon, and questions about the hearer's wealth, will together lead a hearer quickly to the global hypothesis that a request for money is being made. Details of these macrostrategies will be discussed in Chapter 6.

Both for local and for global pragmatic strategies we should assume the presence, not simply of relevant textual or contextual information, but also of very rich information which we may summarize as nonverbal. In addition to featuring such surface signals as pitch, intonation, stress, loudness, speed, and similar phonological or phonetic properties, oral discourse will be accompanied by much nonverbal behavior—for example, gestures, facial expressions, and position of the body. This information alone may sometimes provide the hearer with sound hypotheses about the wants and opinions of the speaker, and may therefore constitute rather powerful signals for the interpretation of threats, accusations, compliments, or congratulations. With the pragmatic strategies we are, so to speak, on the boundary between what we may call the contextual strategies on the one hand and the textual ones on the other. Thus, contextual strategies make systematic searches among cultural, social, and interactional information relevant to the discourse and the communicative situation and their understanding. This search, we assumed, is hierarchical: Wider scope information limits the search for more particular information at a lower level. Within a given culture and society, we already may know that certain interactions and certain speech acts will not occur, and within a given social situation we know that certain speech acts or discourse types are rare, or are typical. It is under the control of these contextual strategies that the textual strategies operate. We have seen that the strategic understanding of speech acts already involves several kinds of textual information. We will now survey some specifically textual strategies, that is, the strategies used for semantic comprehension.

### 3.6.5. Semantic Strategies

Crucial in a model of discourse comprehension are the semantic strategies. They establish what a discourse means and what a discourse is about, that is, its intensions and its extensions or reference. Although in general a discourse is produced only within a pragmatic and social context in which it may have various functions as a speech act or interaction type, the semantic strategies yield the necessary informational content for these social functions. Similarly, surface structure strategies do not have a goal in themselves, but are geared toward establishing a representation of these semantic contents and pragmatic or social functions. In other words, syntactic strategies for sentence analysis are subservient to semantic strategies for sentence understanding, and these in turn are subservient to semantic strategies of discourse understanding, on the one hand, and to the pragmatic strategies mentioned earlier, on the other. We see again a picture of hierarchical ordering for strategic discourse comprehension. This is as it should be. Strategies pertain to overt or mental action and hence involve goals and their effective realization. In discourse comprehension we will assume that this goal consists in a fast, correct, and adequate understanding of the discourse, that is, the construction of a textual representation in episodic memory, and, of course, the establishment of links between a textual representation and other episodic memories (among which are other textual representations).

However, semantic understanding of a discourse involves rather different kinds of tasks, and each of these requires its appropriate strategies. We made a distinction earlier between intensional and extensional understanding. Although this distinction comes from philosophy and logic, it also has its use in linguistics and cognitive discourse-processing models. That is, a language user wants to know not only what an utterance means, but also what it refers to, what it is about, or what it describes. This may be some state of affairs, a situation, an episode, a series of events or actions, as well as the things and persons participating therein, and their properties. As soon as these events, actions, etc. are not merely conceptual or abstract, but realized in some possible world, we will speak of facts. Roughly, then, we assume that clauses or sentences refer to facts of some possible world, and discourse to specific collections of such facts, such as episodes.

These units out in the world, such as things, persons, actions, events, or facts, are relevant for a cognitive model only if they are represented in memory. Epistemologically speaking, this means that cognition is constitutive for such world properties: An object, a person, an action, an event, or a fact does exist as such only in some biophysical way, but as units they are seen, distinguished, understood, and talked about only through their permanent or more episodic representation as concepts in memory. In the next chapter we will discuss this issue in more detail. We will assume here that although meanings and referents in a cognitive model are both of a conceptual nature, we still may make a distinction between a meaning representation, which is tied to language, and a representation of a fragment of the world. Thus a distinction may be made between the meaning of the phrase *the boy*, referring to John, and our conceptual representation of that person John, which involves much more than the concept of 'boy'. Similarly, we may not be able to assign a specific meaning to the article *the* in that phrase but merely a function, namely, that the person referred to (John) is already known to the hearer.

Against this theoretical background we shall now describe some semantic strategies. According to the linguistic and cognitive theories of discourse, it makes sense to distinguish two sets of related strategies, local and global ones. The local strategies establish the meanings of clauses and sentences and the meanings and functions of relations between sentences. The global strategies determine the global meanings of fragments of the discourse or of the discourse as a whole. These two kinds of strategy must, of course, interact: In order to know what a discourse is about globally, we usually need at least some information from the local (sentence) level; conversely, in order to know the precise meaning and function of individual sentences and their mutual connections, we must have an idea about the global meaning or theme of a discourse. This is not only true for meaning but also for reference.

Beginning with global strategies, we must first take into account the fact that information about the overall theme of the discourse does not merely come bottom up from local meanings of words and sentences. We often make a guess about the theme of a discourse on the basis of inferences from specific sociocultural and interactional situations. In class, in a business meeting, at the breakfast table, or in parliament, as well as in a newspaper or a psychology textbook, there are a limited number of discourse types and pragmatic contexts, and hence a limited number of possible themes. According to the hierarchy hypothesis, a language user will always first make guesses or at least have implicit expectations about these possible themes. That is, he or she has a representation of a class of possible themes. Then, these themes may be explicitly signaled to the hearer in many ways, by announcements, agendas, invitations, prefaces, titles, headings, etc. In Chapter 6 we will discuss these macrostrategy signals of the communicative situation. Again, this also holds for reference. If some objects, persons, events, actions, or episodes are available to the language users (directly or via pictures, film, etc.), then they may be cognitively represented, which may lead to the inference of an actual theme. This is what the discourse is globally *about*.

The other information that makes the inference of global meanings and reference possible must come from the discourse itself. This information is basically also semantic: It is the meaning of words, sentences, and sequences that enables the inference of macrostructures. Of course, as for all the inference strategies discussed so far, we also need other cognitive information from world knowledge, beliefs, opinions, attitudes, interests, or goals of the hearer or of the speaker, as believed to exist by the hearer.

Contrary to the macrorules postulated in earlier cognitive models (van Dijk, 1977a, 1980b; Kintsch & van Dijk, 1978), the macrostrategies operate on partial semantic information. Instead of a full sequence of relevant information from sentences, even one or a few sentences (or their underlying propositions) may be enough to derive a macrostructure. There are many cues that guide this very crucial set of macrostrategies: titles and subtitles, summaries, leads, thematic sentences, introductions, and announcements in the text itself, and so on. These may be signaled in written text by specific position, typeface, and type size, in oral discourse by pauses, stress, and intonation. One strategy, for instance, says that if a discourse gives information about the various conditions of some action or event, we may assume that the discourse fragment as a whole will be about that action or event.

Local discourse strategies consist, in part, of the sentence comprehension strategies discussed earlier in this chapter. In our next chapter we will try to show that sentence comprehension involves the strategic construction of propositions, that is, cognitive representations of facts as discussed earlier. Propositions have a fixed schema, depending on the kind of dominant predicate involved, featuring the various participants and their modifiers. Propositions organize lower level conceptual information, that is, the atomic propositions that underlie meaningful words and phrases.

For a discourse model we are particularly interested in the ways in which sentences (or propositions) are related. We have assumed before that one of the fundamental semantic properties of discourse is that it is coherent. The themes or macrostructures discussed earlier define the global coherence of the discourse. Locally, coherence must be established by the interpretation of relations between sentences, the so-called connection relations. Theoretically we know that these relations involve conditional relations between propositions, denoting conditional relations between facts in some possible world. This means that if a hearer assumes that the discourse refers to an understandable fragment of the world, for instance, an episode consisting of some events and actions, then that part of the discourse will be understood as coherent in principle. However, this is not enough. Discourse not only must satisfy the various connection conditions, but must also exhibit a number of complex correspondence rules. That is, we may not describe some episode by arbitrarily joining together the sentences describing aspects of such an episode. We need, first of all, some principles of ordering. These may involve, for instance, the rule that first events are represented first, unless a different order of the events is marked (e.g., with *Before . . . , Earlier, . . .*), or that more general, more encompassing events, objects, or places come before their component objects or properties. Then, we have various types of selection principles. Neither semantically nor pragmatically is it necessary to describe all properties of some event or object. Hence, a discourse will limit itself to partial descriptions, which may vary in degree of completeness and level of abstraction. It follows that the strategies of a discourse understander not only involve correctly establishing the relationship between the sentences as they reflect relationships in our knowledge of reality, but also involve interpreting the selection and ordering evidenced in the discourse.

Finally, it goes without saying that at the local level as at the global level, a language understander will establish coherence relationships as effectively and hence as quickly as possible. It is therefore unlikely that he or she will wait with the interpretation of the relation between $S_i$ and $S_{i+1}$ until the full sentence $S_{i+1}$ has been interpreted. It is plausible that the hearer will try to establish links with $S_i$ after interpreting the first phrases of $S_{i+1}$, for example, the subject or topic. Experimental results reviewed in Chapter 2 support these speculations. In fact the well-known phenomenon of topic–comment articulation is precisely the linguistic manifestation of this strategy: It allows the reader to rapidly know which of the previously mentioned participants is relevant again in the construction of the following proposition. Inferring coherence on the basis of shared arguments among propositions is a powerful strategy for quickly establishing a coherence relation between sentences (Kintsch & van Dijk, 1978). Similarly, explicit connectives will be the most obvious signals of such relationships, this time not between details of propositions (their participants) but between the propositions as wholes. Also crucial at this local level of discourse comprehension is the role of knowledge and beliefs about possible, probable, or likely relations between the facts in the world. Given a sentence referring to some fact, the hearer may already have well-founded expectations about the possible facts that may be mentioned later—although, naturally not about all facts, because then the discourse would be pragmatically trivial. These expectations and their role in the strategic establishment of local coherence will be discussed in more detail in Chapter 5.

### 3.6.6. Schematic Strategies

Whereas the strategies for text processing mentioned in the preceding subsection have their counterparts in rules of grammar, we must assume that discourse also exhibits other kinds of conventionalized structures. Well known, for instance, are the typical schematic structures of narrative. Although in the recent debate about the psychological reality of such structures, it has sometimes been maintained that they do not exist or do not influence discourse processing, or that they can be explained in terms of action, we assume that such schematic structures not only are relevant in an abstract discourse theory, but also should feature in a cognitive model. This means that members of a given culture know for several discourse types what their global organization is: In a story we know that a narrative typically begins with a category like setting, after which we may expect a complication. Such schematic categories organize the macrostructural content of a discourse. They are, so to speak, the macrosyntax for the global meaning. Similarly, we know that argumentative discourse may consist of premises and a conclusion, and that a scientific report is traditionally analyzed in terms of conventionalized categories. These stereotypical categories may sometimes have their basis in properties of communicative interaction, but they have become conventionalized and therefore exhibit their own structural features. For some very specialized types of discourse, comprehension strategies are unfamiliar to many readers and must be taught explicitly, for example, for understanding forms and public documents (Holland & Redish, 1982) or legal discourse papers (Charrow, 1981; Radtke, 1981; Danet, 1980, 1983).

For a theory of discourse strategies such schematic structures are rather important. That is, when we begin to read a discourse, we try to establish as soon as possible what the initial theme or macrostructure is. However, we also want to establish as soon as possible the global function of that section and its theme within the discourse as a whole. That is, we make a hypothesis about the schematic or superstructural category involved (e.g., introduction, or preface, or a lead in a newspaper). As usual, the strategy may make use of a number of surface structure indicators—announcements, subtitles, indications about the type of discourse, source of the discourse (newspaper, book of stories, scientific journal), and so on.

The strategies may run both top down and bottom up: Guessing the function of a macroproposition would be bottom up, whereas partial knowledge of the discourse type and hence of the schema would be top down.

Schematic structures often occur in a transformed way. That is, the actual discourse may somehow be different from the canonical structure. A reader will then not be able to work top down and simply apply the schema, but will have to determine from the global content of the relevant part of the text what the global schematic function is. In that case, however, there is an expectation that a category that normally comes first, for instance the setting in a story, will come later.

Another problem is that not all discourse types have a conventionalized superstructural schema. Thus, an advertisement in a magazine can have nearly any form, so that schematic interpretation is either difficult or irrelevant here. This point will depend on further empirical research into schematic structures of discourse.

Note finally that schematic structures need not be confined to the macrolevel, nor are they solely concerned with semantic structures. A rhyme schema in a poem, for instance, has the same theoretical nature, but organizes prosodic, phonological, and graphical structures. In those cases where the rhyme schema has become conventionalized, for example, in a sonnet, it permits top-down processing. Metrical structures, as they have been studied in poetics and rhetorics, are another example of nonsemantic schemata, though they tend to pertain to the discourse as a whole. Once again, their role in processing should not be underestimated. Their stereotypical or conventionalized nature encourages top-down processing and makes it easier to apply comprehension strategies, thereby facilitating semantic comprehension.

### 3.6.7. Stylistic and Rhetorical Strategies

The very notion of language and discourse strategy seems to be closely related to the object of study for stylistics and rhetoric. In addition to the correct manner of speaking regulated by the grammar, rhetoric in classical times was the art that prescribed the most effective way of public speaking. This effectiveness had several implications. The central aspect was, of course, persuasion: A speaker, for instance, in parliament or in court, should try to convince the public or the judge that he had a good case so that they would judge positively, believe him, and finally accept his arguments. This ultimate goal had to be brought about by specified good ways of speaking, for which rhetorics formulated rules and strategies (Lausberg, 1960; Corbett, 1971). Most of these apply to the local organization of discourse, for example, at the morphophonological, syntactic, and semantic levels. It is here where such prosodic features as rhyme, alliteration, repetition, and figures of speech based on contrast, metaphor, or irony were formulated. Some of these devices are currently studied in the field of stylistics.

For our discussion it is important to stress that in principle any kind of discourse, and especially the more persuasive types, exhibit various kinds of rhetorical structures. Even everyday conversation has many of them. This means that understanding discourse implies at least implicit recognition of rhetorical devices. A processing model for comprehension, therefore, will have to specify what strategies a language user applies to recognize these structures and to relate them somehow to the semantic representation. In many cases this may not be conscious, and most naive language users will not be able to recognize a rhetorical device as such, but we may assume that their postulated effectiveness presupposes interaction with the semantic and pragmatic representation of the discourse. Although surface structures and detailed semantic structures are usually not well remembered, or are remembered only occasionally in specific situations, the rhetorical structures are somewhat of an exception. Because they embody a special or original way of saying things, they may contribute to a better organization of the semantic representation of the discourse and hence to better recall and, therefore, to a better interactional effect. Related to this function would be the esthetic effect of the discourse: Somebody has said something very well. This means that a textual representation is connected with an evaluation, which again is an assignment of additional structure that enables better retrieval of the information. Literature is a prototypical case in this respect, and literary passages are in general read specifically for evaluation and therefore are perhaps easier to recall or recognize (Dillon, 1978; Groeben, 1982). For semantic rhetorical structures such as metaphor, metonymia, or irony we may assume additional processing in order to be able to understand also their literal meaning, although the precise way in which people understand metaphors is still poorly understood (but see Glucksberg, Gildea, & Bookin, 1982). It appears, however, that additional semantic structure is assigned at the local level to the discourse, which also makes the passage more accessible for retrieval. In particular, the use of devices that relate the semantic representation to personal experiences or to episodically or emotionally relevant information (vividness in a description, for instance) assign additional structural relations in episodic memory, so that the discourse can be better recalled (Keenan, MacWhinney, & Mayhew, 1977). We can only guess about the precise strategic processes involved in the decoding, interpretation, and further semantic or episodic integration of such rhetorical structures. But as with schematic structures we should assume that they play an important role in efficiently establishing the semantic representation. In Chapter 7 we will see, for instance, that rhetorical devices may be used to signal the macrostructures of a text. They may point to what is important or specifically relevant. Thus, a metaphor or the elaboration of a thematic contrast may highlight the theme that is most important for the speaker, and in this way the hearer or reader has an additional means of detecting such important parts of the discourse (Carbonell, 1981).

Under the style of a discourse we understand the specific variation of the grammatical and other schematic or rhetorical rules or devices that characterizes that discourse, speaker, discourse type, or context. Here we typically are concerned with the *use* of rules (Labov, 1972a, 1972b; Enkvist, 1973; Sandell, 1977; Scherer & Giles, 1979). Such a specific use may indicate some properties of the actual situation, such as the personal situation of the speaker (angry, happy) in the social context or the communicative interaction. In principle, stylistic variation presupposes some form of underlying identity or similarity: We can say the same thing in different ways. This may mean the same global theme, the same semantic representation at the local level, or the same local or global speech act. Variation in surface structure, given this semantic or pragmatic identity, may then be used to indicate the various contextual aspects which consciously or unconsciously may be used to communicate to the reader or hearer more than just the content—for example, to communicate that we are angry, that we are polite, informal, confidential, or that we know what social context (e.g., school or street) we are talking in. Hence, stylistic variation is extremely important for the interactional interpretation of the discourse, because it may signal intentions, purposes, strategy, attitudes, and the relationship of the speaker to the hearer. The variation is usually defined in terms of phonological (free) variation, such as pronunciation, lexical choice from different registers, and syntactic variation (length, complexity).

The strategic effects of stylistic variation and specific choice are undoubtedly highly complex. Whereas differences in syntactic complexity will, as is well known in reading research, affect ease of decoding and hence of semantic understanding, and the choice of difficult words will require more memory search as well, the other stylistic choices should rather be taken as indications of the contextual information conveyed, whether intentionally or not. A choice of polite words will categorize the discourse and hence the speech act and the speaker as 'now being polite', which has consequences on the interaction of speaker and hearer: The hearer may be more willing to change his or her cognitive set, believe the speaker, or perform the actions requested. Such a stylistically indicated contextual interactional strategy presupposes that a language user knows what kind of stylistic variation is polite, formal, friendly, familiar, aggressive, or defensive. If we assume that language users not only have world knowledge but also, closely associated, language knowledge, we would assume that each lexical expression is paired with its stylistic value, as is indeed the case in dictionaries. But this would just be the word level and would say little about larger discourse structures. Of course, a discourse may be interpreted strategically as being polite on the basis of the use of polite words, but it may contain themes that would not fit such an interpretation at all. Hence, although stylistic choice is an indication about the interactional relationship or attitude of the speaker toward the hearer, the rest of the semantic and pragmatic information should be consistent with these surface structure signals in order for the hearer or reader to construe a correct interpretation.

From this intuitive description of the possible strategic uses of stylistic features of a discourse it again appears that strategic discourse comprehension is an extremely complex process, involving the processing of a large amount of data. From the text itself we need an account of local and global semantic and pragmatic strategies, an account of schematic categories, and finally an account of stylistic and rhetorical strategies which pertain to the various other levels of the discourse. At the same time, the language user must strategically decode various types of contexts, in hierarchical order, and match this analysis with the appropriate analysis of the discourse itself. Only then can partial and tentative hypotheses be made about the meaning or function of a sentence, a sequence of sentences, or the discourse as a whole. Previous discourse models have seriously underestimated the complexity of this job.

## 3.7. THE REPRESENTATION OF STRATEGIES

We have tried in this chapter to present a consistent and comprehensive view of discourse processing. In succeeding chapters we shall elaborate this view in much more detail. It is, however, a long way from the broad, general, theoretical outline we have given here to a worked out information-processing model of comprehension. We shall show how such models can be created for various aspects of discourse comprehension—with certain simplifying assumptions and by sacrificing some of the comprehensiveness of the theory as discussed here. The first step toward the formulation of such specific models is to find a suitable representation system for strategies.

Fortunately, we can turn to other areas and other fields where formalisms have been developed which are highly appropriate for our problems. We suggest that strategic comprehension processes can best be modeled as production systems. Production systems (Newell & Simon, 1972) are, in general, deductive or inductive inference systems that use patterns or rules to guide decision making (Waterman & Hayes-Roth, 1978). The rules are antecedent–consequent pairs. The antecedent of the rule is matched to some input condition (the data), and the match results in the execution of some consequent action (a modification of the data). As Newell and Simon point out, the term production derives originally from symbolic logic, but basically the same idea was used in Markov processes, the rewrite rules of transformational grammar, and some early programming languages such as SNOBOL.

The components of a production system are a data base and a set of production rules which match the data base. If only a single production matches the data, the corresponding action is executed. Usually the world is not so simple, however, and productions require a control system. The task of this system is to select or activate relevant productions and data elements, filtering out an often huge number of irrelevant things. A production system also has to have some conflict resolution procedure in the event that, in spite of this selection, the response set is still ambiguous or multiple. Various control structures have been used. For example, one can consider productions as competing actors or as cooperative beings. In either case, their interaction must be scheduled carefully. Schemes for doing so range from the obvious and simple to the exotic ("Petri-net nodes"); in many cases, knowledge sources and frames provide the desired guidance (for a detailed discussion see the papers in Waterman and Hayes-Roth, 1978).

Pattern-directed inference systems range from the supersimple to the highly complex with the computing power of a Turing machine, and it is our task to explore briefly whether the strategic model of discourse comprehension proposed here can be modeled via a production system, and what such a system would be like.

The stimulus–response theory of behavioristic psychology was an early, extremely simple, form of a production system. It was much too tightly constrained by the requirement that both the antecedents and the consequents of the rules had to be observable. The TOTE hierarchy of Miller, Galanter, and Pribram (1960), as well as the earliest generation of production systems in cognitive psychology (Newell, 1972; Klahr, 1973), were still very tightly constrained, although in other ways.In recent years, however, production systems of astonishing complexity have been constructed. In natural language processing we mention the English language interpreter ELI developed by Riesbeck (1978) and used as a front-end parser for the story-understanding programs SAM and PAM. Also for story understanding, Simmons (1978) developed a production system to transform English text into a propositional representation, which is then analyzed into a network of causal relationships. In these programs we already encounter the central problem of all such systems: how to deal with the large number of productions that are necessary to perform any reasonably interesting task. Even if computation time increases only linearly with the number of productions that have to be checked against the data, systems become unwieldly very quickly and the danger of a computational explosion is never far off. Anderson (1976) in his production system simulation of human memory uses special techniques to limit the number of data elements and rules that are considered at any time (via a spreading activation network). In what is today perhaps the most complex use of production systems, knowledge engineering (Feigenbaum, 1977), the selection of active rules is guided by knowledge sources, hence the "intelligent" character of these systems. In any case, production systems are used successfully today for tasks that in their complexity rival discourse understanding. Are they also suitable for our task?

From the discussion earlier in this chapter we can derive some crucial properties of strategies which an adequate representation must reflect: Strategies are flexible and operate on many different kinds of input; they must be able to function with incomplete, partial input; they must operate in parallel on several different levels of analysis, the results on one level affecting the processes on the other; they are fundamentally nondeterministic and often produce a large number of alternative outcomes varying in plausibility. Although these requirements produce demands on production systems that are not easily met, it appears that work currently progressing in artificial intelligence and cognitive psychology is at least well on the way toward a solution. No other formalism is nearly as completely worked out as production systems to meet the requirements of strategies.

Part of the flexibility requirement of strategies is that they must work top down as well as from the bottom up. Normally, production systems are antecedent driven: The left side of the production rule, the antecedent, is matched to some data element, producing some kind of result. Productions can also work backward, however: Matches can be performed on the consequent, producing an antecedent. A sequence of such backward chaining steps may then generate the given input situation, much as one proves a mathematical theorem by working backward. Strategies usually must work with incomplete, partial information. The need for partial matching is widely appreciated among designers of production systems (Joshi, 1978; Hayes-Roth, 1978), though definitive solutions for all the problems are not yet at hand. Joshi observes that except for logical systems and a few well-structured domains, all inferences are made in a context of incomplete information. If we have a rule $ABC \rightarrow X$, but are given only $A$, a number of problems arise. First of all, $A$ may be a component of other rules, too, and hence an ambiguous response set may be generated. In Joshi's production system, disambiguation is achieved in two ways. First, there is a metarule that selects that rule that differs in the fewest number of elements from the complete input pattern. Second, there is an interesting weighting rule, in which the components actually matched contribute positively (though in different amounts) and elements not matched contribute negatively to the weight of a production. Other schemes are developed to deal with those cases where an input in order to be matched completely requires matching to the antecedents of more than one production.

Weights, whether for validity, reliability, or some sort of proximity measure in semantic space, can readily be incorporated into production systems. Thus, strategies retain their probabilistic character.

Strategic systems are probably best suited to deal with the ever-threatening ruin of production systems—the computational explosion. For efficient computation, both the strategies and the data have to be divided into a small set of active elements and a large set of quiescent ones. The psychology of memory provides some guidelines to tell us what data are active at any time in discourse comprehension. We shall return to that question in detail in Chapter 10 of this book. The question of how knowledge is used, that is, which production strategies are active at any time, will be taken up in Chapter 9. Here it is sufficient to indicate that the solutions which computer scientists have suggested for this problem can readily be applied to strategic systems as defined here. One of the principles is to use global selective filters to prevent irrelevant productions from being compared to condition patterns (e.g., McDermott, Newell, & Moore, 1978); we have described the funneling function of higher order cultural and social strategies in similar terms. Another principle that has been proposed in this connection is that higher order representations should be preferred to lower level ones (Hayes-Roth, 1978); we have already discussed this issue with respect to strategies and shall report an experimental study that is relevant to it in Chapter 9. The efficiency, almost necessity, of using multi-level representations and multilevel processes is repeatedly stressed in the literature on production systems (e.g., Hayes-Roth, Waterman, & Lenat, 1978:593); it is, of course, an integral feature of our system of strategies. The main problem for production systems is complexity reduction; strategies are designed for that purpose.

Most major problems, discourse comprehension certainly included, cannot be solved by a set of predefined rules. Instead, they require a flexible, dynamic, multilevel system, that is, a strategic one. In the next chapters we shall describe the strategies that are used at the various levels of discourse processing, starting with the construction of a propositional representation for a text, and ending with its macrostructure. In Chapter 9 we shall then return to questions of knowledge use which were touched upon in this section.

## 3.8. A SAMPLE ANALYSIS: THE *NEWSWEEK* TEXT

### 3.8.1. General Introduction to the Analysis of This Text

In this chapter and in the following chapters we will illustrate our arguments and proposals with an analysis of the processes involved in the comprehension of a specific text. For this purpose we have chosen a text "Guatemala: No Choices" from *Newsweek* (March 1, 1982, p. 16), which is reprinted on the front endpapers of this volume. This text exhibits most of the properties involved in natural, every-day discourse understanding, in all its complexity of textual, cognitive, and contextual relationships. In the appropriate chapters we will analyze the relevant structures of this text as assigned by an imaginary reader. We will hand-simulate the analyses of the various units and levels, the strategic processes taking place during this analysis, and the representation of the text in episodic memory. This means that we have to make explicit not only the various structural properties of the text itself, but also the knowledge of the reader about the (kind of) situation and events denoted by the text and about the communicative context in which the text is understood. It goes without saying that in making this knowledge explicit we try to construct an ideal, average, reader, but we will also specify how different interpretations can result from different strategies and different previous knowledge or other presupposed cognitive information. Also, it is obvious that our analysis cannot possibly be complete. For each complex unit or level of analysis we will merely give a partial description of structures and processes, with a general emphasis on the *strategies* used in comprehension.

We have chosen this text as an example not only in order to enhance the ecological validity of our model, but also to deviate from the tradition of using simple stories or simple descriptive paragraphs in discourse comprehension modeling. Our sample text is characteristic in the process of forming and changing political knowledge about the world, a process all of us are engaged in when using media messages. For such texts, readers will also need further cognitive information, such as ideologies, attitudes, and opinions, intricately linked to the process of comprehension (Carbonell, 1978).

### 3.8.2. An Overview of the Strategies Involved in Comprehension

In this chapter our analysis will be limited to a description of the various kinds of strategies involved in the comprehension of this *Newsweek* text. In the following chapters we will spell out these strategy types; what is important here is the way in which they interact. Each strategy may variously call on others to obtain the necessary information.

*Sociocultural strategies.* The reader of this text participates in a communication process which is embedded in a larger sociocultural context. For our example this means that we presuppose that a reader forms the *general goal* of acquiring relevant information about the world, including information about political events. The general motivation for this intermittent activity of information seeking may just be interest, or, more specifically, the use of the information in informal everyday conversation, the use of the information in specific social positions, or the use of the information in the process of making political decisions. This general goal may be enacted in different, strategically relevant ways. A person may watch, occasionally or regularly, the news on television, and/or read the newspapers, and/or read a weekly, and/or listen to the radio, and/or read political studies, and/or participate in everyday conversation about news events. The specific ways in which the goal is enacted will depend on a number of factors, such as the availability of the various media, the amount of information needed, the overall use of the information, and so on. In our case, then, we assume that it is a strategy of this person to read (part of) the weeklies, thereby possibly compensating for the lack of news or background information in the other media or types of communication. Input to this strategy may be such information as the reader's socioeconomic position, cultural group, and specialized political interests. For instance, our reader may be middle class, interested in international news, especially about Central America and its relations with the foreign policy of the United States government, and might use this information in a process of political decision making concerning a stance toward the actions of the United States in Central America.

*Communicative strategies.* Within this sociocultural context a person may engage in specific communicative acts, such a reading a weekly. Such an act will, under the scope of the more general goal of 'seeking political information', establish a specific goal based on more specific motivational and decision-making processes. This goal in our case would be something like 'Read this week's *Newsweek*', a communicative action which is consequent upon buying the weekly (or receiving a copy on subscription). Next, the communicative strategy may be specified. For instance, the reader may be interested in reading any news, or just foreign news, or just specific features, or just news about Central America or news about Guatemala. Obviously, the consequences of these strategies will be different. If there is no specific goal, such as 'I want to know the latest news about Guatemala', then our text will be read with a different cognitive set than when the reader does have such a specific interest. Let us assume for the moment that our reader does not have this kind of more specific goal, but just reads the weekly to obtain varied political information. We will also assume that our reader is a middle-class American, with an average knowledge, mostly obtained via the media, about political affairs in general and the international political situation in particular, say a student of psychology. Such a reader would not have specific interests for special information, as would a political activist, a politician, or a business person having business contacts with Guatemala. Having gone through the acts involved in realizing the overall strategy of seeking political information from the media, having selected a specific weekly, and having started to read through, in any order, this issue of *Newsweek*, a reader will then come to this specific page. At this point, even before reading the title of the report, which act may in itself result in the decision to read or skip this article, the reader may have the following cognitive set-up for the actual understanding process involved in reading this text:

1. *General communicative goals*
   1.1. Seeking political information
   1.2. Reading a weekly
   1.3. Reading *Newsweek*
   1.4. Reading all domestic and foreign political articles
2. *Activated knowledge* (sample)
   2.1. General political knowledge, about American foreign policy, for example, United States aids anti-communist regime in Central America.
   2.2. Political knowledge can be obtained from the media
   2.3. Weeklies summarize the week's main news items
   2.4. *Newsweek* is a weekly
3. *Activated beliefs, opinions, or attitudes* (sample)
   3.1. I disagree with the policies of the administration
   3.2. In particular, I disagree with the policy regarding Central America
   3.3. I do not like *Newsweek* in general, but
   3.4. I think *Newsweek* gives relatively complete and balanced information
   3.5. Some articles in *Newsweek* are also critical of the administration

In other words, our reader will start reading the article with an already complex goal and with activated knowledge about political events, opinions about the policy of the United States, and about the political stance or the journalistic quality of the weekly.

*General reading strategies.* Before actually reading the text of the article, the reader may follow various overall reading strategies. In the case of our sample text, these strategies may operate as follows:

1. Read the headline. Try to establish the global topic of the article. Within the framework of activated political information, activate knowledge and opinions about Guatemala and news about Guatemala. Decision: interesting or not interesting within the overall goal of seeking political information.
2. Estimate the length and reading time available for reading of this article. If decision on Point (1) is positive, and if decision about length and reading time is positive, read the text.
3. If (1) or (2) is negative, see if there are other features of the text that would make reading interesting, for example, the picture within the text, or the author of the text (at the bottom of the article).
4. Start reading the text, and specify the topic of the text as implied by the first paragraph, and confirm or disconfirm the earlier decision: continue reading or stop reading.

*Local comprehension strategies.* Having decided to read the text, the reader will start reading the first clauses and the first sentences. From the understanding of the title, and against the background of more general knowledge and opinions about political reports (the word *report* is mentioned above the title), the reader already knows (*a*) that the text is about Guatemala and (*b*) that in Guatemala there are no (political?) choices. The reader will therefore have addressed the more specific knowledge about Guatemala (e.g., country in Central America, bordering with Mexico, Honduras, El Salvador, and Belize), including the personally more variable episodic knowledge, with information about the actual political situation in Guatemala (e.g., that it is a country ruled by the military in which human rights are grossly disrespected). The provisional macroproposition 'There are no political alternatives in Guatemala' will be fed into the monitoring Control System, and the relevant information about Guatemala will be activated as a current situation model in episodic memory. Local information will be processed under the overall control of this macroproposition, the episodic model, and the other communicative goals mentioned here.

With all this information in mind, and especially on the basis of an assumption about the relevant macroproposition, the reader will now start the analysis of the first sentence:

(1)     *Compared with the relative shades of gray in El Salvador, Guatemala is a study in black and white.*

At this point several strategies will come into action. Neglecting for the moment the strategies of graphical analysis—letter identification—and morphemic analysis, we assume that a first strategy will establish the meaning of the initial words or phrases—*compared*, or *compared with*. The activation and actualization of the meaning of this expression also yields information about the grammatical category (verb) and hence about the semantic function of the expression (a predicate), which again provides the functional semantic schema for the clause or sentence. That is, the predicate 'to compare (with)' requires two arguments, namely, two individuals that are compared, and possibly a third argument specifying the dimension of comparison. This activated propositional schema will therefore generate constraints about the occurrence of these arguments. And, finally, the first position of the verb, its mode marking (*compared*), and the absence of a (first position) subject or agent will constrain the overall syntactic and semantic organization of the sentence, in which a first clause is subordinate to the second, and hence the first proposition has a function in the second. In other words, the first words of the first clause already provide much information about the semantics of the clause and the whole sentence and provide the necessary structural and semantic constraints.

The next phrase, *The relative shades of gray,* is more complicated for the understanding process. Its literal meaning does not fit into the meaning structure of the previous verb nor with the meaning of the macroproposition or the overall register of political language and its usual meanings and referents. Thus, either definite interpretation of this phrase is suspended or a hypothesis is set up about the nonliteral (e.g., metaphorical) interpretation of this expression. But the latter is possible only if we know what the "bearer" is of the metaphorical property, and therefore understanding of the next phrase *in El Salvador* becomes imperative. This phrase both ties in with the general political knowledge activated and is related to the more specific knowledge about Guatemala activated by the macroproposition expressed by the headline. However, the reader may still be unsure about the precise (metaphorical) meaning of *relative shades of gray,* as no obvious property of a country is usually rendered with a color metaphor, except maybe the color metaphor of *red* for 'communist'. In other words, full interpretation will have to await further information from the sentence.

The next clause does start with a subject in topic position, *Guatemala,* which at the same time matches with the subject/topic of the macroproposition, so that there is a local manifestation of the meaning of the macroproposition. Moreover, the propositional schema activated by *compared* can now be further filled in: The comparison is between El Salvador and Guatemala, but such that the latter is the main argument in the comparison; a property of Guatemala is compared with a property of another country. Next follows another metaphorical phrase: *a study in black and white.* Again, a precise meaning might not yet be available, although the color metaphor *black and white* does have the more conventional meaning of 'marked contrast'. As the article is interpreted under the general scope of 'political news', the metaphor will first be translated into a specific political meaning, such as 'political contrasts are marked', which will in turn provide some more meaning to the metaphor in the first clause. But, still, even within the semantic domain of politics the precise meaning of the metaphorical expression may remain vague. We may have social, economic, or cultural contrasts. From this example we see on the one hand that the words and phrases of a sentence may already provide constraints about its further meaning, but on the other hand that strategies sometimes do not yield sufficient information for a final interpretation. For the processing model this means that this information, even in its partial analysis, must be kept in the short-term memory buffer, and that information from a next sentence is expected to provide the missing link.

Indeed, the next sentence immediately provides this missing link in a first adverbial noun phrase: *on the left*. This conventionalized spatial metaphor may be interpreted as providing political information—namely, information about parties and groups of a specific political signature, such as "liberal," "socialist," or "communist." Such an interpretation is confirmed in the rest of the first clause of the second sentence, namely, by the phrase *extreme Marxist-Leninist groups*, which fits well with the actualized political information in general and with the more specific knowledge about the political contrasts in Central America. The phrase *on the left*, in its topical position, at the same time sets up the expectation—already present in the short-term memory buffer: $(compare)(x, y)$—that groups on the right will also be mentioned, which is confirmed in the third sentence. The rest of the paragraph provides the details necessary for the interpretation of the metaphor in the first sentence: Gray is the political middle, and black and white is the opposition between the extreme political left and the extreme political right. It goes without saying that in order to provide such interpretations, the reader must have detailed political knowledge and in particular must know something about the political spectrum in countries of Central America.

*Local coherence strategies.* From our description of some of the comprehension strategies operating in the interpretation of the first sentence, we already gleaned some properties of the next kind of strategics involved, namely, those establishing relations between clauses and sentences. Whereas the two clauses of the first sentence are functionally coherent due to the explicit expression of the function of 'comparison', which is a well-known functional or rhetorical type of local coherence between clauses or sentences, the relation between the first two sentences also has a functional nature: The second sentence *explains* or *specifies* what has been said in metaphorical terms in the first, namely, by giving further information about the political contrasts in Guatemala. Indeed, the phrase *on the left* should be understood as referring to the political situation in Guatemala, not to that in El Salvador, and this interpretation is due to the (*a*) topic and subject functions of *Guatemala* in the previous sentence, (*b*) the fact that *Guatemala* occurred in the main clause there, and (*c*) the relevance of the discourse referent Guatemala with respect to the macroproposition. The local coherence strategy, therefore, will link the initial phrase *on the left* with the concept 'Guatemala' in the previous main proposition, a hypothesis confirmed by the subsequent sentences.

The same holds for the strategic interpretation of the third sentence, satisfying the expectation about a left–right description of the political spectrum generated by the first two sentences. At that point, the information from the first sentence may no longer be present in the short-term buffer, but only its general implication, namely, that there are marked political contrasts in the situation in Guatemala and that this is different from El Salvador. This means that the reader will expect that El Salvador will come up again for explication of the comparison, which indeed is the case in the relative clause in the fourth sentence.

*Macrostrategies.* Implicitly we already discussed the next type of strategies, namely, the macrostrategies, which aim at establishing a topic, gist, or macro-proposition for the text as a whole and for the first part of the text in particular. The communicative context already provides constraints on the domain of possible overall meanings, in our case 'politics'. Next, the headline of the article specifies that the text is a discourse about a specific country; the macropredicate, though vague, provides some idea about the political predicament of the situation in that country.

The initial sentences of the text then start out to provide the relevant specifics. The first thus leads to a macroproposition 'The situation in Guatemala is compared to that of El Salvador', which dominates the first part of the text. Next, the black and white metaphor, spelled out with the left–right opposition, explains why 'there are no choices' in Guatemala, which therefore confirms the macroproposition. Not only at the level of words, clauses, and sentences, but also at the level of macro-structures, a considerable amount of world knowledge must be activated in order to derive the relevant macroproposition or to confirm first guesses as derived from title, communicative setting, and context.

*Schematic strategies.* Although we will in general study schematic strategies at the global level, our example also exhibits "schemata" at a more local level, schemata which are often called rhetorical. Thus, making comparisons or spelling out opposition or contrast is a typical rhetorical device, here signaled by metaphors and the use of phrases such as *on the left* and *on the right* in initial positions of adjacent sentences. That is, such schemata assign specific, functional, structure to semantic elements of these sentences.

At the global level, schematic superstructures are supposed to assign an overall organization to this article. That is, the successive macropropositions, represented by, for example, paragraphs, may have conventional functions, such as Introduc-tion and Conclusion. In newspaper discourse, these superstructures will involve such categories as Headlines, Lead, Events, Backgrounds, Context, or Comments (van Dijk, 1981b, 1983a,b).

Thus, the first paragraph is typically a general *summary* of the article, present-ing the main facts: the political contrasts in Guatemala, the consequences of this contrast (i.e., that there is no easy solution), and finally the difference with El Salvador. The second paragraph then gives *historical background,* namely, of the relations between Guatemala and the United States, typically marked by past tenses, and the *consequences* of this historical background for the actual situation. The third paragraph then *specifies* the actual situation of the relationships between the United States and Guatemala. Next, the fourth paragraph summarizes the actual events, namely the activities of the Guatemalan government to fight the guerrilla by arming itself from various sources. In fact, this is still a *preparatory condition* for the main events, namely, the actual fighting and repression going on, mentioned in the next paragraphs. These events are also presented in a schemalike fashion: A description of the actions of the government and the army, as well as of death squads, is followed by a description of the actions and preparations of the guerrillas. This binary opposition is in fact the macrostructural specification of the black and white metaphor given in the beginning. Finally, the last paragraph specifies a number of *conclusions* from the situation for the American foreign policy toward Guatemala.

We see that news reports have a number of recurring, conventional categories, such as a summary or lead, historical backgrounds, a series of main events, including preparations and consequences, and overall (political) conclusions. On the whole the perspective dominating both the macrostructure and the superstructure is the American one, because the conclusions, marking the pragmatic relevance of the text, pertain to American foreign policy. Note that these conventional categories holding for news discourse are not derivable from the local or global semantic structure, or from knowledge about the political events or actions described. They are conventional structures of news discourse per se, but of course are linked to the macrostructures and hence to the possible meanings of the sentences of a paragraph dominated by a macroproposition. There is nothing in the facts themselves that would make it natural to give a summary first and to give a conclusion last. A semantic mapping would at most motivate a historical ordering in the description of the facts, or a causal ordering, going from motivation and goal to the events and their consequences.

The strategies used to derive relevant superstructures again combine information from various sources. First, top down, the knowledge about the communicative event and hence about the specific type of discourse already specifies a possible schema. Next, a segmentation into paragraphs will suggest both a macrostructural and a superstructural organization. Third, the macropropositions themselves will be assigned provisional functions, for example, that of general summary—as expressed also by the title—for the first macroproposition, expressed by the first paragraph. Fourth, there will be local indicators, such as the change to past tense in the second paragraph, functioning as the "historical background" category.

*Knowledge use strategies.* Finally, we have a number of strategies handling the complex flow of knowledge required in the individual steps of the various strategies. At the relevant points we have mentioned the various knowledge components needed. To establish the communicative situation and set up a global communicative goal, it was already necessary to draw upon our knowledge about political affairs, news, weeklies, and a specific episodic knowledge (about Central America) in case the reading goal is specifically geared toward obtaining information about a certain country or region. Obviously, the knowledge involved is vast, resulting from the many sources that have led to our political knowledge of the world. Hence, it seems plausible that a reader will activate, not all knowledge about political affairs, or about international news or about weeklies, but only that knowledge which is immediately necessary for carrying out the acts necessary to reach the established goal. In other words, we will assume that only a few relevant concepts will be actually activated, but not the full schemata or scripts dominated by them.

Thus, we may expect that the overall control system will be fed with propositions such as 'Newsweek is a weekly featuring articles with political information about the current situation in the world', which will guide the expectations about the discourse genre and the possible contents of the text. At the same time, this general information will activate the search for a more specific *episodic model* featuring our previous experiences and our previous reading about some concrete person, issue, country, or event. As soon as we have read the word *Guatemala* in the headline, this search can be more specific, activating our general and episodic knowledge about that country, and, in particular, our more recent memories about the current political situation in that country. Again, the general theme 'political affairs' guides this activation, ruling out, for instance, expectations about the cultural situation in that country. Hence, knowledge search, whether general or episodic, is guided by the overall goal, by the relevant macrostructural information, and by our episodic knowledge about what kind of information we can expect at a given time about a certain issue or individual object.

This all takes place in a more general preparatory phase of understanding. At the local level of comprehension, semantic and episodic knowledge will be addressed in a more specific way, according to the suggestions made in our cursory analysis. In our case, for instance, we will have to specify further knowledge about the two countries being compared, about the actual situation in each country, about the political concepts used to describe this situation, and so on. We assume that only that knowledge is activated which is relevant for the derivation of overall and more local topics, and which is necessary for the interpretation of individual propositions and for the establishment of local coherence relations. Thus, in order to interpret *on the left* in the second sentence, the access to general political information will be such that information about the political organization of groups or parties is activated, which also allows the generation of the expectation after 'the left' is mentioned that 'the right' will be mentioned as well.

In fact, newspaper discourse uses a number of structural categories that are specifically meant to organize the use of relevant knowledge. Thus, categories such as historical background, context, or explanation may serve as reminders for the search in semantic or episodic memory for those readers who have this kind of background knowledge, whereas, at the same time, for readers who do not have this knowledge, a situation model is specified in which the events described are more meaningful.

### 3.8.3. Conclusion

From the highly informal description of a number of strategies used in the comprehension of this text we can draw several conclusions. First, there indeed seem to be hierarchical relations among the strategies: Some strategies will dominate others. Second, the various global types of information act as top-down processing strategies for the comprehension of local information. Third, information for specific strategies, such as the macrostrategies, may come from many sources, such as textual cues (title), contextual information (about the weekly), and already present episodic or semantic memory presuppositions (the actual situation in Guatemala, general knowledge about that country). Fourth, at the local level we have forward interpretation strategies, which provide constraints for the specific meanings to come, as well as backward interpretation strategies, which specify the meaning of expressions that only were assigned partial interpretations. And, fifth, knowledge will be called on, in a number of knowledge use strategies, by all interpretation strategies in such a way that it provides precisely the relevant information at each point, leaving the more general information at the level of the control schema. At the same time, though, these strategies will link the textual representation with the situation model: The model will be updated with the new (or forgotten) information that is expressed by the text. It is this updating strategy that finally satisfies the overall communicative goal of the reader—namely, to obtain new political information. Just as knowledge is activated dependent on the micro- or macrolevel of processing, we may assume that knowledge will also be updated in a similar strategic fashion: Main facts, as represented by the macropropositions, will be assigned a specific function in the situation model, whereas possible details may be added if they are relevant for further processing (e.g., use in conversation).

After this introductory discussion of the various kinds of strategies operating in the interpretation of the *Newsweek* text, our next chapters will for each strategy type specify in more systematic detail how the strategies actually operate. We now have a first idea about their mutual relationships, and we also know that strategies are already operating before the text has even been seen, or before the first words of the text have been read, and that the outcome of these preparatory, communicative, and contextual strategies—specifying, among other things, the overall goal of the reading act—heavily determines the choice of the more local or global textual strategies of comprehension.

*Chapter 4*

# Propositional Strategies

## 4.1. PROPOSITIONS

In Chapter 2 we saw that many discourse comprehension models involve the assignment of propositions to sentential surface structures. In our own text-processing model (Kintsch & van Dijk, 1978) it was also assumed that comprehension consists, among other things, in the formation of a coherent sequence of propositions, a so-called textbase. In this chapter we would like to examine the first set of strategies involved in the construction of such a propositional textbase. More specifically, we would like to focus our attention on the formation of complex propositions as they are expressed by the clauses and sentences of a discourse, and as they represent facts in some possible world. In the next chapter we will then turn to the strategies that enable a language user to establish coherence relations between such complex propositions and hence between the sentences of the discourse. Before we discuss the various propositional strategies, we must, however, briefly assess the nature of propositions in a cognitive model. Whereas we have several notions, in philosophy, logic, and linguistics, of the semantic unit of a proposition, what remains to be made explicit is how it also functions as a cognitive unit.

### 4.1.1. The Notion of Proposition in Philosophy and Linguistics

Because the literature on propositions is too vast to even succinctly account for here, and because the notion is mostly discussed in relation to the notions of meaning, reference, and truth value, we shall only mention some of the milestones. (For a general history of the notion of proposition and related notions, see Kneale & Kneale, 1962, especially pp. 49ff.)

Although Frege (1962) does not use the notion of proposition itself, his distinction between *Sinn* and *Bedeutung*, both for words and sentences, has been fundamental for later discussions of the subject. Whereas *Bedeutung* for him is the truth value of a sentence (or clause), *Sinn* would be the (nonsubjective) thought (*Gedanke*) of the sentence as it determines this truth value. Whitehead and Russell (1910) use the notion of proposition but do not define it. Strawson (1952:3ff.) uses the term "statement" instead and emphasizes that a statement—which is related to truth values and which can be inconsistent with or implied by other statements—is not identical with a sentence nor with the meaning of a sentence, because both may be used to make identical statements even if they are different, and the converse, depending on context. Reichenbach (1947:5ff.) does not make a distinction between proposition, statement, and sentence, but prefers to use the term proposition and takes it as the fundamental unit of language and logic, with the defining criterion that only propositions can be true or false. What is referred to by a proposition or sentence, he calls a "situation" or "state of affairs," rejecting Carnap's (1942:18) identification of situation and proposition. Surprisingly, Reichenbach also rejects as spurious the distinction made by other logicians between sentences and propositions, although admitting that different sentences, for example, actives and their corresponding passives, may be "equi-significant." Carnap (1947:26ff.) appears to be more subtle. Distinguishing between extensions and intensions, he identifies, as usual, the extension of a sentence with its truth value, and the intension with the proposition expressed by it. Like Frege, he warns that a proposition is not some subjective meaning, nor a linguistic expression (a sentence), but an objective conceptual structure (which should not be identified with a "mental occurrence"). In that sense, a proposition is as objective as the abstract, general meaning of a word. However, confusion arises again when he identifies a proposition with something that is "actually the case," exemplified by some individual having some property. As we will see in what follows, it is only with Montague (1974) that this confusion was clarified: A proposition, then, is indeed a conceptual structure, a function, which is "exemplified" (in Carnap's terms) by its instantiations, that is, values, in some possible world. Interesting for our discussion are Carnap's further remarks about *facts* (1947:28), made in referring to a paper by Ducasse (1940). Although he does not admit fácts as a technical term, he identifies a fact with a true proposition, which is both complete and specific, and of course contingent. We will see briefly in what follows that this raises the problem of the referential correlate of negated propositions. Carnap then takes issue with Russell (1940), in which Russell *does* identify a proposition with the meaning (or signification) of a sentence but localizes it in the mind (namely, as psychological or physiological occurrences, such as images), a position which the (semi)positivist Carnap cannot, of course, accept: propositions are objective entities, logical types. Quine (1953:108, 156) follows a similar road, although he would prefer to avoid propositions. He agrees with Frege that propositions are neither statements nor values of statements, but at most their meanings. Battling against such things as meanings and intensions in general, Quine (1960:192ff., 201ff.) grudgingly admits propositions—if only to have something to be the content of sentences like *John believed that* . . . , but maintains that this makes sense only for meanings of "eternal sentences" the truth values of which do not depend on contextual factors such as speaker and time. In Quine (1974:36), he reverts to a rather stern externalist (extensional, if not positivist) position, relegating ideas, meanings, and propositions to the realm of vague, useless, or incomprehensible objects.

From this brief survey of some of the major philosophers and logicians, it emerges that there is not only disagreement, but also confusion. It has been remarked (e.g., White, 1970:13ff.) that many of the philosophers have made rather vague uses of the term (see also Linsky, 1967:7). Proceeding from the various proposals, we will maintain in what follows that a proposition is an abstract, theoretical construct, which is used to identify the meaning, or what is expressed by a sentence under specific contextual restrictions (speaker, time, place), and which is related to truth values. One of the reasons for the multiple confusion is that propositions have been tied too closely to truth values, however. That is, they have been identified with assertions as speech acts, and with the realization of assertions in declarative sentences. Although we will touch upon some of these issues, we cannot go into the details of an abstract, philosophical or logical, definition of propositions.

The use of the notion of proposition in linguistics is more recent than in philosophy and logic, from which it was adopted widely at the end of the sixties (although linguists will in general continue to speak of semantic representations). As is well known, until the sixties the influence of behaviorism on linguistic theories had precluded a systematic study of meaning. Early structuralism was mainly concerned with surface structures, and it was the well-known paper by Katz and Fodor (1963) that tried to provide transformational grammar with a semantic component. Semantic analysis, then, became pervasive in linguistics by the end of the sixties, particularly within the branch of transformational grammar called "generative semantics," mainly through the work of scholars such as McCawley, Lakoff, and, more independently, Fillmore. Again we mention only some major approaches.

Ogden and Richards (1923) speak of propositions in terms of a "complete thought," as the object of beliefs, expressed by a sentence, and related to truth and falsity, in contrast to the meanings of isolated words.

Katz and Fodor (1963) account for meanings of sentences in terms of meanings of lexical items plus projection rules based on syntactic structures, but do not discuss propositions as such. Thus, for years grammatical theory continued to speak of semantic interpretations. Readers in semantics, such as Steinberg and Jakobovits (1971), included philosophers and logicians, but an independent linguistic definition of propositions was not undertaken. This is understandable because, just like word meanings, sentence meanings in linguistics were hardly ever related to extra-linguistic aspects such as truth and falsity, so that the notion of proposition, traditionally linked with truth values, did not become relevant. As soon as an appropriate metalanguage for linguistic semantics was sought in philosophy and logic, however, the notion of proposition also became current in linguistics, for example, Katz (1972:38ff.); Lyons (1977; 1981:119ff.). This is particularly true of linguistic work in the seventies based directly on logical semantics (see, e.g., Keenan, 1975, and Hintikka, Moravcsik, & Suppes, 1973).

In rather rough terms, then, we can say that a proposition is usually taken as the meaning of a (declarative) sentence. This meaning has a composite nature: It is a construction of the meanings of the component expressions—the words or phrases of the sentence. This construction is the output of the semantic interpretation rules, and follows the well-known Fregean principle of functionality: The interpretation of composite expressions is a function of the interpretation of its component expressions. We will see in what follows that this principle not only holds in philosophy, logic, and linguistics, but essentially also in a cognitive model of interpretation.

Whereas a part of philosophy and especially linguistics indeed defines the proposition in terms of the meaning of a sentence, and hence provides a conceptual or intensional semantics, modern logic has initially preferred to define the proposition in referential, denotational, or extensional terms. That is, propositions, or the sentences expressing them, are related to truth values. A proposition, then, is something that can be true or false. For several of the more recent theories of logics, these truth values have been made relative, for example, with respect to possible worlds, situations, language users, or contexts. Contextual semantics has been advocated mainly following Montague (1974)—who spoke of "formal pragmatics," however—for example, by Cresswell (1973). From this perspective, a proposition is usually defined as a set, namely, the set of possible worlds in which it is true. In more sophisticated terms, finally, we can say that a proposition is a function from possible worlds to truth values. This definition is that of Montague (1974:153). Indices for place, time, or other contextual features may be added as further arguments of the function. Thus, the proposition *The boy is ill* is something (formalized by the notion of a function) which for some possible worlds (time, place, etc.) may be true or false. Units like *The boy* or *ill* are not propositions because they cannot, by themselves, be true or false.

There are many philosophical and logical intricacies which we cannot discuss here. For our purposes it is sufficient to know that we have intensional and extensional approaches to the notion of a proposition—and sometimes even combinations of these. To cut short a long discussion, we will abstractly take a proposition as an intensional unit, corresponding to the meaning of a sentence in linguistic theory, and to the conceptual representation of a sentence in a cognitive model of language comprehension. Of course, since we do not hold the view that "meanings" or "concepts" are inherently tied to natural language, propositions defined as some form of a conceptual representation figure more generally in models of comprehension, for example, in the comprehension of real or pictorial images or in the comprehension of other semiotic systems. We will limit our discussion, however, to propositions as they are expressed by natural language.

### 4.1.2. The Propositional Schema

As we have suggested, a proposition is a composite unit. Traditionally, it was analyzed in terms of a *predicate* and one or more *arguments*. In extensional terms, a predicate is understood to refer to properties or relations, and arguments to individuals, such as things or persons. Since we take a proposition as an intensional or conceptual unit, its component predicate and argument(s) should also be intensional: A predicate is a concept of a property or relation, and an argument a concept of an individual. It would be nice if natural language would respect this distinction in the surface structure of the sentence, that is, in the respective expressions of predicates and arguments. But the situation in this respect is confusing: We cannot simply say that predicates are expressed by verbs, and arguments by nouns or noun phrases. In the sentence *The boy is ill,* the noun phrase *the boy* certainly expresses an argument, and—in referential terms—it is used to denote an individual, for instance John, but at the same time it expresses the predicate 'boy' and is thus related to a property of John. Logically speaking, therefore, the sentence would be analyzed as (at least) two atomic propositions—namely, 'boy(a)' and 'is ill(a)'— usually connected by a conjunction ("&") into a compound proposition. In that case the expression 'a', a so-called argument constant, is interpreted as referring to the individual, for instance, John. In other words, what appears to be a single sentence, consisting of one clause, may logically express several atomic propositions. If a proposition, then, is defined as "the" meaning of a sentence, we should remember that the proposition may be composite, that is, itself consist of several other (atomic) propositions. Only sentences like *He is ill,* in which the pronoun *he* has a similar function as the logical expression 'a', would express an atomic proposition.

Sentences are usually much more complex, and feature not only verbs, verb phrases, nouns, and noun phrases, but also adjectives, adverbs, modal expressions (such as *maybe, should*), connectives, and so on. Moreover, they often consist of several clauses, and not just of one clause. The logical analysis of these various categories of expressions, as well as of the syntactic or morphological structures (such as tense morphemes), has met with extremely difficult problems which we cannot discuss here. The adequate logical representation even of atomic propositions has become so complex that at this stage of development it would not be wise to use logical systems as representation formats for propositions in a cognitive model.

Among the many elements of sentences that are still lacking a satisfactory logical analysis, we, for instance, do not yet know how to account for the so-called *semantic roles* or cases characterizing the internal semantic structure of a sentence, such as agent, patient, object, instrument, goal, or source. Following the seminal paper by Fillmore (1968), many linguists now adopt this kind of functional semantics, among others, Dik (1978), Anderson (1971), and Jackendoff (1972). The cases or semantic functions we use here are merely illustrative. We will not try to give a formal account of them.

Thus, if we would represent the meaning of the sentence *John gave the book to Peter* in terms of logical propositions, namely, as 'Gave to (a, b, c) & John = a & book (b) & Peter = c', such semantic roles remain implicit in the ordering of the arguments. In fact, the same ordering could be used to express many other semantic role relations. As an ad hoc (ad hoc because there is still no explicit formal semantics for such expressions) device we could add argument labels, such as agent and patient, to the argument places representing these semantic roles. Similarly, we can devise a *schema* in which the various semantic categories of the meaning of a sentence are represented as the nodes in a tree-like structure (Figure 4.1):

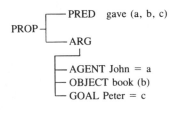

**Figure 4.1**

For reasons of simplicity we will henceforth use such a kind of schematic representation for propositions, and call this a *propositional schema*. Note that the proposition represented in Figure 4.1 is composite: It consists of several atomic propositions. The definite article *the* does not have a separate semantic representation; it only expresses that individual 'b' is known or identifiable by the hearer, and therefore has instead a pragmatic or cognitive function. In other words, not all expressions in the surface structure express only semantic properties of the sentence; they may also express pragmatic, stylistic, rhetorical, cognitive, interactional, or social properties.

In addition to the categories introduced in the schema of Figure 4.1, we will need some others in order to do an elementary semantic analysis of English sentences. First, each category may have a subordinated modifier category or modifier (MOD), under which adverbs and adjectives are represented. Second, we need a circumstance kind of category (CIRC), under which various time, place, or other complementizers can be represented, as well as the possible world in which the sentence is interpreted. To represent a sentence like *Yesterday, John inadvertently gave the old book to Peter in the library,* we would then have something like the schema of Figure 4.2:

```
            ┌PRED gave (a, b, c)
            │  └MOD inadvertently
            │
            ├ARG
            │  ├AGENT John = a
      PROP─┤  ├OBJECT book (b)
            │  │
            │  └MOD old (b)
            │  └GOAL Peter = c
            │
            └CIRC
               ├TIME yesterday
               └PLACE in the library
```

**Figure 4.2**

This schema, however, is not yet adequate—even for our simplified way of representing propositions—because not all terminal elements are atomic propositions. If 'inadvertently' is predicated of the predicate terminal 'give (a, b, c)', we need also a constant to represent the action of giving. The same holds for the circumstance categories: They have the whole action as their scope, that is, they localize the action in time and place. Figure 4.2, then, is a simplified representation for the schema in Figure 4.3:

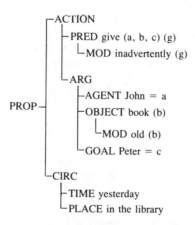

```
            ┌ACTION
            │  ├PRED give (a, b, c) (g)
            │  │  └MOD inadvertently (g)
            │  │
            │  └ARG
            │     ├AGENT John = a
      PROP─┤     ├OBJECT book (b)
            │     │
            │     └MOD old (b)
            │     └GOAL Peter = c
            │
            └CIRC
               ├TIME yesterday
               └PLACE in the library
```

**Figure 4.3**

The general category action dominating the predicate and argument categories is necessary for various reasons. It determines, for instance, the nature of the predicate (e.g., an action verb) and the kind of argument categories involved (e.g., agent). Note that the terminal categories of the circumstance category are not propositional.

They merely localize the complex proposition dominated by the action category. In this respect circumstance acts like modal categories (which make propositions out of propositions). Strictly speaking, the action part of the schema is only a propositional function: It is true or false only if we add time and place categories (e.g., as expressed by the verb tense and the location adverb). A propositional function is, so to speak, an incomplete proposition: It cannot, as such, be true or false. It will typically contain free variables, as in $f(x)$ or $g(x, y)$. If we add quantifiers which bind the variables or substitute constants for the variables, we obtain a proposition. In our example, a full proposition should also contain information about circumstances, for example, as expressed by tense or adverbs. Although, as we suggested, the schema of Figure 4.3 is still far from complete from a linguistic point of view and far from adequate from the point of view of a logical semantics, we will henceforth use this kind of representation for the abstract structure of propositions. In what follows, we will discuss the cognitive relevance of this representation.

### 4.1.3. Facts

Although we now have an approximate analysis of propositions in intensional terms, we still need some further insight into the extensional aspect of propositions. What do propositions, as expressed by clauses or sentences, refer to? Earlier we mentioned that propositions are usually connected with truth values. Such an approach has serious difficulties for the interpretation of natural language sentences. First, a truth functional account would have difficulty providing interpretations for nondeclarative sentences as they are used to perform requests, commands, congratulations, or promises. Such sentences, however, also express propositions. The notion of truth or falsity is linked, it seems, not so much with the meaning, and hence with the propositions, expressed by a sentence, but rather with the pragmatic aspect of declarative sentences, which are mostly used to perform assertions. They refer to a state of affairs, which is a semantic aspect, and at the same time their use implies—in certain appropriate contexts—the act of asserting that this state of affairs indeed holds in some possible world. Similarly, a request also expresses a proposition, but it is performed pragmatically so that the hearer will act in such a way that some state of affairs will be brought about. Second, whereas predicates are interpreted as things like properties or relations, and arguments as individuals, we lack a corresponding possible world unit which is the referent of a proposition, for example, something that is called a "state of affairs." However, since the notion of state of affairs seems rather static, and propositions may also denote events, actions, or processes, we will use the notion of a *fact* as the referent of a proposition.

The notion of fact has had little attention from philosophers and logicians, let alone from linguists (who are seldom interested in extralinguistic entities). We have already mentioned that Carnap (1947:28) informally uses the notion, identifying it with a true proposition (plus some further contextual constraints). Prior (1971) explicitly examines whether besides propositions we need the notion of fact and concludes negatively. We use the notion of fact as being equivalent to the German notion *Tatsache,* which Wittgenstein (1960) distinguished from *Sachverhalt.* A *Sachverhalt,* indeed, would in our terms be the referent of a propositional function, which we may call a possible fact. It may be expressed linguistically by an incomplete *that*-clause: *that John is ill,* or *John's being ill.* A *Tatsache,* a fact, is directly tied to the parameters of some specific possible world and situation. Both for linguistic and for logical reasons, the notion of fact also seems necessary to provide an adequate formal semantics for, say, nominalizations. The discussion about the relevance of facts is rather complex, and we will not try to defend the notion here. Its relevance in the theory of discourse has been emphasized in van Dijk (1977a).

Since our notion of proposition, represented by a schema, is rather different from that in logic or philosophy, we elsewhere have used the term FACT (with capital letters in order to distinguish it from possible world entities, i.e., facts), as the cognitive correlate, the representation, of facts. In order not to confuse our readers, we have here reverted to the classical notion of proposition, though adapting it to our needs. In what follows, we will also use the same, abstract notion of proposition in a cognitive model.

Although the notion of fact has no satisfactory philosophical and logical analysis, and there may be doubts about its usefulness besides either the notion of a proposition itself or besides the truth values 'truth' and 'falsity', we think it has a number of intuitive and formal advantages. Some of these will be discussed when we consider the cognitive aspects of propositions and facts. Formally speaking, facts are fragments of possible worlds. They are, as we see from the intensional analysis of their corresponding propositions (Figure 4.3), combinations of some state, process, action, or event, on the one hand, and some time, place, or other circumstantial parameters, on the other. Hence, the "same" event may become a fact in various worlds or situations. In other words, a possible world is a set of facts. Again, we will ignore a number of technicalities regarding the formal account of facts, mentioning just one aspect of interest: Negated sentences do not denote negative facts, but should be taken as pragmatic denials about the existence, that is, actualization, of a fact in some possible world.

The notion of fact has some philosophical (epistemological and ontological) intricacies which we can only hint at here. It might be argued, for instance, that facts do not exist, as such, in some possible world: There is no physical or biological reality defining a fact, as seems to be the case for properties, relations, or individuals. Facts, in that respect, only exist for human subjects: They are, so to speak, constructions of individuals and their properties and relations. In that case, they would have a cognitive, conceptual, and hence an intensional nature, which makes them equivalent with propositions. However, this argument does not hold. First, properties, relations, and individuals also are conventionalized, cognitively based, discrete entities assigned to some possible world(s). Just as their existence is postulated when we abstract from their cognitive projection, we may postulate the existence of their combination into some fact. So, facts are indeed, epistemologically, constructions based on cognitive operations, but we will in general be able to abstract from this cognitive basis and just postulate that facts exist out there for all practical purposes. If we witness an accident, we assume that the accident happened out there and that it would also exist if we had not seen it. That we call such a physical event an *accident,* thereby distinguishing it from other events, is a conventional, cultural, linguistic, and cognitive aspect of facts. The same, indeed, holds for things like cars, of which we would hardly deny the existence either. Here we come to age old philosophical controversies, which we will not further explore. For our purposes—that is, for the linguistic and cognitive interpretation of discourse—facts will be postulated as entities in possible worlds, and taken as the referents of propositions. That is, car accidents exist no less than cars as ontological units.

This does not mean that facts are fixed discrete entities of some possible world. Their projected or construed nature, on the basis of abstract propositions or "real" cognitive processes of interpretation, allows facts as such to be split into component facts, or the same event to be described or understood at several hierarchical levels. Thus, as part of the event we call an accident, we may have the event 'that I drove my car into another car', or 'that my bumper touched the other car', etc., or, at a higher level, 'that I had a traffic problem', or 'that I ruined myself'.

This philosophical digression does not imply that facts only exist in what we would usually call possible worlds. Take, for instance, the so-called propositional attitudes, such as knowledge, beliefs, opinions, or attitudes about facts. The sentence *I think that John gave the book to Peter* of course also denotes a fact, but in that case it denotes a cognitive fact, that is, a certain state of mind of the speaker. Such states of minds need not be expressed explicitly: *John is stupid* need not refer to an external or objective fact, but may be used to express and denote the opinion of the speaker about John. This brings us back to our philosophical query: In principle the "same" fact may always be seen, interpreted, or understood in different ways by different subjects, and hence facts would not be out there anyway. This is correct, but again ignores the kind of epistemological abstraction involved in the postulation of facts: As soon as a state of affairs, event, or action exists for everybody, that is, if the individual cognitive contexts are no longer relevant, then facts do exist externally. In other words, facts—related to the notion of truth—become social constructs, being open to verifiability criteria, such as observation. Hence, propositional attitude sentences denote subjective facts and other sentences denote intersubjective or social facts. This leaves open the possibility for individual and cultural variation in the construction of the world, as it should be.

Next, a remark about the referential nature of modalized sentences or propositions. A sentence like *Maybe John is ill* of course does not denote a fact in the same way as the sentence *John is ill.* Rather, the speaker considers the possibility that 'John is ill' is true (is a fact in our own possible world). In formal terms this simply means that, for the speaker, there is at least one possible world (imagined situation) in which the fact 'John is ill' exists. This formulation is slightly different from the usual formal semantic interpretation of the modal expression 'it is possible that'.

We have considered the issue of the referential nature of propositions or of the clauses and sentences expressing them, and we have introduced the notion of fact as their possible world referent. In so doing, we have followed the direction usually taken in philosophy, logic, and linguistics, namely, to assign an interpretation to given sentences or propositions. That is, we went from words to worlds, as is usual for semantic interpretation rules. There is little explicit theorizing, however, about the reverse aspect of this relationship: How do we express some given fragment of reality in language, that is, how do we go from worlds to words? Although in abstract terms there may hardly be anything relevant to say, it is obvious that a cognitive model of discourse processing will also have to account for this aspect. Instead of an interpretational semantics, as we may call all those types of semantics that assign meanings and referents (including truth values) to expressions, we now encounter the necessity of devising a *representational semantics*. Given some individuals, properties, or relations as they combine into facts, we want to know how these facts are semantically represented, that is, how propositions are formed and how propositions are expressed in natural language discourse. Of course, in some sense this is again an interpretation problem, but now it is not words but worlds which are interpreted. This aspect is especially crucial for an adequate production model of discourse, to which we will turn in Chapter 8, for in order to know how discourse is produced, we must know how propositions are formed. In the remarks about cognitive processing of propositions in what follows we will therefore also have to look at the role that propositional schemata play in the interpretation of the world, that is, in the identification or construction of facts. Specifically, we will pay attention to the problem of how collections of facts become represented in collections of propositions.

We now have the theoretical machinery to attack a number of issues related to the comprehension of sentences in discourse. We know that sentences express propositions, and that propositions represent facts in some possible world. Both propositions and facts may be composite, in the sense that they may consist of other propositions and facts. Hence, we should postulate atomic propositions and therefore also atomic facts as their referents. Also, we have seen that a proposition can be represented with a propositional schema, featuring a predicate, a number of arguments (with appropriate functions), and various circumstances. However, propositions (and hence, facts) do not come alone: They are organized in ordered sequences, and these constructions have variable expressions in the sentences of the discourse. It is this construction problem which we will analyze, both abstractly and cognitively, in the rest of this chapter.

## 4.2. COMPLEX PROPOSITIONS

We have argued that most sentences of natural language express composite propositions. In logical terms this means that the propositions are compounds, consisting of a number of atomic propositions. These compounds are defined and semantically interpreted in terms of connectives, such as conjunction, disjunction, or conditionals of various sorts. In logical formulas the component propositions are then of the same level: The compound is a coordinated structure. In natural language sentences this may be different. We have both coordinated and subordinated structures: One clause may either have the same function as another clause, as in coordinated sentences, or it may have a function within the other clause, for example, as a noun phrase in the subordinate clause of a complex sentence. In logical terms this would mean that one proposition is placed in argument position of another proposition. Again, it should be recalled that a simple clause or sentence in natural language mostly expresses a proposition that is logically speaking composite, that is, consists of several atomic propositions, as we have seen in the proposition schema introduced in the previous section. This means that, in order to avoid confusion, we should carefully distinguish between complexity at the surface structure level; defined in terms of clauses, and complexity at the semantic level, defined in terms of propositions. For sentential clause structure, we will therefore use the general term composite sentence to denote any sentence that consists of more than one clause, compound sentence to denote sentences of which all clauses are of the same rank, and complex sentence to denote sentences of which at least one clause has different rank, that is, in which there is at least one subordinate clause and a corresponding main clause in which the subordinate clause has a syntactic function. At the semantic level we will use in principle the same terms composite, compound, and complex for propositions.

## 4.2.1. Clause Structure and Propositional Structure

For our discussion the relationships between clausal or sentential structures and propositional structures are of crucial importance. Our schema was devised such that one simple clause corresponds to one propositional schema, consisting of an ordered set of atomic propositions, and one fact, which is the referent of the clause in some possible world. Thus, as soon as we have composite sentences we will also expect composite schemata; one schema may be coordinated or subordinated with respect to another schema, as in sentences such as:

(1)    *The professor hired an assistant who had written a dissertation on discourse comprehension.*

We assume that the (complex) proposition expressed by the second clause will be embedded into the modifier category of the argument category patient which has the atomic proposition 'assistant(b)' as its terminal filler. This assumption is based on the interpretation that the second clause is used to further identify the assistant—as would be the case if a definite article *the assistant* had been used—or to specify a property of some person, as in (1).

Both intuitively and formally, Sentence (1) denotes one fact, namely, the action of hiring somebody who has certain properties. This fact is complex because the property of one of the arguments is described in terms of another (previous) fact. But the sentential structure of (1) suggests that this embedded fact indeed has no independent function other than to specify a (main) fact.

At this point, however, we should view sentential surface structure not only as an expression of underlying semantic structures, but at the same time as an expression of pragmatic functions. That is, the notions of main clause, main proposition, and main fact seem to be related to that of the pragmatic act of an assertion. The pragmatic act of an assertion, however, also has a number of cognitive properties. Basically, for example, the pragmatic conditions must be satisfied that the speaker knows $p$, believes that the hearer does not know $p$, and wants the hearer to know $p$. The use of (1) signals that the speaker wants to assert something about the act of hiring. Although this is true in some sense, it could be maintained that the speaker also asserts something about the assistant, hence about the fact that the assistant had written some dissertation. It follows that if we want to establish links among sentences, propositions, and facts, both from a semantic and from a pragmatic point of view, we will have to introduce the concept of *importance* or *focus*. In that case, even if Sentence (1) denotes one complex fact, and hence several single facts, and even if the speaker is using (1) in some context as an assertion, and thereby speaking about one complex fact or several single facts, a distinction may indeed be made between facts that are pragmatically and hence cognitively more important and those that are less important. In other words, the proposition or fact consisting of the (concept of) *hiring* is in focus here and appears to have more relevance in communication than the act of writing a dissertation. Of course, the syntactic, semantic, pragmatic, and cognitive hierarchies involved may be variable in different contexts. That is, several surface structure types may be used to change the focus of importance:

(2)    *The professor hired an assistant. She had written a dissertation on discourse comprehension.*

(3)    *The assistant who had written a dissertation on discourse comprehension was hired by the professor.*

(4)    *The assistant who was hired by the professor had written a dissertation on discourse comprehension.*

From these examples we may observe that with varying surface structures we obtain at the same time various semantic and pragmatic interpretations. In (2) we have two independent sentences, coordinated without a connective in a discourse. Hence, we have two (related) assertions, and apparently also reference to two independent, but related, facts. In (3) and (4) we again have complex sentences, complex propositions, and complex facts within one act of assertion, but the hierarchies are different from those in (1). In (3) it is still the fact consisting of the act of hiring which is most prominent, but now—intuitively—the assertion seems to be rather about the assistant than about the professor. Or, rather, it is the assistant who is now in the focus of attention, and therefore the *topic* of (3). In sentence or assertion (3) the fact of having written a dissertation on discourse comprehension is again merely used to identify, specify, or qualify one of the participants in the main fact. This situation is reversed in (4): Here the main fact denoted, and hence the focus in the assertion, is the act of having written a dissertation, and the fact of having been hired is just a specification of the participant. Note also that in (3) and (4), as opposed to (2), the propositions that are expressed by the restrictive relative clauses may be *presupposed,* semantically by the sentence or pragmatically by the speaker. That is, they are assumed to be information already available to the hearer, either from previous text or from context.

From this brief discussion about complex sentences and complex propositions we may conclude that syntactic and semantic structures may be systematically related to pragmatic and cognitive structures. That is, the clause structure not only expresses which propositional structure is involved, but also how we should see the facts, and hence what is asserted in the communicative context, what is known, unknown, or presupposed, what is more important and less important or requires more or less focus of attention.

## 4.2.2. Relations among Propositions

Interesting for our discussion in all this is that there are variable ways to communicate about the same facts. The very construction of complex facts or sequences of facts may depend on pragmatic and cognitive criteria and is signaled by surface structure. Thus for a theory of discourse comprehension it is of primary importance to know how semantic information is placed in or distributed across several sentences. In what follows, we will examine in more detail how cognitive factors may determine these variations in the construction of facts and their corresponding cognitive representations. First, we must have a more general, abstract, picture of the relationships among sentences, their (propositional) meanings, facts, speech acts, and some cognitive features such as knowledge and importance.

In order to understand fully just what is going on when a sentence—or a speaker uttering it—expresses several propositions or refers to several facts, we should examine in somewhat more detail the examples given earlier and give some further examples. Returning to Examples (1) and (2) we see that in both cases two (complex) propositions and two facts are involved. Yet, the relationship between the propositions and between the facts seems to be different. Intuitively, it seems that this relation is closer in (1) than in (2): In (1) the fact consisting of writing a dissertation merely functions as a property of a participant in another fact, whereas in (2) the facts are much more independent. Apparently, sentences and discourse may express by their clausal structure different relationships or different degrees of closeness between facts. Let us try to spell out these degrees:

    0. *No relation.* This zero case, in which there is no relation between the facts, would characterize forms of listing or incoherent discourse.

    1. *Indirect coherence.* The facts are part of the same possible world episode. Thus, they may share the same time, place, or argument, and will be part of the same macrofact, as denoted by a macroproposition and expressed by noncontiguous sentences.

    2. *Direct coherence.* As in Degree 1 (indirect coherence) but in addition the facts are temporally and/or conditionally related, denoted by separate claus-

es or sentences which are linearly ordered. The relation is expressed only one way, for example, by sentence adverbials such as *therefore, then, so, as a result,* etc.

3. *Coordinated connection.* As in Degree 2 (direct coherence) but now the facts are mutually related, as cause and consequence, and form one (ordered) pair, triple, *n*-tuple of facts, hence together one composite fact, presented as a unit, mostly by a compound sentence and explicit coordinating connectives.

4. *Subordinate connection.* As in Degree 3 (coordinated connection) but now the facts are no longer sequentially but hierarchically ordered: One fact is taken only as a specification (e.g., a condition) of the other, as is typically signaled by a complex sentence with full embedded clause in adverb position.

5. *Integration.* As in Degree 4 (subordinate connection) but now it is no longer the case that one fact is (re-)presented as conditioning or determining a whole other fact, but rather as determining only one aspect of the other fact, for example, as a specification of the manner of action or the property of a participant. Typically expressed by (restrictive) relative clauses.

6. *Reduction.* As in Degree 5 (integration) but now the fact no longer has the function of a modifier, but is reduced to a noncomplex, atomic property, as typically expressed by adjectivization (such as *expected, fallen,* etc.).

We see that these different relations existing between facts have typical expressions in the surface structures of the discourse. This means that it is the discourse structure, and hence the speaker using this as interpretation indications, that suggests how the facts talked about should be identified and related by the hearer. Of course, there may be other factors, pragmatic or cognitive ones, that may establish other relations between the facts for the hearer. To this kind of comprehension variation we will return in what follows. With this abstract analysis of fact relationships we now can see that Sentences (1) and (2) express Degrees 5 and 2 of the hierarchy, respectively. The intermediate Degrees 3 and 4 would be expressed by sentences like the following:

(5)    *Susan wrote a dissertation about discourse comprehension and was (there-fore) hired by the professor.*

(6)    *After (Because) she had written a dissertation about discourse comprehension, Susan was hired by the professor.*

From the examples given and the hierarchy of fact relations they express we see that a sequence of facts may gradually be merged into one composite or complex fact. As soon as the temporal or conditional nature of the relationship between the facts as wholes get lost, as in the integration case, the fact may be reduced to a complex or even simple property. It is in this sense that we may say that Sentence (1) is really about *one* fact, the action of hiring an assistant. It would be theoretically inadequate to maintain for such a sentence that one of the facts is part of another fact: Writing a dissertation is not part of the fact of hiring an assistant. Rather we should say, perhaps, that the restricted relative clause expresses a proposition of which the referential function is to identify, specify, or qualify a participant individual of a fact. In that case a modifier proposition would denote not a fact but a property. Another option would be to accept reference to one, complex, fact, but such that the relation between the main fact and the subordinated fact only exists via the individual in the main fact, which is asserted to participate in two facts. Note that in unrestricted relative clauses we have a different situation: There we certainly have two independent facts as *referents,* but only integrated surface structure to signal the referential identity of the participating individuals. Finally, it might be argued that the fact-relation hierarchy may be related to a similar hierarchy at the pragmatic level: We may have degrees of assertiveness. The more facts are signaled to be integrated, the less they will be asserted—and often the more they will be presupposed to be known. And similarly for the cognitive importance: More integration will signal less relative importance of a fact.

As the propositional schema discussed is related to clauses in the surface structure and facts as referents, this discussion about the relations between sentences and the world also holds for the relations between propositions. The resulting picture is that we have coherent sequences of propositions, also called *episodes,* composite propositions consisting of connected pairs, triples, . . . , *n*-tuples, and complex propositions of different kinds. (Episodes are sequences of propositions dominated by a macroproposition, van Dijk, 1982b.) Whereas these distinctions are abstract, we should now consider how a cognitive model accounts for the comprehension processes and the strategies operating on or with such propositional structures.

## 4.3. PROPOSITIONS AS COGNITIVE UNITS
## AND AS STRATEGIES

### 4.3.1. The Notion of Proposition in Psychology

The account given in the previous pages of the notion of propositions has been rather abstract, following predominantly a number of philosophical and linguistic criteria for semantic analysis. We have noticed before, though, that this kind of approach has also characterized much work in psychology and artificial intelligence. In part because of a lack of serious alternatives, the proposition has been taken as a fundamental unit in cognitive semantics: Surface structure input is assigned propositional interpretation. Again, we cannot give a full account here of the use of the notion of proposition in psychology. Earlier notions are those of "idea," "thought," "Gedankeninhalt," etc., although already in James (1950:283ff.) we find the notion of a proposition, taken as a combination of subject and predicate. In modern cognitive semantics, it appears most of all in work on semantic memory (Kintsch, 1972, 1974). Clark and Clark (1977) make use of it extensively, but in most work in psycholinguistics and memory one fails to find it in the subject indices. Whereas some researchers (e.g., Norman & Rumelhart, 1975) use the notion of proposition, others (e.g., Schank & Abelson, 1977) prefer conceptual schemata of another type. Although Schank further analyzes predicates (concepts) into protopredicates, his conceptual dependency schemata also involve functional relations. In general, it can be said that there is no fundamental distinction between propositional representation formats and networks or graphs of various kinds, although the latter are not usually associated with a formal semantics, and hence do not have unambiguous interpretations. Of course, simple concept– relation– concept structures will not do—they fail to represent a host of linguistic aspects of propositions, such as adjectives, sentential adverbs, modalities, and so on (see also Woods, 1975). Our schema differs from such networks, in that it represents the formal structure of propositions.

The problem of cognitive relevance or the psychological reality of propositions is, however, rather complex. We have discussed some of the issues involved in Chapter 2, but it cannot be our task here to fully unravel the intricacies of that problem. In a sense we will take propositions for granted as theoretical units of a cognitive model, but we will formulate a number of typical psychological operations—namely, strategies—for the (re-)construction of propositions as part of the process of discourse understanding.

Our claim that propositions are suitable units for a cognitive model is made in spite of repeated warnings from philosophers and logicians to the contrary. As we have seen in the first section of this chapter, several philosophers and logicians have argued that, even if propositions can be taken as the meaning of (declarative) sentences, they should not be identified with mental objects of some kind, but rather treated as abstract constructs. That is, they have argued against the identification of a proposition with the full set of subjective cognitive representations an individual may have when producing or hearing a sentence. In one respect, one need not quarrel with such an antisubjective approach to cognitive meanings: The conditions on interaction and communication indeed require that meanings not be purely subjective, ad hoc, or arbitrary; through a process of episodical learning we must make abstractions and generalizations. This also holds for propositions taken as cognitive units. In this respect, propositions are indeed conceptual representations of what we may call possible facts. On the other hand, if we understand a particular sentence, uttered in a specific situation, and intended to refer to one specific fact, the propositional representation has, of course, a different nature: Instead of a structure of general concepts, we will have a structure of instantiated concepts—specific individuals and their properties, here and now. In that case further memorial or perceptual categories may be associated with the proposition—further knowledge, beliefs, opinions, episodic memories, and so on. This structured but fuzzy set will constitute the actual (hearer's) meaning assigned to a sentence in a specific context. Here we encounter the usual distinction between context-free and context-sensitive meanings, or between sentence meaning and language user's meaning, or between general and specific meaning. Both are cognitively relevant, and, as a result of learning, our general meanings will be derived from specific meanings. Since we are engaged in the actual strategic processes of understanding it is obvious that we need both kinds of meaning. First, we will still deal mainly with more abstract propositions, later these will appear to be further instantiated and enriched with subjective information. Ultimately we aim at a model of subjective understanding, but we recognize that such a model also needs a more objective, intersubjective component, accounting for generalized, abstract knowledge about language meanings, possible worlds, and possible facts.

From a theoretical and methodological point of view there is no a priori reason not to adopt propositions as theoretical units of a cognitive model. Although it is wise in general not to introduce uncritically notions from philosophy, logic, or linguistics into psychological theories of language understanding, we should remember that in all these disciplines the proposition has always been assumed to account for meanings of sentences. Although philosophers and linguists will usually abstract from the precise cognitive nature of such meanings, their theorizing is also very much determined by intuitions and hence by a number of cognitive criteria. For instance, decisions about sameness or difference of sentence meanings, as represented by identical or different propositions, are made on the basis of their intuitive knowledge of the language. In this respect, a psychologist devising a comprehension model would not approach the problem in a very different way. Second, if a cognitive psychologist ignores considerations about the neurological basis of language understanding and memory, the cognitive model also remains rather theoretical and abstract. That is, there is a certain freedom in the theoretical language used to describe cognitive phenomena. Just like the linguist, therefore, the psychologist will aim at an adequate format for semantic representations. Only, instead of formal interpretations, the psychologist will be interested in real interpretations, that is, in cognitive processes of comprehension. If such processes can be formulated in terms of propositions, so much the better, because it makes a long tradition of philosophical and linguistic thinking available to the psychologist. Third, both for the linguist and the psychologist there is the severe constraint of surface structure expression. For both it is relevant to introduce as abstract or underlying theoretical units only those which directly or indirectly manifest themselves in various surface structures. So, in the same way as we couple lexemes with discrete words, we will be inclined to introduce complex semantic units to be coupled, by interpretation rules, with clauses or sentences. And, finally, original proposals from philosophy and logic for the construction of propositions have undergone serious revisions in the last 10 years from linguists and psychologists alike, revisions that expressly try to account for well-founded semantic intuitions about meaning.

Thus, in the preceding discussion we did retain the notion of proposition, but at the same time adopted the usual functional analysis in terms of semantic roles or cases. At the same time we have tried to build in some more hierarchical structure, and we have proposed to represent this in a propositional schema, taken as a semantic representation of denoted facts in some possible world. We will now argue that indeed some form of propositional schema must be part of a cognitive model of discourse comprehension, and of comprehension in general for that matter. In particular, we will examine how cognitive strategies operate in the formation and transformation of such propositional schemata.

## 4.3.2. The Strategic Construction of Propositions

When we try to understand the world, that is, states of affairs, events, actions, or processes, or the discourse about these, we usually do not proceed in an arbitrary, haphazard, or ad hoc way. If we want to translate or decode the various surface structures of words and worlds, we had better have available handy rules or other operations to accomplish such a complex task. This is well known at the level of objects: We make socially and culturally relevant categorical distinctions in the continuous flow of pure reality. Despite their variations in form and color, we therefore distinguish and appropriately categorize cars, chairs, and salami, so that we can recognize instances of the same type of thing when we see or use them. Specifically, we form concepts which represent these discrete distinctions in things and properties of the world and we have learned to couple these with natural language expressions. Thus, each concept may grow into a hierarchical schema, a frame, representing the more important constant and variable properties which through experience have collected around such a concept.

Similar remarks hold not only for things, properties, and relations, but also for the processes, events, actions, and states in which such things and properties participate, that is, for facts. Unlike the number of objects and their properties or relations, taken as types, the number of possible facts is infinite. This follows directly from the theoretical considerations given in the previous section. Although many of the facts, or rather fact types or fact concepts, we are confronted with in our daily routines may be similar or identical, we are also constantly confronted with many new facts. The question then is: How do we handle these facts? How do we know a fact when we see one? How do we distinguish or isolate one fact from another fact? And, how do we represent facts in memory?

We will assume henceforth that this understanding of what is going on in the world, this fact analysis, has a strategic nature. That is, operations of understanding are involved which are fast, flexible, dependent on existing cognitive structures (such as knowledge, attitudes, but also goals, plans, or interests), respecting of cognitive constraints such as short-term memory capacity limitations and long-term memory retrievability conditions (usability of information), and which allow variable input data. We will assume that the first (semantic) goal of such a strategy consists in the construction of a propositional schema. In other words, we understand and thereby construct facts by setting up, strategically, a propositional structure. Although such propositional structures allow rule-governed variations, we assume that there are strategically preferred or stereotypical fixed or schematic versions. Such stereotypical schemata, derived from episodic experiences, account for the vast amount of straightforward fact analyses.

We can only speculate about the precise nature of these proposition formation strategies; there are few experimental techniques to assess them. Intuitively, we might assume that first a number of central participants are identified, possibly with the focus on just one or two. Next, an analysis is made of the biophysical transformations (movements, doings) which define the processes, events, or actions in which these individuals participate, at the same time affecting other individuals (persons, objects). In order to be able to learn and interact, though, we are less concerned with the identification and understanding of individuals: We want to keep track of the changes of the world, of changing properties, events, and actions. The cognitive focus of the facts we understand, hence, must be the predicate. In other words, we only assign a fact to the world or some situation when we assign a predicate to a number of individuals. There seems to be a double process at work here. First, there is the construction and maintenance of routine propositions for the usual facts of observation and everyday (inter)action: familiar objects, persons, places, and their familiar properties and relations. Against the background of these episodically stored routine propositions we have the construction of new facts, and hence new propositions which are relevant enough on the basis of our goals and interests. These new facts represent our registration of what happens in the world. Of course, most of these new facts are still very mundane, and hardly relevant for specific treatment and memory storage and retrieval, let alone for communication, for example, in the form of stories.

From this extremely informal and intuitive discussion we may conclude that the strategic construction of propositions, representing the cognitively relevant understanding of the facts of the world, seems to follow the propositional schema from bottom to top: We establish, or, from previous fact understanding, have already represented, some possible world, time, place, and other circumstances (street, room, town, etc. and summer, Sunday, afternoon, etc.). These serve to localize the state of affairs, events, or actions. Next we have or make a representation of one or more individuals (objects, persons) within this situation. And, finally, against this background of routine scanning we then notice new properties or relations, that is, events or actions, in which these individuals are participating. Relative to each other and to the nature of the predicate concept applied, the individuals are then assigned their respective roles, for example, as agent, patient, or instrument. Thus, if a person is seen to bring about some doing intentionally, then that person is assigned to the agent category. The order of role assignments is presumably strategically controlled: If in some situation and by previous observation or events the focus of attention is on some specific individual, it seems plausible to assume that this individual will be assigned a role first in the state, action, or event. Of course, the kind of strategies we have described informally here by definition do not account for all understanding. In some cases, for instance, we may first have the assignment of a predicate type to some event and only then the assignment of individuals and situation: If we hear a specific sound, we may interpret it first as a crash and then assign individuals such as cars, thereby interpreting the whole event as an accident.

What we have described here as the strategic interpretation of reality in terms of facts by the construction of propositional schemata, essentially holds also for sentence and discourse understanding. Or rather, we should say, our general understanding strategies will follow principles which are similar whether the inputs are real states, events, or actions, or whether the inputs are a pictorial or linguistic representation of these. One essential difference, though, is that such expressions are already precoded, they already exhibit an understanding of reality, and it is the task of the hearer or reader to reconstruct the intended propositions and hence the denoted facts (Hörmann, 1976).

As we will see in more detail in the next chapter, surface structures of sentences and discourse provide indications for this kind of strategic understanding: Word order, morphological structure, and syntactic categories help build the propositional schema. Circumstantial information will initially be taken to be identical with that of previous text or will be inferred from context. First noun phrases, which often express topic function, will denote the individual currently in the focus of attention, who is often identical with the individual in a previous proposition/fact. Then, the predicate is interpreted as the new central information about the property, event, or action defining the new fact, after which subsequent noun phrases and complementizers will fill in the rest of the participant roles. If the background or circumstances change for the new fact, these will often be mentioned first, for instance, as sentence adverbials. In other words, the stereotypical ordering of English sentences expresses or indicates what strategies are preferentially followed in the routine construction of propositional schemata, and it seems reasonable to assume that these strategies are similar to those followed in direct interpretation of the world in observation and action. In other words, all understanding takes place by strategically applying the grid of a stereotypical schema to the incoming data, and we assume that this schema is something like the propositional schema we have discussed. The same holds, of course, for languages other than English, except that the way in which the schematic grid is made to overlay the data is different, each language having developed its own linguistic devices to achieve that purpose.

## 4.3.3. Psychological Implications

Some of the assumptions made here about the cognitive nature of propositions have been experimentally investigated. The basic idea in this experimental approach has been that if propositions are units they should be processed and represented as such in memory. To assess this unity of a set of concepts, we have several experimental techniques. In Chapter 2 several studies were reviewed purporting to demonstrate the psychological reality of propositions. The methods used for that purpose include free as well as cued recall, reading time, and, above all, priming techniques. A great deal of evidence converges to suggest that propositions are, indeed, effective units in the cognitive system.

Our propositional schema is in some respects similar to other propositional formats proposed in the literature (Kintsch, 1974; Anderson & Bower, 1973; Anderson, 1976, 1980; Frederiksen, 1975; Norman & Rumelhart, 1975), but there are also differences. First, our schema is really hierarchical: It has higher and lower level categories. Second, it contains atomic propositions and not just concepts. This means that the proposition contains a proper representation of variables or constants, which is crucial for a theory of instantiation. Third, a specific modifier category has been introduced—unlike the representation in logic, which takes modifying information as separate, conjoined, propositions. Fourth, the predicate category and the argument (or participant) category are organized at a higher level by a specific predication node, for example, ACTION, PROCESS, STATE, or EVENT. Finally, we introduced a specific circumstance category, organizing not only place, time, and conditions, but also the possible world. The latter category allows us to represent modalities (such as *maybe, certainly*) and to change worlds within complex propositions, for example, after world-creating predicates (such as *to believe, to dream, to pretend,* etc.).

If we assume that clauses are strategically interpreted as propositional schemata, we must now examine how complex sentences and sentence sequences are understood in terms of propositions. We have seen in the previous section that the facts of the world can be represented in discourse in several degrees of relatedness, ranging from indirect coherence to integration and reduction. That is, language users form sequences of propositions, composite and complex propositions. In the next chapter, we will be concerned with a discussion of the strategies used to assign coherence relations between propositions in sequences, typically those underlying subsequent sentences. Here we will limit ourselves to propositional formation strategies. Our main point is that although language users apply a propositional schema to sentential structures, differences in surface structure will at the same time provide cues for different propositional structures: We have seen in the analysis of the previous section that sentence sequence, compound or complex sentence structure will in principle also lead to similar propositional structures.

The dependence of the propositional organization on the syntactic segmentation of the surface structure of sentences has been amply demonstrated in psycholinguistic experiments (for a review see Fodor, Bever, & Garrett, 1974, and our discussion in Chapter 2). On the basis of these demonstrations, Tannenhaus and Carroll (1975) have formulated a principle which they call the "functional clause hierarchy." This principle says that the extent to which a sentence will be segmented at clause boundaries depends on how complete the information is which it provides. If there is enough in a clause to construct a proper proposition, the clause will be perceived as a unit. In this case the clause boundary functions as a segmentation point. This has been demonstrated by Carroll and Tannenhaus (1978) with the click method. Clicks were perceived at the boundaries of complete main clauses, even when they physically occurred before or after the boundary, but no click-shift occurred at the boundaries of secondary incomplete clauses. Townsend and Bever (1978) made the same point very clearly in a word recognition study. These authors presented subjects with sentences containing two phrases, with the first phrase either being an incomplete subordinate clause or a complete main clause. Test words from the initial clause were recognized more slowly when they came from a main clause than when they came from a subordinate clause, indicating that the main clauses, but not the still incomplete subordinate clauses, belonged to different perceptual units. This effect was especially strong when the incompleteness of the subordinate clause was directly signaled in the text, for example, by an *although* which specifically instructs the reader that he or she is dealing with a subordinate clause that must be interpreted in the context of a main clause yet to come.

In this connection it is important to note that although readers are better able to recall the exact wording of subordinate clauses than main clauses in short-term memory experiments, nonverbatim, propositional recall is better for the content of main clauses (Flores d'Arcais, 1978; Kintsch, 1974; Townsend & Bever, 1978; Singer, 1976; Singer & Rosenberg, 1973). We interpret this finding to mean that retrieval is more efficient for the principal slots in the propositional schema, and subordinate information which is assigned to modifier or circumstance slots is less retrievable.

However, although syntax thus determines the propositional organization in part, these stereotypical ways of handling information may also be influenced by other factors. Typical for comprehension strategies is that they not only consider linguistic input structure, but also contextual information and available cognitive information, such as knowledge, goals, or interests. This means that the same surface structures may lead to different propositional structures in different contexts. This agrees with our intuitions about contextual variations of discourse understanding, but we should make explicit here which processes are involved in this kind of variation. Let us give a simple example. Take, for instance, the following very short discourse fragments:

(7)     *The professor hired a secretary. She has red hair.*
(8)     *The professor hired a secretary who has red hair.*

Let us assume that (7) denotes two facts, namely, the fact that the professor hired a secretary, and the fact that she has red hair. Sentence (8), however, seems to denote one fact, and in the propositional representation of this fact it will be mentioned in the modifier category for the patient that the secretary has red hair. We see that the same world fragment may be interpreted as one or as two facts: Properties may be expanded to full facts, or full facts may be reduced to properties of individuals, as is also signaled in the surface structure. That in (7) the fact that the secretary has red hair is singled out for separate assertion can be interpreted in terms of the relevance or interest of that fact for the speaker (or for the speaker's model of the hearer). In other words, discourse structure will exhibit not only an interpretation of the facts, but also the relevance, importance, or degree of interest of certain properties or relations, thereby assigning fact status to them. A language user having heard (7) may later report about the same fact with a sentence like (8) or even delete the fact about the red hair, in case he or she is not interested in redheads at all, or deems such information sexist or irrelevant. In other words, given some sentence or discourse fragment, the language user will use information from the social, interactional, and cognitive context in order to construct a propositional textbase which need not be congruent with surface structure indications of the speaker. The hearer may upgrade properties to separate propositional schemata or, conversely, reduce various schemata to one schema. These strategies will be called proposition *splitting* and proposition *fusion,* respectively. Of course, these strategies are not absolute, but are defined relative to the structure of input discourse and its propositional formation cues.

Givón (1983) argues that whether some information is assigned a secondary role in a proposition, or more concretely, whether the corresponding phrase is subordinated syntactically, depends above all on the pragmatic aspects of the communication situation. It is not necessarily the case that restricted relative clauses are logically presupposed whereas main clauses are asserted, or that they contain old, known information whereas main clauses are reserved for new information. Counterexamples could easily be constructed. Relativization, instead, is based on a decision to background certain information in the discourse. The main clause is emphasized and is laid open to challenge. The subordinate clause is backgrounded and shielded from direct challenge. Indeed, Givón proposes an operational test, the challenge test: That part of a sentence that can be directly challenged forms the central proposition. Thus, it would be more natural to say *No, she did not have red hair* after (7) than after (8). If this conjecture is true, the challenge test could perhaps be made into a (badly needed) experimental instrument for the investigation of propositional structure.

The strategies for building propositions are very important in a general theory of discourse production and comprehension. They account, first of all, for the fact that the same facts can be represented and described in different ways. Second, they explain why and how the same discourse may in turn be interpreted in different ways at the propositional level. We already know that the same objects, persons, properties, or events may according to knowledge and attitudes be conceptualized in different ways at the lexical (stylistic) level. We now see that this also holds for the very construction of the facts denoted by the discourse.

From the above it follows that language users will use information from the actual sentence, from the representation of the previous part of the discourse, from the interactive context, and from their cognitive set when they construct a propositional textbase. This may mean that what is presented as a new fact may by fusion be inserted into the propositional representation of a fact that is already known or, conversely, integrated information may be upgraded or even split off from the fact now being denoted. Thus, if for our example the hearer already knows that the professor hired a new secretary, the new information about her being a redhead may be represented as a modifier in the extant proposition or a new proposition may be set up. The latter will typically be the case if the hearer believes this separate proposition may be needed for later use, either in understanding the same discourse or in order to form expectations about the course of events, say, if the hearer knows that the professor tends to fall in love with (or hates) redheaded women. That is, assumptions about the relevance or interestingness of states or events will tend to upgrade these to separate fact status, so that for later processing they can become independent conditions in the textbase. In other words, we may assume that if information is upgraded to independent fact status, it will be easier to retrieve it than if it is part of an embedded category in another propositional schema.

Let us now summarize and further specify the propositional strategies involved in discourse understanding:

1. Given some information from or about a fragment of the world, try to establish a propositional schema.
2. Start construction of the schema with the information already present (e.g., in the short-term memory buffer), for example, with circumstantials and (some) individual—as with the topic of the sentence, then the content of the predicate category, and then the respective other participants in the order of their stereotypical occurrence in the predicate schema (some action concepts require only an agent, e.g., *walk,* others only agent and patient, e.g., *fire,* and so on). Follow the suggestions of word order, syntactic categories, or case endings provided by the surface structure.
3. For composite sentences, follow the suggestions of the clausal structure, that is, interpret main clauses as main propositions and subordinate clauses as embedded propositions.
4. If modifier information (e.g., from adjectives) is important or relevant, according to the language user's knowledge, beliefs, opinions, goals, or interests, for special use in further comprehension or interaction, it should be construed in a separate proposition (proposition splitting).
5. If new propositional information is assumed to be not particularly relevant, and if a proposition is actualized with the same participants, try to reduce the new proposition to a modifier or circumstance category in the old proposition (fusion).
6. Known (presupposed) information should be used to retrieve (reinstate) previous propositional schemata from the episodic representation for the text. The new information of the sentence that has such presupposed elements may be treated as in the above strategies: that is, either it is inserted into the old propositional schema (if the new information is not very relevant) or a new propositional schema is set up (if the information is important).
7. For all those surface structure devices which are used to assign specific focus to any element of the proposition, try to follow the splitting strategy (e.g., in case of topicalization, cleft sentences, intonation, etc.).
8. For ungrammatical or incomplete sentential input also follow the above strategies, searching previous sentence and situational context for the missing predicate or arguments.

The search for meaning at this level consists in the construction of propositional schemata. Typically, the strategies that achieve this are not simply based on the completed surface structure of well-formed sentences. Instead, they operate on incomplete or ungrammatical information, and they also use information from the grammatical (syntactic and semantic) structure of previous sentences, as well as represented information about the context, about the speaker, and about the cognitive set of the hearer (knowledge, beliefs, etc.). This means that the strategies do not only operate bottom up from the surface data, but also top down from more general expectations, such as those supplied by text, context, memory, or the previously constructed macroproposition of the discourse fragment. It is also this information which provides the criteria for deciding whether some new information is relevant or important, so that it may be construed as a separate propositional schema, either in a compound with previous ones or in a sequence. When in the next chapter we consider the ways in which strategies establish coherence relations between propositional schemata of a textbase, we will examine particularly how previous propositions can be used to construe subsequent propositions. In Chapter 9 we will consider how knowledge is used strategically in the construction of local propositions, and in Chapter 10 we will analyze in more detail how episodic memory and a general device for strategic control monitors the propositional strategies. There we will also see how missing links (i.e., information necessary for comprehension which is not expressed by the text) are inserted into the textual representation.

## 4.4. A SAMPLE ANALYSIS OF
## THE *NEWSWEEK* TEXT

In the previous chapter we have illustrated our model with an example taken from *Newsweek* (see front endpapers of volume for text of article). We shall return here to this example to examine in more detail the strategic construction of the propositional textbase. Without a full parser, we let the propositional strategies operate on surface structure fragments, that is, on words and word order. We do not provide a full cognitive lexicon, so that meanings and the knowledge associated with them will also be fragmentary. Finally, our analysis will only be illustrated on the first few sentences of the text and will only be semiexplicit, without spelling out all detail of the strategies involved. Let us start with the first sentence, $S_1$:

($S_1$)     *Compared with the relative shades of gray in El Salvador, Guatemala is a study in black and white.*

It has been assumed that propositional strategies usually require a surface structure analysis in terms of *clauses*. That is, each clause of $S_1$ is taken to express one (complex) proposition. Each clause is analyzed in terms of a single or composite verb phrase and a number of noun phrases, in such a way that the verb phrase is taken as the expression of the underlying main predicate of the complex proposition and the noun phrases as the expressions of underlying arguments depending on this predicate. These are, however, more or less abstract conditions on the propositional strategies because strategic interpretation takes place on line with the incoming surface structure input. This means, for instance, that for English, which is a predominantly SVO language, first phrases will mostly be noun phrases, so that a meaning and semantic function may be assigned to these even before the verb, and hence the organizing predicate, has been processed. Thus, various structural and semantic expectations are set up which need verification by further analysis. We further assume that each content word expresses an atomic proposition, which in turn is organized in a complex proposition according to its assigned semantic function (''case''). From semantic memory, each strategic step will draw grammatical information about each word, and its meaning or other world knowledge relevant for understanding.

Since we have no standard representation format for strategies, we will simply try to systematize the strategies, step by step, in a table (see Table 4.1). For each input, given in the left-most column, we specify the data drawn from semantic memory. Thus, in the remaining columns we represent grammatical information (Column A), (semantic) meaning (B), reference (C), further world knowledge (D), semantic function (E), and various kinds of expectations (F) derived from this knowledge with respect to further structure and meaning. The course of on-line processing is indicated by the first column list of numbered entries. The ordering of Columns (A)–(F) in Table 4.1 does not imply sequential processing starting with syntactic factors and proceeding to semantic analyses. As we have emphasized elsewhere in this chapter, strategies are flexible, and, although it is useful for descriptive purposes to distinguish between syntactic and semantic strategies, no fixed processing sequence is thereby implied.

Semantic strategies, as we said, have the construction of propositions as their goal, and they do so by trying to construct a propositional schema, a schema that is preprogrammed. The provisionally assigned semantic functions (E) will enable the insertion of the relevant meaning unit into such a schema. Whereas Table 4.1 represents the strategic operations, Figure 4.4 captures the terminal product, namely, the complex proposition constructed for the sentence as a whole. In the next chapter, we will see how these propositional schemata can be strategically related into a locally coherent textbase, although some of these interpropositional relations already are exhibited here, namely, when clauses, of a sentence express propositions that are connected.

Whereas functional grammars have come up with a number of useful semantic categories to analyze the semantic structure of action sentences, there are still many expressions, for example, in state descriptions, that lack a functional analysis. This means that we had to assign some expressions to ad hoc categories. Thus, the expression *is a study in black and white* in the main clause is in fact a compound predicate, with a proper ''verbal'' part, namely, the usual 'is a', and a ''nominal'' part functioning as a specification of the attribution. We therefore have used the predicate-dependent category attribute as a specific function, in this case for the main nominal part, 'study' and assign 'in black and white' as a whole (because denoting one color property) to a modifying category.

The embedded proposition expressed by the first clause features a predicate

**Table 4.1**

**Propositional Strategies in the Comprehension of the *Newsweek* Text, Sentence S₁**

| Surface structure input data | A. Syntactic category | B. Meaning (fragment) | C. Reference | D. Knowledge (fragment) | E. Semantic function | F. Expectations |
|---|---|---|---|---|---|---|
| 1. *compared with* | Verb (participle) Exp.: sub. clause Impl.: *we/Newsweek* | COMPARE (primitive) | Mental act of author | Confrontation of two objects for (dis)similarity | Pred. (sub.) (Implicit agent) | a. Two objects A & B b. (Dis)similar |
| 2. *the* | Def. article Exp.: NP | — | Known obj. | | | |
| 3. *relative* | Adj. | Moderate in comparison (Link: 1B) | Evaluation of author | See B | Mod | First obj. (Link: 1Fa) |
| 4. *shades* | Noun (plur.) Exp.: Compl.NP | color property | Property ($x_1$) | See B | Obj ($x_1$) | a. color b. object |
| 5. *of gray* | Compl.NP (Link: 4A) | color | Color ($x_2$) Link: $x_1/x_2$ = A? | Undistinct color average, nonextreme | Obj ($x_2$) | a. color-bearing object |
| 6. *in El Salvador* | Compl.NP, Proper N Loc. adverb | location | Country ($x_3$) = A? | Country in Central America Actual civil war | Loc ($x_3$) | end of clause |

136

| LINKS (3,4,5,6) | Complex NP | Reinterpret (3–4) as metaphor | Political situation? | 'Gray' not a property of countries | | |
|---|---|---|---|---|---|---|
| 7. *Guatemala* | Proper N / Exp.: main clause / Subject / Topic (Link: macro) | (Name) | Country ($x_4$) = B? | Country in Central America / Actual civil war / Repression | Obj. | a. Comparison $x_3$ with $x_4$ / b. Property of $x_4$ for comparison |
| 8. *is* | Verb (present) | Has as property | Actual sit. | | Pred | Property of $x_4$ |
| 9. *a study* | (Indef.) NP | Metaphor? | $x_5$ | | Attr | First inspect next phrases |
| 10. *in black* | PrepP/Noun or Adj. / Link: 9A | color metaphor: dark situation? | Actual situation property of $x_4$ | Political situation negative (Link: 7D) | Mod | ? |
| 11. *and white* | (coord.)N or Adj. | color metaphor: reinterpret (10–11): 'marked contrast' | Political contrasts in $x_4$ Link: $x_6$ | Political situation in $x_4$ and Central America | Mod | ? |
| LINK (9, 10, 11) | VP / Focus (Comment) | Shows marked contrasts | Pol. sit. in $x_4$ | Comparison between pol. sit. in El Salvador and Guatemala | | Explanation of (meta-phorical) statement |
| CLAUSE LINK (1–6), (7–11) | Sub.-Main / I. II. | Relation between facts (pol. sit.) | Rel ($f_1, f_2$) | $x_3$ and $x_4$ are both in Central America, have relevant actual political events, and can be compared (Links: 6D, 7D) | CONNECTION (COMPARISON) | Explanation of Comparison |

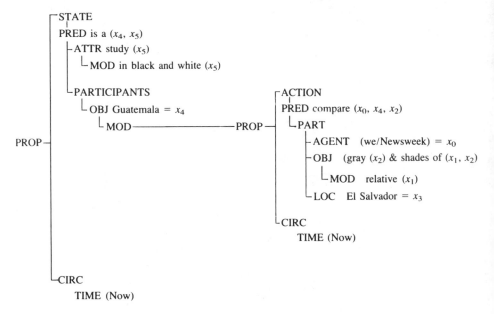

**Figure 4.4.** Propositional structure of $S_1$ of *Newsweek* text.

with an *implicit* agent, namely, 'we', 'I', or '*Newsweek*', denoting the author of the text. We have identified this implicit agent with the constant $x_0$. In other words, this first clause can be interpreted as a conditional, for example, 'If we compare. . .'.

A theoretical problem also exists for expressions with a genitive, such *shades of gray*, which we take as a complex object, described by a conjunction of atomic propositions, in which 'shades of' is a binary predicate. We might also take this latter atomic proposition as a modifier of 'gray'.

Note also that the locative participant—namely, 'El Salvador'—is one of the participants dependent on the predicate 'compare': It is about gray in El Salvador, and not the comparing which takes place in El Salvador, which would place the location in the higher level circumstance category, along with time. We see that for all complex propositions this circumstance category features a time category which has been filled with the pragmatically defined concept (now), denoting the time of speaking/writing, expressed by the present tenses in the sentence. If we inspect Table 4.1 and Figure 4.4, we see that the on-line strategic analysis of the first sentence is rather unsuccessful, mainly because of the unresolved interpretation of the metaphor: A reader does not know yet what the author is trying to convey. What the reader does understand is that two countries are compared, or rather the (political) situation in these two countries, denoted by pictorial expressions, denoting (maybe) an indistinct political situation and a situation of marked contrast or opposition. Strictly speaking $S_1$ is ungrammatical: the Subordinate clause should specify a comparison for the subject in the main clause, namely *Guatemala*, and that would be, for example, El Salvador, and not the situation in El Salvador. So we should have had *Compared with the relative shades of gray in El Salvador, we find a study in black and white in Guatemala.* In that case we have a proper comparison between two properties of these countries. This means that a reader may be rather free in attaching the subordinated clause, and hence its underlying proposition, to the main clause and the main proposition. Thus, the first proposition may be a modifier for 'Guatemala', or a modifier for 'a study in black and white' or even for 'in black and white'. Following the syntactic structure, we have appended the proposition as a modifier to the object 'Guatemala'. Another reading would be rendered by the expression *Compared with El Salvador with its shades of relative gray, Guatemala is . . . ,* which means that the first proposition is itself complex, that is, 'El Salvador' is itself modified, under an implicit predicate 'to have', with the property 'relative shades of gray'.

We assume that after Step 6, the now established links between Steps 3, 4, 5, and 6 result in an unsuccessful literal interpretation for this complex NP, which means that a metaphorical interpretation must be given, based on general knowledge about political situations, and the fact that colors are not usually assigned to countries. The same strategy will be necessary in the second, main clause, but then the reader will already be prepared for a possible rhetorical operation, namely a metaphor, and will probably not first interpret literally at all. Strategically, the first NP of the main clause will be interpreted as representing the *topic* of the sentence, that is, the information already established by the macroproposition expressed by the headline, referring to a country 'about which' some predications will follow. In other words, 'Guatemala' is the first relevant discourse referent, with respect to which other discourse referents may be introduced. Yet, this only holds when we analyze the text in isolation. In general, first position embedded clauses have topical function, for example, of expressing presuppositions. In our case, this may mean that previous articles in the same *Newsweek* issue are about El Salvador, which is indeed the case, and this being so, it is the first clause which exhibits the topic, especially 'El Salvador', and the first occurrence of 'Guatemala' in this text is hence both the new topic and the focus of $S_1$.

Another characteristic feature of this first sentence is the nearly complete lack of knowledge-guided, top-down expectations. There are no general frames or scripts that seem to be activated, nor do the meanings of the words create special expectations. Only the predicate 'to compare' requires two objects to be compared and possibly a feature of comparison. We have seen that these expectations may be satisfied in a rather vague way. That is, we either compare two countries or we compare properties of these countries, such as the political situation, to which the metaphorical expressions refer.

A special column (C) in our analysis is reserved for the *referents* of the expressions. It is assumed that these construct or presuppose elements of the situation model in episodic memory, representing the political situation in Central America, as well as the relations between this situation and the author of the text. As the reader may not immediately come up with this interpretation, the definite assign-

Table 4.2
**Propositional Strategies in the Comprehension of the *Newsweek* Text, Sentence S$_2$**

| Surface structure input data | A. Syntactic category | B. Meaning (fragment) | C. Reference | D. Knowledge (fragment) | E. Semantic function | F. Expectations |
|---|---|---|---|---|---|---|
| 1. *on the left* | PrepP | Lit.: location <br> Met.: location at political spectrum | pol. spectrum in $x_4$ | Frame: political organization of countries progressive parties (left vs. right wing) | Loc | a. Specification of objects/groups parties on left <br> b. On the right |
| 2. *is* | Main verb (present) | existence | state of $x_4$ | | Pred | See 1Fa |
| 3. *a collection of* | NP <br> Exp.: NP | set, class | class of $x_7$ in $x_4$ | See B <br> Non-organized | Quant | Persons or groups |
| 4. *extreme* | Adj. | Pol: having very radical ideas | property of $x_7$ | Frame: politics at the borders of the political spectrum: negative | Mod | Identification of extremely leftist groups |
| 5. *Marxist-Leninist* | Adj. (name) | communist: political ideology | property of $x_7$ | Frame: politics Communist ideology: no private property, no political freedom, etc. | Mod | Noun denoting people |
| 6. *groups* | Noun (plur.) <br> Link: 3A <br> Topic | set of people | people = $x_7$ | Political group | Obj | Specification of nature of groups <br> Link: 1Fa |

| | | | | | | |
|---|---|---|---|---|---|---|
| 7. *led by* | Verb (part.) Pass. Sub. rel. clause Link: 4A | leading/directive action | action of $x_9$ | Frame: political groups (1D) have leaders | Pred Prop: mod | Agent: leader(s) Modifying rel clause |
| 8. *what* | Rel. pronoun Exp. rel clause | | $x_9$ | | | Rel clause |
| 9. *one diplomat* | NP | international political person | $x_8$ (unknown) | Frame: political persons are involved in pol. issues | Agent | Action of agent |
| 10. *calls* | Verb (3rd pers.) | give name | action of $x_8$ | verbal reactions of pol. persons to events/groups (Frame 1D) | Pred | Name or characterization of $x_9$ |
| 11. " " | (Nonverbal) quotes | repeating words of others | utterance of $x_8$ | Newspapers quote politicians (Newspaper script) | ? | Literal quotation |
| 12. *a pretty* | Adj. or Adv. | a. goodlooking or b. degree: high | property | — | Mod | Adj. or noun |
| 13. *faceless* | Adj. | Lit.: without face Met.: without identity | property of $x_9$ | (Frame: politics) Pol. groups can usually be identified | Mod | Noun/NP |
| 14. *bunch of* | NP | unorganized set | set/number | negative property | Attr | Noun |
| 15. *people* | Noun (plur.) | set of humans | $x_9$ | (Frame: politics) Political participants are humans | Agent Link: 5F | ? |

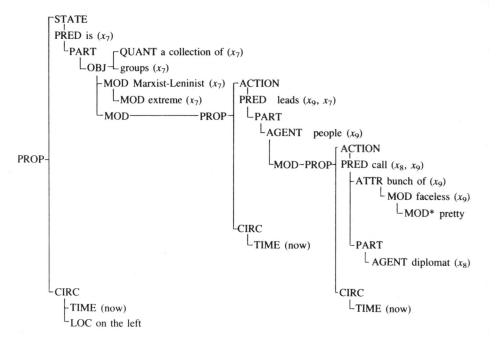

* 'Pretty' modifies a predicate, not an argument.

**Figure 4.5.** Propositional structure of $S_2$ of *Newsweek* text.

ment of meaning and reference may have to wait until the end of the sentence or even until the interpretation of the next sentence. It is in this reference column that we indicate the individual objects or properties referred to, which may in later sentences be coreferred with, either implicitly (by presupposition) or explicitly. The next sentence, $S_2$, is less vague (Table 4.2, Figure 4.5):

($S_2$)     *On the left is a collection of extreme Marxist-Leninist groups led by what one diplomat calls "a pretty faceless bunch of people".*

The previous sentence had introduced two countries and compared them, presumably with respect to their political situation, Thus, a politics frame was activated, which turns out to be crucial for the interpretation of the second sentence. Thus, first we have to know that *on the left* is not just a concrete location identification, but a political qualification of a position in the political spectrum. The associated knowledge is something like 'progressive', 'liberal', or 'socialist'. And the expectation is that 'the right' will also be mentioned. This is particularly the case after the political interpretation of *black and white* in ($S_1$) as 'marked contrast'. The expectation generated from knowledge on the basis of *on the left* is satisfied by *extreme Marxist-Leninist*, which indeed is a political property of some groups on the left.

Text element (7) *led by* sets up an expectation for an embedded relative clause characterizing *groups,* as well as for an agent. A similar syntactic expectation results from (8) *what.*

The quotation marks (11) announce the literal rendering of the words of an utterance. As expected in a news article, important political people verbally react to political events or states of affairs. Characteristically, a newspaper may in this way give evaluations of groups or of events without committing themselves—they just quote somebody else. In this case the diplomat is even unidentified.

Although a consideration of the role of opinions and attitudes in discourse processing is outside the scope of this book, their effect on the text representation that is being constructed cannot be neglected. For the prototypical *Newsweek* reader, the modifier 'Marxist-Leninist' has undoubtedly negative connotations, which are enhanced by the negative implications of the phrase *pretty faceless bunch.* We shall point out later that this negative evaluation plays an important part in justifying the macroproposition suggested by the title of the article, namely, that there are no political choices in Guatemala, with Marxists on one side and death squads on the other.

Although we will not provide a full analysis of $S_3$, we see that the schematic expectation, derived from the phrase *on the left* is indeed satisfied: The group on the right is now mentioned, in the same rhetorical manner. Again, much political knowledge is called for in order to understand and link 'elite', 'dominated', 'CIA-backed coup', etc. In $S_4$ it then becomes fully clear what the 'gray' metaphor of $S_1$ meant, namely, the political center, which does not exist in Guatemala, but still does exist in El Salvador; hence the difference in political situation, and hence the meaning of the macroproposition.

Thus, the interpretation of clauses and sentences by constructing, on line, a propositional schema is guided by information from the previous sentences, and sometimes (as for $S_1$) by information from following sentences. As soon as we have identified a politics frame, and in particular the subsystem of political party relationships, a system of expectations is set up which allows the specific interpretation of expressions of concepts fitting such a frame. Thus, *on the left* will trigger this specific subframe, will easily actualize 'Marxist-Leninist', set up expectations about 'on the right' and 'in the middle' as they indeed appear in next sentences. Within the domain of activated political knowledge (as described in detail by Carbonell, 1979), we then may arrive at a particular macrostatement, as expressed by the title, and which will organize the on-line, that is, linear, description of the political situation characterized as being without choices. The political spectrum information of the schema will provide the information about the possible groups, the comprehension of their typical properties, and the respective evaluations. This is precisely what the first few sentences of this text convey. In the next chapter we will pay some more detailed attention to the coherence links between these sentences, but it has already become clear at this point that propositional strategies for the interpretation of clauses and sentences cannot operate independently: They need information from other sentences, from the macroproposition (titles, headlines, or as provisionally inferred from previous sentences), from the context (knowledge about *Newsweek,* communicative setting), and from more general (political) knowledge.

We have earlier argued that overall sentence structure is a strategic indication for the underlying structure of complex propositions. The textbase does not simply consist of an ordered sequence of discrete (atomic or simple) propositions, but may feature very complex propositions. Depending on the knowledge and beliefs of the reader, there may be strategies that *fuse* propositions even when expressed in one sentence. Also, the relationship between possible propositional structure and the structure of the sentence tells us something about the strategies of the author. In the case of $S_2$, for example, the qualification of the leaders of the Marxist-Leninist groups is provided in a deeply embedded proposition, as is suggested by the embedded clause *what one diplomat calls.* In this way, the negative evaluation is put in focus position of the comment, and hence receives specific attention, even if it structurally has only a low position in the main proposition. This means that the reader may operate such that the embedded qualification comes out much higher, namely, as a direct modifier of the leaders or even of the groups themselves. This is a strategy of upgrading propositions, that is, attaching them to higher level concepts in the propositional schema. Also, in our example it may be possible that a reader engages in proposition *splitting* by taking the embedded qualification as an independent proposition 'They are a pretty faceless bunch of people'. Alternatively, this splitting may happen with 'This is what a diplomat calls them', which would highlight the fact that it is merely an opinion of some unidentified person. In other words, there is no fixed outcome for the final propositional structure: Depending on what we know, believe, or find, we may upgrade or downgrade propositions. The model would predict that the higher the proposition in the schema, and hence in the textbase, the more prominent it will be for macroproposition formation and hence for recall and further use. The indications provided by the structures of the text, therefore, are powerful cues of the cognitive representation, and hence of the beliefs and opinions of the author.

## 4.5. EXPERIMENT 1: PROPOSITION FUSION[1]

How a set of elementary propositions is organized into complex text propositions depends on the organizational strategies that are used. These depend, in turn, on the way the text is written, among other factors. We shall investigate here a specific case where the nature of the surface expression determines the propositional organization, and hence the reader's memory performance. Specifically, we shall

---

[1]This study was performed by Ugo Racheli as part of a Master's thesis at the University of Colorado.

be concerned with proposition fusion: the circumstance under which semantic elements that are realized in the surface structure as two separate sentences are fused to form a single complex proposition.

Suppose we have a sentence S (in the context of some brief paragraph) which expresses the atomic propositions $P_1$ . . . $P_k$ . . . $P_n$. Other things equal, we assume that readers have a strategy to organize these propositions into the complex text proposition $T_1$. In contrast, suppose we have a two-sentence text $S_1$–$S_2$, where $S_1$ is based on $P_1$ . . . $P_n$ and $S_2$ is based on $P_k$. The strategy that takes sentence units as cues for forming complex text propositions would lead the reader to form two separate text propositions, $T_1$ organizing $P_1$ . . . $P_n$, and $T_2$ for $P_k$. $P_k$ would thus be especially emphasized, whereas in the former case $P_k$ would merely fill a slot of $T_1$, or be appended to it as a modifier.

What would be the behavioral consequences of this organizational difference? These depend on the context of the paragraph in which this material is embedded. Because $P_k$ is emphasized and upgraded so that it forms a separate text unit, it becomes more available for later processing, for example, when additional material relevant to that unit occurs in the text, or when it becomes macrorelevant. In such circumstances, signaling out $P_k$, emphasizing it by giving it its own sentence, should facilitate later comprehension processes. However, suppose the paragraph never returns to $P_k$, and $P_k$ turns out not to be an important globally significant piece of the text, but some detail that was misleadingly emphasized. Text propositions containing a single element are certainly not very efficient, unless that element is a very important one for the text as a whole. One of the reader's strategies would be to avoid such constructions. Thus, brief one- (or two-) proposition sentences in a paragraph might produce a conflict situation: On the one hand, there is a tendency to form a new (complex) proposition; on the other hand, there is an opposing strategy to prevent setting up new propositions unless there is enough material there, or unless there are some indications of macrorelevance.

Thus, there are opposing predictions, and it is not clear what the behavioral outcome should be. If a new text unit is formed, one would expect that the material involved would be more available in recall than when it was embedded in some subordinate position in another complex unit. On the other hand, if no new unit is formed, a priori predictions are difficult to make: Possibly, the material from the single sentence will be integrated in the larger unit in just the same way as if it had been expressed within the larger sentence, so that the form of the surface structure would make no difference; possibly, however, this integration into the larger unit would be more difficult now, so that the separate sentence would be recalled less well. This latter outcome could occur when it is not quite clear how to incorporate the single sentence in the larger construction. If $P_1$ . . . $P_k$ . . . $P_n$ are all expressed by a single sentence, the role of $P_k$ vis-à-vis the other propositions may be indicated by the syntax of the phrase expressing $P_k$. For instance, an adjectival modifier calls for appending the proposition to the slot of the schema containing its head noun. However, if $P_k$ was presented out of its proper context, more complex strategies are

**Table 4.3**
**Two Versions of Sample Paragraph with Question for Cued Recall**[a]

---

THE ROBBERY (Paragraph 1)
*Embedded version*
At exactly a quarter past two in the morning, a man entered the isolated convenience store with a *loaded* gun in his hand and asked for all the money in the cash register. In the drawer there were only seventeen dollars and a few cents.

*Separate version*
At exactly a quarter past two in the morning, a man entered the isolated convenience store and asked for all the money in the cash register. The man had a *loaded* gun in his hand. In the drawer there were only seventeen dollars and a few cent.

*Question for cued recall*
What do you remember about the weapon used in the robbery?

---

[a]The critical information is italicized. (Italics were not in the original.)

called for to redintegrate it, requiring more effort, and increasing the likelihood of an encoding failure. Thus, emphasizing $P_k$ by expressing it as a separate sentence might actually lead to poorer recall.

### 4.5.1. Design, Subjects, and Materials

Sixty subjects who were students at the University of Colorado participated in this experiment. Each subject read 12 brief paragraphs, presented in random order, and then was tested for recall on 4 of them. Free recall tests were used for 6 of the paragraphs and cued recall for the other 6. All 12 experimental paragraphs were used. Each paragraph was written in two forms. In the embedded version, a simple clause, usually expressing a single proposition, was embedded into a longer sentence. In the separate version, a separate sentence was included in place of the embedded clause. In all other respects the embedded and separate versions of the paragraphs were alike. The subjects were divided into six groups, such that each paragraph was read by 10 subjects in each version.

Table 4.3 provides an example of the two versions for one of the experimental paragraphs, as well as the question for the cued recall test. (The instructions for the free recall test would have been "List all the facts in the ROBBERY story you remember"—though only cued recall tests were given for this particular story.)

Scoring was done for the presence or absence of the key word—*loaded* in the example in Table 4.3. Close synonyms were accepted.

### 4.5.2. Results

The results are summarized in Table 4.4. Cued recall was better when subjects had read the embedded version of the paragraphs (58%) than when they had read the separate version (42%). This difference was significant statistically both in analyses

**Table 4.4**
**Percentage Cued and Free Recall for the Paragraphs Used in Experiment 1 as a Function of Embedded and Separate Presentation of the Critical Information**

| | Version | |
|---|---|---|
| Paragraph number | Embedded | Separate |
| Cued recall | | |
| 1 | 50 | 20 |
| 2 | 70 | 70 |
| 3 | 90 | 90 |
| 4 | 90 | 70 |
| 5 | 30 | 0 |
| 6 | 20 | 0 |
| | 58 | 42 |
| Free recall | | |
| 7 | 0 | 0 |
| 8 | 20 | 10 |
| 9 | 20 | 10 |
| 10 | 40 | 20 |
| 11 | 80 | 40 |
| 12 | 30 | 10 |
| | 32 | 15 |

over paragraphs ($t$ (5) $= 2.99$, $p < .05$) and over subjects (sign test, $z = 2.40$, $p < .05$). Free recall also was better for the embedded version (32%) than for the separate version (15%), $t$ (5) $= 4.43$, $p < .01$ by paragraphs and $z = 2.18$, $p < .05$ by subjects.

In Paragraphs 2, 3, and 4 the critical information was always a color word (*purple branches, a blue cadillac,* and the *brown robes of monks*). When these paragraphs were written, these color words appeared rather unimportant, somewhat redundant, and quite irrelevant. Nevertheless, subjects remembered these words much better than any other adjectives in these paragraphs, almost irrespective of condition, creating a ceiling effect. We are somewhat puzzled why color words were singled out in this way. The only other case were performance was unusually high occurred in Paragraph 11, where the critical item was very informative and presumably of importance to the text as a whole. In contrast, the critical item was entirely redundant in Paragraph 7, and no subject reproduced it.

For the free recall data, if the critical item was recalled at all, it could be recalled either in a separate sentence or in embedded form. When subjects had read the embedded version, 47% of their recall occurred in embedded form and 53% as separate sentences. For the subjects who received the separate version, these values were 55% and 45%, respectively, A chi-square test does not yield evidence that these proportions are significantly different for the two versions, $\chi_2 (1) = .16$, $p = 31$.

### 4.5.3. Discussion

The finding that recall was worse when a proposition was emphasized by putting it into a separate sentence, rather than embedding it in a larger sentence, indicates that subjects may have used a strategy of proposition fusion in this experiment. For the reasons outlined in the introduction to this experiment—the sentence in question was too short, its content did not appear to be macrorelevant—they chose to integrate the information expressed in the separate sentence into the complex proposition already formed, instead of constructing a new one. This integration was apparently somewhat more difficult when the information to be integrated was expressed in a separate sentence than when it was already embedded into a larger sentence matrix.

If we assume that the critical information was always encoded as part of a superordinate complex proposition, regardless of which version subjects had read, it is not surprising that the form of recall (as separate sentence or embedded phrase) did not depend on the version. The relatively high incidence of separate sentences in recall can be explained by task demands: Subjects were asked ''to list all facts about the paragraph they could remember,'' which encouraged a list-like organization of their protocols, and hence separate recall of facts, in spite of the (presumably) integrated memory organization.

This little study represents no more than an initial exploration of how the memory structures that readers build up depend on the way in which the text they read is written. We have observed here an instance of proposition fusion: Material that was expressed in separate sentences was combined in one complex proposition. In essence, the brief, separate sentences which were used in the experimental texts gave the subjects contradictory cues: On the one hand, they appeared important just because they were separate; on the other hand, they did not lead anywhere. In the end, subjects handled them less well than if they had been misleadingly marked as important, as indicated by their consistently poorer recall. Obviously, this is just one configuration, and other strategies in other contexts need to be similarly investigated before a complete picture can emerge.

# Chapter 5

# Local Coherence Strategies

## 5.1. LOCAL COHERENCE

One of the fundamental properties of discourse is its *coherence*. Linguistic analyses of the notion of coherence in discourse have been provided by van Dijk (1972, 1977a) and Halliday and Hasan (1976), among others, and surveyed in de Beaugrande (1980). Sometimes a distinction is made between "coherence" and "cohesion," the latter being used to account for the more specific grammatical manifestations of underlying semantic coherence.

We will focus our attention here on *semantic* coherence. Other, more general, uses of the term coherence to denote some form of relatedness or unity in discourse might be made. *Syntactic* coherence would in that case refer to the syntactic means to express semantic coherence (for example, uses of pronouns, definite noun phrases, etc.—as illustrated by Halliday and Hasan for cohesion). *Stylistic coherence* would mean that a speaker or a discourse makes use of the same style register, in lexical choice, sentence complexity and length, etc. This notion seems necessary to account for the phenomenon of stylistic breaks. *Pragmatic coherence* would characterize discourse when studied as a sequence of speech acts, since speech acts in sequences are conditionally related and satisfy the same appropriateness conditions holding for a given pragmatic context (a sequence of a polite request followed by an order would be pragmatically incoherent).

Here we shall discuss only conditional (including temporal) and functional semantic coherence. There may be other semantic coherence types, such as those establishing the same perspective (see, e.g., Black Turner, & Bower, 1979, for psychological consequences), the same "level of description" or "degree of specificity" (see van Dijk, 1977a, and Chapter 6 of the present volume for these notions).

Semantic coherence may be local and global. Under local coherence we understand a property of discourse which is defined in terms of semantic relationships between the successive sentences of the discourse. These relationships are both intensional and extensional. That is, we have meaning relations and referential relations between sentences or between constituents of sentences. Roughly speaking, a sequence of sentences can be said to be coherent if the sentences denote facts in some possible world that are related. These fact relationships will often be conditional: One fact will be a possible, probable, or necessary condition for another fact, or a possible, probable, or necessary consequence of another fact. Relationships between facts will usually involve relationships between their defining elements, such as predicates, participants, or circumstances. Thus, time, place, or possible worlds may be identical or have a relation of accessibility to one another. Similarly, we may have identical individuals, as we will often witness in surface structure by coherence expressions such as pronouns. Local coherence relations may also be functional. Whereas the conditional relations are defined in terms of denoted facts, functional relations are intensional: They pertain to meaning relations. Thus, a sentence may be followed by another sentence implying it or implied by it, for example:

(1)    *It is cold today. It has been a lousy winter.*
(2)    *He is very happy. He is in love.*

Both extensional and intensional coherence conditions are not only based on textual information, but are also based on cognitive information, such as world knowledge or episodic memories. So, whereas an abstract linguistic semantics will formulate the general conditions for meaning or reference coherence, we need an additional formulation of the knowledge with respect to which these conditions hold. The most general and abstract definition of coherence can be formulated in terms of relations between propositions as expressed by the sentences of a discourse, relative to some possible world(s), and relative to some set of knowledge or other cognitive information. We may in a cognitive model further specify the culturally, socially, or even personally different contents of memory which make coherence relative to cultures, groups, and persons. The first kind of coherence would then be general and objective and the second kind (inter)subjective. Natural discourse in real communicative situations will be produced, understood, and accepted as coherent relative to the latter, (inter)subjective, conditions of coherence. This does not mean that coherence is arbitrary: Even in the establishment of personally or socially varying coherence in discourse, there are general properties that remain constant. Thus, coherence will always involve relations between denoted facts and relations between denoted fact elements.

Local semantic coherence does not stand alone. We have seen before that linear coherence needs macrocontrol in the form of a theme, topic, or point, as they are theoretically reconstructed as macrostructures. That is, local coherence is to be further defined relative to the global coherence of the discourse. The set of discourse referents will be ordered relative to some central referents such as persons or objects, the set of predicates will be organized according to some major predicates such as macroactions or macroevents, properties of individuals will add up to some global property, and so on. Similarly, sequences of actions or events will have global goals and global motivations. And, finally, there will be some unity of time, place, and possible world for these events and actions and their participating individuals. This is all to be formulated in terms of macropropositions to which we will return in more detail in the next chapter.

## 5.2. UNDERSTANDING SENTENCES

What has been summarized thus far is still fairly abstract: We defined coherence primarily in terms of abstract relations between sentences or between propositions, though relative to some set of propositions, for example, world knowledge or beliefs of speech participants. It is the task of a cognitive model of discourse comprehension to further specify these cognitive coherence conditions, that is, to spell out how a discourse is coherent for a hearer or reader. The cognitive model also will have to specify how this kind of local coherence is actually processed, what memory resources and mechanisms are involved, and what strategies are applied to handle the information involved in the construction of textual coherence. In this chapter, then, we will emphasize these strategic aspects of the establishment of coherence. Whereas in our previous model (Kintsch & van Dijk, 1978) we focused upon the result of the operations in episodic memory, we now want to know how, step by step, this result is established.

Some main features of the previous model will still hold in the model we are presenting here. We assume that sentence surface structures are being processed and, as we have seen in the previous chapter, interpreted as underlying semantic units such as propositions, which in turn are strategically organized in complex propositions and proposition sequences. Relevant information comes both from textual interpretation and from actualization processes for information from episodic and semantic memory (knowledge, beliefs, etc.). Information is processed cyclically in order to keep track of both old and new information and their relationships. That is, relations are established between propositions, then some propositions may be inserted into the text representation in episodic memory, after which new propositions may be admitted to the buffer and new relationships established.

The central assumption of this chapter is that the establishment of local coherence is *strategic*. We do not merely have rules which define the conditions that make sequences of propositions coherent, but also, or rather, we have strategies which process information from various sources in such a way that coherence can be established in an effective and flexible manner. It is not necessary for interpretations of sentences to be completed before beginning to establish coherence links among propositions. Instead, hypotheses about coherence links are made as the propositions themselves are being formed. These hypotheses must be based on partial information. Once the information is complete, a coherent structure has typically already been generated, though there may still be a need to check or revise it. Thus, for instance, the interpretation of a first noun phrase of a sentence may already give rise to some coherence hypothesis.

The information needed for these strategies is not only surface structural or semantic, but may also be epistemic (knowledge based), pragmatic, or may involve knowledge and beliefs about the communicative situation and the sociocultural context. This means that the local coherence strategies are mixed with global coherence strategies, with strategies for the use of knowledge, and with pragmatic and other communicative strategies.

Strategies of local coherence follow a number of global constraints, which we could call *metastrategies*. They are part of the control system of production systems. A metastrategy is a strategy that controls sets of strategies or defines general principles underlying such sets of strategies. They tell us what effective choice should be made among alternative or competing strategies, or what we must do when a given strategy fails. Although some of the principles discussed below also hold for propositional strategies at the sentence level, we have preferred to discuss them here because they are more obvious for coherence establishment. Some of the metastrategies are the following:

1. *Situation normalcy.* If from the representation of the communicative situation there is no evidence to the contrary, assume that all normal conditions obtain. That is, it is assumed that the speaker has full control (is not drunk or drugged, aphasic, schizo, etc.), that the situation is not keyed for a specific discourse type (e.g., poetry or advertisement; see Goffman, 1974), that no learning or other lack of full control of the language is relevant, or that *incoherence* is forced by *situational factors*—as in intended forms of meaninglessness or wanted misinterpretation. The basic strategy in the normal condition, then, is that the speaker or discourse are intended to be coherent and to be interpreted as such.

2. *Referential normalcy.* If no contextual or textual signals have been given to the contrary, assume that coherence should be established relative to our own possible world. That is, the normal postulates (laws, rules, regularities, etc.— possibly variable for cultures) must obtain, and hence the normal relations between facts. In some discourse types, such as science fiction, this normalcy condition is not satisfied. There, we may have other conditions of coherence. Hence, coherence is relative to possible worlds.

3. *Macrodependence.* Sequences are not only locally but also globally coherent. Hence, local coherence depends on macrocoherence as defined by a common macroproposition; all local connections should be matched against their relevance at the global level. Local coherence can therefore be indirect, obtained on the basis of the macroproposition. If no local coherence obtains, check coherence with higher levels of the semantic representation.

4. *Sequential coherence*. If no coherence obtains between immediately adjacent clauses or propositions, apply a *wait-and-see* strategy: necessary information may be mentioned later in the sequence. In general, then, the local strategy of coherence establishment should contribute not only to global coherence, but also to sequential coherence, that is, to the construction of an episode (see Longacre, 1979; Hinds, 1979; van Dijk, 1982b; and Black & Bower, 1980, for linguistic and psychological work on the episode as a unit).

5. *Actual state of text and context*. Local coherence is to be established relative to the actual state of text and context, in other words, relative to what has been said, what has been done in the actual situation, and the plausible cognitive consequences of these, that is, "what can rightfully be supposed by the speaker to to be now known to the hearer."

6. *Propositional coherence*. Coherence is to be established between full propositions (propositional schemata) denoting facts. Component moves in the strategy of local coherence establishment have this kind of propositional coherence as their common goal.

7. *Partial coherence*. If no adequate propositional coherence can be established, maintain the partial coherence results of the component coherence moves (e.g., only argument identity) or accept a mere link with the macroproposition ("theme is the same") or apply sequential wait-and-see (Metastrategy 4).

8. *Maximizing hypotheses*. If coherence strategies fail (partly or wholly), make a best guess about why the propositions are related and see how far it will carry you.

9. *Grammatical evidence*. Just as we have situational and referential normalcy we should expect grammatical or textual normalcy. That is, the hearer or reader may expect that the text will express the coherence relations by a number of signals (pronouns, definite articles, demonstratives, connectives, etc.). If coherence is not standard, this should explicitly be signaled. More specifically, the hearer or reader may expect sufficient grammatical signaling, that is, neither too many nor too few signals (see also Grice, 1967).

From these general principles underlying the strategies to be discussed in what follows, we see that a language user can effectively interpret a discourse in a coherent way if all normalcy conditions obtain. If not, ad hoc means of interpretation, partial interpretation, wait-and-see, or alternative methods of understanding (e.g., asking for clarification) will be applied. We also observe that the various metastrategies force the language user to permanently match three large information systems, namely, knowledge about the actual context, knowledge about previous text, and more general or episodic knowledge of the world. Sometimes these various types of information will mutually corroborate a coherence hypothesis (e.g., a combination of pronouns and gesture-deixis—see Marslen-Wilson *et al.*, 1982) and sometimes it may conflict. In the latter case the weight of the respective information types must be considered, as well as the goals and interests of interpretation.

## 5.3. LOCAL COHERENCE STRATEGIES

Under the more general constraints formulated above we shall now derive some hypotheses about the application of local coherence strategies to sequences of propositions. We will begin with a more or less informal discussion of the strategies involved and then proceed to a more explicit formulation of the complex local coherence establishment strategy.

The assumption underlying the presence of local strategies is that it is most unlikely that language users will process full sentence pairs before establishing some coherence relation. Rather, they will try to relate fragments of a new proposition to the proposition already processed. The argument repetition device which characterized our earlier model (Kintsch & van Dijk, 1978) is just one example of such a local strategy, specifically, a strategy for the establishment of relations between proposition participants.

As a first illustration of the strategies involved, let us take three simple discourse fragments:

(3)    *John went for a hike in the mountains last weekend. He came back with a broken leg.*

(4)    *John went for a hike in the mountains last weekend. He left very early on Friday morning.*

(5)    *John went for a hike in the mountains last weekend. He is crazy about the fresh air and the beautiful views.*

These discourse fragments are initiated by the same sentence but continued by different sentences. Intuitively, the fragments are coherent, or rather, they can be interpreted coherently. Let us assume that the first sentence will be understood as the expression of a first proposition, with 'went' as a predicate, 'John' as an agent, 'in the mountains' as a location, and 'last weekend' as the time specification. The phrase *for a hike* could be taken as part of the predicate 'to go for a hike,' or as a specific goal category. We further assume that, after analysis and understanding, this proposition will be stored in the short-term memory buffer. As we will see in the next chapter, this kind of introductory sentence may have a macrorole as thematic sentence. That is, at the same time there will be a strategic operation that derives this same proposition as a macroproposition for the sequence as a whole. This means that the following sentences might further specify the 'hike in the mountains' theme. Specification is one of the functional coherence conditions (see Meyer, 1975; van Dijk, 1981a; Reichman, 1981). For the role of previous macro-relevant propositions in coherence and coreference establishment, see Cirilo (1981).

We should also assume that the interpretation of the first sentence will have activated the reader's world knowledge about mountain hikes, possibly in scriptlike organization, as well as personal episodic memories about recent hikes (of the reader, of John) and knowledge about John or the particular mountains referred to by the speaker and assumed to be known by the hearer (as signaled by the definite article).

It is against the background of this textual and epistemic information that the second sentence will be read and interpreted.

The standard sentence form of main clauses in English will usually feature a first NP, as is also the case for the three continuing sentences in the discourse. In our example this first NP is a pronoun, referring to a male individual. Such initial NPs, especially definite noun phrases and pronouns, have the strategic function of signaling the sentence topic of the sentence now being processed.

## 5.3.1. Sentence Topics

The notion of "sentence topic" should be carefully distinguished from that of "discourse topic" or "theme," which is to be made explicit in terms of macropropositions (for a discussion of this difference, see van Dijk, 1977a, 1981a).

Sentence topics cannot be fully discussed here. The linguistic and psychological literature about it is vast (see, e.g., Dahl, 1969; van Dijk, 1972, 1977a; Li, 1976; Givón, 1979b; and the survey in Bates & MacWhinney, 1979). We limit ourselves to the coherence functions of sentence topics in strategies. It has been argued elsewhere (van Dijk, 1977a) that a sentence topic cannot simply be described as the part of the semantic representation (or its surface expression, or referent) that the sentence is "about," such that the comment part would contain "what" is said (predicated) about this topical part. Aboutness is a referential function and holds for all expressions of the sentence, also for parts of the predicates. Therefore, the notion of topic can only be appropriately defined in terms of the relations between a sentence and the (con-)text. This is also why such intuitive notions as "given" and "new" information (Haviland & Clark, 1974) have been widely used, although clearly that is not sufficient either. There seems to be a cleft between, on the one hand, adequate formal definitions and, on the other, intuitions and linguistic data from various languages (regarding, e.g., word order phenomena and topic markers).

We consider the "topic" of a sentence to be a discourse function of the sentence, the purpose of which is to exhibit partial coherence with the (con-)textual representation of the previous part of the (con-)text. It is, formally speaking, a choice or selection function, that is, it selects an element (a subtree) from the previous representation, and uses this as the starting point for the construction of the next propositional schema. In this sense it also accounts for the overlap defining semantic relatedness and, at the same time, the continuation with respect to previous discourse. Note, though, that this relationship does not need explicit previous occurrences. We may make inferences, based on knowledge or beliefs, from previous information, and the connection may be established with an implicit proposition (or part of a proposition). This means that topicality also requires a cognitive definition. From that perspective, topics function both as an instruction to search the text representation of the discourse (at a particular moment) and as an indication of how and where to connect propositions of the textbase. Instead of giving a full linguistic discussion of the notion of topic, we will therefore limit ourselves to this cognitive function of sentence topic.

Sentence topics play an important cohesive role in that they relate individuals in different propositions. For instance, the topic may exhibit the relation of identity between denoted individuals, that is, the referent which remains constant across proposition boundaries. Of course, first noun phrases need not always be sentence topics, nor need there be any relation of identity between denoted individuals. Yet, this is often the case, especially for pronouns and definite NPs, so that such a coherence link would be a rather effective strategy to connect propositions. In other words, irrespective of the structure of the proposition, a reader or hearer may assume after having interpreted the phrase *he* that it is used to refer to an individual already known, for instance, by earlier introduction in the discourse. Also, initial *he* usually denotes animate or human individuals, and these will often have the role, in subject position, of the agent or experiencer of the next propositional schema. With this information, the reader or hearer may rapidly search among the participants of the previous proposition to determine whether there is information, for example, as expressed by a noun phrase, used to refer to a male human individual, possibly the agent of an action. In this case, the search is easy and successful: There exists a unique coreferential argument in the previous proposition. The strategy can be more complex, however. Not only does the next sentence yield the standard interpretation strategy for initial NPs, the previous proposition also activates expectations about standard continuations. If an agent is mentioned in a proposition and if this is the initial proposition of an episode and is general enough to function as a macro-proposition, then it is plausible that the same agent will reappear in a following proposition. In other words, *he* was expected. Hence, in this case, the top-down and bottom-up processes match, and the interpretation will therefore be fast.

### 5.3.2. Complex Strategies

Strategies for interpreting the following continuations of our example first sentence are even more involved:

(6) a.    *They were covered with snow.*
    b.    *It was beautiful weather.*
    c.    *It was his happiest weekend this year.*
    d.    *It was very good for his health.*

Whereas *they* in topic position does not meet the agent-individual expectations generated by the first sentence, it is still easy to interpret as there is only one plural individual, which appears in the location slot of the previous proposition. This is not the case for *it*. This pronoun may refer to whole events, to objects, time, place, or to nonhuman animates. As several of these possibilities are allowed by the previous proposition, further reading and interpretation of the sentence is necessary in order to interpret *it*.

The result of the first-NP topic interpretation strategy is the hypothesis that there is a coherence link between the individuals of the respective propositions in (3)–(5).[1] Semantically, this means that a first possible condition to reach the local coherence goal—namely, to establish a relation between the respective propositions as wholes—has been satisfied. There is a plausible relation, because there is referential identity of a human individual having the same role (agent). Further interpretation will have to confirm or disconfirm this hypothesis.

Note that the strategic interpretation of sentence-initial *he* not only yields a fragmentary coherence link between propositions, but also provides a hypothesis about the structure and content of the next proposition. *He* in subject and topic position will, when referring to a human individual, often be an agent of the proposition as well, so that we know that the proposition schema will probably have an agent participant category, and that the predicate will be an action. This information, together with the macroinformation generated by the derived macroproposition incorporating a macroaction, as well as general knowledge about mountain hikes and normal story-telling strategies, will guide the construction of the next proposition.

The subsequent interpretation of a verb phrase is typical for English. This verb phrase will, under the control of the previous information mentioned, generate the standard schema associated with it, with the appropriate participants and time and location specifications. The predicates 'to come back', 'to leave', and 'is crazy about' are all compatible with the earlier interpretation of *he* as a male human individual. *He* fits the agent or experiencer categories for these predicates. The predicate itself needs to be coherently related to the information from the first proposition (and epistemic information from long-term memory). For the predicates 'to come back' and 'to leave' there is an obvious semantic link with the previous predicate: The predicates belong to the same semantic class. The knowledge activated by the first sentence interpretation allows the actions involved in the second proposition to be connected, as consequences or as parts, to the action in the first proposition. The predicate 'is crazy about', does not fit this powerful strategy, but the state description can be combined as a property of the agent in the two propositions.

We see that a first strategic check on the semantic relatedness of the predicates in the subsequent propositions is, as such, not sufficient to establish coherence. Without further information about the participants and the circumstances (time,

---

[1]Although in our example there is indeed a link between individuals in the respective propositions, this does not mean that topic function cannot be assigned to the predicate part of a proposition. This is typically the case in initially stressed NPs and cleft sentences, where the predicate information is known, but the (case) relation of a (known or unknown) individual not yet known as in *JOHN has stolen the books*, or in *It was JOHN who stole the books*, where the structure 'x stole the books' is topic, and 'John = x' is comment.

place) even semantically related predicate concepts need not—as such—be coherent: We need at least a link between the full Action, State, Process, or Event
nodes. Yet, we do assume that the semantic relatedness, although neither necessary
nor sufficient, has a strategic role, namely, in the activation and actualization of
knowledge. In other words, the predicate of the previous proposition will probably
prime some partial meaning of a following predicate, especially in stereotypical
(scripted) situations. Tabossi and Johnson-Laird (1980) demonstrated priming of
meaning due to sentential context. Perhaps this priming effect also holds across
sentence boundaries as long as the information is still active in short-term memory.

   With the interpretation of the verb phrase as the proposition predicate, we have
at the same time the minimal setting up of the propositional schema. The topic NP
already assigned to the agent participant slot and the other participant roles are ready
to receive their content. The predicates of our example do not generate specific
expectations in this respect, however, except for more general time and place
indications, slots that are indeed filled by the subsequent information interpreted
from the next noun phrases. Similarly, the verb tenses coherently continue the time
specification initiated by the first proposition. The specific content of these participant slots is also coherent with the epistemic information activated by both the first
proposition and the second proposition fragment constructed so far: 'a broken leg' is
presupposing a proposition that is coherent with 'taking a hike', whereas 'Friday
morning' is coherent with 'weekend' and 'fresh air' and 'beautiful views' with
information in the 'mountain' frame. In other words, the relevant information for
the interpretation of any of the second sentences is taken from knowledge schemata
that have already been activated by the first proposition interpretation.

   We assume that there is an overall proposition check against world knowledge
about possible facts in the world and situation denoted by the first proposition. In
our examples this check will be positive. It would be more difficult to interpret next
sentences like:

(7) a.    *He came back with one of them.*
    b.    *He is crazy about stamps.*
    c.    *He left very early Monday morning.*

The first fact, if involving reference to a mountain, would not be consistent with our
knowledge about mountains and what humans can do. Thus, although the pronouns
strategically suggest coherence, the proposition in (7a) is not at all possible in our
world. In (7b) we have a possible proposition but it is not coherent with the
information which is part of the 'mountain hike' script. If the hearer still assumes
that the speaker speaks coherently, he or she will expect information about the
relations between stamps or stamp collecting and mountain hiking. And, finally in
(7c) the reference to Monday gives rise to a specific contradiction with the situation
denoted by the first proposition, in view of our knowledge about weekends and days
of the week.

   After the "possible proposition" evaluation—relative to the knowledge about
the situation referred to—we finally reach the interpretation of the overall coherence
link between the respective propositions. As the possible links between facts, and

hence between propositions, are limited in number, the language user can apply a ready-made strategy, that is, to match the proposition with categories such as conditional or functional, featuring cause or consequence in the former case, and specification, explication, or example in the latter. Example (3) allows the interpretation of a causal conditional: The hike caused John to break his leg. In (4) such a conditional is not possible: The second proposition will be functionally interpreted as a specification, at a lower level of description, of the first proposition. Here the first sentence typically has macrostatus: It is a thematic sentence. Such thematic sentences cannot normally be connected with their specification sentences by a connective within a sentence: We may only have semantic or pragmatic specification connectives such as *so,* which are sentence initial, or rather sequence initial. In (5) we have a combined case: The second proposition cannot be taken as a consequence of the first, but rather denotes a possible condition for the first fact. This is a general condition, as may be seen from the present tense. Postponed expressions of conditions, and in our case of motivations, have the functional role of explanations. It follows that these discourse fragments can be accepted as coherent: The propositions can be related according to the possible coherence links existing for propositions, and the propositions involve the details necessary for the connections, such as identical individuals, identical times or locations, related frame or script information, and so on.

Again it appears that the local coherence strategies operate both bottom up and top down: Words and phrases are interpreted bottom up and fitted into the slots of strategically activated schemata—a propositional schema, frame, or script, a macroproposition, connections between propositions, expectations about probable individuals involved, and so on, all of which operate top down to provide categories or expectations about the actual information of the text.

The coherence strategies operate on various types of information. They use syntactic information about word order and syntactic categories, they use semantic information about relations between concepts and coreferential identity, they use epistemic information from specific frames or schemata of world knowledge, as well as knowledge about normal rules and strategies of story telling and about discourse ordering in general, and they require knowledge about relations between actions and their motivations.

Example (3) exhibits a specific problem for the strategies discussed earlier. 'Coming back with a broken leg' may well be interpreted as a possible consequence of 'making a hike in the mountains', but clearly it is not a direct consequence. Thus various strategies of coherent interpretation are open. First, the global check strategy: breaking one's leg is possibly stored as part of the 'mountain hike' script. In that case we may establish superficial coherence if the subsequent propositions are about successive possible propositions of a script. In this case, however, we do not simply have reference to an event, but rather a proposition reduced to modifier status, *broken leg,* presupposing such an event. Less superficial coherence establishment therefore will require the inference that John broke his leg during mountain climbing, which is coherent with the 'mountain hike' script. In order to be able to interpret the sequence coherently we therefore need both the propositions derived from text understanding, as well as a proposition inferred from world knowledge (e.g., Clark, 1977, on bridging inferences). The memory model therefore will have to feature a proposition insertion strategy in order to allow construction of normal, direct, and nonsuperficial connections. Finally, a reader may also activate more specific knowledge about mountain hikes and leg-breaking events, thereby establishing a more specific conditional relation: Although breaking one's leg during a mountain hike is possible, it certainly is not normal. That is also the reason why it is an interesting event underlying the complication category of a story. This means that specific conditions must be satisfied, for example, the fact that John fell or slipped from some height, caught his leg in a crevice, etc. A typical question of the hearer of (3) would indeed be ''What happened?''

Evidence for superficial or sloppy interpretation has been systematically studied by Den Uyl and van Oostendorp (1980). It was questioned whether—as claimed by Kintsch and van Dijk (1978)—in the establishment of coherence and in the integration of old information, there would always be a check with the previous text representation, or whether a check with a script instantiation or a macroproposition would be sufficient, and even more effective than elaborate search and reinstatement from text representation. It appeared that for certain discourse types and certain kinds of fast readers there is indeed some evidence for this kind of superficial coherence establishment.

We see that we may distinguish at least three *levels of coherence establishment* according to the respective depths of interpretation:

1. *Superficial coherence:* A proposition is assumed to be coherent with another proposition if both occur, in a specific order, as possible propositions in the same frame or script.
2. *Normal coherence:* A proposition is assumed to be coherent with another proposition if (1) obtains, and if the two propositions instantiate a direct conditional or functional connection, or if a proposition from world knowledge can be instantiated that establishes such a connection between both propositions.
3. *Full coherence:* A proposition is assumed to be coherent with another proposition if both (1) and (2) obtain, and if further information is inferred from semantic or episodic memory about such propositions and their possible connection.

Depending on the type of text, the reader will for each specific interpretation context (tasks, goals, interests, time, etc.) apply one of these strategies, possibly mixed for the same discourse.

## 5.4. TOPICALITY AND STRATEGIC
## PRONOUN UNDERSTANDING

In this chapter it has been argued that the strategic establishment of coherence between sentences in a text begins with the initial expressions of a sentence, which are linked, as soon as possible, with elements of the representation of previous sentences. In the next section we will experimentally test some of the implications of this hypothesis. We will show that initial noun phrases—in particular, definite pronouns—may be linked with previous information even before the predicate or other information of the sentence has been processed. First, however, we need to discuss the interpretation of pronouns.

The strategic comprehension of pronouns depends on several kinds of information, such as the position, function, and morphology of the pronoun itself, and information about the structures of the sentence, previous sentences, the text, as well as the context, the cognitive representation of these in memory, and, finally, it depends also on various kinds of knowledge. Some of these factors of pronoun understanding have recently been studied in linguistics, psychology, and artificial intelligence. We shall briefly review and critically discuss some of these studies.

Our own experiment (Section 5.5) is limited to the ways in which the interpretation of a pronoun in sentence-initial position is a function of the representation of previous sentences in the text. It has been proposed that such factors as recency, syntactic function (e.g., subject or object), semantic function (e.g., agent or other roles), and topicality play a role in the understanding of pronouns. We will show that of these various factors, *cotopicality* will be the most powerful. That is, a pronoun will preferably be interpreted to refer to individuals that have been earlier referred to by an antecedent having topic function, even if the antecedent occurs several sentences back, even if there are several candidate antecedents, even if the antecedent is not in subject position or does not have agent function, and without regard to whether the antecedent occurs in a main clause or subordinate clause.

### 5.4.1. Some Basic Principles of Pronoun Comprehension

Our view of the processes of pronoun comprehension should be seen as an integral part of our model of strategic discourse comprehension, and in particular as a part of the local coherence strategies of such a model as they have been outlined in this chapter. However, the strategies determining the understanding of pronouns require some more specific principles. As there is much confusion in the literature about these principles, we will briefly enumerate the major ones before we report our experiment, thus marking our views as consonant or dissonant with previous work on pronoun understanding.

A. GRAMMATICAL CONSTRAINTS

Pronouns are linguistic expressions which are interpreted as referring to individuals, such as objects, persons, actions, events, etc. Essentially, we have two types of them, grammatically speaking: *deictic* pronouns, which refer to individuals directly, without the identification of these individuals through textual information, such as antecedents; and *textual* pronouns, which occur with expressions in the same sentence or in previous sentences—the so-called antecedent—which corefer to the same individual as the pronoun. In what follows, we will only be concerned with the interpretation of the latter type of pronouns, that is, the textual ones, although we will later show that in a cognitive model the difference between deictic and textual pronouns is less marked than has usually been assumed. Textual pronouns may be used, and hence may be correctly interpreted, under the following constraints:

1. Textual pronouns occur in constructions with their antecedents. These antecedents may occur in the same sentence, or in previous sentences (if the pronoun is anaphoric; cataphoric pronouns, occurring rarely, have antecedents in following sentences). We may distinguish, therefore, between *sentential* and *sequential* textual pronouns.

2. Sentential pronouns (which are not reflexive) have their antecedents only in previous clauses, or in a following clause that dominates the (subordinate) clause in which a preceding pronoun occurs (the so-called Langacker constraint, 1969). For a discussion of the many other grammatical aspects of sentential pronominalization, see Reibel and Schane (1969).

3. Textual pronouns, in English, must agree in gender and number with their antecedents. It has been assumed that gender and number correspondence is a powerful low-level factor in the establishment of a link between pronouns and their antecedents. In this way *possible* antecedent candidates can be evaluated (see Schwartz, 1981).

4. There are further semantic constraints on possible antecedents. Sometimes pronouns do not corefer, strictly speaking, with their antecedents but with information that is *inferred* from them; that is, antecedents may be constructed (Nash-Webber & Reiter, 1977; Nash-Webber, 1978a; Ehrlich, 1980).

B. TEXTUAL CONSTRAINTS

1. In addition to these grammatical constraints, the use—and hence the interpretation—of pronouns in discourse is constrained in other ways. Some of these constraints are not purely formal, but have a strategic, cognitive nature. Reichman (1981) has shown that pronouns may be used only when they occur in "high focus" within the "context space" activated by the previous sentences. Information that is in lower focus must be expressed by full noun phrases or proper nouns. Marslen-Wilson and Tyler have shown in a number of experimental papers that language users indeed make this distinction (see, e.g., Marslen-Wilson, Levy, & Tyler, 1982; Tyler & Marslen-Wilson, 1982).

2. One of the consequences of the constraint mentioned in (1) is, for example, that pronominalization will rarely occur across paragraph boundaries, which express underlying episodes (Reichman, 1981; van Dijk, 1982b; Hinds, 1979).

3. In terms of our model, pronouns may be interpreted also in relation to implied antecedents that are part of an active macroproposition (van Dijk, 1977a, 1980b).

We shall examine in more detail the cognitive consequences of these textual constraints on pronominalization.

## C. REFERENTIAL CONSTRAINTS

1. Pronouns are typically "referring expressions," denoting individuals (i.e., discrete entities) in some possible world. One of the major confusions, both in the linguistic (e.g., Halliday & Hasan, 1976) and in the cognitive literature (see below) is the assumption that pronouns refer to their antecedents in the text. There is a link of coreference with antecedents, but this means that textual pronouns, just like deictic pronouns, refer to individuals—namely, to individuals referred to and identified by their antecedents.

2. More specifically we could say that pronouns refer to individuals in a *model* constructed due to the interpretation of the text (see van Dijk, 1977a; Stenning, 1978; Nash-Webber, 1978b).

3. Sometimes pronouns do not refer, in a strict sense, to "existing" individuals, but to individuals in nonreal (wanted, intended, counterfactual) models, or the individual identity underlying coreference with an antecedent may be more complex (van Dijk, 1972; Partee, 1978; Nash-Webber, 1978b, and many references given there to the linguistic and logical literature on such forms of pronoun use, which we will ignore here).

## D. COGNITIVE PRINCIPLES

1. Whereas some of the constraints and principles that have been mentioned here have a formal and context-free nature, others should be understood as manifestations of cognitive processes and constraints in the strategic production and comprehension of pronouns, such as textual representations in episodic memory, the role of episodic situation models and other world knowledge, and the capacity limitations of short-term memory.

2. Thus, for instance, the strategy that limits effective pronoun use to cases in which information is "in high focus" (Reichman, 1981, following earlier suggestions by Chafe, 1972, and Grimes, 1975, on "foregrounding") is determined by the limited information capacity of working memory, which contains only immediately preceding clauses or sentences and a current macroproposition (see Kintsch & van Dijk, 1978; Sanford & Garrod, 1981).

3. As suggested earlier in this book (see Chapter 10 for further detail), we make a theoretical distinction between a *representation of the text*, on the one hand, and a *situation model* in episodic memory, on the other. We will assume that pronouns are linked with ("refer to") concepts of individuals in the relevant situation model, namely, those individuals which, by antecedents, have been described and identified during text processing. The specific descriptions of referents are part of the text representation, but the referents themselves are part of the situation model. Thus, we may corefer to individuals in the situation model which have not been introduced by the same definite description in the text representation, but of which the current description is drawn from information in the situation model or from instantiated information from long-term memory.

Clark and Marshall (1978) have emphasized that definite reference, and hence also pronouns, require common and mutual knowledge of speech participants, so that identification of (same) referents is possible. Such an identification presupposes a "reference diary" of significant events in our personal experience, together with more general world knowledge about mutually known referents. Nash-Webber (1978b) also stresses the fact that textual communication has as one of its goals the evocation of entities in a process of discourse model construction. It is not clear, though, whether she clearly distinguishes between the text representation and situation model in our terms, whereas Clark and Marshall do not specify the precise structures and processing functions of their reference diaries. Stenning (1978) does distinguish between "statement set" and "model description" but does not specify the cognitive implications of this distinction.

4. From the principles already mentioned it follows that search for the (unique) referent of a pronoun in a situation model involves, first, a search in working memory for identifying information (expressed in the current or the previous sentence), second, a search through reinstated information from the text representation, in case the first search is not successful, or, third, the instantiation of (and inference from) general world knowledge or other episodic memories in the situation model.

5. The comprehension of a pronoun in a sentence does not take place in isolation. Whatever the strategic operations for fast provisional interpretation, final interpretation is possible only following the interpretation of the whole clause or sentence in which the pronoun occurs (and sometimes even later sentences). And the same holds for the establishment of a coreference link with the antecedents. These also occur in sentences, and only if the two sentences are coherent semantically can pronoun interpretation be completed (see also Tyler & Marslen-Wilson, 1982; Hirst & Brill, 1980).

Against the background of these basic linguistic and cognitive principles for the use and understanding of pronouns, we may now turn to some more specific cognitive strategies of pronoun understanding.

### 5.4.2. Strategies of Pronoun Understanding

Understanding a pronoun in a text involves, as we have seen, the identification of a unique referent in the situation model which is activated or constructed by the previous information expressed by the text. This identification, however, is only possible if we have access to the previous information, which provides the description of the denoted individual. Hence, we must search our memory for this description, usually expressed, sometimes indirectly, by the antecedent. Pronoun understanding presupposes the search for an "initial description" (see Nash-Webber, 1978b) of the referent, but we have seen that inferences, based on context and more general world knowledge, might be applied to this initial description in order to identify the unique referent. Also, there may be more than one previous description of the referent; in a long story, there may be many. Of course, not all these descriptions need be searched for in the text representation. The relevant previous description may be sufficient for identification (e.g., the one given in the directly preceding sentence). We will call this, for reasons of simplicity, the *actual antecedent*, or simply the antecedent, although it should be kept in mind that such an actual antecedent may be an element of a *previous description set* for some individual. Note also that we should distinguish between this selected, or maybe unique, antecedent as a unit of *semantic* information, and the surface structure *expression*, such as a definite noun phrase, of the antecedent. As we are dealing with the strategic establishment of local coherence at the semantic level, here we will take the notion "antecedent" to be a semantic notion. Of course, the strategies involved may well make use of pure surface structure information about antecedents—the position, syntactic function, case endings, (in)definiteness, etc. Most of the experimental work concerns the process of finding antecedents for pronouns, involving various search processes in some kind of previous information. We have already stressed that "finding an antecedent" is *not* the same thing as understanding a pronoun, but only part of that understanding: It provides often necessary information for the identification of a referent in the episodic situation model.

Furthermore, most previous work deals with the understanding of pronouns as part of the understanding of the clause or sentence in which they occur. Variations in the retrievability of antecedents are supposed to lead to differences in reading times for sentences in which pronouns occur, for instance. It is, of course, difficult to single out the process of pronoun understanding as such, which would be the case in a strategic on-line interpretation of pronouns. It is especially the work by Marslen-Wilson and Tyler (Marslen-Wilson, Levy, & Tyler, 1982; Tyler & Marslen-Wilson, 1982) which has investigated this kind of on-line understanding, and production, of pronouns.

The search for antecedents—or, conversely, the influence of previous information, including antecedents, on the understanding of pronouns—involves a number of processes which have been experimentally investigated. We will briefly review some of the major results of this experimental work.

1. *Recency.* Clark and Sengul (1979) found that sentences with anaphoric expressions are understood faster if the referent was mentioned one sentence back than if it was mentioned two or three sentences back. There is a marked discontinuity between search in the first previous sentence and the other previous sentences. In fact, it is the last *clause* that is searched for coreferential antecedents, and the authors argue that this last clause must have a privileged status in working memory (see also Breuker, 1981; Ehrlich, 1980).

According to our model, it is not so much recency per se, but rather the presence of information in short-term memory, or the strategies for activating information from the text representation, the situation model, or world knowledge, which would explain this result. Indeed, what is relevant will often be the last clause (or noncomplex sentence). In our previous model (Kintsch & van Dijk, 1978) it was assumed that the current sentence is kept in the short-term memory buffer to establish coherence. However, as we will see in what follows, both our own experiments and those of others have indicated that the foregrounded status of information may be more relevant than recency. In other words, what is "recent" is not necessarily the previously occurring clause, but rather the information now being processed and its structure, including macropropositions or other inferences from the text.

Chang (1980), who gave probe words after each word in two-clause sentences, found that decision times for words occurring in the final clause are faster than for words in the previous clause, but also that pronouns in the last clause "activate" the meaning of the antecedent in the first clause, which seems to suggest that pronouns are indeed interpreted on-line and not after the input of the whole clause in which they are occurring.

2. *Syntactic structure.* Grober, Beardley, and Caramazza (1978) investigated what they call a "parallel function" strategy in pronoun assignment. In complex sentences of the form NP¹ Aux V NP² *because* PRO . . . , the pronoun was interpreted as being coreferential with the first NP, thus exemplifying a search for the "same" function in the previous clause. Typically, the effects they found are tied to the kind of material used (e.g., using the connective *but* leads to different results), and the role of initial NPs can easily be explained within a functional perspective (role of agents and topics) to which we will turn in what follows (see also Ehrlich, 1980). Schwartz (1981) did not find evidence for a "parallel function" hypothesis for pronoun resolution, which at most may work as an ambiguity resolver. We will provisionally conclude that the effect of surface structures like syntactic ordering is only indirect, namely, when it signals underlying semantic functions, or when explicit cohesion markers signal surface ordering (as in anaphoric expressions such as *the former* and *the latter*.

3. *Verb meaning in previous clauses.* It certainly is the case that pronoun understanding it not only a backward strategy, but also involves forward strategies of structural expectations, as we remarked earlier in this chapter: Readers will expect a story about John to feature the reference to John in first position, topical, agentive NPs (definite expressions and pronouns). This is the top-down aspect of pronoun understanding (see, e.g., Sanford & Garrod, 1981: 141). Hence, the meaning of previous sentences, and inferences based on them, will certainly prepare the understanding of pronouns in various ways.

Caramazza and his co-workers in a number of papers (e.g., Caramazza, Grober, Garvey, & Yates, 1977) have tried to show that the meaning of verbs in antecedent clauses influences the interpretation of pronouns in following subordinate clauses introduced with the connective *because*. Thus the expression *A hit B, because XXX* . . . will favor coreference of *XXX* with *B,* and the expression *A angered B, because XXX* . . . will favor coreference with *A.* They explain the results in terms of the "implicit causality" of the verbs. Similar results are reported by Yekovich and Walker (1978). Ehrlich (1980) has pointed out that this effect cannot be due to the meaning of the verb as such, because the effect does not obtain when *but* is used as a connective. Indeed, what is at stake here are the conditional relations between whole clauses, and the plausibility that a clause is followed by mention of causes, reasons, explanations, or other conditionally or functionally connected information, which also involves the role of agents, and hence of possible coreferents in agent position.

4. *Semantic structure.* In line with the more fundamental observation that connected clauses or sentences should be analyzed in terms of their respective semantic structures, we may assume that semantic roles will indeed have a powerful contribution to make to the strategy of pronoun understanding. If a referent is a person, and if the person has been functioning as an agent in the text during a number of sentences, we may expect that pronouns will corefer to the same agent-person, and hence to the expression having agent function in previous clauses. Breuker (1981) has experimentally tested part of this hypothesis, postulating a functional semantic structure for previous sentences, as we have done earlier in this chapter. He found that the strategic search for coreferents in previous sentences is a hierarchical process in which first the top nodes are scanned, and by spreading activation (with about 50 msec per node) the other possible semantic functions (e.g., object, goal). Schwartz (1981) reports similar results for the role of "experiencer," at least when lower level strategies do not work, as when there is semantic ambiguity, and he stresses that this semantic criterion is important for the final evaluation of coreference assignment.

These results are compatible with our model. Search through previous sentence representations will be predominantly semantic and not arbitrary; top-down search in that case is a plausible strategy. In our experiment, described in what follows, we also find a powerful agency effect. However, we will see that agency is not the predominant information for establishing pronoun references. Agents will often be expressed by first position, topical NPs, and personal pronouns, especially in first position, will first of all be interpreted cotopically, even if their antecedents do not have agent function. We must therefore integrate the role of agency into a more complex model in which topicality is also involved.

### 5.4.3. Topical Strategies

Referents can also be represented in the text by definite expressions or proper names, so the very use of pronouns needs specific explanation. We have argued that this explanation must involve the detailed specification of the processing of discourse in short-term memory. In our previous model (Kintsch & van Dijk, 1978) we have assumed that the short-term memory buffer is limited to a few propositions, and here we have assumed also that pronominal coreference will primarily be based on information from possible antecedents in this buffer.

In more intuitive, or linguistic, terms similar suggestions have been made earlier by Chafe (1972), Broadbent (1973), Grimes (1975), Li (1976), Sanford and Garrod (1981), and Reichman (1981). The idea is that certain information, being coreferred to by later pronouns, will have a privileged position in memory or consciousness. This information is foregrounded, whereas other information may have rather a background role. This may be the case within one sentence, but also in sequences of sentences. Sentence topics usually have this role, and later reference to the referent they denote will, if the referent is still foregrounded, often be handled pronominally (if no ambiguity is possible). This role has also been mentioned in the vast linguistic discussion about notions such as "topic," "comment," and "focus" (see, e.g., van Dijk, 1972, 1977a, 1981a; Givón, 1979b; Li, 1976; Dik, 1978; and Reichman, 1981, for many references), but here we will ignore the intricacies of a linguistic definition of these notions.

Reichman (1981) gives an extensive formal account of the role of coreference in spontaneous discourse. She stresses that the usual predictions about pronoun use in such discourse do not match the facts, and that sometimes there are important cases of nonpronominalization. Not only reference identification is involved but also the topical status of the referent. This status will depend on discourse structure, and in particular on what Reichman calls the "context spaces" established in the text (a notion borrowed from Grimes). Thus, a context space may have various states of availability, between foreground and background, and the referents in the context-spaces may also have various "focus levels." In principle, then, pronominal coreference is restricted to referents of active context spaces, if they have high-level focus (e.g., agency), under specific further conditions (no other competing high focus referents, etc.). Schwartz (1981) found that topicalization is indeed a powerful (especially forward directed) strategy for pronoun understanding. Sanford and Garrod (1981) formulate a number of heuristics of which the first is that the current topic is more likely to be an appropriate antecedent. They mention a study by Purkiss (1978) in which it is shown that pronominal interpretation is faster if the antecedent is in subject (hence topic) function in previous clauses, even if several sentences intervene. Since the now active information is not only provided by the text itself, but also by activated scripts, they assume that an actor, as instantiated by a script, which has an independent topical role in the discourse will be easier to retrieve for pronominal reference than dependent actors in scripts, such as 'waiter' in the 'restaurant' script. Sanford and Garrod (1981: 147ff) report an experiment by Ann Anderson in which she found that even if the text only suggests that a script can no longer be active for temporal reasons, the topical actors are much better available than the dependent actors of the script (even if these had occurred in agent position in the previous sentences). Thus, scripts, too, may be more or less in focus (see also Grosz, 1977).

Only few experimental studies have systematically investigated the topical function of pronouns. Marslen-Wilson, Levy, and Tyler (1982), continuing earlier work on the on-line interpretation of language, report a natural task in which language users could produce pronouns (including deictic ones, by pointing to pictures), definite descriptions, or proper names, and their results are compatible with the theoretical framework given in Reichman (1981): Referents in focus will be pronominalized, others will be identified in other ways. Tyler and Marslen-Wilson (1982) stress the fact that the identification of antecedents will ultimately always depend on a pragmatic check on the plausibility of the continuation of a discourse after a first, scene-setting sentence, even if proper names, pronouns, or just verbs already strategically suggest a preferred antecedent.

The studies that have been cited do provide both theoretically and experimentally better insight into the strategic role of topic (or focus) in local coherence establishment. Yet, some theoretical confusion still remains. Although factors such as agency and topicality cooperate, they should have different roles, and this is the subject of our experiment discussed later in this chapter. Furthermore, the notion of topic (or focus) has been used in a rather vague sense in most studies. And, finally, none of the studies provides a precise processing model for the establishment of local and global coherence.

### 5.4.4. Toward a Model of Topical Coherence Understanding

In what follows we shall specify how our model can account for the role of topicality in local coherence establishment. To begin with, we should differentiate between different notions of *topic* (for details, see van Dijk, 1977a, 1981a). First, we have the linguistic notion of *sentential topic*. This topic is a function assigned to a part of the semantic representation of a sentence, often marked in surface structure by initial position (in English) or by specific topic markers. The topic of a sentence representation marks the way semantic information is distributed in sequences of sentences, such that the topical part, formally speaking, is identical with semantic information expressed or implied by previous sentences of a text representation (and hence "old" information). In cognitive terms, this means that the topic serves to signal with which already established information fragment the current proposition should be connected in short-term memory. We will here ignore the many linguistic details involved in the possible expressions of topics in sentences. A second notion of topic is that of *discourse topic* or *theme* of discourses or discourse episodes as a whole, which we have made explicit in terms of semantic macrostructures. Note that such topics are propositions and *not* functions of semantic representations (that is, of semantic subtrees) of sentences. Of course, macropropositions may themselves be functionally analyzed. Thus, in a story about John's vacation in France, we may have the macroproposition 'John took the train to Paris', and in that macroproposition 'John' may have topic function as defined in the earlier sense, namely, if previous macropropositions also involve 'John' as a macroconcept. Third, there may be an intermediary kind of topic, which we will call *sequential topic*. A sequential topic is also a semantic subtree, for example, representing a participant, such as an agent, but not only for just one sentence, but for a sequence of sentences. Thus, again in the story about John's vacation in France, we may expect many sentences to have 'John' in topic function, even if occasionally other participants may have topic function and then become sequential topics, as for an episode. Often, sequential topics will be assigned to participants that are also represented in a macroproposition, for example, as agents. So we see that the different levels of topicality are related, but they are by no means identical. Thus, if we say for a discourse or episode that its actual topic (or theme, or gist) is that 'John is taking the train to Paris', we are speaking about a macroproposition. But, if we say that 'John' is the topic, this may be the case, at the global level, by the occurrence of 'John' in this macroproposition, by the occurrence of 'John' as a topic for a sequence of sentences (which may also be discontinuous), or, finally, if 'John' is the topic for a given sentence. Strategically, this implies that assumptions about macrotopics will lead to assumptions about sequential topics, which in turn will lead to assumptions about sentence topics. Of course, local information may, bottom up, change these strategic expectations, and in that case we will have reallocations of topic function to other participants (or even actions, events, or locations).

For the cognitive model this means that if we say that some information is now "in focus," we may mean any one of these different topical functions. As we assume that macropropositions control processing in short-term memory, macro-arguments may lead to topical interpretation of sentences, but the same (or a different) sequential topic, derived from the previous sentence and also in short-term memory, may influence this decision as well. The syntactic structure and the meaning of the current sentence will be analyzed in order to establish the actual topical function of the representation, that is, first position, pronouns, agency, etc.

Conversely, as soon as a language user interprets a first position pronoun in a next sentence, the most likely strategy will be to search for the antecedent that also has topical function, because topic continuity is a stereotypical manner of discourse production. If the previous sentence or even earlier sentences clearly mark this topic role, for example, by pronouns or definite descriptions, the language user will prefer a topical antecedent. This will be the case even if other participants have agent function, and even if the antecedent occurs in topically dominant earlier sentences. Of course, if the topic is coupled in addition with the agent function, the strategy will operate on surer grounds, because agency and topicality are often related (e.g., in stories). Thus the strategy can operate more reliably and faster. And the same holds for the expression of topic in subject and first NP position in the antecedent clause. Finally, recency may add to the possible information for the strategy, because it can operate independently of previous structural information, and hence direct the search when structural information is ambiguous or lacking.

Note that the cotopicality strategy for pronoun interpretation operates both when a pronoun is structurally ambiguous and when it is not: The strategy will pick out, preferentially, the topic antecedent from among possible previous NPs. Also, it should be stressed that the cotopicality strategy presupposes that first position pronouns have themselves topic function in their own sentence. This is a strategic assumption: It may turn out that other arguments also have topic function (as signaled by pronouns), as in *He did not want to go out with her,* in which 'her' may also be part of a (complex) topic (see van Dijk, 1977a).

Despite the vast amount of linguistic and psychological work on sentence topics and our earlier proposals on macrotopics and sequential topics, we still do not have an explicit *representation format* for topic functions in sentences. Earlier in this chapter we provided a semantic analysis of propositions in terms of functional categories, but there is no topic information in these representations. This is, of course, correct for context-free representation formats for sentences, because topics can only be properly defined textually. Hence, for sequences of propositions, as they define a textbase, we need to assign specific functions to subgraphs of our representation format. This is necessary for a search strategy in short-term memory; otherwise the search would not *know* which subgraph (e.g., participant) to take as an antecedent for anaphorical expressions such as pronouns.

Such a representation format would, however, presuppose a full-fledged theory about the internal *relevance structure* of sentences, which we do not have: The usual categories are only those of ''topic'' and ''comment,'' possibly with a ''focus'' category for the part of the comment that is the most important new information. Also, there may be degrees of topicality and focus. We will, however, assume provisionally that the relevance structure of the sentence, as assigned to the semantic representation within a textbase, has a *schematic* nature. This schema represents the general cognitive (and hence universal) property that some semantic information is linked with previous information, and that some information is more relevant for the continuation of the discourse than other information, for example, for the establishment of local and global coherence. The schema may be compared with the superstructure schemata (e.g., those of stories) we discuss in Chapter 7; these also assign functions to (macro)meanings. The Relevance structure schema thus assigns functions such as 'topic' or 'focus' to nodes in the semantic representation. In retrieval processes, we assume that first this relevance structure tree, dominating the semantic representation, will be scanned, which may directly produce a relevant antecedent for a pronoun. If it is then found that the semantic category is *also* agent, the strategy is provisionally confirmed, a confirmation which may also use surface structure information of the previous sentence, such as position (first) and syntactic function (subject) or category (noun phrase) of the antecedent.

We have also noted that neither pronouns nor antecedents stand alone: They are integral parts of a complex sentence, and their semantic representation forms part of a complex proposition. Hence, apart from the already powerful information provided for the pronoun interpretation strategy, we may also use the hierarchical structure of the previous sentence or proposition. This means that, all other things being equal, main clauses and dominant propositions will be searched first. We might therefore predict that the most favored position for relevant antecedents for pronouns will be (i) last occurring, (ii) main clause/main proposition, (iii) first position, (iv) subject, (v) agent/person, and (vi) topical noun phrases, in this order of increasing importance. The findings in our experiment are in perfect agreement with this hypothesis. Remember that the strategy only assigns partial coherence, that is, a provisional coherence link for first position pronouns. The definitive interpretation will, of course, be assigned on the basis of the interpretation of the whole clause or sentence, and its coherence links with the previous sentences of the textbase.

We have sketched, informally, a model of topical interpretation for pronouns. The "previous" information was still limited to earlier propositions of the textbase, but the criterion, as we saw, is the accessibility in short-term memory of any kind of previous information, including inferences, and actualized frames, scripts, situation models, and, above all, a macroproposition. Hence, if the search through the actual previous propositions of the textbase, as described here, is unsuccessful, search for antecedents will first be extended to the actual macroproposition, providing information also about possible sequential topics which have been briefly out of focus locally. At this point, currently relevant subgraphs of the situation model or the relevant script, instantiations, as represented in the control system, may be searched. These information packages will specify which participants are possible, can be expected, and, above all, which ones are most important in the present situation, as defined by the situation model. We will come back to the actualization of this kind of information in discourse understanding in Chapter 10. At this point, however, it is important to stress again that the interpretation of pronouns involves the identification of a plausible referent, that such a referent, in our model, is represented in the situation model, and that the textbase fragment currently being processed in short-term memory is only analyzed for the information necessary to identify which possible referent in the situation model is now being talked about. If no other referents (e.g., persons) were involved, search through previous textbase fragments would even be superfluous: The now activated part of the situation model would directly provide "the" referent. If there are more referents mentioned earlier in the text, then both textual information and knowledge will be necessary: The episodic situation model will decide which referent is the only possible one in the actually described fact in the model. Indeed, most of the studies that have been mentioned here stress this pragmatic, or rather epistemic, role in the ultimate interpretation of pronouns, that is, the role of frames, scripts, and inferences (Nash-Webber, 1978a; Garrod & Sanford, 1977; Ehrlich, 1980; Tyler & Marslen-Wilson, 1982; Hirst & Brill, 1980; and Kintsch & van Dijk, 1978).

## 5.5. EXPERIMENT 2: PRONOUN IDENTIFICATION[2]

Within the framework of the theoretical model presented here, and of the earlier studies reviewed, we performed an experiment in which some of the factors contributing to the strategical interpretation of pronouns were varied. Instead of using a reading- or reaction-time method, in which typically only full clauses can be used, we resorted to another way of trying to capture the on-line, strategic interpretation of pronouns. We constructed materials consisting of one or more sentences followed by a new sentence of which only the first word, a pronoun, was given, and asked our subjects to complete that sentence. The pronoun was ambigu-

[2]This study was performed by P. Leseman and F. Lemmens under the direction of T. A. van Dijk at the University of Amsterdam.

ous in the sense that it could refer to several referents, mentioned in the earlier sentence(s). We assumed that if indeed this first pronoun was interpreted cotopically, the sentence would be preferentially completed in such a way that the pronoun would refer to a referent which was earlier referred to by a topical phrase. Because agency, subject function, and main versus subordinate clause position may also be involved, as we saw earlier, our materials were constructed in such a way that the topic antecedent would not always coincide with these other structural features of the previous sentence(s).

According to the model that we have described, subjects will tend to choose a cotopical interpretation for the pronoun, and will show this in their continuations. If other strategically relevant information coincides with the topic-first strategy, then the effects will be larger.

To show that topicality is pervasive, we constructed, as has been mentioned, not only discourses with one previous sentence, but also discourses with a full previous sequence. In such cases, topical coreference should be possible when antecedents are located several sentences back, and even when other candidate antecedents (of the same gender and number) are mentioned in intervening sentences.

### 5.5.1. Method

The subjects were 38 psychology students at the University of Amsterdam who participated in the experiment as part of their course requirements.

Forty discourse fragments were constructed. Sixteen of them consisted of one simple sentence followed by an incomplete next sentence (consisting of a pronoun—*he* or *she,* depending on the gender of the possible antecedents). Sixteen other fragments had a complex previous sentence, 8 with main clause–subordinate clause ordering and 8 with subordinate clause–main clause ordering, such that the previous topic either occurred in the main clause or in the subordinate clause. The remaining 8 discourse fragments consisted of sequences of various length, with the test pronoun occurring 2–4 sentences after the sentence with a topical antecedent, and with the intermediate sentences also having possible antecedents, which, however, did not have a sequential topical role.

Because the strategy of coherence establishment is rather complex and may use information of various sorts, the construction of the materials for this kind of experiment must be carefully undertaken if we are to obtain the effects for the specific variables. That is, there may be many other factors influencing the continuation of some referent. We therefore controlled the discourse fragments for the following factors:

1. *Gender:* Male and female actors were systematically varied in all fragments.
2. *Names:* Different proper names and different definite descriptions were used to refer to antecedent referents.

3. *Length:* Previous sentences or clauses were of approximately the same length and the same semantic complexity for each condition.
4. *Naturalness:* The discourse fragments could easily form partial naturally occurring text or dialogue.
5. *Knowledge/scripts:* The possible situations and the background knowledge (scripts) activated for the understanding of the passages were varied for all conditions.
6. *Other factors:* There may be other factors of semantic structure that may facilitate or inhibit continuation with certain individual referents; thus, presence or absence of an individual in some location now in focus will also influence their presence or absence in a subsequent sentence; similarly, certain actions will often predispose the reader to expect that some action of the same or of another agent will take place immediately afterward, such that a subsequent sentence will either have the same topic or a change of topic. Hence, we constructed sentences that varied in this respect.
7. *Narrative conventions:* The fragments are all supposed to occur in stories, and the local organization of the story may influence expectations about who will do what next, for example, as an expected reaction to some action. Thus, if somebody is said to 'approach' or 'ask something' of somebody else, a natural expectation is a 'reaction' of that other person.

It is certainly possible that other factors may influence the choice of continuation, but we expect that the variation in semantic content as well as intersubject diversity (different knowledge, beliefs, reading habits, interests, etc.) will be neutralized sufficiently across the various conditions.

Table 5.1 shows translations (as literal as possible) of the simple-sentence stimulus materials used. The Dutch sentences are of the form $NP_1-NP_2$. The 16 items are divided into four categories of four sentences each according to a $2 \times 2$ design. The agent and subject are expressed by $NP_1$ in Categories 1 and 2, and by $NP_2$ in Categories 3 and 4. In Categories 1 and 4 $NP_1$ is the topic, and in Categories 2 and 3 $NP_1$ is the comment. Topic role is established here through the use of either a pronoun or a definite description.

Table 5.2 presents the complex sentences which are of the form main clause–conjunction–subordinate clause in Categories 1 and 2, and subordinate clause–conjunction–main clause in Categories 3 and 4. In all cases $NP_1$ is in the first clause, $NP_2$ in the second. Once again, $NP_1$ is the topic in Categories 1 and 4 and $NP_2$ in Categories 2 and 3.

The structure of the sentence sequences is indicated in Table 5.3. A sequential topic is always introduced in the first sentence. As can be seen from Table 5.3, successive sentences vary in number from one to four and either do or do not introduce further competing alternative referents for the final pronoun. Only seven sentence sequences are shown because an error was made in constructing the eighth one. The number of possible, and thus competing, antecedents and the position of these possible antecedents (the most recent clause is still "on stage") have been

**Table 5.1**
**One-Clause Sentences**

|  | Percentage of topic choice[a] |
|---|---|
| CATEGORY 1: Agent/subject + topic −V−O | |
| 1. *The director fired a worker. He−* | 75* |
| 2. *She applied to the director* (fem) *for her resignation. She−* | 92* |
| 3. *The teacher* (masc) *indicated the solution to a student.* He− | 64 |
| 4. *Carla looked foolishly at the woman. She−* | 76* |
|  | 77* |
| CATEGORY 2: Agent/subject−V−topic | |
| 5. *A tourist* (fem) *asked her the road. She−* | 75* |
| 6. *A police officer fined Gerard for speeding.* He− | 50 |
| 7. *A man approached him whistling. He−* | 53 |
| 8. *An aunt gave Mirjam money for the metro. She−* | 50 |
|  | 57 |
| CATEGORY 3: O−V−agent/subject + topic | |
| 9. *Only this therapist* (fem) *she confided in. She−* | 61 |
| 10. *With Hans Theo preferred not to spend his vacation. He−* | 66* |
| 11. *For a certain professor he liked to work eagerly. He−* | 97* |
| 12. *To a passing lady Josje gave away her fur-coat. She−* | 83* |
|  | 77* |
| CATEGORY 4: Topic −V−agent/subject | |
| 13. *With her Francine wanted to write her MA thesis. She−* | 76* |
| 14. *With him only Nico got along well. He−* | 62 |
| 15. *Against him voted an elder* (in church). *He−* | 34 |
| 16. *With her even Margriet could do business well. She−* | 88* |
|  | 64* |

[a]An asterisk indicates a value significantly ($p = .05$) different from chance (50%).

hypothesized as important variables by Kieras (1981b) and Clark and Sengul (1979), respectively.

Each subject was presented with a booklet of 42 pages, of which the first page was empty, the second page contained the instructions, and the next 40 pages contained the various discourse fragments. These fragments were randomized such that each subject had a unique order of fragments, so that no specific order effects would be obtained. Although we expected that after the subjects had read several fragments, they would be able to guess that the experiment is about assigning reference, the random order prohibits detection of the variables involved and the application of a blind strategy. The instructions were as follows: "Here are a

**Table 5.2**
**Two-Clause Sentences**

|  | Percentage of topic choice[a] |
|---|---|
| CATEGORY 1: Main clause/topic –C–subordinate clause | |
| 1. *Harm was very frightened when a man wanted to cross the street. He–* | 83* |
| 2. *Dolores was positively surprised when a girlfriend entered. She–* | 91* |
| 3. *The doorman had not opened the door, because a drunk man wanted to enter. He–* | 82* |
| 4. *Margot prepared for dinner while a girlfriend opened the door for the guests. She–* | 71* |
|  | 82* |
| CATEGORY 2: Main clause–C–subordinate clause/topic | |
| 5. *The teacher* (fem) *gave a passing grade, after Sonja's having answered correctly almost all of the questions. She–* | 58 |
| 6. *A building worker shouted from the scaffolding that he could go and drop dead. He–* | 82* |
| 7. *A gynecologist* (fem) *thought that she had to come urgently for an examination. She–* | 86* |
| 8. *A Jehovah's Witness rang the bell, just as Harold took his coat to leave for his office. He–* | 89* |
|  | 78* |
| CATEGORY 3: Subordinate clause–C–main clause/topic | |
| 9. *Although the police officer clearly gave a stop signal, John thought that he could simply continue driving. He–* | 100* |
| 10. *After a woman had explained the way, she could find the address without any difficulty. She–* | 92* |
| 11. *Although a passing woman gave a warning, Angela thought that nothing could happen. She–* | 100* |
| 12. *When a huge guy blocked the entrance, he split right away. He–* | 100* |
|  | 98* |
| CATEGORY 4: Subordinate clause/topic –C–main clause | |
| 13. *By the time she had had enough of standing up, another woman had already occupied the chair. She–* | 89* |
| 14. *After Ellen had presented herself, the personnel counselor* (fem) *explained the application procedure. She–* | 50 |
| 15. *Just as the athlete thought he would win easily, one of his opponents passed with high speed. He–* | 84* |
| 16. *Just when Victor just thought of the right answer, the supervising teacher snatched away the paper. He–* | 81* |
|  | 76* |

[a]An asterisk indicates a value significantly different ($p = .05$) from chance (50%).

**Table 5.3**
**Sentence Sequences**

| Sentence | Number of sentences intervening | Number of rival antecedents | Last sentence neutral | Choice probability of sequential topic | |
|---|---|---|---|---|---|
| | | | | Observed[a] | Corrected for guessing[b] |
| 1 | 1 | 1 | No | .71* | .42 |
| 2 | 2 | 1 | Yes | .88* | .76 |
| 3 | 2 | 2 | No | .57* | .36 |
| 4 | 3 | 2 | Yes | .89* | .84 |
| 5 | 3 | 3 | No | .55* | .40 |
| 6 | 4 | 3 | Yes | .95* | .93 |
| 7 | 4 | 1 | Yes | .97* | .94 |

[a]An asterisk indicates a value significantly (.05 level) different from chance (which now depends on the number of available response alternatives).

[b]The correction for guessing used is $(p - g)/(1 - g)$, where $p$ is the observed choice probability and $g$ is the guessing probability.

number of fragments from conversations and written texts. Each fragment consists of one or more sentences, followed by the first word of the next sentence. Your task is to complete the next sentence, that is, think of a continuation that is coherent with the fragment. The sentence you should invent need not be funny or original, but it should be a correct and coherent continuation. Don't make very long sentences: keep them as short as possible. Of course it should be clear what you mean. Try to write clearly. Any questions?''

### 5.5.2. Results and Discussion

Two blind judges read the continuations that were generated and decided for each which of the persons mentioned in the first sentence was meant by the personal pronoun that began the second sentence. They based their judgments mainly on the semantic content of the continuation. After the judges worked through the material independently, their decisions were compared and all cases where there was disagreement between them, or where they agreed that the continuation was uninterpretable, were excluded from all further analyses. Thus, 5.2% of the simple sentence continuations, 4.7% of the complex sentence continuations, and 2.0% of the sequence continuations were lost.

The results of the scoring are shown in Tables 5.1–5.3. For the *simple previous sentences* (Table 5.1), we see that the majority of the subjects chose a continuation in which the pronoun corefers with the *topical* noun in the previous sentence. This is especially the case in Conditions 1 and 3, in which the topical noun also expresses the agent and subject functions, in either initial position (Condition 1, 77%) or final position (Condition 3, 77%). But even if the topic is not agent and subject (Conditions 2 and 4), there is some tendency to choose the topic if the topical noun is in first position (Condition 4, 64%). In Condition 2, the topic was preferred in only one case.

If the previous fragment consists of a *complex sentence* (Table 5.2) such that the topical noun phrase occurs either in the main clause or in the subordinate clause, either in first or in last position, the results are even more striking, especially in a main clause that comes last (98%). Note that in this condition the topical noun phrase is also subject and agent (or experiencer).

For the *sequences* (Table 5.3), subjects also preferred to choose as antecedent for the pronoun in the to-be-generated sentence the topical noun in the first sentence, even if several sentences with several intervening noun phrases occurred. This is especially the case for those fragments in which there is no new individual introduced in the last sentence of the sequnce (87% topic choices, versus only 39% when the last sentence is not neutral).

Given a fragment of a text followed by a pronoun that has grammatically ambiguous coreference, subjects exhibited a strong bias in favor of identifying the ambiguous pronoun with the topical noun in the preceding text. This topic bias combined with an agent/subject bias: The topical noun was chosen most reliably when it was also the agent and subject (Conditions 1 and 3 in the simple sentences, and all complex sentences). When the topical noun was not also agent and sentence subject (Conditions 2 and 4 in simple sentences) it was chosen with much less frequency (in only 3 out of 8 sentences was the choice probability significantly different from chance). However, whether the topical noun appeared in first or second position in a sentence, and whether it appeared in a main clause or a subordinate clause, did not affect the data.

The first conclusion from these data is that, whatever the grammatical structure of the fragment, a subject will in general opt for a continuation that has topical coherence. In other words, if it is indicated, by the use of pronouns or definite noun phrases, that an NP has topical function in the previous fragment, the subject will take that hint and associate first position, subject pronouns with a continuation of that topic. Hence the topical coherence strategy in discourse seems to be the strongest force in the (productive) establishment of coreferential coherence. However, we also see that the choice for topic continuity is less prominent as soon as topic and agent/subject functions are dissociated: In that case agentive coreference is also often chosen though usually less than topical coreference. This suggests that the canonical strategy, in which there is cooccurrence of topic, agent, and subject (for human action sentences in stories), also has effects on the coherence role of agents in subject relation: They, too, may function as a plausible continuation.

From these results we may further conclude (*a*) that subject and agent are not the major forces in coreferential interpretation in discourse; (*b*) that recency of the NP does not matter very much if the two NPs occur in the same previous sentence; and (*c*) that the occurrence of the topical antecedent in a main clause or subordinate clause does not affect coreferential choice of the topical NP though recent topical main clauses were the most powerful determinants of choice in this study. On the whole, we get a picture that is rather different from the impression we got from previous experiments on pronoun identification. We see that in discourse it is topical coherence, or at least this aspect of topical coherence (and in the kind of production experiment we did), that is the major force, and not recency or agency.

It should be stressed, furthermore, that in this study the topical role of previous antecedents was established merely by rather superficial features, such as names, pronouns, and definite expressions. In real, complete discourse, many different devices are used to establish the roles of topic and comment (Bates & MacWhinney, 1979: 177, describe 13 grammatical devices), and hence these roles may be much more firmly established, with an even stronger effect on referent determination. In that case, the parallelism between sentence topic, sequence topic, and discourse topic (which according to us is a full proposition, of which the topical NP, or its underlying concept, is a part) will probably even enhance the chances that first position, subject, agent pronouns will be taken to be coreferential with a previous topical NP. From the sequence results we see that even if there are several intervening possible antecedents for a pronoun, subjects will still tend to choose the antecedent that is marked for its sequential topical role, especially in those cases where there is no recency effect (if the immediately previous sentence does not have a competing antecedent).

These conclusions take into account the various structural properties of discourse fragments, such as topical function, subject relation, agent role, position, recency, occurrence in main clause or subordinate clause, and sequential role of a discourse referent. Closer analysis of the materials, although systematically varied according to a number of other possible factors which may influence the choice of a specific discourse referent, would in principle give further hints about the mechanisms involved. The same holds for a protocol analysis of the productions given by the subjects. Although chance variation among subjects certainly exists, some discourse fragments suggest by their semantic content more strongly than others a nontopical continuation.

If we compare, for instance, the one-clause sentences (1) and (2) (Table 5.1), we find that subjects prefer to continue with the NP that is expressed by a pronoun. It seems that pronouns, as may be expected from the literature, have a more powerful influence on topic choice than do definite noun phrases. In part this may be so because expressions like *the director* and, in Sentence (3), *the teacher* need not have occurred earlier: As part of a script they may have been introduced as definite noun phrases which were not topical. Also, between the proper name and the definite NP in Sentence (4) there may be a topic conflict: *the woman* must have been introduced before.

In Category 2 single previous clauses, the subjects chose the topical NP or the agent/subject NP with about equal frequency. Only in Sentence (5) did they opt for the topical NP, probably because the verb *to ask* sets the stage for a reaction from the person asked, which is topical here. In (6) and (7), however, the predicates suggest rather that the current agent will be further described for further action: If $x$ approaches $y$, then we expect that something further is said about $x$.

Category 4 is more problematic, because it is difficult to construct natural examples in which one single previous clause has a topical NP which is neither subject nor agent. This is natural only if the topical NP is patient of some action and the nontopical NP has contrastive function (agent, and subject), which allows topic introduction or change. If we consider (15), the only example where the subjects chose more often the agent/subject than the topical NP (though expressed by a proper noun, not a pronoun), we see that this is a situation where the individual denoted by the topical NP may not be present, so that it is plausible that the nontopical agent/subject is further predicated upon.

For the complex previous sentences, the majority of the fragments are continued by at least two-thirds of the subjects with a topical individual. There are just two cases, namely, (5) and (14), where the choice is random. Both of these have a definite NP as agent in the main clause, which may be sufficiently strong to generate further predication. Note that in (14) the verb *explain* also suggests further information about the act of explaining. In all other examples it is sufficiently clear (by indefinite NPs, subordinate position) that nontopical NPs should not be prominent enough for further predication.

### 5.5.3. Conclusions and Further Speculations

What general conclusions can be attached to the results of this experiment within the more general framework of a complex strategy for local coherence establishment? Let us try to enumerate the major points involved and discuss further their relevance in our model:

1. *Macro-control.* Since we assume that the relevant macroproposition for an episode remains highly available during processing (see Chapter 10), this information is constantly available for strategic comprehension. This allows, for instance, participants of the macroproposition to be coreferentially represented by pronouns. If the use of a pronoun would lead to confusion, for example, if several antecedents could also point to the relevant referent for the pronoun, a full proper name or occasionally a full definite description could be used.

2. *Sequential continuity.* We see that the overall control of the currently active macroproposition manifests itself sequentially in the sentences of the discourse: A macroparticipant will simply be referred to often, and will therefore occur in many, most, or even all sentences, often as an agent in subject function. Yet, it will also be the case that new participants are introduced and further predicated upon. Sometimes, these will only have a secondary role, whereas in other cases they may become part of the macroproposition, for example, as a patient.

Usually, a macroparticipant is also the carrier of the *point of view* in a story. The storyteller identifies his or her point of view with that of the main participant, an identification signaled by the empathic description of feelings and thoughts. Although there will often be coincidence of point of view and thematicality of participants, this need not be the case. A first-person story will locate the point of view with the speaker (unless it is a literary story in which this identification of point of view and speaker role need not always take place), but may still be mainly about the main participant. We may also describe a story about someone from the point of view of someone else, although it is likely in that case that the latter is also involved in the interactions and hence a participant of the macroproposition. One of the topical consequences of the identification of point of view and thematical, sequential, or sentential topicality is the fact that motivations, intentions, and goals for actions can be accessed, as well as interpretations of actions by others, which indeed provides us with the necessary information for thematical agency: We can get a complete picture of the agent, not only a superficial or outside description of his or her actions.

3. *Sentential topicality.* The discussion of sentence topics cannot be dissociated from an anlysis of the role of topical information in the sentence relative to sequential and macrostructural topics. We have seen that discourse will be organized by top-down control of macroparticipants and linear control of sequential topics. The identification of the topical function of semantic units within the sentence depends on the establishment of the textual role of such units, and we have seen that neither agency nor subject position need coincide with topical function in the sentence. From the theoretical literature we know that, semantically, the identity of participants may be involved, and, textually (or contextually), the givenness of the information, whereas, cognitively, the presence of the information in short-term memory is at issue. We now have added a further dimension: Topicality in the sentence may also be determined on the basis of sequential and text topical participants. Note that this is not the same as saying that information is "given" by the sequence or the text, or that a participant can be identified, because in both cases the participant need not have topical functions. On the other hand, the sentential topic need not always be identical with an overall or a sequential topic, but only in those cases in which no clear indication is given of a topic change. Hence, topic continuity is not a rule but part of an expedient strategy.

Topic functions are functions assigned to sometimes complex semantic elements of a sentence relative to the semantic information (and hence also the topicality of previous elements) of discourse. They represent grammatically the cognitive process of expanding and linking information in discourse representations, on the one hand, and keeping or reinstating concepts in short term-memory for the assignment of new information, on the other. Strategically this general definition of topic has various consequences, though.

First, it may mean that readers want to maintain macroparticipants in short-term memory, taking them as central referents which by virtue of that role will have the strongest claim for local topicality. Second, the same holds for sequential topics. Third, the semantic structure of previous sentences will generate expectations about who will be on next—to use a theatrical metaphor often used in this kind of discussion. Fourth, there will be an effect of topic continuity from immediately previous sentences, which at the same time provides the useful cognitive effect of recency (as we have observed for last main clauses in our experiment). Fifth, the frequent cooccurrence of position, grammatical relation (subject), and agency with topicality will favor a strategy in which such sentential elements are assigned topic function. Sixth, surface expressions such as pronouns and definites will have the same effect, and some languages even have specific morphemes to express topicality. These various kinds of information will cooperate in the strategic assignment of topic function in a sentence, and we see that purely grammatical features are systematically linked with conditions on effective information processing in general and coherence assignment in discourse in particular. Many of the extant discussions on the topic–comment articulation of sentences are limited to only one or a few of these grammatical or cognitive features. Yet, although the notion of topic is rather complex, we have assumed that its basic function should be sought in the cognitive processing of textual information at the semantic level, that is, in the establishment of local coherence, and that the various grammatical signals related to this are a strategically handy indication of this function, both in production and in comprehension.

## 5.6. ANALYSIS OF THE *NEWSWEEK* TEXT

For an illustration of some of the local coherence strategies discussed in this chapter, let us turn again to our *Newsweek* text (see front endpapers). In the previous chapter, we gave provisional propositional analyses of the first two sentences of this text. At that point, we ignored a precise analysis of the propositional *relations,* and especially the relations holding between coordinated or sequentially ordered propositions. This characterization is less problematic for embedded propositions; they have in theory the same function as the category in the main clause they specify. Thus, relative clauses will in general be modifiers of arguments, nominal clauses will have direct participant functions, and adverbial clauses will usually modify or specify the time, location, or conditional categories of the circumstantial.

Overall local coherence of propositions is more complex. We have seen that there are two fundamental types of propositional coherence, namely, *conditional* and *functional* coherence. The first is defined in terms of referential relations: Propositions are coherent if they denote facts (in some possible world) that are related. This relation will often be one of conditionality (involving temporality, causality, etc.). Functional coherence, which is often defined in intensional (meaning) terms, is a propositional link in which one proposition—as a whole—has some function with respect to another, for example, an immediately previous one. Such a function may be one of 'specification', 'example', 'comparison', 'contrast', 'generalization', etc.

In the *Newsweek* text $S_1$, the first complex proposition expressed by the first clause, may be not only a dependent modifier of the object 'Guatemala' in the main clause (proposition), but also an implicit if-clause and hence a conditional: 'if we describe the situation in El Salvador in terms of gray, then we may say that . . . '. At the same time, though, there is a functional relation, expressed in surface structure by the verb *compare,* hence a comparison. Coherence links of comparison presuppose not only two or more objects or properties compared, but also a basis of comparison, in our case 'the political situation', predicated on here in metaphorical terms only.

The relation between $S_1$ and $S_2$ is also functional. If $S_1$ is interpreted metaphorically as 'marked political contrasts' (for Guatemala), then $S_2$ *specifies* this situation by describing the situation on the left, and $S_3$ by describing a situation on the right. In formal semantic terms this means that $S_2, S_3$ . . . *imply* $S_1$, and this means that $S_1$ expresses a (metaphorical) macroprosition for the first paragraph.

In Table 5.4 we have indicated the various coherence links between the complex propositions expressed by the sentences of the text. We have, for reasons of simplicity, not done so for each clause within the sentences as well, since these will mostly be characterizable in terms of functionally embedded propositions as indicated earlier. We see from this table that most of the coherence links have a functional nature, which makes this kind of text typically *expository* rather than narrative, in which conditional (e.g., causal) links are typical. Indeed, it is a description of a situation, featuring groups and events, not a description of a sequence of causally related actions only, although these may well be part of a political report.

The strategic understanding of these overall propositional connections is rather complex. Sometimes the first words of a sentence may already indicate that we will have a specification, an example, a contrast, or a generalization, but sometimes such an assumption must wait until nearly the whole sentence has been interpreted. Conditionals are much easier to comprehend strategically, because they will usually be marked with explicit connectives, such as *because, since, then, but, before,* etc., often in first position. This will often be the case for interclausal relations within sentences, which we have left unanalyzed here. Therefore, in Table 5.4 we also indicate which expressions may serve as cues for overall sentential coherence relation establishment.

It has been stressed in the previous sections of this chapter that partial coherence links, such as referential identity, are only one dimension of overall propositional coherence. Thus, forms of argument repetition which we studied in our earlier work (Kintsch, 1974; Kintsch & van Dijk, 1978) are merely possible strategies within a more embracing strategy of coherence establishment: This strategy captures the fact that in related facts we often have identical participants.

Both in our theoretical account of the previous sections and in the experiment reported in the last section we have shown that local coherence strategies, within the global strategy of full propositional coherence establishment, may establish links between component predicates or arguments of the respective propositions, and that often this strategy will select identical agents or identical topics to be coreferring to the same individual. Table 5.4 therefore will also specify which arguments are thus linked, and what the structural basis of the strategy is. Also it will mention the surface structure cues defining the cohesion expressing this underlying (partial) coherence. Again, we will ignore interclausal partial coherence in order to simplify our analysis.

The coherence picture we obtain when we inspect Table 5.4 is the following:

**Table 5.4**
**Local Coherence Strategies in the *Newsweek* Text, $S_1$–$S_{11}$**

| Sentences | Conditional coherence | Functional coherence | Cues | Partial coherence | Strategy | Cohesion cues |
|---|---|---|---|---|---|---|
| $S_1/S_2$ | | Specification | *black and white /on the left* | *Guatemala/ on the left* | Topic/Topic (Loc/Loc) | Ø |
| $S_2/S_3$ | | Contrast | *on the left/ on the right* | *on the left/ on the right* | Topic/Topic (Loc/Loc) | PrepP in initial position Identity: *on the* |
| $S_1/S_3$ | | Specification | *black and white /on the right* | *Guatemala/ on the right* | Topic/Topic (Loc/Loc) | Ø |
| $S_2$–$S_3/S_4$ | | Contrast | *on the left, extreme; on the right, elite/political centrists* | on the left; on the right/ of the political center | Topic/Topic (Loc/Loc, Agent) | PrepP |
| $S_1/S_4$ | | Specification | *black and white /political centrists* | Guatemala/ political center | Topic/Topic (Loc/Loc, Agent) | Ø |
| | | | | Guatemala/ Guatemala | Topic/Focus (Loc/Loc) | Identiy |
| | | | | El Salvador/ El Salvador | Focus/Focus (Loc) | Identity |
| $S_1$–$S_4/S_5$ | | Conclusion (Evaluation) | Quotes Macroprop. | *The situation in G.* | Comment/Topic (macro-topic) | Def. art. |
| | | Comparison | *more than* | G/G  ES/ES | Topic/Topic (Loc) | Identity |
| | Consequences | | *declares* | *G,ES; Central America/Latin American* | Topic/Comment (Loc/Mod) | Partial Identity Inclusion |
| | | | | *American diplomat/?* | Topic/Topic (Agent/Agent) | Identity |
| | | | | *diplomat* | | Ref. identity? |
| $S_5/S_6$ | | Continuation | quotes | (same utterance) | Contiguity | quotes |
| | | Explanation | *much more* | entrenched elite/ | Focus/Topic | Def. art. |

184

| | | (Evaluation) | reactionary | the oligarchy | (Agent/Agent) | Paraphrase |
|---|---|---|---|---|---|---|
| TITLE/ S6 | | Repetition (partial) | no choices/ choices far fewer | choices/choices | Focus/Topic | Identity |
| S3,S6/S7 | Consequence/Reason | TOPIC CHANGE | Relation with US: relevant topic for Newsweek | oligarchy/ oligarchs | Topic/Topic (Agent/Agent) | Identity (quasi) |
| | | | | Guatemala/ Guatemalan on the right/ right wingers | Topic/Topic (part) (Loc/Mod) Topic/Topic (Loc/Agent) | Identity (quasi) (Noun/Adj.) Identity (part.) |
| S3,S4/S7 | | Generalization | Semantic implication: victms of terror/human right abuses | | | |
| S7/S8 | Consequence/Reason | Explanation | joy about election R./ideological kinsman, friend | The oligarchs/they | Topic/Topic (Agent/Agent) | Pronoun |
| | | | | Reagan/Reagan | Focus/Focus | Identity |
| | | | | Guatemalan/ Guatemalan | (Mod/Mod) | Identity |
| S7–S8/S8 | Consequence | Contrast (unexpected) | joy, kinsman/ disappointed but | Guatemalan, olig./ the Guatemalans | Topic/Topic (Agent/Exper.) | Def. art. |
| | | | | Reagan/Reagan | Focus/Topic (sub) | Identity |
| S7–S9/ S10 | Consequence/Reason | Explanation | hate human rights protests persistent demands for moderation | Reagan/Reagan /Carter/Carter | Focus/Topic | Identity |
| | | | | | Focus/Topic | Identity |
| | | | | Guatemalans | Topic/Topic | Identity |
| S9–S10/ S11 | Consequence | Conclusion | quotes | US/US | Mod/Mod | Identity |
| | | | | Guatemalan/G. olig./regime | Mod/Mod | Identity |
| | | | | | Topic/Topic | Def. art. |

The first sentence is of a thematic nature, predicting something very general about the situation in two countries. The following sentences all specify this situation in the two countries. At the same time, a contrast is built up between the different political forces, and this contrast is marked in the subsequent sentences (by the appropriate characterization —on the left, on the right, in the political center—in initial topical position). A conclusion of this situation is given in $S_5$, which makes a comparison and at the same time provides a consequence and its following explanation. After this description of the initial situation (see the superstructure analysis in Chapter 7 for details), we go to the actual events, the relations between the United States and the Guatemalan regime, and the actions of the regime and the guerrillas. There, causal relations between events play a role, such as the cause for the regime's disappointment.

Note that our analysis has been a more or less linear, on-line analysis, linking each new sentence with previous sentences. However, the reader will at the same time build up a *hierarchical structure* of coherence relations in the textbase. Thus, $S_2$–$S_4$ specify $S_1$, and are therefore functionally subordinated to it, whereas $S_5$ is a same-level paraphrase of $S_1$ and the title proposition. It should be stressed, however, that the propositional hierarchy is not based on argument repetition. If that were the case, $S_7$ would be subordinated to $S_3$, but these sentences are at the same level: $S_3$ provides historical background, and $S_7$ gives information about the actual situation (relations with the United States). At that point there is no strict functional coherence, but a *topic change*, dominated by another macroproposition: 'Relations with the U.S. are bad', even if $S_7$ specifies more about the oligarchical regime. The specification, moreover, is not a local connection, but a global one: It constructs an overall property of one of the agents of the macroproposition (see Chapter 6, for details). In that case only the argument repetition provides local coherence between the subsequent sentences and, more abstractly, between the subsequent paragraphs and their dominating macropropositions.

There are hardly any surface structure coherence cues for overall connection, except *but* in $S_9$. Therefore, the reader must rely on semantic cues. The general concept of 'contrast', implied by $S_1$, can be strategically specified by concepts such as 'on the left', 'on the right', etc. The comparison, explicit in $S_1$ and implied in the following sentences, is only expressed in $S_5$ and $S_6$ by such expressions as *much more serious than* and *much more reactionary*. Similarly, a generalization function can be detected when concepts imply each other, as in the relation $S_3, S_4/S_7$ ('terror/'human rights abuses'). The conditional relations, such as reason– consequence in the second paragraph, are rather marked by relationships between events or actions, such as identical or conflicting goals.

On the whole, it could be said for local coherence between participants of respective propositions, indicated in the partial coherence column of Table 5.4, that unlike in stories, we do not primarily have identity of one or a few participants, for example, of agents. Rather, the argument repetition strategy here works for the concept of 'Guatemala', and for the respective groups involved—the oligarchical regime, the guerrillas, and the United States Government—and their respective representatives or qualifications—'on the left', 'on the right', Reagan, and a number of 'spokesmen'. The strategies for establishing local partial coherence are therefore more complex than in the simple stories used in many experimental and artificial intelligence models. A respectable amount of world knowledge is required to be able to identify participants as members of the various groups involved. We must know that 'the oligarchy' in $S_6$ is identical with the 'entrenched elite of the right' in $S_3$, that Jimmy Carter was the U.S. president, and was succeeded in office by Reagan, that Reagan is conservative, that the 'businessmen's group' in $S_8$ will be part of, or sympathetic to, the right-wing oligarchy in Guatemala, and so on. Only our knowledge and in general the 'politics' frame enables us to establish the necessary coreferential "series" (cf. van Dijk, 1977a), which are only in part expressed by such surface cues as nominal or adjectival identity, pronouns, and definite articles.

If we inspect the strategy column in Table 5.4, we observe that most of the coreferential expressions are part of the topics of their respective sentences, and also that coreference is established with previous arguments also in topic position (or part of topical expressions), so that our general hypothesis that much coreference can be strategically retrieved cotopically seems confirmed. But, on the other hand, the strategy is not so straightforward: Antecedents will often be part of a previous locative or a modifier, which, unlike previous agents, are not canonical semantic functions for topic functions. Thus, the phrase *on the left* has topical function only if it presupposes a country, Guatemala, and that the political situation or spectrum has been topicalized before, as indeed has been done metaphorically in $S_1$. But such a strategy, as we saw, requires much world knowledge. This knowledge is both of the semantic and of the episodic kind. The semantic knowledge involves such general information as the distinction between left- and right-wing parties and their respective interests, information about the countries in Central America, the locus of power in the United States and the interests of American foreign policy. The episodic knowledge would consist of our more personal knowledge, from the media or from conversations, about the actual situation in Central American, and in El Salvador and Guatemala in particular. It is the general knowledge about news, about weeklies, about *Newsweek,* and the macroinformation from the headline that activate these knowledge domains, and that allow the metaphorical interpretation of $S_1$ and the establishment of full and partial propositional coherence. The knowledge involved also sets up a schema for this kind of discourse type and its local and global coherence: Expect opposed 'parties' and their conflicting strategies, expect 'allies' for each of the parties, expect 'members' or 'spokesmen' for these parties, and expect a number of 'actions' parties will perform in order to realize the goals that are consistent with their overall interests (or "life goals" or "themes"—see Schank & Abelson, 1977), and expect actions that oppose the realization of the goals of the opposed parties. This is precisely the coherence series we find in this article, and it also explains why we need few functional coherence cues: The cues are provided by this kind of *coherence schema*. Furthermore, it explains how and why we can easily change lower level topics without immediate full or partial (participant) connections between subsequent sentences, as would be found in simple stories about one agent-hero, where besides coagency and cotopicality recency might also work as a strategy.

In the following chapters we will see that the various local coherence strategies need further constraints from macrostructures and schematic superstructures. These will, among other things, also specify how the component paragraphs are coherently interpreted in the text as a whole.

Furthermore, it should be stressed that local coherence is not simply a property holding for consecutive sentences in a discourse. In many of our examples from the *Newsweek* text it appears that there are discontinuities: The fourth sentence may cohere with the first and not with the third, especially if this first sentence has thematic (macrostructure) functions. Similarly, following sentences may introduce new discourse referents, especially at topic change positions (e.g., at paragraph boundaries), which may require further specification in a number of sentences before links are established with already established discourse referents.

It is obvious that without a large amount of intelligently organized knowledge (and beliefs), there is no way this text can be understood, even at this local level of analysis. We will try to systematize this kind of knowledge in more detail in Chapter 9. There we will also show that the coherence schema mentioned here derives from general knowledge frames about politics and civil war, and especially from the situation model we have about Guatemala. The respective propositions of our text are *updating* this situation model, guided by the coherence schema.

# Chapter 6

# Macrostrategies

## 6.1. THE NOTION OF MACROSTRUCTURE

In the previous chapter it was argued that discourse coherence should be accounted for at both the local and the global level. Local coherence has been defined in terms of relations between propositions as expressed by subsequent sentences. Global coherence is of a more general nature, and characterizes a discourse as a whole, or larger fragments of a discourse. Notions used to describe this kind of overall coherence of discourse include topic, theme, gist, upshot, or point. All these notions say something about the global content of a discourse, and hence require explication in terms of semantic structure. The notion of *macrostructure* has been introduced in order to provide such an abstract semantic description of the global content, and hence of the global coherence of discourse (van Dijk, 1972, 1977a, 1980a).

Macrostructures are not the only global structures of discourse. For at least certain discourse types, it is useful to speak also about the *schematic* structure. Thus, stories can be characterized by a narrative schema, and argumentations have usually been analyzed in terms of argumentative schemata, for example, the syllogism of Aristotelian logic. Such schematic structures, which we call *superstructures*, provide the overall form of a discourse and may be made explicit in terms of the specific categories defining a discourse type. Macrostructures, then, are the semantic content for the terminal categories of these superstructural schemata. Although the cognitive understanding of macrostructures and superstructures is an integrated process, we will discuss superstructural strategies separately in the next chapter.

In an abstract, linguistic, semantics of discourse, macrostructures are defined by rules, the so-called *macrorules*. It is a fundamental principle of both linguistic and logical semantics that the interpretation of certain units be defined in terms of the interpretation of their constituent parts. Thus, the definition of macrostructures by means of macrorules must also be based on the meanings of the sentences of a discourse, that is, on the propositions expressed by them. As macrostructures are, by definition, also semantic units they must also consist of propositions, namely, *macropropositions*. A macroproposition, thus, is a proposition that is derived from the sententially expressed propositions of a discourse. In other words, macrorules are semantic mapping rules: They relate proposition sequences with proposition sequences at a higher level, and thus derive the global meaning of an episode or a whole discourse from the local, sentential meanings of the discourse.

Macrorules are recursive. Given a sequence of macropropositions, they may apply again and thus derive a still higher level of macrostructure. It follows that the resulting macrostructure of a discourse is a hierarchical structure, consisting of several levels. Hence, the notion of macroproposition is relative: It is defined relative to the sequence of propositions (local or global) from which it is derived by a macrorule.

The macrorules that have been defined in the theory of discourse are the following:

1. DELETION: Given a sequence of propositions, delete each proposition that is not an interpretation condition (e.g., a presupposition) for another proposition in the sequence.
2. GENERALIZATION: Given a sequence of propositions, substitute the sequence by a proposition that is entailed by each of the propositions of the sequence.
3. CONSTRUCTION: Given a sequence of propositions, replace it by a proposition that is entailed by the joint set of propositions of the sequence.

These brief definitions of the rules neglect many formal details and further constraints. We see, however, that the rules are a form of reduction rules: They delete propositions or replace sequences of propositions by a single (macro)proposition. At the same time they assign a further organization to the meaning of a discourse: Sequences are no longer organized only at the local level, by linear relations of coherence as discussed in the previous chapter, but also by higher level conceptual units.

Figure 6.1 sketches the formal structure of a textbase. The macrostructure is the subgraph labeled with M nodes. The P nodes form the microstructure. For short discourses, we should also provide for the possibility that the local and the global meaning coincide. In that case Rule 1 (DELETION) applies vacuously: All the propositions of the text are then also relevant at the global level. Obviously, the notion of semantic macrostructure is only needed for more extended discourses, to which such notions as topic, upshot, or gist apply.

Our account is still missing a number of fundamental features. For one thing,

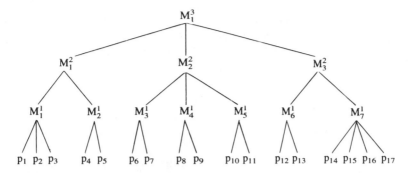

**Figure 6.1.** The formal structure of a textbase.

the rules presuppose that a discourse is fully explicit, that is, that it expresses all propositions that are interpretation conditions for following sentences. However, it is well known that natural discourse is not explicit in this way. Many propositions need not be expressed, as the speaker may assume that they are known to, or can be inferred by, the hearer. Just as for the establishment of local coherence, the rules presuppose that a number of propositions can be supplied by the knowledge set of a language user. Thus, this knowledge set, $K$, indicates when a proposition is an interpretation condition for other propositions. For the GENERALIZATION rule, $K$ specifies when a concept is a superconcept for other concepts. Similarly, $K$ specifies when a sequence of propositions jointly entails a higher level proposition as is required for the CONSTRUCTION rule. The sequence ⟨'X goes to the airport', 'X checks in', 'X waits for boarding',...⟩ entails the macroproposition 'X is taking a plane', given the appropriate world knowledge in the form of frames or scripts. Typically, a discourse will only express some propositions of such a sequence, so that additional propositions from $K$ are necessary to derive the macroproposition. Hence, macropropositions are abstractly derived from sequences of propositions relative to some set of propositions, $K$, representing the world knowledge of language users.

## 6.2. MACROSTRUCTURES AND DISCOURSE UNDERSTANDING

Whereas the abstract account of macrostructures given in the preceding section may be relevant for a linguistic semantics of discourse, it is insufficient for a cognitive model of understanding. Even though the cognitive notion of knowledge appeared to be necessary in the abstract account, a cognitive model will have to be much more complex. In addition to, or instead of, the rules defined we will need at least the following:

1. A definition of the actual *processes* by which macrostructures are derived from sentences of a discourse

2. A specification of the *strategies* used to effectively handle the sometimes vast amounts of information necessary in the application of such processes
3. An explication of the various types of information used by these strategies, henceforth called *macrostrategies*
4. A specification of the *memory* constraints on macrostrategies
5. A characterization of the memory *representation* of semantic macrostructures and their relations with other discourse and episodic representations
6. A specification of the *knowledge* types and strategies necessary for the application of macrorules and strategies
7. An explication of the role of macrostructures and macrostrategies in the cognitive account of *local coherence* assignment
8. An explication of their role in the understanding of *superstructures*
9. A specification of the relevance of macrostructures in processes of *retrieval* and *(re)production* of discourse
10. A specification of the role of macrostructures in the performance of a number of *discourse-related tasks,* such as summarizing, question answering, problem solving, or learning (i.e., the formation or transformation of knowledge, but also of beliefs, opinions, and attitudes)

Some of these specifically cognitive properties of macrostructures were already built into our previous discourse-processing model (Kintsch & van Dijk, 1978). Although the account of macrostructures given in that model was still predominantly static or structural, it predicted at least some experimentally confirmed ideas about the organization of discourse in episodic memory and the major characteristics of related retrieval, recall, and summarization. Lacking was a more dynamic or strategic approach, in which the precise processes are specified by which a macrostructure is actually inferred from text and knowledge. Similarly, the various textual and contextual cues used by the language understander to apply such strategies have not been systematically discussed. And, finally, this abstract, structural description of macrounderstanding could hardly provide a sound explication of individual differences and differences in tasks, goals, or interests in the formation of macrostructures.

This last point needs further comment. Linguistic semantics has usually proceeded from the hypothesis that the meaning of expressions should be specified independently of contextual and personal variations, which were left to psycho- and sociolinguistics. Hence, for a given language community and in a specific period, the meaning of words and of sentences was assumed to be a more or less abstract, stable, or at least intersubjectively invariant, conceptual structure, characterizing the language system as opposed to actual language use. The global meanings of discourse as defined in terms of semantic macrostructures similarly had this abstract, invariant nature: A nonambiguous text was assigned a single macrostructure. Such an assumption is inadequate in a cognitive model of language use: The actual understanding of a discourse will depend on the variable cognitive features of language users and on the context. In other words, depending on different interpretation strategies, different knowledge, beliefs, opinions, attitudes, interests, or goals, each language user will assign his or her own macrostructure to a discourse. Different readers will find different meanings prominent, important, relevant, or interesting, and will assign different topics or gist to the discourse. This may seem obvious by now, but psychology has been uncomfortably close to linguistics in trying to provide more abstract and generalized models of language understanding. This is not wholly incomprehensible from a methodological point of view: A cognitive model will not specify how John or Mary understand a discourse, but try to formulate general principles. Similarly, adequate verbal communication is possible only if language users have meanings and knowledge in common. Therefore, an adequate cognitive model of macrostructures should specify the general principles followed by all language users in understanding the global meanings of discourse, and show how individual differences presuppose sufficient common information to make communication adequate. Whatever the individual cognitive make-up of a language user, he or she can not assign completely arbitrary or disparate macrostructures to a discourse. The speaker's intentions as expressed by the text or reasonably ascribed to the speaker by the hearer on other grounds will play a normative role in the derivation of macrostructures.

### 6.2.1. The Linguistic and Cognitive Reality of Macrostructures

It has hitherto been assumed that macrostructures are structures of discourse, just as both linguistics and psychology usually speak of the meaning "of" words or sentences. In a cognitive model such a way of speaking is not quite adequate. It is more appropriate to account for meanings, and hence also for global meanings, as being *assigned* to a discourse by language users in processes of understanding or interpretation. But, strictly speaking, this is also true for morphophonological and syntactic structures as they are assigned to the phonetic string of an utterance. Hence, phonological, morphological, syntactic, and semantic structures assigned to a sentence or discourse by abstract rules or cognitive operations, are—as a shorthand—said to be structures "of" these sentences or discourses. There is no reason to make an exception for the global meanings which we explicate by means of semantic macrostructures.

One possible argument against this assumption might be that macrostructures are only inferred from a discourse—if they "exist" at all—and therefore do not belong to the meaning representation of a discourse, but at most to a cognitive model. The criterion used here would be that, unlike the meaning of words or sentences, macrostructures are not directly expressed by expressions of the discourse, and therefore cannot be part of the linguistic meaning of a discourse. This argument is wrong, however, not only for a cognitive model of discourse understanding, but even for a linguistic semantics (if it still makes sense to make a clear distinction between these two). First of all, macrostructures are often directly expressed in the discourse, for example, in titles, thematic sentences, and words or in summaries. Second, their presence in the meaning of a discourse is often signaled in other ways: Pronouns, connectives, adverbs, topic–comment articulation, word order, and so on, often presuppose previous underlying macropropositions and their elements (macropredicates or macroarguments), and cannot be accounted for solely in terms of the meanings of individual previous sentences. Third, the local coherence of discourse, as established between subsequent sentences cannot be fully explained only in terms of local relationships between propositions: Higher level meanings are necessary to establish some form of global organization or control. And, finally, there is no serious reason why an account of such empirically relevant notions as topic, theme, gist, or upshot would fall beyond the boundaries of a linguistic or cognitive semantics, any more than other implied meanings, signaled by sentence structures and sequence structures, such as presuppositions, would be deemed to be outside the scope of semantics.

Of course, this argument does not imply arbitrary extensions of either linguistic or cognitive semantics. Thus, we would not say, for instance, that any personal association connected with the understanding of a discourse would be part of the meaning of a discourse. Similarly, we would not take the vast amounts of knowledge presupposed or implied by the meaning of a text to be part of the semantic representation of that text. Although we do not consider it a wise strategy to circumscribe precisely the scope of linguistic semantics, and certainly not of cognitive semantics, we provisionally assume that the meanings of a discourse should be expressed or signaled, directly or indirectly, by the surface structures of the text. Semantic macrostructures are signaled directly by thematic sentences or words, connectives, pronouns, etc., or else they are expressed indirectly by sequences of sentences.

For a cognitive model such methodological issues may be much less relevant because meanings are constructed out of various knowledge units, that is, cognitive structures. In other words, understanding a discourse is a process of inference making at all levels, both at the levels of word, phrase, and sentence meanings and at the more global level of macrostructures. As Slobin (cited in Bates & MacWhinney, 1982: 187) put it: "Language evokes ideas; it does not represent them." From that perspective, the macrostructure of a discourse is the conceptual global meaning assigned to it. This assignment is based both on textually manifested surface and meaning structures on the one hand and on various knowledge or other purely cognitive structures on the other.

### 6.2.2. Macrostructures as an Organizational Device

Semantic macrostructures of discourse in a cognitive model not only are meant to account for notions such as topic or gist or to explicate aspects of global coherence. They have also been postulated for more fundamental cognitive reasons. Macrorules are also rules of information reduction and organization. Large sequences of complex semantic structures, such as sentences, pictures, natural scenes, or actions, cannot be properly handled without higher level structures of some kind.

When we understand a text, we no longer have access to all previous sentences we have read, and the same holds for the everyday understanding of events and actions, of which the multiple details can only be partially retrieved. If, however, large sequences of semantic structures of this kind can be subsumed by macrorules under a few hierarchically structured macropropositions, and if such macrostructures are a sufficient basis for the further understanding of the discourse, the events, or the actions, then the extremely complex task of keeping some order in the vast amounts of semantic details can be managed. That is, we have (*a*) a common semantic basis to connect (sometimes apparently incoherent) sequences; (*b*) a relatively simple semantic structure which may be kept in short-term memory; (*c*) a device for the hierarchical organization of the sequences in episodic memory; (*d*) an important cue for the actualization of knowledge for longer stretches of discourse, events, or actions; (*e*) powerful retrieval cues for the sometimes necessary reactivation of semantic details; and (*f*) an explicit construction defining the essential, the most important or relevant semantic properties of a discourse or episode. This information is needed for later cognitive tasks (learning, recall, action planning), as well as for monitoring and controlling further discourse processing.

Macrostructures in discourse understanding are far from a luxury: Without them these complex tasks could not possibly be performed. It is therefore striking that, although macrostructures of some kind have been adopted in some models of discourse comprehension (Bower, 1974; Cirilo, 1981; Cirilo & Foss, 1980; Reder & Anderson, 1980; Lehnert, 1980a, Schank & Lehnert, 1979; Vipond, 1980; Graesser, 1981), there are still models that only operate at a local linear level. Note also that macrostructures cannot simply be replaced by hierarchical structures of knowledge, such as frames or scripts. The latter are indeed structures of knowledge and have a general and sometimes stereotypical nature, whereas macrostructures are structures of the discourse itself and therefore are often unique. Thus, although macrostructures are formed with the help of hierarchical knowledge structures, they are by no means identical with them. Only the concepts defining a macroproposition are inferred with the help of world knowledge. We know that going to the airport, checking in, boarding, etc., together are concepts that at a higher level may be organized in the action concept of taking a plane, and we know that dogs, cats, and canaries are instances of pets, and finally we know that many properties or actions which are part of our everyday behavior are merely preparatory or component details of more important states, events, or actions. A crucial aspect of complex understanding, therefore, is higher level concept formation, organization, and hence reduction. This means that the communicative or interactional goals of a discourse or sequence of actions cannot be planned or understood just in terms of final results or terminal states—that is, locally, as those of final sentences or actions—but only as goals of higher level propositions, speech acts, actions. In other words, macrostructures cannot be replaced by some other concept, say, by the notion of goal as it is often used in accounts of action or action discourse and story understanding. Only global purposes or goals, that is, plans, would qualify in this respect, and they are defined in macrostructural terms.

After these more or less general preliminaries and methodological caveats, we are now able to address the question of how language users actually infer macrostructures.

## 6.3. CONTEXTUAL MACROSTRATEGIES

### 6.3.1. Possible Topics and Discourse Types

Given the central importance of macrostructures in the processing of complex information, it is imperative that language users try to make intelligent guesses about what a discourse fragment is about. That is, they will use effective strategies to derive a macroproposition. Unlike macrorules, operating on full sequences, such strategies may only need some hints to make powerful predictions. This is possible only when all relevant information is used to arrive at such hypotheses—not only textual information, but also contextual, as well as much world knowledge. Once inferred in this bottom-up manner, a hypothesized macroproposition may be used as a top-down device to understand subsequent sentences, which, of course, also provide a check on the correctness of the hypothesis.

Not all discourses are equally predictable. But even if the individual sentences are not predictable in detail, many discourses have topics or themes that are more or less stereotypical. Since there are so many regularities in events and actions, the discourses about them may be macrostructurally regular, too. Thus, in news stories we may expect that if the Russians do such and such the Americans will act so and so (Carbonell, 1978). That is, once given a certain theme about some event we may predict what will happen. This is also true of trivial literature (romantic stories, crime stories, spy stories, and so on), and even in psychological research reports. In other words, our knowledge about conditions and consequences in the world will often provide us with expedient expectations about the course of a discourse. Clearly, some discourse types may picture some world of their own, which is not always similar to the real world: A happy ending may be conventionally expected in the text even if in real life we know better.

On the other hand, most discourse types will not be predictable in this way. For obvious pragmatic reasons, most of the information provided needs at least to be new in some way. That is, a discourse will often be about the unpredictable or the unexpected. Everyday stories and news stories will be about the funny, dangerous, or otherwise interesting actions and events of life. A psychological paper or a textbook must provide us with information we did not know and cannot easily predict. Of course, we often have mixed cases: Given an account of an unexpected event or action, our knowledge of the world may supply us with expectations or predictions about what plausibly may follow.

Thus, one type of macrostrategy is based on our knowledge of the world: Because discourse is about real or fictitious possible worlds, about which we already have large amounts of knowledge and beliefs, we know what to expect.

Another set of strategies pertains to our knowledge about certain discourse types. We know what kind of actions or events are typically described in various discourse genres: In news stories we expect political events or actions, or otherwise important events such as disasters, but not a description of uninteresting, trivial everyday actions or events. Thus, it seems that most discourse types have constraints on the set of possible topics, a set which we may call the *topic set* of a discourse type. Clearly, this set is fuzzy, and depends on sociocultural norms, values, and interests. What is interesting or reportable here and today will not be elsewhere or tomorrow.

Topic sets are not limited to discourse types. They may also be associated with a culture or subculture, a communicative context or situation, with roles, functions, or positions of social members, and finally with age, sex, or personality of speakers. Since relevant actions and events differ across cultures, we will speak or write about different things than will the inhabitants of some African village. Similarly, different topics will come up depending on whether we are at the breakfast table, in a restaurant, in a streetcar, in court, or in a linguistics class. We talk about different things with friends or with strangers, with a doctor or with a policeman, with children or adults, with men or with women.

This is all rather obvious. But, strangely enough, there is a lack of systematic research in linguistics, sociology, or anthropology into these topic sets. We have, of course, sound intuitions about the kinds of topics that may be raised during a party or a conversation with a stranger on the bus, but very little is known about the constraints and rules for choosing, introducing, maintaining, and changing a topic, for depth of detail, length, and so on. In classical poetics and rhetorics there has been some attention to the study of *loci communes*, that is, stereotypical topics or themes, both in literature and in public speech (topic analysis—"Toposforschung" of Curtius, 1948). Also, we know that there are many themes—both general ones (death, love, etc.) and particular ones (Faust, Don Juan)—that occur through the literature of a given culture, but little is known about our everyday topics in various situations with various persons. It is a stereotype that certain men will, in informal situations, preferably talk about women, sports cars, business, tax deductions, and so on. It is also well known that each culture has topical taboos: Sex has been the major one in our culture at least for situations with relative strangers.

As discourse is essentially and constitutively part of sociocultural interactions, it will manifest the distribution, variation, and constraints on attention, interests, goals, or styles of such encounters in the form of different topic sets. For our discussion this means that language users can make hypotheses about what will or may be said by whom in what situation, at least globally speaking, that is, at the level of macrostructures. These constraints are so strong that we are seldom completely surprised by the topics chosen in particular situations. And if a stranger on a bus suddenly starts to tell about his or her sex life, or income tax problems, we will usually feel highly uncomfortable: If talk is possible at all in such a situation, then it will be limited first of all to topics related to the bus ride, then perhaps to stereotypical issues (weather), important events (a murder in the town), or other public issues, and only lastly will it extend to personal topics—primarily actual behavior and appearance. Hence, it seems from this example that the topic set is ordered: There will be a hierarchy defined in terms of topic likelihood or acceptability. This probability measure affects our expectations of topics for a specific discourse or discourse fragment, and hence the confidence with which a macroproposition is derived hypothetically even before the discourse or the discourse fragment has begun.

The strategies or strategy steps based on the various types of information that we have informally discussed can be called *contextual* (see also Chapter 3). That is, even without particular information from the discourse itself, language users establish at least topic sets for each communicative situation—topic sets that are progressively constrained by the culture, the social situation, the specific cummunicative event or speech act, the various social dimensions (roles, positions, status; sex, age, etc.) of the speaker, and, finally, the personal characteristics (goals, interests, plans, personality, etc.) of the speaker.

Whereas we have a more or less clear picture of the kinds of information handled by contextual macrostrategies, we still lack insight into their precise forms, order, and other cognitive constraints. Although we cannot go into it here, it is obvious that the selection of possible topics of discourse in the widest sense depends on the organization of our cultural knowledge. Similarly, we probably do not have ready-made lists for topics on the bus, at a party, or at the breakfast table, because the length and the number of such lists would make practical, and hence strategical, use impossible for most situations. Nor is it clear how we know that some topic is not acceptable for a given communicative situation. A negative list does not seem a sound possibility either, although we may have a rather short list of taboos for certain types of situations.

As a basis for contextual macrostrategies we therefore should start at a somewhat more specific level, namely, at the level of the sociocultural and communicative situation. These situations are fairly well defined by type of social context, possible interactions, kinds of agents, and by place or set of objects. The most likely topics for those situations, then, will be those pertaining to the typical events and interactions of such situations. In some cases, such topics are obligatory: In class, in court, or when visiting a doctor we have to say certain things and will usually not be allowed to say others. Giving a talk or giving testimony inherently constrains the possible topic sets for such situations. Besides the typical objects or events which may characterize these situations and which therefore become possible topics, the goals, interests, opinions, or attitudes of the participants will indicate what the particular range of topics should be.

In light of the preceding remarks, we shall now try to systematize the various pieces of contextual information used to derive possible topics or topic sets for discourse or discourse fragment in Table 6.1. This list will be more or less ordered, but depending on the communicative context, a language user may simply skip the most general (cultural) levels. The information categorized in Table 6.1 determines the possible (or impossible) topics of speakers. In order to understand a discourse, a

**Table 6.1**
**Contextual Information for Macrostrategies**

1. *General cultural knowledge*
    a. General activities, goals of cultural group (e.g., agricultural)
    b. Specific events or actions (e.g., rites)
    c. Specific biophysical circumstances (e.g., climate, landscape, animals, plants)
    d. Specific objects (e.g., manufactured instruments)
2. *Sociocultural situation* (part of 1)
    a. Situation type (e.g., breakfast, bus ride, visit, court trial, marriage)
    b. Participant categories
        (i) Functions (bus driver, judge, doctor)
        (ii) Roles (mother, friend)
        (iii) Social properties (sex, age, etc.)
        (iv) Individual properties (character, interests, goals)
    c. Typical events and interactions (help, consult, pay)
    d. Conventions (laws, rules, habits)
3. *Communicative situation* (part of 2)
    a. Overall goals of communicative interaction
    b. Global and local speech acts
    c. Actual referential context (presence of persons, objects)

hearer or reader must represent such speaker-oriented contexts or situations, either on the basis of general knowledge—as in (1) and (2)—or on the basis of actual contextual analysis—as in (3). If speaker and hearer do not share knowledge about the various categories, partial comprehension may be the result. At the global level this means that although individual sentences may be understood, the hearer may fail to grasp what the discourse as a whole is about: Without the general, higher level subsuming concepts, no macroproposition may be formed, and the same holds if some presupposed sociocultural event, action, or situation is presupposed by the speaker but is unknown to the hearer.

## 6.3.2. Strategies for Topic Introduction

The idea underlying the information specified in Table 6.1 is that discourses and their topics do not come out of the blue. Language users must be assumed to be continuously active as social members and as persons in the global and local interpretation of their environment. They apply categories to the situations and interactions they witness or are participating in. Discourses, thus, are primarily seen as functional parts of the communicative, and more general social and cultural, goals of groups and individuals. The topics chosen for such discourses will reflect this functional role both semantically and pragmatically. It is not necessary for a language user to go through the whole list of information for each discourse, or to make complex searches through culturally or socially determined knowledge and beliefs: At the moment of speaking or hearing the language understander will usually possess some representation of the global and local context. In the bank we do not start to construct a context only after the teller has addressed us. We already know we are in the institution of a bank, where we can or should perform such and such actions, that certain categories of people are present, and that the interactions may follow some stereotypical script (e.g., cashing a check). The question "May I see some identification, please?" in that case will not be unexpected at all, but will be partly predictable from the general situation and the script, as well as from previous actions (if we already have shown some identification, we no longer expect this topic to come up again). Thus, the language user as a social member will in general already have a partial representation of the structures mentioned in (1) and (2) of Table 6.1, and sometimes also part of (3), especially if (3) involves communicative interactions which are stereotypical interactions of a given sociocultural context ('going to the bank').

There may be varying degrees of freedom or boundedness for topic sets. Informal, familiar, private, and noninstitutional discourses, for instance, conversations and letters among friends, are practically free: Any speaker may introduce any topic when respecting the local coherence of the conversation (topic change rules). On the other hand, topics in the classroom, in court, at the doctor's, or in church are much more bound, or even completely fixed.

Topic introduction is subject to two kinds of constraints. First, the topics may be determined by the sociocultural situation and communicative context of interacting speaker and hearer, as in the examples that have been given. The other constraint comes from the medium and discourse type involved: Stories, news stories in the press or on television, or novels may be about many things, but the general constraint is that the events reported must be interesting to the audience of the discourse.

Thus, the extremely rich contextual information to be processed for possible topics in a situation is now reduced to a manageable size: The hearer already has a representation in episodic memory of the context, and only has to specify what the interaction goals and therefore the most likely communicative goals are. From there, he or she may make educated guesses about the most likely speech acts, and hence about the global topics, as well as about the specific discourse types. Hierarchically dominant will be those topics that are interactionally bound, and the referential freedom, within a given interaction or speech act type, will be further constrained by beliefs about the speaker's interests (or the speaker's beliefs about the hearer's interests), the degree of familiarity or intimacy, or recent actions or events.

Although these considerations properly belong to a sociology or social psychology of discourse, a cognitive theory of discourse understanding must incorporate a model of language users within the sociocultural and communicative situation, from which interactional and referential constraints can be derived for possible topic sets. The strategies we have informally discussed may now be summarized as follows:

*Contextual Macrostrategy I:* GENERAL CONTEXT DEPENDENCE
Limit semantic searches to the general cultural context of the speaker.

*Contextual Macrostrategy II:* ACTUAL SITUATION DEPENDENCE
Limit topic search to the general properties of the actual situation.

*Contextual Macrostrategy III:* INTERACTION DEPENDENCE
Decide which topics are directly functional for the actualization of the interactional and pragmatic goals of the speaker.

*Contextual Macrostrategy IV:* DISCOURSE TYPE
Decide which topics are characteristic for the discourse type(s) expected in this interactional context.

*Contextual Macrostrategy V:* REFERENTIAL FREEDOM
Given I–IV, decide what objects or events can be talked about by whom in a given speech act and discourse type.

These strategies have been formulated in a very general way. Details were given earlier, as well as some examples of the determinacies and constraints involved. Perhaps Strategy V is superfluous, as it seems to follow from I–VI. However, it is meant to specify those possible topics that are not yet specified by the previous strategies. Thus, Strategy V will limit the possible choice of topics in an everyday conversation, for example, or in a story, depending on the social and personal characteristics of the speaker or the speaker–hearer relationship.

The contextual strategies do not operate alone. They have been discussed merely to show that discourse and hence discourse topics depend to a large extent on the properties of the global or local context. It will be the discourse itself that supplies the ultimate decision about the actual topics, and hence also about the necessary match between text and context.

## 6.4. TEXTUAL MACROSTRATEGIES

Whereas the contextual macrostrategies set up anticipatory expectations about possible discourse topics, the various properties of the text itself provide the definite decisions about the actual topic. Of course, contextual and textual strategies go hand in hand. If a contextual strategy determines a very specific topic, as in highly stereotypical situations, the textual strategies will have a much easier task. This dependence may even be so strong that if text and context do not topically match, the hearer may misunderstand the actualized topic of the discourse.

### 6.4.1. Structural Signals

In order to understand the textual strategies of language users in setting up a topic, both in production and in comprehension, we should recall the nature of semantic macrostructures. These consist of fairly high level macropropositions derived from propositions expressed in the text together with information from world knowledge. In principle, therefore, macropropositions need not show directly in the surface structure of the text, but must be inferred from semantic interpretations of words, phrases, clauses, sentences, or sentence sequences. The major strategy must be a form of semantic inference. Yet, to facilitate such inference discourse usually signals intended macrostructures. As language users will bring to bear different sets of knowledge, beliefs, etc., on the interpretation, it is likely that different macrostructures may be derived. In order to constrain this kind of personal variation in interpretation, speakers use devices to limit the possible global interpretations. One obvious way is to explicitly tell in the discourse itself what the main topics are, that is, by expressing the macropropositions. Such expressions, which we will call topical or thematic, may occur at various locations of the discourse, but preferably at the beginning or end of the text as a whole or at the beginning or end of the relevant episodes or paragraphs.

Topical expressions have specific surface structures: Not only will they typically precede or follow a discourse, or occur at the beginning or end of paragraphs, but they are also expressed in independent sentences, or signaled by larger print, italics, bold type, and are separated from other expressions by pauses or blanks. Highlighting topical sentences can be very effective: For instance, children who were unable to use topic sentences efficiently in finding titles for a paragraph were helped substantially when the topic sentence was graphically highlighted (Williams, Taylor, & Ganger, 1981). Topical expressions may have various lengths, ranging from a sequence of sentences to individual sentences, clauses, phrases, or words. Thus, an initial summary (e.g., the lead in a newspaper story) or a final summary will typically consist of a sequence of sentences, whereas titles will consist of one clause or phrase, and captions of one phrase or one word. Finally, even within nontopical sentences topical expressions, such as key words, are used in order to help the reader infer macropropositions for previous or coming discourse segments.

The initial or final position of topical expressions follows from their semantic functions. At the beginning they help the hearer to form a hypothesis about the topic of the discourse or the episode, so that the following sentences can be interpreted top down relative to that macroproposition, whereas in the final position, topical expressions serve to check, remind, or correct the already established macropropositions of the hearer, as well as to repeat what was already known, so that the hearer has not only hierarchically dominant information but also recent information to search for when the topic is needed in subsequent tasks.

There are differences between unplanned spoken discourse and planned written discourse as far as use of topical expressions. Whereas written discourse forms will very often have titles and subtitles, spoken discourse will have recourse to various forms of topical announcements (e.g., Jefferson, 1978; Quasthoff, 1980): "Did I tell you that story about . . ."; "Did you know that . . . ." Also, spoken discourse may use intonation and stress to underline important or prominent concepts. Furthermore, the communicative situation will be less ambiguous due to the rich contextual information, such as gestures and other paratextual signals, as well as a better mutual understanding of the communicative situation. Finally, topics in spoken discourse, especially in unplanned conversation, have less complexity and are generally shorter than in written discourse, so that there will be less doubt about what the actual topic is. Longer forms of spoken discourse, especially the mono-logical types such as lectures or public address, will tend to have properties of written discourse: (preannounced) titles, summaries, and so on.

The kinds of expressions discussed here do not always express full mac-ropropositions, let alone full macrostructures. In general, only summaries will express macrostructures, whereas titles sometimes express only the top macro-proposition. Other expressions may only refer to major concepts in the macro-propositions, as is the case with captions in news stories. In that case, the result of the strategy is not a macroproposition, but only a fragment thereof, or at least a hint for the actualization of relevant knowledge. Topical expressions, indeed, have a double function in this respect. On the one hand they provide concepts that may constitute macropropositions, and on the other hand they are the input for knowl-edge use strategies (see Chapter 9): They activate domains of knowledge, frames or scripts necessary to understand subsequent sentences and to apply macrorules.

### 6.4.2. Syntactic Strategies

Syntactic signaling is mainly used to indicate local importance and works only secondarily to indicate global importance. Thus, topic–comment or focus assign-ment to sentence structure is not so much an indication of global importance or relevance as it is a rule-governed means of connecting and distributing information between the sentences of a discourse. Just as with phonetic stress distribution, signaling is often based on contrast. Cleft sentence structure in particular is a preferred syntactic means of drawing attention to non-normal and hence locally important information. Topicalization and passive structure may be used for a similar purpose. Another natural way to foreground information is provided by the clausal structure of sentences, especially by the distinction between superordinate and subordinate sentences. However, hierarchical sentence structure also serves to indicate information distribution, like the other syntactic means discussed. In gener-al, first clauses are presupposed, whether subordinate or superordinate. This tends to assign more importance to the final, asserted clause. However, one cannot simply identify importance with newness, that is, with assertion or focus. If the normal rule, the rule defining canonical preferred structures, is that new or focused infor-mation in English comes in final, stressed position, then deviations from this rule may be used to mark contrast, and hence breaches of expectations, indicating local relevance.

Basically, these functions are local ones, however. Syntactic structures may indicate global, thematic importance only indirectly, via cumulative inference. If 'John' plays a prominent role syntactically in several sentences, for example, if 'John' regularly occurs as the sentence subject and in topic position, then he may also be a sequential topic, which may lead to the strategic hypothesis that he is the main character for the text as a whole, hence an agent in the macroproposition.

### 6.4.3. Topic Change Markers

Topical expressions pertain both to macrostructures for the discourse as a whole and to topically coherent parts of discourse, so-called episodes. An episode is a sequence of sentences dominated by a macroproposition. A number of authors have used the "episode" concept, or similar ones such as "paragraph," both in linguistics (e.g., Longacre, 1979; Hinds, 1979; van Dijk, 1982b) and in psychology (Black & Bower, 1980; Haberlandt, Berian, & Sandson, 1980). Episodes may be marked in different ways. A well-known surface structure mark is paragraph indentation, or a pause in spoken discourse. Besides these surface structure signals, an episode will often be introduced in semantically conspicuous ways. Since by definition each episode is subsumed by a different macroproposition, we may expect different agents, places, times, objects, or possible worlds to be introduced at the beginning of an episode. Thus, one way to signal topics in a discourse is to signal topic change, namely, the transition from one topic to another in different episodes. Examples of topic change markers at the beginning of new episodes are:

1. Change of possible world: *X dreamt, pretended, . . . that . . .*
2. Change of time or period: *The next day, . . . The following year . . .*
3. Change of place: *(In the meantime) in Amsterdam, . . .*
4. Introduction of new participants
5. Full noun phrase reintroduction of old participants
6. Change of perspective or point of view
7. Different predicate range (change of frame or script)

The general strategy, thus, is that if some sentence no longer can be subsumed under a current macroproposition, a new macroproposition will be set up, of which the change markers are the respective partial expressions.

Macropropositions as exhibited in the different episodes of a discourse must also be properly connected, just as propositions expressed by sentences are connected. This means that their connections may be directly expressed, for example, by connectives, by conjunctions, or adverbs. In addition to the list of episode markers given here we characteristically find *macroconnectives* such as sentence-initial *but, however, on the contrary, moreover,* etc. at the beginning of episodes. Not only do macroconnectives signal new macropropositions, they also assign the necessary coherence structure to the macrostructure as a whole. This structure may be the usual conditional one (cause, consequences), or it may be functional as well. Subsequent episodes may give a specification, an example, a contrast, etc., of the previous episode. In that case they will be hierarchically subordinate to the previous episode.

### 6.4.4. Semantic Strategies

With the discussion of topic change markers which may be used to set up new macropropositions, we have already introduced a number of purely semantic strategies for macrostructure inference. Whereas macropropositions may be directly expressed, they can be properly inferred only from underlying semantic representations. Hence, it is the meaning of words, phrases, and sentences that will provide the major cues for the derivation of topics.

Given the specific monitoring role of macropropositions, we must assume that language users will try to derive the relevant macroproposition of a passage as soon as possible—though they may not always be able to do so, as we shall show in Section 7 of this chapter. If possible, they will not wait until they have already understood, locally, a full sequence of sentences, but start to make macrohypotheses as soon as one sentence, or even one clause, has been interpreted. In some cases, partial macrointerpretation may even occur after one phrase. If a story starts with the sentence: *John . . . . ,* it may be provisionally assumed that the story will be about John, so that we already have one participant for the macroproposition. Yet, a full macroproposition—that is, a topic or theme in our terms—can be derived only with a clause expressing a proposition, so that possible world, time, place, and kind of predicate (action, event), or other participants—and participant roles—are known. If initial clauses or sentences are relatively general, they may be provisionally taken as topical, in the sense discussed earlier. At the other extreme are those initial sentences that merely express one, relatively unimportant, detail of a sequence, such as *It was a beautiful day.* In between are initial sentences that at least introduce participants, time, and place, where the predicate concept will give a first idea about the kind of state, action, or event involved, and hence also about the more global state, action, or event concept that might figure in the macroproposition:

(1)    *John wondered where he would spend his holidays that year.*
(2)    *Mary hadn't seen her grandma for a long time now.*
(3)    *Listen, Harry, are you free tonight?*

From such initial sentences much information can already be inferred about possible topics for the discourse. Not only may predicates be interpreted as states, actions, or events to be subsumed under more general ones, but also our world knowledge tells us which of these states, actions, or events are typical motivations or conditions for others. Finally, various circumstantials of the first sentence or first clause will provide cues for the establishment of the possible world, time, and place categories of a macroproposition.

The various macrohypotheses thus derived from the semantic structure of the first clause or sentence must be confirmed by the interpretation of subsequent clauses and sentences. According to the strategies for local coherence establishment, a fast check will be made about the assumed sameness of place, time, and participants. In case of coreferential identity we have a first confirmation of the macrostructural relevance of these categories. For the interpretation of a predicate in the next sentence, a strategy will establish whether this next predicate can be subsumed under the same more global predicate tentatively inferred from the predicate in the previous sentence, as in 'going on a holiday' in (1) or 'going out' in (3).

If no predicate can be derived yet, the two predicates together may yield enough information for the derivation of a macropredicate in the second sentence, such as 'going to the beach' in the following sequence:

(4)     *It was a hot day today. They hadn't been to the beach for a long time. . . .*

If the sequence of sentences that cannot be subsumed under a tentative macroproposition grows longer, the hearer or reader might have problems. Only local coherence may hold in that case, but no monitoring macroproposition will be there to relate the respective propositions at a higher level. Strictly speaking, this will result in partial interpretations, and the language user will then resort to a wait-and-see strategy: As soon as a sentence is interpreted which provides cues for a topic, the partially interpreted proposition sequence may be retrieved or—post hoc— assigned a macrostructural role.

It is obvious that in any case the function of organized world knowledge is crucial in the inference of macropropositions. If states, actions, or events are mentioned that are part of a knowledge frame or script, it will be easy to derive a macroproposition by instantiating the general proposition covering the script or part of the script. But also more general knowledge, as we suggested earlier, about conditional relations between events, actions, or states of affairs, will be drawn from world knowledge in order to derive expectations about what kind of information may subsume the sequence as a whole.

### 6.4.5. Schematic Strategies

Finally, besides the surface structural and semantic information discussed so far, schematic or superstructural information may strategically help the derivation of macropropositions. This is because, first of all, many schematic structures, such as those of a narrative, have a normal or canonical ordering, and second, because the schematic categories have global semantic constraints. If, indeed, the beginning of a story is schematically organized by a setting, for example, we also know that the first macroproposition(s) may denote a state description, introducing participants, place and time specifications, and backgrounds or motivations for the events or actions that follow. In the next chapter we will study in more detail this link between semantic and schematic global strategies.

### 6.5. MACROSTRATEGIES IN ACTION: SOME EXAMPLES

In order to make the theory of macrostrategies more concrete we shall examine a number of examples here. We shall return, of course, to our news report on Guatemala and provide a detailed analysis of its macrostructure. However, we also want to consider some rather different types of texts. First, we shall analyze the beginnings of some literary texts, to show how macrostrategies operate on the basis of the semantic content of the first few sentences in these stories. Finally, after turning to our *Newsweek* text we shall discuss a quite different example, namely, a conversation, where the communicative and pragmatic context must be reconstructed from the situation.

### 6.5.1. Literary Discourse

Our first examples are drawn from an anthology of short stories (Pickering, 1978):

(5) *Sunlight on his face woke him, but made him shut his eyes again; it streamed unhindered down the slope, collected itself into rivulets, attracted swarms of flies, which flew low over his forehead, circled, sought to land, and were overtaken by fresh swarms. When he tried to whisk them away he discovered that he was bound. A thin rope cut into his arms* . . . [Aichinger, "The Bound Man," p. 1].

(6) *We got up at four in the morning, that first day in the East. On the evening before, we had climbed off a freight train at the edge of town and with the true instinct of Kentucky boys had found our way across town and to the race track and to the stables at once. Then we knew we were allright. Hanley Turner right away found a nigger we knew* . . . [Anderson, "I Want to Know Why," p. 9].

(7) *"You are full of nightmares," Harriet tells me. She is in her dressing gown and has cream all over her face. She and my older sister, Louisa, are going out to be girls together. I suppose they have many things to talk about—they have **me** to talk about, certainly—and they do not want my presence. I have been given a bachelor's evening. The director of the film which has brought us such incredible and troubling riches will be along later to take me out to dinner. I watch her face* . . . [Baldwin, "This Morning, This Evening, So Soon," p. 15].

(8) *Beginning: in the middle, past the middle, nearer three quarters done, waiting for the end. Consider how dreadful so far: passionless, abstraction, pro, dis. And it will get worse. Can we possibly continue?* . . . [Barth, "Title," p. 38].

The first two stories begin, rather typically, with a 'getting up in the morning' scene. Instead of a normal continuation in (5) about the usual routine following the moment of waking up, we have a description of the cause of this event, namely, the sunlight. A possible macroproposition which could be inferred from the first sentence therefore is not (yet) confirmed by the next sentences. In (6) we have a flashback to the previous day instead of a description of the getting up in the morning script.

Thus, in (5) the story starts with an environmental description: sunlight and flies. By Macrorule 1 (deletion), such descriptions, if not directly functional for the rest of the story, will be deleted. Important is only the fact that somebody woke up and that he discovers that he is bound by a rope. It is therefore doubtful whether a macroproposition, except 'He woke up', is being formed for the beginning of (5). At most we might also have 'He was bothered by flies'. That proposition may be more or less functional with respect to the fact that the person discovers that he is bound, namely, by being unable to chase away the flies. Only the proposition that he was bound is out of the normal and hence interesting, and it will therefore be taken as a provisional macroproposition (probably presignaled already by the title of the story: "The Bound Man"). And, indeed, the following sentence starts to give a description of the way he was bound by a rope. We discover that besides the strategy of finding an interesting macroproposition that would subsume subsequent propositions, we have a strategy that directly deletes information from the macro-structure, under the assumption that this will probably just be descriptive detail of the circumstances. If necessary, such information may later be retrieved in case it appears to be more relevant than was originally assumed by the reader (e.g., if the rest of the story is about flies).

In (6) we have a typical change of scene, namely an explanation of 'how we got to the city (in the East)', which by Macrorule 3 (construction) can be taken as a normal condition for 'being in the city now,' which is again a circumstance descrip-tion of the place of subsequent actions. Such a macroproposition may be used as a normal part of the complex macroproposition under the category of location. Then, an idea is given of the reasons for coming to the city: the horse races. And finally, from the first noun phrase of the first sentence, being a subject and expressing an agent, the expression *we* introduces the possible agent for the macroproposition— specified in a later sentence with at least one participant ('Hanley Turner') in this group, and a possible coparticipant ('a nigger') introduced with an indefinite de-scription in object (patient) position. From these two examples we see that in literary prose we sometimes need to apply a wait-and-see strategy before we are able to derive a strategically useful macroproposition: Environmental description, explanations, or backgrounds may come first, possibly with the introduction of at least one macroparticipant.

In (7) the initial scene starts with the beginning of a 'going out' script, in which two women and a central participant ('I') are being introduced. Since the plans of the participants are explicitly expressed, we may assume that propositions such as 'I am going out with a film director' or 'I'll have my bachelor's night' can be derived as topics, as well as 'She (my friend) is going out' as a parallel topic. It cannot yet be decided which of these themes will dominate the rest of the story. This means that in addition to what we have assumed earlier, the beginning of a story may give rise to alternative or parallel macropropositions, which later can be confirmed or not.

Example (8) is more troublesome. The abstractness of the description as yet hardly allows the derivation of a macroproposition: We have no idea what the passage could be about. This is typical for literary prose and poetry, and it will turn out later that this description is about the act of writing itself. In that case, the later information should provide the theme so that earlier information can be picked up as one aspect of the theme, for example, 'that it is difficult, or unsatisfactory.' Maybe we have, instead of a precise initial macroposition, just some emotional impression, possibly categorizable under such concepts as 'difficult action'.

### 6.5.2. A Macroanalysis of the *Newsweek* Text

The role of macrostructure formation for news discourse is absolutely crucial, more so than for stories which we read for our entertainment or for conversations (to which we turn in the next section). The general communicative function of news is to create or update situation models: We want to know new things about situations about which we have heard or read before, or about new situations, often linked with or similar to previous ones. The news input, however, is vast, and we need to select: Macrostructure formation is the primary mechanism enabling us to do so.

Newspaper discourse is organized in such a way that it presents powerful cues to the reader for the inference of macrostructures: Headlines, initial position, bold print, lead or initial thematic sentences—all express the macrostructures of the text, as intended by the journalist. Of course, each reader may apply his or her own strategies of macrostructure formation and the resultant macrostructure may be rather different from the one expressed in the headlines or leads of the newspaper text. But this will presuppose specific knowledge, interests, and goals. The average newspaper reader will for the majority of news articles just follow the cues as presented by the text.

Our *Newsweek* text (see front endpapers) exhibits some of the features mentioned above. It has a headline: *Guatemala: No Choices,* and a (metaphorical) initial position thematic sentence, followed by a high-level first paragraph describing the general political situation in Guatemala as compared to that in El Salvador. We may assume that the reader knows the general schema of news discourse (to which we will turn in the next chapter) and constructs his or her first macropropositions on the basis of these cues: title, initial position sentence, and first paragraph. These, therefore, are expected to present the most important, summarizing information, which will be specified progressively in the body of the article.

Headlines or titles, as in our example, present some information about the relevant macrostructure, but this information will often be partial or vague. In our text, the reader may safely infer that the text will be about Guatemala, and therefore that Guatemala will be the major discourse referent of the text. However, the expression *no choice* is vague, and would lead only to a macropredicate such as 'there is a problem (in G)', or 'there is a predicament'. We have seen that the first sentence of the text does not yield very much more than the overall interpretation that Guatemala is compared with El Salvador, and that the political situation in Guatemala is a 'black and white' one. This calls for specification in more concrete political terms, and these are indeed provided in the next sentences.

In addition to these textual cues, many readers will also have an existing model about the political situation in Guatemala which will play a role in the process of macrostructure formation. The reader's opinions, beliefs, and ideology are also relevant, and we shall point to their effects, even though we cannot model these aspects of the comprehension process explicitly.

In Table 6.2 we have outlined a plausible processing sequence illustrating the strategic derivation of the macrostructure for the *Newsweek* text, starting with the rather vague macroproposition from the headline of the article and from preknowledge about the situation. In the first column we present the expressed propositions, as constructed by the local interpretation processes. These constitute the input to the macrostrategies. In Column A we list possible higher level macropropositions. Note that the macroproposition does not always change when a new text proposition is formed: The text may simply be confirming the existing macroproposition (e.g., the same macroproposition dominates $S_{12}$–$S_{15}$). Topic changes result in new (provisional) macropropositions. Apart from the local meaning of words and sentences, the reader will also use other information in the text to infer a topic change, such as paragraph boundaries, subtitles, or any changes in place, time, participants, or type of action.

Macropropositions, just like any other kind of propositions, are organized schematically. Hence, the reader will inspect the text cues and the local semantics in order to find the major possible categories for a macroschema, such as the macropredicate, the respective macroparticipants, and the time or location of the whole macroevent.

Similarly, macropropositions once formed need to be linked coherently, just like the local textbase. Hence, functional and conditional relations among macropropositions must be established, yielding a specific *macrotext level*, that is, a sequence of macropropositions of the same level of generality. This level may again be the input for the application of further macrorules, and produce a still higher level, and so on until the general topic of the text is derived. In Table 6.3 we therefore apply the macrostrategies again on the information yielded by the macrostructure obtained from the first-level strategies described in Table 6.2.

In order to know which information does need a place in a macroproposition schema, the reader must apply strategic macrooperations. In our text, for instance, the reader must decide that the reference to Brazil, France, South Korea, or Romania is irrelevant at a higher level, and that this information can simply be reduced to '(arms from) several countries'—which is precisely one of the macrostrategies, namely, generalization. Similarly, the reader will have to decide on line which information is probably subsidiary and not a likely candidate for being taken up in a macroproposition, so that deletion becomes possible. For instance, it seems irrelevant that the right-wingers in Guatemala hired marimba bands and set off firecrackers on the night Reagan was elected. Such information may be deleted right away, or be taken as an instance of a scriptlike, culture-specific way of showing happiness, which is a relevant aspect of the theme of the text: They welcomed the election of Reagan, at least at first. We see that, although macrostrategies use operations similar to the formal macrorules, they do so only provisionally, and with a limited and variable input, both from the text and from general world knowledge. It is this world knowledge—about politics, news, *Newsweek,* and the situation in

**Table 6.2**
**Macrostrategies in the Comprehension of the *Newsweek* Text**

| Propositional input as expressed by sentences | Provisional macro-operation | A. Provisional macroproposition(s) | Specific macrocues | B. Knowledge, beliefs opinions, attitudes |
|---|---|---|---|---|
| Title: GUATEMALA: NO CHOICES | ZERO (SELECTION) | There are no (political) choices in G. (1)<br>There is no solution to the problems in G.<br><br>(Overall macroproposition) | Title/Headline<br>First position<br>Bold, large type | 1. POLITICS frame<br>2. Guatemala frame<br>3. Central America episodic model<br>4. Guatemala ep. model<br>5. US foreign policy ep. model<br>6. Att.: PRO US-policy or AGAINST US-policy |
| $S_1$ | GENERALIZATION or ZERO | (Metaphorical interpr.)<br>The political situation in G. is more extreme than in ES (2) | First sentence<br>Mention of important referents (G.,ES) | Specify B.3,4 |
| $S_2$ | DELETION GENERALIZATION | There are unorganized communists on the left (3) | Opinion diplomat is irrelevant | 7. Specify B1 and B5: COMMUNISM frame |
| $S_3$ | DELETION | On the right is an elite who has the power and who was helped by US (4) | History and specif. names are irr. | 8. Epis. knowl: history of G.<br>9. CIA frame |
| $S_4$ | DELETION GENERALIZATION | Political center has been murdered by regime in G., but still exists in ES (5) | Specifics irr. (30,000 victims) | 10. B1 specified: FASCIST frame Mass murders<br>11. Spec. B3: sit. in ES<br>12. Opinion: typical fascist actions |
| $S_5$ | ZERO DELETION | = (2) | Opinion diplomat irrelevant | |
| $S_6$ | ZERO | = (4) and (1) | REPETITION<br>End of paragraph | |

*(continued)*

211

**Table 6.2** (*Continued*)

| Propositional input as expressed by sentences | Provisional macro-operation | A. Provisional macroproposition(s) | Specific macrocues | B. Knowledge, beliefs opinions, attitudes |
|---|---|---|---|---|
| $S_7$ | DELETION | G. regime first welcomed election of Reagan (6) | History and details irrel. Referent: Reagan New paragraph (head) | 13. Ep. model B5: Carter's policy 14. B6: Att. PRO/AGAINST Reagan |
| $S_8$ | DELETION CONSTRUCTION | G's regime had counted on R's administration's help (7) | Names and details irr. | 15. US government frame (White House) 16. BUSINESS frame: relations with conservative regime |
| $S_9$ | ZERO | G's regime now disappointed about R.'s adm. (8) | General predicate (conclusion about actual situation) | 17. B5: US foreign policy favors more moderate conserv. |
| $S_{10}$ | GENERALIZATION | G's regime does not like demands from US for political moderation (8) | | 18. =B17 |
| $S_{11}$ | DELETION | US has no influence in G. (10) | Opinion diplomat irr. | 19. B1: if a country criticizes other country, then there will be loss of influence |
| $S_{12}$ | GENERALIZATION CONSTRUCTION | G's regime acts negatively towards US represent. (11) | New paragraph Head | 20. B15: Congress frame |
| $S_{13}$ | CONSTRUCTION | =(11) | All actions of G's regime are blocking US goals | 21. B7: COMMUNISM frame B10: FASCISM frame |
| $S_{14}$ | CONSTRUCTION | =(11) | | 22. Ep. model: R. sent Walters to G. |

| | Operation | Description | Note | Rules / Frame |
|---|---|---|---|---|
| $S_{15}$ | CONSTRUCTION | =(11) | | 23. B5: US usually backs anti-communist wars |
| $S_{16}$ | DELETION | G's regime thinks they fight a US war alone (12) | Opinion irr. | |
| $S_{17}$ | DELETION/ZERO | G's regime will fight also without US help (12) | | |
| $S_{18}$ | DELETION | =(12) | REPETITION New paragraph | 24. WAR script PREPARATIONS: arms |
| $S_{19}$ | CONSTRUCTION | G's regime acquired arms from many countries (13) | After $S_{18}(=S_{17})$ Initial sentence of new paragraph | 25. Military industry B24 (WAR SCRIPT) |
| $S_{20}$ | CONSTRUCTION, or SELECTION | =(13) Also Israel helps (14) | but, principal | 26. Israel frame 27. Ep. model: Israel even helps fascist regimes with weapons 28. Att. how can anti-fascist country help fascist regimes? |
| $S_{21}$ | CONSTRUCTION | = ($S_{14}$) | Details of weapons from Isr. | 29. B24. Weapons. |
| $S_{22}$ | CONSTRUCTION | = ($S_{14}$) | Other details of military aid | 30. B24. Personnel training |
| $S_{23}$ | CONSTRUCTION DELETION | G. uses US military equipment (14b) | Result of no embargo | 31. B5 (US foreign policy) B24 (Weapons) |
| $S_{24}$ | ZERO | (see A9) Difficult relation between G's regime and R. adm. (15) | Still New paragraph | 32. B10: US prefers moder. |

*(continued)*

213

**Table 6.2** (*Continued*)

| Propositional input as expressed by sentences | Provisional macro-operation | A. Provisional macroproposition(s) | Specific macrocues | B. Knowledge, beliefs opinions, attitudes |
|---|---|---|---|---|
| | | (see A5): G's regime commits mass murders (16) | Reintrod. Reagan | |
| $S_{25}$ | GENERALIZATION | | First sentence new paragraph | 33. . B10: FASCIST frame Mass murders |
| $S_{26}$ | CONSTRUCTION (consequence) | (16) | Specification of numbers | B10 |
| | | (16) | Detail of murders in media | B10 |
| $S_{27}$ | CONSTRUCTION (component acts) | (16) | Agents of murders | B10: Death squads, right wing, government backed (34) |
| $S_{28}$ | CONSTRUCTION | (16) | Victims also from US | B10 |
| $S_{29}$ | CONSTRUCTION | (16) | Innocent victims | B10,B33 |
| $S_{30}$ | CONSTRUCTION | (16) | Murderers blame opponents | B10 Try to blame victim (35) |
| $S_{31}$ | CONSTRUCTION DELETION | (16) | Details irr. | B10 |
| $S_{32}$ | ZERO | (16) | Repetition | B10 |
| $S_{33}$ | ZERO/DELETION | (16) does not daunt guerrilla opponents (17) | New paragraph Head: *Hydra* Change of disc. referent: guerrilla | 36. B4 Guerrilla frame. |

| | | | | |
|---|---|---|---|---|
| S$_{34}$ | GENERALIZATION or CONSTRUCTION | Guerilla now joined forces (18) | | B36. Condition of success for guerilla: unite |
| S$_{35}$ | CONSTRUCTION (component acts) | (17) | Details of fight irr. | B36. Bombing |
| S$_{36}$ | CONSTRUCTION or GENERALIZATION | Guerilla backed by Communist countries (19) | | B7, B36 COMMUNISM frame Guerrilla backed by communist countries |
| S$_{37}$ | CONSTRUCTION | (19) | Details of aid | B7, B24 WAR script Ep. model: Soviet help |
| S$_{38}$ | CONSTRUCTION | (19) | Fights/results | B36. Guerrilla frame Regime fights back |
| S$_{39}$ | CONSTRUCTION | (19) | Fights/results | B36 |
| S$_{40}$ | ZERO | (1) | New par. TITLE Referent: US | B5 (US policy) |
| S$_{41}$ | GENERALIZATION | (2) No centrist solution, like in ES (20) | Referent: centrists | B1–B5 El Salvador, Christian Democrats Ep. model: situation in ES |
| S$_{42}$ | GENERALIZATION or CONSTRUCTION | Also political center is massacred (21) | Details of reason for 20. | B10: Fascist murders |
| S$_{43}$ | CONSTRUCTION | (21) | Details of murders | B10 |
| S$_{44}$ | CONSTRUCTION | (21) | Reaction to (21) | B1, B10, B5 |
| S$_{45}$ | CONSTRUCTION | (21) helps left (22) | Conclusion | B1, B4, B7. Popular support. |
| S$_{46}$ | GENERALIZATION | Will US help G's regime? (23) which is brutal? (=A5, A16, A21) | Final sentence TITLE: What choice? | B5, B23 (US backs anti-comm) |

**Table 6.3**
**Higher Level Macrostrategies for the *Newsweek* Text**

| First level macropropositions | Provisional macro-operations | Second level macropropositions | Knowledge and beliefs | Higher level macropropositions |
|---|---|---|---|---|
| $M_1$ | ZERO | $M_1^2$ There are no political choices in G. | 1. US foreign policy frame | $M_1^n$ There are no political choices in G |
| $M_2$ | ZERO | $M_2^2$ Situation in G. more extreme than in ES | 2. General and episodic about G. and ES. | $\emptyset$ |
| $M_3$ | DELETION/ZERO | $M_3^2$ On the left is a communist guerrilla | 3. POLITICS frame 4. COMMUNISM frame | $M_2^n$ On the left is a communist guerrilla. |
| $M_4$ | ZERO | $M_4^2$ On the right is elite with power, backed by US | (1) 5. FASCIST frame | $M_3^n$ On the right is elite with power, backed by US. |
| $M_5$ | DELETION | $M_5^2$ Political center has been murdered by regime. | (5) | $M_4^n$ Regime murders opponents |
| $M_6$ | DELETION | $\emptyset$ | | |
| $M_7$ | DELETION | $\emptyset$ | | |
| $M_8$ | DELETION | $\emptyset$ | | |

| | | | | |
|---|---|---|---|---|
| $M_9$ ($M_6$, $M_7$, $M_8$) | ZERO | $M_6^2$ Regime opposed to US demands for moderation | (1), (3) | $\emptyset$ |
| $M_{10}$ | ZERO | $\emptyset$ | (1) | $\emptyset$ |
| $M_{11}$ | ZERO | $M_7^2$ Regime acts negatively against US | (1) | $M_5^n$ Regime in G. opposes actual US policy ($M_6^2$, $M_7^2$) |
| $M_{12}$ | GENERALIZATION | $M_7^2$ Regime fights guerrilla | 6. WAR frame. Weapons | $M_6^n$ Regime fights guerrilla |
| $M_{13}$ | CONSTRUCTION | $M_7^2$ (preparation) | (1) | |
| $M_{14}$ | CONSTRUCTION | $M_7^2$ (preparation) | | |
| $M_{15}$ | ZERO | $M_6^2$ (consequence) | (1) | $M_5^n$ |
| $M_{16}$ | ZERO | $M_8^2$ Regime commits mass murders | (5) | $M_4^n$ |
| $M_{17}$ | GENERALIZATION | $M_9^2$ Guerrilla fights back | 7. Guerrilla frame | $M_7^n$ Guerrilla fights back |
| $M_{18}$ | CONSTRUCTION | $M_9^2$ (condition) | (7) | $M_7^n$ |
| $M_{19}$ | ZERO | $M_{10}^2$ Guerrilla backed by communist countries | (4), (7) | $\emptyset$ |
| $M_{20}$ | ZERO | $M_{11}^2$ No centrist solution like in ES | (3) | $M_8^n$ There is no centrist solution |
| $M_{21}$ | ZERO | $M_5^2$ | (3) | $M_4^n$ |
| $M_{22}$ | DELETION | $\emptyset$ | | $\emptyset$ |
| $M_{23}$ | ZERO | $M_{11}^2$ Will US back brutal regime? | (1) | $M_3^n$ |

Central America—which provides the necessary information that the marimba bands and the firecrackers are most unlikely to further organize the information of the text as a whole (as would be the case, perhaps, in a local newspaper covering the events of Reagan's election night). In Table 6.1 we therefore need a further column (3) specifying at least a fragment of this general knowledge, the kind of frames and scripts involved, or the stereotypical scenes that may occur in many scripts, such as the MOPs discussed by Schank (1979b).

Macropropositions ultimately organize sequences of propositions of the textbase in episodic memory. Such sequences we have called *episodes* (van Dijk, 1982b). Often, they are signaled in surface structure by paragraph indentation in written discourse, or pauses in spoken discourse, as well as by the subheadings we mentioned earlier, or the change, at the semantic level, of participants, places, time, or type of action. Also, new episodes may be signaled by specific grammatical words, such as *still* in $S_{24}$ of our text, by full definite expressions instead of pronouns (see Marslen-Wilson *et al.*, 1982), or nominalizations of previous macropropositions, such as 'the wholesale killing' in $S_{33}$ of our text.

In Table 6.4 we present summaries expressing the three levels of the macro-

---

**Table 6.4**
**Possible Summaries for *Newsweek* Text**

1. *Long summary.* Because the political situation in Guatemala is more extreme than in El Salvador, there are no political choices. There are unorganized groups of communists on the left, and on the right is an elite helped to power by the U.S. Unlike the situation in El Salvador, the political center has been murdered in Guatemala. Although the regime first had welcomed Reagan's election and had counted on aid from his administration, they are now disappointed because of the continuing U.S. demands for political moderation. Therefore the U.S. has little influence in Guatemala and the Guatemalan regime frustrates U.S. diplomacy. The regime will fight the guerrillas without U.S. help, and has acquired arms from many countries, in particular from Israel, adding to the U.S. military equipment they already have. The relations between the U.S. and Guatemala are strained especially because of the mass murders committed by the Guatemalan regime. The actions of the regime, however, have not daunted the guerrilla groups, which have now joined forces and receive aid from communist countries. There is no centrist solution in Guatemala, like the one that may be possible in El Salvador, because the political center has been massacred by the regime, which, of course, will help the guerrillas. Will the U.S. continue backing this kind of brutal regime?

2. *Short summary (second level).* Since the political situation in Guatemala is more extreme than in El Salvador, there are no political choices. On the left are communist guerrillas, and on the right an elite, backed by the U.S., whereas the political center has been murdered by the regime. The recent U.S. demands for political moderation have been ignored and the regime frustrates U.S. policy. They continue to fight the guerrillas on their own, committing mass murders. The guerrillas, backed by communist countries, fight back. Therefore, there does not seem to be a centrist solution like in El Salvador, but will the U.S. support a brutal regime?

3. *Shortest (higher level) summary.* In Guatemala there are no political choices. On the left are communist guerrillas, and on the right an elite regime, backed by the U.S., which has murdered its (centrist) opponents. The regime, ignoring U.S. demands for moderation, continues on its own to fight the guerrillas who, however, resist successfully. A centrist solution is impossible.

structure derived in Tables 6.2 and 6.3. Obviously, these are not the only summaries that could be derived from these textbases: Any paraphrase would in principle be acceptable, with wide stylistic variations, though actual readers summarizing a text would normally imitate the style of the original article.

Similar remarks need to be made with respect to the macrostructure that we have derived in Tables 6.1 and 6.2: This is only one possible macrostructure, derived from our analysis of the text with an objective attitude, that tries to be faithful to the intentions of the author. Quite different macrostructures (and eventually summaries) would result if a reader with strong political opinions subjectively interprets the text (e.g., imagine how ideologically committed readers, such as participants on the right or left in the Guatemalan civil war would summarize this text).

### 6.5.3. Conversation

Finally, let us briefly examine an example of natural, spontaneous, everyday conversation. The fragment has been supplied for analysis by Schegloff (1979). The first part of the conversation between two girls who have known each other for a long time is about teachers they used to have at the same school before Bee went to another school. Then, Bee starts to talk about a teacher she has now:

```
(9)                        (0.2)
  198   Bee:  nYeeah, `hh This feller I have-(nn)."felluh" ; this ma:n.
                                         (iv-)
  199         (0.2) t!`hhh He ha::(s)- uff-eh-who-who I have fer
  200         linguistics [is   real]ly too much, `hh[h=
  201   Ava:              [Mm hm?]                    [Mm[hm,
  202   Bee:                                             [=I didn` notice it
  203         b`t there`s a woman in my class who`s a nurse `n. `hh she
  204         said to me she s`d didju notice he has a ha:ndicap en I
  205         said wha:t. Youknow I said I don`t see anything wrong
  206         wi[th im, she says his ha:nds.=
  207   Ava:    [Mm.
  208   Bee:  =`hhh So the nex` cla:ss hh! `hh fer en hour en f`fteen
  209         minutes I sat there en I watched his ha:n(h)ds hh
  210         hh `hhh=
```

This is just the beginning of the conversation, which continues about the way the teacher holds his fingers around the chalk and the fact that the woman in the class has experience with handicapped people.

Important for our observations is that this kind of story does not come from nowhere. It is triggered by other thematic elements in the conversation—here, for instance, the kind of experiences, teachers, classes, etc., the girls have or have had in their schools. Under that general conversation topic, we may have a more local topic, namely, a story about a particular teacher. This story is introduced with the filler expression *n Yeeah* in Line 198, which marks, after the 0.2 pause, the continuation of the same global conversation topic and which may also introduce a next subtopic. This subtopic is actually introduced with the reference to the major participant (as an object for discussion) of the story: *This feller*, a term which is then corrected to *this man*, perhaps because the story about him (being handicapped) requires the more neutral concept of man as 'feller' may be interpreted negatively. Another repair hastens to add that he is a linguistics teacher, which is a necessary detail in the topic of the conversation as a whole (type of classes and teachers are usually given), before the story may mention the specific of this teacher (*He ha::(s)*). Then Bee opts for a more dramatic introduction of the main predicate of the story: Instead of saying that he has handicapped hands, she traces back to the discovery of the relevant facts (*I didn' notice it b't there's a woman in my class . . .*), introducing another participant (the nurse) in the story, and then a reported dialogue with that woman about the hands of the teacher. For the hearer (Ava) this means that she has been able to establish a main participant for the macroproposition (a linguistics teacher), and that there is something noticeable about him. But only in Line 204 is the central predicate—namely, that he has a handicap—actually expressed. Both for this embedded story and in the conversation as a whole, this thematic predicate is interesting and therefore also marked in the (reported) conversation with extra stress. The interestingness is enhanced by the incredibility tag *I said wha:t* and its motivation (*I don't see anything wrong*) upon which the nurse in the reported dialogue finally introduces the topical item (*ha:nds*), also with particular stress and a long vowel.

From these few observations we see that in natural conversation a new topic may be introduced (*a*) after a pause, (*b*) after specific boundary or linking signals (*Yeah*), (*c*) by first introducing the major referent of the episode, and then (*d*) the major predicate or other participants. Typically, all those topical elements are signaled by heavy initial stress (on first consonant or syllable) or lengthened vowels. Also, in stories, instead of telling what happened from the actual perspective, the storyteller may dramatize the events by relocating the perspective to the time and place at which they occurred, by introducing the relevant topic in a reported conversation, and by rhetorical devices, such as the incredibility tag, perhaps used to make the reported event more interesting (while unbelievable). Together, these devices signal for the hearer that we have the following approximate macroproposition for this story: 'We had a linguistics teacher with handicapped hands'. Notice, also, that the story is organized in terms of narrative categories (Clark, 1983). Thus, Lines 198–199 function as a proper setting for the story, then from Line 202 onward we have the complication, and, finally, in Line 208 a transition to the resolution (Bee's seeing that the man is indeed handicapped) and from Line 219 onward (a segment not reproduced here) an evaluation of the teacher, his handicap, and the consequences for the class (*they're usually harder markers*).

As in this conversation we already have a partial macrostructure ready ('my teachers') the fragment in question need not be oriented toward this general topic participant. Conversely, had the topic been 'handicapped people I know', then the fact that it was a college teacher would become more prominent. Also, in our example the central predicate of the macroproposition is not announced but dramatically and rhetorically delayed to make the story more effective. Often, in everyday stories, the teller will first bring up the interesting topic of the story, so that other speakers will become interested and thus willing to yield the floor for some time (notice, too, that in our example Bee can continue at length, encouraged only by *Mmhhmms*'s of Ava, or a question concerning the major property of the topical participants—*Why, what's the matter with his hands?*). Such announcements and floor reservation strategies also have the important cognitive function of providing a macroproposition around which the details of the story can be organized (for details see Jefferson, 1978).

### 6.5.4. Conclusions

What conclusions can we draw from our analysis of the textual properties that may be used as devices in the strategic construction of macropropositions? Although we have examined only three types of discourse, the general principles of textually based comprehension strategies emerge fairly clearly:

1. At all levels, textual information and contextual information are closely intertwined. The properties of the communicative context (goals, speech acts, participants) constrain the range of possible topics.
2. The communicative context also constrains the possible discourse types, which are associated with sets of probable or possible topics.
3. Many discourse types feature anticipatory or initial expressions of parts of the macrostructure, for example, in announcements, titles, summaries, or leads.
4. Initial sentences sometimes have a thematic nature, expressing either a first macroproposition or settings, preparations, plans, or motivations which are either fragments of such a macroproposition or a basis for their inference from world knowledge (e.g., by frames or scripts).
5. Initial sentences feature propositions with participants, especially the main agent, and sometimes time and location, that may be strategically taken as those of the first macroproposition.
6. In some discourse types, for example, artificial (literary) or everyday stories, rhetorical devices may be used to delay the relevant categories of the macroproposition, such as its predicate, in order to arouse interest or suspense.
7. If no direct macroproposition can be strategically derived, macrorules (e.g., deletion) may be applied provisionally on the assumption that such local propositions are irrelevant or only a component of the state, event, or action occurring in the macrostructure.
8. If no conclusion at all can be made on the basis of preliminary contextual or initial textual information, a wait-and-see strategy is applied. The pro-

cessed propositions may be reinstated from episodic memory to be used as elements for the derivation of a macroproposition signaled later in the text.

9. Discourse types may be associated with stereotypical schematic structures which are associated with constraints on possible macropropositions, for example, the setting of a story with introductory descriptions of location, time, circumstances, and above all the cast of discourse participants.

If these principles are correct, a number of more specific conclusions may be drawn for processing properties of different types of texts in different contexts. A general prediction would, of course, be that if more of the contextual and textual signals are available to the hearer or reader, comprehension will on the whole be easier and hence faster. A second prediction is that local information strategically subsumed under a macroproposition can be retrieved, and hence recalled longer and better. Third, if during the comprehension of initial sentences a macroproposition must be provisionally derived (and, to do so, also relevant episodic and general knowledge), the first sentence of a discourse will usually take longer to process than following sentences of the same length (e.g., Den Uyl & van Oostendorp, 1980; Haberlandt, Berian, & Sandson, 1980). This effect will obtain, in principle, for each initial sentence of the various episodes of the text. Fourth, texts that have topics that are unexpected for the given discourse type or communicative context will initially be more difficult to process (because the relevant expectations and hence the macrostrategies are thwarted).

## 6.6. EXPERIMENT 3: INTEREST AND LEVEL OF DESCRIPTION AS MACROSTRUCTURE CUES[1]

Several experimental investigations of macrostrategies were mentioned in Chapter 2, for example, studies involving titles, thematic sentences in initial position, and frequency of mentioning. We know that titles and subtitles may influence the formation of macrostructures (Schwarz & Flammer, 1981, among others), that initial sentences are often effective cues for macropropositions (as, e.g., in Kieras, 1980b), and that pre- and post-questions and reminders can also play an important role (for a summary of this work, see Ballstaedt, Mandl, Schnotz, & Tergan, 1981). Experiment 3 adds two more demonstrations to this list: It shows that the surprisingness—and hence interestingness—of an element contributes to the likelihood that this element will be perceived as macrorelevant, and that changes in the level of description have the same effect.

An interest strategy was first postulated by Schank (1979a). Everything else being equal, an interesting item is more salient than an uninteresting one. Interest,

[1]This experiment was performed by W. H. Walker. A full account can be found in W. H. Walker and W. Kintsch, *Interest and elaboration as macrostrategies*, Technical Report, University of Colorado, 1981.

of course, may be based on many different factors. Interest is no more than a common sense term—though a useful one—which needs to be defined for technical purposes (Kintsch, 1980a). Of the many possible sources of interest we have selected suprisingness here: An otherwise uninteresting item can be made interesting by putting it into a surprising context. We predict, therefore, that if a text element occurs in a surprising context in a text, it will be rated as interesting and will be likely to be included in the macrostructure of the text, in preference to comparable uninteresting elements.

How shifts in the level of elaboration may signal macrorelevance has been described above. The tendency to perceive elaborate material in a text as macrorelevant may simply be a special case of the Gricean conversational postulate to say only as much as necessary (Grice, 1975). If one says more, this might mean that the elaborated item is destined to play some important role later on in the text's macrostructure.

An operational test of whether or not subjects perceive a text element as macrorelevant was obtained by giving subjects incomplete texts and asking them for plausible continuations. Specifically, subjects did not have to complete the text in full detail, but had merely to say in a sentence or two how they thought the text could plausibly continue. That is, subjects were asked, in effect, to complete the macrostructure of the text. If they used the critical text element in this completion, they thereby assigned macrorelevance to that element. If they did not use it, they presumably did not think it was important enough for the text as a whole.

In two different experiments we varied the surprisingness and the level of description of a concept which appeared toward the end of a page-long text fragment. Subjects then gave continuation responses.

### 6.6.1. Method and Materials

In Experiment 3, 60 college students from the University of Colorado served as subjects. Six text fragments were written according to a $3 \times 2$ factorial design. The first factor was condition, the second setting. The three experimental conditions were the basic text, an elaborated version, and a surprising version. The basic text consisted of a narrative about two boys walking around and encountering some simple objects and events, including the target item. In the elaborated text the target item was described in some detail, whereas in the basic version it was merely mentioned by its name; the two versions were otherwise identical. In the surprising version the target item appeared out of context, whereas in the basic and elaborated versions it was appropriate to the story context.

The texts were set either in the Rocky Mountains or in downtown Manhattan. In the Rocky Mountain texts, the two boys are hiking up a mountain and encounter either a mountain goat (in the basic and elaborated version) or a bus (the surprise). In the City texts, the two boys come across a bus (in the basic and elaborate versions) or a mountain goat (in the surprising version).

The texts were incomplete, stopping one sentence after the target item was introduced. Each subject received a booklet with one of the incomplete texts. After they had read it, the narrative's incompleteness was pointed out to them and they were asked to complete it. They were told that we were interested in how well they could predict the end of the story. They were to write down two or three sentences indicating how they thought the story would continue. It was emphasized that they did not actually have to complete the story, but merely indicate the gist of the completion. The subjects were not allowed to reread the text fragments at this point.

After completing the story, each subject was asked to rate either the surprisingness or the interest value of the target item in the context of the story. Ten subjects read and completed each fragment. Half rated the surprise value and half rated the interest value of the targets. Ratings were done by marking a 7-point scale, the end points of which were labeled "quite interesting" and "quite uninteresting." These labels were further explained as "As interesting/boring as things in a little story like this can be." Similarly, surprisingness was rated on a scale whose end points were "quite surprising" and "quite unsurprising," with the explanation that this meant "As surprising/predictable as things in a little story like this can be."

### 6.6.2. Results

Table 6.5 shows the results of this study. We see, first of all, that putting the target item into an inappropriate (indeed, bizarre) context had the desired effect: It made it surprising ($F (2,24) = 25.47, p < .001$) and it made it interesting ($F (2,24) = 6.69, p = .005$). The elaborated and basic versions, on the other hand, did not differ significantly from each other in either surprisingness or interest.

Making the target item surprising almost guaranteed that it would be included in the continuations subjects wrote. Elaborating it also significantly increased the likelihood that it would be perceived as macrorelevant, though in this experiment the effect of the elaboration was less pronounced than that of surprisingness.

These results were exactly as expected. A bus in the city and a goat on the mountain were not very salient, but merely elaborating the descriptions of these objects somewhat made them appear macrorelevant. Putting the bus onto the mountain and the goat into the city made almost everyone think that the story must be about them in some way.

**Table 6.5**
**Surprisingness, Interest, and Macrorelevance in Experiment 3A**

|                                           | Basic text | Elaborated text | Surprising text |
| ----------------------------------------- | ---------- | --------------- | --------------- |
| Surprisingness rating                     | 2.70       | 2.90            | 6.40            |
| Interest rating                           | 3.40       | 3.60            | 5.90            |
| Probability of inclusion in continuation  | .35        | .70             | .95             |

### 6.6.3. Replication

Although the results of Experiment 3A are indisputable, it is not clear how generalizable they are as they are based on only three versions of two texts. Furthermore, our manipulation of surprisingness was rather extreme. The experiment was therefore replicated with new texts and somewhat more subtle, realistic manipulations: The target items were embedded in a context that was unpredictable, but not bizarre, and the degree of elaboration used was reduced from two additional sentences to one.

Otherwise, Experiment 3B was designed and run exactly like the previous experiment. Another group of 60 subjects participated. The basic text consisted of a story about a young woman observing animals in a zoo. In the primate house she either sees a young chimpanzee (in the basic and elaborated version) or a small leopard (in the surprising version). These targets reverse their roles when the woman visits the cat house.

To use a chimp and a leopard as the target items proved to be a poor choice: It seems that everybody regarded them as so interesting that whether or not they appeared in a predictable context made little difference. As Table 6.6 shows, the interest ratings did not replicate the pattern of results obtained in the first experiment. The surprisingness ratings were as expected, though even in the inappropriate context the target items were not considered very unusual, and an analysis of variance did not yield a significant $F$ value for these ratings. Although the ratings thus were not sensitive enough to confirm our experimental manipulations as they had done in Experiment 3A, the continuation responses indicated that subjects nevertheless were significantly more likely to include the target item in their continuations when it was elaborated or when it occurred in the less predictable context (all $p < .05$).

### 6.6.4. Discussion

These experiments demonstrate that subjects do indeed employ an interest and a level-of-description strategy in forming macrostructures. As our subjects had to work with relatively short and simple texts which provided an insufficient number of alternatives for constructing a macrostructure, the target items were chosen with

Table 6.6
**Surprisingness, Interest, and Macrorelevance in Experiment 3B**

|  | Basic text | Elaborated text | Surprising text |
|---|---|---|---|
| Surprisingness rating | 2.80 | 2.80 | 3.70 |
| Interest rating | 4.70 | 3.10 | 4.20 |
| Probability of inclusion in continuation | .25 | .50 | .55 |

relatively high probabilities even in the base condition (by about a third of the subjects in the first experiment, and by about a quarter in the second). Nevertheless, elaborating these target items in quite minor ways—only a few words describing a bus are sufficient—greatly increased the chances that these items would be perceived as macrorelevant. Similarly, predictability in context played a role: If a text element is completely out of context, as in Experiment 3A, this is considered almost a sure sign for its global importance. But even when it is not terribly surprising but merely somewhat unusual (Experiment 3B) it tends to be seen as macrorelevant. We thus can add interest and level-of-description to our list of macrostrategies that have been experimentally confirmed. We must point out, however, that as far as interest strategies are concerned the present investigation is extremely limited: We have only been concerned here with interest caused by surprisingness, that is, by contextually determined interest. Interest may have numerous other sources, ranging from inherent interest of topics (such as those discussed in books advising journalists on what makes news in our society, e.g., Gans, 1979) to interest generated because one has already learned certain things about a topic and wants to know more (Walker, 1981).

It is worth noting as an aside that the interest strategy for macrostructure formation can sometimes produce surprising and quite undesirable results. Hidi, Baird, and Hildyard (1982) have shown that under certain conditions the practice of including interesting bits and pieces of information in a text (as educators are often told to do, in order to capture the attention of their pupils) can backfire: The exciting anecdote is strategically chosen for the macrostructure formation, and the points that were really important to the teacher are neglected. Similarly, in Kintsch and Bates (1977) the jokes were the best remembered elements from a lecture on history given to a class of college students. It seems that one has to use some care in exploiting the interest strategy pedagogically: It helps if important points in a text are interesting, but to include interesting but irrelevant detail in a text or in a lecture may just confuse the macrostrategies.

## 6.7. EXPERIMENT 4:
## PRIMING MACROPROPOSITIONS[2]

According to the model we have outlined here, the construction of a macrostructure is an integral component of text comprehension processes. Whenever certain conditions are met, the macrostrategies become engaged and macropropositions are formed. Thus, in the canonical case, once text units such as a paragraph have been read, the macropropositions for that text fragment are formed. Indeed, after a single reading of a paragraph on some familiar topic people can write reasonably accurate summary sentences. If a summary sentence is expressed in the

---

[2]This experiment was performed by R. Guindon and is reported more fully in R. Guindon and W. Kintsch, *Priming macrostructures,* Technical Report, University of Colorado, 1982.

paragraph, their inspection times, importance ratings, and thinking aloud protocols show that they recognize it as such (Kieras, 1980b; Kieras & Bovair, 1981). Similarly, after reading a well-formed story just once, or listening to it, people are able to produce adequate summaries (e.g., Kintsch & Kozminsky, 1977). However, in all these cases subjects are specifically asked to form summaries. What happens, though, in normal reading, when there are no explicit instructions to form summaries? A less intrusive experimental method is required to answer that question.

A procedure that suggests itself is the priming method of Ratcliff and McKoon (1978). We have mentioned their work before: Subjects read a few sentences and then were given a yes–no recognition test for some words from these sentences. Reaction times revealed a priming effect: If two successive test words on the recognition test came from the same sentence, the reaction time to the second word was 110 msec faster than when the word was not preceded by a same-sentence word. Two words belonging to the same atomic proposition yielded an additional 20 msec priming effect. The interpretation of this effect is that the sentence, as well as the proposition, are effective memorial units: The first member of a test pair accesses and activates this unit, so that the second member can be processed more rapidly.

This methodology appears suitable to investigate macrostructures, too. According to our model, the macropropositions should form very strong memory units, and hence produce substantial priming effects. This priming effect should be greater than that observed for micropropositions, because macropropositions are formed and stored in memory with a greater probability than micropropositions. Hence, priming effects should be obtained for almost all subjects for macropropositions, but only some of the time for micropropositions—at other times the respective microunit would not be available in memory. Specifically, then, if we have a paragraph containing an explicit macrostatement, two words from that macrostatement should yield a larger priming effect than two words from elsewhere in the text. This hypothesis will be tested in what follows, together with the further hypothesis that two words belonging to the microstructure of the text would produce a larger priming effect if they came from the same sentence than if they did not, as observed by Ratcliff and McKoon (1978).

However, this result would only show that if a macrostatement is explicit in a text, subjects pick it out and assign it a special role, as they should. It could not tell us anything about the even more interesting case in which the macropropositions must be inferred from the text. The priming method can be applied for this purpose too, however. If the macrostatement from the previous paragraph is deleted, subjects will presumably infer something like it. Hence, the test words from the macrostatement would be harder to reject on a recognition test than the other distractor words, leading to a higher false alarm rate as well as slower response times. In order to show that this effect is indeed due to the macrostructure and not merely to general similarity of the test words to the words in the original paragraph, two kinds of distractor words must be used: words totally unrelated to the paragraph to yield a baseline, and words related to the paragraph but only to words that play a

**Table 6.7**
**Sample Text and Words for the Recognition Test**[a]

---

*Text*

Extra powerful shoulders that could *give* a decathloner an advantage in throwing the discus and shot can slow him in the sprints and hurdles. Thus, he must try to keep tight tapered calves of a sprinter even as he *builds* up strong *hands* for throwing the discus, shot, and javelin, and a barrel chest to pump *air* for endurance. A decathloner must *develop* a well-rounded athletic *body* that avoids overspecialization.

| | *Test Words* | | |
| Condition | Priming word | Primed word | Correct response |
|---|---|---|---|
| MACRO | *develop* | *body* | yes/no if implicit |
| MICRO-SAME | *builds* | *hands* | yes |
| MICRO-DIFFERENT | *give* | *air* | yes |
| RELATED | *train* | *feet* | no |
| UNRELATED | *contribute* | *family* | no |

[a]The explicit version is shown; the implicit version is identical except that it lacks the last sentence expressing the macroproposition.

role in its microstructure. The latter should be harder to reject than unrelated control words because of general similarity effects; the macrostructure words should be even harder to reject, because they both are similar to the paragraph in general and play a role in very accessible memory units—the macropropositions.

Thus, an experiment was designed to evaluate these hypotheses. Table 6.7 shows a sample text with its corresponding test items. In the explicit condition, subjects read this text—and others like it, as will be described in what follows—just as it is shown here, and immediately afterward they were given a recognition test with words from the paragraph as well as suitable distractor words. Neglecting for the moment various filler items used for control purposes, the important test items were the ones labeled MACRO, MICRO-SAME, and MICRO-DIFFERENT in Table 6.7: In the first case, both the priming and the primed word belong to the macrostatement, which in this sample is the last sentence of the paragraph; in the second case, the word pair belongs to another sentence which is part of the microstructure of the text; in the third case, the word pair comes from different sentences of the microstructure. If subjects treat the last sentence as an expression of the paragraph's macrostructure, MACRO words should be recognized faster and more accurately than MICRO-SAME words, recognition for which should in turn be better than for the MICRO-DIFFERENT words.

Another group of subjects received the implicit version of the text shown in Table 6.7: the same paragraph without the macrostatement. Thus, these subjects had not seen the MACRO word before, but had presumably inferred it. Hence it should be more difficult for them to respond ''no'' to the MACRO word than to the UNRELATED and RELATED control words.

Both the explicit and implicit conditions are tests of the hypothesis that macropropositions are formed during reading, except that in one case a facilitatory effect is involved and in the other an inhibitory. Note that the test is nonintrusive: Subjects are merely given a recognition test, they are not concerned specifically with macrostructures, global relevance, or the like.

In the experiment reported in what follows, we actually employed four groups of subjects instead of just two as explained here. Essentially, we did the same experiment twice, except that the first time we made sure subjects formed macrostructures, whether they read the explicit or implicit versions. We asked them to write a summary statement after reading each paragraph and before taking the recognition test. We did this to calibrate the experimental method: How big are the various priming effects when we know that macrostructures have been formed? Then we repeated the experiment, but this time subjects were not alerted to form macrostructures—they were merely given some paragraphs to read followed by a recognition test. If the subjects formed macrostructures they did it all on their own. How do the priming effects compare in this spontaneous case with the ones obtained when we forced subjects to form macrostructures?

### 6.7.1. Method

Four groups of 16 students each served as subjects. The students were fulfilling a course requirement at the University of Colorado.

Twelve texts were used—eight from Miller and Kintsch (1980) and four from Kieras (1980a). The text shown in Table 6.7 was one of the 12. Texts were approximately 60–120 words long. Each contained a summarizing statement either at the beginning or at the end. This summarizing statement was deleted from the implicit version of the texts but present in the explicit versions.

For each text, six pairs of test words were used. The first member of a pair was always the priming word and the second the primed word. Reaction times and false alarm rates to the primed words were the data of experimental interest. Five of the word pairs are illustrated with examples in Table 6.7; the sixth was a filler pair, sometimes requiring a yes, sometimes a no response. All test words were content words. Syntactic class was matched within the different categories. Primed words were equated within each text for word frequency, and equated for length over all paragraphs.

A study–test recognition memory paradigm was used. Each subject received three practice texts before the experimental texts. Tests were administered immediately after each text was read. The order of the 12 texts was randomized for each subject. The order of the test items was semirandom, subject to certain constraints to assure that the critical test items (MACRO and the two MICROs in the explicit condition; MACRO, RELATED, and UNRELATED in the implicit condition) appeared in comparable positions and contexts.

Texts were presented on a CRT screen under computer control. Reading times were self-paced but limited. Summaries were written on a sheet of paper provided by the experimenter and were restricted to two lines in length. Recognition responses were made by pressing YES and NO buttons, with instructions to respond as quickly and accurately as possible. Correct responses were followed by the next test word; for incorrect responses, the word ERROR appeared briefly on the screen.

## 6.7.2. Results

The results of the experiment are shown in Table 6.8. The data shown in this table are based on correct responses to the primed word only. Parallel analyses were also performed for those cases in which the responses to both the primed and priming word were correct. These analyses were identical in essential respects to the ones reported here: Correlating means over experimental conditions yields an $r$ = .994, with an average overall difference of 18 msec. No outlayers were excluded in Table 6.8, but data trimming did not change the results in notable ways. Hence, these supplementary analyses will be neglected here.

Statistical tests on the data shown in Table 6.8 revealed that all adjacent reaction time means were significantly different, except the means for MICRO-SAME and MICRO-DIFFERENT, in both the explicit and implicit conditions. The tests used were correlated $t$-tests, exluding data points where one or both members of a pair were missing. Furthermore, all adjacent proportions in Table 6.8 differ significantly, as ascertained by chi-square tests. A 5% significance level was used throughout.

Consider the. main question: Did subjects behave differently when they wrote down an explicit summary statement after reading and when they did not?

As Table 6.8 shows, writing or not writing a summary sentence had almost no effect on the data. The means in the table correlate $r$ = .955, with a difference between the grand means of a mere 5 msec. We can safely conclude that whatever subjects were doing on the recognition tests, it was the same whether or not we forced them to form an explicit macrostructure.

Strong and statistically significant macrostructure priming effects were obtained in both the explicit and implicit conditions. In the explicit condition, primed macrowords were recognized 176 msec faster on the average than primed microwords. On the other hand, there was no evidence that microwords primed with a word from the same sentence were recognized any faster than microwords primed with a word from a different sentence: No significant differences were observed with or without a written summary, and the overall difference averaged out to only 3 msec.

Miss rates mirror the reaction time data: The miss rate for macrowords was 3.5%, but averaged 21% for microwords. Once again, the expected difference in favor of MICRO-SAME words did not materialize. Indeed, the miss rates for MICRO-DIFFERENT words were significantly lower in both conditions.

Turning to the results of the subjects in the implicit condition who did not read a summary statement in the text but had to infer one, we again find strong evidence for the importance of the macrostructure: It is really hard to respond ''no'' to a macroword. About two thirds of the time the macroword is falsely recognized as

Table 6.8
**Recognition Latencies in Msec and False Alarm Rates for Different Classes of Primed Words as a Function of Experimental Conditions**

| | Written summary | | | No written summary | | |
|---|---|---|---|---|---|---|
| | MACRO | MICRO-SAME | MICRO-DIFFERENT | MACRO | MICRO-SAME | MICRO-DIFFERENT |
| *Explicit* | | | | | | |
| Correct recognition— latency | 811 | 918 | 963 | 805 | 1048 | 1006 |
| Misses (%) | 4 | 22 | 14 | 3 | 20 | 9 |
| *Implicit* | MACRO | RELATED | UNRELATED | MACRO | RELATED | UNRELATED |
| Correct rejection— latency | 1399 | 1261 | 1044 | 1334 | 1223 | 1009 |
| False alarm | | | | | | |
| Percentage | 67 | 22 | 4 | 63 | 27 | 8 |
| Latency | 1114 | 1421 | 1580 | 1075 | 1229 | 1397 |

having been in the paragraph (compared with a false alarm rate of 6% for unrelated distractors), and even if it is rejected, a 340 msec average increase in response latencies indicates just how hard it is to reject such items. That this effect was truly due to the role of these items in the macrostructure and not to general similarity effects is apparent if one considers the RELATED distractor items: They are harder to reject than UNRELATED items (an error rate of 24.5% versus 6% for unrelated distractors, and a priming effect of 218 msec), but not nearly as hard as macroitems. Thus general similarity effects alone, although important, do not explain all the effects observed with macrowords.

Because of the high error rates in the implicit condition, it was possible to analyze the response times for errors, that is, for incorrect acceptances. These means are shown in the last row of Table 6.8. Macrowords again play a special role: They are accepted faster than words that are merely similar to some detail to the text, which in turn are accepted faster than unrelated words.

### 6.7.3. Discussion

The data presented here strongly support the idea that macrostructures are formed during reading, whether they are stated explicitly in the text or not, and whether subjects are asked to do so or not. For these texts at least, macrostructure formation appeared to be an almost automatic process: Readers formed macrostructures because their natural reading strategies led them to do so, not because the experimental task required it in any way.

The reaction time method used here proved to be a useful tool for investigating this process, both because it does not involve complex and strange instructions and, especially, because it is not intrusive. Macrostructures are investigated without the subject being aware of it, minimizing potential distortions from experiment-specific strategies.

Although the data are clear on the main points at issue here, our failure to replicate Ratcliff and McKoon's (1978) finding that greater priming effects are obtained within atomic propositions than between propositions needs some comment. There were many differences between these two experiments: Our texts were longer and much more complex, reaction times were considerably longer, and error rates were much higher. In other words, the task was much more difficult here than in the Ratcliff and McKoon study. Furthermore, the differences bewtween our materials and those of Ratcliff and McKoon appear very substantial in retrospect, so that our failure to replicate their results is perhaps not surprising. First of all, our sentences were often very long and complex. The priming and primed word did not always form a close pair as in the example shown in Table 6.7. In one case, for instance, the sentence was "When Eisenhower was Grand Marshall of the Tournament of Roses he was trapped in a *bathroom* at tournament headquarters by a jammed door and rescued just in time by a *clerk*." The priming word from this sentence was *bathroom*, with *clerk* as the primed word. It is perhaps not surprising that the priming effect in cases like this was no larger than for between-sentence words. There were also some problems with a few of the primed words in the DIFFERENT condition, which turned out to be too closely related to the theme of the paragraph (such as *wind* for a text on hanggliders, *boots* for a paragraph on cowboys). Indeed, if one does a post hoc analysis deleting those items that are objectionable for one reason or another, the significant difference in the wrong direction between the false alarm rates disappears, and a modest priming effect of 67 msec for MICRO-SAME versus MICRO-DIFFERENT appears. Obviously, such an ad hoc analysis lacks force, but it leads us to question our data in this respect. Our necessarily more complex materials are not sufficiently comparable to the Ratcliff and McKoon study.

The evidence we have presented here that people form macrostructures during reading, whether or not the experimental instructions induce them to do so, provides strong support for one of the main claims of our model: that comprehension processes are global as well as local, that one guides the other, and that one cannot be understood while neglecting the other. We do not want to imply, however, that what we have observed here will always be found in text comprehension. There surely are situations where for one reason or another local processing is minimal, indeed degenerate, while reasonably adequate macrostructures are being formed (e.g., the work on skimming newspaper reports, Masson, 1979). On the other hand, in situations where top-down processes are ineffective and the local decoding processes are extremely resource consuming, it is quite possible that understanding is only, or primarily, local, at least on first reading (which is what Schnotz, Ballstaedt, & Mandl, 1981, observed when their subjects were trying to summarize a rather difficult essay). The reaction time method used here can probably be fruitfully employed to investigate further the interaction of local and global processes in comprehension. Easy and difficult texts, stories and essays, skimming and memorizing, need to be studied. And finally, the exact point in the text where macropropositions are formed should be determined.

# Chapter 7

# Schematic Strategies

## 7.1. SUPERSTRUCTURES

Both in classical rhetorics or poetics and in current theories of discourse it has been assumed that certain types of discourse exhibit conventional structures that go beyond those usually accounted for in a grammar. Such structures may characterize several levels of discourse. Well known, for instance, is the metrical organization of phonological, graphical, and morphological structures, as accounted for in separate metrical theories. In part, such structures are abstract and even language independent. Similarly, we may have rhetorical structures grafted onto the syntactic structures of sentences and sentence sequences or onto semantic structures, as in metaphor, metonymia, irony, or other figures of speech.

Such additional organizational patterns may also be relevant at the level of the discourse as a whole. That is, certain parts of the discourse may have specific functions which are conventionalized in well-known categories. Even in everyday, nontechnical language a discourse may have an introduction and a conclusion. Classical tragedy was thus partitioned into five acts, whose respective theatrical or narrative functions were described as early as Aristotle's *Poetics*. Rhetorics similarly made distinctions between the parts of a public speech. Argumentational structures, as we know from classical logic (dialectica), were distinguished in the theory of the syllogism, namely, into different kinds of premises and a conclusion, distinctions which later were further refined in the philosophical theory of argumentation (Toulmin, 1958), and which in various forms reappear not only in everyday arguments, but also in scholarly discourse such as psychological articles (Kintsch & van

Dijk, 1978). Perhaps best known, both in current theory of discourse and in psychology, are the narrative structures that characterize stories in our culture, namely, the categories of Setting, Complication, Resolution, Evaluation, and Coda (Labov & Waletsky, 1967), or variations thereof. The pioneering work on narrative structures was that of Propp (1968), with later developments due to Barthes (1966), Bremond (1973), van Dijk (1972, 1976), and others. This work is surveyed in Gülich and Raible (1977) and van Dijk (1980c) (see also Chapter 2).

Typical of all these structures is their schematic nature: They consist of conventional categories, often hierarchically organized, that assign further structure to the various levels of discourse. Sometimes the categories will only affect surface structures, as in metrical or prosodic patterns, but semantic or even pragmatic units are often schematically organized as well. As in all these cases the structures seem to go beyond the usual linguistic or grammatical organization of discourse, that is, to be somehow additional or grafted onto the linguistic structures, we call them *superstructures*. For stylistic reasons, sometimes we will also use the term *schematic structures*, although the term schema is much more general, and is also used for linguistic patterns or knowledge organization. In order to distinguish the various kinds of superstructures, we will add the respective adjectives, and speak of metrical, rhetorical, argumentative, or narrative superstructures. We may similarly characterize the level of linguistic description they operate on—for example, narrative schemata are semantic superstructures. Finally, the scope of the structures may encompass a single sentence, a sequence of sentences, or the text as a whole; thus, rhetorical alliterations are mostly within the scope of sentences, whereas narrative structures are inherently textual.

The intent of this chapter is not to go into the intricate details of the various theories about superstructures of discourse. Thus, we must refer to classical and modern work in rhetorics, poetics, narrative theory, argumentation theory, and so on, for a discussion of the different units, categories, and rules defining schematic structures. Here our focus shall be on the *cognitive* properties of such postulated schemata. In particular, this chapter will conclude our discussion of the strategic aspects of discourse structure and the process involved in their comprehension. In other words, we must investigate in what ways superstructure schemata actually can and do play a role in comprehension, storage, and retrieval of discourse. A straightforward hypothesis, for instance, would be that under certain circumstances superstructures may facilitate comprehension, storage, and retrieval of discourse. This assumption is dictated by the current paradigm in cognitive psychology, according to which information processing takes place in multiply organized chunks: Sentences and discourses are understood and stored on the basis of their units, categories, and levels. Thus more structure often is correlated with additional or more complex processing, which results in better structured representations, and hence in better retrieval. Since the general principles, rules or strategies, categories, and units, for each language and culture are learned by the language users, these organizational patterns become preprogrammed, so to speak, which also facilitates understanding. In this respect the two extremes may be, on the one hand, arbitrary lists of nonsense words and, on the other, highly conventionalized discourses, such as children's stories or news stories. As we will see in more detail in Chapter 10, the highly complex task of understanding, storing, and retrieving discourse necessarily requires that the language user assign an optimal structure to the discourse, and that such structures be strategically organized in known categories. Thus, the schematic categories of a story may function as the conventionalized discourse functions for semantic macrostructures, namely, as a possible form for the global content of the story. For this reason schematic superstructures are sometimes compared to the syntax of sentences: They are, so to speak, the macrosyntax corresponding to the macrosemantics we have discussed in the previous chapter.

We have assumed that superstructures are not merely the theoretical constructs of linguistic or rhetorical models of discourse, but that they should somehow also feature in cognitive models of discourse processing. In other words, some principles, categories, or units are cognitively relevant. This cognitive relevance—which is a notion with intended vagueness—may be specified in varying degrees of strength. It may mean that all rules, categories, or units are known and used as such in processing. On the other hand, the assumption might be made that some of them are merely constructs of the theory and that only a few, in a specific format, are cognitively real. In this respect, we can learn from the fate of generative transformational sentence grammar and the early hypotheses about the psychological reality of its units, rules, and transformations. A psychological model may get valuable suggestions from a more abstract structural theory, but it should specify further why and how the processing principles, units, and categories are learned and used, and what the specific memory constraints are that require them. In the previous chapters, for instance, we have seen that the theoretical distinction of units and rules of various levels of discourse may not always be respected by the strategies of comprehension. Similarly, we should not assume that the strategic comprehension of schematic structures necessarily follows the levels or categories of an abstract theory of superstructures.

Finally, we assume that during comprehension superstructure categories are assigned on the basis of the textual and, above all, the semantic information (i.e., from the bottom up), while, at the same time, assumptions about the canonical structure of the discourse, expectations, are generated from the top down about the plausible or possible global semantic content of subsequent episodes in the discourse. In the next section of this chapter we will try to spell out what strategies language users apply in constructing superstructural schemata.

## 7.2. SCHEMATIC STRATEGIES

The assignment of superstructures necessarily has a strategic nature. A language user does not normally wait until the end of a full episode or until the end of a complete discourse before deciding about the schematic functions of the local or global information. And, conversely, once some category of a schema has been assigned, knowledge about the canonical structure of the schema allows the language user to anticipate information in the text, which will then facilitate reading and comprehension. We shall review some experiments in this section, and report a new one in the next, which show that superstructure schemata do indeed facilitate comprehension and recall.

As in previous chapters, we assume that the input information for the strategies is both contextual and textual. Language users have conventionalized knowledge about the relations between contextual and textual structures on the one hand and schematic structures on the other. Let us elaborate this claim in more detail.

### 7.2.1. Cultural Information

Contextual information encompasses our knowledge of the whole range of communicative behavior. Language users interact as members of a specific culture, as participants in social situations, as well as at an interpersonal, pragmatic level, and each level has associated with it a variety of conventionalized discourse types and schematic constraints. Poems, stories, psychological articles, courtroom discourse, etc., are discourse types that are characteristic of culturally variable communicative events. Telling a story, pleading a case, giving a lesson, or writing a paper—each is restricted to situations with specific participants, specific goals, norms, and values. This means, conversely, that the participants in a given situation may expect a range of possible discourse types, some of which may have a conventionalized schema. Once the type of context and the probable type of text is known, strategic guesses can be made about the most probable superstructure schema (Gumperz & Hymes, 1972; Bauman & Scherzer, 1974; Sanches & Blount, 1975; Freedle, 1979; Chafe, 1979).

The cultural aspect of these very general and basic strategies of comprehension resides in the fact that the context types, text types, and schemata may vary according to culture. Both from studies in the ethnography of communication and from experimental studies it has become clear that narrative schemata, for instance, may be very different from one culture to another. As early as 1932 Bartlett had demonstrated that our comprehension, representation, and recall of an American Indian story is severely restricted by our lack of knowledge of the narrative schemata underlying such stories. We shall return to some more recent experimental evidence in what follows.

### 7.2.2. Social Context and Interaction

Within this broader cultural framework, language users participate in communicative events in more or less conventionalized social settings. Features of the interactional context may be systematically linked with schematic discourse structures, in such a way that, once given contextual information of this kind, the language user may make plausible inferences about the actual categories of the schema. The most obvious example is the schematic structure of everyday conversations (Sudnow, 1972; Psathas, 1979). The constraints on successful interaction are mirrored in the conventionalized schematic categories of ongoing talk. Conversations will differ depending on such features as the shared knowledge of the participants, their status, age, or other social parameters. The presence and style of, say, the category of greeting or leavetaking, as well as the local management of opening and closing a topic section, also depend on social factors. Thus, it is a contextual constraint that participants will greet each other only if they have not seen each other for some time, and the length of such an introductory category will often be proportionally linked with time of separation and intimacy of the relationship. Cultural differences pertaining to such hierarchical social relations as rank and status will also help determine the complexity, length, style, and content of the category of greetings. Once participants know these social parameters, they will be able to anticipate whether introductory turns of the conversation belong to the polite opening ritual or to the central topic section of the talk. Similarly, not only the global contents but even the narrative schema of a story may depend on properties of the social context: A speaker may want to convey a recommendation, suggestion, or even a command to a listener by telling a story (Kirshenblatt-Gimblett, 1974). In that case an evaluation and a coda may be obligatory categories in the story.

### 7.2.3. Pragmatic Information

Since discourses as a whole may be used to perform global speech acts, the interactional context will allow plausible inferences about the possible speech acts being performed by the speaker. Not only are there systematic links between such global speech acts and their global semantic content, but the very presence or ordering of schematic categories may also depend on this pragmatic information. Thus, for instance, it is not very plausible for a global request to be located mainly in the introductory category of a conversation; instead, we expect it to be part of the topic section. The same holds true, as we have mentioned, for a possible recommendation in or via a story: It will typically not be part of the setting, the complication, or the resolution, but rather be part of the evaluation or of the coda, taken as a conclusion to the story as a whole. Conversations, letters, and similar exchanges have specific speech acts at conventionally determined places, such as greetings at the beginning and wishes at the end.

Both context types and text types may be inherently linked with speech act sequencing and pragmatic schemata, as in everyday conversation. Hence, some text types are not merely defined in terms of surface structure style or semantic content and their schemata, but above all in pragmatic terms. Argumentative discourse is a case in point. Premises and conclusions are schematic categories which not only are linked through a semantic chain of implication, entailment, implicature, or practical inference, but also involve speech acts of asserting, assuming, and drawing conclusions. Similarly, an advertisement, for all its freedom from surface and semantic

structure, will at least implicitly feature the speech act of a request, recommendation, or invitation, often at the beginning or end of the text, and often accompanied
by (pseudo)argumentation.

From such contextual information the language user draws strategic inferences
about plausible contexts and text types and hence about possible schemata or their
categories. In all but the highly predetermined text–context dependencies of institutional settings, such as courtrooms, classrooms, or parliaments, definite decisions
about the actual discourse type and their schemata must of course come from the
textual information itself. Not only does there exist a considerable amount of
freedom in the kind of discourse possible in each context, but we may also have
various transformations of the superstructural schemata, such as deletions, permuta-
tions, substitutions, additions, or recombinations. Johnson and Mandler (1980)
have discussed transformations of the story schema in more detail. Each well-
established schema has a fundamental *canonical form,* with respect to which the
transformations can be defined. It is the canonical form that defines precisely the
strategic nature of schema application in a cognitive model: In normal circumstances the language user will assume that a discourse exhibits a canonical schema,
and that this schema is directly available from knowledge about discourse types in a
given culture. Thus, for stories, the strategic hypothesis will simply be that the first
episode of the story is information that belongs to the setting. Textual information
may confirm or disconfirm this hypothesis. If, for instance, the macrostructural
information does not fit an expected schematic category, then a bottom-up process
of matching the presented global content with another category will take place. If a
story begins with the description of a murder, it may typically be assumed that the
episode is not part of the setting, but rather of the complication. In part, such an
inference may again be stereotypical: Knowledge about crime stories allows us to
link murders or similar crimes directly with the complication of the story. In other
circumstances further inferences are necessary: If some action or event, for a given
culture and a given reader or listener, can be taken as interesting (e.g., funny,
dangerous, uncommon, and so on), then it may be assigned the category of a
complication if it is not consistent with the norms, values, goals, or expectations of
the participants described or of the participants in the storytelling event.

Readers use various strategies for inferring the schematic categories of texts
from their *semantic macrostructures.* Thus, if according to the macrostrategies
described in the previous chapter a language user infers a macroproposition from the
first sentence(s) of the discourse, the next strategic step will be the assignment of
the specific superstructure function of that macroproposition. If the first sentences
of a story describe the time, place, participants or, in general, a situation, then the
first macroproposition(s) may be assigned to the setting category. Similarly, disrup-
tive events or actions—at the global level—may be assigned to the complication
category, whereas reactive actions of some important participant in the story, which
are aimed at solving a problem or reestablishing a desired situation, may be assigned to the resolution category. We may assume that top-down and bottom-up
processes interact strategically here. Assumptions about the plausible schema de-

rived from contextual information or from previous textual information will be combined with local semantic information in order to form and confirm hypotheses about the actual schematic category.

Whereas semantic macrostructures, which are the global content of superstructural schemata, play a decisive role in the strategic inferencing of schematic categories, we may also have various *surface structure signals* for such inferences. Titles and subtitles, as well as various forms of announcements, often explicitly mention the text type and hence the possible schema involved. Thus, for certain discourse types, headings in printed text sometimes state the topic and/or the schematic category. A characteristic example is provided by scholarly discourse, which typically exhibits such headings as *Introduction, Theoretical Framework, Experiment,* and *Conclusion.* Similarly, we have schema category expressions in initial and final sentences of episodes, such as *This story takes place in . . . , We may conclude that . . . , Before I start with . . . ,* and so on.

Because schematic categories organize semantic and pragmatic macrostructures, and because macrostructures are derived from local semantic structures (and world knowledge), lexical expressions of local semantic content may also be signals for schema categories, typically so at the beginning and the end of episodes. An expression such as *Suddenly,* for instance, will often indicate the beginning of a complication episode, whereas *Thus* may introduce a conclusion section. Sometimes formulaic expressions are used for the contents or speech acts subsumed by a schema category. *Once upon a time . . .* not only opens a children's story but also indicates the setting category. The formulaic structure of official letters, documents, and institutional discourse may also be linked with schematic categories.

Finally, the phonetic, morphological, graphical, and paratextual features of ongoing discourse may hint at special categories: Leads in news stories are often printed in bold type; complications in stories may be introduced with higher pitch, loudness, or stress; and initial greetings and final greetings, (i.e. the closings in conversation) have similar surface or paratextual properties.

What has been said here about such well-known schematic structures as those of stories or argumentations also holds, mutatis mutandis, for other kinds of schemata and their strategic processing. Metrical and prosodic schemata are limited to very specific discourse types, often literary or ritual, and are indicated by special contexts (e.g., literary or esthetic ones). Inasmuch as such schemata constitute a further organization of surface structures that is uncommon in other discourse types, they can be perceived immediately and recognized as such on the basis of specially learned cues. In part, this is also true of many rhetorical operations, such as alliteration, rhyme, parallelism, and semantic figures such as metaphors. All these literary, esthetic, or rhetorical schemata, and their categories, do not have specific meanings as such, but may have various functions, for example, a persuasive function in the communicative context where they may influence the "acceptability" of the discourse. It may be assumed, and it has been demonstrated experimentally, that these additional forms of organization allow a better representation in episodic memory and hence better retrieval: Surface structures which normally are forgotten quickly can be inserted into nontrivial categories of a schema. It is a well-known fact, from classical poetics and rhetorics onward, that metrical, prosodic, and rhetorical figures have not only an esthetic or persuasive function but also a mnemonic one (Groeben, 1982).


## 7.3. SCHEMATIC ANALYSIS OF THE *NEWSWEEK* TEXT

It has been argued in this chapter that many types of discourse have a conventional global schema or superstructure. Such a superstructure provides a kind of overall functional syntax for the semantic macrostructures. That is, macropropositions and the episodes dominated by them may be assigned to a conventional schematic category determining their function within the discourse as a whole. Thus, many discourses have some kind of *introduction* and *conclusion* category.

News discourse, as it appears in news stories in newspapers, television programs, or news weeklies, also can be assigned a conventional superstructure. Empirical research on such news discourse schemata is still in its initial stage (Thorndyke, 1979; Findahl & Höijer, 1981; Larsen, 1982), and systematic descriptive and comparative research is necessary to establish the various categories of the 'news' schema (van Dijk, 1981b, 1983a, 1983b). Before we give a schematic analysis of the *Newsweek* test (see front endpapers), we will briefly discuss some of the major categories of news discourse schemata.

One of the most obvious initial categories of news is that of *headlines*. We have seen in the previous chapter that such headlines are typical strategic cues for the derivation of macrostructures, of which they usually express a fragment. Often, there is not just one headline, but also a super- and a subheadline, above and below the main headline. We ignore whether these represent different aspects of the macrostructure. In principle, we will assume that all headline propositions represent macroinformation. The communicative function of headlines is clear: They attract attention (also due to larger and/or bold print), summarize the macrostructure of the text, and hence serve as a cue for the reader's strategic decision-making process as to whether he or she will or will not read the text. Also, headlines are the minimal information about the respective events of the news, so that they constitute the basis for the process of skimming the paper.

Often the headline category will be followed by a *lead,* consisting of one or a few sentences, expressing the macrostructure of the text. Leads will also often be printed in larger or bold type, and along with the headline they typically occur in initial position. Leads do not only summarize the text, but also serve as an *introduction*. Thus, arguments introduced in the lead may be coreferred with, even in pronominal form, by expressions in the proper text of the news discourse (i.e., in the "body"). Both headline and lead form the overall *summary* information of the news discourse.

News discourse may be characterized as a specific kind of *story,* hence the frequent use of the term *news story*. They are stories in the sense that they are about relevant (interesting, important) events and actions, which are often events and actions disrupting the goals of persons, groups, or societies. Yet, news does not have the conventional superstructure of everyday stories, which indeed may have summarizing announcement categories (as in *Did you hear about John's accident?*), but which further will be primarily organized by a conditionally ordered set of categories, such as complication and resolution, possibly followed by an evaluation and a coda. News stories, instead, have a *relevance structure*. That is, their main schematic categories are ordered by communicative importance. So, we first have the headline, with the shortest possible summary, then the lead with a proper summary, and then we expect the major events constituting the "news" of the day. Hence, we will simply postulate an *event* category, featuring propositions (or macropropositions) denoting the most important news events. This category may well be discontinuous. That is, fragments of it may be interspersed throughout the text, so that more important events (in the interpretation of the journalist) come first and less important ones come last. The latter may, in fact, typically be placed at the end, in part for technical reasons: When the editor cuts the journalist's text to fit the available space, only the least important information will get lost. Newspaper news will therefore hardly have important categories (e.g., the conclusion) in the end. These will, on the contrary, occur in the lead.

Although we now have the core of a news discourse schema, many news stories will be more complex, especially if relatively much information is reserved for the event (this complexity is due to many factors; see Galtung & Ruge, 1970; van Dijk, 1981c). Thus, first the text may refer to previous information given about the same event (cued by phrases like *As we already reported yesterday/in an earlier edition . . .* ). This *previous information* category has an obvious function in our processing model: It typically activates the situation model the reader already may have about the same event/situation. In other discourses as well (e.g., in everyday conversation, in continuing lectures, at the beginning of new chapters in a book, and so on) we find such reminders of previous information, which have typical intertextual functions.

Next, each event may itself be placed within a *context*. This context may first of all be *historical*. The news in that case specifies, sometimes also as a reminder, the events that have led to the actual events. Then, the context may also be *actual*. In that category we will typically find further information about the cooccurring events or situations of an event (e.g., the visit of the American president to Europe will be the context for the reported event of a demonstration in Europe against U.S. policy in Central America). We see that some of the context factors may be actual conditions, but this need not be the case. Actual events may just be parts of a wider context of events or situation. Similarly, events and their context will often be described against some *background*. Thus, demonstrations in Europe against the visit of the American president may take place against the background of anti-American attitudes among many young Europeans. Backgrounds typically place an event in a larger perspective. They will describe the socioeconomic situation of a country about which some political event has been reported, or describe living conditions in a ghetto in which riots have taken place.

Sometimes both context and backgrounds have the overall function of an *explanation*. They provide the factors the readers must know in order to understand why and how the events reported have taken place. In terms of our processing model, context and background precisely provide, for the nonexpert reader, the necessary situation model details plus general semantic memory frames necessary for understanding. An explanation need not remain implicit in the context and background category, though. It may also be explicit, namely, when the journalist explicitly indicates *which* of the factors of the context and background are causally or structurally linked with the actual events.

Events usually have consequences, which we may therefore expect news stories to mention in a *consequences* category. Such a category will often make explicit why the events are so important, why they are relevant to us, how they affect our country, our economy, or that of our important allies or enemies. Consequences may themselves be events or situations (as results), but they also may be the verbal or other *reactions* of relevant persons, for example, of people who are politically important. The *comments* category, therefore, is an important one in international news. This category is also one that can be flexibly used by the newspaper to give implicitly its own opinions about the events, for example, by selecting or editing the comments of specific political persons. Of course, the same holds for the specification of context, backgrounds, and the very description of the events: News discourse is not just a description of some events, but a subjective reconstruction of events, or rather of several discourses (reports, international news agency telexes, communications, press conferences, etc.) about such events (see van Dijk, 1981c, for details).

What we have described are some major categories of news stories in (Western) newspapers; there are, of course, many local, national, or international variations on this schema. Thus, the ordering may be somewhat different, some categories—such as context and background—may be optional, and further categories may be given. For example, some newspapers will, perhaps as part of context or background, provide biographical sketches of newly introduced important persons (e.g., in a footnote—as *Le Monde* does). There are also variations in format among the different news media. Television news has its own format (see Glasgow University Media Group, 1977, 1980), as do weeklies. Weeklies—such as American *Time* and *Newsweek*, German *Der Spiegel*, French *l'Express* and *Le Nouvel Observateur*, Italian *Espresso*, and Dutch *Haagse Post* (HP), all in magazine format—do indeed seem to have a slightly different news schema. In contrast to the daily newspapers and television news, weeklies do not report actual news. Instead, they provide articles with much more context, background, consequences, and perhaps *evaluations* a category which in the newspaper is often reserved for the editorials, which are expressly separated from the news—in keeping with the ideology that "facts" and "opinion" are two different things. Because weeklies are read in a different way than newspapers, skimming is less important, so that leads will occur less often, or perhaps as part of special "boxes". Although first sentences may function partly as such summarizing thematic sentences, they often just give some striking detail (e.g., a description of an interesting situation, action, or event, or the comment of some important politician). *Time* used to have a style (imitated, e.g., by *Der Spiegel*) in which first sentences would start with some intimate detail about the actions of some important person, in order to give some inside flavor to the article. Also, weekly articles will have definite length more often than newspaper articles, hence they may well have important information, such as conclusions, at the end.

If we now turn to our *Newsweek* text (see front endpapers), we observe that many of the hypothetical categories that have been discussed here indeed feature in the superstructural schema. In Table 7.1, we have listed the macropropositions from our analysis given in the previous chapter, and we have strategically, that is, on line and on the basis of flexible information input, assigned schematic categories to each. Because the strategic comprehension process of superstructure categories does not take place only at the macrolevel, but also at the word, clause, and sentence levels, we also indicate in Table 7.1 which local information cues may be relevant for superstructure formation. Thus, changes of paragraphs, marking changes of episode and hence of macroproposition (global topic), will often also be cues for changes in superstructure category. Similarly, a change from present tense to past tenses will often mark the beginning of a historical background category.

Strategic comprehension of schematic categories often involves top-down processing. We do not know to what extent readers have conscious knowledge about the news schema, but we assume that they have learned such a schema after the many thousands of news texts read during their adult life. Probably we would be aware of the schematic categories only when they are missing, although some of them might not be necessary or constitutive categories, but rather categories defining good reporting in quality newspapers. We thus assume that the communicative context will activate specific expectations about the type of discourse involved, and therefore also some implicit expectations about possible overall schemata for the news.

Another reason for our hypothesis that the categories mentioned earlier do have some cognitive relevance and not only abstract structural reality, is the fact that several of them have direct communicative functions, such as the headline and the lead, whereas others have immediate processing function correlates: The previous information category, as we suggested, activates situation models; context reminds or constructs further new details for such a situation model so that the information about actual events can be understood; and backgrounds may activate specific semantic memory frames or scripts. Consequences or evaluation, finally, indicate the pragmatic and hence communicative relevance of the news item for the reader or the reader's reference groups. In other words, the categories are not arbitrary, but have communicative, social, and cognitive relevance.

We assumed earlier that schematic superstructures assign textual functions to macropropositions. We also assumed that such interpretations take place strategically, that is, on line with the linear interpretation of subsequent sentences and the

**Table 7.1**
**Schematic Strategies in the Comprehension of the *Newsweek* Text**

| Macropropositions (see Table 6.2) | Superstructure category | Cues | Knowledge and beliefs | Comments |
|---|---|---|---|---|
| 1. There are no political choices | Headline | First, top position Large, bold type | NEWS schema | |
| 2. The political situation in G is more extreme than in ES | Lead | First sentence | Abstract, high level info | The Lead may here be extended to include $M_1$ to $M_5$ |
| 3. There are unorganized communists on the left | Background | Introduction of participants | Specification of general situation | Here, the Background is given in the Lead if we assume that the Lead is not limited to $M_1$. |
| 4. On the right is an elite in power, helped by the US | Background Historical Context | Past tense for Hist. Background | Specification of actual political situation in G. and of the historical antecedents of the actual situation | Again, we see that superstructure categories may be 'distributed' or 'discontinuous' through the text. |
| 5. The political center has been murdered by the elite in G, but still exists in ES. | Background Historical Context | Past tense. *last 15 years* | Specification of the pol. sit. | |
| 6. G regime first welcomes election of R. | Previous Events | New paragraph Past tense New participants | Situation model of previous events in G. | The *Event* category can be split up in Previous Events or Conditions for the *Actual Events*, and in *Consequences*. |
| 7. G's regime had counted on R's administration's help. | Previous Events | See above | | |

| | | | | |
|---|---|---|---|---|
| 8. G's regime now disappointed about R's administration | Actual Context (Reasons) | Composed tense Topic: Guatemalans | Description of the actual situation | The Actual Context can be specified for the role of its 'factors' on the actual events. Here they are *reasons* for action. |
| 9. G's regime does not like demands from US for political moderation | Actual Context (Reasons) | Same Topic | Relation US–Guatemala | |
| 10. US has no influence on G's regime | Actual Context | Comment | Verbal reaction of diplomat | |
| 11. G's regime now acts negatively towards US representatives | Actual Events or Previous Events | New paragraph | Details of actions of regime | The Actual events may still have 'past events' as their part, and we might assign this and the previous macropropositions also to Previous Events |
| 12. G will fight also without US help | Actual Events | End of paragraph and New paragraph | Description of actual political actions/fights | |
| 13. G acquired arms from many countries | Actual Context (Preparatory Actions) | Composed tenses | Description of preparatory actions. (WAR script, WEAPON frame). | If this information is the main information of the text, then it could also be 'Actual Events'. |
| 14. Also Israel helps | Actual Context | Present tense New participant | Politically interesting information: special role of Israel | Idem. |
| 15. Difficult relations between US and G | Consequence | New Paragraph Re-instatemenet US Present tense | Description of possible actions of US as a reaction | Here the Consequence partly preceded the Actual Events (the murders) |
| 16. G's regime commits mass murders | Actual Events or Previous Events (main actions) | New paragraph Composite Tense | Description of past terrorism of regime | Again, if information is new, it would be Actual Events, otherwise Previous Events |

*(continued)*

**Table 7.1** (*Continued*)

| Macropropositions (see Table 6.2) | Superstructure category | Cues | Knowledge and beliefs | Comments |
|---|---|---|---|---|
| 17. This does not daunt guerrilla | Actual Events (main reactions) | New paragraph New referents | Description of the actions of opponents | Part of the Actual Event category may have a proper *Narrative* structure, with Complicating Actions/ Events and Resolution Reactions. |
| 18. Guerrilla now joined forces | Previous Events | *Earlier this month* | | |
| 19. Guerrilla backed by communist countr. | Actual Context | Hypothetical Past tense | As in $M_{13}$ and $M_{14}$ help of actions are conditional actions | |
| 20. No centrist solution like in ES | Comment (Evaluation) | New paragraph Present/Future tense | Possible reactions of US Opinion statement | Comments of *Newsweek* mingled with those of diplomats |
| 21. Mass murders favor the left | Consequence/ Comment (Evaluation) | Future tense | Possible consequences mentioned. | If this is a fact, then it is Consequence, if an opinion then it is a Comment. |
| 22. Will US help G's brutal regime? | Comment/Conclusion | Hypothetical: *could* | Evaluating/Predicting future reaction of US | The major final Comment which is most relevant for the future policy and events could be called a *Conclusion* or *Coda*. |

macropropositions inferred from these. Yet, for the moment we ignore the precise locus of schematic superstructure formation. Part of it is top down, as we saw, triggered by communicative context and expected text type, and hence immediately available. But some other categories may be triggered by purely local information (e.g., paragraph change) or triggered only after the formation of macropropositions to which they assign functions. We will provisionally assume that the process will use information from all these levels but predominantly operates at a macrolevel. Therefore, we provide macropropositions as input in Table 7.1.

If we inspect Table 7.1, we first observe that some macropropositions, due to their complex propositional structure, may have several functions at the same time. Thus, $M_4$ says something about the political background in Guatemala, but also specifies some historical contexts (the CIA-backed coup) of the actual U.S. involvement and the power of the conservative elite. Similarly, $M_{11}$ may be interpreted as specifying actual events, namely, the Guatemalan reactions to American diplomacy, or rather (because past actions are involved) as being about the previous events of the actual events (strain in relations between the United States and Guatemala). Again, $M_{13}$ may be seen as part of the context (the general armament sources of the elite) or as a preparatory condition of the main events (fighting the guerrillas). And, finally, $M_{21}$ may be a statement about likely consequences, derived from general political knowledge about Central America, or be an evaluative comment, implying that it is wrong—or at least not desirable in terms of U.S. policy—that the guerrillas be strengthened. It is not problematic that macropropositions—or at least their component simple propositions—have different functions. But we still lack unambiguous criteria for the differentiation of some categories, despite our attempts at definition given earlier. Further descriptive work will have to specify such criteria.

In Figure 7.1 we have tried to capture the overall resulting schema of the *Newsweek* text. We see that on the whole the superstructure indeed organizes the respective macropropositions of the text, sometimes dominating just one, in other cases a whole sequence. The order of the macropropositions, as expressed by the sentences in the text, roughly corresponds to the terminal categories of the superstructure. Sometimes, though, there may be *transformations,* as we also know from narrative theory. Thus consequences may be spelled out first—due to the relevance criterion—and only then their reasons or causes given.

We have argued that macropropositions serve as the input to the schematic structure, although actual processing may be more complex. Indeed, even local propositions may suggest possible schematic categories. Thus, as we suggested earlier, $M_4$ is based on $S_3$, which expresses different propositions, some about the actual situation, some about the historical context. Embedded clauses, especially temporal or relative ones, may, together with tense changes denoting time change, be used as local cues for the derivation of the appropriate superstructure categories.

It is probably appropriate to repeat here some of the remarks we made in Chapter 1 about the boundary conditions of our model. We do not claim that readers of the *Newsweek* article will form a macrostructure organized schematically as

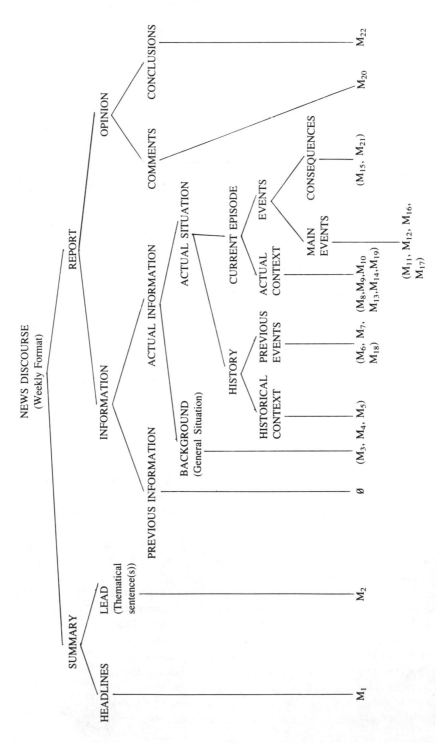

**Figure 7.1.** Schematic superstructure representation of the *Newsweek* text.

shown in Figure 7.1. This figure shows what could happen—for a reader who is sufficiently motivated and has sufficient resources, as well as a greater than average familiarity with news report schema. An actual, given reader in some specific situation will form a macrostructure that may be not only quite different from the one we have derived for this text (depending on the reader's knowledge, opinions, and political attitude), but also much more sketchy and incomplete. Furthermore, its schematic organization, too, will merely reflect some of the distinctions which we have indicated in Figure 7.1. Complete processing of the available information is an idealization we use in illustrating our model—not something we expect from an actual reader.

## 7.4. PREDICTIONS AND IMPLICATIONS OF THE THEORY OF SCHEMATIC SUPERSTRUCTURES

It is an axiom concerning memory that organization, especially meaningful organization, aids retention. Schematic superstructures provide additional organization to a text, therefore such structures should make it easier to remember a text. The additional structure should also be useful in the very process of comprehending. Since comprehending implies finding an appropriate organization for a text, the more possibilities there are for organizing a text, the easier this task should be. Hence, the theory proposed here makes the general prediction that schematic superstructures should facilitate comprehension as well as memory for text.

We may specify this general statement in a number of ways. First of all, superstructures must be not only in the text, but also in the reader's or listener's mind. One must know about conventional schemata before one can use them. Some of these schemata are learned very early. For instance, Poulson *et al.* (1979) obtained strong evidence that 4-year-old children already had some knowledge of the conventional narrative schema and were actively employing this knowledge in story understanding.

At a general level, there is much evidence from the work on story grammars that superstructures facilitate comprehension and memory. Open questions remain, however, and many details need to be worked out. Thus, one would expect that the use of surface signals to indicate the schematic categories of a text would be helpful, but as yet no systematic studies of this problem are available (but see Section 7.5). Similarly, one would expect a canonical schematic organization to be easier to detect in a text and hence make the text easier to comprehend and remember than transformed superstructures. The only experimental studies bearing on this prediction involve some very radical transformations, namely, the random reordering of whole paragraphs. If this reordering is done carefully so that the local coherence of the text is not disrupted (e.g., by avoiding the occurrence of pronouns without referents, a frequent result when sentences are scrambled), some rather surprising results are obtained, which superficially seem to contradict the prediction just made. Thus, Kintsch, Mandel, and Kozminsky (1977) had subjects summarize simple, well-formed stories (from Bocaccio's *Decameron*) which were read either in the original, canonical form or with their paragraphs randomly reordered. Their subjects were able to summarize these stories equally well whether or not they had been scrambled. However, this does not mean that the canonical ordering was of no help to the subjects, as they did take longer to read the scrambled stories than the well-ordered ones. It thus appears that, given these simple, schema-conforming stories, subjects were able—albeit with an extra effort—to overcome the confusion caused by presenting the paragraphs in random order and to mentally assign the paragraphs to their proper schematic categories. The basis for this assignment could be the content of the stories and whatever schematic signals still remained in them (i.e., other than order, normally a potent cue). Knowing what schematic categories to expect in a story made it possible to reorder the scrambled text.

Confirming this interpretation was the finding that subjects always wrote their summaries in the canonical order, whether or not the text they had read was in that order. One would, of course, predict that texts that lack a conventional schematic superstructure, or that have a structure unfamiliar to the reader, would be more sensitive to paragraph scrambling.

The Kintsch, Mandel, and Kozminsky (1977) study illustrates how careful one must be in interpreting experimental results. On the face of it, the main result—that scrambled stories are summarized as well as normal ones—suggests that superstructures are superfluous. But, if one considers the fact that the scrambled stories were harder to read, together with other internal evidence discussed in the original report (the story that corresponded least well to a simple narrative schema was the one subjects had the most trouble with in the scrambled form), the true implications of these results become apparent: What we see here is not the lack of a story-schema effect, but, on the contrary, a very powerful effect that permits readers to overcome the deficiencies of the scrambled presentation order.

Anectodal evidence suggests that readers may have a tendency to impose schematic orderings on texts that are not really appropriate. The superstructure that people are most familiar with and handle most easily is the narrative schema (Graesser, Hoffman, & Clark, 1980). Thus, a narrative organization is sometimes superimposed on texts that are not stories (a news report, for instance, may be understood as a story) (Thorndyke, 1979; Larsen, 1982).

Schematic superstructures are learned; some, such as the story schema, are learned very early, others only through specialized training (e.g., various literary text types). Superstructures are, therefore, culture specific. What happens when one reads a text for which one does not know the appropriate schema has been shown in several studies, including Kintsch and Greene (1978). In this study, American college students were asked to summarize a Grimm's fairy tale, which corresponded closely to their expectations about narratives, and an Apache Indian story, which completely violated them. For the former, subjects wrote good summaries; in contrast, the latter with its unfamiliar narrative structure, was summarized very badly, often with whole sections missing. Such poor summaries rarely occurred when the subjects knew the schema according to which the story was constructed—the slots of the schema were there and had only to be filled in. It is interesting to note that the difficulties subjects had with the Indian folktale were at the macrolevel only: When the sentences of the two stories were rated for comprehensibility out of context, that is, just as separate sentences, those from the Indian folktale were judged to be just as easy as those from the Grimm's fairy tale. Steffensen, Jogdeo, and Anderson (1980) reported a study that makes a similar point, although they investigated a culture-specific action schema rather than a culture-specific text structure. Wedding ceremonies in the United States and in India are very different, and American students found it easy to remember a description of an American wedding but not of an Indian wedding, whereas for Indian students the results were reversed (see also Freedle, 1979; Chafe, 1979).

The question in all of these studies, as well as in the story grammar literature as a whole (see our review in Section 2.8), is the extent to which these results are due to the influence of textual superstructures per se, or, alternatively, to nontextual factors, such as action schemata. Clearly, culture-specific knowledge about wedding ceremonies was the source of the performance differences in the Steffensen *et al.* study. In the Kintsch and Greene work both the textual superstructure (a familiar narrative schema) and the content of the stories favored the Grimm's fairy tale: As is proper for stories in our culture, the fairy tale was about human actions and was thus temporally and causally coherent; the Indian story, on the other hand, lacked a temporal–causal organization. Differences between the two, therefore, may be due to either textual (narrative schema) or nontextual factors (the structure of actions).

All work on stories suffers from this confounding, as we saw in Chapter 2 in our discussion of the story grammar controversy. We have, of course, strong theoretical reasons to assume that superstructures must play an important cognitive role, as we outlined earlier. The culturally determined ordering of the descriptions in a story, their completeness and level of detail, principles of perspective in story-telling, and even the narrative categories go beyond the actions themselves. We know more about action descriptions than we know about actions. But, stories are so closely tied to actions that it is almost impossible to unconfound text and action structure experimentally within that context. However, one can avoid this problem, at least partially, by looking at other types of text. In particular, descriptive texts are often not as tightly constrained by their content as action texts. Thus, in laboratory experiments such texts might provide a clearer picture of the psychological effects of schematic superstructures. An investigation involving descriptive texts and their rhetorical schemata is reported in what follows.

## 7.5. EXPERIMENT 5: THE ROLE OF RHETORICAL STRUCTURE IN DESCRIPTIVE TEXTS

A variety of conventional patterns can be found in descriptive texts (Kieras & Bovair, 1981; Meyer & Freedle, in press). Readers are not nearly as familiar with them as with the narrative schema, but college students will have at least an implicit understanding of such rhetorical forms as arguments, definition, classification, illustration, and procedural descriptions. Descriptive texts—essays—are rarely pure examples of one or another of these forms, but rather combine these and other structures in multiple, unpredictable ways. Nevertheless, the ability to recognize these rhetorical structures in an essay may be of considerable help to the reader and may permit him or her to organize the text more easily. Suppose, for instance, that a student is reading a chapter in a science textbook. He or she realizes (not necessarily consciously) that a paragraph is organized according to some known rhetorical form, say as a "definition", perhaps because the author announced specifically "We are now going to define X," or perhaps because of more subtle, indirect cues. We are assuming that the student at this point calls up a rhetorical schema 'definition', and organizes the paragraph around that schema. The student knows that definitions are often of the form genus + differentiae (class + special characteristics), and hence looks for the genus in the text, as well as for primary and secondary characteristics. These immediately become the macropropositions of the text, to which the other propositions in the text can be subordinated. Thus, rhetorical structure allows for a certain amount of top-down processing, and, although it is quite likely that a similar organization of the text could have been achieved through a more careful analysis of the text propositions themselves, laborious bottom-up inferencing can in this way be bypassed.

The task of the essay writer, then, is to make sure that the right kind of rhetorical schema is triggered by the text, in which case the reader should arrive at an optimal organization of the text, congruent with the author's intentions. One way to achieve this goal is to use rhetorical forms in their canonical order and to signal the various categories as clearly as possible. On the other hand, if the author hides the rhetorical structure of a text through the use of some transformations (sensible ones, not random reorderings) and in addition omits all rhetorical signals, the reader would probably still comprehend the text if it is simple enough and deals with some familiar topic, but would be more likely to miss a few points or misrepresent the author's intentions.

Two experiments investigating this prediction have recently been completed in our laboratory (see Kintsch & Yarbrough, 1982, for more detail). Good and bad texts were constructed which were identical in their content, but differed in their rhetorical organization. If students use rhetorical strategies as suggested here, then the good texts ought to be easier to comprehend than the bad ones, because it should be easier to form appropriate macrostructures for the former. However, whether or not an essay is well organized rhetorically should have little or no effect on the local processing of the text, because, according to our theory, rhetorical structures have their effects at the macrolevel. Therefore, comprehension tests that are sensitive to the macrolevel should reveal the effects of rhetorical structure whereas tests that are only related to microprocesses should not.

We have chosen direct questions about the macrostructure as a means of assessing the macroprocesses in our experimental subjects. Thus subjects were asked "What is this text about?" and "What are the main ideas the author wanted to get across?'' On the other hand, a cloze test provides a way to assess micro-processes. If every fifth word in a paragraph is omitted and subjects have to guess what it is supposed to be, their performance is determined primarily by how well they understand each sentence or phrase in its local context and should be fairly independent of their success or failure to achieve global organization of the text.

We did not try in this study to distinguish what makes for good or bad rhetorical form. Thus, we did not differentiate between the effects of canonical ordering and various kinds of rhetorical signals in the text.

It is possible that good rhetorical form is most useful when the text is rather complex at the macrolevel; for simple, straightforward texts, macrostructures can be generated even without their help. Therefore, we included a second factor in our experiment, namely, the structural complexity of the text. For each rhetorical category we wrote one paragraph that was structurally simple (e.g., a straightforward classification) and one that was always structurally complex (e.g., involving sub-classifications). We tried to keep the simple and complex texts comparable in terms of familiarity of the topic, sentence complexity, and other such variables, but, of course, they differ on many dimensions in unknown ways. Therefore, a simple main effect due to complexity would be of little interest. Indeed, it would be surprising if people's ability to answer questions about the main ideas in a text would not be influenced by the structural complexity of the text. However, the question of whether complexity interacts with rhetorical form is of real interest.

## 7.5.1. Method and Procedure

In the first experiment, four rhetorical structures were employed: classification, illustration, comparison and contrast, and procedural description. For each structure, a simple and a complex paragraph were prepared. The texts were written to conform as closely as possible to their respective rhetorical schemata. They were then transformed to make them less schema conforming. The transformation involved the reordering and deletion of rhetorical signals from the text. An example of a text in good rhetorical form is given in Table 7.2. It is a simple illustration with the topic stated in the first paragraph, and then an example provided in each of the following four paragraphs. These paragraphs are also arranged in their logical order. In Table 7.3, the transformed text is shown. The order of paragraphs is no longer canonical, and two rhetorical signals present in the original text have been deleted (the *next* of Paragraph 4 has been replaced with an uninformative *usually*, and *finally we find* in the last paragraph has been changed to *it should be noted that*). One more word had to be changed in order to make the text in Table 7.3 coherent (*more*—replaced by *rather*— would have been strange in the first sentence because no basis for the comparison has yet been specified).

The texts were from 205 to 420 words long. The good and bad versions were always equally long. The content of the good and bad versions was identical except for 4.6 words, on the average, which were changed as explained in the preceding paragraph.

**Table 7.2**
**An Example of a Simple Classification Text in Good Rhetorical Form**

---

In order to obtain an understanding of how man has evolved it is often helpful to analyze him in relation to the other primates. One major way of seeing this relationship is by examining locomotor patterns.

The most developmentally constricted form of locomotion is called vertical clinging and leaping. All prosimians fall into this form. In this pattern the animal normally clings to the branch with its head above its limbs. In its predominant locomotive form the animal pushes off from the branch or tree with its hind limbs and springs or leaps to the next.

A developmentally more advanced form is quadrupedalism. As the name suggests all four limbs are involved in this pattern. Macaques and howler monkeys typify this form.

Next is ape locomotion which is characterized by arm swinging and/or occasional linked branch-to-branch swinging, climbing, and knuckle walking. The gibbon, orangutan, and chimpanzee locomotive patterns are characterized by this form.

Finally, we find bipedalism which is the characteristic locomotive form of man: Bipedalism includes standing, striding, and running. This form completes an adaptive developmental sequence which began sometime in the deep past with vertical clinging and leaping.

---

For each text, there were two questions. The first was always "What is this essay about?" A correct answer for the text shown in Tables 7.2 and 7.3 would have been "types of locomotion" or some paraphrase thereof. The second question asked for the main points in each text, for example, "What are the four major points made?" for the text in Tables 7.2 and 7.3. A correct answer in this case would be to list in some way the four types of locomotion described in the article, either in general terms (bipedalism) or by example (walking). The number of main points was not always the same for different texts (but was identical, or course, for the good and bad versions).

**Table 7.3**
**An Example of a Simple Classification Text in Poor Rhetorical Form**

---

A developmentally rather advanced form is quadrupedalism. As the name suggests all four limbs are involved in this pattern. Macaques and howler monkeys typify this form.

It should be noted that bipedalism is the characteristic locomotive form of man: Bipedalism includes standing, striding, and running. This form completes an adaptive developmental sequence which began sometime in the deep past with vertical clinging and leaping.

In order to obtain an understanding of how man has evolved it is often helpful to analyze him in relation to the other primates. One major way of seeing this relationship is by examining locomotor patterns.

The most developmentally constricted form of locomotion is called vertical clinging and leaping. All prosimians fall into this form. In this pattern the animal normally clings to the branch with its head above its limbs. In its predominant locomotive form the animal pushes off from the branch or tree with its hind limbs and springs or leaps to the next.

Ape locomotion is usually characterized by arm swinging and/or occasional linked branch-to-branch swinging, climbing, and knuckle walking. The gibbon, orangutan, and chimpanzee locomotive patterns are characterized by this form.

---

 For the cloze test, every fifth word in the good versions of the texts was deleted and replaced by a line. The same words were then deleted from the poor versions.

Each subject received either all eight good texts or all eight bad texts, and was tested either with the cloze test or with the macrostructure (topic or main idea) questions.

### 7.5.2. Results

The main results of the experiment are shown in Figure 7.2. Subjects were much better at answering topic or main idea questions when they read the rhetorical-ly good versions of the paragraphs (51% correct) than when they read the poor versions (26% correct). This difference was highly significant statistically.

As expected, the answers to the complex texts were less likely to be correct than the answers to the simple texts (42% versus 35%), but the interesting finding was that there was no sign of an interaction between complexity and the presence or absence of rhetorical structure. An analysis of variance yielded an $F < 1$ for this interaction. Rhetorical structure was just as helpful with the simple texts as with the complex ones.

The pattern of results was completely different when comprehension was as-sessed with the cloze test. Rhetorical form was simply irrelevant as far as the subjects' ability to guess the deleted words was concerned. Subjects guessed 40.7% of the words correctly in the good versions and 41.7% in the poor versions. Struc-tural complexity was similarly unrelated to cloze performance: 41.5% correct

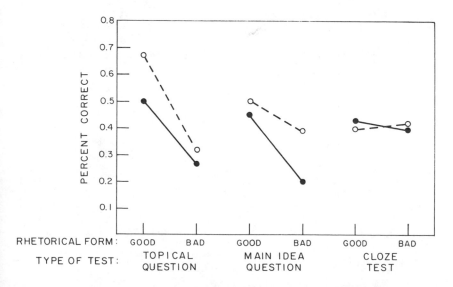

**Figure 7.2.** Percentage correct on topic and main idea questions as well as on cloze tests as a function of good and bad rhetorical form and structural complexity. (The open circles represent the structurally simple paragraphs, the closed circles represent the complex paragraphs.)

guesses on the good versions did not differ statistically from 40.9% on the poor versions.

### 7.5.3. Experiment 5B—A Replication

In a second experiment, two different texts were used, a simple and a more complex definition. Again, we wrote these paragraphs so that they corresponded ideally to the rhetorical form of a definition, and then transformed them to conceal as well as possible their rhetorical structure, without changing either the content or the integrity of the text itself. Thirty-two subjects participated in this experiment, and the procedure was in essential respects identical to that of the first experiment. The results for the definitions were very much as in the previous case, as shown in Figure 7.3. Good rhetorical form greatly facilitated performance on the topic and main idea questions. Indeed, the poor version of the complex paragraph was almost unintelligible to our college student subjects, with only 6% of the main ideas identified correctly. Complexity also produced the expected main effect, in that subjects did much better with the simple paragraphs. But, once again, complexity did not interact with rhetorical form. For the cloze test the presence or absence of

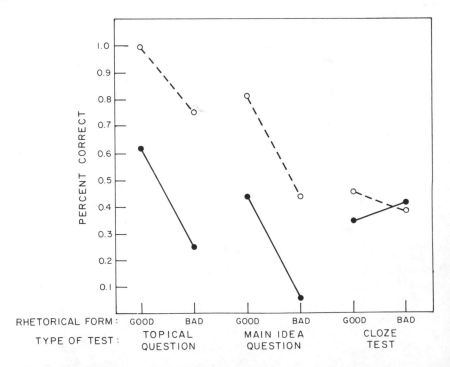

**Figure 7.3.** Percentage correct on topic and main idea questions as well as on cloze tests as a function of good and bad rhetorical form and structural complexity. (The open circles represent the structurally simple paragraphs, the closed circles represent the complex paragraphs.)

rhetorical structure was inconsequential (41.0% correct for the good forms versus 40.5% for the bad forms). Cloze performance was marginally better for the simple than for the complex texts.

### 7.5.4. Discussion

The implications of these two studies are quite clear. Good rhetorical form can significantly enhance the comprehension of descriptive passages at the macrolevel. Our college student subjects had presumably enough experience with the rhetorical structures used in these experiments that they had formed representations thereof (schemata) which matched the input in those cases where it was well structured rhetorically. Once such a schema was activated by a suitable input, it guided the subjects to form appropriate macrostructures.

It is not clear what happened when the rhetorical structure was absent. Perhaps subjects did not form macropropositions at all, more likely they generated inappropriate ones, picking out some salient detail from the text, rather than the main idea that we, as the authors, had intended to convey. The fact that most of the errors in answering the questions were incorrect responses rather than omissions is not informative in this respect, since it most likely reflects task demands: If subjects are asked to state two main points, they will give two responses, even if they have to make them up on the spot.

Meyer, Brandt, and Bluth (1980) reported some free recall data which support the present results. In their study, texts that were well organized rhetorically were recalled better than loose, list-like structures. According to our interpretation, this result is to be expected because rhetorical schemata play a role in the macrostructure formation and free recall depends to a considerable extent on the macrostructure.

In free recall, however, micro- and macroprocesses are confounded in ways that are hard to extricate. Indeed, a model-dependent analysis such as that of Kintsch and van Dijk (1978) is necessary for that purpose. In the present experiments, a clearer separation between macro- and microprocesses has been achieved. Rhetorical form was shown to have large effects on the former, but none on the latter. This finding has important implications for comprehension testing. One first has to have a very clear idea what aspect of the comprehension process is to be evaluated, and then a test must be constructed that is adequate for that purpose. This obvious point is often not appreciated in practice. One frequently sees cloze tests being used to validate readability tests, for instance. Then it is argued that texts with a good readability score are easier for students to read. Such claims reflect superficial and inadequate analyses of the problem of comprehension testing. No progress can be made in this area until testing procedures are based on a detailed understanding of the psychological processes involved in comprehension. There is no unitary process "comprehension" that could be measured once and for all if we could but find the right test. Comprehension is a common sense term which dissolves upon closer analysis into many different subprocesses. Thus, we need to construct separate measurement instruments for macroprocesses, knowledge integration, coherence, parsing, etc., as discussed in these chapters. A test for one level may have no bearing on another, as we have just shown in these experiments. Comprehension is just a convenient term for the aggregate of these processes; it is not to be reified, not to be tested for.

Results like the present ones (Kintsch & Yarbrough, 1982) and those of Meyer *et al.* (1980) are less ambiguous with respect to the psychological role of schematic superstructures than are the studies in the narrative domain. As we have seen, the difficulty in the latter studies is to unconfound textual structure from the structure of the content itself. Stories are about actions and readers know a lot about the structure of actions, inside or outside of stories. The content in descriptive texts is much less constrained. Temporal and causal relations play a decisive role in stories (see the discussion of Johnson & Mandler, 1980) but are absent in some types of descriptive texts. This is not to say that content does not constrain the form of an essay, but the constraints are certainly much weaker than in the case of stories. Hence demonstrations that rhetorical superstructures affect comprehension and memory in these cases can be accepted with some confidence.

*Chapter 8*

# Production Strategies

## 8.1. PROBLEMS OF A PRODUCTION MODEL FOR DISCOURSE

It is well known that most work done in psycholinguistics is about comprehension. In this respect the psychology of discourse is no exception. Our earlier model of discourse is also mainly about comprehension. Production was an issue limited to some aspects of reproduction, mainly in the framework of recall experiments. How language users go about producing a new discourse, either monological or as part of a dialogue, is a problem we know little about (but see Clark & Clark, 1977: Chapters 6 and 7; Butterworth, 1980; Gregg & Steinberg, 1980). In this book we will not even attempt to supply an adequate answer to this important question of language use, but will merely formulate a number of specific problems and some suggestions about the strategic aspects of discourse production as they seem to emerge from the previous chapters on comprehension.

A first observation in this respect is the restatement of an insight, which grew over at least 10 years of psycholinguistic research, that processes of production are not simply the reverse of processes of comprehension (Hirsch, 1977; Olson, Mack, & Duffy, 1981; Rubin, 1980). The application of early ideas from generative transformational grammar suggested that the grammar was a model of linguistic competence, and that such a model was neutral regarding the production or comprehension processes of language use. Although this assumption may have some validity for the account of such abstract objects as sentential or textual structures as such, it certainly does not hold for the cognitive model itself in which analysis and synthesis are related yet complementary processes (Fodor, Bever, & Garrett, 1974: 388ff.; Garrett, 1980: 212ff.). From the point of view of our strategy model this is of course a truism. The initial data and the goals of the processes are different, and, therefore, the strategies themselves must be different: Comprehension, which has surface structures as input and semantic or pragmatic representations as a cognitive goal, makes rather different demands on the system that does production, which starts from some knowledge or beliefs, or from some semantic or pragmatic representation and has surface structure expression as its goal.

Yet it does not seem wise to go to the other extreme and postulate completely separate processes. The first reason for this caveat is economical: It seems highly implausible that language users would not have recourse to the same or similar levels, units, categories, rules, or strategies in both the productive and the receptive processing of discourse: In both they handle surface structures and semantic representations, and many of the rule-governed and the strategic relations between these will feature both in production and in comprehension. Second, we have seen on many occasions that comprehension is not simply a passive or bottom-up process. Much of our understanding is active, top down, constructive, and predictive: Given some contextual and textual information, a language user may derive inferences about what to expect, at least from a semantic and stylistic point of view. Therefore, it will be interesting for the production model to specify which structures and principles have a more general nature, characterizing discourse processing in either direction, and which strategies are typical either for production or for comprehension. In trying to account for the step-by-step moves of the actual processing, it is precisely in this strategic approach that we may discover some of the particularities because it differs essentially from an abstract, structuralistic model.

### 8.1.1. The Input Problem

The study of production has been somewhat of a stepchild in the development of the psychology of language (Butterworth, 1980). Why do so many psychologists prefer to study comprehension rather than production? The answer lies largely in historical trends both within psychology and within linguistics. Psychologists have a long-standing interest in general questions about comprehension, not only of language but also in other areas such as perception. Linguists, on the other hand, have primarily been concerned with the structure of utterances and have developed sophisticated theories about these structures. Thus, psycholinguists had a reasonably well-understood independent variable for their experiments: the structure of the language input. They could then concentrate on what happened to that input during processing. Even the grammer itself is, despite claims to the contrary, biased toward analysis: It usually starts off with phonetic strings and phonological, morphological, and syntactic structures, which are interpreted by the semantic component. This bias is in part due to the historical development of linguistics itself: Both structuralism and the influence of behaviorism favored the analysis of observable phenomena, and hence of surface structures, leaving to psychology the account of such vague cognitive phenomena as meaning. Against this background it was natural that the psychology of language would be concerned primarily with analysis, decoding, interpretation, and hence with comprehension, rather than with production.

Within psychology, the experimental approach has its own requirements. The need for adequate control demands input that can be precisely specified, and so, again, words, phrases, sentences, or discourses are taken as the point of departure, rather than some unknown semantic representation or vague structures in memory.

### 8.1.2. Methods and Concepts for Studying Discourse Production

Whereas our intuitions about the processes underlying the surface formulation of sentences do not seem to be very strong (with the possible exception of conscious, stylistically determined, lexical choice), our intuitions about discourse production are much stronger. Especially in complex written discourse production, we may well be conscious of or even reflect about what to say and how to say it. Systematic protocol analysis of these thoughts may thus provide interesting data for the production model (Hayes & Flower, 1980).

The production of meaningful and contextually adequate linguistic utterances should be viewed as a complex task which needs planning. Whereas at the sentence level this planning may be more or less automatic, complex discourse seems to require a kind of planning that is similar to the planning of complex actions, and it would therefore be instructive to make interesting cognitive generalizations that cover both kinds of processing.

There exists a considerable body of theorizing and experimentation about the notion of planning and decision making relevant to discourse production. In their classic book about plans, Miller, Galanter, and Pribram (1960) established a connection between planning and linguistic production—though, of course, still formulated in terms of abstract generative-transformational grammars. After Miller, Galanter, and Pribram (1960), the notion of a "plan" was generally adopted in the psycholinguistics of speech production, both at the syntactic level and for the articulatory execution (Fodor, Bever, & Garrett, 1974; Clark & Clark, 1977). Clark and Clark (1977:228ff.) also discuss "discourse plans," in which they treat mainly conversational turn taking and descriptions.

The development of AI-models of language processing, though also biased toward understanding (the computer can hardly be expected to say something by itself), allows a more constructive approach to language and discourse processing. Programs can be and are designed to simulate the steps involved in production, for instance, in the task of question answering (Lehnert, 1980b).

The recent interest within both artificial intelligence and psychology in the representation of knowledge and beliefs is beginning to make feasible the much needed study of initial structures in the process of production. If language users form, formulate, and express some "idea," such an idea will come from their knowledge or beliefs. We know something about the structure of this idea, we know how to represent it, how to retrieve it from memory, and therefore we are finally able to go beyond informal intuitions in the study of language production.

The growing insight into the role and mechanism of both episodic and short-term memory helps us to specify further the basic features of initial internal representations as well as the short-term memory constraints on production. That is, what we have learned from comprehension processes about the limitations of the short-term buffer must also hold for production processes. From this perspective it is nearly trivial to state that it is impossible for a language user to first construct a long sequence of propositions which will then constitute the input to the surface structure formulators.

From this last point the notion again emerges that a strategic approach to production is imperative: There exists a flexible mechanism which at the same time constructs semantic representations, lexical expressions, and their syntactic and phonological structures, taking into account various kinds of information, such as knowledge, goals, local and global constraints at various levels, and other contextual information of the communicative setting.

Thus, even if we still know little about production processes, our insight into more general or comparable cognitive mechanisms allows us to make plausible guesses about the principles of production and to develop a number of hypotheses and experimental techniques to test these. In the next sections we will single out some of these hypotheses for closer inspection.

## 8.2. INTERACTIVE AND PRAGMATIC PRODUCTION STRATEGIES

### 8.2.1. Actions

The production of discourse should first of all be seen as the planning and execution of various actions as part of the social and cultural management of communicative interaction. A full account of the planning and execution strategies of action and interaction would require a separate monograph; here we can only mention some of their basic principles. Zammuner (1981), whose concept of "cognitive maneuvers" is akin to our strategies, has provided a more detailed account which is highly compatible with the suggestions we are making here.

As discourse production involves the planning of actions and interactions, the theory of actions is directly relevant to our discussion. We have reviewed the relevant notions from action theory in Chapter 3 and do not want to repeat this discussion here. However, we shall briefly reintroduce some crucial terms.

We need to distinguish between the observable properties of actions and the properties of the cognitive representations of actions. Actions have consequences—their *goals*. Actions are represented cognitively as *intentions,* and their goals as *purposes*. Goals are constrained in that they must be consistent with the *motivations* of the agent (his or her wishes, wants, preferences, knowledge about possible actions). Purposes are based on this motivational system.

Usually we are not concerned with a single action but with action *sequences* as well as with *macroactions*. *Plans* are the cognitive representations of global actions. *Strategies* play a role because we not only want to achieve global goals, but want to do so in an effective manner.

Against this theoretical background, we can begin our discussion of the strategic processes involved in discourse production.

## 8.2.2. The Strategic Planning of Production

First we need a strategy for deciding whether a desired change in a situation can and should be brought about by some action. A next strategy will analyze the possible actions of the agent (the abilities), the possible alternatives, and estimated effectiveness of these alternatives with respect to the realization of some global goal. Thus, if we do not want another person to take a trip to Italy, for example, because we will miss that person too much or are concerned about his or her health, we will in general not prevent him or her from going by applying bodily force, but will have recourse to verbal interaction, such as a letter or a conversation. That is, in most cases where the interpretation and reasons for our own actions are not obvious from nonverbal actions alone, discourse will be involved, taken as an inherent part and form of social interaction. Yet, we have many possible discourses that may ultimately have the effect that some listener will not go to Italy. We may warn someone, request or command, or just affirm that we do not like it. That is, as part of the complex system of interaction, people will form concepts of verbal macroactions, that is, plans for global speech acts. It is exactly at this point where the actual production of discourse begins, given a representation of the situation, of the action context, of one's own motivations and goals. Macroplanning is a feature of production that has been neglected in the sentence production literature. Whereas the notion of speech act planning does occur (see, e.g., Clark & Clark, 1977), the formation of macroplans was hardly discussed, although in our opinion it is one of the basic planning and control aspects of production. Butterworth (1980:164) mentions macroplans but fails to identify them precisely, either in semantic or pragmatic terms. Van Dijk (1980a) gives more details on macroplanning of discourse.

A plan may be formed to change the situation in the desired direction, and this plan may be the global representation of a macro speech act. The strategy used in the choice and local execution of such a speech act will first of all involve a more specific analysis of the situation. If the listener is a friend, commands are out. If we do not want to exhibit our own wishes or wants too much, requests may be too direct. If we are concerned about the well-being of our speech partner, a suggestion, advice, or warning may be more appropriate. Hence, the formation of a pragmatic (macro-)plan depends on a systematic scanning of the situation for those features that determine the possible and effective use of a speech act, such as to advise, suggest, or warn. For our purposes we will assume that this pragmatic plan controls the rest of the production process. This control is strategic: Sometimes possible component actions will—on the basis of knowledge and experience—be derived top down from this global plan; on the other hand, actual actions will be evaluated constantly in order to see whether the change in the situation is or will be possible according to one's purpose. Similarly, various kinds of information will be admitted to the strategy: Sociocultural constraints, analyses of one's own motivation or that of the listener, as well as the semantic and surface structures of the ongoing discourse will be given as input to the strategy. The actual—and changing—state of the hearer, crucial in order to bring about the desired change of knowledge, beliefs, opinions, and their possible action consequences (as decided, planned, and executed by the hearer in the same way as described above) will be monitored by parallel analysis of his or her doings, that is, intended actions and nonconscious activities, such as nonverbal communication (gestures, facial expressions, and so on). The result of this monitoring will provide the necessary feedback information for the system of discourse production. Given all this information and its analysis by the speaker, decisions may be made about the more specific content and surface structures as well as about the actual execution of the discourse.

It should be stressed at this point that the strategic planning of speech acts at this global level—using the various kinds of cognitive and contextual information described here—does not yield pragmatic information. That is, it is not likely that a language user will decide to use advice or a warning independent of the semantic content of the discourse. Macro speech acts also have a global propositional content, that is, a macroproposition. This macroproposition is also derived from the analysis of the interaction context and its cognitive counterparts. The conclusion 'I do not want her to go to Italy', which may be the input to the discourse production system as a whole and determine the choice of the most appropriate and effective global speech act, also yields the theme or topic of the discourse, and hence the macrostructural content for the global speech act. Again, we see that strategies have variable, fragmentary input, flexible operations, and multiple outputs. We now have two closely related macrostructures, formed during interaction, for the further formation of the actual discourse, namely, a pragmatic plan and a semantic plan, for instance, 'I am giving her advice' and 'She should not go to Italy'. Together with further cognitive and contextual information about the listener and the ongoing speech situation, this very specific *discourse plan* will be the hierarchical schema that controls the local, linear, that is, "lower," levels of discourse production.

What we have described here is an idealization. Actual behavior in language production may sometimes come close to this idealization, especially in writing and with difficult texts, where conscious, orderly planning is almost a necessity. Ordinarily, discourse plans will be much more sketchy, more vague, and not necessarily conscious at all. In many types of conversation the control is almost entirely local and data driven: The plan may be no more than a general decision to keep up the conversation. Even in writing we observe similar phenomena: in some of the poorer essays or chapters we have to read which jump from one random thought to the next, or in certain types of literary prose where the discourse plan affects only some very high level of organization and is well hidden from the reader. We do not claim that the picture we have presented of careful, deliberate discourse planning accurately depicts what people do. At present, however, our need is to explore theoretically via our intuitions as we do here, and eventually also experimentally, what people can do and how discourse production works in such idealized, simplified situations.

### 8.2.3. Discourse Plans

The execution of a global speech act is, in all respects, a strategic enterprise. There is an overall goal, and it is the task of the speaker to strategically bring about a change in accordance with this goal on the basis of continuously fluctuating local information. In other words, the choice of local speech acts is not only determined by the macro speech act, but also by the previous speech acts and the reaction to these of the hearer. Especially in nondirected everyday conversation the hearer is able to influence fundamentally the pragmatic and semantic plans of the speaker, such that even these global plans may be changed during speaking. If our global plan is to invite somebody to go to the movies with us, then local information from the hearer may be such that we give up this plan before its full execution. Thus, a global plan will depend on local information for its effective execution. Each response from the hearer will require its own reaction from the speaker because each local speech act must be defined with respect not only to the overall speech act, but also to the local action context. The strategy involved must therefore be that a speaker tries to effectively reach his or her goal while taking into account this local information.

Subject to these local constraints, the central strategy remains to successively realize the subgoals that may lead to the final, overall goal. Here we meet the inverse of those operations encountered in the previous chapters. Whereas macrostrategies are operations that derive macrostructures from local information by deletion, generalization, and construction—for both semantic and pragmatic structures—we now expect global information to be *specified* for the local levels. That is, details are *added,* general statements are *particularized,* and complex actions are *analyzed* into their respective components. Typical, for instance, is the execution of a series of preparatory, component, and terminating speech acts. If, for the execution of a global speech act, prior information about the hearer's state of mind is necessary, then a number of preparatory speech acts will be executed. Some of these will have a purely ritual function, that is, defining how speech interaction is initiated in such encounters. Thus, greetings, questions about mutual health, and so on, will typically open everyday conversations between speech partners who meet after a certain period of time. Genuinely preparatory speech acts are those that establish the mutual information for the speech participants relative to their respective goals. Such interactional planning has been discussed by Clark and Clark (1977), Beattie (1980), and Castelfranchi and Parisi (1980).

Thus, if we do not want somebody to go to Italy, we might first of all, in a state of epistemic uncertainty, try to ascertain whether the hearer is indeed planning to go, for example, by such questions as ''Are you still planning to go to Italy this summer?'' The most direct strategy, but often not a very wise one if one knows that the hearer really likes going there, would simple be to directly state the advice: ''Well, don't go.'' Of course, this will usually be insufficient, because the speaker knows that the hearer will want to have good reasons. Thus, the speaker will try to establish those grounds by making a number of statements so that the hearer may know what the disadvantages are of going to Italy. If these are disadvantages for the speaker (e.g., that the speaker will miss the hearer), then a request would be more appropriate than advice. For the advice it should be shown that the action would have unwanted consequences for the hearer. Hence, assertions will be made to spell out such consequences: hot weather if the hearer does not like heat, many tourists if the hearer is known to dislike touristy places, work that will not be finished if the hearer has work to finish, and so on. At this local level, it may then be the case that each of these strategic points made by the speaker needs its own justifications. That is, the assertion ''It is very hot there during the summer'' may be challenged by the hearer and may need to be backed up, for example with the further assertion ''In Sicily temperatures during the summer are usually between 30 and 40 C.'' We see that even at the local level strategies may be necessary to make a relevant move, to change the knowledge or opinion of the hearer about a particular point. One such step may in some cases extend to a full embedded discourse, like a story. For our example, this would be a story by the speaker about his or her personal experiences during a summer vacation in Italy. The evaluation and the coda of such a story, giving the emotional and the pragmatic conclusion of the narrative, then provide, in an indirect way, the assertion that is meant to influence the opinion of the hearer about this aspect of going on a vacation to Italy. This is a proper rhetorical device for the strategic specification of speech acts at the local level: The assertive claim is the same, but the persuasive function, and hence the effectiveness which defines the strategy, may be considerably different. That is, here we typically have added information which, as such, is not relevant (my experiences need not be relevant for your vacation plans), but which may provide more interesting, better grounded premises for the general conclusion. Gazdar (1980) has described more completely such surface manifestations of underlying pragmatic conditions.

It should be noticed that also a strategic use may be made of the global or local advice speech act itself: If the speaker for some reason wants to dissimulate his or her own preferences, then a direct request grounded with ''I don't like it'' may not be powerful enough. In that case, a strategy aiming at establishing a belief that not going is for the benefit of the hearer may be more effective. This strategy is so common in everyday interaction that speakers sometimes are not even aware of it themselves. It is well-known in therapeutic practice, for instance, that people learn to recognize these strategies during their interaction with others, especially in those cases where they may lead to interpersonal conflicts.

The successive local speech acts have a preparatory function so that often it will not even be necessary to accomplish the main speech act in a conversation because the hearer already knows what the overall goal of the speaker is. That is, often the overall speech act will be *indirect*, leaving the possible overall interpretation to the hearer. This apparent freedom of the hearer to assign his or her own interpretation to the global action of the speaker also has strategic relevance: It seemingly leaves open the possibility of drawing other conclusions without appearing to be uncooperative. Such strategic games people play need not be spelled out here: They are well known from the sociological literature on strategic interaction. For our own discussion it means that under the general control of an overall goal, speakers will plan and execute local actions that take into account the final state of previous actions as well as the wishes, wants, preferences, and beliefs of the hearer and which respect the more general principles of cooperative interaction.

In monological discourse, such as in a lecture, a scholarly article, or a news story, the specification of global speech acts is, of course, less dependent on the direct interaction with the hearer or reader. Yet, speakers or writers will implicitly take into account possible objections of the hearer/reader and specify matters in such a way that these are taken care of first.

Another difference between the monological and the dialogical forms of discourse planning is that in written monological discourse, planning may be more conscious, more explicit, and its execution better controlled by the overall plan. In everyday conversation, a speaker may have such an overall plan, but the information from or about the hearer may be such that the plan must be changed, or the local speech interaction may be such that the speech partners get lost in a local interchange. Thus, speakers may forget the overall plan and will typically say things like "What was I talking about?", "What did I want to ask?", etc. Or, local goals may suddenly take over and dominate the rest of the conversation. Thus, in our Italy example a long argument may develop about the unpredictability of the weather or ways to cope with a hot climate. For a speaker it may suddenly become more important to defend his or her credibility on some point of assertion than to execute the original global speech act. Hence conversations will in general be more locally conditioned than the production of written discourse.

Finally, it should be noted that the ultimate goal of verbal interaction is to speak or write in such a way that the knowledge, beliefs, or opinions of the hearer are transformed according to the wishes of the speaker, often with the further goal that the hearer will act on that basis according to the wishes of the speaker. This perlocutionary aspect of speech acts and interaction requires permanent analysis of the assumed state of the knowledge, beliefs, opinions, attitudes, and emotions of the hearer. Similarly, an assertion or opinion, or the conditions for an action will only be acceptable if they are coherent with the information in these cognitive systems. If this is not obviously the case, the speaker must choose a strategy of cognitive coherence establishment, either by specifying the coherence link or by first changing the other information. For the establishment of more or less superficial knowledge, beliefs, or opinions, the argumentative specification of new facts or a correction showing the incoherence may be sufficient if the new information is defensibly well grounded. It is well known from the social psychological literature, however, that more fundamental beliefs, opinions, or attitudes cannot thus be changed logically: They will need additional and more varied, persuasive information. The strategy in that case will preferably be to show that what is proposed is still coherent with these more fundamental ideas, or that even more basic beliefs and attitudes require a change in the specific ones to make the information acceptable. In our Italy example, we may appeal to the rather central value 'that one should do one's duty' when it is argued that some project, say, should be finished first before one takes a vacation in Italy. Instead of establishing a coherence link with other beliefs or opinions, the speaker here shows that some proposition, for example, 'I want to go to Italy' is incoherent with these beliefs and opinions and should therefore be changed. As soon as the speaker recognizes that the main goal, namely, that of dissuasion, cannot be reached, a more modest goal can be set up (e.g., going to Italy only for a short time). That is, if there is a conflict of interests, the compromise strategy will be followed.

The amount of information processed in the production of a global speech act is enormous. When we then realize that the choice of a particular speech act (together with its content and its stylistic surface structures) must depend on all this information and still be planned within fractions of a second, the conclusion must again be that without powerful mechanisms of organization, reduction, higher level control, and especially expedient and fast strategies, this task cannot be accomplished with the available information-processing resources. In the next two chapters we will examine in more detail what the consequences are for the cognitive model that is to accommodate this great amount of information processing. Here we have argued that discourse production, first of all, is the production of some global speech act, and that the goals of this act are controlled by the overall goals of the interaction in a given communicative context and by the norms and values of the actual (sub)culture. The global speech act then controls the production of local speech acts, namely, by a number of specification operations that generate necessary preparatory and component speech acts. The definite choice of such speech acts depends on local pragmatic coherence constraints and the features of the actual local action context. Part of this action context is the set of beliefs we have about the actual knowledge, beliefs, interests, opinions, or attitudes of the hearer. The strategy followed, then, is first to realize the subgoals that contribute to the realization of the global goal. Depending on the situation and the cognitive set of the hearer, a speaker may choose an elaborate but perhaps too complex strategy, with the risk of losing the hearer's interest or of getting trapped in side arguments, or, alternatively, a more direct, but riskier, strategy. This strategic choice will depend not only on the importance of the realization of the goal or on the cognitive state of the hearer, but also on more general principles of interaction, such as politeness, frankness, openness, honesty, and so on. In other words, a permanent strategic choice must be made between an optimal realization of one's goals and an optimal confirmation of one's social esteem. The interaction and pragmatic production strategies are summarized in Figure 8.1.

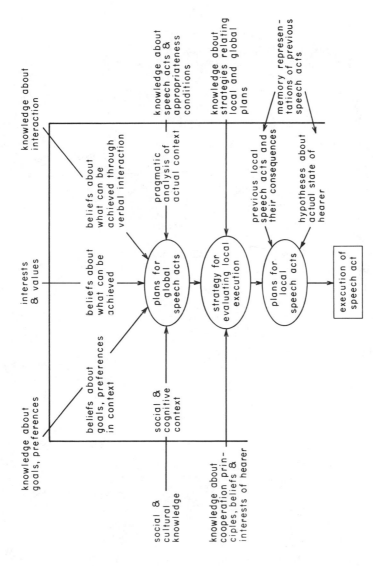

**Figure 8.1.** The interaction of strategies in discourse production.

## 8.3. SEMANTIC PRODUCTION STRATEGIES

Unlike most accounts of production processes, we began our discussion with the production of speech acts as they are accomplished by the utterance of discourse in social contexts. That is, according to the views of most interesting linguistic theories, language and discourse are not merely seen in terms of forms and their meanings, but primarily in terms of social interaction, upon which syntax and semantics are functionally dependent. This means that meaning production and its surface expression should not be viewed as an autonomous process. And, indeed, we have seen that at both the local and the global level, semantic representations are constructed as the content for the speech act of a discourse. Similarly, surface structures, such as those accounted for by phonology, morphology, and syntax, are not only expressions of underlying meaning but may directly express pragmatic and other interactional features (e.g., Gazdar, 1980; Givón, 1979b). In technical terms this implies that we cannot merely have a pragmatic component which yields information as input for the semantic component, which in turn yields information that is the input for the syntactic component, and so on. Certain conditions of speech acts and their appropriateness may be directly expressed in intonation, emphatic particles, word order, or gestures. Thus, our conceptual analysis of the production process in terms of various subcomponents should not be viewed as a representation of the successive phases of production. On the contrary, our strategic approach stresses the fact that interactional, pragmatic, semantic, and surface structure information may closely cooperate in the production process. This also holds for the semantic aspects of production. Semantic strategies may have pragmatic, contextual, surface structural, and epistemic (i.e., knowledge-dependent) structures as their input.

Semantic production strategies should be accounted for in terms that are similar to those of discourse comprehension. Basically, we assume that semantic macrostructures (a topic or theme) are formed and that semantic representations for the respective sentences of a discourse are construed under the control of these macrostructures. In other words, the semantic macrostructure of a discourse may be viewed as a global semantic production plan. At least for more complex, written discourse types, this view is intuitively appealing: When we produce a discourse, we will know what it is about in global terms before we start to produce the first sentence. In rather free discourse types, such as spontaneous everyday conversation, such a semantic plan may be less obvious or even nonexistent for the conversation as a whole. In that case, several loosely related topics may exist in successive order. The topic for such conversation episodes may be construed more or less continuously. Yet, even then the speech participants need to know, in order to contribute coherently to the conversation, what the actual topic of such an episode is. So, the basic principles of semantic production also are assumed to hold for such discourse types, with the provision that the plan may have a more local, less stable, and more interaction-controlled nature.

### 8.3.1. Strategies for the Semantic Macrostructure

The strategic interpenetration of pragmatics and semantics has been discussed in the previous section. In order to construct a pragmatic plan for the execution of a global speech act, a language user must generate at the same time a macrostructure which constitutes the content of this global speech act. We do not simply generate the idea of wanting to produce a warning or a request without at the same time generating the propositional content of such a global speech act.

This topic must be construed from information in memory. More specifically, we assume that the information that constitutes the possible topic for a discourse resides in episodic memory. Most discourses are not about our general semantic knowledge, but rather about more specific, particular experiences with persons, objects, actions, or events. Perhaps only in textbooks, encyclopedias, or other didactic discourse forms, does the topic production depend mainly on long-term, general knowledge and beliefs. Our knowledge about 'your going to Italy this summer' has a more episodic nature, and therefore we should look for the origins of topic formation in the episodic representation of our knowledge of the world. The same is true for our knowledge, beliefs, opinions, or wants with respect to what the hearer should know, believe, or do as a result of our discourse. Hence, under the control of interactional and pragmatic information, defining the goals of the discourse, the language user will select from episodic memory a topic for the discourse. Such a topic may be directly read off from what we know, as when we want to give information, or else may be construed from conceptual units that are otherwise represented. That is, taking again our earlier example, we may not have a proposition such as 'I do not want you to go to Italy', but perhaps only the proposition 'John is going to Italy this summer', and some opinion related to this fact. Only in the process of expressing this opinion through textual communication is the relevant macroproposition formed.

In order to better dissociate the episodic information in memory from the actually planned macrostructure, we should carefully distinguish between these two types of semantic or conceptual information. By a semantic macrostructure we understand the propositional structure that will actually be expressed through the sentences of the text and their meanings, whereas the episodic information is in principle language and discourse independent: It may also be expressed by other means, for example paratextually or by nonverbal communication, or not be expressed at all. In this sense, it is only a form of proto-semantic representation: It forms the information from which semantic macrostructures are construed. We will simply refer to it as "episodic information." In Chapter 10 we will give further arguments for this distinction between textual and other forms of semantic information in episodic memory.

The precise strategies underlying the formation of semantic macrostructures can only be speculated about at this moment. It cannot simply be said that one or more arguments, such as persons or objects, are selected for attention and that some global property, event, or action is then predicated of these. This may be the case, but more often than not what is really interesting from a communicative point of view is to state (or ask, request, order, etc.) something new and interesting like your vacation in Italy—which would emphasize instead the production priority of predicates. We may even talk about vacations in general, thereby changing the possible participants. There does not seem to be a general strategy that holds for all forms of topic production: Sometimes it will primarily be a concept for a person or object, or a concept for a property, relation, event, or action, whereas often the combination of some thing or object and some property or event will be selected as a whole. It will, however, be assumed that only the full propositional structure thus generated may be the input for macrostructure formation for a particular discourse.

Propositions that are possible candidates for a macrostructural role in discourse production need not occur as such in episodic memory; they might first need construction. Such a construction process may involve a proper derivation of a more global proposition from more detailed information in memory: We may have bits and pieces of experiences which hitherto had not been unified by some higher level proposition. We may observe or undergo some action or event, and understand these locally, without realizing that we were part of a 'hold up', a 'seduction', or a 'revolution'. Coherent discourse production may force a language user to first organize such partial experiences into some more global representation, so that the discourse about them has some clearly identifiable topic. During everyday spontaneous conversation this global interpretation may occur at the same time as, or even somewhat later than, the respective production steps.

### 8.3.2. Strategies for the Microstructure

Important for a cognitive model of discourse production are, of course, the strategies involved in the specification of such macrostructures, as derived from episodic information, into the respective semantic representations of the sentences of the discourse. In other words, we have here a linearization problem: We have some global topic, but must start somewhere and continue coherently. Once this problem has been solved, the speaker or writer can have recourse to familiar and even automatized strategies for expressing these semantic representations in surface forms.

As we have assumed in the previous section for the specification strategies of pragmatic macrostructures, we will also assume here that, basically, semantic production depends on the application of inverse macro-operations. That is, given some macroproposition for a discourse as a whole, information will be added, particularized, and analyzed. The resulting propositions may still be fairly general and may need further applications of the same processes. That is, talking about our vacation in Italy, we may particularize the concept of 'Italy' by giving the places we visited, and analyze the actions into preparatory, component, and consequent actions, such as taking a train to Rome or visiting some museum or participating in a political event. At that point we may add details drawn directly from episodic memory, even if these are irrelevant for the rest of the story—for instance, that we had the best ice cream in Florence.

If specification operations are indeed some form of inverse macro-operations they can be formulated in a rather straightforward way: enumerate elements from sets, analyze actions into component actions, particularize general predicates, and so on. Yet, this is only one aspect of the complex strategy of going from topic to subtopic and from there to individual semantic representations. What we also need, as part of the linearization problem, is an appropriate order for these semantic representations. That is, we should effectively construct a relevant textbase for the discourse. The ordering problem for information in discourse has received some attention, for example, in the literature on descriptions: Linde and Labov (1975) (see Clark & Clark, 1977:232, for a summary), Levelt (1982), and Jarvella and Klein (1982). Levelt (1982) also interestingly mentions the medieval and classical rhetorical notions of ordering, such as the relations between "world" and "discourse" ordering. Here we extend the notion of ordering to all relevant levels of discourse production.

Ordering strategies differ from one discourse type to another. For instance, a news story will begin with some rather general, summarizing information, directly actualizing part of the macrostructure as the first part of the text, after which the specifications are given. In normal stories we will begin with details about location, place, participants, and their properties. In literary narrative we may begin in medias res, that is, with the specification of the complication of the story. Hence we see that a first constraint on ordering is determined by the schematic superstructure. In the previous chapter we have seen that such a canonical or transformed schema may be construed or retrieved from memory. In the formation and specification of macrostructures the schema will act not only as a further organization of the macrostructure, but also as a global form, determining which information comes first. For each category of the superstructure schema we may then specify the contents of the relevant episode. More specifically semantic are the strategies for ordering semantic information within episodes. Both for lower level macrostructures and for the semantic microstructures, then, we may have the following ordering strategies:

1. In the *description of processes, events, and actions,* follow the natural order unless contextual, pragmatic, rhetorical, or cognitive constraints necessitate another order (see below). Under the natural order we understand the ordering of propositions that is parallel to the temporal or conditional order of the facts.
2. In the *description of objects, persons, or states of affairs,* follow an order which is from more general to particular, from higher to lower, from sets to elements, from wholes to parts, and so on.
3. In the *description of whole facts,* first specify some minimal description of discourse individuals and then the additional properties or relations of these individuals. (This is necessary for the appropriate reidentification of individuals.)

4. Follow the *presuppositional structure* of the discourse, that is, always first specify the facts (individuals and their properties or relations) presupposed by later facts described in the discourse.
5. It is possible that the ordering strategies 1–4 can all be expressed as manifestations of more abstract underlying strategies. If the macrostructure is represented as a semantic network with propositions as the nodes and relations among propositions as the connections, general linearization strategies might be formulated on the graph structure, as was done in Levelt (1982). The simplest strategy would be to follow a path, if there is one, with specifications for what to do at choice points, how to handle loops in the network, and how to do all of this within the limitations imposed by human short-term memory. The seminal work of Levelt might show us the way to a formal theory of linearization strategies in discourse production.
6. If *deviations* from the natural order, as specified in Strategies 1 and 2, are necessary, mark these explicitly, for example, by time, condition, or spatial expressions from which the hearer/reader can reconstruct the natural order.

Deviations from natural ordering principles are common, though. They may be summarized under the following categories (van Dijk, 1977a):

1. *Cognitive reordering.* Often it is not the proper ordering of the facts, but rather our perception, understanding, recognition, evaluation, or production of facts, which is relevant. Under the scope of verbs expressing such mental acts as 'see', 'think', 'remember', 'dream', 'understand', etc., the facts may be presented later than the respective mental facts under whose scope they are presented.
2. *Pragmatic reordering.* For the appropriate and effective execution of speech acts, some semantic information may need to be specified in a different order than the natural order, for instance, so as to mark pragmatic relevance. This, in an expression such as "Can you please shut the window. It is cold in here," the specification of a semantic and pragmatic condition comes later, so that the upshot of the request, which is the main speech act, can be presented first. We will call this a (pragmatic) primacy strategy. If information is presented at the end of a text or episode, although properly belonging to an earlier position in the natural order, we will call this a recency strategy. Whereas primacy strategies are important for the establishment of information that must dominate the comprehension of later information (as such, the lead in a newspaper story), recency strategies are aiming at better recall due to the specific location of new information in episodic memory.
3. *Rhetorical reordering.* Related to pragmatic reordering strategies are the rhetorical reordering strategies. They do not specifically aim to stress pragmatic relevance, but will in general involve transformations of the natural or even of the usual textual ordering which aim at greater effectiveness. The esthetic function of reorderings in literary narrative are one example in

kind. Reordering may also be used to enhance suspense in stories (such as the final identification of the murderer in a detective story).

4. *Interactional reordering.* Also related to pragmatic reordering strategies are those ordering strategies that depend on the properties of the communicative and interactional context. For reasons of cooperation, such as politeness, modesty, strategic effectiveness, we may delay necessary information or give later conclusions first. Thus, in a request for money, we will not usually follow the pragmatic reordering and ask for the money first and then specify our reasons, but introduce the request with some conditions. Sometimes this ordering may coincide with the natural order or with the cognitive ordering, but this need not be the case: Conclusions from argumentation may come first if this is interactionally relevant. In general, we expect information that is probably difficult for the hearer to accept to be presented later in the discourse (assuming a communicative situation in which cooperation principles rather than conflict principles are followed).

It goes without saying that both the normal ordering strategies and their systematic reorderings as determined by cognitive, pragmatic, rhetorical, and interactional criteria need further specification, discourse analysis, and experimental verification.

Although we now have some elements for an informal model of semantic production, featuring specification strategies for semantic macrostructures and ordering strategies for local semantic information, the picture is still far from complete. What has remained implicit is the role of knowledge, beliefs, or opinions, both in the speaker and in the hearer (as represented by the speaker), as well as some further consequences of the pragmatic and interactional constraints on discourse production.

We know from the model of discourse comprehension that much of the information necessary to understand a text remains implicit, although presupposed by sentences of the text, and that this information is, if necessary, supplied by the episodic or more general knowledge of the hearer or reader. In the next chapter we will examine in more detail the strategies applied in using this knowledge during discourse processing. In production, however, this means, in general, that a strategy is followed according to which all information directly known to the hearer need not be explicitly expressed, although indications of its presupposed nature may be necessary to signal its role in understanding. The same holds for obvious inferences for such knowledge items. In principle, then, only new information must be given—either in assertions or in other speech act contexts. This newness, to be sure, applies to full facts, not to individuals or their properties as such: That is, we may tell a story about people we already know, or tell known events or actions about persons we do not know, and so on. Also, in order to be able to introduce these new facts, some known propositions may be explicitly stated in order to place information or to recall these known facts to the hearer. We know or may infer that people usually open doors in order to enter a house, but a story may still mention the

fact that "Peter opened the door," first of all, to specify the instantiated fact of a
more general knowledge script, and second, in order to describe at least some
features of what was going on, so that the hearer knows where we are in description
of the sequence of facts. Again, discourse analysis and psychological experiments
will be necessary in order to establish how much of the directly available or inferable knowledge must be at least or at most presented in a text. This variation will
depend on context (e.g., knowledge about the hearer's knowledge), the discourse
type, or the rhetorical effectiveness of the discourse. We will return in somewhat
more detail to this issue in the next chapter.

## 8.4. STRATEGIES FOR ESTABLISHING
##      LOCAL COHERENCE

In this and the next section we will briefly turn to a series of more specific
strategies for the semantic production of discourse—those determining the local
coherence of the textbase. We have examined some strategies that specify the
semantic information of the discourse and its ordering principles in the textbase
under the control of contextual information and of pragmatic and semantic macrostructures. We have seen that the knowledge that the hearer is assumed to have
plays an important role in the decisions about what information to leave implicit and
what information to include in the discourse. Although we thus have a first idea of
what to put into a textbase and in which approximate order, we still do not know
how the various propositions of the textbase are semantically related by the speaker.
That is, once a proposition is produced, there are severe constraints on the production of the next proposition. What are these constraints? In other words, what are
the precise expansion strategies for textbases?

Let us assume, first of all, that a speaker selects from the more or less ordered
set of information as it is stored in episodic memory—and produced under the
control of macrostrategies of specification—one proposition, by introducing it into
the short-term memory buffer. Next, we assume that this proposition will be the
input into the sentence formulation strategies to which we will turn in what follows:
That is, a syntactic form will be construed on the basis of the semantic (and
pragmatic) information as well as lexical and phonological expressions. During
these operations, the semantic representation will be kept in the short-term memory
buffer because this information will be necessary in the strategic establishment of
coherence with the next proposition. The easiest strategy would then be to select
from episodic memory a proposition that is semantically coherent with the proposition already stored in the short-term memory buffer—again under the control of the
macroproposition that is relevant for this episode, also stored in the short-term
memory buffer. This selection strategy for next propositions would, for instance,
search for a proposition that satisfies the following conditions:

1. It should be a specification of the same macroproposition.
2. It should respect the ordering principles for textbases.

3. It should be conditionally or functionally related to the previous proposition (the one already in the short-term memory buffer).
4. It should either feature an identical discourse referent and introduce a new predicate, or feature the same predicate for different discourse referents, and the time, location and possible world should be identical or be explicitly changed.

Once found, a proposition satisfying these conditions will also be added to the short-term memory buffer and then given to the sentence formulation mechanism. Part of the coherence conditions may explicitly instruct this mechanism to express surface structure signals, such as connectives, pronominalization (or pro-verb production), definite articles, tense and location marking, definite articles or demonstratives, and so on.

Although this direct search strategy for coherent propositions does not seem basically wrong, it is still too structural and not strategic enough. It may be the case that the next proposition does not occur ready-made in episodic memory at all. At least for some production processes we should rather assume that the next proposition is construed in short-term memory, out of information which indeed is in episodic memory, but under the control of the semantic structure of the actual proposition (and of the relevant semantic and pragmatic macrostructures). It may even be the case that there is a feedback from the surface structure of the actual proposition as it is sententially expressed. This construction hypothesis for coherence establishment during production is more flexible than the direct actualization hypothesis. Given a proposition like 'John went to Italy this summer' as the first proposition (with a more or less macrostructural function) of a story, we may, of course, directly actualize a stored proposition such as 'John had an accident in Rome', but we may also construct a next proposition such as 'John didn't like it, because he had an accident', in which the first proposition may not directly occur in episodic memory at all, but rather is now constructed on the basis of a knowledge-determined inference: 'People who are involved in accidents do not like them'. In other words, a more active construction strategy allows the speaker to start from given information in the short-term memory buffer, such as a concept for a discourse referent, and then combine relevant information in episodic memory with world knowledge and assumptions about the knowledge, beliefs, interests, and goals of the hearer. If we merely actualized our ready-made episodic memory information, we would be unable to strategically modify it so as to make it relevant for the actual local context of production. Also, we should assume that a speaker will sometimes suddenly realize implications or associations of a currently produced proposition which were not in episodic memory but which are also currently inferred. Another argument for the construction hypothesis for local coherence establishment is the sentence formulation mechanism. Instead of having a full new proposition ready for expression, a speaker may start, strategically, with the first noun phrase, functioning as subject and topic of the next sentence, without yet knowing exactly which new information, in the form of a predicate phrase, and functioning as comment of the next sentence, should be actualized from episodic memory.

Hesitation phenomena after initial pronouns or other topical noun phrases seem to indicate that even during production of next sentences semantic information is still sought for in episodic memory. This is in accordance with the comprehension strategy which already begins to interpret the noun phrase at the beginning of next sentences.

## 8.5. PROPOSITIONAL PRODUCTION STRATEGIES

The establishment of local coherence during discourse production takes place, as we have seen in the previous section, by a number of strategies regulating the retrieval or construction of subsequent propositions on the basis of episodic information, and under the control of a macroproposition, the current speech act, and other contextual information relevant for the present local production process. This means that the production of meaning is not simply the actualization of propositions from memory, to be expressed via the sentence formulation mechanism.

In general, each proposition must be constructed under textual and contextual constraints of coherence and relevance, and only seldom do such propositions occur ready-made in episodic memory. Both semantically and pragmatically the primary goal of discourse is to say something about reality or to affect it in a particular way. Hence, we may have concepts about this reality in memory, for example, concepts of persons, objects, places, events, or actions we know about. Presumably, these fragments of episodic knowledge about reality organize into schematic clusters, say, around persons or events. To be able to express this knowledge, or our beliefs or opinions about them, the conceptual richness that may be used to refer should somehow be fixed. That is, particular meanings must be selected that specify the particular properties of a person, object, or event. We may have a lot of knowledge about the concept 'John', but when we want to refer to John through the expression of a discourse term, we need to use meaningful expressions, such as *brother, lawyer, crook,* or pronouns. In other words, during the production of propositions, a language user must select a specific meaning which is coherent and relevant with respect to text and context.

It seems difficult to specify just one type of strategy for this kind of textually and contextually bound formation of propositions. The canonical form of a proposition, reflecting the abstract structure of a fact in some possible world, is, of course, only an approximate schema for the strategies involved. It tells us how to complete a proposition once initiated with one of its concepts, but it does not say where to start the construction of the propositional frame. However, despite this still rather obscure aspect of textual meaning production, there are some suggestions for strategic effectiveness. In fact, surface structures provide us with clues regarding this kind of underlying semantic strategy. Thus, it is well known that the canonical topic–comment structure of many languages has a strategic value: It suggests how language users go about linking new information, or now actualized or relevant information, with old, previously actualized, information.

Against this background, therefore, we will assume that the basic strategy for textual meaning production consists in the selection of one or more arguments, to which a series of predicates are systematically applied. These arguments will usually be discourse referents such as persons or objects, and the predicates will usually be properties or relations between these persons or objects. For each subsequent proposition of a textbase, the strategy is to start the new proposition schema with the already actualized individual concept. Thus this concept has topic function, and is in many languages also expressed as the first noun phrase, often as a subject, of the next sentence expressing this proposition. The next step, then, is to retrieve the predicate denoting the property or relation in which this given argument is involved. This predicate is associated with a propositional schema or predicate frame, which provides the typical participants and their roles associated with the predicate. If these other participants were not introduced before, they must then be introduced, either explicitly or implicitly. If one or more of the other participants was already introduced, the predicate merely gives the relation holding between them.

A next aspect of the strategy of proposition production is to follow some preferred order. That is, certain participant roles are reviewed first. If the discourse referent is a human being, first its role as an agent will be preferred in production. Hence, sentence topics will often be, not only subjects of sentences, but also agents or causes of the predicate schema. If they are no longer agents, then two strategies are possible: Another agent may be introduced so that the previous agent can become, for instance, patient; alternatively, the discourse referent remains topic, and hence is introduced first to establish strategic coherence, but his different role is specifically signaled through different pronouns, intonation, or prepositions, as in *John went to Italy last summer. He was surprised by the vast numbers of tourists.*

Finally, the state of affairs, action, or event thus propositionally produced must be situated, that is, put into some possible world, time, and location, sometimes accompanied by specific conditions. Again, there are several possible strategies here, depending on (con-)text. In case the possible world, time, and location are known (i.e., previously introduced or known from context), these parameters may remain implicit or are only signaled marginally, as by the verb tense or a pro-adverb. If introduced they will typically be specified last, in the preprositional complements of the sentence. If an explicit change of possible world, time, or location is necessary, this will preferably take place first, and in the surface structure this strategy will exhibit itself in preposed adverbial phrases: *The next day . . . , Somewhat later . . . , Maybe . . . ,* etc.

These strategies for proposition production can now be summarized in the following way—and in the order indicated:

1. Introduce possible world, time, and location—if these remain constant, keep them implicit or signal them marginally—if they change, signal the change explicitly
2. Introduce main participant persons first, agents first—if main participants already introduced, signal marginally (pronouns)

3. Introduce predicate for this participant (these participants)
4. Actualize the typical propositional role schema (case structure) of this predicate
5. Introduce the (other) participants in their respective case roles, persons first, objects next, and time and location last

Of course, as we suggested before, these semantic strategies in the gradual construction of propositions may show in surface structure: Typical word order, intonation, case endings, tense markings, prepositions, etc., will in general follow the construction of the schema. That is, the way the speaker gradually builds up the sentence should reflect the way he or she also gradually builds the underlying semantic representation. Characteristic for the strategic approach is this mingling of phonological, morphological, lexical, syntactic, and semantic strategies: We do not first have a complete proposition which is then given as input to the surface structure formulators.

Also characteristic for a strategy is the fact that there exists a typical, preferred ordering for the construction process, but not a rigid one. According to principles already examined in the context of proposition ordering in textbases, we may have specific orderings under the influence of stylistic, rhetorical, cognitive, pragmatic, or interactional factors. However, as hearers must be able to apply their comprehension schemata, effective communication presupposes that these deviations be explicitly marked, for example, by different intonation, specific pronouns, case endings, and so on.

We will not pursue the analysis of possible production strategies for propositions beyond these few indications. They are outside of the scope of this book and are being examined in detail in current psycholinguistic studies (Clark & Clark, 1977; Butterworth, 1980; and Rosenberg, 1977, provide some details). More interesting from our perspective is the distribution problem for propositions. In Chapter 4 we saw that propositions may have variable degrees of complexity. We may have complex or compound propositions, or a sequence of propositions featuring the same set of atomic propositions. Depending on a number of factors, such as importance or pragmatic relevance, we may have proposition collapsing or splitting in comprehension. The opposite will take place in production. The speaker may have a set of propositions, but during the process of production, these may be either split up or combined. That is, a proposition may be inserted into the modifier category for some participant, or may itself become a participant, typically so in object positions for verbs of saying, feeling, thinking. etc. Thus, if for any reason the information of a proposition is relatively important, for semantic, pragmatic, or other contextual reasons, the proposition will either be independent or dominant with respect to other propositions. This is another reason why we cannot simply say that discourse production takes place on the basis of a set of ready-made propositions: sometimes the propositions should be construed out of other propositions in memory, and nearly always the speaker must strategically decide how to make larger or smaller constructions out of propositions. Again, this process of proposition combination will show in the surface structure, for example, in the clause structure of sentences and the relations between sentences. It follows that if a proposition contains information about known, presupposed, inferable, stereotypical, relatively unimportant, or other less prominent features of a person, object, action, or event, this proposition will strategically be downgraded as an embedded proposition in the surface structure, and appear as an adjective, adverb, or relative clause. Similarly, the ordering of propositions will follow the principles that also hold for the units within the sentence or proposition: Known, previously introduced, presupposed, less relevant, or world, time, or location introducing or changing propositions will come first (and in subordinate position and appropriately marked with connectives: *While he was driving to New York, John had an accident*).

## 8.6. SOME CONSEQUENCES FOR SENTENCE PRODUCTION STRATEGIES

Production strategies for sentential surface structures are beyond the scope of this book. Yet the previously discussed strategies of textually dependent proposition and proposition sequence production appeared to be closely linked also with surface structure strategies. The main conclusion of what we have observed for the respective levels of discourse production is not only that these levels strategically presuppose each other, but also that many of the underlying strategies show up again in surface structure. Of course, this is as it should be: The hearer or reader has the surface structure to begin with in order to work out the underlying semantic and pragmatic strategies, and the information from the communicative context will not always be sufficient to help. Hence the speaker must organize his or her utterance in such a way that the hearer receives enough cues to figure out, not only grammatically or correctly, but also effectively, how the utterance should be interpreted. Current functional approaches to grammar try to account for sentential structures in the light of this role of the utterance in communicative interaction (Dik, 1978; Givón, 1979b).

In fact, the functional dependence of surface structures upon the underlying semantic and pragmatic representations and their cognitive and social processing holds not only for sentential surface structures and their production or comprehension, but also between sentential structures on the one hand and sequential and whole textual structures on the other. Let us briefly summarize some sentential surface strategies that depend on and determine textual structures:

1. *Intonation:* In spoken discourse, sentence intonation—combining elements of stress, pitch, tone, volume, vowel quality, rhythm, and speed—not only depends on underlying semantic and pragmatic structures, but

(a) Sentence and clause boundaries, and hence (complex) proposition or proposition sequence structure
(b) Initial and final episode boundaries, and hence the onset and termination of relevant macropropositions
(c) Locally and sometimes also globally important concepts
(d) Contrastive meaning

2. *Word order:* Besides the typical expression of semantic roles (cases), word order may signal the following textual properties (see Givón, 1979b):
   (a) Topic–comment structures
   (b) Presuppositional structures
   (c) Change of possible world, time and place parameters (when adverbials are in first position)
   (d) Topic introduction and change, as in extraposition or topicalization phenomena (*John, I haven't seen him. As for Mary, . . .* , etc.)
   (e) Topic reminders, same but with backwards extraposition
   (f) Discourse topic arguments and sentence topics: sentence topics will preferably be sequential and textual discourse referents ("important individuals")

3. *Definite and indefinite noun phrases:* As is well known, textual functions include signaling that concepts or individuals referred to are supposed to be, in the case of definites, known, having been previously introduced in the discourse, or, in the case of indefinites, unknown and nonintroduced.

4. *Pronouns:* As in (3), but with the concept still identifiable in the short-term memory buffer.

5. *Predicates (verbs) in general:* These signal same or different knowledge frame, hence local and global coherence.

6. *Verb tenses:* Indicate same or different time parameters, with respect to previous propositions, as well as changes in perspective and verb aspect (in English or Spanish; some languages have special morphological structures for these).

7. *Emphatic particles* (as in German *doch, ja, halt,* etc., and in Dutch and Greek): Establish semantic and pragmatic relationships with previous or following sentences, propositions, speech acts, or turns, for example, signaling conclusions, expectations, surprise, etc. (Franck, 1980).

8. *Connectives:* Express relations between propositions and relations between speech acts, mostly denoting conditional relations between facts (e.g., cause and consequence).

9. *Adverbials:* Express (change of) time, place, etc. parameters, also for sentence sequences—see also (2c).

10. *Clausal sentence structure:* The subordinate and superordinate hierarchical structure of clauses signals presupposition and pragmatic and semantic relevance or importance.

This list is only partial, and for each point the phenomena could be described in further detail and examples given. For this, however, we refer to the literature mentioned earlier on the phonology and syntax of textually relevant sentence structures. For our present discussion it is only relevant to recall that during the production of sentential surface structures the language user will not simply have recourse to an autonomous syntax and phonology: At nearly each point a decision must be made about the semantic, pragmatic, interactional, and textual relevance of lexical items, word order, intonation, and the presence of certain words (e.g., adverbs, connectives, or particles) or morphemes. On full analysis there are probably few surface structure items that are not produced in order to signal a semantic, pragmatic, cognitive, social, rhetorical, or stylistic function. Thus, at this level, little is left of the old Saussurian arbitrariness in the relations between expressions (signifiers) and their meanings (signifieds). For production strategies this important linguistic fact is crucial: Nearly all underlying (semantic, pragmatic, etc.) information can be mapped onto surface structures and parallel paratextual action. Cognitively or interactionally important, relevant, previously introduced elements may be produced first (either canonically or by topicalization or extraposition), or given special stress; changes in time, place, macroproposition, discourse referent, etc. can be marked directly, and so on. That is, the sentence not only expresses its own meaning but also the multiple links it has with the whole text and communicative context. Typical for the strategic approach, then, is that the surface structure formulator need not wait with its operation in short-term memory until the full semantic or pragmatic representation has been formed. Instead, the coherence relations or the cognitive prominence of semantic units allow the language user to start with adverbials, connectives, or initial noun phrases, signaling sameness or difference of the time or place parameters, sameness or difference of the individual, and the overall relations between the propositions or speech acts. The rest of the sentence will then fill out the details of this picture: precise predicate, other participants, and so on, in decreasing order of importance and closeness to the predicate.

The relation between surface structures and their semantic, pragmatic, or interactional functions, on the one hand, and their relevance for cognitive production and production, on the other hand, cannot be too strict. Some languages have quite varied surface structures, and it remains to be seen whether this will always directly presuppose different comprehension and production strategies. For instance, in VSO languages the textual relevance of first noun phrases should have a different aspect, or require processes of topicalization and extraposition, depending on text and context, and the same holds for the few OVS languages. Note also that in those cases where the main verb comes last (e.g., in German or Dutch composite verbs) both comprehension and production sometimes require rather complex short-term memory processing. Further work regarding these relationships between the (functional) structures of sentences in different languages and their cognitive processing is necessary—especially taking into account the textual relevance of these functions.

## 8.7. SOME PRODUCTION STRATEGIES FOR
## THE *NEWSWEEK* TEXT

In our previous analyses of the *Newsweek* text we gave a semi-explicit simulation of a number of comprehension strategies, thus modeling the comprehension of a reader of this text. A simulation of production has a number of additional problems to solve. We do not have a full-fledged production model, and we can only speculate about the specific strategies involved. We do, however, assume that the basic principles of complex information processing must be the same in both production and comprehension, and against the background of that hypothesis we have formulated a number of production strategies. We will try to illustrate some of these in a partial production simulation of some fragments of the *Newsweek* text.

A strategic production model for the *Newsweek* text involves a partial simulation of the author, namely, *Newsweek's* correspondent in Guatemala City, mentioned at the bottom of the text (neglecting the desk editors at the U.S. office of *Newsweek*). Furthermore, a journalist does not write his or her article on the basis of direct knowledge of the situation in Guatemala, but on the basis of indirect knowledge which is inferred from other discourses, such as government reports and press conferences, previous information from the local press, talks with participants, and so on. In other words, the situation model of the author is itself the result of a large number of text-processing operations on different occasions. This may mean, among other things, that the ultimate stylistically relevant choice of lexical items is not simply based on corresponding concepts of the author, but also may reflect lexicalization in these antecedent discourses.

### 8.7.1. Sociocultural Strategies

As we have emphasized elsewhere, discourse production must be understood in its sociocultural background. Assuming for the moment that the journalist is an American, it follows that he will participate in the general cultural values, norms, and ideologies of American society, and in those of his professional group in particular. Thus, although not explicitly stated, it must be assumed that the murder of thousands of people by the Guatamelan regime is an act that is evaluated negatively according to the norms of the author, and which the author also implicitly ascribes to the United States government since he specifies that therefore the government will be, and has been, in a dilemma whether it should back such a regime. On the other hand, he also presumes and participates in an ideology about communism, which specifies that communists are not an acceptable alternative group for the assumption of power in Guatemala. We have shown that the text suggests that the author implicitly accepts this general ideology. Presumably, the readers of the article are expected to share it, too.

### 8.7.2. Communicative Strategies

Within the general framework of sociocultural strategies determining the ways the reporter will see, interpret, and evaluate a political situation and hence also the ways he can be expected to write about it, we have a number of more specific *communicative* strategies. The author has a specific communicative task, namely, writing a status report about the situation in a country which is now on the interest list of the press. This means that he must write a text that is acceptable to his editors and, ultimately, to his readers.

The strategies involved here are general ones, but they dominate, even at the local stylistic level, all other production strategies. Some plausible strategies might be (see, e.g., Gans, 1979; Tuchman, 1979):

1. Write about situations and events the editors and readers are interested in.
2. If you write about still unknown situations and events indicate why these would be interesting for the editors/readers.
3. Separate descriptions of facts and expressions of opinions. If opinions are described, do so by attributing them to relevant participants—neutral local observers, diplomats, or other credible sources.
4. Do not only report new events, but also summarize previous events, and specify the general and actual context as well as the background of the situation and the events.
5. Specify general political situations as much as possible in terms of concrete interesting actions of participants (see S7, S12–S15).
6. Specify the political implications of the situation for the U.S., both the U.S. government's policies and U.S. citizens.
7. Take the perspective of an outside, neutral observer, and do not side with controversial groups or participants, especially not with those who threaten basic values, norms, and interests.
8. Try to substantiate facts with proof-like statements, such as precise numbers, credible sources, own observations, etc.
9. Assume some but not too much general knowledge of the reader about the country and the political situation there.
10. Respect the specific format rules (style, length, deadlines, etc.) for this kind of report.

These are just a few examples of general communicative strategies. Some of them are specific versions of Grice's (1967) cooperation principles, for example, those of "relevance," "truth," and "manner." Our text, taken on the whole, indeed seems to exhibit these strategic principles, as we will see in more detail in what follows. The principles explain such features as the description of backgrounds and history (typical for weeklies), the frequent citation of diplomats, the numbers, the specific attention for U.S. participants, the scanty information about the communist guerrillas, the international political implications (such as arms sales), and some perfectly irrelevant but pictorial details such as *The President's plane was just preparing for take-off just as Walter's landed* ($S_{15}$).

Added to the more general sociocultural strategies of knowledge and belief management, the communicative strategies provide a finer grid for the desired or expected kinds of information to be supplied in the text, as well as the perspective and style of reporting these.

To provide an explicit cognitive account of how such strategies work is not an easy task, however. Consider the first principle (write about interesting events), which would require a very complex retrieval strategy. Although the press does have the overall function of agenda setting (Gans, 1979; Tuchman, 1979), it would be too easy to assume that we just have a corresponding list of interesting items. There must be complex evaluation procedures which for any situation and event yield the information now needed for expression.

### 8.7.3. Pragmatic Strategies

Globally speaking, a news report will usually and predominantly have the nature of an *assertion*. This means that the author wants to or must provide information which is such that the reader (*a*) does not have it (all) yet, (*b*) is probably interested in having it, and (*c*) is likely to believe that it is true. This also holds for the more local speech acts of the text, which also predominantly are assertions. Only, in that case, it may well be that some facts are already known by some readers. Hence, assertions may serve as reminders for some readers and as information for others.

Yet, a news report is not only an assertion but may also indirectly function as an *advice, suggestion,* or *recommendation*. This advice (namely, not to side with a brutal regime) in our text is the pragmatic point of the communicative interaction, on the one hand aiming at a direct influence on U.S. policy and on the other hand aiming at the (trans)formation of opinions among the reading public about such policy. These overall pragmatic goals provide further constraints on the strategic choices occurring in discourse production.

### 8.7.4. Macrostrategies of Production

Under the overall control of the information yielded by the cultural, social, communicative, and pragmatic strategies, the author will be able to effectively *plan* the text itself. We have assumed that this plan consists of the macrostructure of the text. The intention to write a report about the 'actual situation in Guatemala' will be the major argument for the superordinate macroproposition for the text. With this information in the control system, the author will activate his episodic situation model about Guatemala. For a journalist on location we assume that such a model will be relatively rich. The journalist knows much more than would be relevant to write. Hence, the necessity of the sociocultural, communicative, and pragmatic constraints: It is necessary to select the relevant, interesting, new, and important information. Relevant in our case are the political relationships between Guatemala and the United States; important is the fact that the actual regime commits mass murders, and that there is a communist guerrilla element; and new is the political development as seen in the light of the recent developments in El Salvador. From these constraints, the journalist may indeed form a general macroproposition of the type metaphorically expressed by the first sentence of the text: 'Compared to the moderate situation in El Salvador, the one in Guatemala is much more extreme'. As the situation in El Salvador, extensively reported in the press and in the same issue of *Newsweek,* may be presupposed, the main next macrostructural step is the description of the situation in Guatemala, specifying why it is much more extreme than that in El Salvador. On the basis of general world knowledge and specific knowledge about Central America, the journalist will therefore next activate the necessary semantic components covered by the predicate 'extreme', namely, extremely opposed political groups and their respective goals and actions. Thus, the next step in the semantic macroplan is to introduce these groups, as indeed is the case in the first macropropositions (and the first sentences) of the text, and then to give historical background and context about these groups and their relations with the United States. This latter point is especially important in satisfying the communicative and pragmatic relevance criterion: Macropropositions must be formed in order to organize the various events and actions of the relations between Guatemala and the United States. These also will consist of historical backgrounds, context, previous event type, and actual events, as specified by the news schema discussed in the previous chapter. It follows that the overall production plan consists of at least three interwoven plans: a pragmatic plan, defining the overall speech act; a schematic plan, defining the overall ordering, organization, and functional categories of the text; and a macrosemantic plan, providing the overall content.

It thus appears that a processing model for discourse production will have to include a planning component that is considerably more complex than envisaged by some current theories of writing (e.g., the discussion of planning in Hayes and Flower; 1980, neglects the distinction between different levels of planning). By embedding such a model in a more general theory of discourse processing, additional factors and constraints become apparent which are important for an understanding of production processes. It should be stressed that in actual production some steps in the formation and execution of these plans may be strategically made only during actual writing: We do not assume that the journalist already has a complete triple plan before writing the first sentence, but we do assume that in writing rather complex texts at least parts of these plans must have been formed. If not, the author would not know what kind of information to retrieve from the episodic situation model, or what kind of information to present first. Another strategically relevant point is the actual process in activating fragments of the situation model. Although we may assume that situation models are also hierarchically organized and feature macropropositions to organize the vast amount of detailed knowledge we have about situations, it is not necessarily the case that the writer will access the model *only* from top to bottom. Some detailed information may be more relevant, important, interesting, or new, especially within the framework of the overall communicative strategies specified earlier. Thus, although the refusal of Guatemala's president to see Reagan's emissary Walters, the role of Israel in the arms sales, or the gruesome act of beheading a large group of peasants may be details relative to the overall political situation, and hence relative to the respective macropropositions formed, they may nonetheless be interesting enough to guide direct retrieval. It follows that besides the formation of a semantic macroplan, the journalist may already have retrieved propositions which satisfy the communicative criteria and which he or she therefore wants to report. In that case, the formation of local propositions, or larger parts of the actual textbase, will sometimes precede the formation of overarching macrostructures.

The semantic formation processes therefore involve the following strategic steps:

1. Activate the situation model 'Guatemala' and corresponding semantic (more general) information about politics, Central America, and political conflicts.
2. Activate the situation model about the knowledge of the average reader, and compare with own model of Guatemala: Decide what the reader does not yet know.
3. Activate or apply the various cultural, communicative, and pragmatic strategies so that information becomes available which decides which information from the writer's situation model satisfies the criteria (relevance, importance, interestingness, newness, etc.) of the communicative context.
4. Form an overall theme or topic for the information that is to be communicated.
5. Activate or apply the news schema and the relevant categories into which further, lower level, local and global propositions can be fitted.
6. Derive more specific macrostructures from the overall topic, beginning with those of the initial schematic categories of the text form.
7. Keep more detailed propositions in store (that is, as parts of a fragmentary textbase already formed) until the relevant macroproposition, episode, and schematic category are executed at the local level.

In other words, the formation of the textbase to be expressed takes place from top to bottom, although some bottom information may already be available, and this formation process takes place by reading off the situation model under the constraints of communicative and pragmatic strategies. Of course, part of this reading off strategy may be sustained by external memory procedures, such as the consultation of notes or the sketch for an overall semantic plan for the text.

## 8.7.5. Local Semantic Strategies

Constrained by global communicative, semantic, and pragmatic plans, the writer will next start to generate specific semantic material for the higher level categories and topics that have been established. Again the situation model will be addressed under the constraints of this higher level information. At the same time, the writer will activate at each step general frames and scripts necessary for the understanding of local semantic propositions and their connection in the textbase.

The formation of the initial propositions of the textbase is a complex strategy which involves steps such as the following:

1. Specify the macropropositions with information from the situation model which satisfies the communicative principles.
2. Follow the ordering, in episodes, of the macropropositions as determined by the news text schema.
3. Use information from previous sentences, and hence the topic–comment distribution of semantic information.
4. Presuppositional constraints: specify participants before specifying actions of these participants.
5. Conditional coherence: first specify causes, reasons, or other conditions of events, then the events, then the consequences of these events.
6. Functional coherence: respect normal orderings for descriptions of complex situations, such as general–specific, abstract–instantiation, whole–part, etc.

On the basis of such strategies, the writer will perhaps start with a headline, satisfying the text schema and summarizing the main topic. Next, a thematic initial sentence will be necessary to function as a lead, to be specified in the next sentences. According to schema we then should derive some historical background, context, and previous events, followed by the description of actual events. The presuppositional constraints determine, among other things, that the text first mentions the initial joy of the Guatemalan elite about the election of Reagan, followed by a functional explanation of this event, and only then the causes of the actual disappointment and its consequences. The first step will lead to the formation of propositions, selected from episodic situation models, which may be interesting for the reading public. Instead of a rather high level proposition 'they were glad about the election of Reagan', the episodic model may be inspected for more concrete facts implying this high-level information, namely, the information about marimba bands and firecrackers, or about the business relations of White House aide Deaver with Guatemala.

Of course, the various principles and strategies mentioned earlier still leave a lot of freedom in the actual formation of a textbase fragment to be expressed. Thus, the description of the relationships between the Guatemalan regime and the U.S. diplomats could have come after the description of the mass murders and the fights with the guerrillas. However, the relevance criterion for news discourse might determine an ordering in which first of all the relations with the United States should be given.

Note, finally, that in principle each new episode should be initiated with a proposition of a rather high (thematic) level, after which specifications may follow.

This is indeed the case in our text, except maybe for $S_7$ and $S_{12}$ which provide more specific details.

Whereas the description of actions and events will locally be heavily influenced by conditional ordering, we still ignore the precise ordering in the description of situations, such as political situations. We have indicated some functional principles, but they do not account for all local connections. Thus, is there a constraint saying that 'on the left' groups should be presented before the 'on the right' groups? It seems as if for this kind of text, the most powerful production strategy at the local level is that of *general–specific* relations, where general propositions are often paragraph initial, thematic ones. In $S_{36}$ we see that also the *assertion–argumentation/backing* relation may be followed: a general assumption followed by facts proving it. And finally, we observe for this text that first some general or actual context or facts are presented, followed at the end of the paragraphs by the opinions or conclusions of spokesmen. Although we herewith have tracked some local semantic formation strategies, a lot of descriptive research and experiments remain to be done to assess the major relevant production strategies at this level.

### 8.7.6. Formulation Strategies

Once a partial textbase has been formed, the writer will strategically have to formulate sequences of local propositions in actual sentence forms. We cannot describe these strategies in detail. We may assume, though, that just as the language user has propositional schemata, he or she also has *clause and sentence schemata* to work with in a strategic way. Thus, the semantic relations in the propositions need to be expressed by specific word order, case endings, and clause hierarchies. At the same time a process of *lexicalization* will select appropriate lexical items to express the concepts of the propositions in the textbase.

However, this selection of clause and sentence schemata and the use of lexicalization strategies is not free. First, it is bound by the *style register* determined by text type and communicative context: The author must use words that belong to the repertoire of news discourse. If not, as in *bunch of people* in $S_2$, the words occur in a quotation. Next, it may be constrained by rhetorical devices, such as comparisons, metaphors, irony, and fixed expressions, as in the metaphor of $S_1$, *kinsman* in $S_8$, *giving the cold shoulder* in $S_{13}$, and so on. Third, the semantic distribution of information constrains the *topic–comment* structure of the respective sentences, and hence word order. Similarly, focusing will put important phrases in first position, such as *on the left* and *on the right* in $S_2$ and $S_3$. Fourth, main propositions will be expressed in superordinate, first position clauses, with modification in second position or embedded relative clauses. And, fifth, all these stylistically relevant choices of possible formulations for underlying propositions will be monitored by the higher level cultural, communicative, and pragmatic controls, providing the overall evaluations and opinions that underlie the selection of specific words, word orderings, and clause structure. Thus, the selection of *extreme* in $S_2$, the negative quotation in the same sentence, the neutral *deposed* in $S_3$, the patient role of the political middle in El Salvador in $S_4$, and the metaphor *hydra* in $S_{40}$, clearly express the overall opinions and ideologies of the writer and the reading public.

## 8.8. TOWARD A PROCESS MODEL OF DISCOURSE PRODUCTION

So far in this chapter we have concentrated on the strategic aspects of discourse planning at various levels, from the most global down to the propositional. A general cognitive model of discourse production will have to include more components than just these strategies, of course. It is therefore instructive to place production strategies within the context of a general model, even though we can do no more here than sketch such a model.

Recent work is in fair agreement as to what the outlines of a process model of discourse production must be. Both Hayes and Flower (1980) and Collins and Gentner (1980) have provided task analyses of the process of discourse production in writing that can serve as a guide in that respect. Writing has been chosen in part for its practical significance in education, and in part for its greater explicitness, on which we have repeatedly commented. Hayes and Flower distinguish three components in their model of writing: a task environment, a memory structure, and the actual process of writing. The first serves essentially in a control function and comprises the writer's motivation, the characteristics of the intended audience, and the topic to be written about. For simplicity, we shall assume these to be constants in a writing episode. The writer's long-term memory, which provides the writer with a source for new ideas to write about, can similarly be regarded as a constant for our purposes, so that we can focus on the actual process of writing. Hayes and Flower distinguish four subprocesses here: generating ideas, organizing them, translating the ideas into words and sentences, and editing what has been written or thought about. Each of these, of course, is a complex psychological process in its own right, and part of our task here, and that of future investigators of writing processes, will be to unpack these complexities. Eventually, we would like to have explicit process models where we now have no more than code words such as translating and editing.

Idea generation stands for the process of generating ideas from the writer's long-term memory under the constraints of the task environment. The generation process need not be direct, however, in that whatever material is dredged up from memory may be subjected to expansion and alteration via inference processes. In what follows we shall elaborate somewhat on the process of idea generation from memory.

Organization is a very important part of writing. Many of the strategies that have been discussed here deal with organizational processes. Expert writers know that organization and planning is crucial and spend as much as two-thirds of their writing time on organization (Atlas, 1979), whereas novices do much less organizing, to the detriment of the writing they produce. Nevertheless, detailed models of this component of the writing process are rare, in part because the organization problem differs so much for different writing tasks. It is not clear exactly where the general principles are to be found. For the restricted domain of linearization, though, some progress has been made toward designing explicit process models. We refer to the work of Levelt (1982) who asked subjects to describe graphs of interconnected color nodes which formed patterns of varying complexity. On the basis of the protocols he collected, Levelt was able to distinguish some fairly general principles of linearization. Thus, he could specify strategies people use in describing these graphs, based on general principles, such as to minimize short-term memory load. (Strategies of, for example, choosing short branches before long branches, choosing the least complex branch first, and taking on loops with priority were found to be global strategies related to short-term memory economy, whereas other strategies observed were of a more local character.)

As we have suggested, it might eventually be possible to relate the linearization strategies observed in this simplified experimental situation to actual writing processes. In the simplest kind of stories the linearization problem is trivial, because the macrostructure itself specifies a (canonical) causal–temporal sequence. However, in more complex stories as well as in expository prose, problems that are formally similar to Levelt's graph descriptions are encountered. Will the same, or any, general principles be found to underlie the subjects' production strategies? We have argued repeatedly that comprehension strategies are often based on short-term memory constraints (Kintsch & van Dijk, 1978; Kintsch & Vipond, 1979; Chapter 10), and it would seem plausible that the situation is similar with respect to production.

The translation phase of writing involves expressing ideas verbally. Once more, we are dealing with a strategic process and it would appear likely that sentence production strategies are at some level related to sentence comprehension strategies. Clearly, empirical work in this area is needed.

Reviewing and editing is the final process discussed by Hayes and Flower (1980). It is a process that can be studied especially well with the tools of protocol analysis, as Flower and Hayes have shown. Their data led them to distinguish a locally controlled editing process, which often interrupts other ongoing processes, from a review process that is subject to higher level control. These higher level control processes differ among individuals and for experts and novices. Thus, some writers follow the processing order generate–organize–translate–review, whereas others do not. Identifying people's strategies in this respect, and examining them for their effectiveness or ineffectiveness, appears to be of some pedagogical value.

### 8.8.1. Experiments on Idea Generation

How idea generation works as a subcomponent of writing (or discourse production in general) is a problem if great complexity which we as yet do not know how to investigate in detail. It might be useful in this situation to investigate a pure idea generation process outside the writing framework. We have, of course, no guarantee that idea generation in writing, when it is interacting with other processes as sketched here, shares many interesting features with the pure process we have studied, but neither do we have information to the contrary, and it would seem worth a try. One does not necessarily, maybe not even usually, write down ideas as they are retrieved from memory. But there are some natural writing situations that come fairly close to that; for example, when answering an essay question asking for factual information on some topic, or when reporting an accident in a newspaper. At the other extreme, of course, would be certain literary forms of writing, where the basic ideas are few and simple, but what is done with them is elaborate and interesting. Most writing will be somewhere between these two extremes. We propose to model the case where ideas are simply retrieved from memory but are not then transformed or changed.

Operationally, the situation we have in mind is as follows. Suppose we ask a subject to tell us everything he or she knows about some topic (e.g., 'the role of nuclear energy in our energy needs, now and in the future'), simply saying out loud everything that comes to mind, without editing or organizing. We assume that what the subject is doing in this task is to retrieve from memory information in response to these instructions. There may, of course, be times when the subject does not comply with instructions and engages in editing and organizing, but as Flower and Hayes demonstrated, such instances can be identified in the protocols and excluded. We want to get at memory retrieval in its simplest, purest form. We assume that this retrieval process is identical in character with the memory retrieval that has been studied extensively in memory laboratories everywhere for the last two decades. Specifically, we propose to use a retrieval model designed for laboratory data to describe out task. In the usual episodic memory task the subject is presented with some items to be remembered (usually words, but not always) and is later asked to recall them. Learning the items consists in associating them with the particular experimental context, and that context is the retrieval cue that is later used to recall them. In our present situation, the retrieval cue is not an association with an experimental context, but an association with some topic. Formally, the context is a node to which the to-be-remembered items, which may themselves be interassociated to some extent, are connected. In our situation, the topic is a node or network of nodes to which other items have been associated in the past. The question is, however, the same in both instances: How do the context node(s), or the topic node(s), manage to retrieve the nodes that are associated with them?

We propose to use the model for memory retrieval suggested by Raaijmakers and Shiffrin (1981) and Raaijmakers (1979), to answer that question in part (Kintsch, 1982b).[1] Their model serves as a reasonable first approximation of the

[1]The Raaijmakers and Shiffrin model accounts for many or most of the laboratory phenomena about memory known today. It is probably as close as one can come to a true consensus model of memory. It is, however, not the only model of such scope and empirical adequacy: Metcalf and Murdock (1981) start with quite different assumptions about the memory system but account for more or less the same phenomena. It is quite conceivable that a knowledge retrieval model could be built around the principles of the Metcalf and Murdock model.

quite complex automatic aspects of the retrieval process. Essentially, it describes what happens when a given retrieval cue is used to retrieve information from memory, what factors contribute to a successful retrieval, how the very act of retrieval dynamically changes the memory structure itself as well as the retrieval cue. The main part of this operation—the retrieval itself—is unconscious, automatic, and not subject to strategic control. Thus, the strategic aspects of the process can be isolated and highlighted, allowing us to ask more precise questions than before. Strategies enter into this process in the control of the retrieval cue: How the retrieval is composed in the first place, how it is changed in response to successful information retrieval or to failure, is a strategic process. By unconfounding it from other aspects of the memory retrieval process we can study it.

First, however, we need to examine the empirical situation and the kind of data it yields. This was done in a doctoral thesis at the University of Colorado by Caccamise (1981). Caccamise gave subjects—32 college students—an index card with one of four topics printed on it and instructions to start talking about that topic, saying everything that came to mind, without regard to organization, repetitions, or proper syntax, but sticking to the topic that was specified. Of the four topics, two were of a general nature and two were more specific (e.g., "Discuss our energy needs and energy sources, now and in the future" versus "Discuss the role of nuclear energy in our energy needs, now and in the future"). Of each pair of topics one was familiar (about the educational system) and the other was less familiar (the energy needs example). In addition, some of the subjects were told that their prospective audience would be a fifth-grade class that was about to begin studying energy sources, whereas for other subjects no audience was specified, thus implicitly assuming an adult audience of peers.

Caccamise scored her protocols in terms of propositions and then derived various measures for them. The most important ones were the total number of (different) propositions, the cumulative number of propositions as a function of time, the number of chunks defined by argument overlap, various organizational measures the details of which need not concern us here, the rate of idea repetition, and the frequency of unassociated ideas. The results of these analyses convincingly demonstrate the usefulness of the experimental paradigm Caccamise employed. There were large and regular differences between the familiar and unfamiliar topics (the specific–general variation had no effect because subjects found ways to generalize the supposedly specific topics). Familiar topics produced almost twice as many ideas (not including repetitions) as unfamiliar ones and a correspondingly larger number of chunks. The average number of ideas per chunk, however, proved to be approximately constant, with about 2.5 propositions per chunk. On the other hand, all organizational measures devised by Caccamise indicated a better, more structured organization for the familiar topics. This was especially clear when one considered the number of unrelated ideas that were produced: About five times as many propositions that were not related by argument overlap to other propositions were produced for the unfamiliar topics than for the familiar ones. Subjects not only retrieved less when the topic was unfamiliar, what they retrieved was also much less interrelated and organized. It was not that they did not try hard: Indeed, the total number of ideas produced was about the same in the familiar and unfamiliar conditions, except that many more were repetitions of earlier ones when the topic was unfamiliar.

Of considerable interest are Caccamise's results for those cases when the intended audience was specified to be children. As others have also observed in more conventional writing tasks (Atlas, 1979), people are surprisingly poor at taking audience constraints into account. On the surface, everything looks normal: When addressing children, the same number of ideas was produced, the same number of chunks, and once again, a constant 2.5 propositions per chunk. However, the structure of the ideas produced is much poorer than in the adult case: There is less complexity, less interrelatedness, many more dangling, isolated propositions. The whole process takes about twice as long, but whereas pauses usually occur at meaningful boundaries (i.e., where the content changes) when people are generating ideas for an adult audience, here they tend to be distributed more randomly. Caccamise concluded that the audience constraint did not serve as an integral part of the retrieval cue subjects were using (in which case it would have assured that only material suitable for children was retrieved), but rather was enforced later on by a special editing process (indicated also by many comments subjects made). This editing process may have destroyed the normal orderly flow of ideas, resulting in a highly disorganized idea set that would require careful reorganization and review before it could be turned into a suitable textbase, especially for the audience in question.

### 8.8.2. A Computer Simulation of Idea Generation

Once we know that we can get orderly data with our experimental procedures, how can we describe them with the Raaijmakers and Shiffrin model, as suggested in the preceding section (Kintsch, 1982b)? The solution we have chosen involves constructing a computer simulation of the model to see whether the empirical results obtained by Caccamise can be mimicked at least qualitatively by the processes assumed here. If so, a more detailed analysis of production strategies can begin: Different strategies can be built into the model, their overall results can be observed, and they can be verified by further empirical research using protocol analysis. This project was carried out by Walker (1982), in another doctoral dissertation from the University of Colorado.

To describe Walker's work we must say at least a few more words about the Raaijmakers and Shiffrin (1981) model. First, why this model and not an alternative one? The answer to that question has at least three parts. It is one of the few models around that is sufficiently formalized. In addition, it works quite well, accounting for the standard laboratory phenomena of episodic memory experiments with word lists, and quite a few subtle ones as well. Most importantly, it appears to be somewhat of a consensus model, incorporating the major features of memory models of the past decade into one sensible whole: There is the crucial role of the retrieval cue (as Tulving & Thompson, 1979 among others have emphasized); there is an associative memory network which has been an important characteristic of recent memory models, as, for instance, in the work of Anderson and Bower (1972); and there is a place for some kind of redintegrative process which many memory theorists have insisted upon, for example, the pattern completion of Kintsch (1974). All these important principles are integrated in the Raaijmakers and Shiffrin model.

The model assumes an associative network with complex nodes containing sensory, semantic, and associative information. These nodes could be word concepts as well as propositions. The connections among nodes are associations varying in strength. Retrieval from this network requires a probe cue to be held in short-term memory. The probe consists of an array of cues: context cues, task constraints, and other relevant cues. In our situations, the other cues are the topic specified for the retrieval task. However, the probe changes during the retrieval process in a strategically controlled way: As items are retrieved they may be added to the probe, displacing other items from the array. One of the main questions that concerns us here are the strategies controlling this process.

The memory net itself is dynamic, too, and changes in response to the retrieval operations. Specifically, the associative strength between every item retrieved and the content of the probe is augmented as a consequence of the process of retrieving. This generates the kind of output interference observed in memory experiments as well as in idea generation experiments.

The probability that an item is retrieved is a function of the relative strength of the association of the item with the probe cues as compared to other items. The retrieval operation is always successful, in that it always results in the implicit retrieval of an item. That item, may, however, not be produced overtly if its absolute strength is too low. Thus, for a response to occur two things are necessary: An item must be *retrieved* (depending on its relative strength), and the retrieved item must actually be *recovered,* that is, produced (depending on its absolute strength). This interplay between retrieval and recovery processes, as well as the dynamics of the retrieval process, enable the model to account for much of the data in the memory literature. We cannot dwell here on the reasons for the various properties of the model, nor on the actual details of the model. Suffice it to say that we shall be concerned primarily with three parameters of the model: the number of cumulative retrieval failures (i.e., a retrieved item cannot be recovered) and re-retrievals before purging the probe; the number of cumulative retrieval failures and re-retrievals before stopping; and the strength increment between a cue and a retrieved item. The model has other parameters which are not of interest here and can be pretty much treated as constants.

Walker deliberately refrained from making ad hoc adjustments in this model when he applied it to the idea generation paradigm. It was of interest how a straight episodic list-learning model would do in this new situation. Instead of a small list of items with their interassociation matrix and a context cue, Walker gave the model an associative net constructed from 100 nodes. No attempt was made to model any specific semantic field, however. Instead, the connections in the 100 × 100 association matrix were inserted at random, subject to certain constraints. With association strengths varying from 0 to 100, Walker looked, for instance, at nets with high or low average strength values, various distributions of strength values, and, especially, at nets with clusters in which associations within a cluster were relatively high compared with associations between clusters. Indeed, cluster overlap was systematically varied.

The outcome of these explorations was highly positive. Clearly, the model would mimic response patterns like those obtained by Caccamise, and it would do so for reasonable parameter choices. Idea generation curves as a function of time were especially interesting. In their simplest form these have been studied since Bousfield (1953) by many investigators, and Walker could show that his model yielded the smooth, decelerating cumulative output curves familiar from the literature. In addition, he studied individual output curves, which are not smooth but highly scalloped, and their dependence on model parameters. Similarly, he showed what factors in the model combine to generate high rates of idea repetition. Most importantly, and quite nontrivially, Walker showed that the model behaved reasonably when confronted with clusters. The model retrieved items from clustered nets much like people retrieve information from their semantic memory, which is also highly structured. In particular, the cluster structure of semantic memory constantly overlaps: Nodes often pertain to more than one script or frame, and they enter into various organizational structures. Yet people rarely get confused by this: When 'doctor' is encountered as part of the 'surgeon' frame very different associations are produced than when it is encountered as part of the 'dentist' or 'anthropologist' frame. Walker showed that the retrieval model also has the ability to slice up the network in many different overlapping ways, without getting lost.

Thus, the model passed the first test. It can mimic qualitatively what we know happens when people generate ideas. We cannot go into the details of Walker's work here and must refer the reader to the original source. However, we must comment on Walker's further work with the model, which goes much beyond a mere feasibility study. Once we know that the model gives qualitatively the right results for proper parameter choices, we can start experimenting with the model. This is a lot easier than experimenting with people, and it gives readily interpretable results as we can examine in detail the factors that produced them. It does not, of course, replace experimenting with people, but it can be an all important guide for experiments with people.

The experiments Walker did involved trying out various strategies for constructing, maintaining, and updating the retrieval probe. Efficient idea generation requires a person to operate somewhere between the extremes of being completely inflexible and simply probing memory with the initial topic as the probe over and over again, and being completely flexible and letting retrieval be guided entirely by the items already recovered. Even if we find the ideal compromise between these extremes, questions arise about how the local retrieval data should be combined with the topic constraints. How many items are kept in the probe? How are they changed? Cue replacement could be entirely on the basis of recency, as in a push-down stack where the lowest item is lost; alternatively, replacement could be random; or it could be intelligent in some way or another. Focusing strategies might involve replacing that item in the probe array that is least related to the rest, whereas divergent thinking strategies might involve the opposite, always replacing the most interrelated and therefore most redundant item in the probe. Walker showed that the consequences of such strategies could readily be explored with his model. Some strategies give qualitatively reasonable results, whereas others simply do not work (i.e., they result in protocols quite unlike those of real subjects). Thus, a pool of strategies can be isolated that are plausible. Empirical observation can now concentrate on this plausible subset of idea generation strategies: The model gives us some idea of what to look for; protocol analyses can then check out the theoretically plausible strategies.

Most importantly, Walker's model permits us to distinguish those aspects of idea generation processes that are a consequence of the inherent retrieval dynamics of the memory system from those that arise as a consequence of higher order control processes. The model does not include a control component, and hence cannot account for the corresponding behaviors. There were several such discrepancies between model and protocols obtained from real subjects which illustrate the operation of control processes in production. People often used a hierarchical retrieval strategy: Instead of entering the memory structure with the specified retrieval cue (e.g., "tell me all the different cars you know") and then exploring this structure randomly, guided only by the dynamics of the automatic retrieval process, they employed a two-stage strategy. They first did not search for cars at all, but for fields related to cars (e.g., parking lots, family cars, foreign cars); once a field is retrieved, it is added to the original retrieval cue and the search for elements in this field begins—as described by the model. When the field is exhausted, control is shifted back to search for another field, and the process repeats. Each retrieval process (for fields where cars are likely to be encountered, and for actual cars within each field) are probably as described by the model, but the model lacks a control component that arranges these subprocesses in sequence.

Another example of where the model fails because it lacks the right control processes occurs in the retrieval of scriptal information. The time course of retrieval from a script (e.g., "tell me all that happens when one visits a supermarket, or doctor's office") is quite different from retrieval from categorical structures: The retrieval rate is constant (whereas it is negatively accelerated for categories), and group and individual functions are alike (whereas scalloped individual functions contrast with smooth group functions in the case of category member retrieval). Once again, the control of the retrieval cue that is necessary to produce such a process goes beyond the basic retrieval dynamics specified by Raaijmakers and Shiffrin. These control functions had to be added to the retrieval model before it could adequately account for idea generation data—a task that according to Walker appears quite feasible. Thus, we are not saying that idea generation (or text production) is "just" automatic memory retrieval; that is merely one component of a considerably more complex process. It is, nonetheless, an important component, and in order to study the other components we need to know what aspects of such behavior can be ascribed to it.

At the beginning of this chapter we raised the question of why work on discourse production has lagged so far behind work on discourse comprehension. We may end the chapter on a positive note. It appears that we now have a theoretical framework within which the study of discourse production can be very fruitful. The work that is needed to fill out this framework has barely begun, of course. We need much more precise models of various production tasks and a much more extensive empirical data base than we now have. But at least we are beginning to see what such models would have to be like, what factors they would have to take into account, and we are beginning to gain some understanding of what sorts of experiments should be performed and what observations need to be collected.

*Chapter 9*

# Strategies for the Use of Knowledge

One of the major contributions of psychology and artificial intelligence to the study of discourse processing is the recognition of the fundamental role of the language user's world knowledge in production and comprehension. In the previous chapters we have observed that processing strategies continuously need information from long-term memory in order to construct or specify semantic and pragmatic representations of discourse. In other words, much of the information needed to understand a text is not provided by the information expressed in the text itself, but must be drawn from the language user's knowledge of the person, objects, states of affairs, actions, or events the discourse is about. We have seen that part of this knowledge is of an episodic nature, that is, is inferred from knowledge in episodic memory as it is gradually construed on the basis of our previous experience. Other knowledge, derived from this episodic knowledge through learning processes of abstraction, generalization, decontextualization, and recombination, has a more general and more stable nature, and can be used in order to perform a great variety of cognitive tasks. Although knowledge is of course socioculturally variable, it is sufficiently general to allow for intersubjective language use and communication.

Without this general picture of the world and its underlying regularities, it would be impossible to understand words, to understand meaningful combinations of words in sentences, to understand the fact-dependent relations between sentences, or to understand a discourse as a whole. Understanding a discourse, that is, assigning it a meaningful interpretation, in many respects coincides with understanding the fragment of some possible world the discourse is about. If we cannot make sense of the facts, and their combination, referred to by the words, sentences, or episodes of a discourse, we will often say that the discourse itself makes no sense. Since, however, language users know of each other that they share much of this knowledge about the socioculturally construed world and the social contexts they are members of, they may leave much of this presupposed knowledge implicit in their discourses. That is, it is assumed that a reader or hearer can supply necessary missing links or background while understanding the discourse. Thus, in their comprehension strategies language users continuously have to consult this stock of world knowledge—first, to understand the text itself, and, second, to construct a picture of the world fragment the text is about.

But if comprehension implies finding a suitable knowledge structure that fits the to-be-comprehended material, we must not forget that actions and events, as well as the discourse about them, are always new in some respects. Hence the preestablished knowledge schemata will in general not fit the new event or the new discourse precisely. They can provide a basis or a background for comprehension, but no more. Everything really new and unexpected must be constructed on the basis of this background information. Therefore, knowledge schemata cannot be rigid, but must accommodate many possible variations in the observed or textually presented objects, persons, and events. Somehow, for the purpose of comprehension, whether we are comprehending discourse or events and scenes, we need a memory organization that is flexible and responsive to contextual demands.

As yet, the nature of that organization is only poorly understood in cognitive science, nor is there enough known about how such knowledge systems are used. We cannot solve these very deep problems here. Knowledge organization is a problem beyond the scope of this book. However, we cannot avoid these problems altogether. As we have already argued, the use of knowledge is an integral component of discourse comprehension. We cannot talk about strategies of discourse comprehension and neglect this central aspect. Therefore, we must consider, if only in a preliminary way, the problem of knowledge organization. In the next section, we shall review current thinking about the structure of knowledge, and raise some questions concerning the use of knowledge. Against this background we shall then present our current ideas about the strategies for knowledge use in discourse comprehension. We cannot investigate the process without some idea of the nature of the structure. Until more satisfactory, explicit models of knowledge structure become available, this whole discussion must remain tentative. But tentative or not, it is too important to be neglected.

## 9.1. KNOWLEDGE SYSTEMS

We shall first review proposals about the organization of knowledge from psychology and artificial intelligence. From these, a number of issues of a general nature can be discerned. They will give us at least some idea what a theory of knowledge representation might look like.

### 9.1.1. Psychological Approaches:
### Concepts and Categories

Philosophers, and in their wake psychologists, have explored in great detail several issues concerning the representation of knowledge. However, this work has typically had a very narrow focus which restricts its usefulness for present purposes.

Philosophers have been interested in how general concepts are abstracted from concrete instances. The predominant notion has been that general concepts are defined via some sort of summary description that applies to the class as a whole, stating the necessary and sufficient properties for class membership. Psychologists at first accepted that definition. It was employed in a great deal of experimental work on categorization, which very successfully described how people classify artificial concepts and how they learn to do so (e.g., Bruner, Goodnow, & Austin, 1956; Bourne, 1966). However, as soon as psychologists turned to natural concepts, all kinds of problems arose with the notion of necessary and sufficient characteristics, which eventually led to the abandonment of the classical view (Smith & Medin, 1981). It has recently been resurrected in the form of predicability hierarchies (Keil, 1979), but it is not clear how this new approach can avoid in the long run the problems that plagued the older theories.

For the most part, psychologists today have given up on the classical definitional approach and have developed models of categorization in which optional, non-necessary characteristics play an important role. Smith and Medin (1981) have provided a sensitive review of this research area. The theories in question range from feature models and dimensional models which retain the old idea that concepts need to be described via a summary of their properties, but differ from the classical view in that they take into account nonessential features (or dimensions), to models in which concepts are entirely (or partly) characterized via exemplars. As Smith and Medin have shown, quite sophisticated models can be built in this way, which account for a large number of empirical phenomena in their domain.

The trouble with these models, for our purposes, is that they are too narrow to be of much use. Most of them deal with the classification of objects, often in very narrow and specialized domains, such as animal names and kinship terms. Keil's ontological concepts are a bit broader (including "events", for instance), but he does not make very fine distinctions. There is some work on verb categories (most notably Miller & Johnson-Laird, 1976), but on the whole this research falls short of providing us with a model for a knowledge system that could support discourse comprehension. The basic problem is that this work has been concerned with only one way in which concepts function—their categorization. But there are other things one needs to do with concepts besides putting them into categories. Specifically, they are needed as a foundation for constructing text representations. The traditional approach from philosophy and psychology is of little use to us here.

If we turn to linguistics, the situation is not much improved. The linguist's "lexicon" is typically designed within the classical framework to provide definitions for words, their essential properties. The sort of general world knowledge with its fuzziness that invariably intrudes upon these neat definitions when human language use is studied is ignored or ruled outside linguistics. Not until·the advent of artificial intelligence did knowledge systems and the problems of knowledge use receive the scholarly attention they deserve.

## 9.1.2. Semantic Decomposition: Levels of Cognitive Units

A central issue with respect to the use of concepts is that of semantic decomposition. In its classical form the notion implies that understanding a concept means accessing the elements from which it is composed, that is, decomposing it semantically (e.g., Katz & Fodor, 1963; the processing implications are clearly spelled out in Schank, 1972). Thus, the mind was thought to work by putting together and pulling apart a relatively small number of semantic primitives, perhaps corresponding to cognitive primitives (Bierwisch, 1969; Miller & Johnson-Laird, 1976), somewhat like matter being composed of a small number of chemical elements. This position is currently untenable for both theoretical and empirical reasons (Fodor, Garrett, Walker, & Parkes, 1980; Kintsch, 1974). Understanding a concept does not necessarily involve decomposing it into constituents, be they semantic primitives or not. Chunks are the normal units of information processing both in perception (see, e.g., many studies on word and letter or phoneme identification in reading and listening reviewed in Section 2.1) and in comprehension (e.g., Fodor *et al.*, 1980; some of the studies referred to in what follows show that schemata can function as units).

But although we must face up to the existence of internally complex psychological units such as a macroproposition, to cite another example, we must not lose sight of the fact that the system is indeed a multilayered one. There is no such thing as compulsory decomposition into elements, but nevertheless the elements are as real as the chunks, and often processing does indeed involve the elements rather than the chunks as wholes. There is really nothing strange about this state of affairs, and in areas other than semantics, where this issue has created a surprising amount of confusion, identical situations have long been accepted. Thus, although many semanticists automatically decompose word meanings in their analyses, phonologists consider phonemes, syllables, and words as separate units of analysis, each with its own justification. Although the properties of a word cannot be reduced to those of its constituent list of phonemes (see the studies on word perception reviewed in Chapter 2), the phoneme nevertheless remains a useful and important unit of analysis. In semantics, too, we must learn to deal with units of varying size, from atomic elements to complex schemata.

Note, however, that this multilayered nature of the system greatly compounds the problems for the theorist. Consider the notion of 'concept'. At its own level, it is related to a multitude of other concepts, forming semantic fields of various sorts. It also enters into a variety of propositional relations, thus participating in higher order chunks. At an even higher level, overlapping and criss-crossing schemata pertain to the concept. At the same time, the concept itself can be decomposed into a set of features, dimensions, or attributes, depending on one's theory, conceivably even into an elementary set of semantic-cognitive primitives. How are these various levels coordinated: What determines whether a process reaches up a level or goes down one? What are the relevant constraints in such a system? We simply cannot answer these questions now.

### 9.1.3. The Contribution of Artificial Intelligence: Frames and Scripts

Building machines to perform complex cognitive functions very soon demonstrated to people interested in artificial intelligence the crucial role of knowledge in cognition. Suddenly, the structure of knowledge systems became an important issue in cognitive science. The only thing psychology and philosophy had to offer— associative networks (e.g., Anderson & Bower, 1973)—were found to be inadequate. An extremely influential early attempt to construct a knowledge system was the semantic network of Quillian (1968). As in an associative network, the nodes were concepts. The concepts were not defined explicitly by features or essential properties, as in the work we considered earlier, but implicitly by their position in the semantic network and their relations to other concepts. But unlike an associative network where the relations among concepts vary merely in strength, qualitatively different relations were admitted in Quillian's semantic net. Relations among nodes were labeled, rather than unlabeled as in an associative network: Thus, *coffee* is related to *bean, drink,* and *cup* in qualitatively different ways, not just in terms of associative strength.

There is no need to describe here Quillian's proposal, nor the work that derived from it. Suffice it to say that working with large semantic nets proved to be cumbersome, and people soon began to detect structure within such nets. Frames (Minsky, 1975; Bobrow & Winograd, 1977; Fahlman, 1979; Charniak, 1977) scripts (Schank & Abelson, 1977), and schemata (Rumelhart & Ortony, 1977) were discovered. Though there are differences between these concepts (e.g., scripts refer to stereotyped action sequences), the basic idea is the same. A schema (script, frame) is a knowledge structure which ties together information in memory. It is a label with slots that stand in some prearranged relation to each other. Each slot accepts information of a given type. "Information" here may mean concepts, propositions, or even other schemata. One can think of the slots of a schema as variables, which can be replaced with specific instances. This is precisely what happens when a schema is instantiated in discourse comprehension: Specific information fills the appropriate slots of a schema. The instantiated schema will in this way be one of the knowledge sources that contribute to the strategic construction of a text representation in episodic memory. However, contrary to other approaches in artificial intelligence, we do not believe that the instantiated frame or script is identical with a textual representation. We have suggested earlier in this chapter that most discourses will on the one hand presuppose general knowledge, but on the other hand will usually bring new information, including information that is not simply an instantiation of a frame or script. So, in a story about events in a restaurant we may expect some propositions that are instantiations of frame or script knowledge (e.g., 'Peter ordered a steak', 'Mary signaled the waiter', or 'Peter left a big tip'), but we may also expect propositions about interesting, nonscriptal properties of participants, about actions and events that are not stereotypical, or that are organized by other frames or scripts, such as the 'quarrel' or 'fire' scripts. This means that although general knowledge does contribute to the local and global coherence of the text representation, other factors are also involved, such as (a) local coherence relations based on conditioning, for example, when event or action sequences and their goals are involved (activating general and episodic knowledge about actions of participants), (b) global coherence, involving the construction of (often unique) macropropositions, and (c) textual schemata, such as narrative ones, which assign some superstructure to the text. It follows that the contribution of general knowledge to the coherence involves general knowledge or metaknowledge about likely sequences of events and actions, about motivations and goals, about plans and interests, on the one hand, and procedural knowledge about discourse strategies and discourse structures, on the other. We conclude that the use of knowledge in discourse comprehension is much more complex than the simple instantiation of scripts, script tracks, or script scenes. What we would like to emphasize is that some fragments of instantiated general knowledge are flexibly used in a strategic manner to understand and represent new, unique information provided by the text, which is organized also according to other principles, such as those of the various textual structures and strategies discussed in the previous chapters, as well as on the basis of episodic experiences.

As we will detail in the next chapter, we propose a two-step use of general knowledge: After the activation of certain concepts on the basis of some input word or clause, some general knowledge fragment (e.g., of a frame or script) is activated and instantiated with the specific constants (*Peter, Mary*) of the text. This instantiation will in turn activate, and its information be added to, specific episodic memories about the same or similar situations, namely, the situation model. It is the thus activated or constructed information in the situation model that forms the knowledge base for understanding the text. For instance, we may activate or construct a situation model 'Fire in a restaurant', involving general information about restaurants, and general information about fires, added to personal experiences with such or similar fires.

In terms of the local–global distinction that has played such an important part in this book, schemata can be found at either level. There are global schemata, such as the narrative schema discussed at length in Chapter 7, but also very local ones, such as propositional schemata and verb frames. Our own proposal for a propositional schema was discussed in Chapter 4. Verb frames have been widely used since Fillmore (1968), both in linguistics and in artificial intelligence. Verb frames organize concepts, in that they assign them to certain case roles, as agents, patients, instruments, and so forth. Thus, we are able to understand *John gives Mary a book* as *John* is the agent of the action *give, Mary* is its patient, and *book* the object. But whereas verb frames organize concepts, the frames themselves may be organized in higher order structures. Charniak (1981) points out that verb frames form an *is-a* hierarchy, not unlike the well-known is-a hierarchy for nouns. Just as a 'dog' is a 'mammal', and thus may inherit the property of having a 'head' from its superordinate, verbs, too, may inherit properties in an is-a hierarchy. If we know that 'reading' is a *transitive act* and that transitive acts have agent and patient slots, then we do not need to store that information with 'reading.' Instead, we can deduce it from the superordinate node when it is needed. All we have to be concerned about with 'reading' are the properties that are specific to it, for example, that one reads a text. Charniak shows that this solves one of the long-standing embarrassments of case theory, namely, the question of how many cases there are. No one has been ever able to show how many cases there are and exactly what they are. In Charniak's analysis this is not a surprise: Probably there are only a few general cases such as agent and patient which apply high up in the verb hierarchy; but as one goes down in the hierarchy, more and more specialized verbs appear, with more and more specialized cases (which might as well remain nameless). Thus, there is no need to worry about the case of *in French* in Charniak's example *Frederica read a book in French*. The case analysis can be useful, even though the slots in the case frames do not come from a closed set. If we leave the field of verb frames and consider schemata in general, there is little reason to suppose that we can come up with a finite, fixed set of slots that schemata can have. In each domain there are probably some slots that apply with some generality, just as agent, patient, instrument, etc. in the domain of verb frames, but as schemata become more specific, special purpose slots must be added. It is difficult to see how formal theories of schema-based knowledge systems could be possible in view of this ad hoc component. One would wish for constraints.

Before continuing with a more detailed discussion of some of the problems encountered in working with schema-based knowledge systems, we need to ask ourselves to what extent such systems are real, or at least plausible psychologically. Recently, a certain amount of experimental work has been reported which indicates quite clearly that something like a schema is a viable notion psychologically, and not just a useful construct in artificial intelligence.

Most of this work has been concerned specifically with the script concept, and a lot of diverse evidence has been obtained that scripts indeed function as psychological units. Black and Bower (1979) have shown that script-based episodes in stories are treated as chunks in memory. This conclusion was further supported by Black, Turner, and Bower (1979), who showed that subjects tend to list the actions of a script together, and that they make recognition errors among them. Like chunks, scripts are retrieved as a unit, and the time to retrieve them is independent of the number of actions in the script, just as it is independent of the number of items in a chunk (Anderson, 1980; Smith, Adams, & Schorr, 1978).

Scripts are not just sets of actions, but ordered sets. If the actions of a script are presented out of order, subjects tend to reorder them (Black, Turner, & Bower,

1979). Furthermore, the usual kind of similarity effect is observed in retrieving script-related actions: Retrieval speed depends on how close the actions are to each other, and how central they are to the script (Galambos & Rips, 1982). How textual information is integrated with knowledge in reading script-based text has also been studied by Sanford and Garrod (1981:146) and Bellezza and Bower (1982). The latter suggests that scripts serve a dual role, both as cognitive cueing structures and as guides for the allocation of attentional resources during comprehension.

There is good evidence for the existence of substructures in scripts. Subjects cluster script actions together in a regular way, distinguishing fixed *scenes* within a script (Bower, Black, & Turner, 1979) and marking them linguistically with a single word ('ordering', 'eating' in the restaurant script, but not, e.g., 'counting the money' which is merely part of a 'paying' scene). Abbott and Black (1980) have argued that the script structure is hierarchical and presented evidence that script actions in the context of a narrative activate their superordinates in the script hierarchy, but not the other way around. Thus, when we encounter the word *restaurant* in a text, we do not think of 'ordering', 'eating', and 'paying', but if we hear these words which are subunits of a script, the script label 'restaurant' will be activated.

In conclusion, it appears that we now have good evidence that scripts with their subordinate actions form psychological units (chunks) in much the same way as do other concepts that have been studied traditionally within psychology. Indeed, scripts are only too similar to our familiar categories. Like them, they cannot be defined precisely, but are fuzzy by their very nature; they cannot be used in simple, fixed ways but are highly flexible and context dependent.

Most of the difficulties in designing knowledge systems derive from this flexibility that concepts, scripts, and schemata share. We have seen the shift that took place within psychology in the last decades in the way we think about concepts: From the neat, clean definitions via necessary and sufficient properties we have moved to context-dependent feature sets and exemplars. Scripts (and with them schemata and frames) have undergone very much the same evolution, having changed from fixed, prepared structures to context-sensitive entities that are constructed in response to some task demand. The 'restaurant' script of Schank and Abelson (1977) is the classical representative of the former view. Situational variety in classical scripts was accounted for by special "tracts." For instance, in addition to the general 'restaurant' script, Schank and Abelson had special tracks for 'French restaurant', 'fast food', etc. But there really is no end to special tracks—every application of the restaurant track requires its own special track. At this point the script as a fixed knowledge structure is no longer useful. Instead, we must consider how context-sensitive scripts can be generated on demand out of some flexibly organized knowledge system. Schank's MOPs ("Memory Organization Packets") are an attempt to design such a system (Schank, 1979b). It is, however, easier to recognize the need for a flexible, dynamic knowledge system than to construct such a system. Many of the problems involved have not yet been solved satisfactorily (nor even recognized), and we can do no more here than to indicate some of the issues and problems involved in constructing flexible knowledge systems.

### 9.1.4. Levels of Cognitive Units

Neither concepts nor schemata can be defined in the strict sense. The case against definition has been made repeatedly and with a variety of arguments (especially Fodor *et al.*, 1980; Kintsch, 1980b; Smith & Medin, 1981). But definitional systems, because they are clear and orderly, are so much easier to work with than dynamic, flexible systems the properties of which are not very well understood. Theories about knowledge require constraints and structures to theorize about. If the meaning of a concept cannot be specified once and for all by some small set of semantic elements, if it requires instead a large, open set of complex statements, theories will be much more difficult to formulate. However, given the situational lability of concepts as well as schemata, we have no choice but to learn to work with complex, messy interactions.

The problem is compounded by the fact that we are not dealing with a single knowledge system, but with a multileveled system. Psychologically relevant knowledge units exist at the levels of features, concepts, propositions, and schemata. Features and concepts are generally considered noncontroversial, and we can take them as given. The evidence for propositions has been summarized at several points in this book (especially Chapters 2 and 4). Similarly, the reality of schemata has concerned us repeatedly throughout this book, most specifically in the previous section. Interactions among these levels, however, produce a whole new set of problems.

There are other questions, too, equally formidable ones. Are knowledge representations abstract, propositional, or do they involve imagery? How can we ever identify the internal structure of a knowledge system from behavioral data alone? Clearly, all we can strive for is a model, a theory, and as with all theories, we cannot know whether it is the only one or even the best one. In fact, we know that it is not the only possible one—there are always more theories, especially vague ones. The problem for us is not to attain the impossible—the ultimate, right theory; rather, it is a much more modest one: to achieve a good theory of knowledge representation, one that is useful in explaining the important facts that need explaining, and one that does it in a sensible, natural way (Anderson, 1976; Pylyshyn, 1973; Kieras, 1980b). That is hard enough without becoming involved in controversies about undecidable issues.

In spite of the many questions that we have to leave open at this time, it is possible at least to sketch the overall outlines of a knowledge system. First of all, the system must have many levels, with nodes from one level forming often overlapping chunks at higher levels. In such a system it is possible that the elements of two chunks are not directly associated but only associated indirectly via their chunk nodes. The notion of chunk has long been familiar in psychology (Miller, 1956;

Simon, 1974); indirect associations via control elements also have been used for some time (Müller, 1911; Estes, 1972). Because chunks at some point have to be created from elements that reside in short-term memory simultaneously, chunk size is limited to about four elements (following Broadbent, 1975). Hierarchical chunking structures are used to overcome this limitation (Mandler, 1967).

Before we consider how such structures are used in comprehension we need to make one more point about the term "knowledge system." Usually, when we talk about knowledge we mean decontextualized, generalized information as opposed to context-embedded, unique personal experience. That is, we mean semantic memory as opposed to episodic memory in the terminology of Tulving (1972). Although that distinction is useful for many purposes, it is quite misleading here because any kind of information in long-term memory can be used in comprehension, whether it is generalized knowledge or a special episode. Furthermore, the structure of episodic memory must exhibit the same multilevel character as the structure of general knowledge. For present purposes, therefore, we do not want to make a distinction between the two: Knowledge, as the term is used here, is simply everything we know, whether it is generalized information distilled from many experiences, or the memorial records of a single, unique experience.

## 9.2. KNOWLEDGE USE IN METAPHOR COMPREHENSION

A particularly interesting use of knowledge occurs when phrases have to be understood nonliterally. Specifically, consider the construction of propositions. We assume that every time a proposition is completed, a knowledge check is made to determine how it is to be interpreted. This interpretation determines what inferences, if any, follow from a given proposition. A problem arises because a great many expressions that we encounter are not used literally. How do we understand metaphors and other nonliteral expressions which must fail this knowledge check? We certainly do understand such expressions, and not as esoteric rarities which require a lot of overt problem-solving activity, but naturally and readily.

The classical processing theory has been that metaphors are first rejected as semantically anomalous, and then reinterpreted on the basis of some special strategies to yield appropriate interpretations. There have even been some attempts to build explicit process models of this kind, specifying how the initial anomaly judgment and the later reinterpretation occur (e.g., Kintsch, 1972, and Miller, 1979, for metaphors, Clark & Lucy, 1975, for indirect requests). Any such two-stage notion of metaphor interpretation implies that nonliteral expressions require more extensive processing than literal expressions: The latter simply pass the knowledge check and that is that, whereas some kind of extra processing has to occur for anomalous expressions. There is, however, no evidence that this is the case. Metaphors (Ortony, Schallert, Reynolds, & Antos, 1978), idioms (Swinney &

Cutler, 1979), and indirect requests (Clark, 1979) are understood as easily and as directly (Glucksberg, Gildea, & Bookin, 1982; Gibbs, 1982) as comparable literal expressions. (These conclusions hold for conventionalized or semiconventionalized metaphors—more extensive problem-solving activities are presumably required for new creative metaphors, such as those used in some forms of modern poetry—van Dijk, 1972; van Dijk & Petöfi, 1975; Ching, Haley, & Lunsford, 1980; Groeben, 1982.)

Let us review what we know today about metaphor understanding: First of all, people can tell what is a literal expression, what is a good metaphor, and what is plain nonsense (or could be interpreted in a meaningful way only with much special-purpose processing)—the fact that metaphor boundaries are once again fuzzy can come as no surprise any more; second, people have no more trouble understanding good (conventionalized) metaphors than they do literal expressions. This suggests that they probably use the same or similar comprehension strategies with metaphors as with nonmetaphors, and that pretty much the same amount of calculation is involved in processing óne or the other.

What may be wrong about the classical conception may not be so much how metaphors are understood, but rather how literal expressions are understood. The knowledge check that occurs with literal expressions is not in itself sufficient, but must be followed up with further processing—very much as is the case with metaphors, the difference being that the check is positive in one case and negative in the other. Although the further processing of literal and nonliteral expressions is not identical, it is similar in many ways. Let us start with metaphors. We assume, first, that an expression like *prices are soaring* is checked against the knowledge base and that anomaly is detected (hence, we know that we are dealing with a metaphor). Next, we have to determine what the implications of the proposition *prices are soaring* are, which is done through the application of certain comprehension strategies. Although our picture of precisely what such strategies involve is still incomplete, some important cases have been described by Carbonell (1981). Carbonell has studied some of the more frequent types of metaphors described by Lakoff and Johnson (1980), among them the *more-is-up, less-is-down* metaphors of which we just have cited an example. He considers why such metaphors are used (e.g., to transfer knowledge from a relatively well-understood domain to a poorly understood one) and what strategies we use in understanding them. His main point is that these strategies can be ordered and form an expected invariance hierarchy. Metaphors are mostly used to say something about goals and plans, often about causal structures and functional attributes, sometimes about temporal orderings, attributes, and tendencies, rarely about social roles or structural properties, almost never about descriptive properties and object identity. In interpreting the metaphor we check for implications in the order just given, from goals downward; if information is found in a category, we take that to be the implication of the metaphor and stop. Thus, in *John is a fox* we stop as soon as we find the tendency ascribed to foxes of being sly; we do not go down to the physical attribute and conclude that

John has pointed ears. In contrast, not knowing anything about giraffes other than their size and perhaps clumsiness, we have to go all the way to the level of physical descriptions when we interpret *John is a giraffe.*

Thus, Carbonell has at least a partial theory of metaphor understanding and the strategies involved. We cannot do justice to his work here, and many serious questions remain. For instance, Carbonell's invariance hierarchy must somehow respond to context effects because how a metaphor is interpreted can be strongly influenced by context. Furthermore, there may be various other metaphor comprehension strategies, relying on quite different operations (such as asymmetrical similarity judgments, as suggested by Ortony, 1979). There is certainly more to be known. But, at the minimum, Carbonall has specified at least some comprehension strategies that account for how some metaphors are understood.

We would like to suggest that very similar comprehension strategies must be used in the understanding of literal expressions. A literal expression is not understood simply by noting that it is semantically acceptable. People apparently do that, just as they note that metaphors are semantically unacceptable, but that alone is not enough. Metaphors pick out one or more implications of semantically anomalous propositions to form the basis of an interpretation. With semantically regular propositions, context does the same thing. In either case, comprehension strategies are needed to determine exactly how the proposition is to be interpreted. The concepts that we use in our language are just not precise enough by themselves. Usually, a speaker can trust tbe context to give them precision so that they convey the intended meaning, whereas at other times a metaphor might be used to point the hearer in the right direction. This property of language has been appreciated for some time, for instance, by Weinreich (1966) who introduced the concept of "transfer features": A sentence context transfers features to a concept used in that sentence to give it its full meaning. Consider, for instance, the verb *turn,* as in *the wheel is turning, the weather is turning, the car turned a corner, Joe turned on his accuser, he turned around, he turned pale, he turned eighty, he turned the doorknob, he turned into a father, he turned a hose on the fire.* What *turn* means in these phrases is determined by the context provided by each phrase. It is not enough for a knowledge check to determine that *wheel* is an appropriate argument for *turn,* and hence that the proposition is semantically acceptable, but it has to provide the necessary specification— a process not totally unlike what happens in metaphor understanding (van Dijk, 1972).

Consider another example, provided by Bierwisch (1982), involving the meaning of *money* in the following sentences: *John lost his money as he was not aware of the hole in his pocket* and *John lost his money by speculating on the stockmarket.* What *money* means in the two sentences is quite different, and determined by the context. Again, merely concluding that *money* is a semantically appropriate argument for *lose* does not get us very far, though it is part of the story.

Somewhat paradoxically, when we ask what strategies are involved in specifying concepts when they are used literally, we know even less than when we ask about their use in metaphorical contexts. A considerable amount of work needs to be done before we achieve a detailed understanding of these processes (but see Ching *et al.*, 1980, and van Dijk & Petöfi, 1975, for some relevant attempts).

## 9.3. REDINTEGRATION, REMINDING, AND PARTIAL MATCHES

The main problem concerning knowledge use is that the knowledge base that we use in comprehension is huge. It must be huge in order to avoid errors. Small knowledge systems make errors. Only a huge, interactive, redundant system permits us to react to the world adaptively. The problem, then, is how we can retrieve the right piece of information from such a system.

This is a complex problem which must be addressed in parts. First, let us consider the actual mechanism of memory retrieval. We have argued in Chapter 8 that the laboratory research on memory has provided a reasonable model for this mechanism. We refer here to the memory retrieval model of Raaijmakers and Shiffrin (1981) and its adaptation to knowledge retrieval by Walker (1982). However, what we have is merely a model for that part of the retrieval process that can accurately be called a "mechanism," but not for the strategic processes that control this mechanism. The question of whether the Raaijmakers and Shiffrin model is really the right one, or even the best one available, is not crucial for us here. It surely is a good first approximation, and it undoubtedly is not the last word. The main problem for us is that this model is but a single component of a knowledge retrieval system. First of all, it does not deal explicitly with the multilayered nature of the system, though Walker (1982) has made some beginnings in dealing with chunks within the framework of that model. Second, it only tells us what happens when a given retrieval cue is used to tap into memory. What remains largely unexplored are the strategies used to establish this cue in the first place, and to change it in response to the outcome of the retrieval process, and the use to which the retrieved information is then put. In the idea generation paradigm studied by Walker, these strategies were relatively simple. When we are concerned with knowledge use in comprehension, much more complex strategies need to be considered.

Knowledge is needed in comprehension to fit into it the new information, in order to provide a structure for organizing it, that is, for making sense of the new information. But the existing knowledge structure never quite fits the new information. Some important pieces are always missing in the puzzle, and others do not fit at all. In the terminology of computer science, we always have to perform a partial match.

The problem has been recognized for a long time in psychology. Classical statements are Hamilton's law of redintegration and Höffding's law of totality (Hamilton, 1859; Höffding, 1891). In this century, Selz (1939) had some highly original thoughts about this problem. (See the monograph and text edited by de Groot and Frijda (1981) on Selz and his work.) His notion of pattern completion, however, remained without much impact on psychology. More recently, cognitive scientists have become interested in these problems again, mostly under the influence of artificial intelligence, such as Schank's concept of "reminding" and the work on pattern-directed inferences in computers (Schank, 1979; Waterman & Hayes-Roth, 1978).

How can partial matches be successful in a knowledge system that is as huge and as complexly organized as the human one? Brute force is probably part of the answer. Matching is one of the elementary cognitive operations, and is apparently performed efficiently and effectively by the brain. However, brute force can hardly be the whole answer. Strategies are needed to reduce the enormous amount of computation that must be performed in comprehension. Techniques employed in artificial intelligence for similar purposes can give us some idea of what they might be.

Intuitively, we make a distinction between active and quiescent knowledge. At any point in the comprehension process, a certain area of knowledge appears to be readily available and actively participating in the process, while other fields of knowledge remain quiescent, which frequently leads us to overlook important and interesting relations between the new information and old problems and questions that somehow were never brought into contact with it. In most current artificial intelligence programs this would happen because the new information is not matched with all of the existing knowledge system, but only with an active subset thereof. The active subset can be selected in various ways. Spreading activation in a semantic network has often been invoked for that purpose (Quillan, 1968; Collins & Loftus, 1975; Anderson, 1976). There is good evidence that the spread of activation is a plausible model psychologically. At the very least, it seems that activated information is matched first, before the more remote possibilities are tried, or is otherwise given some advantage if the matching occurs in parallel. But there may be other processes, in addition to or instead of spreading activation, that limit the amount of knowledge that is being considered at any time. A useful strategy appears to be based on a bias for global over local matches: If possible, find a match at the level of schemata, which will take precedence over lower order matches and guide them to the exclusion of matches that do not conform to the schema. Such a global bias appears to be an efficient device for avoiding unnecessary analyses, and in the last section of this chapter we shall present some experimental data that show that people actually use such a strategy in discourse comprehension. Other strategies to achieve the same purpose rely on the principle of first making a rough, approximate match, and then following up only those elements that passed this initial criterion. We have excellent evidence that people use such a strategy in making recognition judgments in laboratory experiments (Atkinson & Juola, 1974) and probably also in a host of other similar decision situations (see the discussion on two-stage decision models in Kintsch, 1977a). The same strategy appears to be useful in knowledge utilization. In the ACT production system, for instance, a certain number of likely candidates are first selected and put on the agenda (the APPLYLIST) for the actual matching (Anderson, 1976). This is done crudely but effectively by the criterion of argument overlap: If at any time working memory contains the concepts A, B, S, and V, then all productions with A, B, S, and V on the condition side are put on the APPLYLIST for futher consideration. Which production of those selected then applies first depends on a number of other factors, such as its strength (an index of how recently and successfully it has been applied) and its specificity. Joshi (1978) uses argument overlap recursively to select relevant rules and facts in his inference system.[1] Given certain rules, a set of relevant facts is determined as discussed here, then the set of rules is augmented by adding those that share arguments with the new expanded fact set, and so on, until a local closure is obtained.

## 9.4. STRATEGIES FOR KNOWLEDGE USE IN DISCOURSE

The general strategies for knowledge utilization find their counterparts in discourse strategies. Given the kind of knowledge structure we have been discussing here, it would seem that a global bias could be used effectively to restrict the matching process. As soon as a match, or rather a partial match, is established at the schema level, all lower order matches could be constrained to be congruent with it. At least, this would be a good first hypothesis which could save a lot of processing time and resources. If that first hypothesis is counterindicated, other, unexpected possibilities have to be tried, of course. This strategy will be further explored in Section 9.6.

In selecting an appropriate schema (or rather in constructing one, as we shall emphasize in what follows), devices like the APPLYLIST or Joshi's (1978) "Local Context Closure" could play a role to limit the number of alternatives that must be considered. Basically, the idea is to use a two-stage decision strategy: First reject all candidates that do not appear to be applicable on some rough criterion, then worry about the rest. Knowledge utilization strategies interact here closely with the macrostrategies. Whatever concepts and propositions have been identified to be of global significance for the text (on the basis of the strategies discussed in Chapter 6) also must hold the clues as to the appropriate knowledge structure which is to be applied globally for the interpretation of the text. Thus, if we have identified as the macroproposition of a text fragment 'John is taking the train to Paris', we thereby have also identified a knowledge source for the organization of the text.

In our example, the required knowledge structure would be a script 'taking a train'. At least it would be for some of us, who on the basis of past experience have developed such a script. For many American readers, however, the problem would

---

[1]Rules and facts parallel the distinction between procedural and declarative knowledge which is often made (e.g., Anderson, 1976). It is useful to keep declarative and procedural knowledge apart. The former provides a basis for computations without actually changing the system: Changes can have wide and sometimes unthought-of repercussions in a complex interacting network, and need to be made with care. A special procedural component operating on the declarative knowledge base can be made responsible for taking actions, thus providing a much needed buffer between thought and action.

be more complex, since they do not always have recourse to a 'train' script, if they never hav taken a train and perhaps never have read much about taking trains either. Assume, however, that our hypothetical reader has taken a train once—to Baltimore. We would not want to suppose that a generalized, decontextualized 'train' script resulted from that single experience, but our reader probably remembers quite well the highpoints of the trip. From that specific memory episode a schema can now be constructed: The events that are still part of that memory episode become slots for textual information of a similar type. Our reader organizes and hence understands John's trip on the train to Paris by putting it into correspondence with the reader's own, vaguely remembered, train trip to Baltimore. Propositions in the text that partially match propositions in memory are put into the framework or schema provided by the reader's memory. The fact that the reader's memory about that train trip to Baltimore may contain many things that could not possibly happen to John on his way to Paris never intrudes. The reader does not expect the same things to happen to John on his train ride; rather, he or she merely notes whatever correspondences there are. Needless to say, this process is not necessarily or even usually conscious.

Even if our reader never had taken a train, he or she could still construct quite easily a schema to understand the text about John's trip. The reader will have a general schema and/or personal experiences about other types of public transportation, say about riding a bus. General problem-solving procedures can now be applied to construct a schema for John's train trip in analogy to whatever is known about riding the bus.

The point of these examples is that the schema used for discourse comprehension is always constructed. The raw material may be general, decontextualized knowledge, or some personal experience (or a mixture of the two), or merely some remotely similar knowledge structure or experience that is transferred to the present situation via analogy. When we talk about a general schema or script for taking trains, all we mean is that we know a lot about trains, that this knowledge is general and context independent, and that some parts of it are used in constructing a coherent text representation. Which parts, specifically, is quite unpredictable and changes from text to text (or experience to experience). The text selects the schema slots it needs. The unused portion of the knowledge does not necessarily become a part of the text representation. It may, if it is needed to fill a gap in the text (conditions under which this is known to occur have been discussed in Section 2.7) or if the reader for whatever reason chooses to elaborate the text. It is possible to read a great deal into a text, and cases are legion when readers have done exactly that. Certain text types (especially poetry) even encourage the reader to do so. But, in general, readers stick pretty much to the text and the inferences that are necessary for its coherence. Specifically, we claim that it is not the case that all slots in a schema that could be created on the basis of one's knowledge are indeed created (and assigned default values) when a schema is activated and used in understanding a text. The experimental results discussed in Section 2.7 form the basis for this claim.

To return to our train example, if our reader with a given knowledge base about trains, say a very rich one, reads two texts, one about John's first-class trip on the train to Paris, and one about Martha's journey on the Transsiberian Railroad, obviously he or she will not only construct two different macrostructures for these two texts, but will actually use two somewhat different schemata in doing so: The texts will require different pieces of knowledge, in different combinations, so that two different schemata will be generated according to these diverging text demands from the same knowledge base. Note the contrast between this notion of context-dependent knowledge utilization and the application of preexisting, fixed scripts with 'first-class' and 'Transsiberia' tracks.

The three cases of knowledge use we have discussed so far—using general knowledge to construct a schema, adapting a personal experience, and schema generation through analogical reasoning—all have in common that they are not specific to any particular type of text, but represent general strategies that are employed as needed in many different types of situations. Specialized knowledge utilization strategies are, however, often of great importance in understanding certain types of texts, mostly of a technical nature. An example that has been studied in some detail concerns understanding word arithmetic problems (Kintsch & Greeno, 1982; see also Section 10.5).

## 9.5. KNOWLEDGE USE IN THE *NEWSWEEK* TEXT

In this section we shall provide some examples of the kinds of knowledge structures that are necessary for understanding the *Newsweek* text and of the strategies involved in activating and using them. In a sense, what we are doing here is no more than reviewing what has been done with this text in the earlier chapters: What kinds of knowledge structures were used in interpreting the text? How do they interact across levels? How are they kept active in memory?

### 9.5.1. The Lexicon and the Construction of Propositions

The lexical information needed to build propositions has been (partially) indicated in Columns A and D of Table 4.1: The former contains (a sketch of) the syntactic information that is required, and the latter identifies relevant bits of knowledge about the word concepts that are being processed. Neither has been formalized in any way, because we are still lacking a systematic theory of knowledge structures.

Nevertheless, it is of some interest to look at these entries a little more closely, so that we can at least see what sort of things an eventual formal theory of knowledge will have to deal with. Take the first word pair of the text: *compared with*. We have identified it as a verb and supplied an implicit agent ('we', or '*Newsweek*'). Furthermore, we can strategically identify it as belonging to a subordinate clause, hence generating a syntactic expectation, as shown in Table 4.1. The semantic frame of COMPARE must look something like this:

## (1) COMPARE (AGENT, OBJECT1', OBJECT2', PROPERTY)

where the prime after OBJECT 1 and 2 indicates that more than a single object may be involved. PROPERTY either is a property of the objects being compared ("Compared with apples, peaches are sweeter"), or is ascribed to the objects, thus requiring a metaphorical interpretation (as the colors gray and black-and-white are ascribed to countries in the first sentence of our text). Furthermore, we need to associate a meaning postulate with (1) to the effect that the OUTCOME of COMPARE is either a similarity or dissimilarity. This superficial analysis gives us all we need to know about *compare* to understand the first sentence. Note that the knowledge here is quite context independent.

Consider next the word *gray* from the same sentence. When it appears in the text we can assign it a particular syntactic function and we can identify it as a color term (as such, it would be defined linguistically with respect to other color terms as well as cognitively by a certain perceptual act and sensory experience), but we do not know which of its semantic aspects to activate (e.g., whether the sensory experience, or some association we might have with it). That can only be done when we come to the next word group in the text: *in El Salvador*. At this point the reader realizes that the literal meaning of *gray* is not called for—countries do not have colors. Thus, some other aspect of *gray* needs to be found that fits the situation. The title of the article and its context control this process, suppressing inappropriate readings (e.g., the *gray* as referring to rainy weather, which would be appropriate in another context, for example in a sentence like *Scotland was gray*), and constraining *gray* to refer to the political situation in a country, thereby priming the reading of *gray* as 'indistinct' or the like. Note that *gray* is not precisely the same in this context as 'indistinct' or any other concept—if such a perfect paraphrase existed the author of the article might have preferred it to the use of the metaphorical *gray*.

Compared with our first example, the strategic use of knowledge in interpreting *gray* is certainly very complex. It is both context dependent and subject to top-down effects. As we have emphasized throughout this chapter, the strategies for knowledge use have to be fine tuned and sophisticated, and will not be very easy to formulate explicitly.

One of the points that we have emphasized is that knowledge use strategies must furnish only the relevant knowledge and not overburden the system by retrieving irrelevant information. This can be illustrated by considering the processing of the word *Guatemala* in the first sentence of our text. Although most readers probably do not know very much about this country, the typical reader might know a great deal more than what is needed here. The knowledge about Guatemala that is actually activated here is quite specific and deals only with the political struggles in that country: The participants (right/left), their goals (destruction of the other side), causes (lack of consensus, oppression), actions (preparatory actions such as buying arms, main actions such as fighting and murdering). Only the participant information, of course, would be activated in the first sentence, the rest would be added as the respective sections of the text are being read. Thus, we have a successive growth of the active knowledge base about Guatemala as the article is being processed.

As a final example, consider the expression *led by* in the second sentence (Number 7 in Table 4.2, the guerrillas are led by a faceless bunch of people). It is interesting because it illustrates nicely the interplay between top-down and local processes in assigning lexical meaning to words. The verb *to lead* is almost as multifaceted as *to turn* which we discussed earlier. We know from the word identification literature (see Section 2.1) that initially a very broad context-independent meaning of *lead* is activated as the word is read, but then top-down processes take over to guide the further interpretation of the word. At that point in the process, a 'politics' frame is active at the macrolevel which together with the previous word *groups* constrains the meaning of *lead:* Political groups have leaders, and it is in that sense that *lead* is interpreted. Note that from a processing standpoint, what happened here is not very different from what happened with the word *gray:* An initial superficial identification of the word is followed by a context-dependent selection of its relevant aspects—regardless of whether these are metaphorical as with *gray* or literal as with *lead.* The amount of processing involved is comparable.

### 9.5.2. Macrostructure Formation

Scripts and frames need to be put together from the reader's knowledge base to support the process of macrostructure formation. As we see in Table 6.2, the first frame used by the macroprocesses is the 'politics' frame. Although the word *political* was not part of the title of our article, the contextual, communicative, and schematic strategies of the reader will probably have inferred that the "choices" mentioned in the title are political choices, and hence that the article is about politics (in Guatemala). This provisional topic choice together with the content of the first sentence produces the first macroproposition, as described in Section 6.5: 'There are no political choices in Guatemala', activating a 'politics' frame as the relevant organizational schema for the propositions of the text. Activating this frame means that from the reader's wide knowledge of politics, certain pieces of information are selected because they match pieces of the text, and are then used as a framework for establishing a coherent textbase. Specifically, what we need to know first is that there are political groups on the left, right, etc., with certain general characteristics; that there are certain political persons (first the unnamed diplomat, later congressmen, presidents, etc.); and that there are certain political actions (like 'leading groups' and 'dominating a country'). As we have seen, this frame knowledge is needed not only for the establishment of coherence relations and of a macrostructure, but also for the purely local processes of concept identification. It determines what aspects of the knowledge that we have associated with a concept will be used in interpreting the text.

Once a frame is activated it may be further specified by the text. For instance, Macropropositions (3), (4), and (5) specify the 'politics' frame by indicating the status of certain political groups.

The other two large-scale knowledge systems that are required for understanding the *Newsweek* text are about U.S. foreign policy and about civil war. Their role is very much like that of the 'politics' frame. They serve to constrain local interpretations, as we have shown. They guarantee coherence [e.g., by assigning to Macroproposition (13)—Guatemala acquires arms from other countries—the role of "preparatory act" in the 'war' script]. Finally, these frames are basic to macrostructure formation: The macropropositions are, indeed, instantiations of slots in the frame. Thus, to cite just a few examples from the 'civil war' frame, $M_5$ 'Political center has been murdered' instantiates one of the action slots in that frame (terror against political opponents); $M_7$--'The regime had counted on Reagan's help'—and $M_9$--'Guerrillas backed by communist countries'—instantiate another action slot in the same frame (help friends); $M_{13}$, already mentioned, instantiates a preparatory act in the 'war' frame, and so on.

Note, however, that we do not simply retrieve the 'war' frame from knowledge and then fill its slots with textual information, but that we construct the frame on the spot from knowledge components under the control of the text itself. Thus, a certain slot is created because an appropriate macroproposition has been formed. Frame construction and macrostructure formation are intertwined, and merely form different aspects of the same process.

Another type of knowledge that is important in macrostructure formation is of a schematic nature. In this case, the 'news report' schema is relevant. We have discussed this in some detail in Chapter 7 and need not repeat this discussion here. Suffice it to say that the activation conditions for this schema lie in the nature of the text being read and the super-headline "Special Report."

However, not only knowledge of various types plays a role in discourse understanding, but also opinions, attitudes, and emotional responses. Indeed, their role is especially notable in the *Newsweek* text analyzed here. We have repeatedly stressed this role in previous sections, pointing out, for instance, that the very title of the piece—"Guatemala: No Choices"—presuppose a U.S. perspective and U.S. values. Thus, attitudes are anything but negligible in understanding this discourse. However, since theoretical work in that area is at present even less well developed than with respect to knowledge use, and since it is outside the scope of this book, we cannot do here much beyond pointing out, informally, the enormous significance and the nontrivial nature of these problems (van Dijk, 1982b).

### 9.5.3. The Control System

At several points in this book we have claimed that knowledge structures that are activated at various levels during discourse comprehension fulfill a control function. Indeed, we often have used the term *control system* to refer to this active knowledge segment. Although a full discussion of this notion must be deferred until Chapter 10, we want to illustrate this notion by means of the *Newsweek* text. Suppose we have arrived at the words *led by* in the second sentence of our text—the example we used in the preceding section. What comprises the control system at this point in processing?

First of all, there is the global context which guides the higher level strategic choices of the reader: the whole sociocultural context, as well as the specific context of reading *Newsweek*. Next, there are more specific knowledge structures that we have assumed to be activated at this point: first of all, the 'news report' schema, then the 'politics' frame as discussed above. Next, we need to deal with the text itself: The first macroproposition is available at this time and controls the ongoing text processing. Also activated is whatever knowledge is needed at that moment for the local text processing, namely, the understanding of the current phrase *led by*. Thus, the control system at that moment in time consists of:

(2)    a.  American values, norms, and ideology
        b.  reading *Newsweek*
        c.  'news report' schema
        d.  politics
        e.  *led by*

Saying that (2) is activated and forms a control system means that this information is much more available than other information in the reader's long-term memory. It is recency tagged and therefore can be readily retrieved via these recency tags, independent of content-based retrieval cues which would be required for the retrieval of other, nonactivated sections of the reader's long-term memory. Thus, this active section of memory forms a surround for the actual comprehension processes, controlling and guiding them. As outlined in more detail in the next chapter, we assume that actual processing occurs in a working register which has ready access to the control system as discussed here and to a limited capacity short-term store which contains the most recent text fragments that are being processed. Specifically, in our example we would have in the short-term store the immediate preceding propositions $S_1$ (as outlined in Table 4.1) and the text fragment currently being processed ("On the left is a collection of extreme Marxist-Leninist groups. . . ."). Once a decision is made that the new text fragment cannot be incorporated into $S_1$, $S_1$ is dropped from the short-term buffer and a new proposition, in this case $S_2$, is formed. Of course, $S_1$ remains readily accessible on the basis of recency cues, just as other information in the control system. In effect, $S_1$ becomes part of that control system. However, whereas some information in the control system is relatively permanent (2a), (2d), mere recency will soon become insufficient to retrieve $S_1$ as other interfering text propositions are constructed in the course of reading, and subsequent retrieval must be achieved on the basis of content-based retrieval cues.

We have, perhaps inappropriately, anticipated quite a bit of Chapter 10 here. The sketch of the memory processes involved in discourse understanding will be elaborated and explained there. However, since we shall not return to the *Newsweek* example in Chapter 10 (on the grounds that such a discussion would be too speculative, given the extreme complexity of this text; although important to illustrate our points in previous chapters it would become overwhelming at the present level of analysis), we felt it important to indicate here, at least in a rough way, how the control system would function in reading the *Newsweek* text.

## 9.6. EXPERIMENT 6: GLOBAL BIASES IN KNOWLEDGE UTILIZATION[2]

One of the strategies we have suggested for making knowledge utilization more efficient was to control the application of local strategies through global constraints. In comprehending a text, the reader or listener must respond to constraints at various levels, from global ones down to constraints at the lexical level. Global constraints could be used to restrict the range of local alternatives that will be considered.

Specifically, suppose that some sentence $S$ out of context partially matches some number $n$ of knowledge structures $K_1$, $K_2$, . . . $K_i$, . . . $K_n$, and that $K_i$ provides the best partial match and is hence chosen most often to interpret the sentence when it is presented out of context. Suppose, furthermore, that some context $C$ partially matches the knowledge structures $K_j$ . . . $K_n$ but does not match $K_1$ . . . $K_i$, where $K_i$ is the previously preferred knowledge structure. We hypothesize that in comprehending $S$, the context $C$ prevents activation of $K_1$ . . . $K_i$, so that when $S$ is interpreted in the context of $C$, the interrelation will now be based on $K_j$ . . . $K_n$, that is, on those knowledge structures that are appropriate for $C$ as well as $S$; specifically, the previously favored $K_i$ will now be neglected.

We present here a partial test of this hypothesis. A full test would require a demonstration of the activation or inactivation of various knowledge structures during comprehension. This has not yet been done, but we have tested an implication of the hypothesis: If knowledge is active during comprehension, it should influence the nature of the continuation responses readers make when they are given an incomplete text and are asked to provide an appropriate continuation. If a reader expects the text to continue in some particular way, we conclude that the organization that the reader has formed at that point in the comprehension process is the source of his or her expectations. Continuations reveal the constraints under which the comprehension processes operate.

Consider the critical sentence $S$; if subjects read $S$ out of context and are asked what they expect might come after $S$ in some unspecified text, they will generate some common answers. What these answers are is determined by the propositions used in $S$ and by the lexical items in $S$, that is, by sentence-level constraints.

Suppose $S$ is embedded into a text that can be organized around some conventional frame, and that $S$ itself fits into that frame. We hypothesize that if readers are asked for their expectations after reading $S$ in a frame-context, they will respond

[2]This research was supported by Grant MH 15872 from the National Institute of Mental Health. We thank Craig Yarbrough for his help.

with statements derived from the constraints of the overall thematic organization of the text, rather than from the sentence alone. On the other hand, if $S$ is embedded in a text that is not suitable for organization in terms of some superordinate frame, then the reader's expectations will be determined by the sentence-level constraints alone, just as in the case where the sentence is presented alone.

Readers will always form expectations easily, because they always operate under some constraints in the comprehension process. The critical prediction is that these constraints will be global ones if subjects are able to form global, frame-based organizations, but local if a text is too ill structured for frame-based organizational processes.

Consider the following sentence: "Last year, Eva Benassi became seriously ill with peritonitis." A group of subjects will state how this sentence could be continued after reading it out of context. A second group of people will read a short paragraph that is lacking in structure and that does not have a clear-cut topic, and they, too, will continue the target sentence. We hypothesize that these two groups of subjects will respond with similar expectations about how the text would continue: In both cases, these expectations should reflect the sentence-level constraints effective at this point in the comprehension process, with some intrusions from the paragraph content when the sentence is read in the context of an unorganized paragraph. On the other hand, if the same target sentence is embedded in a paragraph discussing miracles, the subjects' continuations should reflect the overall organization of the paragraph in terms of a 'miracle' frame, and should therefore be quite different from the earlier two cases.

### 9.6.1. Experiment 6A

Three texts were developed. They appear in the appendix to this chapter. Each of the 32 students was given a booklet containing three fragments, one from each of the texts ("Eva," "Complaints," and "Brakes"), and one from each of the conditions (sentence alone, sentence framed, and sentence unframed). Subjects were instructed to read each text carefully, and then to write down, in a sentence or phrase, what they thought would be a likely continuation of the paragraph fragment they had just read. They were told that there were no "correct" answers, but that the experimenter was interested in their intuitions about these texts. They were also asked to rate their confidence in their response on a 5-point scale, and, finally, to write down a word or brief phrase that in their opinion best indicated the topic of the text. Enough time was given to complete this test.

The subjects' responses were assigned to three classes: those related to the sentence-based constraints, those related to the paragraph theme as well as sentence constraints, and other responses (including failures to respond). Five percent of the responses fell into this third category, which will be neglected in all further analyses. For the "Eva" paragraph, sentence-based constraints would lead subjects to respond with something that was in some way related to her illness (a description, consequences, or treatment), whereas theme-based constraints would elicit something about miracles. Similarly, for the ''Brakes'' text, the sentence alone would elicit continuations concerned with driving a car or with wildlife, whereas in the frame context something about accidents was appropriate. The third text, ''Complaints,'' was somewhat different: Out of context, the normal continuation would deal with some further specification of the complaints (explanation, justification, etc.); in context, however, if subjects were correctly organizing this text as a part of the method section of an experimental report, the continuation should deal with the results of the experiment. Of course, this kind of organization could be expected only to the extent that upper-class undergraduates are familiar with the conventions of the 'psychological report' schema.

The predicted shift in the expectations away from the sentence-level constraints in the presence of a higher order organizational principle (knowledge frame or report schema) was indeed obtained in the experiment (Figure 9.1, Table 9.1). For the ''Eva'' text, the results almost perfectly corresponded to the predictions: All subjects continued with something about 'illness' when they read the sentence alone, and all but one did so when the sentence was read in the unframed context. In contrast, all subjects mentioned miracles in their continuation in the framed continuation. The ''Brakes'' text gave similar results, though they were somewhat attenuated. The ''Complaints'' text showed that the subject population in this experiment was not really familiar with the 'report' schema: The schema effect in this case was considerably reduced, compared with the other two texts. In all cases, however, the obtained interaction effects were statistically significant, with $\chi^2(2) = 19.63, 14.47$, and $16.07$ for ''Eva,'' ''Complaints,'' and ''Brakes,'' respectively, all significant at tbe .001 level.

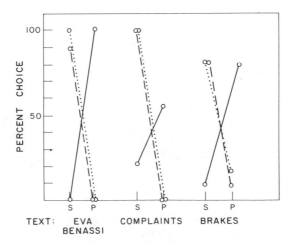

**Figure 9.1.** Percentage of choices of sentence (S) and paragraph topics (P) for continuation responses for three texts in Experiment 6A and three context conditions: alone (dotted line), unframed (broken line), and framed (continuous line).

**Table 9.1**

**Percentage of Continuations Involving Sentence Topic or Paragraph Topic as a Function of Context**

| Contextual condition | Continuations | | |
| --- | --- | --- | --- |
| | Sentence topic | Paragraph topic | Unclassifiable or no response |
| Alone | 93 | 0 | 7 |
| Unframed | 90 | 3 | 7 |
| Framed | 10 | 81 | 9 |

Table 9.2 shows the average confidence ratings that subjects gave to their responses as a function of text and experimental condition. The most interesting thing here is the absence of a main effect for condition: Averaged over the three texts, subjects gave equally high ratings to their continuation responses, whether they worked from the sentence alone or with the framed or unframed text. This is instructive: Readers who do not have a global organization are not necessarily lost—they merely drop down a level and work with the more local constraints of the text. Unfortunately, this conclusion needs to be tempered a bit, because of the presence of a significant text $\times$ conditions interaction in the confidence ratings, $F$ $(4, 81) = 4.23$, $p = .004$, which limits the generality of the claim just made. The interaction reflects mostly the low confidence subjects had in the framed condition when they read the ''Complaints'' text—they were not at all sure about the use of the 'report' schema! Presumably, with graduate students or faculty one could get cleaner results with this text.

The final measure collected in this experiment was topic generation. As Table 9.3 shows, this measure parallels the expectation data in Figure 9.1, but is considerably less sensitive. Subjects gave much clearer data when asked to state their expectations than when asked to state a topic. The proportion for ''other or no'' responses is .37 for the topic responses, compared with .08 for the expectation responses. Similarly, the frame versus no-frame interaction, although still present,

**Table 9.2**

**Mean Confidence Ratings**

| Contextual condition | Text | | | Average for three texts |
| --- | --- | --- | --- | --- |
| | ''Eva'' | ''Brakes'' | ''Complaints'' | |
| Alone | 3.09 | 2.64 | 2.62 | 2.78 |
| Unframed | 2.80 | 2.28 | 2.91 | '2.66 |
| Framed | 3.10 | 4.08 | 2.00 | 3.06 |

**Table 9.3**
**Percentage of Topic Choices Appropriate to Sentence and Paragraph Topics as a
Function of Context**

|  | Topic choice | | |
|---|---|---|---|
| Contextual condition | Sentence alone | Paragraph topic | Unclassifiable or no response |
| Alone | 71 | 4 | 25 |
| Unframed | 21 | 3 | 76 |
| Framed | 6 | 81 | 13 |

is reduced in magnitude, with a corresponding reduction in the statistical significance level (only "Eva" is still significant at the .001 level; "Complaints" is
significant at the .01 level, and "Brakes" only at the .05 level). Also, although the
expectations were practically identical in the sentence alone and the unframed
conditions (Table 9.1), the topics were perceived to differ. This certainly was the
case for the "Complaints" text ($p = .0002$), but occurred to some extent also with
"Eva" ($p = .165$) and "Brakes" ($p = .102$). Clearly, stating expectations was a
better method for our purpose than choosing a topic.

Experiment 6A confirms the chunking hypothesis: If readers have available a
global principle of organization such as a paragraph topic, they tend to base their
expectations on it, rather than merely on local sentence properties. On the other
hand, if they cannot discern a global framework, they readily fall back on the
sentence and use it to form some ideas about where the text is going. However,
these conclusions are based on the responses of relatively few subjects, and on only
three texts. Furthermore, the method of analysis used leaves open a number of
questions, especially about the continuations in the unframed condition: If they are
unable to form a paragraph theme, readers revert to the sentence level—but with
longer and more varied texts it would be surprising if they always chose to concentrate exclusively on the last sentence they had read. Thus, a replication of Experiment 6A was performed with new and more varied texts and a somewhat different
scoring scheme, in order to find answers to the questions raised here.

### 9.6.2. Experiment 6B

Ten different texts were constructed on a variety of topics, both narrative and
descriptive. Each text was written in three versions; only the last sentence was the
same in all three versions. In the alone condition, the text consisted of the critical
sentence alone. In the framed condition, the target sentence came at the end of a
paragraph 100–150 words long which had a clear, easily identifiable theme (this
was verified informally by having several people identify the themes of the 10
paragraphs). Finally, in the unframed condition, the target sentence came at the end
of a 100–150 word long paragraph that was globally incoherent, that is, that did not

possess an easily identifiable theme but consisted merely of a sequence of loosely related or unrelated sentences.

Sixty-two subjects participated in the experiment in groups of 4–6 persons, 22 in the alone condition and 20 each in the other two experimental conditions. Each subject received a booklet which contained all 10 texts, plus several practice texts. All texts in a booklet were presented in the same context condition. Subjects were assigned randomly to the three context conditions. Subjects in the unframed condition were warned that the texts they had to work with were sometimes strange, but were asked to do as well as they could. Subjects were asked to reach each fragment carefully and to write down in a sentence or phrase, what they thought a likely continuation of the paragraph fragment might be. The subjects were told to think of themselves as the author of each text and to produce what would be the most logical continuation. The continuations were not to be generalizations or predictions but rather actual anticipated sentences or phrases. The subjects were informed that the experimenters were interested in their intuitions about the texts and that there were no correct answers. For 'each fragment, subjects were also asked to give a confidence rating—ranging from 1 (no confidence) to 5 (very confident)—to their written continuations.

The continuations produced by the subjects were scored by comparing them with the words in the target sentence: If a continuation involved only content words that already appeared in the target sentence or words that were judged to be closely related thematically to the target sentence, the response was assigned to the category sentence-alone. If a response contained content words unrelated to the target sentence alone, it was classified as sentence-plus. In the framed context, this additional material could either be related to the paragraph topic, or it could be something else, either some detail from the earlier sentences in the paragraph, or an extra paragraph intrusion. In the unframed context, of course, all sentence-plus responses must belong to the latter two categories, and in the alone condition only intrusion responses could be made.

A single judge performed the scoring, with a second judge checking it. In 2% of the cases responses could not be scored, or were missing.

The results of the experiment are shown in Table 9.4. If readers have a well-

**Table 9.4**
**Percentage of Continuations Based on Sentence Alone and Sentence-Plus-Paragraph as a Function of Context**

| Context condition | Basis of continuation | | |
|---|---|---|---|
| | Sentence alone | Sentence-plus-paragraph | Unclassifiable or no response |
| Alone | 93 | 3 | 4 |
| Unframed | 69 | 30 | 1 |
| Framed | 10 | 89 | 1 |

formed paragraph to work with, their continuation responses are predominantly based on material derived from that paragraph as a whole. Indeed, in such cases, of the 89% of the responses in the sentence-plus-paragraph column, 83% were based on the paragraph theme, the other 6% on some other detail from the paragraph. In only 10% of these framed context cases was the paragraph theme neglected and the text continued on the basis of the last sentence only. Of course, if subjects were given only that last sentence, that was all they could do and did in fact do; in only a few cases (3%) did they use extraneous material unrelated to the sentence. Subjects in the unframed condition were intermediate between these extremes: For the most part, they ignored the ill-formed, disorganized paragraph and concentrated on the last sentence, just like subjects who only had this sentence to work with. On the other hand, we also find many responses that are based wholly or partially on the paragraph. Thus, in 11% of all cases a continuation was based on some salient detail picked up from an earlier sentence in the paragraph, and in 19% of the cases subjects used material from the target sentence as well as from earlier sentences in the paragraph.

As in Experiment 6A, there was a slight tendency to be more confident of continuation responses in the framed context than in either the alone or unframed context, but once again the difference was small and did not reach statistical significance, $t(60) = 1.73, p = .09$. The mean confidence ratings in the alone, unframed, and framed conditions were 2.46, 2.42, and 2.63, respectively.

### 9.6.3. Discussion

The results of these two experiments can be summarized quite simply. If subjects read an incomplete text and are asked to write down a likely continuation for it, their responses depend on how much context they have, and how good that context is. If they are working with a good, well-formed paragraph that has a clearly discernible frame-based theme, they use that theme for continuing the text. If, on the other hand, they are given an ill-formed, disorganized paragraph, they do not have a frame to base their continuations on and must rely instead on some salient detail that they find in the paragraph. Most often, they simply use the last sentence, but sometimes they pick up a detail in an earlier sentence, or try to integrate the last sentence with earlier material in the paragraph. If all they have is a single sentence, they use it to construct a continuation. The important point here is that in all these cases subjects produce continuations readily, and with about the same level of confidence. They have a bias for the paragraph theme; however, if they do not have such a theme, they are by no means lost, but just revert to some sentence-level detail.

This simple observation has some theoretical significance, in that it allows us to identify an important constraint in discourse processing. The task of constructing a continuation for an incomplete text can be considered as an indicator for the way the reader is organizing the text at that moment. The semantic units of a text are organized on the basis of some propositional schema, and that propositional schema provides a basis for constructing a plausible continuation of the text. Thus, if one reads a paragraph about 'miracles', the knowledge involved very likely is about 'miracles', which has many possible elements, among them a lot for 'instances of miracles'; if we then see a sentence that might be the precondition of a miracle (Eva's dying of peritonitis), we might very well regard it as part of the description of a miracle, and continue the text accordingly.

On the other hand, if a reader receives an incoherent paragraph that cannot be organized globally, some other basis for a continuation response must be found, for example, the last text proposition, or an earlier text proposition that contained some salient detail.

Thus, one can conclude that readers have a bias for global over local principles of organization when producing continuations of incomplete texts. Local constraints are, of course, not neglected; otherwise the continuations subjects produced would have been of an unsuitable level of generality and locally inappropriate, which they were not. But the global constraint biased the local ones: Of the many possible local continuations, the global constraints picked out certain ones and suppressed others, even when they were the most prominent ones in isolation. Although our production task doesn't permit us to conclude exactly which knowledge structures were activated in comprehension, it nevertheless supports the original hypothesis indirectly. Direct knowledge activation during comprehension will be needed to further investigate this problem.

In concluding, we should point out that we have discussed this experiment here from the perspective of knowledge utilization, but that we could have stressed equally well another aspect of this study: the demonstration of the strategic role of propositions in the comprehension and production of discourse. As we have emphasized with respect to the *Newsweek* example in the previous section, global knowledge utilization and macrostructure formation are part of one and the same process.

## APPENDIX: TEXTS USED IN EXPERIMENT 6A

Text 1: "Eva"
Sentence alone:
   Last year, Eva Benassi became seriously ill with peritonitis.
Unframed:
   Settled amidst wooded hills in the back country of Ohio is the town of Plattsville. Its high school was opened only a few years ago. Eva Benassi was one of the students in its first freshman class. Last year, Eva became seriously ill with peritonitis.
Framed:
   While most miracles that the Church acknowledges occurred in times past, quite a few are claimed in our own days. Ardent prayer sometimes helps miraculously in all kinds of misfortunes. Last year, Eva Benassi became seriously ill with peritonitis.
Text 2: "Brakes"
Sentence alone:
   John Park stepped hard on the brake when he saw his first moose.

Unframed:

John Park and his family were among the 2.4 million visitors who visited Yellowstone Park last year. Yellowstone has more active geysers than any other place in the world as well as abundant wildlife. Most attractions in the park can be visited by car. John Park stepped hard on the brake when he saw his first moose.

Framed:

Many automobile accidents occur when they are least expected. Sudden, unpredictable stops are a case in point. John Park and his family drove all the way from Chicago to see the wildlife in Yellowstone Park. He stepped hard on the brake when he saw his first moose.

Text 3: "Complaints"

Sentence alone:

Many students complained about the length of the session.

Unframed:

Highway accident rates have reached higher levels than ever before during the past decade, especially in the Rocky Mountain States where snow and mountain roads make driving difficult. Skilled drivers must be able to handle all kinds of road conditions, even ice. All high school students in five Rocky Mountain states were given a compulsory 2-hour lesson in driver education. Many students complained about the length of the session.

Framed:

An experiment was performed to investigate the accuracy and speed with which people can detect different types of printing errors while proofreading. Errors occurred either in the beginning, middle or end of words, half of which were function words and half content words. Twenty college students participated in a 2-hour experimental session during which they were required to proofread a 5000-word text. Many students complained about the length of the session.

# Chapter 10

# The Cognitive Model

In the previous chapters we examined in some detail the various processes involved in discourse comprehension. We now turn to the question of how all this can happen in real time. It is worthwhile at this point to remind ourselves just how complex "all this" really is. It borders on the miraculous how many subtasks people perform, how many points they keep track of, and how many constraints they respect when comprehending discourse—all normally without apparent effort, in a routine manner:

- An incoming stream of sounds must be interpreted as phonemes, phoneme combinations as morphemes, and structured morpheme combinations as clauses. Meaning must be assigned to these various structures within a few seconds per phrase as a maximum, and between 100 and 200 msec per lexical item at the fastest speed.

- At the same time, clauses must be connected in sentences, coherent connections among sentences must be established, and global macrostructures must be derived in order to determine the topic or theme of a passage.

- These interpretations depend on general or episodic world knowledge, which must be searched for, selectively activated, and instantiated. Knowledge-based inferences are necessary to establish local and global coherence.

- In addition and at the same time, the hearer must scan the communicative context for a large variety of data about the typical social situation, the speaker, the interaction types, and the speech act conditions. The interpretation of these data, once again, depends on memory (e.g., episodic memories about the speaker).

- These various levels of interpretation are not independent but must be linked. Surface signals may be relevant not only for standard lexical or syntactic interpretation, but will also be used to express macrostructures, speech act types, and various interactional properties. The same holds for the other relations between syntax, semantics, and pragmatics.

- While busy with all this, the hearer must keep track of various pieces of information needed to control the interpretational processes, such as the interactional frame (e.g., 'this is a lesson', 'this is a trial'), the macro speech act, the semantic macrostructure, schematic superstructures, and possible other overall features, such as stylistic and rhetorical ones.

- Not only knowledge must be activated in the execution of these processes, but also opinions, attitudes, values, and emotions, for example, to evaluate the content or intention of the discourse.

- Finally, but still simultaneously, the hearer has to keep track of his or her own wishes, interests, goals, and plans, which exert a monitoring function on all the other components of the comprehension process.

Somehow, we as scientists describing it have made a process that our intuition tells us is quite simple and elegant look very complex. However, as we have shown in the previous chapters of this book, all these factors do indeed influence comprehension and are involved in it in some way: The phenomenal simplicity of discourse comprehension hides a great deal. Furthermore, the complexity of discourse comprehension as we have analyzed it here does not necessarily exceed that of other human actions not involving language. If we would analyze an action such as walking across a crowded campus to a lecture in the same detail as we have analyzed discourse comprehension here, the level of complexity encountered would probably not be hugely different from that found in discourse comprehension. Even seemingly simple behaviors require complex descriptions and theories.

The problem for the cognitive theorist is to design a system in which all of the subprocesses of discourse comprehension can occur and be coordinated, without violating known constraints on human information capacities.

The most important constraints which we are concerned with here are memory and processing constraints. Perceptual constraints are much better understood and need not be considered here. Processing constraints have only recently been investigated in discourse comprehension and are as yet poorly understood (for some initial work, see Britton, Meyer, Hodge, & Glynn, 1980, and also Experiment 3, Section 6.6). It appears that in principle cognitive processes can operate in parallel and under certain circumstances without interfering with each other (for a review of the relevant literature, see Kintsch, 1977a:Chapter 3). This parallel processing capacity is limited, however, in two ways, through resource and data limits. Data limits occur when a person cannot do something, no matter how favorable the circumstances (e.g., people cannot jump 100 m, nor can they solve expert physics problems without the appropriate knowledge base). Resource limits occur when something could be done in principle but not in the actual situation (e.g., the subjects in Experiment 3 could derive macrostructures, but for some difficult texts they were unable to do so on first reading because they were overloaded by the other components of the comprehension task). Resource limitations can be circumvented by automatizing behavior. Thus, a comprehension strategy that must be applied consciously and requires a special effort is of limited usefulness, because in many actual comprehension situations insufficient resources would be available for the application of such a strategy. On the other hand, well-practiced, fully automatized strategies can run off in parallel without overloading the system.

Research on the processing constraints of discourse comprehension will undoubtedly become a major focus of discourse studies in the coming years. Although we have certainly not done justice to this problem with this highly superficial discussion, we do not intend to follow it up here. Instead, we shall turn to the topic of memory constraints.

Memory constraints are of two types.[1] First, there is the well-known limitation of short-term memory. Short-term memory capacity is limited to about four chunks in certain types of short-term memory experiments (Broadbent, 1975), or to about two items in free recall experiments where fewer resources can be devoted to short-term memory maintenance (Glanzer & Razel, 1974). Mandler (in press) claims that consciousness is limited to a single idea. Clearly there is no room in the short-term memory box for all the information that must be processed and maintained in discourse comprehension, however we want to chunk it. Equally clearly, most of what is going on in discourse comprehension is not conscious, and thus there is no reason to put it into the short-term memory box. What, then, is the role of short-term memory in comprehension?

The second form of memory constraints that concern us here arise from limitations on retrievability. In order to retrieve an item from memory, the retrieval cue must match, at least partially, the encoded item. The cue must be appropriate for the encoding. The efficiency of memory is determined not by either encoding or retrieval alone, but by the encoding–retrieval interaction. This is the principle of encoding specificity of Tulving and Thomson (1973).

The view we take of encoding here is a very simple one. Memory is a by-product of processing—one remembers what one does. The depth of processing and its elaboration are important because deeper, more elaborate processes leave more traces that can later be recovered. Variable encoding leaves traces that can be matched by more retrieval cues. Thus, the nature of the encoding processes makes a great deal of difference for how well some experience will be recalled later: Elaborate, semantic, meaningful encoding, and the embedding of experiences in a rich,

---

[1]The question of whether it would be better to have a model with a single memory store rather than to retain the short-term–long-term distinction we shall disregard, because even in a single-store model some provision must be made for an active, conscious core.

accessible matrix ensure memorability. Imagery plays a crucial role. We shall later show that discourse comprehension quite naturally generates favorable conditions for memory encoding.

A retrieval cue is effective if it partially matches an encoded memory episode. That memory episode may then be retrieved and reinstated in short-term, active memory. However, retrieval effectiveness is usually not merely a matter of an isolated cue being successful or not, but of operating within a retrieval system. In such a system, a retrieval cue not only leads to the recovery of some desired information in memory, but at the same time another retrieval cue is generated that allows more extended information recovery. Memory episodes which are integrated into such systems are therefore much more likely to be retrievable than unorganized, isolated memory traces. In what follows, we shall show that discourse comprehension, by its very nature, leads to the establishment of well-integrated retrieval systems, and hence to superior memory, especially when compared to memory for unorganized word lists as used in classical studies of memory.

Before we can consider these problems, however, we must add yet one further complication to our picture of discourse comprehension—a complication that becomes very important when we are dealing with questions of memory. The point is simply that, as far as memory is concerned, the purpose of discourse comprehension is not usually memory for the discourse, but memory for what the discourse is about. This obvious fact has far-reaching consequences which we need to consider in some detail before we can investigate further the memory dynamics of discourse comprehension.

## 10.1. FROM THE TEXT REPRESENTATION TO THE SITUATION MODEL

Most discourse processing models assume that during comprehension a language user gradually constructs a representation of the text in episodic memory. This textual representation features, in principle, both surface, semantic and pragmatic information, as well as schematic superstructures. This text representation, it is further assumed, has a hierarchical nature, such that microstructures, organized by their linear connections form the terminal categories.

At various times in previous chapters we have pointed out the limitations inherent in this view. In very general terms, the problem is that a text representation involves not only text elements, but also knowledge elements. How many of these become part of the text representation? In other words, is the text representation the kind of rich, elaborated structure that our intuition as well as our experiments tell us it can be, or is it more text bound? Where do we draw the boundaries? In this book, we have consistently opted for keeping the text representation relatively uncontaminated and unelaborated: Only those inferences become part of it that are necessary to establish coherence at the local or global level. Others have hypothesized much richer text representations, including the discourse and its context as well as the internal knowledge brought to bear during interpretation. Graesser (1981), for instance, has demonstrated how texts can become elaborated inferentially during comprehension. We propose that these elaborations, except for the ones that are textually necessary as outlined in Chapter 5, are not part of the text representation proper but of a model that the hearer or reader constructs about the situation denoted by the text. It is this model which supplies and collects all the relevant information for the adequate comprehension of the text. We have already introduced this model informally and referred to it repeatedly, but we have not yet discussed it in any systematic way.

The distinction between a situational representation and a text representation is not an entirely new one. In our own work (van Dijk, 1977a) it evolved via the notions of "facts," "possible worlds," and "discourse models." Similar notions were used by others, such as "reference diaries" by Clark and Marshall (1978), "discourse referents" by Karttunen (1976), "discourse entities" by Nash-Webber (1978a), "reference nets" by Habel (1982), the "text-world theory" of Petöfi (1980), the "discourse representations" of Kamp (1981), and the "mental model" of Johnson-Laird (1980). Although differing in detail, all of these notions are motivated by the same insight: that to understand the text we have to represent what it is about. If we are unable to imagine a situation in which certain individuals have the properties or relations indicated by the text, we fail to understand the text itself. If we do not understand the relations between the local facts and the global facts to which the text refers, we do not understand the text.

These claims follow directly from our discussion of the role of knowledge use in discourse comprehension. Using knowledge in discourse comprehension means being able to relate the discourse to some existing knowledge structure, which then provides a situation model for it. The process is one of being reminded of past situations, be they specific episodic or generalized semantic ones (Schank, 1979). Many of the discourses we interpret are about objects, persons, places, or facts we already know from past experience. In memory, these experiences form part of (overlapping) clusters of similar experiences. To the extent that they are episodic, they are, of course, subjective and differ from person to person. Thus, each person has subjective experiential clusters about the town he or she lives in, the house, friends, place of work, and major life events. Similarly, each person shares, to some extent at least, other clusters of experiences about such items as countries, towns, historical events, political events, or well-known people. At the other extreme, as decontextualization sets in, these experiences become entirely general or almost so, such as one's knowledge of arithmetic or chess.

We assume that during understanding such clusters are retrieved and form the basis for a new model of the situation. Sometimes this model is directly ready for use, sometimes it must be constructed from several partly relevant existing models. It has been suggested (Carbonell, 1982) that reasoning by analogy provides powerful procedures for transforming existing but ill-fitting models into models that are adequate to the demands of a particular task. Thus, the understander is reminded by the text of some prior experience, and then uses that experience to construct a model of the present situation. Usually this requires transforming the old experiential structure in some way, and Carbonell has discussed various operators that can be used to gradually transform an existing structure into a new one based on means–ends analyses. In this respect discourse comprehension is a problem-solving task.

The situation model that is constructed in this way is the basis for the interpretation of the text. It features all the knowledge that is left implicit in the text or otherwise presupposed. General knowledge is treated exactly like specific experiences in this respect: Both may form the basis for situation models, and hence for the encoding of new experiences.

### 10.1.1. Why a Situation Model Is Needed

We now turn to a number of specific linguistic and psychological arguments to demonstrate that situation models are not merely plausible constructions, but are indeed necessary to account for the phenomena of discourse comprehension and memory.

*Reference.* In philosophy and linguistics it has been the custom to distinguish between "meaning" and "reference" (see Chapter 4). We use words or referential expressions to refer to various types of elements, such as individual things or properties, relations, and facts (truth values) in some possible world. Such a distinction has been lacking in psychology. The situation model fills this gap. The world, as it is referred to, is not cognitively relevant: What we see or think about is again some construction, namely, the situation model. It is the representation of that fragment of the world the text is speaking about. Of course, the text will leave unsaid much of this fragment, mainly because the hearer already has a lot of knowledge about it. On the other hand, the main (semantic and pragmatic) function of the text is to enrich the model: to get to know things. This holds not only for semantic information in assertive contexts, but also for threats, promises, and excuses: These speech acts inform us about the wants, wishes, beliefs of the speaker with respect to our actions.

This means that besides the properly "semantic" situation model, we also need a *communicative context model,* representing speech acts and their underlying intentions, as well as other information about speaker, hearer, and the context. We may assume that it is this communicative context model that forms the link between the situation model and the text representation: The text representation is, so to speak, the semantic "content" of the communicative act, of which the situation model is the referential basis. We will not be able to further explore here the precise nature of this communicative context model, though, nor its relations with the text representation or the situation model.

*Coreference.* Expressions in discourse do not refer to other expressions or their underlying concepts in a text, but to individuals in the situation model. The expression *my brother* and *the lawyer* may have different conceptual meanings, but may both refer to the same individual, say John. The situation model provides the representation of this same individual. The notion of coreference would make no sense in a cognitive processing theory of comprehension if we did not have this ability to coordinate the text representation with a situation model. Johnson-Laird and Garnham (1980), Clark and Marshall (1978), Karttunen (1976), and Webber (1978a) have elaborated this argument further, and it has been discussed here in Chapter 5.

*Coherence.* In our earlier work we have stressed that both local and global coherence depend on relations between propositions. Roughly speaking, a textbase is locally coherent if the facts referred to are connected, for example, by conditional or temporal/causal relations. Again, the real facts in the world are irrelevant for a cognitive theory, so we need a representation of them, that is, a model. If in the model of tbe situation as it has been constructed by the hearer the represented facts are connected, then this fragment of the text is coherent.

*Situational parameters.* Similar arguments can be given for the role of possible world, time, and location parameters in discourse. We have seen that these often remain implicit in the individual sentences of a text. Sometimes they will simply be presupposed, inferred from context information, or mentioned only once in the text so that further sentences are interpreted under their scope. In a textual representation this kind of localization of propositions is not easy, and sometimes is impossible, to account for. In a model this would be straightforward: The model is precisely defined by such circumstance parameters—it is indeed a "model of the situation."

*Perspective.* Discourses may have different and changing perspectives or points of view (Black, Turner, & Bower, 1979). That is, the facts or the situation are seen, interpreted, described, and talked about by different persons, from different points of view, etc. Yet, we know that the same facts are being described. This intuition can easily be accounted for if we have some stable point of reference, hence a model of the situation which is more or less independent of the actual discourse and its point of view.

*Translation.* Translation is not merely an operation that takes one surface form into another, and not even one that takes one text representation into another, but, rather, one that relates text representations via a situation model. This is easy to overlook when the two languages largely share the same knowledge base, which therefore can be left as implicit in the second language as it was in the first language. But when this is not the case, for example, when the cultural code of the source language is widely different from that of the target language—then translation requires an explicit situation model before it can be meaningfully completed. This point has been emphasized by Hutchins (1980), who translated a discourse among Trobriand Islanders involving an argument about land rights. The discourse is patently meaningless ("primitive," "alogical"), unless one related it to the underlying situation model—the land rights and customs on the Trobriand Islands, which are entirely foreign to us, but which were implicitly assumed by the participants. Then the discourse can be seen as what it really is: a complex, coherent, logical piece of reasoning.

*Individual differences in comprehension.* It is well known that two people can receive the same information but derive from it two very different messages. In part, this may involve the construction of somewhat different text representations. Thus, in Chapter 6 we discussed how goals and interests could lead readers to construct diverse macrostructures for the same text. Normally, there are fewer possibilities for distorting the microstructure of a text. However, interpretational differences need not be at the level of the text representations at all, but rather can be at the level of situation models. We hear the same message, but what we take it to mean is another thing. Literary texts often do not constrain the situation model very tightly, giving the reader great latitude in constructing his or her own model. Debates about what a classical text "means" are therefore frequently not about the text proper, but about the situation model to be constructed from it.

*Level of description.* Ideally, texts are suitable for their audience: They presuppose just the right amount so as not to bore the reader with superfluous information, but without omitting necessary information that the readers do not have available. This leads to great economy in communication, as long as the required knowledge base is shared. If it is not—a situation in which, as Hutchins (1980) points out, anthropologists and children are likely to find themselves quite frequently—then the level of discourse must be changed: The situation model to be used must be conveyed in the discourse, together with the information to be communicated.

*Memory.* There are some clear-cut demonstrations in the psychological literature that under certain conditions people remember the situation model but not the text representation. Usually this involves conditions in which the text representation is very difficult to construct, perhaps because many very similar sentences are used, creating massive amounts of interference, so that the comprehender skips the text representation and concentrates entirely on the situation model, which typically is nice and simple (e.g., Bransford & Franks, 1972; Potts, 1972; Barclay, 1973). Thus, it is easy to remember that "hawks are smarter than bears which are smarter than lions which are smarter than wolves"—but it is almost impossible to remember a bunch of comparative sentences with these arguments in various combinations. The only function these sentences serve is to permit the listener to construct an appropriate situation model, but not a textbase (which would be an extremely impoverished one in any case).

An alternative way of showing that the situation model is remembered but not the textbase involves giving subjects sentence pairs in which there are minimal distinctions in the textbase (say, a difference of a single preposition) but very large ones in the situation model (the single preposition makes the situations described very different ones). In this case, too, subjects confuse the sentences, but not the situations (Bransford, Barclay, & Franks, 1972; Garnham, 1981).

Conversely, there are situations where people remember the text but have no situation model at all, as when children are taught to chant Hebraic texts or the Koran without understanding what they are saying. Typically, however, long-term memory is poor in the absence of understanding, that is, a situation model, as is demonstrated, for instance, by the well-known findings of Bransford and Johnson (1972). There are strong theoretical reasons why memory should be better for the situation model than for the textbase itself: Retrieval is most likely to occur if a memory episode is embedded within some larger structure which can serve as a retrieval system. Situation models, by their very nature, tend to be embedded in such systems and form a part of a larger model, whereas the textbase itself is more loosely associated with these structures, often via the corresponding model. In those cases, retrieval of the textbase would require the activation of the model, but not vice versa. This is, of course, not true in all cases, because it certainly is possible to retrieve a textbase via some textual cue directly, but this seems to be the exception rather than the rule. Furthermore, the textbase proper, once it has fulfilled its main purpose as a stepping stone toward the situation model, will rarely be reactivated, whereas the corresponding model, if the information it contains is of any importance at all to the individual, may be subject to extensive use and updating, as we shall see in what follows. This retrieval practice will greatly strengthen the retrievability of the model (Hogan & Kintsch, 1971) whereas the textbase proper experiences no such advantage.

*Reordering.* When people are told stories in which the order of events has been disarranged, they often retell the story in its canonical order (e.g., Kintsch, Mandel, & Kozminsky, 1977). There are two ways to explain this phenomenon, both of which implicate the situation model. First, it may be that in retelling people reconstruct the story from the situation model that they had formed when they heard it in scrambled form: As they had available the appropriate knowledge schemata, they were able to construct a canonical model from the scrambled input, and in retelling they simply work from that model rather than from the text representation proper. Alternatively, it might be the case that the text representation itself was unscrambled and put into the correct order, in spite of the disorderly input. However, the only way this unscrambling could be done was to construct a situation model in canonical form, and then to use this model to rearrange the textbase. In either case, the reordering of scrambled narratives presupposes the construction of a situation model.

*Crossmodality integration.* It is frequently the case that information from textual and nontextual sources must be integrated. The situation model, which may be modified either through direct perception and action or through a discourse, forms a much needed link between modalities.

*Problem solving.* The situation model plays a particularly significant role when some sort of action is to be taken on the basis of reading a text, such as in problem solving. The basis for problem solving is not the textbase directly, but the model derived from it. Problem-solving techniques, such as mathematics and logic, apply to the model, but not to natural language itself. Logic, therefore, is not an appropriate formalism for the representation of language. Language merely provides the cues that indicate what sort of a model needs to be constructed, and comprehenders interpret these cues strategically, as we have shown in the previous chapters. The situation model which is the result of this interpretational process provides the basis for further cognitive operations, such as formal, logical reasoning, as well as other types of inference and problem-solving activities. In the final section of this chapter we shall describe a case where the situation model provides the base for the application of arithmetical operations as occurs in solving word problems in arithmetic.

*Updating and relating.* These are two of the most important functions for which the situation model is used. Text representations are related to other elements in memory—general knowledge as well as personal experiences -to a large extent via their corresponding models. Thus, they participate in the memory network which determines their further use via the models that were created from them. Specifically, it is not always the case that each text leads to the construction of a new and separate situation model. Rather, very frequently an already existing model is modified on the basis of a new text. This occurs, for instance, in knowledge updating on the basis of news reports. Thus, what we now remember about such highly publicized events as, for instance, Watergate is a frequently updated, often modified situation model that integrates many different experiences, and includes not only declarative statements, but also opinions, attitudes, emotions—and even a moral, perhaps. Given the immense importance of knowledge updating, experimental research as well as theoretical work in this area is merely in its initial stages. Some interesting work on memory updating on the basis of news reports has been done by Larsen (1982) and Findahl and Höijer (1981), and the theoretical implications of updating have been explored via a simulation program by Kolodner (1980).

*Learning.* Last but not least, the concept of a situation model is required as a basis for learning. Learning from text is not usually learning a text. Learning can best be conceptualized as the modification of situation models. Exactly which modifications deserve the name "learning," how such modifications are brought about, what the mechanisms and constraints are, are questions beyond the scope of this book. Yet, learning theory, after a long hiatus is once more coming to the forefront within cognitive science (e.g., J. R. Anderson, 1982). All we can hope is that the theory of discourse comprehension that we have presented here will provide a firm basis for investigating how learning from text proceeds. For both theoretical and practical reasons, this is potentially one of the most important directions this type of research could take.

## 10.1.2. Why Textbases Are Needed, Too

The reasons why a situation model is needed, summarized in the preceding section, make convincing reading. Indeed, they make such a strong argument for a situation model that one is tempted to radically simplify the model of discourse comprehension by throwing out altogether the text representation proper. Do we really have to bother with a multileveled propositional textbase?—Could we not merely have the words on the one hand and the situation model on the other? What role does the text representation play?

Let us first discuss a few reasons why surface structure representations are necessary components of a textbase:

1. Discourses do not merely express meanings or refer to facts and their elements and relations, they do so in a specific, linguistic way. For several reasons it is necessary to store episodically these surface structures. For grammatical operations beyond the sentence boundary, the precise surface structure of a previous sentence may still be relevant.
2. Discourses may have a specific *style:* Even if the facts we speak about are the same, the way we speak about them may be different. Such stylistic features will receive semantic, pragmatic, and interactional interpretations; and language users, throughout a text and also long after, will have access to this particular style and its features, directly or through retrieval of their relevant semantic or interactional functions.
3. Discourses may have a number of rhetorical operations, at each level. Again, these are not so much intended as indicators or expressors of facts, but rather as communicative devices to make the discourse more effective. And again, language users may have separate recall of such rhetorical devices as rhyme, alliterations, metaphor, etc.

However, as we have seen throughout the previous chapters, comprehension processes cannot be restricted to surface structures but involve conceptual processes based on propositional representations:

1. Discourses sometimes have a specific superstructure schema. Whether canonical or transformed, the schema will often be independent of the facts denoted, and pertain rather to the global ordering of macrosemantic or macropragmatic information.
2. Also at the global level, as we observed in previous chapters (see, e.g., Chapter 8), there are possible (re)orderings in the presentation of propositions, according to cognitive, pragmatic, stylistic, rhetorical, or interactional constraints. Again, these reorderings are not so much dependent on the facts, as on the way these are presented to the hearer.
3. What has been said earlier about perspective also holds the other way around: If the facts are the same, we may still describe them from various points of view, and people do have access to these different perspectival descriptions.

Thus, the need for the text representation proper is twofold: On the one hand, it is a necessary station on the way toward the situation model. At least in this theory, we simply could not construct explicitly a situation model without the intervening structure of the propositional text representation. It is doubtful whether other theories can circumvent this intermediate stage, without introducing some notational variant through the back door. On the other hand, however, we need to separate the text representation from the situation model because the representation of the text and the representation of the situation do not always coincide. The text representation may very well have its own, distinct existence in memory. Just as one normally remembers the situation the text refers to rather than the text itself, one *can* and often does remember the text per se—its organization, its macrostructure which may but need not share important features with the structure of the situation. For cognitive scientists it is crucial to be clear about what we attribute to the text and derived structures which are text specific, such as the propositional textbase, and what we attribute to the world. It will not do to confuse the two.

### 10.1.3. On the Representation of Situation Models

We have mentioned a number of arguments in favor of situation models. Such arguments at the same time provide criteria for an adequate theory of situation models: The criteria should allow the various phenomena and processes to be formulated in terms of the structure and the use of such models. Here we cannot aim at a complete theory of episodic situation models, but some suggestions might nevertheless serve as preliminaries for such a theory. We have seen that a situation model is an integrated structure of episodic information, collecting previous episodic information about some situation as well as instantiated general information from semantic memory. Also, in discourse comprehension, the situation model should allow updating, and, finally, situation models should form the basis for learning. Since the previous inputs, as well as the generalized output, and the way the information is used in variable tasks, will always be rather different in structure, we must assume that a situation model also has a *schematic* nature. Just like scripts or frames, it should allow for variable terminal categories. This is an expedient hypothesis, for it allows us (a) to instantiate (part of) scripts or frames to become the backbone of a situation model, and, conversely (b) to proceed easily from a situation model to a more abstract, decontextualized script or frame through a process of learning. Indeed, if we have once taken a plane, we will not yet have a script, but a unique situation model of that episode (see Schank & Abelson, 1977, for an episodic illustration of the formation of scripts in children). Later experiences of the same kind will complete, correct, and further fill in such an experience-based schema. In other words, the situation model is different from a frame or script in that it is much more personal, based on one's own experiences, and therefore it will feature all kinds of details which, in learning, will be abstracted from. Let us assume for the moment, then, that such an episodic trace of previous information is about a complex event, that is, about some episode, like a car accident. Either because we have participated in such an accident, or because we have seen one, or because we have heard a story about one, we will have formed a representation of such a complex event. Later events of the same kind will, in part, remind us of that earlier event. According to our theory of complex information processing, this earlier experience will probably no longer be available in all its details. More probably, the earlier event will merely be retrievable at a macrolevel. In other words, a situation model will mainly be formed—and updated—by previous macropropositions (from perception, action, or discourse) plus some occasional details.

It is rather tempting to hypothesize that the structure of situation models is formed by a frame similar to the *propositional frame* we have discussed in Chapter 4: at the top a predicate, filled with the information 'having an accident,' and followed by a list of participants, for example, in such a way that the agent role can be filled by the person him- or herself: 'I', possibly followed by other participants. The event is then localized in place, time, and conditions. Note that the macro-proposition representing previous information may be less complete, and, for in-stance, not feature these other participants or further circumstantial information. The situation model, however, would have a full schema, and later experiences can fill in these still "empty" categories. Since we have assumed that a propositional schema has atomic propositions as its terminal units, further experiences about similar events (accidents) can simply be added, as propositions, to these terminal categories. Of course, we may assume that these propositions are somehow or-dered. First, there may be a recency ordering, which places the newest information in each category on top of the stack. But there may also be a relevance ordering: We will surely better remember our own accident of 5 years back than one we read about in the paper 5 days ago (which might even be understood without accessing these personal memories about our accident). In any case, the information under some final categories may in its turn become so complex that it will itself be summarized again in some macroproposition: We may group experiences of acci-dents in some class, and the same for likely locations of accidents. Note that details of each situation can be easily inserted into such a model frame: Further properties of participants can be inserted under the final participant categories, and the same holds for the properties of the event itself, of the location. Similarly, we have inverse macrorules which allow us to specify the macroevent into preparatory or conditional events, component events, and consequences.

This kind of format for the situation model can easily be retrieved and fits well with our other assumptions. When understanding a text, we first of all want to establish a provisional macroproposition. That macroproposition will be an excel-lent retrieval cue to find the macroproposition dominating the complex situation model. And, conversely, the many information chunks obtained from the current text will be neatly inserted into the respective relevant categories of this situation model, at different macrolevels.

It may further be assumed that recent or frequent use of a situation model will allow the understander to retrieve relatively more details of the previous situation. Also, as soon as the situation model is used more frequently, all the different details in its terminal categories cannot be—and usually need no longer be—available for later understanding. In that case, generalization and decontextualization—that is, learning—takes place: We form a frame or script for this kind of situation. With further use, such a general script or frame (or MOP) may be much easier to handle, by simple instantiation, and may supply all relevant instantiated details together with the new information about the actual situation. In that case, only some recent, or very relevant, past experiences may still be needed for retrieval from previous states of the situation model. Thus, in order to be able to take the subway in New York I simply need a 'taking a subway' script or frame, if I have one, and supply now relevant specific information about the situation. But at the same time, I may—even if I take the subway daily—be reminded of yesterday's trip when I met this strange man, or last year's when there was a fire in the subway. If I do not have a frame or script, I may well be reminded of the rather vague and remote (i.e., macro-) information from the model I built when some years ago I took the subway in New York, or from situations that were similar (taking the subway in Paris).

Another point concerns the possible uniqueness of situation models. Are they only models of one unique situation, about which we just acquire further information (e.g., the actual civil war in El Salvador), or is a situation model a flexible schema allowing for a collection of *similar* situations? The latter alternative seems more plausible: that episodic memory is not just an unorganized collection of a myriad of situation models, but, rather, that similar experiences are grouped together. This does not mean, though, that we are not able to selectively retrieve some specific situation from memory: We may do so either by selectively retrieving details from the terminal categories of the situation model or by retrieving the textual or other representation we had about that specific event—if still retrievable. Only an integrated conception of situation models allows efficient search of similar information, and possible generalization in processes of learning. The theory of macrostructures provides us with the strategic processes for the organization and retrieval of various events under the same macropropositions.

As yet, we know very little about the conditions that favor or inhibit the construction of situation models from texts. Earlier we reviewed some studies that suggest that if texts are very confusing, though the situation they describe is simple, readers will dispense with the text representation and concentrate on the model. One would imagine accordingly that simple texts describing complex and obscure situations would invite concentration on the textbase at the expense of the model.

## 10.2. A FRAMEWORK FOR A PROCESS MODEL

With the discussion of the situation model, we now have all the parts that we need to consider in building process models of discourse comprehension. It is, of course, senseless to suppose that there can be a single process model of discourse comprehension. In Chapter 1 the inherent vagueness of the term "comprehension" was discussed. There are many modes in which discourses may be comprehended. All we can do here, therefore, is merely to present a framework for a processing model, instructions, so to speak, for building such a model in some concrete, well-constrained situation. Comprehension models for specific, concrete situations can and must be explicit, complete, and testable. However, the general framework that we are concerned with here must necessarily remain vague and underdetermined as it must apply to the whole variety of behaviors that we label discourse comprehension. We shall outline the framework we propose here and then, in Section 10.5, show how it can be used to design a specific process model in a concrete experimental situation.

We are merely summarizing here what has already been said or implied in various places in this book. Figure 10.1 illustrates the essence of the processing model we are proposing. It contains once more the multiple levels of representation and processing that are involved in discourse comprehension and that have figured importantly in all our discussions so far. This time, however, the question is how these multiple levels are processed and coordinated in real time. The moment-to-moment flow of processing in comprehension is represented in the figure by the central circle. Surrounding this stage we have a variety of interacting memory systems.

Basically, there are three major classes of surround systems. First, there is a *sensory register* which briefly holds the incoming perceptual information and makes it available to the central processor. Standard current formulations of this process

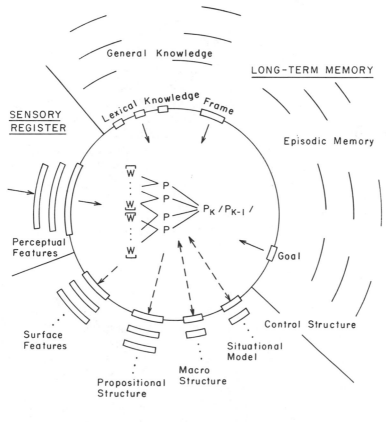

**Figure 10.1.**   A sketch of the operation of the memory system in discourse comprehension. The circle represents working memory, containing words and propositions; $P_k$ is currently under construction while the previous proposition $P_{k-1}$ is held in the limited capacity buffer.

are entirely adequate for our purposes (for a review of this literature, see Kintsch, 1977a; Chapter 3). Note that at any point in time only certain perceptual features are available to the processor.

Second, there is the comprehender's *long-term memory*. For our purposes we do not need to make a clear distinction between general knowledge on the one hand and personal experiences on the other. As we have stressed repeatedly, one may serve as a relevant knowledge source in comprehension as well as the other. They differ only in the conditions under which they are retrievable, not in the way they are used in comprehension. Several of these knowledge structures are presumed to be active at each moment, for example, the lexical knowledge required by the words being processed and larger knowledge systems forming scripts or frames which serve as the basis for the propositional structure that is being generated. Chapter 9 was devoted to exploring the details of the processes by means of which knowledge is used in comprehension. We have also added to long-term memory, somewhat arbitrarily, the comprehender's goals and purposes, wishes, interests, and emotions, namely, the active control structure.

The third component is the memory representation that is being constructed, the *episodic text memory* as well as the *situation model*. As far as the episodic text memory is concerned, we distinguish surface memory, the propositional textbase, and the macrostructure. Other relations within and across the different memory areas in Figure 10.1 have not been represented explicitly. The memory representations of the text that are being constructed can be thought of as push-down stacks, with always new elements being added at the boundary, pushing the older elements farther and farther away. Thus, retrieval by recency cues alone of these elements is workable only for the last few in each stack. However, the items in the stack are not only ordered by recency, they are heavily interrelated among each other (at least the propositional representations and the model of the situation), and they are also coordinated with corresponding elements in the parallel structures. Thus, items can be retrieved not merely via recency cues, but also via their relationships with other items, both within the same stack and in parallel stacks. Because the situation model is the most heavily interrelated and integrated structure, it remains most retrievable when recency cues are no longer effective. At the other extreme, verbatim surface memory is retrievable only via recency cues, via coordinated propositions, or by some partial matching that makes available surface memory chunks. A real retrieval system for surface memory is lacking. The propositional structure, including the macrostructure, on the other hand, is a coherent, interrelated network, where one proposition leads to another, forming an effective retrieval system.

Surrounded by these memory systems we find in the center of Figure 10.1 the *central processor*. All cognitive operations take place in this processing unit. Thus, in order to modify any element from one of the memory systems that were described before, the element must be brought into the central processor. Retrieval is the only operation that can be performed on memory elements outside it.

The central processor consists of a core and a boundary. Although there are no limits on the amount of processing that can be done in the central register (except for resource limits, as mentioned briefly earlier), there are serious limits on how much information can be maintained in an active state in the working register. These are the well-known capacity limits of short-term memory. As Figure 10.1 indicates, we assume that in general short-term memory is able to maintain the chunk that is currently being processed, plus some carry-over information from the previous chunk to establish coherence. The current chunk consists of the complex proposition $P_k$ which contains a number of atomic propositions $P$, as discussed in Chapter 4. Each of the atomic propositions was derived from certain text fragments, denoted $W$ in Figure 10.1. In general, as we have shown in Chapter 4, a complex proposition $P_k$ often corresponds to some phrase or sentence unit at the linguistic level. Hence, what we find in short-term memory at any point in time during comprehension is the surface representation of the most recent one or two phrases or simple sentences, and the atomic propositions derived from it which are bound together on the basis of some knowledge schema to form the propositional unit $P$. In addition, a short-term buffer contains some residual information from the previous text proposition, $P_{k-1}$: In general, this will not be the whole unit, including all its subordinated atomic propositions and the actual linguistic forms from which these were derived, but some stripped-down version of $P_{k-1}$. As $P$ is based on a knowledge structure (a frame or script constructed for that purpose, as discussed in Chapter 9), an efficient strategy would be to carry over only the main slots of $P_{k-1}$, deleting inessential information such as that assigned to modifier positions in the schema.

One cannot be more precise about the principles governing the operations of this buffer at this point, because they may be strategy controlled and differ to some extent in different situations. However, consider the following example. Suppose we have comprehended the sentence *On a stormy afternoon, Lucy overturned her new sailboat just outside Sausalito harbor* as an 'accident', arriving at the following complex proposition (so as not to distract from the main issue, the notation here is entirely informal);

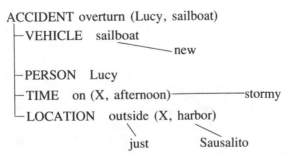

Suppose that the buffer is limited to three atomic propositions (a reasonable number in light of some of the estimates obtained in previous work using the Kintsch & van Dijk, 1978, model). In that case, the top three slots in the complex proposition would be retained—specifying the nature of the accident, and the vehicle and person involved. Modifiers would be discarded, and in this case also the time and location slots. Also discarded are the linguistic surface expressions from which the propositional information was computed. (Discarded here means merely discarded from short-term memory—traces will, of course, be laid down in episodic text memory.) Thus, if the next sentence *She got away with a scare, but the expensive new boat was badly damaged* is read, it now can be interpreted in terms of the accident proposition still available in short-term memory, establishing coherence between these two sentences. If more previous information is needed to interpret an incoming sentence, a reinstatement search of episodic text memory must be made to retrieve it. In our example, if the text continued not with Lucy and her boat, but about the afternoon, which—it will be remembered—was not retained in an active state, for instance, *On the same afternoon, three other boats sank in the bay,* a reinstatement search for the time slot would be necessary. Because that search has as its target the immediately preceding sentence, it would certainly be successful and probably would require few resources, unlike a search for information several sentences away, where recency cues can no longer be relied on for retrieval.

As has been pointed out many times here, texts are not processed merely in the context of some schematic representation of the previous sentence or phrase; there are many other factors that actively affect processing. These we have put at the boundary of the short-term memory central processor and the surrounding memory systems. The term *control system* will be used for these active elements. At any point in time, various knowledge structures are active in comprehension. They are not part of short-term memory, but they influence it. The same is true of the goals and interests that control the whole comprehension episode, and most importantly for the textbase itself. The most recently constructed macroproposition influences ongoing processing at other levels at all times quite directly without having to be brought into short-term memory by some retrieval operation. Like an active knowledge structure it is directly available to the process. Similarly, the most recent component of the situation model is directly available and constrains and controls the processes that are going on centrally. Of course, when new macropropositions are formed, or new versions of the situation model are constructed, these processes occur centrally, too, though once more under the influence of the previous model or macroproposition which participates in the new constructions from its position on the boundary of the system.

Why have we put this control system at the boundary and not made it a full member of the inner circle? Mostly because we would like to think of the central processing unit as having some of the properties of short-term memory as well as of consciousness. We know that many more elements have to participate in discourse processing than there is room for in a capacity-limited short-term memory, even if we are most generous with our estimates. Theoretically, this might be a good argument for the claim that the capacity-limited short-term store of the traditional memory literature has no place in a model of discourse comprehension. That, however, would destroy much of the predictive power of our model, in the earlier Kintsch and van Dijk (1978) version as well as in its present form, as will be shown in Section 10.5. Furthermore, it would be hard to reconcile such a step with the data on short-term memory use in discourse comprehension, as we shall argue in the next section of this chapter. A better solution to our dilemma appears to be the one we have chosen, namely, to combine features of short-term memory and consciousness in the tradition of William James. Consciousness, according to arguments by Mandler (in press), contains one idea at a time. In the context of discourse comprehension it appears quite reasonable to identify an idea with a (complex) proposition. Consciousness, however, always has been considered to have a boundary where ideas are available quite directly, but of which one is not actually conscious. This is clearly the case with knowledge structures in discourse comprehension: They are used, but one is not normally conscious of them. Similarly, goals, and even the topic and main themes of the text itself (the macrostructure and the situation model), are not actually in consciousness, though they actively influence the way we understand the discourse, and though they can be brought into focus any time. What we are normally conscious of are the words and their meaning. Hence we suggest that the central processing unit in Figure 10.1 consists of an active, conscious, but strictly capacity-limited core, and a boundary area containing the control system where memory structures affect processing in the core without being directly conscious and without being subject to capacity limitations. Knowledge structures beyond that boundary, that is, beyond the active macropropositions, frames, and goals, can participate in discourse processing only if they are successfully retrieved.

Our discussion of Figure 10.1 raises numerous questions. However, there is little point in pursuing these questions in a general way here, because they are probably not answerable at a general level. What we need to do is to investigate experimentally short-term memory processes in discourse comprehension in specific, well-constrained situations, and to build specific, explicit models for those situations. Only in that way is there some hope of coming to grips with these endlessly complex phenomena. But in order to build specific models we first need the general framework, if we want to avoid ad hoc solutions.

We need to remark briefly on the relationship between the present processing model and our previous one presented in Kintsch and van Dijk (1978). The 1978 model can be considered as a specific submodel within the present framework. Essentially, it is not a different model, but rather a simplified version that omits and shortcuts much of what we want to explicate here. Now, we are explaining in detail how complex propositions are constructed, what is retained in short-term memory and why. All these processes are treated as functions of how knowledge is used in comprehension. In our previous model, we have circumvented these problems via some formal rules and statistical approximations. Likewise, all processing was assumed to occur in cycles, whereas now we assume that all words are processed on line, though cycles still play a role in short-term memory use, as complex propositions are usually formed in short-term memory at sentence and phrase boundaries, just as in the 1978 model. Indeed, for some purposes the 1978 model might still be quite satisfactory, for example, if one is not concerned with some of the fine grain of the processes, but is content with relatively gross analyses of memory, forgetting, summarizing, and the like. Thus, the present work does not necessarily replace the 1978 model, for all its limitations.

## 10.3. SHORT-TERM MEMORY USE IN
##       DISCOURSE PROCESSING

In this section we want to argue that the classical short-term memory concept as it has evolved from many laboratory studies with nondiscourse materials is a useful explanatory concept for understanding discourse processing. Thus, we want to provide a justification for our choice to give short-term memory a central place in the processing model for discourse.

Traditionally, the two main features of short-term memory have been its capacity limits (Miller, 1956; Simon, 1974; Broadbent, 1975) and quick access which does not require complex retrieval schemes (Sternberg, 1966). However, when we use the term short-term memory as in Figure 10.1, we assign it not only storage functions, but also processing functions: It is both a central working register and a store for maintaining information. The term *working memory* is often used for this type of active short-term system (e.g., Baddeley & Hitch, 1974). The capacity limits in such a dual function system cannot be defined with respect to only one of its functions; instead, the two functions—process and storage—must be thought of as competing for capacity. In a memory span test where processing is minimal, most of the available capacity can be devoted to storage (and hence a memory span of $7\pm2$ items is obtained), whereas in a free recall test encoding for long-term retention must compete with short-term storage (resulting in a much smaller short-term capacity, around 2 items). Similarly, if processing is minimized, approximately equal estimates for the short-term memory capacity of children and adults are obtained, but adults are much more efficient processors in general, so that in most tasks where storage must compete for resources with processing, adults can maintain more items in short-term memory than can children (Chi, 1976; Huttenlocher & Burke, 1976). Similarly, there are no significant differences in the short-term memory capacity of good versus poor readers when traditional memory span measures are considered (where reading skills are quite irrelevant), but if memory span is measured within a reading task, comprehension scores and memory span are highly correlated (Daneman & Carpenter, 1980). For instance, readers' ability to identify pronoun referents in a text several sentences back correlated $r = .90$ with their *reading span,* a measure which Daneman and Carpenter defined as the maximum number of sentences for which subjects are able to recall accurately the last word.

One would also expect good short-term memory to be correlated with good long-term memory. Long-term memory depends heavily on how well the to-be-remembered material was organized, that is, encoded in interrelated memory chunks. In order to form a chunk, separate items have to be brought together in short-term memory (e.g., Kintsch, 1970; Jacoby, 1974; Shiffrin & Schneider, 1977). Hence, better short-term memory means bigger chunks and better long-term memory.

Experimental studies concerned with the use of short-term memory in discourse comprehension are still rare, but there is a small body of information available. First, there is the well-known work of Jarvella (1971, 1979), which established the relevance of sentence and clause boundaries for the short-term retention of discourse. Jarvella used a running memory span measure; that is, a sequence of sentences was interrupted at some point and the subject was asked to recall verbatim as many words as could be remembered. Subjects usually recalled the last clause, and sometimes the one before that, with sharp breaks in recall performance occurring at the clause boundaries, indicating that the syntactic structure of sentences was used by subjects in scheduling the discourse for short-term maintenance. On the average, somewhere between one and two simple sentences were retained verbatim in short-term memory. Glanzer, Dorfman, and Kaplan (1981) obtained similar estimates. Indeed, simple sentences in these experiments appear to function much like items such as single words in traditional list-learning experiments, where comparable estimates for the number of items retained in short-term memory have been obtained (Glanzer & Razel, 1974).

Glanzer et al. (1981) also demonstrated that procedures that are traditionally used to interfere with short-term memory retention have their expected effects when the material to be retained is discourse. In one of their experiments, subjects read eight sentences, but had to do addition problems after each sentence before they were allowed to proceed to the next one. One would expect this intervening activity to interfere with short-term retention and hence to force subjects to rely on retrieval from (long-term) episodic text memory, which might lead either to poorer comprehension or to longer reading times if the subjects are compensating. The latter effect was actually observed in their experiment. Glanzer et al. also had subjects do a counting task while they were reading the sentences. This had even stronger effects on performance, lengthening reading times as well as lowering comprehension scores. Thus, short-term memory appears to play a role in discourse that is very similar to what is normally found in laboratory experiments with word lists.

This similarity does not merely reflect the fact that Glanzer et al. were doing a laboratory experiment, too, albeit one involving discourse, for the same conclusions follow from some observations reported by Levelt and Kelter (1982) who were working in a much more naturalistic situation. These authors studied how shopkeepers in Nijmegen answered simple questions that were put to them over the telephone: The wording of the answer tends to reflect the wording of the question. Levelt and Kelter investigated in some detail the memory dynamics in this situation. How does the respondent remember the form of the question (because remembered it must be if it is to be used as a model for the answer)? By adding various irrelevant statements after a question, they could demonstrate that the form of the question is normally retained in short-term memory, but if short-term memory is interfered with, the form may occasionally still be retrievable from long-term memory, which leads to a greatly diminished congruence effect in answering the questions. (Control experiments ruled out the possibility that the congruence is not a true memory phenomenon, but merely the result of plausible reconstruction in the context of the situation in which the questions were asked.)

Thus, short-term memory in these discourse studies appears to have much the same properties as in list-learning research. What we do not yet know is actually what the information is that is being held in short-term memory. The literature suggests an acoustic coding bias, but it is clear that although it is easiest and usually preferred to maintain information in short-term memory in an acoustic-phonological form, this is by no means necessary. Imagery or abstract semantic information may be retained in short-term memory if the task requires it (this material is reviewed in Kintsch, 1977a). This is probably also the situation in discourse. Jarvella, Glanzer *et al.*, and Levelt and Kelter have examined only verbatim memory, and as far as these studies are concerned it is quite possible that what is retained in short-term memory is a linguistic surface structure, probably phonologically coded. Glanzer *et al.* explicitly entertain this possibility. Our model, of course, requires that in addition to the surface structure, short-term memory also contain a propositional representation of a discourse fragment.

As one cannot test for propositions directly, but must necessarily work through the medium of language, it is hard to separate experimentally the two levels of representation. A study by Fletcher (1981), however, suggests that short-term memory is not merely a matter of maintaining surface forms. He shows that propositions predicted by the Kintsch and van Dijk (1978) model to be retained in the short-term buffer are in fact in short-term memory, even when they come from a previous clause. Correspondingly, propositions from the same previous clause that according to the model are not held over in the buffer are unavailable in short-term memory. It is hard to see how this selective short-term retention of information from a clause could be explained without recourse to an analysis in terms of propositions.

Because Fletcher's work is of particular importance here, we shall review it in some detail. Fletcher (1981) worked with the same set of texts that were used by Miller and Kintsch (1980) in their recall and readability study. As part of that study, computer simulations were run for each text according to the Kintsch and van Dijk model. Among other things, these simulations specified which propositions were in the short-term buffer at each point in the comprehension process. Fletcher devised several experimental tests to evaluate the accuracy of these predictions. Two procedures were used: cued recall and recognition. In both cases, subjects read a text which was displayed phrase by phrase on a screen and was interrupted at predetermined intervals for a short-term memory test. On cued recall tests, a content word from the text just read was repeated and the subject was asked to respond with the content word that followed it in the text. On recognition texts, an old–new recognition response was required. Cue words were selected either from the last cycle (which is always assumed to be available in short-term memory according to the model), the next-to-the-last cycle, or an earlier cycle. Words from earlier cycles were not predicted by the model to be in the buffer and, indeed, were chosen so that, according to the model, they would never even be selected for the buffer; these words formed the long-term memory control material. Words from the next-to-last cycle were of two kinds: words from propositions that were maintained in the buffer at the time the interruption occurred, according to the model, and words from propositions not in the buffer according to the model. If the model was right, the

**Table 10.1**
**Recall, Recognition and Response Time for Words from Text[a,b]**

| | Percentage correct | | |
| --- | --- | --- | --- |
| | Cued recall | Recognition | Response time (msec) |
| Last cycle | 61 | 91 | 1234 |
| Next-to-last: in buffer | 45 | 70 | 1385 |
| Next-to-last: unselected | 27 | 67 | 1462 |
| Prior cycles: unselected | 30 | 68 | 1478 |

[a]After Fletcher, 1981.
[b]The top two lines are predicted to be available in the short-term memory buffer, the bottom two lines are not.

latter should behave exactly like the long-term memory control words from earlier portions of the text, because they had to be retrieved from long-term memory just like the earlier words. On the other hand, words from propositions predicted to be still in the buffer should have an advantage, just like the words from the final cycle, because both are available in short-term memory at the time of testing.

Table 10.1 shows that these predictions were generally confirmed in Fletcher's experiments. Words no longer in the buffer from the next-to-the-last cycle were comparable to the long-term memory control words: Cued recall performance, recognition, and response times are almost identical for the last two lines of the table. In contrast, words from the next-to-the-last cycle that the model predicts to be still available in the buffer led to better recall and recognition, and to faster response times, as one would expect. These measures, however, were not quite up to those for the words from the very last cycle: Here even better recall and recognition were observed, and response times were even lower. Though both types of words referred to propositions available in the buffer, the words themselves were available in the buffer only for the last cycle in which the whole phrase or sentence was still maintained; for the next-to-the-last cycle, all that the buffer contained were some especially important propositions which were retained for the sake of providing a coherence link between processing cycles—the actual surface forms were no longer active in short-term memory. Thus, responses for words from the final phrase were especially accurate and quick because they could be based either on surface memory or on the propositional representation, whereas for the next-to-last cycle only the latter was still available in the buffer. This interpretation is strengthened by another observation reported by Fletcher. On the recall test, almost all correct responses for the last cycle were verbatim correct, while for previous cycles a substantial proportion of the correct responses were only gist correct (2% paraphrases in the last cycle, 22% in the others).

One might ask why items predicted to be held in the buffer did not lead to a correct response with a probability close to one, rather than the more moderate values shown in Table 10.1. For one, of course, the way the buffer contents were selected in the Kintsch and van Dijk model can be considered no more than an approximation. More significantly, as soon as we are dealing with average data, as we must in these experiments, precise predictions become impossible. Even if we had the perfect model of comprehension, and perfect knowledge about the knowledge and strategies available to an individual subject, we could still only approximate average group performance.

Fletcher's work strongly suggests that short-term memory in discourse comprehension does not merely maintain surface structures, but, in addition, also includes structurally important text propositions which are needed to establish a coherent text representation at the conceptual level. However, further research is required before this highly significant issue can be regarded as settled.

## 10.4. RETRIEVAL FROM EPISODIC
   ## TEXT MEMORY

One could summarize the previous section quite succinctly by saying that short-term memory in discourse processing is more or less the same as we know it from the traditional memory literature. The chunks in discourse are, of course, not the same as in a list of nonsense syllables, but the number of chunks that can be held, the way they are affected by interference, etc., are comparable. At first glance, this is clearly not so when we look at long-term memory for discourse. Text memory is very much better than memory for lists of words or nonsense syllables. Whereas people are able to recall not much more than half a dozen words from a list of random words, they can recall more than ten times as much after reading a page of coherent text. This obvious discrepancy might lead one to think that the memory theory derived from list-learning experiments would be irrelevant as far as memory for discourse is concerned. An argument can be made to the contrary, however (Kintsch, 1982b): Classical memory theory explains quite well why memory for discourse is so much better than memory for lists. The key lies in understanding the ways in which the text representations generated during comprehension function as efficient retrieval structures.

The Kintsch and van Dijk (1978) model did not include an explicit account of retrieval processes. Whatever predictions it made about memory were based on the plausible and widely shared hypothesis that what is processed more extensively will be better recalled. Certain text propositions reside in short-term memory longer than others, because they were selected to be maintained for coherence establishment on the basis of their structural prominence in the textbase. These propositions are recalled better in proportion to the amount of extra processing that they have received. In addition, some propositions are processed further because they are macrorelevant and form the basis from which the macrostructures is generated. This extra processing again is reflected in an increased likelihood of recall. As we have just outlined in the previous section, the present model shares these assumptions with the earlier one, except that it shifts the basis on which propositions are selected for the short-term buffer from a statistical approximation (the "leading edge strategy" of the 1978 model) to the way in which frames and schemata organize a text, that is, to the knowledge structures that are being used to interpret it. With this modification, recall predictions can be derived from the present model in much the same way as in the 1978 model and in Miller and Kintsch (1981).

However, memory is certainly not merely a matter of differential strength of encoding. Interacting with these encoding processes, retrieval plays a dominant role. A model for the retrieval process follows quite directly from the nature of the textbase itself as well as from the availability and structure of the situation model, which we will disregard for a moment here, although what we say about search in the textbase applies equally well to search in the situation model. Indeed, the nature of the textbase dictates, at least in general outlines, the form of the model. Given any text element, what can be retrieved from that starting point are the elements directly connected to it. Retrieved elements then become the starting points of new retrieval operations, so that after many such operations two elements in the text representation (macropropositions, text propositions, or atomic propositions, even phrases if we want to study verbatim memory) may be connected by a long retrieval path with many intermediate nodes. If a textbase is fully coherent, this implies that starting anywhere in the textbase all elements can be retrieved, in principle. However, if each retrieval operation is probabilistic, retrieval failures accumulate as the number of nodes that must be traversed along a path increases. Exactly what the restrictions in this network retrieval are is not yet known. However, specific submodels embodying different sets of restrictions can easily be devised and are subject to empirical text.

We provide two illustrations. First, consider a free recall model that is entirely top down. That is, retrieval always starts at the top node and proceeds to lower nodes in the text representation. Let $r$ be the probability that a retrieval operation is successful. Then, a proposition $P$, which is related to the top node via $k$ intervening macropropositions $M$ and by no other path, will be retrieved with probability $r^k$. If the target proposition in question can also be reached via a second path involving $j$ intervening macropropositions, the retrieval probability would be $r^k + r^j - r^{k+j}$, assuming path independence.

This sketch can be filled in in various ways. Let us assume, for instance, that the retrieval probability is $r$ for connections between macropropositions $(M-M)$ and between macropropositions and text propositions $(M-\mathcal{P})$, but that different retrieval probabilities are involved for operations within the propositional schema itself. For instance, it would seem highly plausible that atomic propositions $P$ that fill a slot in the schema are retrieved with a probability $s$ which is greater than the probability $t$ of retrieving propositions that do not fill a slot but are merely added to the schema, for example, as modifiers. Furthermore, one might want to provide for the possibility that connections among propositions at the same level can also be used for retrieval, say with some probability $c$. For example, if we consider the textbase fragment shown here, we may obtain the following retrieval probabilities for the atomic propositions $P_1-P_3$:

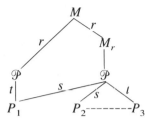

$$pr \text{ (retrieve } P_1) = rt + r^2s - r^3st$$
$$pr \text{ (retrieve } P_2) = r^2s + r^2tc - r^4stc$$
$$pr \text{ (retrieve } P_3) = r^2t + r^2sc - r^4stc$$

We simply follow each path from the top node to the target proposition, multiplying the probabilities along the way. Paths probabilities are then added and their intersection subtracted, assuming independence of path.

If $P_1-P_3$ are successfully retrieved, with the probabilities just calculated, then their encoding strength determines the probability that they can be actually recalled. Specifically, if a proposition $P$ has resided in short-term memory during $i$ processing cycles, its recall probability given successful retrieval is assumed to be

$$p(\text{recall}/i) = 1 - (1 - n)^i$$

where $n$ is the probability of successfully encoding a microproposition during any one processing cycle. In words, this formula means that recall occurs if at least one of the chances an item had to be encoded was successful. Similarly, if the proposition $P$ has participated in the construction of $j \geqq 1$ macropropositions, its recall strength will be

$$p(\text{recall}/j) = 1 - (1 - m)^j.$$

Where $m$ is the probability of successfully encoding a macroproposition during any one processing cycle. $P(\text{recall}/i)$ and $p(\text{recall}/j)$ are additive and independent. Exactly the same encoding assumptions were made in Kintsch and van Dijk (1978). Thus, the 1978 model can be considered a limiting case of the present model where $r = s = c = 1$. Obviously, somewhat different assumptions about retrieval probabilities could be made with equal plausibility. We have no data set that is extensive and detailed enough so that we could empirically explore which retrieval assumptions are most adequate.[2] If, however, such data were available, alternative models like the one sketched could be tested against each other.

For a second illustration, consider how cued recall would work in this model. Again, we could construct various alternative models: The textbase specifies the

---

[2]The Miller and Kintsch (1980) data which were used to evaluate the 1978 model are useless for present purposes. In order to apply the present model we would need to have some idea about the kind of knowledge structures used by the subjects in understanding the text. Various experimental possibilities suggest themselves, for example, pretraining, or having control subjects state their expectancies at various points in the text.

connections among whatever elements we are concerned with, and we could explore plausible assumptions about how well different types of connections support retrieval. Thus, to use our example again, if we know that $P_2$ has been recalled, we could calculate the conditional probabilities that $P_1$ and $P_3$ would be recalled with different sets of assumptions. If we had a suitable data set, such analyses might tell us quite a lot about retrieval processes in discourse.

However, the main use of the model is not (or at least not yet) in this quantitative testing of specific hypotheses about retrieval processes in discourse, but in providing us with a qualitative explanation for the most salient phenomenon in discourse memory—its general excellence. If we look at the retrieval model that we have arrived at here, it is no longer a puzzle that memory for text is so good. The kind of structures that are being built during discourse comprehension are very efficient retrieval systems. The material is organized into chunks which are constructed in correspondence with preexisting memory units, and the chunks are richly interconnected—the coherence requirement for both the micro- and macrostructure of the textbase assures that. Furthermore, the chunks are organized hierarchically by the macrostructure, and related to, and hence accessible from, similar chunks in the situation model.

That is exactly the kind of system that memory theory leads us to expect would be ideal for retrieval. It is not, of course, the kind of system that subjects in the usual laboratory experiment construct. The subjects in traditional list-learning experiments are faced with an unfamiliar task, with unfamiliar materials, and are forced to devise encoding strategies on the spot often without a corresponding situation model. All they can do is to rely on some general but weak encoding strategies, and the result is far from optimal for retrieval. When faced with a simple text on some familiar topic, however, subjects are in a very different situation. They can rely on rich background knowledge and they can bring to bear well-practiced—indeed, automatized—comprehension strategies. The result is a textbase that is also an efficient retrieval system. These subjects are expert comprehenders: They have the right knowledge and the required strategies highly available and well practiced. Like experts in other fields, their memory reflects their expertise.

Memory for text must, therefore, be compared with other types of expert memory that have been studied in the laboratory, such as the memory feats of experienced telegraphers (Bryan & Harter, 1899), the skills of experts in mental calculation (Müller, 1911; Hunter, 1962), the memory performance of chess players (de Groot, 1966; Chase & Simon, 1973), laboratory subjects who were trained in the use of mnemonic devices (Bower, 1972; Chase & Ericsson, 1981), and, above all, the ancient art of memory that was practiced by orators in classical antiquity (Yates, 1966). In light of such comparisons, text memory does not appear extraordinary at all. These mnemonists were experts in the use of their particular mnemonic technique, but they were as poor as anyone else when they had to remember material outside their field of expertise. Ordinary readers are experts in that sense, too: They are good at remembering simple, familiar texts for which they have had lots and lots of practice, but their memory fails them as soon as they are faced with a text that they cannot understand properly, perhaps because they lack the proper knowledge base, as in reading a technical discourse on an unfamiliar subject, or perhaps because they have not developed the right strategies, as when dealing with unusual forms of discourse, such as in reading poetry.

In order to follow up the parallel between text memory and expert memory in more detail, we need to review some of the principal characteristics of expert memory. A paper by Chase and Ericsson (1981) provides an excellent account of these characteristics. Chase and Ericsson have studied a subject in the laboratory who learned to memorize sequences of over 80 random digits on a single hearing. A memory span of more than 80 digits seems puzzling in view of the well-known limitations of short-term memory. The span is often considered a measure of short-term memory, and it would seem strange that short-term memory could be expanded in this way. Chase and Ericsson showed, however, that no miraculous expansion of short-term memory was involved at all. The short-term memory capacity of their subject was completely normal and unchanged: The chunks that he formed always consisted of 3–4 digits; the phonemically coded rehearsal groups that he used never exceeded 5 or 6; order errors occurred as soon as more than 3 or 4 groups had to be tracked (which eventually forced him to invent a hierarchical organization schema to overcome this limitation). Thus, the working capacity of Chase and Ericcson's subject was no different than that of ordinary people who can remember no more than 7 or 9 items on a digit span test.

The feat was not one of short-term memory at all, but consisted in the efficient use of long-term memory. It was mostly a matter of chunking and building an efficient retrieval system, Chase and Ericsson discovered. The trick was to use a chunking mechanism to bind stimulus traces to a hierarchical semantic structure. Chase and Ericsson's subject invented a complex set of strategies to encode digit sequences. For this purpose, he used a knowledge base that he was very familiar with and interested in: His hobby was running, and he encoded the digit strings in terms of running times which then served as unique retrieval cues for the string. Much like the orator in Cicero's Rome, he deposited the to-be-remembered numbers in particular places in his semantic structure about running times. Classical orators were taught to remember speeches by segmenting them into scenes, encoding each as a vivid pictorial image, and depositing that image at a distinctive place along a well-memorized route. Retrieval could then occur by mentally wandering along that route, picking up the respective images along the way. This binding to a retrieval structure occurs in working memory and is a form of chunking: A rich, well-organized knowledge base about running times permits the immediate recognition of relevant patterns which are then bound to semantic features in the running time structure (e.g., 1-mile time, near world record). The semantic features were interassociated and formed a retrieval structure that led the mnemonist from one place in memory to the next, making available at each location the digits deposited there.

The prerequisites for such a retrieval structure are two. First, there must be a rich knowledge base, such as the elaborate network of running times that Chase and

Ericsson's subject had available. Second, all storage and retrieval operations must occur rapidly and effortlessly. Speed is crucial, because otherwise short-term memory would quickly become overloaded. Therefore, a very large amount of practice is required before these operations become sufficiently automatized.

There are several striking analogies with text memory. Text memory is very good when there is an elaborate knowledge base to support it. Comprehension strategies are highly overlearned, they are fast and automatic. Text elements are bound to prior knowledge structures in that propositional schemata and are used to chunk the text. Hierarchical macrostructures form efficient retrieval systems. At least, such is the case when simple, familiar texts are to be remembered. When texts are read for which an appropriate knowledge base does not exist, memory becomes poor—just as when experts are given materials to process outside their areas of competence. The texts we remember so well are often simple narratives for which we are very well prepared indeed, whereas descriptive texts tend to be harder to remember (Kintsch, Kozminsky, Streby, McKoon, & Keenan, 1975; Graesser, Hoffman, & Clark, 1980). When readers do not know what they are reading because the authors have cleverly hidden what they are talking about (Bransford & Johnson, 1972), memory fails. A paragraph about washing clothes written in such a way that the readers could not figure out what the text was about and hence could not activate the appropriate knowledge was remembered just as badly as if subjects had been given a list of random words (3.6 out of 14 idea units). A title which told the reader what the text was about and therefore permitted the normal operation of comprehension strategies greatly improved memory for the same paragraph (8 idea units recalled). The un-understood paragraph was recalled so poorly because without relevant knowledge structure and without an appropriate macroproposition (as expressed by a title) no retrieval scheme could be established. Subjects still understood the sentences at a local level and stored information in memory, but it was stored in an incoherent form and hence remained irretrievable (Alba, Alexander, Harker, & Carniglia, 1981). A prerequisite for a coherent text representation is the ability to construct a coherent situation model. Without that, memory for text is stored in disjoint bits and pieces which can no more be retrieved than a list of random words.

Some preliminary experimental results confirming the interpretation of text memory that we have offered here have been reported in Kintsch (1982b). If propositions are used for chunking a discourse, they should behave like other memorial units. Specifically, the effectiveness of a text fragment as a retrieval cue should depend on chunk boundaries: An element may be better able to retrieve material from within the same chunk than material across a chunk boundary. This is a classical result which has been obtained in other situations where experts have employed a chunking strategy. Chase and Ericsson (1981), for instance, have observed this phenomenon in their investigation of the chunking that their memory expert employed for remembering strings of random numbers. They were able to determine quite accurately what kinds of chunks were being used (through protocol analysis as well as other converging experimental results). Thus, they could select small groups of digits in such a way that they did or did not coincide with a chunk boundary. When one of these digit groups was presented, their subject had to recall the digits that had followed it in the original string. This he was very well able to do, as long as the cue and the digits following it belonged to the same chunk. However, when the recall cue fell at a chunk boundary, so that the digits to be recalled belonged to a different chunk, his performance dropped significantly. The chunks determined from the protocol analyses were apparently also functioning as recall units.

With discourse, we can also predict where the chunk boundaries are, depending on the propositional analysis of the text. Hence, following Chase and Ericsson, we would expect a text fragment that forms the beginning of a chunk to be a good retrieval cue for the remainder of the chunk, but a text fragment that coincides with a chunk boundary to be less effective in retrieving the succeeding text across the chunk boundary.

Five subjects listened to 250-word sections from a nontechnical psychological research report. After each section, a phrase 6–19 words long from the passage just read was repeated, and the subjects had to recall orally the words immediately following that phrase in the original text. Recall was to be verbatim if possible, otherwise subjects were encouraged to say anything they could remember. We shall give only two examples here to illustrate the qualitative nature of the results, pending a more extensive experiment.

In the first example, the recall cue ended in the middle of a phrase. To complete a propositional chunk the words immediately succeeding it are necessary. Hence, they should be recalled well:

CUE: *This discrepancy reflects not only our*
CONTINUATION: *society's concentration of formal educational effort. . . .*

Below are some illustrative responses from subjects in this study:

RESPONSE (a): *society's concentration of effort. . . .*
RESPONSE (b): *society's focus on formal education. . . .*
RESPONSE (c): *the shift in concentration of educational research. . . .*

Obviously, in all three of these cases the subject's response more or less completed the propositional unit. Furthermore, the completions were largely verbatim. In (a) the response is entirely verbatim except for some omissions; in (b) we have both an omission and a synonym; only (c) is less precise, but even here two of the principal content words are reproduced verbatim. Such performance is quite remarkable, considering that the subjects had heard this text only once, and that after hearing the passage used in the recall test subjects had listened to another 150 words of potentially interfering text. Clearly, subjects were not recalling from short-term memory, by any reasonable definition of that term. It appears that the phrase used as a cue partially matched a memory chunk at a very early level of analysis, making available the chunk as a whole at that level. Thus, not only the meaning but also most of the wording of the continuation was retrieved. Whether the omissions represented encoding or retrieval failures we cannot specify at this point.

Now let us consider a recall cue that completes a chunk and therefore forces the subject to retrieve the next one. In this case, the problem is not merely to redintegrate a chunk on the basis of a partial match, but to (partially) match a chunk in memory, and then retrieve via the textbase hierarchy the next chunk:

CUE: *As shown primarily by the work of Schaie,*
CONTINUATION: *a peak of intellectual performance occurs later for current adult cohorts. . . .*

Some sample responses are:

RESPONSE (d): *some abilities don't reach their peak until sometime later.*
RESPONSE (e): *a peak occurs much later than previously believed and no decline in intelligence.*
RESPONSE (f): (after a long pause) *He was finding results that differed from previously held ideas.*

These responses are quite different in character than (a)–(c): Responses (d) and (e) are more of a paraphrase of the original phrase than a verbatim reproduction. The fact that these responses are less verbatim suggests that the process of retrieval did not tap directly into the text representation as in the first example, but that the appropriate continuation was located indirectly via the superordinate macroproposition that connects the two chunks to which the cue and the continuation belong. This process is less likely to retrieve the actual wording of the continuation, because the process of retrieval involves the propositional level, whereas in the previous case matches at both the linguistic and the propositional level occurred. To reach the linguistic level after retrieving the appropriate microproposition requires one further fallible retrieval step.

In (f) we are clearly dealing with a reconstruction: The subject was apparently unable to retrieve the successor proposition, but instead generated a partial reconstruction, probably via the macroproposition that dominated this portion of the text, which was something like 'Old research shows X–in contrast–Schaie shows Y'. Response (f) was unusual: What happened more frequently when no successor proposition could be retrieved was that subjects gave no response at all. Indeed, in about one-third of all cases no responses were given to cues that straddled a chunk boundary, whereas no failures to respond occurred when a cue tapped directly into a propositional chunk.

In spite of the preliminary nature of these data the conclusion seems warranted that cued text recall shows much the same chunking effects as cued digit recall in a memory expert. It will, of course, require a great deal more data to definitely confirm our claim, but what data we have so far is in good agreement with it: Discourse memory—at least under ideal conditions which insure adequate comprehension—is by its very nature a kind of "expert" memory. We need not postulate new, as yet undiscovered, principles of memory to explain the fact that discourse memory is so much better than what we normally observe under laboratory conditions in list-learning experiments. The principles of memory are the same in both cases; it is just that the process of comprehending a discourse creates conditions that are very favorable for remembering. The well-structured, multilevel, coherent textbase that is the result of the comprehension process quite naturally functions as an efficient retrieval system so that just reading or listening to a text assures a respectable level of recall. Of course, this does not mean that it would be impossible to achieve even better recall for discourse as a result of special memory encoding procedures (e.g., as described in Levin, 1982). Under natural conditions, discourse recall is certainly not perfect, especially for subordinate details that are not macrorelevant, and various mnemonic tricks can be used to improve it. For instance, it appears plausible that the use of imagery would greatly improve discourse memory without having any effect on comprehension per se, that is, on the construction of the textbase (except, perhaps, in cases where the imagery might help generate a good situation model). Comprehension and recall are correlated only up to a certain point: Beyond that, memory improvement can still occur without affecting comprehension.

## 10.5. A PROCESSING MODEL FOR UNDERSTANDING AND SOLVING WORD ARITHMETIC PROBLEMS

To end chapter and book, we present a specific, explicit, complete processing model for a simple, well-defined comprehension problem. Our discussions throughout have been general, emphasizing the flexibility with which the many subcomponents of discourse comprehension can interact in different situations and for different purposes. As was pointed out in the beginning of this book, there is no unitary psychological process "comprehension," and a general theory of comprehension is more like a set of instructions for building specific comprehension models in specific situations. At this point, we want to take our instructions and see how well they work when applied to a simple, but realistic and significant, comprehension problem: how children, from kindergarten to third grade, understand and solve word arithmetic problems. This work is by Kintsch and Greeno (1982), and what we want to do here is to show in detail how it was derived from the general principles of discourse comprehension presented in this book.

Word arithmetic problems are ideally suited for this purpose. First of all, we are dealing with a well-specified task: The reader's purpose, what is going to be done with the information obtained from the text, is unambiguous. This greatly restricts the range of strategies that we need to consider. Furthermore, the strategies to be used for understanding word arithmetic problems are very unusual ones: They are so unusual that they must be taught in school (though we shall see that by our analysis this is really not quite true—instead of being taught explicitly, most of the strategies necessary are left to be discovered by the student in the course of trial-and-error problem solving). The very fact that such specialized comprehension strategies are involved is an advantage for the model because these strategies are very distinct and easier to describe than widely used all-purpose strategies which we tend to take for granted. Finally, for all its simplicity, the problem is a significant one. Doing word arithmetic problems is not an easy task for these children, even though they know very well how to add and subtract: To determine from a discourse what operations to perform on which numbers is often quite confusing. The task of our model is to show exactly what steps are involved in this determination, and what the sources of confusion are.

**Table 10.2**
**Types of Word Problems in Riley, Greeno, and Heller (1982)**

---

CHANGE
  Result Unknown
  1. Joe had 3 marbles.
    Then Tom gave him 5 more marbles.
    How many marbles does Joe have now?
  2. Joe had 8 marbles.
    Then he gave 5 marbles to Tom.
    How many marbles does Joe have now?

  Change Unknown
  3. Joe had 3 marbles.
    Then Tom gave him some more marbles.
    Now Joe has 8 marbles.
    How many marbles did Tom give him?
  4. Joe had 8 marbles.
    Then he gave some marbles to Tom.
    Now he has 3 marbles.
    How many marbles did he give to Tom?

  Start Unknown
  5. Joe had some marbles.
    Then Tom gave him 5 more marbles.
    Now Joe has 8 marbles.
    How many marbles did Joe have in the beginning?
  6. Joe had some marbles.
    Then he gave 5 marbles to Tom.
    Now Joe has 3 marbles.
    How many marbles did Joe have in the beginning?

COMBINE
  Combine Value Unknown
  1. Joe has 3 marbles.
    Tom has 5 marbles.
    How many marbles do they have altogether?

  Subset Unknown
  2. Joe and Tom have 8 marbles altogether.
    Joe has 3 marbles.
    How many marbles does Tom have?

COMPARE
  Difference Unknown
  1. Joe has 8 marbles.
    Tom has 5 marbles.
    How many marbles does Joe have more than Tom?
  2. Joe has 8 marbles.
    Tom has 5 marbles.
    How many marbles does Tom have less than Joe?

  Compared Quality Unknown
  3. Joe has 3 marbles.
    Tom has 5 more marbles than Joe.
    How many marbles does Tom have?
  4. Joe has 8 marbles.
    Tom has 5 marbles less than Joe.
    How many marbles does Tom have?

  Referent Unknown
  5. Joe has 8 marbles.
    He has 5 more marbles than Tom.
    How many marbles does Tom have?
  6. Joe has 3 marbles.
    He has 5 marbles less than Tom.
    How many marbles does Tom have?

---

Fortunately, a model of word problem *comprehension* does not have to start at the beginning but can build on a large amount of research and theory on word problem *problem solving*. Empirically, there is an excellent data base, showing which problems are difficult, when children can solve them, etc. Theoretically, there exist well-developed models for how the children solve these problems. However, these models do not start directly with the text, but with a problem representation derived intuitively from the text. Certain operations are then performed on this problem presentation, leading to the solution of the problem in ways that simulate the childrens' solutions. Specifically, the model that we rely on here is that of Riley, Greeno, and Heller (1982). What we attempt to do is to fill in the missing step in this model that takes us from the text that the children read to the problem representation that their model is concerned with.

The main problem types Riley *et al.* were concerned with are shown in Table 10.2. Change (1) and Combine (1) are problems all first-graders in their sample could solve, whereas Change (3), Combine (2) and all the compare problems were quite difficult for the first-graders. Even in the second-grade children still had a lot of trouble with Compare (3) (for more detail see Table 10.17). Why do the three problem types vary in difficulty? Why do problems within a type differ?

## 10.5.1. The Propositional Analysis

The first step in the model is to derive a propositional textbase from the verbal input. This is a particularly simple task in the present case because all the problems in Table 10.2 are constructed from just a few sentence frames. Indeed, there are only 10 frames, which are listed in Table 10.3. The following conventions are observed in Table 10.3 and in what follows: X stands for a person (either Joe or Tom our examples), Y for an object (always marbles here), N for a number, P for a proposition, and S for a set. Associated with each propositional frame is a meaning postulate that indicates how the proposition is to be used in building the kind of

**Table 10.3**
**Propositional Frames and Their Meaning Postulates**

| | Frames | | Meaning postulates |
|---|---|---|---|
| 1(a) | Existential–singular: Joe, Tom | $j(x)$  $t(x)$ | $S_x$ |
| 1(b) | Existential–plural: marbles | $m(y)$ | $S_y$ |
| 2. | Have | HAVE (X,Y) | $S_{X,Y}$ |
| 3. | Quantity (number or "some") | $N(Y)$ | $S_{Y,N}$ |
| 4. | Give | GIVE(X-AGENT, X-PATIENT,Y) | (See Table 10.4) |
| 5. | More-than | MORE $(y_i y_j)$ | (See Table 10.6) |
| 6. | Less-than | LESS $(y_i y_j)$ | (See Table 10.6) |
| 7. | Now | NOW(P) | $S_{RESULT}$ |
| 8. | Then | THEN($P_1$, $P_2$) | $S1_{START}$, $S2_{TRANSFER}$ |
| 9. | Beginning | PAST(P) | $S_{START}$ |

**Table 10.4**
**The SET Schema**

| | |
|---|---|
| *Object:* | Y (marbles) |
| *Specification:* | X (a person, or two persons) |
| *Quantity:* | N (a number or SOME) |
| *Role:* | subset, superset; startset, transferset, resultset; matchset, remainder, whole |

knowledge structures that need to be built here: sets. The schema for a set is shown in Table 10.4: A set has a *label*, namely, the proposition from which it has been derived; furthermore, it has four slots: for a *specification* (in terms of ownership), an *object*, a *quantity*, and a *role*. Note that the first two slots are entirely ad hoc in the sense that they are tailormade for the particular problem set Riley *et al.* worked with. Equally well, the entire problem set could have been worded differently, for example, in terms of red and green apples, or marbles on the floor and in the pocket, without any essential changes in the model. The important slots of the set schema are quantity and role—the first because it is the defining feature of a set, the second because it specifies the relationship of the set with other sets.

Thus, if we have some X (say, Joe), we can form a set with owner X and otherwise unspecified slots, which we denote by $S_X$. Similarly, for Y. A HAVE proposition gives us more information, because it specifies both the owner and the object, just as a Quantity proposition gives us the object and number. The meaning postulate for GIVE is quite a bit more complex, because we are no longer dealing with a single set, but with a triplet of sets: a start set, a transfer set, and a result set. Specifically, the GIVE proposition corresponds to a set that has the role of transfer set, the owner specified by the patient of the GIVE proposition, and the object also as specified by the GIVE proposition. The problem context then must provide suitable start and result sets: If sets marked as start and result sets exist with the same owner as the transfer set, then the TRANSFER-IN schema applies, which is characterized by a restriction on the quantity slot of the result set, which must be equal to the sum of the quantities associated with the start and transfer sets. If, on the other hand, the owner of the transfer set is not the same as the owner of the start and result sets, the TRANSFER-OUT schema is obtained, as indicated in Table 10.5.

The roles of start, transfer, and result sets may be marked more or less explicitly in a problem. Sentence order is a sufficient cue (*Joe has three marbles. Tom gives him five more marbles. How many marbles does Joe have?*), but roles can be marked more explicitly by specifying the temporal relationships among sets with *now*, *then*, and *in the beginning* (*In the beginning Joe has three marbles. Then Tom gives him five more marbles. How many marbles does Joe have now?*)

The MORE-THAN schema is similar to the TRANSFER schema in that the complete schema involves three sets. If we say "Joe has 5 more marbles than Tom," the elementary propositions involved are Joe $j(x_1)$, Tom $t(x_2)$, marbles $(y_1)$, HAVE $(x_1y_1)$, HAVE $(x_2y_2)$, MORE-THAN $(y_1y_2)$, and $5(y_1)$. The three sets in-

**Table 10.5**
**The TRANSFER-In and TRANSFER-OUT Schemata**

| | |
|---|---|
| *TRANSFER-IN:* | *TRANSFER-OUT* |
| *S-start:* | *S-start:* |
|   Object:  Y |   Object:  Y |
|   Spec:  HAVE(X-PATIENT,Y) |   Spec: HAVE(X-AGENT,Y) |
|   Quantity: $N_A$ |   Quantity: $N_A$ |
|   Role: start |   Role: start |

                    *S-transfer:*
                       Object:  Y
                       Spec: GIVE(X-AGENT,X-PATIENT,Y)
                       Quantity: $N_B$
                       Role: transfer

| | |
|---|---|
| *S-result:* | *S-result:* |
|   Object:  Y |   Object:  Y |
|   Spec: HAVE(X-PATIENT,Y) |   Spec: HAVE(X-AGENT,Y) |
|   Quantity: $N_A + N_B$ |   Quantity: $N_A - N_B$ |
|   Role: result |   Role: result |

volved consist of some unspecified number of marbles Joe owns (the *whole set*), some unspecified number of marbles owned by Joe and matched by Tom's marbles (the *match set*), and the 5 marbles that Joe owns in addition to the number matched by Tom's marbles  (the *remainder set*). Table 10.6 summarizes the MORE-THAN as well as the LESS-THAN relationships.

What we are saying here is that understanding the propositions HAVE, GIVE, MORE-THAN, etc., in the context of arithmetic word problems implies an ability

**Table 10.6**
**The MORE-THAN and LESS-THAN Schemata**

| | |
|---|---|
| *"$x_1$ has $n_r$ more marbles than $x_2$"* | *"$x_1$ has $n_r$ less marbles than $x_2$"* |
|   *S-whole:* |   *S-whole:* |
|     Object:  $y_1$ |     Object:  $y_1$ |
|     Spec: owned by $x_1$ |     Spec: owned by $x_2$ |
|     Quantity: $n_m + n_r$ |     Quantity: $n_m + n_r$ |
|     Role: whole |     Role: whole |

                    *S-match:*
                       Object:  $y_2$
                       Spec: owned by $x_1$ and $x_2$
                       Quantity: $n_m$
                       Role: match

| | |
|---|---|
|   *S-remainder:* |   *S-remainder:* |
|     Object:  $y_3$ |     Object:  $y_3$ |
|     Spec: owned by $x_1$ and not $x_2$ |     Spec: owned by $x_2$ and not $x_1$ |
|     Quantity: $n_r$ |     Quantity: $n_r$ |
|     Role: remainder |     Role: remainder |

to construct from them sometimes rather complex set-schemata. The appropriate schematic superstructure of these word problems is in terms of sets. Once we have the propositions of the textbase, we must know how to generate the right kind of set relations to organize them into a coherent textbase.

## 10.5.2. The Schematic Superstructures

The knowledge of the set schemata that we need comes with the text propositions in the form of associated meaning postulates, as we have just seen. Schematic strategies use this knowledge, generating a superstructure for the organization of the text propositions in terms of interrelated sets. Formally, strategies are modeled as productions. Table 10.7 shows the four schematic strategies that are needed to understand the 14 word problems in Table 10.2. Each strategy has a name, a condition—the occurrence of a particular type of proposition in the textbase—and an action—the set it creates via the meaning postulate which is associated with the proposition which is the condition for the action. In each case the set that is generated is incomplete with respect to the schema, so that one or more requests for additional information have to be set up (e.g., for the number in the quantity slot, or for information on the role of the set). MAKE-SET is thus triggered by a quantifier proposition in the context of a HAVE proposition and generates a set with owner

**Table 10.7**
**Schematic Strategies**

| Name | Condition | Action |
|---|---|---|
| 1. MAKE-SET: | $N(y)^{\wedge}HAVE\ (x\ y)$ | S–Object: $y$<br>Spec: $x$<br>Quantity: $N(y)$<br>Role: PAST(P) - start<br>      THEN(P,P') - start<br>      NOW(P) - result |
| 2. MAKE-TRANSFERSET: | $N(y)^{\wedge}GIVE(x\text{-}AGT\ x\text{-}PAT\ y)$ | S–Object: $y$<br>Spec: $x$-pat<br>Quantity: $N(y)$<br>Role: transfer<br>REQUEST: $S_{start}$, $S_{result}$ |
| 3. MAKE-SUPERSET: | $N(y)^{\wedge}HAVE(x_i\ \&\ x_j\ y)$ | S–Object: $y$<br>Spec: $x_i\ \&\ x_j$<br>Quantity: $N(y)$<br>Role: superset<br>REQUEST: $S_{x_1,sub}$, $S_{x_2,sub}$ |
| 4. MAKE-REMAINDERSET: | $N(y_i)^{\wedge}MORE/LESS\ (y_iy_j)$ | S–Object: $y_i/y_j$<br>Spec: $x_1/x_2$<br>Quantity: $N(y_i)$<br>Role: remainder<br>REQUEST: $S_{whole}$, $S_{match}$ |

and object as specified by that proposition. Quantifier propositions in the context of GIVE generate transfer sets as indicated, with requests for the quantity slot and suitable start and result sets. The context of a HAVE proposition with joint owners generates a superset (with corresponding requests for the two subsets, of course). A MORE/LESS-THAN proposition, in the context of a quantifier, generates a remainder set, with associated requests for the missing elements of the schema.

Note that the schematic strategies presuppose two conditions: First, the appropriate knowledge schema must be available—if the child does not know what GIVE or MORE-THAN means, that is, does not have associated with it the right meaning postulate, then these problems cannot be solved. Second, however, this knowledge must be active and in the form of a production: The reader must know precisely which cues in the text are supposed to trigger particular knowledge structures. It is not enough to have the knowledge, it must also be used at the right moment.

### 10.5.3. Macro-operators

For the word problems in Table 10.2 macro-operators play a relatively minor and fairly subtle role. The texts are short, and written in such a way that their microstructure and macrostructure is essentially identical. There is no redundant or irrelevant material to delete, there are no occasions to use the construction operator. One could easily rewrite these problems, however, embedding them into a longer text and introducing both problem-irrelevant information and redundancies. Word problems could in this way be made much more difficult. In that case, the child would need to learn strategies for the use of the deletion operator, for example, to delete all propositions that do not contribute directly to the establishment of the schematic superstructure. In other words, it would be necessary to acquire task-specific macrostrategies, which may run counter to normal reading strategies. One would suppose that embedding an arithmetic problem into an interesting story would interfere with the operation of these task-specific macro-operators: The child would have to learn to disregard what is normally important in a story (goals, conflicts, interesting complications), and to look at it merely in terms of sets and their associated quantities. (For some similar kinds of interference effects, see Hidi, Baird, & Hildyard, 1982.)

However, even in the prepared problem set we are dealing with here, the macro-operation of generalization has still an important though subtle role to fulfill. What needs to be done is to strip the names and objects used in these problems of all their individuality and treat them merely as labels for sets. Whether it is my enemy Joe who has the marbles or my dear friend Lucy does not matter, and if instead of marbles Lucy has the cutest little kittens it still does not matter. This abstraction is of crucial importance in learning to do arithmetic (or other types of formal reasoning), and cannot always be taken for granted, especially when the outcome of the arithmetic operation is of emotional importance to the problem solver. Thus, the macro-operation of generalization plays a subtle but significant role even in degenerate, prepared school problems of the kind we are dealing with here. In a realistic, real life context, macrostrategies would assume an even more important role.

### 10.5.4. The Problem Representation and Arithmetic Operations

The schematic operators construct the microstructure of the text, which in our special case is also its macrostructure, except for the kind of abstraction mentioned above. The textbase for these word problems consists, therefore, of a number of set units which contain in their slots the propositions of the text, and which are interrelated with each other, forming higher order units, such as the TRANSFER-IN schema, or the MORE-THAN schema. Thus, we obtain a hierarchical structure with various complex schemata at the top, set schemata at the next level corresponding to the propositional schemata of Chapter 4, and atomic propositions in the slots of these set schemata. This organization is, of course, specifically generated for the purpose of doing arithmetic operations, but in principle it is no different from the organization of a narrative, for instance. In that case, too, we have atomic propositions bundled together via macropropositions in accordance with a narrative schema.

The reason for constructing such a single-minded textbase for word problems is that the situation model that has to be generated is a set structure. The stiuation model is simply the problem representation in terms of sets—much as it was envisaged by Riley *et al.* Corresponding to the textbase unit Set A, for instance, we have a conceptual representation Set A' that is nontextual. Set A is a text structure that organizes certain atomic propositions in a schematic way; Set A' is an abstract structure, specifying a certain set, with a certain number of elements, and a certain role in the larger schema.

Arithmetic operators apply to this problem representation. Once again, these operators are productions, the condition for which is a certain constellation of sets. For instance, if a problem representation consists of a superset and a subset with known quantities, and another subset with an unknown quantity, the production SUBTRACT is triggered, which computes the unknown quantity and uses it to answer the problem. Table 10.8 shows various other constellations which give rise to arithmetic operations, exactly as in Riley *et al.* Note that in addition to the true arithmetic operations ADD and SUBTRACT, there are various counting operations which children can and do use in solving these problems. Young children use counting to solve several problem types before they have a concept of set, which is a prerequisite for true addition and subtraction. The first four change problems and the first combine problem can be solved by counting operations, whereas the remaining problems presuppose true arithmetic operations. Riley *et al.* discuss these matters in appropriate detail.

Note that the situation model—that is, the problem representation—in part simply mirrors the textbase. The textbase has its slots filled with propositions, while

**Table 10.8**
**Calculational Inferences**

(a) *Counting operations*

|              | Start | Transfer-out | Transfer-in | Result |
|--------------|-------|--------------|-------------|--------|
| COUNT-ON     | X     |              | X           | ?      |
| COUNT-BACK   | X     | X            |             | ?      |
| COUNT-BACK   | X     |              | ?           | X      |
| COUNT-ON     | X     | ?            |             | X      |
| (CONVERT)    | ?     |              | X           | X      |
| (CONVERT)    | ?     | X            |             | X      |

(b) *Arithmetic operations*

|          | Superset | Subset A | Subset B |
|----------|----------|----------|----------|
| ADD      | ?        | X        | X        |
| SUBTRACT | X        | X        | ?        |

at the level of the problem representation we have merely a label, a role designation, and a number. However, quite frequently the textbase unit may be incomplete, for example, because there is no proposition to fill one of the slots of the schema so that the quantity or role slots remain unspecified. Nevertheless, these slots must be filled in in the corresponding problem representation: Inferences must be used to decide what the missing values for the role and quantity slot are. Thus, the problem representation is a double of the propositional textbase, but it contains additional, inferred information that is not part of the textbase proper—which is of course one of the reasons which we gave in Section 10.1 for introducing a situation model in the first place.

### 10.5.5. Examples of the Operation of Schematic Strategies

In Tables 10.9–10.16 examples are presented of how this model works for the problem set of Table 10.2.

*Change problems.* Consider Change (1) (Table 10.9). *Joe has three marbles* contains four atomic propositions: Joe = $x_1$ and marbles = $y_1$, HAVE $(x_1, y_1)$, and $3(y_1)$. The notation for *three marbles* we have chosen here has the virtue of simplicity and is quite adequate for present purposes (though of course not for the purposes of a logician or semanticist). In the second sentence, *Tom* is introduced by another atomic proposition, and so is the second *marbles*. However, we do not need a new atomic proposition for *him* ( = *Joe*), because we are dealing with a definite description that refers to an earlier entity, unlike *five more marbles,* which does not refer to the earlier marbles. *How many marbles* in the final sentence is also treated as an indefinite description, requiring a separate atomic proposition.[3]

[3]Note that the convention used in Kintsch (1974) of omitting explicit existential propositions would produce considerable confusion here because we need to be specific about which marbles we are talking about.

**Table 10.9**
**Change (1)**

| ACTION | | SHORT-TERM MEMORY |
|---|---|---|

$P_1$   $j(x_1)$      $\rightarrow S_1$   ⎡Object: $P_2$ ──────► M
$P_2$   $M(y_1)$           │   Spec: $P_1{}^{\wedge}P_3$ ─────►J
$P_3$   $HAVE(x_1 y_1)$    │   Quantity: $P_4$ ──────3
$P_4$   $3(y_1)$ ────────┘   ⎣Role:          /start/

$P_5$   $THEN(P_3\ P_8)$   $\rightarrow S_2$   ⎡Object: $P_7$ ──────►M        $S_{1_?}$
$P_6$   $t(x_2)$           │   Spec: $P_6{}^{\wedge}P_8$ ─────►J
$P_7$   $M(y_2)$          │   Quantity: $P_9$ ──────►5
$P_8$   $GIVE(x_2\ x_1\ y_2)$   │   ⎣Role: $P5$ ──────────transfer
$P_9$   $5(y_2)$ ────────┘   REQUEST: $S_{start}$//
                       $S_{result}$

$P_{10}$   $M(y_3)$       $\rightarrow S_3$   ⎡Object: $P_{10}$ ──────►M      ⎡$S_{1_{start}}$
$P_{11}$   $HOWMANY(y_3)$ ┘   Spec: $P_{12}$ ──────►J      $S_{2_{transfer}}$
$P_{12}$   $HAVE(x_1\ y_3)$    Quantity: $P_{11}$ ──────►*    REQUEST: $S_{result}$//
$P_{13}$   $NOW(P_{12})$      ⎣Role: $P_{13}$ ──────►result

        CALCULATE: Count-on                 ⎡$S_{1_{start}}$
                                           $S_{2_{transfer}}$
                                           ⎣$S_{3_{result}}^{*}$

We assume propositions to be constructed on line, as soon as all the necessary linguistic information is available. Whenever a proposition is obtained that is a condition for one of the schematic strategies, that strategy is triggered, and all the propositions from the current sentence are used to fill the slots of the set that resulted from that strategy. Thus, in Table 10.9, $P_3$ and $P_4$ is the condition for a MAKE-SET operation and results in Set $S_1$, which has $P_1$ and $P_3$ as its specification, $P_2$ in the object slot, and $P_4$ in the quantity slot. Note that there is no proposition to fill the role slot of $S_1$. The slots of the set schema have two entries: The first is a text proposition, and derived from it (indicated by an arrow) is the corresponding element of the problem representation (M for *marbles,* J for *Joe,* the number *3*).

In the next sentence, $P_9$ in the context of the GIVE proposition $P_8$ triggers a MAKE-TRANSFERSET, with the result of $S_2$. The transfer set $S_2$ carries with it automatically requests for a start and result set. Set 1 can be identified as the start set on the basis of two cues: initial position, and the *then* of the second sentence ($P_5$). At this point the role of start set can be assigned to $S_1$—but only to the problem representation of $S_1$, not to the textbase itself. In order to indicate that the start role of $S_1$ was inferred later and not when $S_1$ was first set up, we have enclosed "start" within slashes in $S_1$.

$P_{11}$ and $P_{12}$ are the condition for another MAKE-SET, generating $S_3$. Although the MAKE-set operation by itself does not fill the role slot of $S_3$, the presence of a request for a result set as well as specific linguistic cues (sentence order and *now*) indicate that $S_3$ must be a result set. Note that in the quantity slot of

**Table 10.10**
**Change (3)**

| ACTION | SHORT-TERM MEMORY |
|---|---|

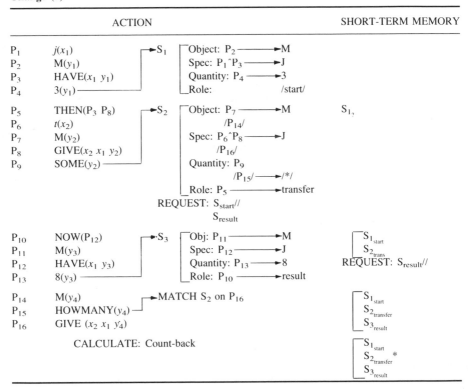

$S_3$ we have the proposition HOWMANY (MARBLES) in the text representation, but a * indicating a calculation goal in the problem representation. The pattern $S_{J,3,start}$– $S_{J,5,trsf}$– $S_{J,*,res}$ is the condition for a COUNT-ON operation, which supplies the solution of the problem.

The construction of the propositions for Change (3) (Table 10.10) is in all respects the same as for the previous problem. Again, we have only one *Tom* and one *Joe*, but several different *marbles*. The schematic operators are also used in much the same way as in Change (1), but note that the quantity slot in $S_2$ is filled on the textbase side by $P_9$--SOME(MARBLES), but is empty in the problem representation. The fourth sentence of the problem triggers another MAKE-TRANS-FERSET, but the set that is created is the same as $S_2$; hence $P_{14}$–$P_{16}$ are subsumed under $S_2$, thereby assigning a calculation goal to the problem representation of $S_2$. Change (5) (Table 10.11) proceeds analogously.

*Combine problems* (Tables 10.12–10.13). A different operator is triggered in the combine problems. In Combine (1), a quantifier proposition in the context of a HAVE proposition with joint owner ($P_{10}$–$P_{11}$) is the condition for a MAKE-SU-

**Table 10.11**
**Change (5)**

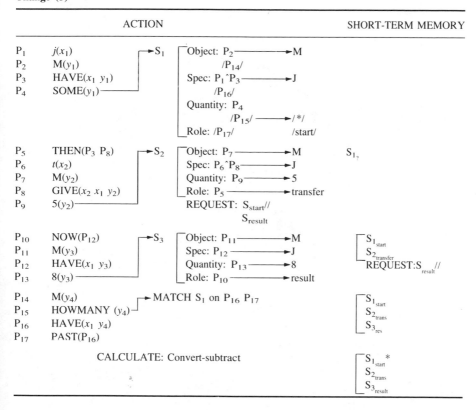

| ACTION | | | SHORT-TERM MEMORY |
|---|---|---|---|

$P_1$   $j(x_1)$    → $S_1$   Object: $P_2$ ──────► M

$P_2$   $M(y_1)$               /$P_{14}$/

$P_3$   $HAVE(x_1 \; y_1)$   Spec: $P_1{}^{\wedge}P_3$ ──────► J

$P_4$   $SOME(y_1)$ ───────       /$P_{16}$/

                         Quantity: $P_4$

                              /$P_{15}$/ ──────► /*/

                         Role: /$P_{17}$/       /start/

$P_5$   $THEN(P_3 \; P_8)$ → $S_2$   Object: $P_7$ ──────► M      $S_{1_?}$

$P_6$   $t(x_2)$            Spec: $P_6{}^{\wedge}P_8$ ──────► J

$P_7$   $M(y_2)$         Quantity: $P_9$ ────► 5

$P_8$   $GIVE(x_2 \; x_1 \; y_2)$   Role: $P_5$ ──────────► transfer

$P_9$   $5(y_2)$ ──────────   REQUEST: $S_{start}$//

                                 $S_{result}$

$P_{10}$   $NOW(P_{12})$ → $S_3$   Object: $P_{11}$ ──────► M      $S_{1_{start}}$

$P_{11}$   $M(y_3)$         Spec: $P_{12}$ ──────► J       $S_{2_{transfer}}$

$P_{12}$   $HAVE(x_1 \; y_3)$   Quantity: $P_{13}$ ────► 8     REQUEST:$S_{result}$//

$P_{13}$   $8(y_3)$ ──────────   Role: $P_{10}$ ──────► result

$P_{14}$   $M(y_4)$         → MATCH $S_1$ on $P_{16}$ $P_{17}$    $S_{1_{start}}$

$P_{15}$   $HOWMANY \; (y_4)$ ┘                      $S_{2_{trans}}$

$P_{16}$   $HAVE(x_1 \; y_4)$                         $S_{3_{res}}$

$P_{17}$   $PAST(P_{16})$

            CALCULATE: Convert-subtract      $S_{1_{start}}^{*}$

                                            $S_{2_{trans}}$

                                            $S_{3_{result}}$

PERSET. With it come two requests for subsets, one for each of the joint owners. The previously established sets $S_1$ and $S_2$ satisfy these requests and the role of subset is assigned to them in the problem representation, which sets the condition for the arithmetic operator ADD.

In Combine (2) a superset is established first, carrying with it a request for appropriate subsets. Sets $S_2$ and $S_3$ can be identified as such merely on the basis of the specification slot. However, a slight rewording of the second and third sentence in Combine (2) could provide a more direct linguistic cue to their subset roles: *Joe has three of these* would be the condition for a special subset operator, which would directly establish the subset roles of $S_2$ (and $S_3$) and thereby obviate the necessity for an inference. Indeed, Riley *et al.* report that such slight rewording makes the problem somewhat easier to solve—presumably because it supplied the children with an extralinguistic cue that was missing in the original version.

*Compare problems.* In Compare (1) (Table 10.14), two roleless sets are established first. These are then assigned roles as whole and match sets on the basis of

**Table 10.12**
**Combine (1)**

| ACTION | | SHORT-TERM MEMORY |
|---|---|---|

$P_1$  $j(x_1)$    → $S_1$  ⌈ Object: $P_2$ —→ M
$P_2$  $M(y_1)$          Spec: $P_1$^$P_3$ —→ J
$P_3$  HAVE($x_1y_1$)     Quantity: $P_4$ —→ 3
$P_4$  $3(y_1)$           ⌊ Role:       /sub/

$P_5$  $t(x_2)$     → $S_2$  ⌈ Object: $P_6$ —→ M     $S_{1_{j,?}}$
$P_6$  $M(y_2)$          Spec: $P_5$^$P_7$ —→ T
$P_7$  HAVE($x_2$ $y_2$)    Quantity: $P_8$ —→ 5
$P_8$  $5(y_2)$          ⌊ Role:       /sub/

$P_9$  $M(y_3)$    → $S_3$  ⌈ Object: $P_9$ —→ M     $S_{2_{t,?}}$
$P_{10}$  HOWMANY ($y_3$) ⌐ Spec: $P_{11}$ —→ J&T
$P_{11}$  HAVE($x_1$&$x_2$ $y_3$)    Quantity: $P_{10}$ —→ *
                      ⌊ Role:       super

REQUEST: $S_{j,sub}$//         Reinstate $S_1$
           $S_{t,sub}$//

CALCULATE: Add            ⌈ $S_{3_{j\&t,super}}$ *
                          $S_{1_{j,sub}}$
                          ⌊ $S_{2_{t,sub}}$

**Table 10.13**
**Combine (2)**

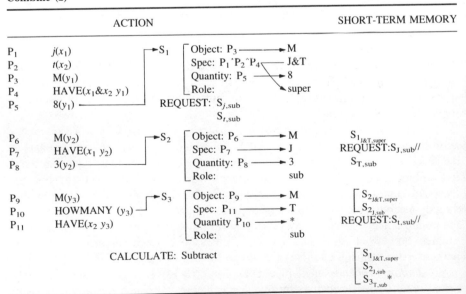

| ACTION | | SHORT-TERM MEMORY |
|---|---|---|

$P_1$  $j(x_1)$     → $S_1$  ⌈ Object: $P_3$ —→ M
$P_2$  $t(x_2)$          Spec: $P_1$^$P_2$^$P_4$ —→ J&T
$P_3$  $M(y_1)$        Quantity: $P_5$ —→ 8
$P_4$  HAVE($x_1$&$x_2$ $y_1$) ⌊ Role:       super
$P_5$  $8(y_1)$      REQUEST: $S_{j,sub}$
                    $S_{t,sub}$

$P_6$  $M(y_2)$   → $S_2$  ⌈ Object: $P_6$ —→ M     $S_{1_{J\&T,super}}$
$P_7$  HAVE($x_1$ $y_2$)     Spec: $P_7$ —→ J     REQUEST:$S_{j,sub}$//
$P_8$  $3(y_2)$          Quantity: $P_8$ —→ 3     $S_{T,sub}$
                    ⌊ Role:       sub

$P_9$  $M(y_3)$    → $S_3$  ⌈ Object: $P_9$ —→ M     ⌈ $S_{2_{J\&T,super}}$
$P_{10}$  HOWMANY ($y_3$) ⌐ Spec: $P_{11}$ —→ T     ⌊ $S_{2_{J,sub}}$
$P_{11}$  HAVE($x_2$ $y_3$)     Quantity $P_{10}$ —→ *     REQUEST:$S_{t,sub}$//
                    ⌊ Role:       sub

CALCULATE: Subtract       ⌈ $S_{1_{J\&T,super}}$
                             $S_{2_{J,sub}}$
                            ⌊ $S_{3_{T,sub}}$ *

**Table 10.14**
**Compare (1)**

| ACTION | | | SHORT-TERM MEMORY |
|---|---|---|---|

| | | | |
|---|---|---|---|
| $P_1$ | $j(x_1)$ | ┌►$S_1$  ⌈ Object: $P_2$ ──► M | |
| $P_2$ | $M(y_1)$ | Spec: $P_1{}^\wedge P_3$ ──► J | |
| $P_3$ | HAVE($x_1\ y_1$) | Quantity: $P_4$──► 8 | |
| $P_4$ | $8(y_1)$ ─────────┘ | ⌊ Role: /whole/ | |
| | | | |
| $P_5$ | $t(x_2)$ | ┌►$S_2$  ⌈ Object: $P_6$ ──► M | $S_{1_{J,?}}$ |
| $P_6$ | $M(y_2)$ | Spec: $P_5{}^\wedge P_7$ ──► T | |
| $P_7$ | HAVE($x_2\ y_2$) | Quantity: $P_8$──► 5 | |
| $P_8$ | $5(y_2)$ ─────────┘ | ⌊ Role: /match/ | |
| | | | |
| $P_9$ | $M(y_3)$ | ┌►$S_3$  ⌈ Object: $P_9$ ──► M | $S_{2_{T,?}}$ |
| $P_{10}$ | HOWMANY ($y_3$)─┘ | Spec: $P_{11}$ ──► J | |
| $P_{11}$ | HAVE($x_1 y_3$) | Quantity: $P_{10}$──► * | |
| $P_{12}$ | MORE($y_3 y_2$) | ⌊ Role: $P_{12}$ remainder | |

REQUEST: $S_{J,whole}$//          Reinstate $S_1$
$\qquad\qquad\quad S_{T,match}$//

CALCULATE: Subtract

$$\begin{bmatrix} S_{1_{J,whole}} \\ S_{2_{T,match}} \\ S_{3_{J,remainder}} \end{bmatrix} *$$

their ownership when the remainder set is constructed. Note that what is inferered is entirely a conceptual structure belonging to the problem representation— not a set of propositions in the textbase. The final two problems (Tables 10.15–10.16) introduce no new devices, though the by now familiar operators are combined here in novel ways. In all of the compare problems, the final outcome is a MORE-THAN pattern, with a whole set, a match set, and a remainder set, and a calculation goal assigned to one of these. We can either assume that these patterns are by themselves conditions for the appropriate arithmetic operations, or that the whole– match– remainder pattern gets converted into a super–sub–sub pattern, the usual condition for addition and subtraction.

What these examples demonstrate is, first of all, that the model works as we claimed it did. One can indeed specify comprehension strategies at various levels that result in the construction of a text representation and a situation model that are suitable for the problem-solving task. As Kintsch and Greeno (1982) pointed out in their original report on this work, such a demonstration has some interesting implications. It tells us, for instance, why some problems are harder to solve than others. Different problem types require different knowledge structures and different strategies for the application of that knowledge. Change problems, for instance, require that the child know about the TRANSFER schema, which is simple and concrete and, apparently, is quite within the grasp of even the kindergarten children. The SUPERSET schema and especially the MORE-THAN schema are much less available and might require some special training, both at the level of concrete

**Table 10.15**
**Compare (3)**

| ACTION | | | SHORT-TERM MEMORY |
|---|---|---|---|
| $P_1$ | $j(x_1)$ | → $S_1$ ⎡Object: $P_2$ ⟶ M | |
| $P_2$ | $M(y_1)$ | Spec: $P_1\char`^P_3$ ⟶ J | |
| $P_3$ | $HAVE(x_1\ y_1)$ | Quantity: $P_4$ ⟶ 3 | |
| $P_4$ | $3(y_1)$ | ⎣Role:      /match/ | |
| | | | |
| $P_5$ | $t(x_2)$ | → $S_2$ ⎡Object: $P_6$ ⟶ M | $S_{1,?}$ |
| $P_6$ | $M(y_2)$ | Spec: $P_5\char`^P_7$ ⟶ T | |
| $P_7$ | $HAVE\ (x_2\ y_2)$ | Quantity: $P_8$ ⟶ 5 | |
| $P_8$ | $5(y_2)$ | ⎣Role: $P_9$      remainder | |
| $P_9$ | $MORE(y_2\ y_1)$ | REQUEST: $S_{T,whole}$ $S_{J,match}$// | |
| | | | |
| $P_{10}$ | $M(y_3)$ | → $S_3$ ⎡Object: $P_{10}$ ⟶ M | ⎡$S_{1,match}$ |
| $P_{11}$ | $HOWMANY\ (y_3)$ | Spec: $P_{12}$ ⟶ T | ⎣$S_{2,T,remainder}$ |
| $P_{12}$ | $HAVE\ (x_2\ y_3)$ | Quantity: $P_{11}$ ⟶ * | |
| | | ⎣Role:      whole | REQUEST: $S_{T,whole}$// |
| | | CALCULATE: Add | ⎡$S_{3,T,whole}$   * |
| | | | $S_{1,J,match}$ |
| | | | ⎣$S_{1,T,remainder}$ |

**Table 10.16**
**Compare (5)**

| ACTION | | | SHORT-TERM MEMORY |
|---|---|---|---|
| $P_1$ | $j(x_1)$ | → $S_1$ ⎡Object: $P_2$ ⟶ M | |
| $P_2$ | $M(y_1)$ | Spec: $P_1\char`^P_3$ ⟶ J | |
| $P_3$ | $HAVE(x_1\ y_1)$ | Quantity: $P_4$ ⟶ 8 | |
| $P_4$ | $8(y_1)$ | ⎣Role:      /whole/ | |
| | | | |
| $P_5$ | $M(y_2)$ | → $S_2$ ⎡Object: $P_5$ ⟶ M | $S_{1,?}$ |
| $P_6$ | $HAVE(x_1\ y_2)$ | Spec: $P_6$ ⟶ J | |
| $P_7$ | $5(y_2)$ | Quantity: $P_7$ ⟶ 5 | |
| $P_8$ | $MORE\ (y_2\ y_3)$ | ⎣Role: $P_8$      remainder | |
| $P_9$ | $t(x_2)$ | $P_9\char`^P_{10}\char`^P_{11}$ | |
| $P_{10}$ | $M(y_3)$ | REQUEST: $S_{J,whole}$// | |
| $P_{11}$ | $HAVE(x_2\ y_3)$ | $S_{T,match}$ | |
| | | | |
| $P_{12}$ | $M(y_4)$ | → $S_3$ ⎡Object: $P_{12}$ ⟶ M | ⎡$S_{1,J,whole}$ |
| $P_{13}$ | $HOWMANY\ (y_4)$ | Spec: $P_{14}$ ⟶ T | ⎣$S_{2,J,remainder}$ |
| $P_{14}$ | $HAVE\ (x_2\ y_4)$ | Quantity: $P_{13}$ ⟶ * | $P_9\char`^P_{10}\char`^P_{11}$ |
| | | ⎣Role:      match | REQUEST: $S_{T,match}$// |
| | | MATCH $P_{10}=P_{12}$, $P_{11}=P_{14}$ | |
| | | CALCULATE: Subtract | ⎡$S_{1,J,whole}$ |
| | | | $S_{3,T,match}$   * |
| | | | ⎣$S_{2,J,remainder}$ |

**Table 10.17**
**Some Processing Characteristics of Word Arithmetic Problems**

| | Change | | | Combine | | Compare | | |
|---|---|---|---|---|---|---|---|---|
| | 1 | 3 | 5 | 1 | 2 | 1 | 3 | 5 |
| *Knowledge base used* | | | | | | | | |
| Transfer | X | X | X | (X?) | | | | |
| Superset | | | X | X | X | X | X | X |
| More-than | | | | | | X | X | X |
| *Processing statistics* | | | | | | | | |
| No inferences | 0 | 0 | 0 | 2 | 2 | 2 | 2 | 2 |
| Reinstatements | 0 | 0 | 0 | 1 | 0 | 1 | 0 | 0 |
| *Short-term memory load* | | | | | | | | |
| Average chunk size | 1.67 | 2.25 | 2.25 | 1.67 | 2.00 | 1.67 | 2.00 | 2.00 |
| *No* requests | 1 | 1 | 1 | 0 | 3 | 0 | 1 | 1 |
| *No* unattached propositions | 0 | 0 | 0 | 0 | 0 | 0 | 0 | 3 |
| *Proportion correct* | | | | | | | | |
| First grade | 1.00 | .56 | .28 | 1.00 | .39 | .28 | .17 | .11 |
| Second grade | 1.00 | 1.00 | .80 | 1.00 | .70 | .85 | .80 | .65 |

operations and of abstraction. As we have mentioned before, skill in solving these problems is not merely a matter of having the right knowledge. The model also specifies what sort of strategies (condition–action pairs) the skilled problem solver needs in order to apply this knowledge.

However, the examples discussed so far do not yet do justice to the full power of the model. There is an obvious problem: If problem difficulty were merely a matter of the right knowledge and the right strategies, then all the problems within a given problem type should be equally difficult, because exactly the same schemata and strategies are used for all change problems, for all compare problems, and so on. The problems within each type differ only in the order in which the information is presented, but nevertheless this is a major factor in problem difficulty: As Table 10.17 shows, differences in problem difficulty exist not only between types, but also within types, with the most difficult version within a type being from two to four times as hard as the easiest version for the first-graders. Some of these intratype differences are due to the fact that in some problem versions counting operations can be used, whereas true arithmetic operations are needed for others, as has been argued by Riley *et al.* However, even if we take this undoubtedly important factor into account, differences in problem difficulty remain which the model so far has not accounted for. The reason for this is that we have not yet considered the constraints that are imposed on the comprehension and solution process by the capacity limits of the human information-processing system.

## 10.5.6. Real-Time Processing Constraints

Of primary concern at this point are the short-term memory constraints discussed in Section 10.3. However, we need here specific assumptions instead of the general discussion presented there. We assume that short-term memory can hold a single chunk, but that certain properties of that chunk are related to memory load. A chunk is defined as an element at any of the levels of analysis considered here: It may be a solitary atomic proposition, or a set of such propositions bundled together by a set schema, or even several set schemata forming a higher order structure, such as a TRANSFER or SUPERSET schema. Thus, if Set A is held in short-term memory and a new, unrelated Set B is formed, Set A will be displaced from short-term memory by Set B, so that retrieving it at a later time would require a reinstatement operation. On the other hand, if Set A is held in short-term memory and a Set B is generated such that both A and B are part of some larger unit (say a TRANSFER schema), and both A and B can be jointly retained in short-term memory. Thus, at the end of compare problems, the whole set structure involving three sets is available in short-term memory, so that it can cue one of the arithmetic operators. One of the properties of short-term memory is therefore chunk size, measured in terms of component sets.

Another factor determining memory load is the number of active requests for missing information that have to be carried along. These are requests for sets to fill the roles in some higher order schema (as when a GIVE proposition establishes a transfer set but no suitable start or result set is available in the short-term buffer). The number of such requests that have to be kept active during processing provides another measure of short-term memory load.

Let us now consider once more the examples we have discussed, keeping track of how the processing occurs in real time subject to the constraints just mentioned. The right-hand columns of Tables 10.9–10.11 summarize what happens with the change problems. For Change (1), the first sentence leads to the formation of $S_1$ with owner J and quantity 3. As the second sentence is read, $S_{1\ J,3}$ is held in the buffer, while $S_2$ is formed. As $S_2$ is a transfer set, it occasions requests for start and result sets. The request for the start set can be satisfied immediately (indicated in the table by double slashes after $S_{start}$), as $S_1$ is still available in the buffer and is a suitable candidate. The request for a result set, on the other hand, must be carried along in an active state. Hence, for the third processing cycle, the short-term buffer contains the (partial) TRANSFER schema construction $S_1$–$S_2$, plus an active request. When $S_3$ is formed during that cycle, that request can be satisfied. For the final processing cycle we have in the buffer a complete TRANSFER schema, filled with the information from the text, which triggers the calculation operator COUNT-ON, providing the solution to the problem.

Change (3) and (5) proceed similarly, except that in each case there is a fourth sentence which does not lead to the formation of a new set but rather to a match to an old one.

In Combine (1) (Table 10.12) $S_2$ displaces $S_1$ from the buffer, because at that point in the process $S_1$ and $S_2$ are separate chunks: We do not (yet) know what their relationship is. Hence, when a superset is formed during the third processing cycle and two requests for subsets are activated, only $S_2$ is still available in the buffer to satisfy one of these requests. To retrieve $S_1$ requires a reinstatement search of episodic text memory. The condition for this search would be that there is no more text input, but still a left-over, active request. Note that in assigning the roles of subset to $S_1$ and $S_2$ inferences are made: There are no direct cues in the text that trigger this role assignment.

Combine (2) (Table 10.13) requires the same inferences, but the problem is formulated so that there is no need for a reinstatement search. The short-term memory load is, however, substantially greater in this case.

The compare problems (Tables 10.14–10.16) are processed similarly. Consider the processing of Compare (5). A set $S_1$ of 8 marbles belonging to *Joe* is created. Next, MORE-THAN creates a remainder set, and $S_1$ is recognized as the corresponding whole set; a flag goes up for the missing match set. For the first time in these problems we encounter a case where not all propositions can be assigned to slots in the schema: $P_9$–$P_{11}$ are connected to $P_8$, but there is no quantifier proposition which would trigger a MAKE-SET operation, creating a set of Tom's marbles and a home for $P_9$–$P_{11}$. Thus, these dangling propositions must be carried along in short-term memory until a place can be found for them in the text structure. This occurs in Cycle 3, where they can be assigned to the match set. The whole pattern is completed, the MORE-THAN schema is converted into a SUPERSET schema, the arithmetic operation SUBTRACT is triggered, and the problem is solved.

Table 10.17 summarizes some statistics relevant to problem difficulty in this problem set: the kind of knowledge structures required, the number of inferences that have to be made, the number of reinstatement searches required, the short-term memory load in terms of the average chunk size, the number of requests and the number of unassigned propositions that have to be carried along in the buffer during comprehension. Some empirical indications as to problem difficulty are also provided from the data presented in Riley *et al.* Quite obviously and not surprisingly, the nature of the knowledge structure makes a great deal of difference. As the number of inferences is strongly correlated with knowledge structures, it is hard to tell how much they contribute to problem difficulty. However, the evidence mentioned earlier that combine problems can be made easier by rewording them so that set roles do not have to be inferred but are indicated by linguistic cues suggests that inferences do matter (as they did with completely different texts in Miller & Kintsch, 1981). Reinstatements, however, do not appear to add to problem difficulty at all in Table 10.17. This observation contrasts strongly with the Miller and Kintsch results just alluded to, where reinstatements proved to be a major source of problem difficulty. The reason for this discrepancy is easy to see: The present problems were so short that long-term memory searches were trivial. Even without a proper retrieval cue, the reader could retrieve the first sentence on the basis of temporal cues. With the considerably longer texts of Miller and Kintsch, temporal cues become less useful and reinstatement becomes a resource-demanding operation.

The most important source of problem difficulty within each problem type was clearly short-term memory load according to Table 10.17. Even the second-graders had some trouble with those versions of change and combine problems that made large demands on short-term memory, in spite of the fact that their behavior on other versions of these problems clearly showed that they were familiar with the requisite knowledge structures and strategies. For the more difficult compare problems, this probably was not the case, but once again whether or not a problem was expressed in a way that was friendly with respect to short-term storage requirements made a substantial difference. The only problem with our analysis is that according to the model the memory load is identical for Change (3) and Change (5), whereas there exists a clear difference behaviorally. This discrepancy probably reflects an unwarranted assumption we have made: We assumed that an indefinite quantifier proposition—SOME($y$)—functions as a condition for a MAKE-SET operation. It is plausible, however, that children might not treat "some marbles" in quite the same way as "five marbles," and fail to construct a corresponding set. To the extent that this might have happened, the memory load for Change (3) and especially Change (5) would increase substantially, because unattached propositions would have to be carried along over much as three cycles in Change (5). Thus, we suggest that the (surprising) difficulty children have with Change (5) is due to confusion over indefinite quantifiers.

According to this analysis, there are, therefore, two reasons why failures to solve word arithmetic problems occur: because of a lack of knowledge, and because of lack of resources. Important research questions arise at this point concerning the interaction between short-term memory capacity and the degree to which schema use is automatized, and hence would make fewer resource demands, leaving the reader free to deal with problems of short-term memory. Without sufficient automatization, one would expect that the knowledge use strategies would divert too many resources from the short-term memory maintenance required by these problems, thereby introducing a source of error and problem difficulty. Although we cannot explore these contingencies here, a model like the present one at least sets the stage for the study of such questions.

This brief description of the model for understanding word arithmetic problems must suffice here. More detail is provided in the original publication. We would like to point out, however, that some of the properties of this model pertain to the behavior to be modeled, and are not features of our general theory. The present model is extremely bottom up, data driven; whatever planning and goal setting is done happens right away when the decision is made to deal with a certain problem set and certain operators. Even slight generalizations (as envisaged by Kintsch & Greeno, 1982) would introduce more top-down processing, a deeper semantic analysis of the problem situation than was necessary here, and more complex, flexible strategies. Here we modeled a data-driven process; the techniques we used could also be applied to modeling more complex understanding processes than children's problem solving.

It would, of course, be silly to claim that the model we have sketched here is the correct one, or the only one possible. All we have done here is to work out in detail one possible model—one that follows straightforwardly from the general theory of comprehension presented in this book and that fits in well with the problem-solving model of Riley *et al.* (1982). We have just seen that this model predicts rather well problem difficulty in the set of problems considered here, and hence has at least some empirical support. We have also seen that this model raises some interesting questions, both research questions and questions concerning teaching methods and educational practice (Kintsch & Greeno, 1982, discuss some of these questions more fully). But none of this means that we have found the right or the ultimate solution. Obviously, there are alternative formulations, involving possibly very different assumptions both about discourse comprehension and problem solving. For the sake of scientific progress such models must eventually be developed and tested against each other. What we have done here is merely to take a first step: to work out in detail *a* complete and principled model of how children understand and solve word arithmetic problems. Our main point was to show that the general theory presented here permits such an explicit formulation. Eventually, when alternative theories and alternative models have reached comparable stages of development, the task of deciding among them can be undertaken.


## 10.6. EPILOGUE

In concluding this book we want to reflect briefly on the nature of the enterprise that we have been engaged in. What is the use of developing a general theory of comprehension strategies? It belongs neither to linguistics nor psychology, is neither fish nor fowl. From the very beginning it was clear that the theory could not cover all aspects of comprehension processes, and hence must remain partial, though we have tried to be comprehensive within the boundary conditions we set for ourselves. It was also clear that despite of our efforts, many details of the theory must remain vague. Indeed, what we have presented is not so much a theory as a framework for a theory. We have tried to define the principles needed to construct a theory, given a particular comprehension situation. There can be no theory of comprehension that is at once specified and general because there is no single, unitary process 'comprehension'. Every time we look at discourse comprehension, it is a little bit different. What one needs to deal with this situation is a framework for studying it, a set of principles and analyses that can be applied to concrete cases. The application will always work out a little differently in each case, but because the same building blocks are used every time, we can go beyond ad hoc, arbitrary miniature models, which might be very simple and even elegant, but which merely serve to deceive us about the real complexity of comprehension processes.

Not only do new situations require new and different models, but different theoretical purposes also lead to the construction and use of different models. Thus, if our purpose is to study how knowledge is used in solving word arithmetic problems, a different level of analysis is required than when our purpose is merely to predict average recall performance for subjects who read a story. The latter goal is well served by the Kintsch and van Dijk (1978) version of our model, which is well suited for that particular purpose, though entirely inadequate for some other purposes.

Similar things can be said about notation, for example, the kind of propositional representations we have employed here: There is no need to make it more complex than required. If one needs a rough analysis of a text into idea units, quite a superficial notation will suffice; the more subtle the goals of the analysis, the more sophisticated the notation must become. Within the general framework there are many possible approaches. It is neither necessary nor desirable to deal with the problem always at its full level of complexity. As long as we have a general framework we can know where and what we have been simplifying, and can judge whether these simplifications were appropriate.

How does one evaluate the adequacy of the general framework for understanding language comprehension that we have developed here? Although some global, informal evaluations with respect to what is known about discourse comprehension in the literature and from our own intuitions are certainly possible, formal, precise evaluations are not—by its very nature, the theory *has* to be too flexible, too general for that. Thus, the main criterion of success, we suggest, becomes our ability to derive fruitful situation- and task-specific models from the general theory, as well as experimental tests of various principles and implications of these models. Thus, the methods of experimental psychology can provide an empirical evaluation, albeit in a somewhat unconventional way. The theory as a whole is too general to be subject to direct experimental tests, but the accumulation of observational and experimental evidence relative to certain of its points will eventually verify or disconfirm the theory. The experiments reported here, are no more than a beginning. There is very much more that can and should be done, compared with the modest results we have achieved so far. Basically, what we have consists of a series of demonstrations that processes that should occur in a certain way according to the theory can indeed be observed under appropriate, carefully controlled laboratory conditions. Thus, in Chapter 5 we showed that discourse effects, to which we have assigned great importance in the discussion of local coherence establishment, can indeed exercise a dominant influence on pronoun identification. In Chapter 6 (Experiment 4) we arranged conditions in such a way that two macrostrategies—involving interest and level of descriptions as cues for macrorelevance—can be seen to operate. In Chapter 7 we showed that the presence of a clear-cut rhetorical structure may facilitate the formation of macrostructures. All these cases are basically demonstration experiments: We arrange experimental conditions—the nature of the text as well as the tasks the subjects perform—in such a way that certain theoretically interesting behaviors can be observed in relatively clear form; such experiments are demonstrations of the control we are able to exercise over the subject–text interaction, and thereby, by implication, of our knowledge about comprehension processes. Other experiments reported here are, however, of a quite different nature: They are not so much tests of the theory, but are plainly and frankly exploratory. Often the theory gives us no more than an indication where and how to look for potentially interesting phenomena. Thus, in Chapter 4 we reported some exploratory work on strategies for proposition construction. We did not know enough to make precise predictions, but we did know enough to make some observations that go beyond common sense and may be the starting point for a more systematic mapping out of this potentially important field of investigation. Similarly, the use of the priming methodology to investigate the real-time course of macrostructure formation (Chapter 6) was exploratory, yielding some important insights and opening up a promising territory. Much the same could be said about the study of global biases in knowledge use (Chapter 8). This use of experiments as tools for theory-guided exploration, complementing the more traditional function of experiments as tests for theoretical predictions, must become more and more widespread and more important as theories in cognitive science become more complex and less directly testable.

In the immediate future, we see several ways in which this work can develop further. One was implicit in the preceding paragraphs: Now that we have what we think is an acceptable framework for discourse comprehension, research on the details of comprehension processes becomes more feasible, and much more of it is needed to deepen out understanding of these processes. Such work must be both theoretical, involving the construction of specific, explicit models for well-defined situations, and experimental, as suggested above. The second line of development involves expansion beyond the constricting boundaries that we have respected here, to a more detailed consideration or parsing processes, for instance, or to the burgeoning field of ''hot cognition'' (opinions, attitudes) that has fascinated us so much here. Finally, a third line of development will be the construction of an explicit cognitive bridge toward the communicative context: the situational and sociocultural context of discourse processing.

# References

Abbot, V., & Black, J. B. *The representation of scripts in memory.* Technical Report, Department of Psychology, Yale University, 1980.

Abelson, R. P. Differences between belief and knowledge systems. *Cognitive Science,* 1979, *3,* 355–366.

Adams, M. J., & Collins, A. A schema-theoretic view in reading. In R. O. Freedle (Ed.), *New directions in discourse processing.* Norwood, N.J.: Ablex, 1979.

Alba, J. W., Alexander, S. G., Harker, L., & Carniglia, K. The role of context in the encoding of information. *Journal of Experimental Psychology: Human Learning and Memory,* 1981, *7,* 283–292.

Anderson, J. M. *The grammar of case.* London: Cambridge University Press, 1971.

Anderson, J. R. *Language, memory and thought.* Hillsdale, N.J.: Erlbaum, 1976.

Anderson, J. R. *Concepts, propositions, and schemata: What are the cognitive units?* Technical Report, Department of Psychology, Carnegie-Mellon University, 1980.

Anderson, J. R. Acquisition of cognitive skill. *Psychological Review,* 1982, *89,* 369–406.

Anderson, J. R., & Bower, G. H. Recognition and retrieval processes in free recall. *Psychological Review,* 1972, *79,* 97–123.

Anderson, J. R., & Bower, G. H. *Human associative memory.* Washington, D.C.: Winston, 1973.

Anderson, J. R., & Reder, L. M. An elaborative processing explanation of depth of processing. In L. S. Cermak & F. I. M. Craik (Eds.), *Levels of processing in human memory.* Hillsdale, N.J.: Erlbaum, 1979.

Anderson, R. C., & Ortony, A. On putting apples into bottles—a problem of polysemy. *Cognitive Psychology,* 1975, *7,* 167–180.

Atkinson, R. C., & Juola, J. F. Search and decision processes in recognition memory. In D. H. Krantz, R. C. Atkinson, R. D. Luce, & P. Suppes (Eds.), *Contemporary developments in mathematical psychology* (Vol. 1). San Francisco: Freeman, 1974.

Atlas, M. A. *Addressing an audience: A study of expert–novice differences in writing* (Technical Report No. 3.) Washington, D.C.: 1979. Document Design Center, 1979.

Baddeley, A. D., & Hitch, G. Working memory. In G. H. Bower (Ed.), *The psychology of learning and motivation* (Vol. 8). New York: Academic Press, 1974.

Baggett, P. Memory for explicit and implicit information in picture stories. *Journal of Verbal Learning and Verbal Behavior*, 1975, *14*, 538–548.

Ballstaedt, S. P., Mandl, H., Schnotz, W., & Tergan, S. O. *Texte verstehen–Texte gestalten*. Munich: Urban & Schwarzenberg, 1981.

Barclay, J. R. The role of comprehension in remembering sentences. *Cognitive Psychology*, 1973, *4*, 229–254.

Barthes, R. Introduction a l'analyse structurale des recits. *Communications*, 1966, *8*, 1–27.

Bartlett, F. C. *Remembering: an experimental and social study*. Cambridge: Cambridge University Press, 1932.

Bates, E., & MacWhinney, B. A functionalist approach to the acquisition of grammar. In E. Ochs & B. Schieffelin (Eds.), *Developmental pragmatics*. New York: Academic Press, 1979.

Bates, E., & MacWhinney, B. Functionalist approaches to grammar. In L. Gleitman & E. Wanner (Eds.), *Language acquisition: The state of the art*. New York: Cambridge University Press, 1982.

Bauman, R., & Sherzer, J. (Eds.). *Explorations in the ethnography of speaking*. London: Cambridge University Press, 1974.

Beattie, G. W. The role of language production in the organization of behaviour in face-to-face interaction. In B. Butterworth (Ed.), *Language productions*. London: Academic Press, 1980.

de Beaugrande, R. *Text, discourse and process*. Hillsdale, N.J.: Erlbaum, 1980.

de Beaugrande, R., & Colby, B. Narrative models of action and interaction. *Cognitive Science*, 1979, *3*, 43–66.

de Beaugrande, R., & Dressler, W. *Introduction to text linguistics*. London: Longman, 1981.

Becker, C. A. Semantic context effects in visual word recognition: an analysis of semantic strategies. *Memory and Cognition*, 1980, *8*, 493–512.

Bellezza, F. S., & Bower, G. H. Remembering script-based text. *Poetics*, 1982, *11*, 1–23.

Bever, T. G. The cognitive basis for linguistic structures. In J. R. Hayes (Ed.), *Cognition and the development of language*. New York: Wiley, 1970.

Bever, T. G. Garrett, M. F., & Hurtig, R. The interaction of perceptual processes and ambiguous sentences. *Memory and Cognition*, 1973, *1*, 277–286.

Bierwisch, M. On certain problems of semantic representation. *Foundations of Language*, 1969, *5*, 153–184.

Bierwisch, M. Poetik und Linguistik. In H. Kreuzer & R. Gunzenhäuser (Eds.), *Mathematik und Dichtung*. Munich: Nymphenburger, 1965. English translation in D. C. Freeman (Ed.), *Linguistics and literary style*. New York: Holt, Rinehart & Winston, 1970.

Bierwisch, M. *Formal and lexical semantics*. Paper presented at the XIII International Congress of Linguistics, Tokyo, 1982.

Black, J. B., & Bower, G. H. Episodes as chunks in narrative memory. *Journal of Verbal Learning and Verbal Behavior*, 1979, *18*, 309–318.

Black, J. B., & Bower, G. H. Story understanding and problem solving. *Poetics*, 1980, *9*, 233–250.

Black, J. B., Turner, T. J., & Bower, G. H. Point of view in narrative comprehension, memory and production. *Journal of Verbal Learning and Verbal Behavior*, 1979, *18*, 187–198.

Black, J. B., & Wilensky, R. An evaluation of story grammars. *Cognitive Science*, 1979, *3*, 213–229.

Bobrow, D. G., & Collins, A. *Representation and understanding: studies in cognitive science*. New York: Academic Press, 1976.

Bobrow, D. G., & Winograd, T. On overview of KRL, a knowledge representation language. *Cognitive Science*, 1977, *1*, 3–46.

Bobrow, S., & Bower, G. H. Comprehension and recall of sentences. *Journal of Experimental Psychology*, 1969, *80*, 455–461.

Bourne, L. E., Jr. *Human conceptual behavior*. Boston: Allyn & Bacon, 1966.

Bousfield, W. A. The occurrence of clustering in the recall of randomly arranged associates. *Journal of General Psychology*, 1953, *49*, 229–240.

Bovair, S., & Kieras, D. E. *A guide to propositional analysis for research on technical prose* (Technical Report No. 8). Department of Psychology, University of Arizona, 1981.

Bower, G. H. Mental imagery and associative learning. In L. W. Gregg (Ed.), *Cognition in learning and memory*. New York: Wiley, 1972.

Bower, G. H. Selective facilitation and interference in retention of prose. *Journal of Educational Psychology*, 1974, *66*, 1–8.

Bower, G. H., Black, J. B., & Turner, T. J. Scripts in memory for text. *Cognitive Psychology*, 1979, *11*, 177–220.

Bransford, J. D., Barclay, J. R., & Franks, J. J. Sentence memory: A constructive versus interpretive approach. *Cognitive Psychology*, 1972, *3*, 193–209.

Bransford, J. D., & Franks, J. J. The abstraction of linguistic ideas. *Cognitive Psychology*, 1972, *2*, 331–350.

Bransford, J., & Johnson, M. K. Contextual prerequisites for understanding: Some investigations of comprehension and recall. *Journal of Verbal Learning and Verbal Behavior*, 1972, *11*, 717–726.

Brazil, D. *Discourse intonation*. Ph.D. dissertation, University of Birmingham, 1978.

Bremond, C. *Le logique du récit*. Paris: Seuil, 1973.

Breuker, J. *Availability of knowledge*. Ph.D. dissertation, University of Amsterdam, COWO, 1981.

Britton, B. K., Meyer, B. J. F., Hodge, M. H., & Glynn, S. Effect of the organization of text on memory: Tests of retrieval and response criterion hypotheses. *Journal of Experimental Psychology: Human Learning and Memory*, 1980, *6*, 620–629.

Broadbent, D. E. *Perception and communication*. New York: Pergamon Press, 1958.

Broadbent, D. E. *In defence of empirical psychology*. London: Methuen, 1973.

Broadbent, D. E. The magical number seven after 15 years. In R. A. Kennedy & A. Wilkes (Eds.), *Studies in long-term memory*. New York: Wiley, 1975.

Bruce, B. Analysis of interacting plans as a guide to the understanding of memory structure. *Poetics*, 1980, *9*, 295–312.

Bruner, J. S., Goodnow, J., & Austin, G. *A study of thinking*. New York: Wiley, 1956.

Bryan, W. L., & Harter, N. Studies on the telegraphic language: The acquisition of a hierarchy of habits. *Psychological Review*, 1899, *6*, 346–375.

Buschke, H., & Schaier, A. H. Memory units, ideas, and propositions in semantic remembering. *Journal of Verbal Learning and Verbal Behavior*, 1979, *18*, 549–564.

Butterworth, B. (Ed.). *Language production* (Vol. 1). London: Academic Press, 1980.

Caccamise, D. J. *Cognitive processes in writing: Idea generation and integration*. Ph.D. dissertation, University of Colorado, 1981.

Cantor, N., & Mischel, W. Traits as prototypes: Effects on recognition memory. *Journal of Personality and Social Psychology*, 1977, *35*, 38–48.

Caplan, D. Clause boundaries and recognition latencies for words in sentences. *Psychological Review*, 1972, *12*, 73–76.

Caramazza, A., Grober, E., Garvey, C., & Yates, J. Comprehension of anaphoric pronouns. *Journal of Verbal Learning and Verbal Behavior*, 1977, *16*, 601–609.

Carbonell, J. G., Jr. POLITICS: Automated ideological reasoning. *Cognitive Science*, 1978, *2*, 1–15.

Carbonell, J. G., Jr. *Metaphor comprehension*. Technical Report, Department of Computer Science, Carnegie-Mellon University, 1981.

Carbonell, J. G., Jr. Learning by analogy: Formulating and generalizing plans from past experience. In J. Michalski, J. G. Carbonell, & T. M. Mitchell (Eds.), *Machine intelligence: An artificial intelligence approach*. Palo Alto, Calif.: Tioga Press, 1982.

Carnap, R. *Introduction to semantics*. Cambridge, Mass.: Harvard University Press, 1942.

Carnap, R. *Meaning and necessity*. Chicago: University of Chicago Press, 1947.

Carr, T. H. Research on reading: Meaning, context effects, and comprehension. *Journal of Experimental Psychology: Human Perception and Performance*, 1981, *7*, 592–603.

Carroll, J. M., & Bever, T. G. Sentence comprehension: A case study in the relation of knowledge and perception. *Handbook of perception (Vol. 8)*. New York: Academic Press. 1976.

Carroll, J. M., & Tannenhaus, M. K. Functional clauses and sentence segmentation. *Journal of Speech and Hearing Research*, 1978, *21*, 693–708.

Castelfranchi, C., & Parisi, D. *Linguaggio, conoscenze e scopi*. Bologna: Il Mulino, 1980.

Cattell, J. M. The time taken up by cerebral operation. *Mind*, 1886, *11*, 220–242.

Chafe, W. L. Discourse structure and human knowledge. In J. B. Carroll & R. O. Freedle (Eds.), *Language comprehension and the acquisition of knowledge*. Washington, D.C.: Winston, 1972.

Chafe, W. L. (Ed.). *The pear stories*. Norwood, N.J.: Ablex, 1979.

Chang, F. R. Active memory processes in visual sentence comprehension: Clause effects and pronominal reference. *Memory and Cognition*, 1980, *8*, 58–64.

Charniak, E. *Toward a model of children's story comprehension*. Ph.D. dissertation, Massachusetts Institute of Technology, 1972.

Charniak, E. A framed PAINTING: The representation of a common sense knowledge fragment. *Cognitive Science*, 1977, *1*, 355–394.

Charniak, E. The case-slot identity theory. *Cognitive Science*, 1981, *5*, 285–292.

Charrow, V. R. *Linguistic theory and the study of legal and bureaucratic language* (Technical Report No. 16). Washington, D.C.: Document Design Center, 1981.

Chase, W. G., & Ericsson, K. A. Skilled memory. In J. R. Anderson (Ed.), *Cognitive skills and their acquisition*. Hillsdale, N.J.: Erlbaum, 1981.

Chase, W. G., & Simon, H. A. Perception in chess. *Cognitive Psychology*, 1973, *4*, 55–81.

Chi, M. T. H. Short-term memory limitations in children: Capacity or processing deficits? *Memory and Cognition*, 1976, *4*, 559–580.

Chiesi, H. L., Spilich, G. J., & Voss, J. F. Acquisition of domain-related information in relation to high and low domain knowledge. *Journal of Verbal Learning and Verbal Behavior*, 1979, *18*, 257–274.

Ching, M. K. L., Haley, M. C., & Lunsford, R. F. (Eds.). *Linguistic perspectives on literature*. London: Routledge & Kegan Paul, 1980.

Cirilo, R. K. Referential coherence and text structure in story comprehension. *Journal of Verbal Learning and Verbal Behavior*, 1981, *20*, 358–368.

Cirilo, R. K., & Foss, D. J. Text structure and reading time for sentences. *Journal of Verbal Learning and Verbal Behavior*, 1980, 19, 96–109.

Clark, H. H. Inferences in comprehension. In D. LaBerge & S. J. Samuels (Eds.), *Basic processes in reading: Perception and comprehension*. Hillsdale, N.J.: Erlbaum, 1977.

Clark, H. H. Responding to indirect speech acts. *Cognitive Psychology*, 1979, *11*, 430–477.

Clark, H. H. Language use and language users. In G. Lindzey & F. Aronson (Eds.), *The handbook of social psychology* (3rd ed.). Reading, Mass.: Addison-Wesley, 1983.

Clark, H. H., & Clark, E. V. *Psychology and language*. New York: Harcourt Brace Jovanovich, 1977.

Clark, H. H., & Lucy, P. Understanding what is meant from what is said: A study of conversationally conveyed requests. *Journal of Verbal Learning and Verbal Behavior*, 1975, *14*, 56–72.

Clark, H. H., & Marshall, C. Reference diaries. In D. Waltz (Ed.), *Theoretical issues in natural language processing*. Urban-Champaign: Center for the Study of Reading, 1978.

Clark, H. H., & Sengul, C. J. In search of referents for nouns and pronouns. *Memory and Cognition*, 1979, *7*, 35–41.

Cofer, Ch. N. A comparison of logical and verbatim learning of prose passages of different lengths. *American Journal of Psychology*, *54*, 1941, 1–20.

Collett, P. (Ed.). *Social rules and social behaviour*. Oxford: Blackwell, 1977.

Collins, A., & Gentner, D. A framework for a cognitive theory of writing. In L. W. Gregg & E. R. Steinberg (Eds.), *Cognitive processes in writing*. Hillsdale, N.J.: Erlbaum, 1980.

Collins, A. N., & Loftus, E. F. A spreading activation theory of semantic processing. *Psychological Review*, 1975, *82*, 407–428.

Corbett, A. T., & Dosher, B. A. Instrument inferences in sentence encoding. *Journal of Verbal Learning and Verbal Behavior*, 1978, *17*, 479–491.

Corbett, E. P. J. *Classical rhetoric for the modern student* (2nd ed.). New York: Oxford University Press, 1971.

Coulthard, M. *An introduction to discourse analysis*. London: Longman, 1977.

Coulthard, M., & Montgomery, M. (Eds.). *Studies in discourse analysis*. London: Routledge & Kegan Paul, 1981.

Cresswell, M. J. *Logics and languages*. London: Methuen, 1973.

Crothers, E. J. *Paragraph structure inference*. Norwood, N.J.: Ablex, 1979.

Crystal, D., & Davy, D. *Investigating English style*. London: Longman, 1969.

Culler, J. *Structuralist poetics*. London: Oxford University Press, 1975.

Curtius, E. -R. *Europäische Literatur und lateinisches Mittelalter*. Bern: Francke, 1948.

Dahl, Ö. *Topic and comment*. Stockholm: Almquist & Wicksell, 1969.

Daneman, M., & Carpenter, P. A. Individual differences in working memory and reading. *Journal of Verbal Learning and Verbal Behavior*, 1980, *19*, 450–466.

Danet, B. Language in the legal process. *Law and Society Review*, 1980, *14*, 445–565.

Den Uyl, M., & Oostendorp, H. van. The use of scripts in text comprehension. *Poetics*, 1980, *9*, 275–294.

van Dijk, T. A. *Some aspects of text grammars*. The Hague: Mouton, 1972.

van Dijk, T. A. Philosophy of action and theory of narrative. *Poetics*, 1976, *5*, 287–338.

van Dijk, T. A. *Text and context*. London: Longman, 1977. (a)

van Dijk, T. A. Semantic macro-structures and knowledge frames in discourse comprehension. In M. A. Just & P. A. Carpenter (Eds.), *Cognitive processes in comprehension*. Hillsdale, N.J.: Erlbaum, 1977. (b)

van Dijk, T. A. (Ed.). Story comprehension. *Poetics*. 1980, *8*, Nos. 1–3. (a)

van Dijk, T. A. *Macrostructures*. Hillsdale, N.J.: Erlbaum, 1980. (b)

van Dijk, T. A. Story comprehension: An introduction. *Poetics*, 1980, *8*, 7–29. (c)

van Dijk, T. A. *Studies in the pragmatics of discourse*. The Hague: Mouton, 1981. (a)

van Dijk, T. A., *Textual structures of news in the press*. Unpublished manuscript, Department of General Literary Studies, University of Amsterdam, 1981. To appear in the *Journal of Communication*. (b)

van Dijk, T. A. *News production as discourse processing*. Department of General Literary Studies, University of Amsterdam, 1981. (c)

van Dijk, T. A. Opinions and attitudes in discourse comprehension. In J. F. Le Ny & W. Kintsch (Eds.), *Language and comprehension*. Amsterdam: North-Holland, 1982. (a)

van Dijk, T. A. Episodes as units of discourse analysis. In D. Tannen (Ed.), *Analyzing discourse: Text and talk*. Washington, D.C.: Georgetown University Press, 1982. (b)

van Dijk, T. A. *Nieuwsanalyse* (News Analysis). Amsterdam: University of Amsterdam, Dept. of General Literary Studies, 1983 (a)

van Dijk, T. A. News. In T. A. van Dijk (Ed.), *Handbook of discourse analysis* (4 vols.). London: Academic Press, 1983. (b)

van Dijk, T. A., & Kintsch, W. Cognitive psychology and discourse: Recalling and summarizing stories. In W. U. Dressler (Ed.), *Current trends in text linguistics*. Berlin/New York: de Gruyter, 1978.

van Dijk, T. A., & Petöfi, J. S. (Eds.). *Theory of metaphor*. Special issue of *Poetics*, 1975, *4*, Nos. 2–3.

van Dijk, T. A., & Petöfi, J. S. (Eds.). *Grammars and description*. Berlin/New York: de Gruyter, 1977.

Dik, S. C. *Functional grammar*, Amsterdam: North-Holland, 1978.

Dik, S. C. *Studies in functional grammar*. New York: Academic Press, 1980.

Dillon, G. L. *Language processing and the reading of literature*. Bloomington, Ind.: University Press, 1978.

Dooling, D. J., & Mullet, R. L. Locus of thematic effects in retention of prose. *Journal of Experimental Psychology*, 1973, *99*, 404–406.

Dressler, W. U. *Einführung in die Textlinguistik*. Tübingen: Niemeyer, 1972.

Dressler, W. U. (Ed.). *Current trends in textlinguistics*. Berlin/New York: de Gruyter, 1978.

Ducasse, C. J. Propositons, opinions, sentences and facts. *Journal of Philosophy*, 1940, *37*, 701–711.

Edwards, W., & Tversky, A. (Eds.). *Decision making*. Harmondsworth: Penguin Books, 1967.

Ehrlich, K. Comprehension of pronouns. *Quarterly Journal of Experimental Psychology*, 1980, *32*, 247–255.

Enkvist, N. E. *Linguistic stylistics.* The Hague: Mouton, 1973.

Erlich, V. *Russian formalism.* The Hague: Mouton, 1955.

Estes, W. K. An associative basis for coding and organization in memory. In A. W. Melton & E. Martin (Eds.), *Coding processes in human memory.* Washington, D.C.: Winston, 1972.

Evans, H. (Ed.). *Handling newspaper text.* London: Heineman, 1974.

Fahlman, J. E. *NETL: A System for representing and using real-world knowledge.* Cambridge, Mass.: MIT Press, 1979.

Feigenbaum, E. A. The art of artificial intelligence: I. Themes and case studies of knowledge engineering. *Proceedings of the 5th International Joint Conference on Artificial Intelligence.* Cambridge, Mass., 1977.

Fillmore, C. J. The case for case. In E. Bach & R. T. Harms (Eds.), *Universals of linguistic theory.* New York: Holt, Rinehart & Winston, 1968.

Findahl, O., & Höijer, B. Studies of news from the perspective of human comprehension. In G. C. Wilhoit & H. de Bock (Eds.), *Mass communication review yearbook* (Vol. 2). Beverly Hills, Calif.: Sage Publications, 1981.

Fletcher, C. R. Short-term memory processes in text comprehension. *Journal of Verbal Learning and Verbal Behavior,* 1981, *20,* 546–574.

Flores d'Arcais, G. B. The perception of complex sentences. In W. J. Levelt & G. B. Flores d'Arcais (Eds.), *Studies in the perception of language.* London: Wiley, 1978.

Fodor, J. A., Bever, T. G., & Garret, M. F. *The psychology of language.* New York: McGraw-Hill, 1974.

Fodor, J. A., & Garrett, M. F. Some syntactic determinants of sentential complexity. *Psychological Review,* 1967, *2,* 289–296.

Fodor, J. A., Garrett, M. F., Walker, E. C., & Parkes, C. H. Against definition. *Cognition,* 1980, *8,* 263–367.

Fodor, J. D., Fodor, J. A., & Garrett, M.F. The psychological unreality of semantic representations. *Linguistic Inquiry,* 1975, *6,* 515–531.

Forster, K. I. Visual perception of rapidly presented word sequences of varying complexity. *Perception and Psychophysics,* 1970, *8,* 215–221.

Franck, D. *Grammatik und Konversation.* Königstein, Ts.: Scriptor, 1980.

Frederiksen, C. H. Representing logical and semantic structure of knowledge acquired from discourse. *Cognitive Psychology,* 1975, *7,* 371–458.

Frederiksen, J. R. Assessment of perceptual, decoding, and lexical skills and their relation to reading proficiency. In A. M. Lesgold, J. W. Pellegrino, S. Fokkema, & R. Glaser (Eds.), *Cognitive psychology and instruction.* New York: Plenum, 1977.

Frederiksen, J. R. Sources of process interaction in reading. In A. M. Lesgold & C. A. Perfetti (Eds.), *Interactive processes in reading.* Hillsdale, N.J.: Erlbaum, 1981.

Freedle, R. O. (Ed.). *New directions in discourse processing.* Norwood, N.J.: Ablex, 1979.

Frege, G. *Funktion, Begriff, Bedeutung.* Göttingen: Vandenhoeck & Ruprecht, 1962.

Galambos, J. A., & Rips, L. J. Memory for routines. *Journal of Verbal Learning and Verbal Behavior,* 1982, *21,* 260–281.

Galtung, J., & Ruge, M. The structure of foreign news. In J. Turnstall (Ed.), *Media sociology.* London: Constable, 1970.

Gans, H. J. *Deciding what's news.* New York: Vintage Books, 1979.

Garnham, A. Mental models as representations of text. *Memory and Cognition,* 1981, *9,* 560–565.

Garrett, M. F. Levels of processing in sentence production. In B. Butterworth (Ed.), *Language production.* New York: Academic Press, 1980.

Garrett, M. F., Bever, T. G., & Fodor, J. A. The active use of grammar in speech perception. *Perception and Psychophysics,* 1966, *1,* 30–32.

Garrod, S., & Sanford, A. Interpreting anaphoric relations. *Journal of Verbal Learning and Verbal Behavior,* 1977, *16,* 77–90.

Gazdar, G. Pragmatic constraints on linguistic production. In B. Butterworth (Ed.), *Language production.* New York: Academic Press, 1980.

Gibbs, R. W. J. A critical examination of the contribution of literal meaning to understanding non-literal discourse. *Text, 2,* 1982, 9–28.

Givón, T. (Ed.). *Syntax and semantics 12: Discourse and syntax.* New York: Academic Press, 1979. (a)

Givón, T. *On understanding grammar.* New York: Academic Press, 1979. (b)

Givón, T. Deductive vs. pragmatic processing in natural language. In W. Kintsch, P. G. Polson, & J. R. Miller (Eds.), *Methods and tactics in cognitive science.* Hillsdale, N.J.: Erlbaum, 1983.

Gladwin, T. *East is a big bird.* Cambridge, Mass.: Harvard University Press, 1970.

Glanzer, M., Dorfman, D., & Kaplan, B. Short-term storage in processing text. *Journal of Verbal Learning and Verbal Behavior,* 1981, *20,* 656–670.

Glanzer, M., & Razel, M. The size of the unit in short-term storage. *Journal of Verbal Learning and verbal Behavior,* 1974, *13,* 114–131.

Glasgow University Media Group. *Bad news.* London: Routledge & Kegan Paul, 1977.

Glasgow University Media Group. *More bad news.* London: Routledge & Kegan Paul, 1980.

Glucksberg, S., Gildea, P., & Bookin, H. B. On understanding nonliteral speech: Can people ignore metaphors? *Journal of Verbal Learning and Verbal Behavior,* 1982, *21,* 85–98.

Goetz, E. T., Anderson, R. C., & Schallert, D. L. The representation of sentences in memory. *Journal of Verbal Learning and Verbal Behavior,* 1981, *20,* 369–385.

Goffman, E. *Interaction ritual.* New York: Anchor Books, 1967.

Goffman, E. *Strategic interactión.* Philadelphia: University of Pennsylvania Press, 1969.

Goffman, E. *Frame analysis.* New York: Harper & Row, 1974.

Gomulicki, B. R. Recall as an abstractive process. *Acta Psychologica,* 1956, *12,* 77–94.

Goodman, K. S. Reading: A psycholinguistic guessing game. In H. Singer and R. B. Ruddell (Eds.), *Theoretical models and processes of reading.* Newark, Del.: International Reading Association, 1976.

Graesser, A. C., *Prose comprehension beyond the word.* New York: Springer-Verlag, 1981.

Graesser, A. C., Hoffman, N. L., & Clark, L. F. Structural components of reading time. *Journal of Verbal Learning and Verbal Behavior,* 1980, *19,* 135–151.

Gregg, L. W., & Steinberg, E. R. *Cognitive processes in writing.* Hillsdale, N.J.: Erlbaum, 1980.

Greimas, A. J. *Sémantique structurale.* Paris: Larousse, 1966.

Grice, H. P. Logic and conversation. Unpublished lecture notes. Partly published in P. Cole & J. L. Morgan (Eds.), *Syntax and semantics 3: Speech acts.* New York: Academic Press, 1975.

Grimes, J. *The thread of discourse.* The Hague: Mouton, 1975.

Grober, E. H., Beardley, W., & Caramazza, A. Parallel function in pronoun assignment. *Cognition.* 1978, *6,* 117–133.

Groeben, N. *Leserpsychologie.* Münster: Aschendorff, 1982.

de Groot, A. D. Perception and memory versus thought: Some old ideas and recent findings. In B. Keinmuntz (Ed.), *Problem solving: Research, method, and theory.* New York: Wiley, 1966.

de Groot, A. D., & Frijda, N. H. *Selz and his work.* The Hague: Mouton, 1981.

Grosz, B. *The representation and use of focus in dialogue understanding* (Technical note 15). Stanford, Calif.: Stanford Research Institute, 1977.

Gülich, E., & Raible, W. *Linguistische Textmodelle.* Munich: Fink (UTB), 1977.

Gumperz, J. D., & Hymes, D. (Eds.). *Directions in sociolinguistics: The ethonography of communication.* New York: Holt, Rinehart & Winston, 1972.

Habel, C. Zur Geschichte von Referenzobjekten. Teil 1: Diskursmodelle. In P. Finke & H. Gust (Eds.), *Sprachen und Welten,* 1982.

Haberlandt, K. Story grammar and reading time of story constituents. *Poetics,* 1980, *9,* 99–118.

Haberlandt, K., Berian, C., & Sandson, J. The episode schema in story processing. *Journal of Verbal Learning and Verbal Behavior,* 1980, *19,* 635–650.

Haberlandt, K., & Bingham, G. Verbs contribute to the coherence of brief narratives. *Journal of Verbal Learning and Verbal Behavior,* 1978, *17,* 419–425.

Hakes, D. T., & Foss, D. J. Decision processes during sentence comprehension: Effects of surface structure reconsidered. *Perception and Psychophysics,* 1970, *8,* 413–416.

Halliday, M. A. K. Categories of the theory of grammar. *Word,* 1961, *17,* 241–292.

Halliday, M. A. K., & Hasan, R. *Cohesion in English*. London: Longman, 1976.

Hamilton, W. *Lectures on metaphysics and logic* (Vol. 1). Boston: Gould & Lincoln, 1859.

Harris, Z. S. Discourse analysis. *Language, 1952, 28,* 1–30.

Hartley, J., & Davies, I. K. Preinstructional strategies: The role of pretests, behavioral objectives, overviews and advanced organizers. *Review of Educational Research, 1976, 46,* 239–265.

Hartmann, P. Text, Texte, Klassen von Texten. *Bogawus, 1964, 2,* 15–25.

Hartmann, P. Textlinguistik als linguistische Aufgabe. In S. Schmidt (Ed.), *Konkrete Dichtung. Konkrete Kunst*. Karlsruhe: Privatdruck, 1968.

Harweg, R. *Pronomina und Textkonstitution*. Munich: Fink, 1968.

Haviland, S. E., & Clark, H. H. What's new? Acquiring new information as a process in comprehension. *Journal of Verbal Learning and Verbal Behavior, 1974, 13,* 512–521.

Hayes, J. R., & Flower, L. S. Identifying the organization of writing processes. In L. W. Gregg & E. R. Steinberg (Eds.), *Cognitive process in writing*. Hillsdale, N.J.: Erlbaum, 1980.

Hayes-Roth, F. The role of partial and best matches in knowledge systems. In D.A. Waterman & F. Hayes-Roth (Eds.), *Pattern directed inference systems*. New York: Academic Press, 1978.

Hayes-Roth, F., Waterman, D. A., & Lenat, D. Principles of pattern-directed inference systems. In D. A. Waterman & F. Hayes-Roth (Eds.), *Pattern directed inference systems*. New York: Academic Press, 1978.

Hidi, S., Baird, W., & Hildyard, A. That's important but is it interesting? Two factors in text processing. In A. Flammer & W. Kintsch (Eds.), *Text processing*. Amsterdam: North-Holland, 1982.

Hinds, J. Organizational patterns in discourse. In T. Givón (Ed.), *Syntax and semantics 12: Discourse and syntax*. New York: Academic Press, 1979.

Hintikka, K. J. J., Moravcsik, J. M. E., & Suppes, P. (Eds.). *Approaches to natural language*. Dordrecht: Reidel, 1973.

Hirsch, E. D., Jr. *The philosophy of composition*. Chicago: University of Chicago Press, 1977.

Hirst, W., & Brill, G. A. Contextual aspects of pronoun assignment. *Journal of Verbal Learning and Verbal Behavior, 1980, 19,* 169–175.

Höffding, H. *Outlines of psychology*. London: Macmillan, 1891.

Hogan, R. M., & Kintsch, W. Differential effects of study and text trials on long-term recognition and recall. *Journal of Verbal Learning and Verbal Behavior, 1971, 10,* 562–567.

Holland, V. M., & Redish, J. C. Strategies for understanding forms and other public documents. In D. Tannen (Ed.), *Analyzing discourse: Speech and talk*. Washington, D.C.: Georgetown University Press, 1982.

Hörmann, H. *Meinen und Verstehen*. Frankfurt: Suhrkamp, 1976. (English translation: *To Mean—to Understand*. Berlin: Springer, 1981.)

Huey, E. B. *The psychology and pedagogy of reading*. New York: Macmillan, 1908.

Huggins, A. W. F., & Adams, M. J. Syntactic aspects of reading comprehension. In R. J. Spiro, B. C. Bruce, & W. F. Brewer (Eds.), *Theoretical issues in reading comprehension*. Hillsdale, N.J.: Erlbaum, 1980.

Hunter, I. M. L. An exceptional talent for calculative thinking. *British Journal of Psychology, 1962, 53,* 243–258.

Hutchins, E. *Culture and inference*. Cambridge, Mass.: Harvard University Press, 1980.

Huttenlocker, J., & Burke, D. Why does memory span increase with age? *Journal of Verbal Learning and Verbal Behavior, 1976, 8,* 1–31.

Ihwe, J. *Linguistik in der Literaturwissenschaft* (2 vols.). Munich: Bayerischer Schulbuch Verlag, 1972.

Jackendoff, R. S. *Semantic interpretation in generative grammar*. Cambridge, Mass.: MIT Press, 1972.

Jacoby, L. L. The role of mental contiguity in memory: Registration and retrieval effects. *Journal of Verbal Learning and Verbal Behavior, 1974, 13,* 483–496.

James, W. *The principles of psychology*. New York: Dover Books, 1950 (Originally published, 1890.)

Jarvella, R. J. Syntactic processing of connected speech. *Journal of Verbal Learning and Verbal Behavior, 1971, 10,* 409–416.

Jarvella, R. J. Immediate memory and discourse processing. In G. H. Bower (Ed.), *The psychology of learning and motivation* (Vol. 13). New York: Academic Press, 1979.

Jarvella, R. J., & Klein, W. (Eds.). *Speech, place and action*. Chichester: Wiley, 1982.

Jefferson, G. Sequential aspects of story telling in conversation. In J. Schenkein (Ed.), *Studies in the organization of conversational interaction*. New York: Academic Press, 1978.

Johnson, N. F. The psychological reality of phrase structure rules. *Journal of Verbal Learning and Verbal Behavior*, 1965, *4*, 469–475.

Johnson, N. J., & Mandler, J. M. A tale of two structures: Underlying and surface form in stories. *Poetics*, 1980, *9*, 51–86.

Johnson-Laird, P. N. Mental models in cognitive science. *Cognitive Science*, 1980, *4*, 72–115.

Johnson-Laird, P. N., & Garnham, A. Descriptions and discourse models. *Linguistics and Philosophy*, 1980, *3*, 371–393.

Jones, L. K. *Theme in English expository discourse*. Lake Bluff, Ill.: Jupiter Press, 1977.

Joshi, A. K. Some extensions of a system for inference on partial information. In D. A. Waterman & F. Hayes-Roth (Eds.), *Pattern directed inference systems*. New York: Academic Press, 1978.

Just, M. A., & Carpenter, P. A. A theory of reading: From eye fixations to comprehension. *Psychological Review*, 1980, *4*, 329–354.

Kamp, H. A theory of truth and semantic representation. In J. A. G. Groenendijk, T. M. V. Janssen, & M. B. J. Stockhof (Eds.), *Formal methods in the study of language*. Amsterdam: Mathematical Centre Tracts, 1981.

Kaplan, R. M. Augmented transition networks as psychological models of sentence comprehension. *Artificial Intelligence*, 1972, *3*, 77–100.

Karmiloff-Smith, A. The grammatical marking of thematic structure in the development of language production. In W. Deutsch (Ed.), *The child's construction of language*. London: Academic Press, 1981.

Karttunen, L. Discourse referents. In J. D. McCawley (Ed.), *Syntax and semantics* (Vol. 7). New York: Academic Press, 1976.

Katz, J. J. *Semantic theory*. New York: Harper & Row, 1972.

Katz, J. J., & Fodor, J. A. The structure of semantic theory. *Language*, 1963, *39*, 170–210.

Keenan, E. L. (Ed.), *Formal semantics of natural language*. London: Cambridge University Press, 1975.

Keenan, J. M., & Kintsch, W. The identification of explicitly and implicitly presented information. In W. Kintsch (Ed.), *The representation of meaning in memory*. Hillsdale, N.J.: Erlbaum, 1974.

Keenan, J. M., MacWhinney, B., & Mayhew, D. Pragmatics in memory: A study of natural conversation. *Journal of Verbal Learning and Verbal Behavior*, 1977, *16*, 549–560.

Keil, F. C. *Semantic and conceptual development*. Cambridge, Mass.: Harvard University Press, 1979.

Kendon, A. (Ed.). *Interaction and gesture*. The Hague: Mouton, 1981.

Kendon, A., Harris, R. M., & Key, M. R. (Eds.). *Organization of behavior in face-to-face interaction*. The Hague: Mouton, 1975.

Kieras, D. E. Good and bad structure in simple paragraphs: Effects on apparent theme, reading time and recall. *Journal of Verbal Learning and Verbal Behavior*, 1978, *17*, 13–28.

Kieras, D. E. *Abstracting main ideas from technical prose: A preliminary study of six passages*. Technical Report, University of Arizona, Department of Psychiatry, 1980. (a)

Kieras, D. E. Knowledge representation in cognitive psychology. In L. Cobb & R. M. Thrall; *Mathematical frontiers of the social and policy sciences*. Boulder, Colo.: Westview Press, 1980. (b)

Kieras, D. E. Initial mention as a signal to thematic content in technical passages. *Memory and Cognition*, 1980, *8*, 345–353. (c)

Kieras, D. E. Component processes in the comprehension of simple prose. *Journal of Verbal Learning and Verbal Behavior*, 1981, *20*, 1–20. (a)

Kieras, D. E. Topicalization effects in cued recall of technical prose. *Memory and Cognition*, 1981, *9*, 541–549. (b)

Kieras, D. E. The role of major referents and sentence topic in the construction of passage macrostructure. *Discourse Process*, 1981, *4*, 1–15. (c)

Kieras, D. E., & Bovair, S. *Strategies for abstracting main idea from simple technical prose* (Technical Report No. 10). University of Arizona, 1981.

Kimball, J. P. Seven principles of surface structure parsing in natural language. *Cognition*, 1973, *2*, 15–47.

Kintsch, W. Models for free recall and recognition. In D. Norman (Ed.), *Models of human memory*. New York: Academic Press, 1970.

Kintsch, W. Notes on the structure of semantic memory. In E. Tulving & W. Donaldson (Eds.), *Organization of memory*. New York: Academic Press, 1972.

Kintsch, W. *The representation of meaning in memory*. Hillsdale, N.J.: Erlbaum, 1974.

Kintsch, W. *Memory and cognition*. New York: Wiley, 1977. (a)

Kintsch, W. On comprehending stories. In M. A. Just & P. Carpenter (Eds.), *Cognitive processes in comprehension*. Hillsdale, N.J.: Erlbaum, 1977. (b)

Kintsch, W. Learning from texts, levels of comprehension, or: why anyone would read a story anyway. *Poetics*, 1980, *9*, 87–98. (a)

Kintsch, W. Semantic memory: A tutorial. In R. S. Nickerson (Ed.), *Attention and performance, 8*. Hillsdale, N.J.: Erlbaum, 1980. (b)

Kintsch, W. Psychological processes in discourse production. In H. W. Dechert & M. Raupach (Ed.), *Psycholinguistic models of production*. Hillsdale, N.J.: Erlbaum, 1982. (a)

Kintsch, W. Memory for text. In A. Flammer & W. Kintsch (Eds.), *Text processing*. Amsterdam: North-Holland, 1982. (b)

Kintsch, W. Approaches to the study of the psychology of language. In T. Bever, J. M. Carroll & L. A. Miller (Eds.), *Talking minds*. Cambridge, Mass.: MIT Press, 1982. (c)

Kintsch, W., & Bates, E. Recognition memory for statements from a classroom lecture. *Journal of Experimental Psychology: Human Learning and Memory*, 1977, *3*, 150–159.

Kintsch, W., & van Dijk, T. A. Comment on se rapelle et on resúme des histoires. *Languages*, 1975, *40*, 98–116.

Kintsch, W., & van Dijk, T. A. Toward a model of text comprehension and production. *Psychological Review*, 1978, *85*, 363–394.

Kintsch, W., & Greene, E. The role of culture-specific schemata in the comprehension and recall of stories. *Discourse Processes*, 1978, *1*, 1–13.

Kintsch, W., & Greeno, J. G. *Understanding and solving word arithmetic problems*. Technical Report, University of Colorado, Department of Psychology, 1982.

Kintsch, W., & Keenan, J. M. Reading rate and retention as a function of the number of the propositions in the base structure of sentences. *Cognitive Psychology*, 1973, *5*, 257–274.

Kintsch, W., & Kozminsky, E. Summarizing stories after reading and listening. *Journal of Educational Psychology*, 1977, *69*, 491–499.

Kintsch, W., Kozminsky, E., Streby, W. J., McKoon, F., & Keenan, J. M. Comprehension and recall of text as a function of content variables. *Journal of Verbal Learning and Verbal Behavior*, 1975, *14*, 196–214.

Kintsch, W., Mandel, T. S., & Kozminsky, E. Summarizing scrambled stories. *Memory and Cognition*, 1977, *5*, 547–552.

Kintsch, W., & Vipond, D. Reading comprehension and readability in educational practice and psychological theory. In L. G. Nilsson (Ed.), *Perspectives on memory research*. Hillsdale, N.J.: Erlbaum, 1979.

Kintsch, W., & Yarbrough, J. C. The role of rhetorical structure in text comprehension. *Journal of Educational Psychology*, 1982, *74*, 828–834.

Kirshenblatt-Gimblett, B. The concept and varieties of narrative performance in East European Jewish Culture. In Bauman & Sherzer (Eds.), *Explorations in the ethnography of speaking*. London: Cambridge University Press, 1974.

Klahr, D. A production system for counting, subitizing and adding. In W. G. Chase (Ed.), *Visual information processing*. New York: Academic Press, 1973.

Kneale, W., & Kneale, M. *The development of logic*. London: Oxford University Press, 1962.

Kolers, P. A. Pattern analyzing disability in poor readers. *Developmental Psychology*, 1975, *11*, 282–290.

Kolodner, J. L. *Retrieval and organizational strategies in conceptual memory: A computer model* (Technical Report 187). Department of Cognitive Science, Yale University, 1980.

Kozminsky, E. Altering comprehension: The effect of biasing titles on text comprehension. *Memory and Cognition*, 1977, *5*, 482–490.

Kozminsky, E., Kintsch, W., & Bourne, L. E., Jr. Decision making with texts: Information analysis and schema acquisition. *Journal of Experimental Psychology: General*, 1981, *110*, 363–380.

Labov, W. *Language in the inner city*. Philadelphia: University of Pennsylvania Press, 1972. (a)

Labov, W. *Sociolinguistic patterns*. Philadelphia: University of Pennsylvania Press, 1972. (b)

Labov, W., & Waletzky, Y. Narrative analysis: Oral versions of personal experience. In J. Helm (Ed.), *Essays on the verbal and visual arts*. Seattle: Washington University Press, 1967.

Lakoff, G. Linguistics and natural logic. *Synthesis*, 1970, *22*, 151–271.

Lakoff, G., & Johnson, M. *Metaphors we live by*. Chicago: University of Chicago Press, 1980.

Langacker, R. W. On pronominalization and the chain of command. In D. A. Reibel & S. A. Schane (Eds.), *Modern studies in English*. Englewood Cliffs, N.J.: Prentice-Hall, 1969.

Larsen, S. F. Memory for radio news. In A. Flammer & W. Kintsch (Eds.), *Text processing*. Amsterdam: North-Holland, 1982.

Lausberg, H. *Handbuch der literarischen Rhetorik*. Munich: Hueber, 1960.

Lee, W. *Decision theory and human behavior*. New York: Wiley, 1971.

Leech, G. N. *English in advertising*. London: Longman, 1966.

Lehnert, W. G. *Affect units and narrative summarization* (Technical Report No. 179). Yale University, Department of Computer Science, 1980. (a)

Lehnert, W. G. *The process of question answering*. Hillsdale, N.J.: Erlbaum, 1980. (b)

Lenat, D. B. *The nature of heuristics*. Technical Report, Xerox Palo Alto Research Center, April 1981.

Lesgold, A. M. Pronominalizations: A device for unifying sentences in memory. *Journal of Verbal Learning and Verbal Behavior*, 1972, *11*, 316–323.

Lesgold, A. M. Variability in children's comprehension of syntactic structures. *Journal of Educational Psychology*, 1974, *66*, 333–338.

Levelt, W. J. M. Linearization in describing spatial networks. In S. Peters & E. Saarinen (Eds.), *Processes, beliefs and questions*. Amsterdam: Reidel, 1982.

Levelt, W. J. M., & Kelter, S. Surface form and memory in question answering. *Cognitive Psychology*, 1982, *14*, 78–106.

Levin, J. R. Pictures as prose learning devices. In A. Flammer & W. Kintsch (Eds.), *Text processing*. Amsterdam: North-Holland, 1982.

Lévi-Strauss, C. L'analyse morphologique des contes russes. *International Journal of Slavic Linguistics and Poetics*, 1960, *3*, 122–149.

Lévi-Strauss, C. *Structural anthropology*. (Translated from the French.) New York: Basic Books, 1963.

Lewis, D. *Convention*. Cambridge, Mass.: MIT Press, 1969.

Li, C. N. (Ed.). *Subject and topic*. New York: Academic Press, 1976.

Linde, C., & Labov, W. Spatial networks as a site for the study of language and thought. *Language*, 1975, *51*, 924–939.

Linsky, L. *Referring*. London: Routledge & Kegan Paul, 1967.

Loftus, E. *Eyewitness testimony*. Cambridge, Mass.: Harvard University Press, 1979.

Longacre, R. E. (Ed.). *Discourse grammar*. Dallas, Tex: Summer Institute of Linguistics, 1976.

Longacre, R. E. The paragraph as a grammatical unit. In T. Givón (Ed.), *Syntax and semantics 12: Discourse and syntax*. New York: Academic Press, 1979.

Lyons, J. *Semantics* (2 vols.). London: Cambridge University Press, 1977.

Lyons, J. *Language, meaning and context*. London: Fontana, 1981.

MacKay, D. G. To end ambiguous sentences. *Perception and Psychophysics*, 1966, *1*, 426–436.

Mandel, T. S. Eye movement research on the propositional structure of short texts. *Behavior Research Methods and Instrumentation*, 1979, *11*, 180–187.

Mandler, G. Organization and Memory In K. W. Spence & J. A. Spence (Eds.), *The psychology of learning and motivation* (Vol. 1). New York: Academic Press, 1967.

Mandler, G. The construction and limitation of consciousness. In V. Sarris & A. Parducci (Eds.), *Perspectives in psychological experimentation*. Hillsdale, N.M.: Erlbaum, in press.

Mandler, J. M. A code in the node: The use of a story schema in retrieval. *Discourse Processes*, 1978, *1*, 14–35.

Mandler, J. M., & Johnson, N.S. Rememberance of things parsed: Story structure and recall. *Cognitive Psychology*, 1977, *9*, 111–191.

Mandler, J. M., & Johnson, N. S. On throwing out the baby with the bathwater: A reply to Black and Wilensky's evaluation of story grammar. *Cognitive Science*, 1980, *4*, 305–312.

Manelis, L. Determinants of processing for a propositional structure. *Memory and Cognition*, 1980, *8*, 49–57.

Manelis, L., & Yekovich, F. R. Repetition of propositional arguments in sentences. *Journal of Verbal Learning and Verbal Behavior*, 1976, *15*, 301–312.

Marslen-Wilson, W., Levy, E., & Tyler, L. K. Producing interpretable discourse: The establishment and maintenance of reference. In R. J. Jarvella & W. Klein (Eds.), *Speech, place and action*. Chichester: Wiley, 1982.

Marslen-Wilson, W., & Tyler, L. K. The temporal structure of spoken language understanding. *Cognition*, 1980, *8*, 1–71.

Marslen-Wilson, W. D., Tyler, L., & Seidenberg, M. Sentence processing and the clause-boundary. In W. J. M. Levelt & G. Flores d'Arcais (Eds.); *Studies in the perception of language*. London: Wiley, 1978.

Masson, M. E. J. Cognitive processes in skimming stories. *Journal of Experimental Psychology, Learning, Memory, and Cognition*, 1982, *8*, 400–417.

Mayer, R. E. Elaboration techniques that increase the meaningfulness of technical text: An experimental test of the learning strategy hypothesis. *Journal of Educational Psychology*, 1980, *72*, 770–784.

McClelland, J. L. On the time relations of mental processes: An examination of systems of processes in cascade. *Psycholgical Review*, 1979, *86*, 287–330.

McClelland, J. L., & Rumelhart, D. E. An interactive activation model of context effects in letter perception: Part I. An account of basic findings. *Psychological Review*, 1981, *88*, 375–407.

McConkie, G. W., & Zola, D. Is visual information integrated across recessive fixations in reading? *Perception and Psychophysics*, 1979, *25*, 221–224.

McConkie, G. W., & Zola, D. Language constraints and the functional stimulus in reading. In C. A. Perfetti & A. M. Lesgold (Eds.), *Interactive processes in reading*. Hillsdale, N.J.: Erlbaum, 1981.

McDermott, J., Newell, A., & Moore, J. The efficiency of certain production system implementations. In D. A. Waterman & F. Hays-Roth (Eds.), *Pattern directed inference systems*. New York: Academic Press, 1978.

McKoon, G., & Keenan, J. Response latencies to explicit and implicit statements as a function of the delay between reading and test. In W. Kintsch (Ed.), *The representation of meaning in memory*. Hillsdale, N.J.: Erlbaum, 1974.

McKoon, G., & Ratcliff, R. Priming written recognition: The organization of propositions in memory for text. *Journal of Verbal Learning and Verbal Behavior*, 1980, *19*, 369–386. (a)

McKoon, G., & Ratcliff, R. The comprehension process and memory structures involved in anaphoric reference. *Journal of Verbal Learning and Verbal Behavior*, 1980, *19*, 668–682. (b)

Mehler, J., & Carey, P. The role of surface and base structure in the perception of sentences. *Journal of Verbal Learning and Verbal Behavior*, 1967, *6*, 335–338.

Metcalf, J., & Murdock, B. B., Jr. An encoding and retrieval model of single-trial free recall. *Journal of Verbal Learning and Verbal Behavior*, 1981, *20*, 161–169.

Meyer, B. J. F. *The organization of prose and its effects on memory*. Amsterdam: North-Holland, 1975.

Meyer, B. J. F. What is remembered from prose: A function of passage structure. In R. D. Freedle (Ed.), *Discourse production and comprehension: Advances in research and theory* (Vol. 1). Norwood, N.J.: Ablex, 1977.

Meyer, B. J. F. *A selected review and discussion of basic research on prose comprehension*. Technical Report, Department of Educational Psychology, University of Arizona, 1979.

Meyer, B. J. F. Brandt, D. M., & Bluth, G. J. Use of top-level structure in text: Key for reading comprehension in ninth-grade students. *Reading Research Quarterly*, 1980, *16*, 72–103.

Meyer, B. J. F., & Freedle, R. O. The effects of different discourse types on recall. *American Educational Research Journal*, in press.

Miller, G. A. The magical number seven, plus or minus two: Some limits on our capacity for processing information. *Psychological Review*, 1956, *63*, 81–97.

Miller, G. A. Images and models, similes and metaphors. In A. Ortony (Ed.), *Metaphor and thought*. Cambridge: Cambridge University Press, 1979.

Miller, G. A., Galanter, E.,& Pribram, K. H. *Plans and the structure of behavior*. New York: Holt, Rinehart & Winston, 1960.

Miller, G. A., & Johnson-Laird, P. N. *Language and perception*. Cambridge, Mass.: Harvard University Press, 1976.

Miller, G. A., & McKean, K. O. A chronometric study of some relations between sentences. *Quarterly Journal of Experimental Psychology*, 1964, 267–308.

Miller, J. R., & Kintsch, W. Readability and recall of short prose passages: A theoretical analysis. *Journal of Experimental Psychology: Human Learning and Memory*, 1980, *6*, 335–354.

Minsky, M. A framework for representing knowledge. In P. Winston (Ed.), *The psychology of computer vision*. New York: McGraw-Hill, 1975.

Montague, R. *Formal philosophy*. Cambridge, Mass.: Harvard University Press, 1974.

Moore, P. G., & Thomas, H. *The anatomy of decisions*. Harmondsworth: Penguin Books, 1976.

Morton, J. Interaction of information in word recognition. *Psychological Review*, 1969, *76*, 165–178.

Müller, G. E. Zur Analyse der Gedächtnistätigkeit und des Vorstellungsverlaufes. *Zeitschrift für Psychologie*. Ergänzungsband V, 1911.

Nash-Webber, B. L. Description formation and discourse model synthesis. In D. Waltz (Ed.), *Theoretical issues in natural language processing* (Vol. 2). Urbana-Champaign, 1978. (b)

Nash-Webber, B. L., & Reiter, R. *Anaphora and logical form* (Technical Report No. 36). Urbana-Champaign: Center for the Study of Reading, 1977.

Nash-Webber, B. L. *Inference in an approach to discourse anaphora* (Technical Report No. 77). Urbana-Champaign: Center for the Study of Reading, 1978. (a)

Newell, A. A theoretical exploration of mechanisms for coding the stimulus. In A. W. Melton & E. Martin (Eds.), *Coding processes in human memory*. Washington, D.C.: Winston, 1972.

Newell, A. Production systems: Models of control structures. In W. G. Chase (Ed.), *Visual information processing*. New York: Academic Press, 1973.

Newell, A., & Simon, H. A. *Human problem solving*. Englewood Cliffs, N.J.: Prentice-Hall, 1972.

Norman, D. A., & Rumelhart, D. E. *Explorations in cognition*. San Francisco: Freeman, 1975.

Ogden, C. K., & Richards, I. A. *The meaning of meaning*. London: Routledge & Kegan Paul, 1923.

Olson, G. M., Duffy, S. A., & Mack, R. L. Applying knowledge of writing conventions to prose comprehension and composition. In W. J. McKeachie (Ed.), *Learning cognition, and college teaching*. San Francisco: Jossey-Bass, 1980.

Olson, G. M., Mack, R. L., & Duffy, S. A. Cognitive aspects of genre. *Poetics*, 1981, *9*, 283–315.

Ortony, A. Beyond literal similarity. *Psychological Review*, 1979, 86, 161–180.

Ortony, A., Schallert, D. L., Reynolds, R. B., & Antos, S. J. Interpreting metaphors and idioms: Some effects of context on comprehension. *Journal of Verbal Learning and Verbal Behavior*, 1978, *17*, 465–477.

Otto, W., & White, S. (Eds.). *Reading expository material*. New York: Academic Press, 1982.

Partee, B. H. Bound variables and other anaphors. In D. Waltz (Ed.), *Theoretical issues in natural language processing*. Urbana-Champaign: Center for the Study of Reading, 1978.

Paul, I. Studies in remembering: The reproduction of connected and extended verbal material. *Psychological Issues*, 1959, *2*, I.

Perfetti, C. A., & Goldman, S. R. Thematization of sentence retrieval. *Journal of Verbal Learning and Verbal Behavior*, 1974, *13*, 70–79.

Perfetti, C. A., Goldman, S. R., & Hogaboam, T. W. Reading skill and the identification of words in discourse context. *Memory and Cognition*, 1979, *7*, 273–282.

Perfetti, C. A., & Lesgold, A. M. Discourse comprehension and sources of individual differences. In M. Just & P. Carpenter (Eds.), *Cognitive processes in comprehension*. Hillsdale, N.J.: Erlbaum, 1977.

Perfetti, C. A., & Roth, S. Some of the interactive processes in reading and their role in reading skill. In A. Lesgold & C. Perfetti (Eds.), *Interactive processes in reading*. Hillsdale, N.J.: Erlbaum, 1981.

Petöfi, J. S. *Transformationsgrammatiken und eine ko-textuelle Texttheorie*. Frankfurt: Athenaeum, 1971.

Petöfi, J. S. Representation language and their function in text interpretation. In S. Allen (Ed.), *Text processing*. Stockholm: Almquist & Wiksell, 1982.

Pickering, J. H. *Fiction 100: An anthology of short stories* (2nd ed.). New York: Macmillan, 1978.

Pike, K. L. *Language in relation to a unified theory of human behavior*. The Hague: Mouton, 1967.

Pompi, K. F., & Lachman, R. Surrogate processes in the short-term retention of connected discourse. *Journal of Experimental Psychology*, 1967, *75*, 143–150.

Posner, M. I., & Snyder, C. R. R. Attention and cognitive control. In R. Solso (Ed.), *Information processing and cognition: The Loyola Symposium*. Hillsdale, N.J.: Erlbaum, 1975.

Potts, G.R. Information processing strategies used in encoding linear orderings. *Journal of Verbal Learning and Verbal Behavior*, 1972, 11, 727–740.

Poulson, D., Kintsch, E., Kintsch, W., & Premack, D. Children's comprehension and memory for stories. *Journal of Experimental Child Psychology*, 1979, *28*, 379–403.

Prior, A. N. *Objects of thought*. London: Oxford University Press, 1971.

Propp, V. *Morphology of the folktale* (2nd ed.). Austin: University of Texas Press, 1968. (Originally published in Russian, 1928.)

Psathas, G. (Ed.). *Everyday language: Studies in ethnomethodology*. New York: Irvington, 1979.

Purkiss, E. *The effect of foregrounding on pronominal reference*. Unpublished undergraduate thesis, University of Glasgow, 1978. (Cited in A. J. Sanford & S. C. Garrod, 1981.)

Pylyshyn, Z. W. What the mind's eye tells the mind's brain: A critique of mental imagery. *Psychological Bulletin*, 1973, *80*, 1–23.

Quasthoff, U. M. *Erzählen in Gesprächen*. Tübingen: Narr, 1980.

Quillian, M. R. Semantic memory. In M. Minsky (Ed.), *Semantic information processing*. Cambridge, Mass.: MIT Press, 1968.

Quine, W. V. O. *From a logical point of view*. New York: Harper & Row, 1953.

Quine, W. V. O. *Word and object*. Cambridge, Mass.: MIT Press, 1960.

Quine, W. V. O. *The roots of reference*. La Salle, Ill: Open Court, 1974.

Raaijmakers, J. G. W. *Retrieval from long term store: A general theory and mathematical models*. Nijmegen: Stichting Studentenpers, 1979.

Raaijmakers, J. G. W., & Shiffrin, R. M. Search of associative memory. *Psychological Review*, 1981, *88*, 93–134.

Radtke, I. (Ed.). *Die Sprache des Rechts und der Verwaltung* (Volume 2 of *Der öffentliche Sprachgebrauch*). Stuttgart: Klett, 1981.

Ratcliff, R., & McKoon, G. Priming in item recognition: Evidence for the propositional structure of sentences. *Journal of Verbal Learning and Verbal Behavior*, 1978, *17*, 403–418.

Ratcliff, R., & McKoon, G. Automatic and strategic components of priming in recognition. *Journal of Verbal Learning and Verbal Behavior*, 1981, *20*, 204–215.

Reder, L.M. The role of elaborations in memory for prose. *Cognitive Psychology*, 1979, *11*, 221–234.

Reder, L. M. Plausibility judgements versus fact retrieval: Alternative strategies for sentence verification. *Psychological Review*, 1982, *89*, 250–280. (a)

Reder, L. M. Elaborations: When do they help and when do they hurt? *Text*, 1982, *2*, 211–224. (b)

Reder, L. M., & Anderson, J. R. A comparison of texts and their summaries: Memorial consequences. *Journal of Verbal Learning and Verbal Behavior*, 1980, *19*, 121–134.

Reder, L. M., & Anderson, J. R. Effects of spacing and embellishment on memory for the main points of a text. *Memory and Cognition*, 1982, *10*, 97–102.

Reibel, D. A., & Schane, S. A. (Eds.). *Modern studies in English*. Englewood Cliffs, N.J.: Prentice-Hall, 1969.

Reichenbach, H. *Elements of symbolic logic.* New York: Free Press, 1947.

Reicher, G. M. Perceptual recognition as a function of meaningfulness of stimulus material. *Journal of Experimental Psychology,* 1969, *8,* 225–280.

Reichman, R. *Plain speaking: A theory and grammar of spontaneous discourse.* Technical Report, Bolt, Beranek & Newman, Inc., 1981.

Rescher, N. *Plausible reasoning.* Assen, Netherlands: Van Gorcum, 1976.

Reiger, C. Spontaneous computation in cognitive models. *Cognitive Science,* 1977, *1,* 315–354.

Riesbeck, C. An expectation-driven production system for natural language. In D. A. Waterman & F. Hayes-Roth (Eds.), *Pattern directed inference systems.* New York: Academic Press, 1978.

Riley, M. S., Greeno, J. G., & Heller, J. L. Development of children's problem solving ability in arithmetic. In H. P. Ginsburg (Ed.), *The development of mathematical thinking.* New York: Academic Press, 1982.

Rosenberg, S. *Sentence production.* New York: Wiley, 1977.

Rothkopf, E. Z. The concept of mathemagenic activities. *Review of Educational Research,* 1970, *40,* 325–336.

Rothkopf, E. Z. Structural text features and the control of processes in learning from written material. In J. Carroll & R. O. Freedle (Eds.), *Language comprehension and the acquisition of knowledge.* Washington, D.C.: 1972.

Rubin, A. D. A theoretical taxonomy of the differences between oral and written language. In R. J. Spiro, B. C. Bruce, & W. F. Brewer (Eds.), *Theoretical issues in reading comprehension.* Hillsdale, N.J.: Erlbaum, 1980.

Rumelhart, D. E. Notes on a schema for stories. In D. G. Bobrow & A. Collins (Eds.), *Representation and understanding.* New York: Academic Press, 1975.

Rumelhart, D. E. Understanding and summarizing brief stories. In D. Laberge & S. J. Samuels (Eds.), *Basic processes in reading: Perceptions and comprehensions.* Hillsdale, N.J.: Erlbaum, 1977.

Rumelhart, D. E. On evaluating story grammars. *Cognitive Science,* 1980, *4,* 313–316.

Rumelhart, D. E., & Ortony, A. Representation of knowledge. In R. C. Anderson, R. J. Spiro, & W. E. Montague (Eds.), *Schooling and the acquisition of knowledge.* Hillsdale, N.J.: Erlbaum, 1977.

Russell, B. *An inquiry into meaning and truths.* New York: Norton, 1940.

Sacks, H., Schegloff, E. A., & Jefferson, G. A simplest systematics for the organization of turntaking for conservation. *Language,* 1974, *50,* 696–735.

Sanches, M., & Blount, B. G. (Eds.). *Sociocultural dimensions of language use.* New York: Academic Press, 1975.

Sandell, R. *Linguistic style and persuasion.* London: Academic Press, 1977.

Sanford, A. J., & Garrod, S. C. *Understanding written language.* New York: Wiley, 1981.

Schallert, D. L. Improving memory for prose: The relationship between depth of processing and context. *Journal of Verbal Learning and Verbal Behavior,* 1976, *15,* 621–632.

Schank, R. C. Conceptual dependency: A theory of natural language understanding. *Cognitive Psychology,* 1972, *3,* 552–631.

Schank, R. C. The structure of episodes in memory. In D. G. Bobrow & A. Collins (Eds.), *Representation and understanding.* New York: Academic Press, 1975.

Schank, R. C. Interestingness: Controlling inferences. *Artificial Intelligence,* 1979, *12,* 273–297. (a)

Schank, R. C. *Reminding and memory organization: An introduction to MOPs* (Technical Report 170). Department of Computer Science, Yale University, 1979. (b)

Schank, R. C., & Abelson, R. P. *Scripts, plans, goals and understanding.* Hillsdale, N.J.: Erlbaum, 1977.

Schank, R. C., & Colby, K. (Eds.). *Computer models of thought.* San Francisco: Freeman, 1973.

Schank, R. C., Goldman, N., Rieger, C., & Riesbeck, J. C. *Conceptual information processing.* Amsterdam: North-Holland, 1975.

Schank, R. C., & Lehnert, W. G. *The conceptual content of conversation.* Technical report #160, Department of Computer Science, Yale University, 1979.

Schank, R. C., Wilensky, R., Carbonell, J. G., Kolodner, J. L., & Hendler, J. A. Representing attitudes: Some primitive states (Technical Report No. 128). Department of Computer Science, Yale University, 1978.

Schegloff, E. The relevance of repair to syntax-for-conversation. In T. Givón (Ed.), *Syntax and semantics 12: Discourse and syntax*. New York: Academic Press, 1979.

Schenkein, J. (Ed.). *Studies in the organization of conversational interaction*. New York: Academic Press, 1978.

Scherer, K. M., & Ekman, P. (Eds.). *Handbook of methods in nonverbal behaviour research*. Cambridge: Cambridge University Press, 1982.

Scherer, K. M., & Giles, H. (Eds.). *Social markers in speech*. London: Cambridge University Press, 1979.

Schmidt, S. J. *Texttheorie*. Munich: Fink, 1973.

Schnotz, W., Ballstaedt, S., & Mandl, H. Kognitive Prozesse beim Zusammenfassen von Lehrtexten. In H. Mandl (Ed.), *Zur Psychologie der Textverarbeitung*. Munich: Urban & Schwarzenberg, 1981.

Schwarz, M. N. K., & Flammer, A. Text structure and title–effects on comprehension and recall. *Journal of Verbal Learning and Verbal Behavior*, 1981, *20*, 61–66.

Schwartz, S. P. *The search for pronominal referents*. Unpublished paper, Yale University Cognitive Science Program, 1981.

Selfridge, O. G., & Neisser, U. Pattern recognition by machine. *Scientific American*, 1960, *203*, 60–80.

Selz, O. *Über die Gesetze des geordneten Denkverlaufs*. Stuttgart: Spemann, 1913.

Shiffrin, R. M., & Geisler, W. S. Visual recognition in a theory of information processing. In R. L. Solso (Ed.), *Contemporary issues in cognitive psychology*. Washington, D.C.: Winston, 1973.

Shiffrin, R. M., & Schneider, W. Controlled and automatic human information processing: II. Perceptual learning, automatic attending and a general theory. *Psychological Review*, 1977, *84*, 127–190.

Simmons, R. F. Some semantic structures for representing English meanings. In J. B. Carroll & R. O. Freedle, *Language comprehension and the acquisition of knowledge*. Washington, D.C.: 1972.

Simmons, R. F. Rule-based computations on English. In D. A. Waterman & F. Hayes-Roth (Eds.), *Pattern directed inference processes*. New York: Academic Press, 1978.

Simon, H. A. The logic of heuristic decision making. In N. Rescher (Ed.), *The logic of decision and action*. Pittsburgh: Pittsburgh University Press, 1967.

Simon, H. A. *The sciences of the artificial*. Cambridge, Mass.: MIT Press, 1969.

Simon, H. A. How big is a chunk? *Science*, 1974, *183*, 482–488.

Sinclair, J., & Coulthard, M. *Towards an analysis of discourse*. London: Oxford University Press, 1975.

Singer, M. Thematic structure and the integration of linguistic information. *Journal of Verbal Learning and Verbal Behavior*, 1976, *15*, 549–558.

Singer, M. Processes of inference during sentence encoding. *Memory and Cognition*, 1979, *7*, 192–200.

Singer, M. Verifying the assertions and implications of language. *Journal of Verbal Learning and Verbal Behavior*, 1981, *20*, 46–60.

Singer, M., & Rosenberg, S. The role of grammatical relations in the abstraction of linguistic ideas. *Journal of Verbal Learning and Verbal Behavior*, 1973, *12*, 273–284.

Slamecka, N. J. Studies of retention of connected discourse. *American Journal of Psychology*, 72, 409–416.

Smith, E. E., Adams, N., & Schorr, D. Fact retrieval and the paradox of the expert. *Cognitive Psychology*, 1978, *10*, 438–464.

Smith, E. E., & Medin, D. L. *Categories and concepts*. Cambridge, Mass.: Harvard University Press, 1981.

Smith, F. *Psycholinguistics and reading*. New York: Holt, Rinehart & Winston, 1973.

Spilich, G. J., Vesonder, G. T., Chiesi, H. L., & Voss, J. F. Text processing of domain-related information for individuals with high and low domain knowledge. *Journal of Verbal Learning and Verbal Behavior*, 1979, *18*, 275–290.

Stanovich, K. E. Toward an interactive-compensatory model of individual differences in the development of reading fluency. *Reading Research Quarterly*, 1980, *16*, 32–71.

Stanovich, K. E., & West, R. F. The effect of sentence context on ongoing word recognition: Tests of a two-process theory. *Journal of Experimental Psychology: Human Perception and Performance*, 1981, *7*, 658–672.

Steffensen, M. F., Jogdeo, C., & Anderson, R. C. The cross-cultural perspective on reading comprehension. Technical Report #97. Center for the Study of Reading, University of Illinois, 1980.

Stein, N. L., & Glenn, C. G. An analysis of story comprehension. In R. O. Freedle (Ed.), *New directions in discourse processing* (Vol. 2). Norwood, N.J.: Ablex, 1979.

Steinberg, D. D., & Jakobovits, L. A. (Eds.). *Semantics*. London: Cambridge University Press, 1971.

Stenning, K. Anaphora as an approach to pragmatics. In M. Halle, J. Bresnan, & G. A. Miller (Eds.), *Linguistic theory and psychological reality*. Cambridge, Mass.: MIT Press, 1978.

Sternberg, S. High-speed scanning in human memory. *Science*, 1966, *153*, 652–654.

Stevens, A., Collins, A., & Goldin, S. E. Misconceptions in students' understanding. *International Journal of Man–Machine Studies*, 1979, *11*, 145–156.

Stockwell, R. P., Schachter, P., & Partee, B. H. *The major syntactic structures of English*. New York: Holt, Rinehart & Winston, 1973.

Strawson, P. F. *Introduction to logical theory*. London: Methuen, 1952.

Strohner, H., & Nelson, K. E. The young child's development of sentence comprehension: Influence of event probability, nonverbal context, syntactic form and strategies. *Child Development*, 1974, *45*, 567–576.

Sudnow, D. (Ed.). *Studies in social interaction*. New York: Free Press, 1972.

Swinney, D. A. Lexical access during sentence comprehension: (Re)Consideration of context effects. *Journal of Verbal Learning and Verbal Behavior*, 1979, *18*, 645–659.

Swinney, D. A., & Cutter, A. The access and processing of idiomatic expressions. *Journal of Verbal Learning and Verbal Behavior*, 1979, *18*, 523–534.

Tabossi, P., & Johnson-Laird, P. N. Linguistic context and the planning of semantic information. *Quarterly Journal of Experimental Psychology*, 1980, *32*, 595–603.

Tannen, D. (Ed.). *Analyzing discourse: Text and talk*. Washington, D.C.: Georgetown University Press, 1982.

Tannenhaus, M. K., & Carroll, J. M. The clausal processing hierarchy and nouniness. In R. Grossman, J. San, & T. Vance (Eds.), *Papers from the parassession on functionalism*. Chicago: Chicago Linguistic Society, 1975.

Thorndyke, P. W. Cognitive structures in comprehension and memory of narrative discourse. *Cognitive Psychology*, 1977, *9*, 77–110.

Thorndyke, P. W. Pattern-directed processing of knowledge from texts. In D. A. Waterman & F. Hayes-Roth (Eds.), *Pattern directed inference systems*. New York: Academic Press, 1978.

Thorndyke, P. W. Knowledge acquisition from newspaper stories. *Discourse Processes*, 1979, *2*, 95–112.

Thorndyke, P. W., & Yekovich, F. R. A critique of schema-based theories of human memory. *Poetics*, 1980, *9*, 23–50.

Todorov, T. *Grammaire du Décameron*. The Hague/Paris: Mouton, 1968.

Toulmin, S. *The uses of argument*. London: Cambridge University Press, 1958.

Townsend, D. J., & Bever, T. G. Interclause relations and clausal processing. *Journal of Verbal Learning and Verbal Behavior*, 1978, *17*, 509–521.

Tuchman, G. *Making news: A study in the construction of reality*. New York: Free Press, 1979.

Tulving, E. Episodic and semantic memory. In E. T. Tulving & W. Donaldson (Eds.), *Organization of memory*. New York: Academic Press, 1972.

Tulving, E., & Gold C. Stimulus information as determinants of tachistoscopic recognition of words. *Journal of Experimental Psychology*, 1963, *66*, 319–327.

Tulving, E., & Thompson, D. M. Encoding specificity and retrieval processes in episodic memory. *Psychological Review*, 1973, *80*, 352–373.

Turner, A., & Greene, E. *Construction and use of a propositional text base*. JSAS Catalogue of selected documents in psychology, MS 1713, 1978.

Tyler, L. K., & Marslen-Wilson, W. The resolution of discourse anaphors: Some outline studies. *Text*, 1982, *2*, 263–291.

Vendler, Z. *Linguistics in philosophy*. Ithaca, N.Y.: Cornell University Press, 1967.

Vipond, D. Micro- and macroprocesses in text comprehension. *Journal of Verbal Learning and Verbal Behavior*, 1980, *19*, 276–296.

Walker, W. H. *Interest as a function of knowledge* (Technical Report No. 109). Institute of Cognitive Science, University of Colorado, 1981.

Walker, W. H. *Retrieval of knowledge from memory*. Unpublished Ph.D. dissertation, University of Colorado, 1982.

Wanner, E. *On remembering, forgetting and understanding sentences*. The Hague: Mouton, 1975.

Wanner, E., & Maratsos, M. An ATN approach to comprehension. In J. Bresnan & M. Halle (Eds.), *Linguistic theory and psychological reality*. Cambridge, Mass.: MIT Press, 1977.

Warren, W. H., Nicholas, D. W., & Trabasso, T. Event chains and inferences in understanding narratives. In R. O. Freedle (Ed.), *New directions in discourse processing* (Vol. 2). Norwood, N.J.: Ablex, 1979.

Waterman, D. A., & Hayes-Roth, F. (Eds.). *Pattern directed inference systems*. New York: Academic Press, 1978.

Webber, B. C. Discourse model synthesis: Preliminaries to reference. In A. K. Joshi, B. C. Webber, & I. A. Sagg, *Elements of discourse understanding*. Cambridge, England: Cambridge University Press, 1981.

Wegman, C. Conceptual representations of belief systems. *Journal for the Theory of Social Behavior*, 1981, *11*, 279–305.

Weinreich, U. *Explorations in semantic theory*. In T. A. Sebeok (Ed.). *Current trends in linguistics* (Vol. 3). The Hague: Mouton, 1966, Pp. 395–477.

Wellek, R. *A history of literary criticism*. New Haven: Yale University Press, 1955.

White, A. R. *Truth*. Garden City, N.Y.: Doubleday, 1970.

Whitehead, A. N., & Russell, B. *Principia mathematica*. London: Cambridge University Press, 1910.

Wilensky, R. *Understanding goal-based stories* (Research Report 140). Department of Computer Science, Yale University, 1978.

Williams, J. P., Taylor, M. B., & Ganger, S. Text variations at the level of the individual sentence and the comprehension of simple expository paragraphs. *Journal of Educational Psychology*, 1981, *73*, 851–865.

Wimsatt, W. K., Jr., & Brooks, C. *Literary criticism*. New York: Random House, 1957.

Winograd, T. *Understanding actual language*. New York: Academic Press, 1972.

Wittgenstein, L. *Tractatus logico-philosophicus*. Frankfurt: Suhrkamp, 1960. (Originally published, 1922.)

Wittrock, M. C., Marks, C., & Doctorow, M. Reading as a generative process. *Journal of Educational Psychology*, 1975, *67*, 484–489.

Woods, W. A. Transition network grammars for natural language analysis. *Communication of the ACM*, 1970, *13*, 591–606.

Woods, W. A. What's a link: Foundations for semantic networks. In D. G. Bobrow & A. Collins (Eds.), *Representation and understanding*. New York: Academic Press, 1975.

Woods, W. A. Multiple theory formation in speech and reading. In R. J. Spiro, B. C. Bruce, & W. F. Brewer (Eds.), *Theoretical issues in reading comprehension*. Hillsdale, N.J.: Erlbaum, 1980.

Woods, W., & Brachman, R. Research in natural language understanding. Technical Report TRI, 3742. Bolt, Beranek & Newman, Cambridge, Mass., 1978.

von Wright, G. H. *Norm and action*. London: Routledge & Kegan Paul, 1963.

Yates, F. A. *The art of memory*. London: Routledge & Kegan Paul, 1966.

Yekovich, F. R., & Thorndyke, P. W. An evaluation of alternative functional models of narrative schemata. *Journal of Verbal Learning and Verbal Behavior*, 1981, *20*, 454–469,

Yekovich, F.C., & Walker, C.H. Identifying and using referents in sentence comprehension. *Journal of Verbal Learning and Verbal Behavior*, 1978, *17*, 265–277.

Yngve, V. H. The depth hypothesis. *Proceedings of the XII Symposium in Applied Mathematics*. Providence, R.I.: American Mathematical Society, 1961.

Yuille, J. C., & Paivio, A. Abstractness and the recall of connected discourse. *Journal of Experimental Psychology*, 1969, *82*, 467–472.

Zammuner, V. L. *Speech production: Strategies in discourse planning: A theoretical and empirical enquiry*. Hamburg: Buske Verlag, 1981.

# Author Index

# Subject Index